ETHICAL CONFLICTS in PSYCHOLOGY

ETHICAL CONFLICTS
IN PSYCHOLOGY

SECOND EDITION

DONALD N. BERSOFF

AMERICAN PSYCHOLOGICAL ASSOCIATION
WASHINGTON, DC

Published by
American Psychological Association
750 First Street, NE
Washington, DC 20002

Copies may be ordered from
APA Order Department
P.O. Box 92984
Washington, DC 20090-2984

In the UK, Europe, Africa, and the Middle East copies may be ordered from
American Psychological Association
3 Henrietta Street
Covent Garden, London
WC2E 8LU England

Typeset in Berkeley by EPS Group Inc., Easton, MD

Printer: Data Reproductions Corp., Auburn Hills, MI
Jacket Designer: Minker Design, Bethesda, MD
Jacket Illustrator: Elena Dvorkina
Technical/Production Editor: Rachael J. Stryker

Library of Congress Cataloging-in-Publication Data
Ethical conflicts in psychology / [edited by] Donald N. Bersoff.—
    2nd ed.
        p.   cm.
    Includes bibliographical references and index.
    ISBN 1-55798-591-X (hardcover : alk. paper).—ISBN 1-55798-599-5
(pbk. : alk. paper)
    1. Psychology—Moral and ethical aspects.   2. Psychologists—
Professional ethics.   I. Bersoff, Donald N.
BF76.4.E814   1999
174′.915—dc21   99-14474
                                                                    CIP

British Library Cataloguing-in-Publication Data
A CIP record is available from the British Library.

Printed in the United States of America
Second edition

Be not too hasty to trust . . . the teachers of morality
. . . they discourse like angels, but they live like men.

—Samuel Johnson, *Rasselas*

◆　◆　◆

To my mother, Mina, and my late father, Irving, who laid the foundation,
and
to my wife, Deborah Leavy, and my children—Benjamin, David, and Judith—who built an
unassailable edifice on that foundation and truly taught me what love and ethics
were all about.

Contents

Preface to the Second Edition

I am gratified by the apparent success of the first edition of this text, published in 1995 by the American Psychological Association. I am hopeful that this revision will be as welcomed as the original. I have kept the same format, presenting judiciously edited articles from a wide variety of sources interspersed with original commentary and citations to other published materials. I have also maintained my original intent—to offer conflicting views about fundamental ethical and moral dilemmas, allowing users of this book to ultimately arrive at their own conclusions about their proper resolutions.

Although the format and intent remain the same, I have incorporated some changes in this edition. Like any anxious author, I read the reviews of the first edition of this text and took them to heart. One important criticism was that the book was too ethnocentric. In response, I have included the Canadian Code of Ethics as well as the Canadian Psychological Association's system for ethical decision making. These additions make the book more useful to colleagues in the North and allow readers to contrast the APA and CPA codes with regard to their readability, helpfulness in guiding ethical behavior, and comparability in regulating professional conduct.

Although I have retained some older articles for historical context, the majority of the materials in this second edition were published within the last decade, and about half were published in the past five years. Much of this newer material represents rapidly changing events in psychology. Thus, readers will find more material on managed care, the merits and demerits of tele- (or cyber-) therapy, and updated information about research ethics, among others.

I am indebted to those at APA for their decision to publish a revised and modernized second edition. Gary VandenBos, Executive Director of the APA Publications and Communications Program, and Julia Frank-McNeil, Director, APA Books, saw the value in a second edition and encouraged me to pursue the project. Development Editor Margaret Schlegel collaborated most closely with me during the book's publication. If not for her gentle insistence on keeping the book within a manageable and affordable length and her reading and rereading early drafts, this text would not be as concise and affordable as it is. Production editor Rachael Stryker significantly improved the text's language and readability.

This project could not have been completed but for the granting of my sabbatical leave by the former dean of Villanova Law School, Steven P. Frankino. Also vital was the financial sustenance of a summer research grant provided by the school's present dean, Mark Sargent. I wish to thank Erik Nabors and Kim Picarello, students in the Law & Psychology Program co-sponsored by Villanova Law School and the Medical College of Pennsylvania—Hahnemann University, who served as my research assistants. Finally, I am thankful for the students who have used these materials in one form or another over the past decade and who have improved its usefulness through their cogent suggestions.

If students, psychologists, and other readers have suggestions for material to be included in what I hope will be future editions, I would be pleased if you communicate with me.

Preface to the First Edition

This book represents the final common pathway of over 3 decades of professional work. My experiences as a psychologist working with inpatients and outpatients, collecting data from human subjects in research, or scrutinizing the research proposals of others while serving on institutional review boards; my work as an attorney defending psychologists against claims of malpractice and unethical conduct, or acting as a consultant to state psychology licensing boards seeking to discipline errant professionals; and my service to the American Psychological Association (APA) as its legal counsel for 10 years and, currently, as a member of its Board of Directors—all of this has taught me that there is a need to better inculcate ethical values and virtues in all those who practice, teach, and do research in psychology. In particular, however, it was my role as an academician—directing programs in law and psychology, discussing and debating ethical issues with colleagues and graduate students, and, specifically, teaching ethics to graduate students—that led me to develop this book.

As a teacher, I found that books providing narrative overviews of ethics, although educational, did not always stimulate lively discussion, sometimes failed to adequately represent several sides to the ethical conflicts and dilemmas that contemporary psychologists face, and did not easily facilitate a career-long commitment to treating clients, employees, academic institutions, or research participants with fidelity and integrity. In actuality, students who read published materials, such as journal articles or book chapters, seemed more inspired to invest in particular topics. However, many of these excellent selections often either were burdensomely long or contained information irrelevant to psychology graduate students who were taking their first course in ethics. Moreover, readings alone could not provide the structure, context, and balance that students needed to comprehend the breadth of issues in the field, to understand the conflicts inherent in ethical decision making, and to integrate this material in a meaningful way.

As a result, for a number of years I experimented in the classroom with a hybrid approach—attempting to combine the best of both worlds. First, I gleaned materials from a wide variety of sources, including psychology journals and books, law reviews, legal decisions, statutes, and official policy documents of the APA. When appropriate, I presented only excerpts of the publications to focus attention on their most relevant and salient points, which allowed for comprehensive coverage over the course of a semester of the major ethical conflicts in psychology.

To the articles previously published, I added original explanatory writings before or after some readings as well as provided introductions to each of the topics. In this book, my comments within excerpted articles are called *Editor's Notes*, or *Ed. notes*, whereas my notes before and after articles are offered as *Commentary*. I added these comments to illuminate the issues raised by readings, to provide thought-provoking questions, and, at times, to direct the reader to other important sources. I found that the topical organization helped to structure learning and the brief introductions to the topics provided readers with an overview and context for both the readings and the notes.

I have used successive editions of these materials since 1990, when I began teaching a course in ethics and professional issues through Hahnemann University's Department of Clinical and Health Psychology. Each year I have revised and improved the materials on the basis of informative and candid critiques by students themselves. Once I felt satisfied that they were indeed inculcating sensitivity and awareness of ethical issues and fostering the kind of ethical decision-making strategies that are respectful of the complexity of such issues, I decided to offer them to a broader audience. This book is the result.

Being fully aware of the professional need for guidance in this area, I also designed this book to be of interest and value to psychologists who have finished their formal training and are engaged in teaching, practice, and research. It is in the conduct of day-to-day professional life in psychology that ethical principles become truly compelling. It is then that perception of and sensitivity to ethical issues become paramount and that ethical decision-making skills are put to the test. Most important, it is in these practical situations that ethical problems fully reveal their ambiguity and in which psychologists may feel at sea. At such times, a book such as this can serve as an anchor—allowing psychologists a brief respite on stormy waters to study the scholarly constellations and landmarks before navigating further on their particular ethical voyage. It is my hope that this book will serve this purpose well.

For psychologists as well as students of psychology, the book is particularly timely, as it reflects the major changes that were made by the APA in 1992 to its ethics code, when it was renamed the *Ethical Principles of Psychologists and Code of Conduct*. I take complete responsibility for my interpretation of the past and current ethics codes and for the views expressed throughout the book, while applauding the APA for courageously publishing a volume that is at times critical of official APA policy. I do wish to emphasize, however, that my past and current affiliations with the APA do not imply APA endorsement of or agreement with the views expressed herein.

I now offer some words of appreciation for those who helped in the development of this book. First and foremost, I owe the greatest debt of gratitude to my students for their thoughtful and honest critiques of the material over the years. I also wish to acknowledge the support of the APA Publications and Communications Program. Executive Director Gary VandenBos encouraged me early on to do this project, despite its unusual format. Julia Frank-McNeil, Director of Acquisitions and Development for APA Books, helped shape the contours of the text during its formative stages and secured helpful, early reviews from colleagues whom I can only thank anonymously. Development Editor Margaret Schlegel not only applied just the right amount and mixture of positive reinforcement and necessary prodding but also provided essential suggestions for improving the book's organization and structure. Production Editor Molly Flickinger significantly improved its language and readability, with the assistance of Sarah Trembath, Production Assistant. Both Stan Jones, Director of the APA Office of Ethics, and Ken Pope, one of the most prolific and thoughtful ethics scholars in psychology, prepared detailed critiques of the content and structure of drafts. Each of these contributions immeasurably enhanced this text. Of course, I am fully accountable for the flaws that remain.

Back home, Steven P. Frankino, Dean of the Villanova Law School, sustained me with research grants for four summers while I wrote, edited, and revised the book. The Medical College of Pennsylvania—Hahnemann University, my other academic setting, provided me with Robin Lewis—one of the most efficient, intelligent, and helpful secretaries that a faculty member could hope for. Finally, I wish to thank Lowell Burket, Adam Rosen, Steve Anderer, Drew Messer, Natacha Blain, and Trudi Kirk, all of whom served as my research assistants during the writing of this text and, as such, did the "scut work"—tracking down the materials, securing readable copies, and obtaining the necessary permissions to reprint—that faculty members assiduously attempt to avoid.

If students, psychologists, or other readers have favorite articles relevant to the issues covered in this text that were not included and serve its goals, I would very much like to hear from them. Please provide me with an appropriate reprint or, at least, a citation to the reference. I will be happy to consider your suggestions for future editions.

Introduction

Ethics is the study of those assumptions held by individuals, institutions, organizations, and professions that they believe will assist them in distinguishing between right and wrong and, ultimately, in making sound moral judgments (Bersoff & Koeppl, 1993; Delgado & McAllen, 1982).[1] Making such judgments requires a number of cognitive, affective, and characterological attributes.

Consider the following situations:

1. A male faculty member is supervising the doctoral research of a female graduate student of similar age. After several months, the student informs the professor that she would like to develop a social relationship with him and asks if they could discuss the matter over dinner.
2. In perusing an academic journal, a young assistant professor discovers that, in an article just published, an older colleague has used the work of another psychologist without proper attribution.
3. A client in serious need of intensive and long-term treatment informs his therapist that although 80% of the therapist's fees are covered by insurance, he is unable, because of severe financial problems, to pay the remaining 20% of the fee and requests that the therapist forgive this copayment for the foreseeable future.
4. An industrial psychologist is told by her employer to use a test of questionable validity to assess applicants for unskilled positions in her factory.
5. A forensic psychologist who has tested a criminal defendant to evaluate whether the defendant may be excused from responsibility for a crime because he meets the test of legal "insanity" is asked by the attorney who has retained the psychologist for a hefty fee to testify that the client is, in fact, insane, although the evidence for that assertion is equivocal.

It is unlikely that all of these hypothetical but realistic situations will arise in the course of any single psychologist's work, but they are assuredly problems that confront the everyday

---

[1] Scholars who study ethics may be divided into two classes. *Descriptive ethicists* are concerned with uncovering and delineating the moral tenets of particular groups. They are like empirical scientists, gathering data about ethical beliefs in an objective and rigorous manner. Once descriptive ethicists have identified and analyzed the basic principles of morality, *normative ethicists* attempt to transform these principles into concrete, behavioral prescriptions designed to guide correct conduct. Thus, normative ethicists are more like philosophers or legislators than scientists. Formal codes of ethics are the expressions of normative ethics.

academician and professional psychologist. Each requires the psychologist facing the particular situation to make a sound and reasoned moral judgment. But to do so requires a myriad of skills and attributes.

The psychologist must first be sensitive to and appreciate the fact that the situation does indeed raise an ethical and moral issue. He or she must then know what published sources are available to help resolve the situations in an ethical and moral manner. These sources include, but are not limited to, (a) the APA's (1992) formal code of ethics; (b) other APA documents that guide teaching, practice, and research; (c) federal and state laws and regulations that affect one's work[2]; and (d) institutional or organizational policies of one's work setting.

For several reasons, however, such didactic knowledge is not enough. First, although there may be codes, guidelines, laws, and policies that will be helpful in making and evaluating an ethical decision, they are often fraught with ambiguity or written in generalized language that may not explicitly help to resolve an ethical conflict. Second, it is the rule, rather than the exception, that at any point in time more than one principle can be applied or argument made for and against adopting a particular course of action. Third, at their base level, codes and laws are grounded in such fundamental moral principles and duties as refraining from doing harm, recognizing the right of others to self-determination, or acting justly. Thus, at some point—although armed with knowledge of the rules and appreciative of his or her moral obligations (and recognizing that there may be conflicting points of view)—the psychologist must determine how he or she wants to be viewed. An ethical decision may ultimately depend on one's character and ability to act maturely, wisely, and prudently.

PURPOSE OF THE BOOK

The essential purpose of any book about ethics in psychology is to introduce readers to the formal and enforceable documents that regulate professional, scientific, and academic conduct. That is an inescapable obligation that this book seeks to fulfill. In this regard, the book will be useful to psychology graduate students in their ethics courses. In fact, because its content is relatively comprehensive and reflects the major contemporary ethical conflicts in psychology, the book can be used as a primary text in these classes. In addition, because it covers the major changes made in 1992 in the APA's Ethical Principles as well as the 1996 revision of the rules and procedures by which complaints of ethical violations are adjudicated, it can help those who are already psychologists keep abreast of these changing issues.

The book's primary purpose, however, is to help readers develop sensitivity to the ethical aspects of their work as present or future psychologists. It is intended to actuate readers to a deeper level of thought regarding these aspects and to leave them more considerate, critical, and skeptical about their own behavior and the ethical constraints under which they are asked to treat, teach about, and investigate human and animal behavior.

---

[2] These laws would include licensure or certification statutes and administrative regulations existing in the jurisdiction in which the psychologist is practicing. Often, these documents contain ethical codes that may vary from that of the APA.

PLAN OF THE BOOK

To accomplish these ends, I have structured and composed this book in a way that should be useful, yet may be unfamiliar, to those in the social and behavioral sciences. I have sought to combine the benefits of historical, classical, and contemporary readings in psychology, law, and ethics with the benefits of narrative structure, engrossing questions and ethical dilemmas, and suggestions for further reading.

The articles, chapter excerpts, legal decisions, statutes, policy documents, original chapter introductions, editor's notes, and commentaries are organized in a logical progression to teach, juxtapose points of view, stimulate discussion, and analyze and examine contemporary ethical conflicts and issues in psychology. Because I have found that students enjoy and profit from discussing ethical conflicts derived from factual situations, I have included many articles that contain vignettes presenting such conflicts and have developed some original ones as well. I recommend that teachers who use this book take full advantage of the provocative nature of these vignettes to explore the underlying and sometimes competing ethical and moral values they evoke.

The materials are organized into 10 chapters. The first chapter, "Ethics Codes and How They Are Enforced," provides a bit of history and an introduction to the myriad ethical issues facing contemporary psychologists. As a resource, it also includes an unabridged version of the current APA Ethical Principles and the Rules and Procedures by which ethical complaints are adjudicated by the APA Ethics Committee, as well as a description of the sanctions the committee may levy should an ethics violation be found. To make it useful to Canadian readers, I have also included the provisions of the Canadian Code of Ethics for Psychologists.

The materials in chapter 2, "How Ethics Are Applied," reveal the disparity between the lofty ideals underlying ethical codes and the extent to which those ideals are translated into the real-life behavior of psychologists. This chapter also raises issues concerning the conflict between codes of ethics and other constraints on psychologists' conduct.

Although chapter 3 has an unassuming title—"Learning Ethics"—it is actually an essential and central part of the book. In fact, some teachers may want to begin their ethics course with this chapter. It presents and defines the fundamental moral principles that should serve as the foundation for any ethical code and offers several different strategies for attempting to resolve ethical dilemmas and conflicts.

Whereas the first three chapters provide a general framework for studying ethical issues, each of the remaining seven chapters examines a central and contemporary topical conflict in ethics. Chapter 4—"Confidentiality, Privilege, and Privacy"—defines these essential terms and then tackles such knotty issues as protecting intimate disclosures by violent clients, by children, or by clients infected with the HIV virus. Chapter 5, "Multiple Relationships," shows how unethical behavior can arise through a variety of interactions between psychologists and clients or research participants, presents opposing views on prohibiting sexual intimacies between clients and clinicians, and offers some strategies for avoiding the almost inevitable problems that dual relationships can create. Chapters 6 and 7— "Psychological Assessment" and "Therapy and Other Forms of Intervention," respectively— cover both traditional issues inherent to these topics and more current ones as well, such as computerized testing and therapy, treating culturally diverse populations, and the move to gain prescription privileges so that psychologists may administer psychotropic medications.

Chapter 8—"Academia: Research, Teaching, and Supervision"—includes material related to research with humans and animals generally but concentrates on the ethical dilemmas presented by deception research with humans. It also raises issues that may confront teachers of psychology, who will find that ethics codes follow them behind the ivy-covered facades of their academic institutions. Chapter 9, "Forensic Settings," may appear to focus on a narrow and specialized topic, but it actually raises issues that will increasingly face professionals and academics in psychology. The text concludes with another subject—"The Business of Psychology"—that will affect growing numbers in psychology, as the government and the courts more often perceive the provision of mental health services as a matter of commerce and profit making than as an aspect of a learned profession serving the public interest.

Readers will note that there is more in this text on psychological practice than on psychologists in science or academia. Psychologists who serve clients in schools, hospitals, clinics, counseling centers, or business organizations appear to have greater opportunities to evoke complaints of ethical misconduct because of the nature of the tasks in which they engage. Nevertheless, the book does pay serious attention to the ethics of those who perform research. I have also included excerpts from those rare articles that discuss the ethics of teaching and of the student–professor relationship.

I believe that this book fulfills its intended goals and hope that readers will find it not only timely, educational, and interesting but also challenging and engaging.

References

American Psychological Association. (1992). Ethical principles of psychologists and code of conduct. *American Psychologist, 47,* 1597–1611.

Bersoff, D. N., & Koeppl, P. M. (1993). The relation between ethical codes and moral principles. *Ethics and Behavior, 3,* 345–357.

Delgado, R., & McAllen, P. (1982). The moralist as expert witness. *Boston University Law Review, 62,* 869–926.

CHAPTER 1

ETHICS CODES AND HOW THEY ARE ENFORCED

Each profession shares many, varied attributes. They include selective recruitment, lengthy periods of education and training, the development of a shared language (including technical jargon), and controlled entrance into practice. A common characteristic of professions, and of occupations that would like to be perceived as professions, is the development and dissemination of a code of ethics that both emphasizes devotion to fundamental values, such as service to the public and concern for the welfare of those the profession serves, and informs the public of the positive qualities of those who pledge to adhere to the code.

Learning about ethics and the particular code of conduct promulgated by one's professional organization is, thus, one of the major and essential components of a student's socialization into the profession. Ethics teach "the way a group of associates define their special responsibility to one another and to the rest of the social order in which they work" (Erikson, 1967, p. 367). The code of ethics itself, which embodies the formal expression of these responsibilities, should, therefore, instruct those who study it how to relate to their colleagues and how to fulfill their professional roles and responsibilities toward those they serve—clients, patients, employers, research participants, students, institutions, and the public at large.

Ideally, a code of ethics should serve as a guide to resolving moral problems that confront the members of the profession that promulgate it, with its primary emphasis on protecting the public that the profession serves. It should be a grand statement of overarching principles that earn the respect of that public by reflecting the profession's moral integrity. Rarely can a profession fully attain this ideal. Realistically, what a code of ethics does is consensually validate the most recent views of a majority of professionals empowered by their colleagues to make decisions about ethical issues. Thus, a code of ethics is, inevitably, anachronistic, conservative, ethnocentric, and the product of political compromise. But recognition of that reality should not inhibit the creation of a document that fully realizes and expresses fundamental moral principles.

This chapter contributes to the socialization of psychologists by introducing readers to the profession's code of ethics—its voice of conscience. I begin by providing a brief history of the development of a code of ethics by the American Psychological Association (APA). Few know that APA established the Committee on Scientific and Professional Ethics 14 years before adopting its first ethics code in 1952. In fact, the development of an APA code was hotly debated in the 1940s and 1950s. One antagonist, eminent psychologist Calvin Hall (1952), argued that an ethics code plays into the hands of . . . . [t]he crooked operator [who] reads the code to see how much he can get away with, and since any code is bound to be filled with ambiguities and omissions, he can rationalize his unethical conduct by pointing to the code and say[ing], "See, it doesn't tell me I can't do this," or "I can interpret this to mean what I want it to mean." (p. 430)

Modern writers (Schwitzgebel & Schwitzgebel, 1980) have also argued that ethics codes are "vaguely formulated and rarely enforced. Therefore they provide almost no specific and tangible guidance to either practitioners or clients" (p. 3). In this chapter, I present in its entirety the current version of the APA ethics document, adopted in 1992 and titled the "Ethical Principles of Psychologists and Code of Conduct." I also present the Canadian "Code of Ethics for Psychologists." After studying this most recent version of the code and the material that follows, the reader may want to ask whether the concerns raised by critics of ethics codes in general pertain to this current revision.

If all the APA ethics code did was tweak the conscience and instruct its adherents about "dos" and "don'ts," it would be no more than a book of etiquette—a style manual for how scientists, academics, and practitioners should behave. But it is more than that. This code is enforced by an ethics committee established by the APA, a major purpose of which is to adjudicate complaints of unethical behavior brought by colleagues and members of the public against APA members. In cases where the committee, as a result of its adjudication, finds that a member complained about has committed an ethical violation, it may levy sanctions itself or, in serious cases, may recommend to the APA Board of Directors that the psychologist be dropped from membership. In some very serious cases, such organizationally imposed discipline may lead to complementary sanctions by state licensing boards or institutional employers. How the committee works, on what factual and documentary bases it relies to review complaints, the range of sanctions it may levy, what protections complainants and those psychologists they complain about have, and the extent to which members may appeal adverse findings are all spelled out in the Rules and Procedures drafted by the ethics committee.

Any set of rules that controls the consideration of complaints, that potentially results in a finding that one has committed an ethical violation, that imposes penalties that consequently may damage one's professional or scientific reputation as well as one's economic security (such as increasing malpractice premiums), or that may result in the loss of one's license to practice or the right to apply for federal research grants must be in accord with fundamental principles of fairness, or due process. As readers scrutinize the APA's Rules and Procedures, they might ask whether they afford more due process than is necessary: That is, does the APA provide too much protection for alleged ethics violators, or not enough?

What kinds of ethical dilemmas do psychologists commonly face? In the remaining nine chapters of this text, I examine the answers to that question in great detail. However, by way of introduction, I have included the last excerpt in this chapter to provide an overview. Interestingly, if the results of the survey described in this excerpt are valid, then of the four most troubling categories of ethical incidents, two pertain to practitioners, one pertains to academicians, and one cuts across both domains. Can you speculate as to what those categories are?

In summary, my purposes in this first chapter are to begin the processes of familiarization and socialization into the ethics of psychology and to introduce the reader to the topics addressed in later chapters of this book.

References

Erikson, K. T. (1967). A comment on disguised observation in sociology. *Social Problems, 14,* 366–373.

Hall, C. S. (1952). Crooks, codes, and cant. *American Psychologist, 7,* 430–431.

Schwitzgebel, R. L., & Schwitzgebel, R. K. (1980). *Law and psychological practice.* New York: Wiley.

Ethical Dilemmas Encountered by Members of the American Psychological Association: A National Survey

Kenneth S. Pope and Valerie A. Vetter

Founded in 1892, the American Psychological Association (APA) faced ethical problems without a formal code of ethics for 60 years. As the chair of the Committee on Scientific and Professional Ethics and Conduct in the early 1950s observed,

> In the early years of the American Psychological Association, the problems of ethics were relatively simple. We were essentially an organization of college teachers. The only ethical problems which seemed to present themselves were those of plagiarism and of academic freedom. (Rich, 1952, p. 440)

The Committee on Scientific and Professional Ethics was created in 1938 and began handling complaints on an informal basis. By 1947, the committee recommended that APA develop a formal code. "The present unwritten code . . . is tenuous, elusive, and unsatisfactory" ("A Little Recent History," 1952, p. 427).

The method used to create the formal code was innovative and unique, an extraordinary break from the traditional methods used previously by more than 500 professional and business associations (Hobbs, 1948). Setting aside what Hobbs termed the "armchair approach" (p. 82) in which a committee of those "who are most mature, in wisdom, experience, and knowledge of their fellow psychologists" (p. 81) would study the various available codes, issues, and literature and then submit a draft to the membership for approval, APA decided to create "an empirically developed code" based on an investigation of the ethical dilemmas encountered by a "representative sample of members": "The research itself would involve the collection, from psychologists involved in all of the various professional activities, of descriptions of actual situations which required ethical decisions" (p. 83). A survey collecting examples of the ethical dilemmas encountered by APA members led to a draft code (APA Committee on Ethical Standards for Psychology, 1951a, 1951b, 1951c) that was refined and approved in 1952 (APA, 1953) . . . .

The 1959 revision, the result of nine drafts over a three-year period, was adopted for use on a trial basis (APA, 1959). The committee anticipated that future revisions would be necessary to address changing conditions of practice[.] . . .

To maintain the unique nature and effectiveness of the code, future revisions were to be based not only on discussion among members but also on "additional critical incidents of controversial behavior" (Holzman, 1960, p. 247). To base revisions on recommendations by ethics committees seemed inadequate because "the energies of ethics committees are so totally devoted to fire fighting that fire proofing or concern with problems that have not yet emerged in the form of complaints must take a lower priority" (Golann, 1969, p. 454). Moreover, if the existing code neglected certain issues or dilemmas, individuals would obviously have no basis on which to file complaints relevant to those issues or dilemmas;

From *American Psychologist, 47*, 397–411. Copyright 1992 by the American Psychological Association. Table 1 has been omitted. Adapted with permission of the author and publisher.

thus there could be extreme discrepancies between the issues brought to the attention of an ethics committee and the issues encountered by the diverse membership. Even if a committee of experts were to develop ethical standards for diverse areas, they would, according to the rationale of the original code, likely overlook problems in implementing those standards that would be obvious to someone whose day-to-day work was in one of those areas.

The conviction that revisions should be based on subsequent critical incident studies was also based on beliefs about empowerment, management style, group process, and allegiance . . . . This conviction reflected the assumption that two ways of developing a revision would produce very different results. In the first approach, unique to psychology, the revision process would begin by actively soliciting through a formal mail survey the observations, ideas, and questions from those working "on the front lines" in diverse specialties, settings, and circumstances. A revision committee would then base its work on the primary data of this survey. In the alternate approach, used by virtually all other professional and business associations, a committee would decide how the code should be revised. The draft would then be circulated or published along with an announcement inviting comments. The first approach . . . was considered to empower individual members by involving them meaningfully at the beginning of the project. The process seemed likely not only to lead to a better revision but also to create and benefit from better group dynamics. . . .

The unique nature of the code was that it was "based upon the day-to-day decisions made by psychologists in the practice of their profession, rather than prescribed by a committee" (Golann, 1969, p. 454). Basing revisions on recent critical incidents provided by the membership was believed necessary to maintain an ethical code "close enough to the contemporary scene to win the genuine acceptance of the majority who are most directly affected by its principles" (Holzman, 1960, p. 250). . . .

References

American Psycholgical Association. (1953). *Ethical standards of psychologists*. Washington, DC: Author.

American Psychological Association. (1959). Ethical standards of psychologists. *American Psychologist, 14,* 279–282.

APA Committee on Ethical Standards for Psychology. (1951a). Ethical standards for psychology: Section 1, Ethical standards and public responsibility. Section 6, Ethical standards in teaching. *American Psychologist, 6,* 626–661.

APA Committee on Ethical Standards for Psychology. (1951b). Ethical standards for psychology: Section 2, Ethical standards in professional relationships. Section 4, Ethical standards in research. Section 5, Ethical standards in writing and publishing. *American Psychologist, 6,* 427–452.

APA Committee on Ethical Standards for Psychology. (1951c). Ethical standards in clinical and consulting relationships: Part 1. *American Psychologist, 6,* 57–64.

Golann, S. E. (1969). Emerging areas of ethical concern. *American Psychologist, 24,* 454–459.

Hobbs, N. (1948). The development of a code of ethical standards for psychology. *American Psychologist, 3,* 80–84.

Holzman, W. H. (1960). Some problems of defining ethical behavior. *American Psychologist, 15,* 247–250.

A little recent history. (1952). *American Psychologist, 7,* 426–428.

Rich, G. J. (1952). A new code of ethics is needed. *American Psychologist, 7,* 440–441.

◆ ◆ ◆

Commentary: *For a more extensive history of the development of codes of ethics see Sinclair, C., Simon, N. P., & Pettifor, J. L. (1996). The history of ethical codes and licensure. In L. J. Bass, S. T. DeMers, J. R. Ogloff, C. Peterson, J. L. Pettifor, R. P. Reaves, T. Retfalvi, N. P. Simon, C. Sinclair, & R. M. Tipton (Eds.), Professional conduct and discipline in psychology (pp. 1–15). Washington, DC: American Psychological Association. The original APA code of ethics, adopted in 1952 and published in 1953, has had many descendants, including the current code's immediate ancestor, published in 1981 and revised in 1989. See, for example,*

American Psychological Association. (1981). Ethical principles of psychologists. American Psychologist, 36, 633–638.

American Psychological Association. (1990). Ethical principles of psychologists (amended June 2, 1989). American Psychologist, 45, 390–395.

The 1989 revision was stimulated by concerns expressed

by the Federal Trade Commission. For a discussion of why the U.S. government was interested in the APA's code of ethics, see chapter 10 ("The Business of Psychology").

The APA ethics code is considered an expression of association policy. Barring an emergency, all APA policy is adopted by its legislative body—the Council of Representatives. The council also promulgates Association Rules (ARs)—regulations for administering the APA's governance structure. AR 20-4.1 states:

> The Ethics Committee shall have the responsibility from time to time of initiating a review of the latest formally adopted version of the ethics code ... and proposing necessary changes or additions. In carrying out such a review, the Ethics Committee may set up such ad hoc committees as it finds necessary.

Coincident with the Federal Trade Commission's investigation, but begun independently of it, the APA in 1986, under the authority of AR 20-4.1, formed a task force to completely revise its ethical principles. Unlike the original 1953 code, the revision was not based on critical incidents gleaned from the field, but was drafted using the "alternate approach" described by Pope and Vetter (1992) in the article excerpted above. The task force produced several review drafts. Reactions were mixed, and a number of controversial issues were raised. After an 8-hour debate the Council of Representatives voted to adopt the now-current and enforceable code (see Ethical Principles of Psychologists and Code of Conduct reprinted on the following pages). For a more complete description of the revision process, see APA Ethics Committee. (1995). Report of the Ethics Committee, 1994. American Psychologist, 50, 706–713; APA Ethics Committee. Report of the Ethics Committee, 1991 and 1992. American Psychologist, 48, 811–820.

Ethical Principles of Psychologists and Code of Conduct

American Psychological Association

INTRODUCTION

The American Psychological Association's (APA's) Ethical Principles of Psychologists and Code of Conduct (hereinafter referred to as the Ethics Code) consists of an Introduction, a Preamble, six General Principles (A–F), and specific Ethical Standards. The Introduction discusses the intent, organization, procedural considerations, and scope of application of the Ethics Code. The Preamble and General Principles are *aspirational* goals to guide psychologists toward the highest ideals of psychology. Although the Preamble and General Principles are not themselves enforceable rules, they should be considered by psychologists in arriving at an ethical course of action and may be considered by ethics bodies in interpreting the Ethical Standards. The Ethical Standards set forth *enforceable* rules for conduct as psychologists. Most of the Ethical Standards are written broadly, in order to apply to psychologists in varied roles, although the application of an Ethical Standard may vary depending on the context. The Ethical Standards are not exhaustive. The fact that a given conduct is not specifically addressed by the Ethics Code does not mean that it is necessarily either ethical or unethical.

Membership in the APA commits members to adhere to the APA Ethics Code and to the rules and procedures used to implement it. Psychologists and students, whether or not they are APA members, should be aware that the Ethics Code may be applied to them by state psychology boards, courts, or other public bodies.

This Ethics Code applies only to psychologists' work-related activities, that is, activities that are part of the psychologists' scientific and professional functions or that are psychological in nature. It includes the clinical or counseling practice of psychology, research, teaching, supervision of trainees, development of assessment instruments, conducting assessments, educational counseling, organizational

From *American Psychologist, 47,* 1597–1611. Copyright 1992 by the American Psychological Association. Adapted with permission of the author and publisher.

This version of the APA Ethics Code was adopted by the American Psychological Association's Council of Representatives during its meeting, August 13 and 16, 1992, and is effective beginning December 1, 1992. Inquiries concerning the substance or interpretation of the APA Ethics Code should be addressed to the Director, Office of Ethics, American Psychological Association, 750 First Street, NE, Washington, DC 20002-4242.

This Code will be used to adjudicate complaints brought concerning alleged conduct occurring on or after the effective date. Complaints regarding conduct occurring prior to the effective date will be adjudicated on the basis of the version of the Code that was in effect at the time the conduct occurred, except that no provisions repealed in June 1989, will be enforced even if an earlier version contains the provision. The Ethics Code will undergo continuing review and study for future revisions; comments on the Code may be sent to the above address.

The APA has previously published its Ethical Standards as follows:

American Psychological Association. (1953). *Ethical standards of psychologists*. Washington, DC: Author.
American Psychological Association. (1958). Standards of ethical behavior for psychologists. *American Psychologist, 13,* 268–271.
American Psychological Association. (1963). Ethical standards of psychologists. *American Psychologist, 18,* 56–60.
American Psychological Association. (1968). Ethical standards of psychologists. *American Psychologist, 23,* 357–361.
American Psychological Association. (1977, March). Ethical standards of psychologists. *APA Monitor,* pp. 22–23.
American Psychological Association. (1979). *Ethical standards of psychologists*. Washington, DC: Author.
American Psychological Association. (1981). Ethical principles of psychologists. *American Psychologist, 36,* 633–638.
American Psychological Association. (1990). Ethical principles of psychologists (Amended June 2, 1989). *American Psychologist, 4,* 390–395.

consulting, social intervention, administration, and other activities as well. These work-related activities can be distinguished from the purely private conduct of a psychologist, which ordinarily is not within the purview of the Ethics Code.

The Ethics Code is intended to provide standards of professional conduct that can be applied by the APA and by other bodies that choose to adopt them. Whether or not a psychologist has violated the Ethics Code does not by itself determine whether he or she is legally liable in a court action, whether a contract is enforceable, or whether other legal consequences occur. These results are based on legal rather than ethical rules. However, compliance with or violation of the Ethics Code may be admissible as evidence in some legal proceedings, depending on the circumstances.

In the process of making decisions regarding their professional behavior, psychologists must consider this Ethics Code, in addition to applicable laws and psychology board regulations. If the Ethics Code establishes a higher standard of conduct than is required by law, psychologists must meet the higher ethical standard. If the Ethics Code standard appears to conflict with the requirements of law, then psychologists make known their commitment to the Ethics Code and take steps to resolve the conflict in a responsible manner. If neither law nor the Ethics Code resolves an issue, psychologists should consider other professional materials[1] and the dictates of their own conscience, as well as seek consultation with others within the field when this is practical.

The procedures for filing, investigating, and resolving complaints of unethical conduct are described in the current Rules and Procedures of the APA Ethics Committee. The actions that APA may take for violations of the Ethics Code include actions such as reprimand, censure, termination of APA membership, and referral of the matter to other bodies. Complainants who seek remedies such as monetary damages in alleging ethical violations by a psychologist must resort to private negotiation, administrative bodies, or the courts. Actions that violate the Ethics Code may lead to the imposition of sanctions on a psychologist by bodies other than APA, including state psychological associations, other professional groups, psychology boards, other state or federal agencies, and payors for health services. In addition to actions for violation of the Ethics Code, the APA Bylaws provide that APA may take action against a member after his or her conviction of a felony, expulsion or suspension from an affiliated state psychological association, or suspension or loss of licensure.

PREAMBLE

Psychologists work to develop a valid and reliable body of scientific knowledge based on research. They may apply that knowledge to human behavior in a variety of contexts. In doing so, they perform many roles, such as researcher, educator, diagnostician, therapist, supervisor, consultant, administrator, social interventionist, and expert witness. Their goal is to broaden knowledge of behavior and, where appropriate, to apply it pragmatically to improve the condition of both the individual and society. Psychologists respect the central importance of freedom of inquiry and expression in research, teaching, and publication. They also strive to help the public in developing informed judgments and choices concerning human behavior. This Ethics Code provides a common set of values upon which psychologists build their professional and scientific work.

---

[1] Professional materials that are most helpful in this regard are guidelines and standards that have been adopted or endorsed by professional psychological organizations. Such guidelines and standards, whether adopted by the American Psychological Association (APA) or its Divisions, are not enforceable as such by this Ethics Code, but are of educative value to psychologists, courts, and professional bodies. Such materials include, but are not limited to, the APA's *General Guidelines for Providers of Psychological Services* (1987), *Specialty Guidelines for the Delivery of Services by Clinical Psychologists, Counseling Psychologists, Industrial/Organizational Psychologists, and School of Psychologists* (1981), *Guidelines for Computer Based Tests and Interpretations* (1987), *Standards for Educational and Psychological Testing* (1985), *Ethical Principles in the Conduct of Research With Human Participants* (1982), *Guidelines for Ethical Conduct in the Care and Use of Animals* (1986), *Guidelines for Providers of Psychological Services to Ethnic, Linguistic, and Culturally Diverse Populations* (1990), and *Publication Manual of the American Psychological Association* (3rd ed., 1983). Materials not adopted by APA as a whole include the APA Division 41 (Forensic Psychology)/American Psychology–Law Society's *Specialty Guidelines for Forensic Psychologists* (1991).

This Code is intended to provide both the general principles and the decision rules to cover most situations encountered by psychologists. It has as its primary goal the welfare and protection of the individuals and groups with whom psychologists work. It is the individual responsibility of each psychologist to aspire to the highest possible standards of conduct. Psychologists respect and protect human and civil rights, and do not knowingly participate in or condone unfair discriminatory practices.

The development of a dynamic set of ethical standards for a psychologist's work-related conduct requires a personal commitment to a lifelong effort to act ethically; to encourage ethical behavior by students, supervisees, employees, and colleagues, as appropriate; and to consult with others, as needed, concerning ethical problems. Each psychologist supplements, but does not violate, the Ethics Code's values and rules on the basis of guidance drawn from personal values, culture, and experience.

GENERAL PRINCIPLES

Principle A: Competence

Psychologists strive to maintain high standards of competence in their work. They recognize the boundaries of their particular competencies and the limitations of their expertise. They provide only those services and use only those techniques for which they are qualified by education, training, or experience. Psychologists are cognizant of the fact that the competencies required in serving, teaching, and/or studying groups of people vary with the distinctive characteristics of those groups. In those areas in which recognized professional standards do not yet exist, psychologists exercise careful judgment and take appropriate precautions to protect the welfare of those with whom they work. They maintain knowledge of relevant scientific and professional information related to the services they render, and they recognize the need for ongoing education. Psychologists make appropriate use of scientific, professional, technical, and administrative resources.

Principle B: Integrity

Psychologists seek to promote integrity in the science, teaching, and practice of psychology. In these activities psychologists are honest, fair, and respectful of others. In describing or reporting their qualifications, services, products, fees, research, or teaching, they do not make statements that are false, misleading, or deceptive. Psychologists strive to be aware of their own belief systems, values, needs, and limitations and the effect of these on their work. To the extent feasible, they attempt to clarify for relevant parties the roles they are performing and to function appropriately in accordance with those roles. Psychologists avoid improper and potentially harmful dual relationships.

Principle C: Professional and Scientific Responsibility

Psychologists uphold professional standards of conduct, clarify their professional roles and obligations, accept appropriate responsibility for their behavior, and adapt their methods to the needs of different populations. Psychologists consult with, refer to, or cooperate with other professionals and institutions to the extent needed to serve the best interests of their patients, clients, or other recipients of their services. Psychologists' moral standards and conduct are personal matters to the same degree as is true for any other person, except as psychologists' conduct may compromise their professional responsibilities or reduce the public's trust in psychology and psychologists. Psychologists are concerned about the ethical compliance of their colleagues' scientific and professional conduct. When appropriate, they consult with colleagues in order to prevent or avoid unethical conduct.

Principle D: Respect for People's Rights and Dignity

Psychologists accord appropriate respect to the fundamental rights, dignity, and worth of all people. They respect the rights of individuals to privacy, confidentiality, self-determination, and autonomy, mindful that legal and other obligations may lead to inconsistency and conflict with the exercise of these rights. Psychologists are aware of cultural, individual, and role differences, including those due to age, gender, race, ethnicity, national origin, religion, sexual orientation, disability, language, and socioeconomic status. Psychologists try to eliminate the effect on their work of biases based on those factors, and they do not knowingly participate in or condone unfair discriminatory practices.

Principle E: Concern for Others' Welfare

Psychologists seek to contribute to the welfare of those with whom they interact professionally. In their professional actions, psychologists weigh the welfare and rights of their patients or clients, students, supervisees, human research participants, and other affected persons, and the welfare of animal subjects of research. When conflicts occur among psychologists' obligations or concerns, they attempt to resolve these conflicts and to perform their roles in a responsible fashion that avoids or minimizes harm. Psychologists are sensitive to real and ascribed differences in power between themselves and others, and they do not exploit or mislead other people during or after professional relationships.

Principle F: Social Responsibility

Psychologists are aware of their professional and scientific responsibilities to the community and the society in which they work and live. They apply and make public their knowledge of psychology in order to contribute to human welfare. Psychologists are concerned about and work to mitigate the causes of human suffering. When undertaking research, they strive to advance human welfare and the science of psychology. Psychologists try to avoid misuse of their work. Psychologists comply with the law and encourage the development of law and social policy that serve the interests of their patients and clients and the public. They are encouraged to contribute a portion of their professional time for little or no personal advantage.

ETHICAL STANDARDS

1. General Standards

These General Standards are potentially applicable to the professional and scientific activities of all psychologists.

1.01 Applicability of the Ethics Code

The activity of a psychologist subject to the Ethics Code may be reviewed under these Ethical Stan-

dards only if the activity is part of his or her work-related functions or the activity is psychological in nature. Personal activities having no connection to or effect on psychological roles are not subject to the Ethics Code.

1.02 Relationship of Ethics and Law

If psychologists' ethical responsibilities conflict with law, psychologists make known their commitment to the Ethics Code and take steps to resolve the conflict in a responsible manner.

1.03 Professional and Scientific Relationship

Psychologists provide diagnostic, therapeutic, teaching, research, supervisory, consultative, or other psychological services only in the context of a defined professional or scientific relationship or role. (See also Standards 2.01, Evaluation, Diagnosis, and Interventions in Professional Context, and 7.02, Forensic Assessments.)

1.04 Boundaries of Competence

(a) Psychologists provide services, teach, and conduct research only within the boundaries of their competence, based on their education, training, supervised experience, or appropriate professional experience.

(b) Psychologists provide services, teach, or conduct research in new areas or involving new techniques only after first undertaking appropriate study, training, supervision, and/or consultation from persons who are competent in those areas or techniques.

(c) In those emerging areas in which generally recognized standards for preparatory training do not yet exist, psychologists nevertheless take reasonable steps to ensure the competence of their work and to protect patients, clients, students, research participants, and others from harm.

1.05 Maintaining Expertise

Psychologists who engage in assessment, therapy, teaching, research, organizational consulting, or other professional activities maintain a reasonable level of awareness of current scientific and professional information in their fields of activity, and undertake ongoing efforts to maintain competence in the skills they use.

1.06 Basis for Scientific and Professional Judgments

Psychologists rely on scientifically and professionally derived knowledge when making scientific or professional judgments or when engaging in scholarly or professional endeavors.

1.07 Describing the Nature and Results of Psychological Services

(a) When psychologists provide assessment, evaluation, treatment, counseling, supervision, teaching, consultation, research, or other psychological services to an individual, a group, or an organization, they provide, using language that is reasonably understandable to the recipient of those services, appropriate information beforehand about the nature of such services and appropriate information later about results and consultations. (See also Standard 2.09, Explaining Assessment Results.)

(b) If psychologists will be precluded by law or by organizational roles from providing such information to particular individuals or groups, they so inform those individuals or groups at the outset of the service.

1.08 Human Differences

Where differences of age, gender, race, ethnicity, national origin, religion, sexual orientation, disability, language, or socioeconomic status significantly affect psychologists' work concerning particular individuals or groups, psychologists obtain the training, experience, consultation, or supervision necessary to ensure the competence of their services, or they make appropriate referrals.

1.09 Respecting Others

In their work-related activities, psychologists respect the rights of others to hold values, attitudes, and opinions that differ from their own.

1.10 Nondiscrimination

In their work-related activities, psychologists do not engage in unfair discrimination based on age, gender, race, ethnicity, national origin, religion, sexual orien-

tation, disability, socioeconomic status, or any basis proscribed by law.

1.11 Sexual Harassment

(a) Psychologists to not engage in sexual harassment. Sexual harassment is sexual solicitation, physical advances, or verbal or nonverbal conduct that is sexual in nature, that occurs in connection with the psychologist's activities or roles as a psychologist, and that either: (1) is unwelcome, is offensive, or creates a hostile workplace environment, and the psychologist knows or is told this; or (2) is sufficiently severe or intense to be abusive to a reasonable person in the context. Sexual harassment can consist of a single intense or severe act or of multiple persistent or pervasive acts.

(b) Psychologists accord sexual-harassment complaints and respondents dignity and respect. Psychologists do not participate in denying a person academic admittance or advancement, employment, tenure, or promotion, based solely upon their having made, or their being the subject of, sexual-harassment charges. This does not preclude taking action based upon the outcome of such proceedings or consideration of other appropriate information.

1.12 Other Harassment

Psychologists do not knowingly engage in behavior that is harassing or demeaning to persons with whom they interact in their work based on factors such as those persons' age, gender, race, ethnicity, national origin, religion, sexual orientation, disability, language, or socioeconomic status.

1.13 Personal Problems and Conflicts

(a) Pyschologists recognize that their personal problems and conflicts may interfere with their effectiveness. Accordingly, they refrain from undertaking an activity when they know or should know that their personal problems are likely to lead to harm to a patient, client, colleague, student, research participant, or other person to whom they may owe a professional or scientific obligation.

(b) In addition, psychologists have an obligation to be alert to signs of, and to obtain assistance for, their personal problems at an early stage, in order to prevent significantly impaired performance.

(c) When psychologists become aware of personal problems that may interfere with their performing work-related duties adequately, they take appropriate measures, such as obtaining professional consultation or assistance, and determine whether they should limit, suspend, or terminate their work-related duties.

1.14 Avoiding Harm

Psychologists take reasonable steps to avoid harming their patients or clients, research participants, students, and others with whom they work, and to minimize harm where it is foreseeable and unavoidable.

1.15 Misuse of Psychologists' Influence

Because psychologists' scientific and professional judgments and actions may affect the lives of others, they are alert to and guard against personal, financial, social, organizational, or political factors that might lead to misuse of their influence.

1.16 Misuse of Psychologists' Work

(a) Psychologists do not participate in activities in which it appears likely that their skills or data will be misused by others, unless corrective mechanisms are available. (See also Standard 7.04, Truthfulness and Candor.)

(b) If psychologists learn of misuse or misrepresentation of their work, they take reasonable steps to correct or minimize the misuse or misrepresentation.

1.17 Multiple Relationships

(a) In many communities and situations, it may not be feasible or reasonable for psychologists to avoid social or other nonprofessional contacts with persons such as patients, clients, students, supervisees, or research participants. Psychologists must always be sensitive to the potential harmful effects of other contacts on their work and on those persons with whom they deal. A psychologist refrains from entering into or promising another personal, scientific, professional, financial, or other relationship with such persons if it appears likely that such a relationship reasonably might impair the psychologist's objectivity or otherwise interfere with the

psychologist's effectively performing his or her function as a psychologist, or might harm or exploit the other party.

(b) Likewise, whenever feasible, a psychologist refrains from taking on professional or scientific obligations when preexisting relationships would create a risk of such harm.

(c) If a psychologist finds that, due to unforeseen factors, a potentially harmful multiple relationship has arisen, the psychologist attempts to resolve it with due regard for the best interests of the affected person and maximal compliance with the Ethics Code.

1.18 Barter (With Patients or Clients)

Psychologists ordinarily refrain from accepting goods, services, or other nonmonetary remuneration from patients or clients in return for psychological services because such arrangements create inherent potential for conflicts, exploitation, and distortion of the professional relationship. A psychologist may participate in bartering *only* if (1) it is not clinically contraindicated, *and* (2) the relationship is not exploitative. (See also Standards 1.17, Multiple Relationships, and 1.25, Fees and Financial Arrangements.)

1.19 Exploitative Relationships

(a) Psychologists do not exploit persons over whom they have supervisory, evaluative, or other authority such as students, supervisees, employees, research participants, and clients or patients. (See also Standards 4.05–4.07 regarding sexual involvement with clients or patients.)

(b) Psychologists do not engage in sexual relationships with students or supervisees in training over whom the psychologist has evaluative or direct authority, because such relationships are so likely to impair judgment or be exploitative.

1.20 Consultations and Referrals

(a) Psychologists arrange for appropriate consultations and referrals based principally on the best interests of their patients or clients, with appropriate consent, and subject to other relevant considerations, including applicable law and contractual obligations. (See also Standards 5.01, Discussing the Limits of Confidentiality, and 5.06, Consultations.)

(b) When indicated and professionally appropriate, psychologists cooperate with other professionals in order to serve their patients or clients effectively and appropriately.

(c) Psychologists' referral practices are consistent with law.

1.21 Third-Party Requests for Services

(a) When a psychologist agrees to provide services to a person or entity at the request of a third party, the psychologist clarifies to the extent feasible, at the outset of the service, the nature of the relationship with each party. This clarification includes the role of the psychologist (such as therapist, organizational consultant, diagnostician, or expert witness), the probable uses of the services provided or the information obtained, and the fact that there may be limits to confidentiality.

(b) If there is a foreseeable risk of the psychologist's being called upon to perform conflicting roles because of the involvement of a third party, the psychologist clarifies the nature and direction of his or her responsibilities, keeps all parties appropriately informed as matters develop, and resolves the situation in accordance with this Ethics Code.

1.22 Delegation to and Supervision of Subordinates

(a) Psychologists delegate to their employees, supervisees, and research assistants only those responsibilities that such persons can reasonably be expected to perform competently, on the basis of their education, training, or experience, either independently or with the level of supervision being provided.

(b) Psychologists provide proper training and supervision to their employees or supervisees and take reasonable steps to see that such persons perform services responsibly, competently, and ethically.

(c) If institutional policies, procedures, or practices prevent fulfillment of this obligation, psychologists attempt to modify their role or to correct the situation to the extent feasible.

1.23 Documentation of Professional and Scientific Work

(a) Psychologists appropriately document their professional and scientific work in order to facilitate provision of services later by them or by other professionals, to ensure accountability, and to meet other requirements of institutions or the law.

(b) When psychologists have reason to believe that records of their professional services will be used in legal proceedings involving recipients of or participants in their work, they have a responsibility to create and maintain documentation in the kind of detail and quality that would be consistent with reasonable scrutiny in an adjudicative forum. (See also Standard 7.01, Professionalism, under Forensic Activities.)

1.24 Records and Data

Psychologists create, maintain, disseminate, store, retain, and dispose of records and data relating to their research, practice, and other work in accordance with law and in a manner that permits compliance with the requirements of this Ethics Code. (See also Standard 5.04, Maintenance of Records.)

1.25 Fees and Financial Arrangements

(a) As early as is feasible in a professional or scientific relationship, the psychologist and the patient, client, or other appropriate recipient of psychological services reach an agreement specifying the compensation and the billing arrangements.

(b) Psychologists do not exploit recipients of services or payors with respect to fees.

(c) Psychologists' fee practices are consistent with law.

(d) Psychologists do not misrepresent their fees.

(e) If limitations to services can be anticipated because of limitations in financing, this is discussed with the patient, client, or other appropriate recipient of services as early as is feasible. (See also Standard 4.08, Interruption of Services.)

(f) If the patient, client, or other recipient of services does not pay for services as agreed, and if the psychologist wishes to use collection agencies or legal measures to collect the fees, the psychologist first informs the person that such measures will be taken and provides that person an opportunity to make prompt payment. (See also Standard 5.11, Withholding Records for Nonpayment.)

1.26 Accuracy in Reports to Payors and Funding Sources

In their reports to payors for services or sources of research funding, psychologists accurately state the nature of the research or service provided, the fees or charges, and where applicable, the identity of the provider, the findings, and the diagnosis. (See also Standard 5.05, Disclosures.)

1.27 Referrals and Fees

When a psychologist pays, receives payment from, or divides fees with another professional other than in an employer–employee relationship, the payment to each is based on the services (clinical, consultative, administrative, or other) provided and is not based on the referral itself.

2. Evaluation, Assessment, or Intervention
2.01 Evaluation, Diagnosis, and Interventions in Professional Context

(a) Psychologists perform evaluations, diagnosis services, or interventions only within the context of a defined professional relationship. (See also Standard 1.03, Professional and Scientific Relationship.)

(b) Psychologists' assessments, recommendations, reports, and psychological diagnostic or evaluative statements are based on information and techniques (including personal interviews of the individual when appropriate) sufficient to provide appropriate substantiation for their findings. (See also Standard 7.02, Forensic Assessments.)

2.02 Competence and Appropriate Use of Assessments and Interventions

(a) Psychologists who develop, administer, score, interpret, or use psychological assessment techniques, interviews, tests, or instruments do so in a manner and for purposes that are appropriate in light of the research on or evidence of the usefulness and proper application of the techniques.

(b) Psychologists refrain from misuse of assessment techniques, interventions, results, and interpretations and take reasonable steps to prevent others

from misusing the information these techniques provide. This includes refraining from releasing raw test results or raw data to persons, other than to patients or clients as appropriate, who are not qualified to use such information. (See also Standards 1.02, Relationship of Ethics and Law, and 1.04, Boundaries of Competence.)

2.03 Test Construction

Psychologists who develop and conduct research with tests and other assessment techniques use specific procedures and current professional knowledge for test design, standardization, validation, reduction or elimination of bias, and recommendations for use.

2.04 Use of Assessment in General and With Special Populations

(a) Psychologists who perform interventions or administer, score, interpret, or use assessment techniques are familiar with the reliability, validation, and related standardization or outcome studies of, and proper applications and uses of, the techniques they use.

(b) Psychologists recognize limits to the certainty with which diagnoses, judgments, or predictions can be made about individuals.

(c) Psychologists attempt to identify situations in which particular interventions or assessment techniques or norms may not be applicable or may require adjustment in administration or interpretation because of factors such as individuals' gender, age, race, ethnicity, national origin, religion, sexual orientation, disability, language, or socioeconomic status.

2.05 Interpreting Assessment Results

When interpreting assessment results, including automated interpretations, psychologists take into account the various test factors and characteristics of the person being assessed that might affect psychologists' judgments or reduce the accuracy of their interpretations. They indicate any significant reservations they have about the accuracy or limitations of their interpretations.

2.06 Unqualified Persons

Psychologists do not promote the use of psychological assessment techniques by unqualified persons.

(See also Standard 1.22, Delegation to and Supervision of Subordinates.)

2.07 Obsolete Tests and Outdated Test Results

(a) Psychologists do not base their assessment or intervention decisions or recommendations on data or test results that are outdated for the current purpose.

(b) Similarly, psychologists do not base such decisions or recommendations on tests and measures that are obsolete and not useful for the current purpose.

2.08 Test Scoring and Interpretation Services

(a) Psychologists who offer assessment or scoring procedures to other professionals accurately describe the purpose, norms, validity, reliability, and applications of the procedures and any special qualifications applicable to their use.

(b) Psychologists select scoring and interpretation services (including automated services) on the basis of evidence of the validity of the program and procedures as well as on other appropriate considerations.

(c) Psychologists retain appropriate responsibility for the appropriate application, interpretation, and use of assessment instruments, whether they score and interpret such tests themselves or use automated or other services.

2.09 Explaining Assessment Results

Unless the nature of the relationship is clearly explained to the person being assessed in advance and precludes provision of an explanation of results (such as in some organizational consulting, preemployment or security screenings, and forensic evaluations), psychologists ensure that an explanation of the results is provided using language that is reasonably understandable to the person assessed or to another legally authorized person on behalf of the client. Regardless of whether the scoring and interpretation are done by the psychologist, by assistants, or by automated or other outside services, psychologists take reasonable steps to ensure that appropriate explanations of results are given.

2.10 Maintaining Test Security

Psychologists make reasonable efforts to maintain the integrity and security of tests and other assessment techniques consistent with law, contractual obligations, and in a manner that permits compliance with the requirements of this Ethics Code. (See also Standard 1.02, Relationship of Ethics and Law.)

3. Advertising and Other Public Statements
3.01 Definition of Public Statements

Psychologists comply with this Ethics Code in public statements relating to their professional services, products, or publications or to the field of psychology. Public statements include but are not limited to paid or unpaid advertising, brochures, printed matter, directory listings, personal resumes or curricula vitae, interviews or comments for use in media, statements in legal proceedings, lectures and public oral presentations, and published materials.

3.02 Statements by Others

(a) Psychologists who engage others to create or place public statements that promote their professional practice, products, or activities retain professional responsibility for such statements.

(b) In addition, psychologists make reasonable efforts to prevent others whom they do not control (such as employers, publishers, sponsors, organizational clients, and representatives of the print or broadcast media) from making deceptive statements concerning psychologists' practice or professional or scientific activities.

(c) If psychologists learn of deceptive statements about their work made by others, psychologists make reasonable efforts to correct such statements.

(d) Psychologists do not compensate employees of press, radio, television, or other communication media in return for publicity in a news item.

(e) A paid advertisement relating to the psychologist's activities must be identified as such, unless it is already apparent from the context.

3.03 Avoidance of False or Deceptive Statements

(a) Psychologists do not make public statements that are false, deceptive, misleading, or fraudulent, either because of what they state, convey, or suggest or because of what they omit, concerning their research, practice, or other work activities or those of persons or organizations with which they are affiliated. As examples (and not in limitation) of this standard, psychologists do not make false or deceptive statements concerning (1) their training, experience, or competence; (2) their academic degrees; (3) their credentials; (4) their institutional or association affiliations; (5) their services; (6) the scientific or clinical basis for, or results or degree of success of, their services; (7) their fees; or (8) their publications or research findings. (See also Standards 6.15, Deception in Research, and 6.18, Providing Participants With Information About the Study.)

(b) Psychologists claim as credentials for their psychological work, only degrees that (1) were earned from a regionally accredited educational institution or (2) were the basis for psychology licensure by the state in which they practice.

3.04 Media Presentations

When psychologists provide advice or comment by means of public lectures, demonstrations, radio or television programs, prerecorded tapes, printed articles, mailed material, or other media, they take reasonable precautions to ensure that (1) the statements are based on appropriate psychological literature and practice, (2) the statements are otherwise consistent with this Ethics Code, and (3) the recipients of the information are not encouraged to infer that a relationship has been established with them personally.

3.05 Testimonials

Psychologists do not solicit testimonials from current psychotherapy clients or patients or other persons who because of their particular circumstances are vulnerable to undue influence.

3.06 In-Person Solicitation

Psychologists do not engage, directly or through agents, in uninvited in-person solicitation of business from actual or potential psychotherapy patients or clients or other persons who because of their particular circumstances are vulnerable to undue influence. However, this does not preclude attempting to implement appropriate collateral contacts with signif-

icant others for the purpose of benefiting an already engaged therapy patient.

4. Therapy
4.01 Structuring the Relationship

(a) Psychologists discuss with clients or patients as early as is feasible in the therapeutic relationship appropriate issues, such as the nature and anticipated course of therapy, fees, and confidentiality. (See also Standards 1.25, Fees and Financial Arrangements, and 5.01, Discussing the Limits of Confidentiality.)

(b) When the psychologist's work with clients or patients will be supervised, the above discussion includes that fact, and the name of the supervisor, when the supervisor has legal responsibility for the case.

(c) When the therapist is a student intern, the client or patient is informed of that fact.

(d) Psychologists make reasonable efforts to answer patients' questions and to avoid apparent misunderstandings about therapy. Whenever possible, psychologists provide oral and/or written information, using language that is reasonably understandable to the patient or client.

4.02 Informed Consent to Therapy

(a) Psychologists obtain appropriate informed consent to therapy or related procedures, using language that is reasonably understandable to participants. The content of informed consent will vary depending on many circumstances; however, informed consent generally implies that the person (1) has the capacity to consent, (2) has been informed of significant information concerning the procedure, (3) has freely and without undue influence expressed consent, and (4) consent has been appropriately documented.

(b) When persons are legally incapable of giving informed consent, psychologists obtain informed permission from a legally authorized person, if such substitute consent is permitted by law.

(c) In addition, psychologists (1) inform those persons who are legally incapable of giving informed consent about the proposed interventions in a manner commensurate with the persons' psychological capacities, (2) seek their assent to those interventions, and (3) consider such persons' preferences and best interests.

4.03 Couple and Family Relationships

(a) When a psychologist agrees to provide services to several persons who have a relationship (such as husband and wife or parents and children), the psychologist attempts to clarify at the outset (1) which of the individuals are patients or clients and (2) the relationship the psychologist will have with each person. This clarification includes the role of the psychologist and the probable uses of the services provided or the information obtained. (See also Standard 5.01, Discussing the Limits of Confidentiality.)

(b) As soon as it becomes apparent that the psychologist may be called on to perform potentially conflicting roles (such as marital counselor to husband and wife, and then witness for one party in a divorce proceeding), the psychologist attempts to clarify and adjust, or withdraw from, roles appropriately. (See also Standard 7.03, Clarification of Role, under Forensic Activities.)

4.04 Providing Mental Health Services to Those Served by Others

In deciding whether to offer or provide services to those already receiving mental health services elsewhere, psychologists carefully consider the treatment issues and the potential patient's or client's welfare. The psychologist discusses these issues with the patient or client, or another legally authorized person on behalf of the client, in order to minimize the risk of confusion and conflict, consults with the other service providers when appropriate, and proceeds with caution and sensitivity to the therapeutic issues.

4.05 Sexual Intimacies With Current Patients or Clients

Psychologists do not engage in sexual intimacies with current patients or clients.

4.06 Therapy With Former Sexual Partners

Psychologists do not accept as therapy patients or clients persons with whom they have engaged in sexual intimacies.

4.07 Sexual Intimacies With Former Therapy Patients

(a) Psychologists do not engage in sexual intimacies with a former therapy patient or client for at least two years after cessation or termination of professional services.

(b) Because sexual intimacies with a former therapy patient or client are so frequently harmful to the patient or client, and because such intimacies undermine public confidence in the psychology profession and thereby deter the public's use of needed services, psychologists do not engage in sexual intimacies with former therapy patients and clients even after a two-year interval except in the most unusual circumstances. The psychologist who engages in such activity after two years following cessation or termination of treatment bears the burden of demonstrating that there has been no exploitation, in light of all relevant factors, including (1) the amount of time that has passed since therapy terminated, (2) the nature and duration of the therapy, (3) the circumstances of termination, (4) the patient's or client's personal history, (5) the patient's or client's current mental status, (6) the likelihood of adverse impact on the patient or client and others, and (7) any statements or actions made by the therapist during the course of therapy suggesting or inviting the possibility of a posttermination sexual or romantic relationship with the patient or client. (See also Standard 1.17, Multiple Relationships.)

4.08 Interruption of Services

(a) Psychologists make reasonable efforts to plan for facilitating care in the event that psychological services are interrupted by factors such as the psychologist's illness, death, unavailability, or relocation or by the client's relocation or financial limitations. (See also Standard 5.09, Preserving Records and Data.)

(b) When entering into employment or contractual relationships, psychologists provide for orderly and appropriate resolution of responsibility for patient or client care in the event that the employment or contractual relationship ends, with paramount consideration given to the welfare of the patient or client.

4.09 Terminating the Professional Relationship

(a) Psychologists do not abandon patients or clients. (See also Standard 1.25e, under Fees and Financial Arrangements.)

(b) Psychologists terminate a professional relationship when it becomes reasonably clear that the patient or client no longer needs the service, is not benefiting, or is being harmed by continued service.

(c) Prior to termination for whatever reason, except where precluded by the patient's or client's conduct, the psychologist discusses the patient's or client's views and needs, provides appropriate pre-termination counseling, suggests alternative service providers as appropriate, and takes other reasonable steps to facilitate transfer of responsibility to another provider if the patient or client needs one immediately.

5. Privacy and Confidentiality

These Standards are potentially applicable to the professional and scientific activities of all psychologists.

5.01 Discussing the Limits of Confidentiality

(a) Psychologists discuss with persons and organizations with whom they establish a scientific, or professional relationship (including, to the extent feasible, minors and their legal representatives) (1) the relevant limitations on confidentiality, including limitations where applicable in group, marital, and family therapy or in organizational consulting, and (2) the foreseeable uses of the information generated through their services.

(b) Unless it is not feasible or is contraindicated, the discussion of confidentiality occurs at the outset of the relationship and thereafter as new circumstances may warrant.

(c) Permission for electronic recording of interviews is secured from clients and patients.

5.02 Maintaining Confidentiality

Psychologists have a primary obligation and take reasonable precautions to respect the confidentiality rights of those with whom they work or consult, recognizing that confidentiality may be established by law, institutional rules, or professional or scientific relationships. (See also Standard 6.26, Professional Reviewers.)

5.03 Minimizing Intrusions on Privacy

(a) In order to minimize intrusions on privacy, psychologists include in written and oral reports, consultations, and the like, only information germane to the purpose for which the communication is made.

(b) Psychologists discuss confidential information obtained in clinical or consulting relationships, or evaluative data concerning patients, individual or organizational clients, students, research participants, supervisees, and employees, only for appropriate scientific or professional purposes and only with persons clearly concerned with such matters.

5.04 Maintenance of Records

Psychologists maintain appropriate confidentiality in creating, storing, accessing, transferring, and disposing of records under their control, whether these are written, automated, or in any other medium. Psychologists maintain and dispose of records in accordance with law and in a manner that permits compliance with the requirements of this Ethics Code.

5.05 Disclosures

(a) Psychologists disclose confidential information without the consent of the individual only as mandated by law, or where permitted by law for a valid purpose, such as (1) to provide needed professional services to the patient or the individual or organizational client, (2) to obtain appropriate professional consultations, (3) to protect the patient or client or others from harm, or (4) to obtain payment for services, in which instance disclosure is limited to the minimum that is necessary to achieve the purpose.

(b) Psychologists also may disclose confidential information with the appropriate consent of the patient or the individual or organizational client (or of another legally authorized person on behalf of the patient or client), unless prohibited by law.

5.06 Consultations

When consulting with colleagues, (1) psychologists do not share confidential information that reasonably could lead to the identification of a patient, client, research participant, or other person or organization with whom they have a confidential relationship unless they have obtained the prior consent of the person or organization or the disclosure cannot be avoided, and (2) they share information only to the extent necessary to achieve the purposes of the consultation. (See also Standard 5.02, Maintaining Confidentiality.)

5.07 Confidential Information in Databases

(a) If confidential information concerning recipients of psychological services is to be entered into databases or systems of records available to persons whose access has not been consented to by the recipient, then psychologists use coding or other techniques to avoid the inclusion of personal identifiers.

(b) If a research protocol approved by an institutional review board or similar body requires the inclusion of personal identifiers, such identifiers are deleted before the information is made accessible to persons other than those of whom the subject was advised.

(c) If such deletion is not feasible, then before psychologists transfer such data to others or review such data collected by others, they take reasonable steps to determine that appropriate consent of personally identifiable individuals has been obtained.

5.08 Use of Confidential Information for Didactic or Other Purposes

(a) Psychologists do not disclose in their writings, lectures, or other public media, confidential, personally identifiable information concerning their patients, individual or organizational clients, students, research participants, or other recipients of their services that they obtained during the course of their work, unless the person or organization has consented in writing or unless there is other ethical or legal authorization for doing so.

(b) Ordinarily, in such scientific and professional presentations, psychologists disguise confidential information concerning such persons or organizations so that they are not individually identifiable to others and so that discussions do not cause harm to subjects who might identify themselves.

5.09 Preserving Records and Data

A psychologist makes plans in advance so that confidentiality of records and data is protected in the event of the psychologist's death, incapacity, or withdrawal from the position or practice.

5.10 Ownership of Records and Data

Recognizing that ownership of records and data is governed by legal principles, psychologists take reasonable and lawful steps so that records and data remain available to the extent needed to serve the best interests of patients, individual or organizational clients, research participants, or appropriate others.

5.11 Withholding Records for Nonpayment

Psychologists may not withhold records under their control that are requested and imminently needed for a patient's or client's treatment solely because payment has not been received, except as otherwise provided by law.

6. Teaching, Training Supervision, Research, and Publishing
6.01 Design of Education and Training Programs

Psychologists who are responsible for education and training programs seek to ensure that the programs are competently designed, provide the proper experiences, and meet the requirements for licensure, certification, or other goals for which claims are made by the program.

6.02 Descriptions of Education and Training Programs

(a) Psychologists responsible for education and training programs seek to ensure that there is a current and accurate description of the program content, training goals and objectives, and requirements that must be met for satisfactory completion of the program. This information must be made readily available to all interested parties.

(b) Psychologists seek to ensure that statements concerning their course outlines are accurate and not misleading, particularly regarding the subject matter to be covered, bases for evaluating progress, and the nature of course experiences. (See also Standard 3.03, Avoidance of False or Deceptive Statements.)

(c) To the degree to which they exercise control, psychologists responsible for announcements, catalogs, brochures, or advertisements describing workshops, seminars, or other non-degree-granting educational programs ensure that they accurately describe the audience for which the program is intended, the educational objectives, the presenters, and the fees involved.

6.03 Accuracy and Objectivity in Teaching

(a) When engaged in teaching or training, psychologists present psychological information accurately and with a reasonable degree of objectivity.

(b) When engaged in teaching or training, psychologists recognize the power they hold over students or supervisees and therefore make reasonable efforts to avoid engaging in conduct that is personally demeaning to students or supervisees. (See also Standards 1.09, Respecting Others, and 1.12, Other Harassment.)

6.04 Limitation on Teaching

Psychologists do not teach the use of techniques or procedures that require specialized training, licensure, or expertise, including but not limited to hypnosis, biofeedback, and projective techniques, to individuals who lack the prerequisite training, legal scope of practice, or expertise.

6.05 Assessing Student and Supervisee Performance

(a) In academic and supervisory relationships, psychologists establish an appropriate process for providing feedback to students and supervisees.

(b) Psychologists evaluate students and supervisees on the basis of their actual performance on relevant and established program requirements.

6.06 Planning Research

(a) Psychologists design, conduct, and report research in accordance with recognized standards of scientific competence and ethical research.

(b) Psychologists plan their research so as to minimize the possibility that results will be misleading.

(c) In planning research, psychologists consider its ethical acceptability under the Ethics Code. If an ethical issue is unclear, psychologists seek to resolve the issue through consultation with institutional review boards, animal care and use committees, peer consultations, or other proper mechanisms.

(d) Psychologists take responsible steps to implement appropriate protections for the rights and welfare of human participants, other persons affected by the research, and the welfare of animal subjects.

6.07 Responsibility

(a) Psychologists conduct research competently and with due concern for the dignity and welfare of the participants.

(b) Psychologists are responsible for the ethical conduct of research conducted by them or by others under their supervision or control.

(c) Researchers and assistants are permitted to perform only those tasks for which they are appropriately trained and prepared.

(d) As part of the process of development and implementation of research projects, psychologists consult those with expertise concerning any special population under investigation or most likely to be affected.

6.08 Compliance With Law and Standards

Psychologists plan and conduct research in a manner consistent with federal and state law and regulations, as well as professional standards governing the conduct of research, and particularly those standards governing research with human participants and animal subjects.

6.09 Institutional Approval

Psychologists obtain from host institutions or organizations appropriate approval prior to conducting research, and they provide accurate information about their research proposals. They conduct the research in accordance with the approved research protocol.

6.10 Research Responsibilities

Prior to conducting research (except research involving only anonymous surveys, naturalistic observations, or similar research), psychologists enter into an agreement with participants that clarifies the nature of the research and the responsibilities of each party.

6.11 Informed Consent to Research

(a) Psychologists use language that is reasonably understandable to research participants in obtaining their appropriate informed consent (except as provided in Standard 6.12, Dispensing With Informed Consent). Such informed consent is appropriately documented.

(b) Using language that is reasonably understandable to participants, psychologists inform participants of the nature of the research; they inform participants that they are free to participate or to decline to participate or to withdraw from the research; they explain the foreseeable consequences of declining or withdrawing; they inform participants of significant factors that may be expected to influence their willingness to participate (such as risks, discomfort, adverse effects, or limitations on confidentiality, except as provided in Standard 6.15, Deception in Research); and they explain other aspects about which the prospective participants inquire.

(c) When psychologists conduct research with individuals such as students or subordinates, psychologists take special care to protect the prospective participants from adverse consequences of declining or withdrawing from participation.

(d) When research participation is a course requirement or opportunity for extra credit, the prospective participant is given the choice of equitable alternative activities.

(e) For persons who are legally incapable of giving informed consent, psychologists nevertheless (1) provide an appropriate explanation, (2) obtain the participant's assent, and (3) obtain appropriate permission from a legally authorized person, if such substitute consent is permitted by law.

6.12 Dispensing With Informed Consent

Before determining that planned research (such as research involving only anonymous questionnaires, naturalistic observations, or certain kinds of archival research) does not require the informed consent of research participants, psychologists consider applicable regulations and institutional review board re-

quirements, and they consult with colleagues as appropriate.

6.13 Informed Consent in Research Filming or Recording

Psychologists obtain informed consent from research participants prior to filming or recording them in any form, unless the research involves simply naturalistic observations in public places and it is not anticipated that the recording will be used in a manner that could cause personal identification or harm.

6.14 Offering Inducement for Research Participants

(a) In offering professional services as an inducement to obtain research participants, psychologists make clear the nature of the services, as well as the risks, obligations, and limitations. (See also Standard 1.18, Barter [With Patients or Clients].)

(b) Psychologists do not offer excessive or inappropriate financial or other inducements to obtain research participants, particularly when it might tend to coerce participation.

6.15 Deception in Research

(a) Psychologists do not conduct a study involving deception unless they have determined that the use of deceptive techniques is justified by the study's prospective scientific, educational, or applied value and that equally effective alternative procedures that do not use deception are not feasible.

(b) Psychologists never deceive research participants about significant aspects that would affect their willingness to participate, such as physical risks, discomfort, or unpleasant emotional experiences.

(c) Any other deception that is an integral feature of the design and conduct of an experiment must be explained to participants as early as is feasible, preferably at the conclusion of their participation, but no later than at the conclusion of the research. (See also Standard 6.18, Providing Participants With Information About the Study.)

6.16 Sharing and Utilizing Data

Psychologists inform research participants of their anticipated sharing or further use of personally identifiable research data and of the possibility of unanticipated future uses.

6.17 Minimizing Invasiveness

In conducting research, psychologists interfere with the participants or milieu from which data are collected only in a manner that is warranted by an appropriate research design and that is consistent with psychologists' roles as scientific investigators.

6.18 Providing Participants With Information About the Study

(a) Psychologists provide a prompt opportunity for participants to obtain appropriate information about the nature, results, and conclusions of the research, and psychologists attempt to correct any misconceptions that participants may have.

(b) If scientific or humane values justify delaying or withholding this information, psychologists take reasonable measures to reduce the risk of harm.

6.19 Honoring Commitments

Psychologists take reasonable measures to honor all commitments they have made to research participants.

6.20 Care and Use of Animals in Research

(a) Psychologists who conduct research involving animals treat them humanely.

(b) Psychologists acquire, care for, use, and dispose of animals in compliance with current federal, state, and local laws and regulations, and with professional standards.

(c) Psychologists trained in research methods and experienced in the care of laboratory animals supervise all procedures involving animals and are responsible for ensuring appropriate consideration of their comfort, health, and humane treatment.

(d) Psychologists ensure that all individuals using animals under their supervision have received instruction in research methods and in the care, maintenance, and handling of the species being used, to the extent appropriate to their role.

(e) Responsibilities and activities of individuals assisting in a research project are consistent with their respective competencies.

(f) Psychologists make reasonable efforts to minimize the discomfort, infection, illness, and pain of animal subjects.

(g) A procedure subjecting animals to pain, stress, or privation is used only when an alternative procedure is unavailable and the goal is justified by its prospective scientific, educational, or applied value.

(h) Surgical procedures are performed under appropriate anesthesia; techniques to avoid infection and minimize pain are followed during and after surgery.

(i) When it is appropriate that the animal's life be terminated, it is done rapidly, with an effort to minimize pain, and in accordance with accepted procedures.

6.21 Reporting of Results

(a) Psychologists do not fabricate data or falsify results in their publications.

(b) If psychologists discover significant errors in their published data, they take reasonable steps to correct such errors in a correction, retraction, erratum, or other appropriate publication means.

6.22 Plagiarism

Psychologists do not present substantial portions or elements of another's work or data as their own, even if the other work or data source is cited occasionally.

6.23 Publication Credit

(a) Psychologists take responsibility and credit, including authorship credit, only for work they have actually performed or to which they have contributed.

(b) Principal authorship and other publication credits accurately reflect the relative scientific or professional contributions of the individuals involved, regardless of their relative status. Mere possession of an institutional position, such as Department Chair, does not justify authorship credit. Minor contributions to the research or to the writing for publications are appropriately acknowledged, such as in footnotes or in an introductory statement.

(c) A student is usually listed as principal author on any multiple-authored article that is substantially based on the student's dissertation or thesis.

6.24 Duplicate Publication of Data

Psychologists do not publish, as original data, data that have been previously published. This does not preclude republishing data when they are accompanied by proper acknowledgment.

6.25 Sharing Data

After research results are published, psychologists do not withhold the data on which their conclusions are based from other competent professionals who seek to verify the substantive claims through reanalysis and who intend to use such data only for that purpose, provided that the confidentiality of the participants can be protected and unless legal rights concerning proprietary data preclude their release.

6.26 Professional Reviewers

Psychologists who review material submitted for publication, grant, or other research proposal review respect the confidentiality of and the proprietary rights in such information of those who submitted it.

7. Forensic Activities
7.01 Professionalism

Psychologists who perform forensic functions, such as assessments, interviews, consultations, reports, or expert testimony, must comply with all other provisions of this Ethics Code to the extent that they apply to such activities. In addition, psychologists base their forensic work on appropriate knowledge of and competence in the areas underlying such work, including specialized knowledge concerning special populations. (See also Standards 1.06, Basis for Scientific and Professional Judgments; 1.08, Human Differences; 1.15, Misuse of Psychologists' Influence; and 1.23, Documentation of Professional and Scientific Work.)

7.02 Forensic Assessments

(a) Psychologists' forensic assessments, recommendations, and reports are based on information and techniques (including personal interviews of the individual, when appropriate) sufficient to provide appropriate substantiation for their findings. (See also Standards 1.03, Professional and Scientific Relationship; 1.23, Documentation of Professional and

Scientific Work; 2.01, Evaluation, Diagnosis, and Interventions in Professional Context; and 2.05, Interpreting Assessment Results.)

(b) Except as noted in (c), below, psychologists provide written or oral forensic reports or testimony of the psychological characteristics of an individual only after they have conducted an examination of the individual adequate to support their statements or conclusions.

(c) When, despite reasonable efforts, such an examination is not feasible, psychologists clarify the impact of their limited information on the reliability and validity of their reports and testimony, and they appropriately limit the nature and extent of their conclusions or recommendations.

7.03 Clarification of Role

In most circumstances, psychologists avoid performing multiple and potentially conflicting roles in forensic matters. When psychologists may be called on to serve in more than one role in a legal proceeding—for example, as consultant or expert for one party or for the court and as a fact witness—they clarify role expectations and the extent of confidentiality in advance to the extent feasible, and thereafter as changes occur, in order to avoid compromising their professional judgment and objectivity and in order to avoid misleading others regarding their role.

7.04 Truthfulness and Candor

(a) In forensic testimony and reports, psychologists testify truthfully, honestly, and candidly and, consistent with applicable legal procedures, describe fairly the bases for their testimony and conclusions.

(b) Whenever necessary to avoid misleading, psychologists acknowledge the limits of their data or conclusions.

7.05 Prior Relationships

A prior professional relationship with a party does not preclude psychologists from testifying as fact witnesses or from testifying to their services to the extent permitted by applicable law. Psychologists appropriately take into account ways in which the prior relationship might affect their professional objectivity or opinions and disclose the potential conflict to the relevant parties.

7.06 Compliance With Law and Rules

In performing forensic roles, psychologists are reasonably familiar with the rules governing their roles. Psychologists are aware of the occasionally competing demands placed upon them by these principles and the requirements of the court system, and attempt to resolve these conflicts by making known their commitment to this Ethics Code and taking steps to resolve the conflict in a responsible manner. (See also Standard 1.02, Relationship of Ethics and Law.)

8. Resolving Ethical Issues
8.01 Familiarity With Ethics Code

Psychologists have an obligation to be familiar with this Ethics Code, other applicable ethics codes, and their application to psychologists' work. Lack of awareness or misunderstanding of an ethical standard is not itself a defense to a charge of unethical conduct.

8.02 Confronting Ethical Issues

When a psychologist is uncertain whether a particular situation or course of action would violate this Ethics Code, the psychologist ordinarily consults with other psychologists knowledgeable about ethical issues, with state or national psychology ethics committees, or with other appropriate authorities in order to choose a proper response.

8.03 Conflicts Between Ethics and Organizational Demands

If the demands of an organization with which psychologists are affiliated conflict with this Ethics Code, psychologists clarify the nature of the conflict, make known their commitment to the Ethics Code, and to the extent feasible, seek to resolve the conflict in a way that permits the fullest adherence to the Ethics Code.

8.04 Informal Resolution of Ethical Violations

When psychologists believe that there may have been an ethical violation by another psychologist, they attempt to resolve the issue by bringing it to the attention of that individual if an informal resolution appears appropriate and the intervention does not violate any confidentiality rights that may be involved.

8.05 Reporting Ethical Violations

If an apparent ethical violation is not appropriate for informal resolution under Standard 8.04 or is not resolved properly in that fashion, psychologists take further action appropriate to the situation, unless such action conflicts with confidentiality rights in ways that cannot be resolved. Such action might include referral to state or national committees on professional ethics or to state licensing boards.

8.06 Cooperating With Ethics Committees

Psychologists cooperate in ethics investigations, proceedings, and resulting requirements of the APA or any affiliated state psychological association to which they belong. In doing so, they make reasonable efforts to resolve any issues as to confidentiality. Failure to cooperate is itself an ethics violation.

8.07 Improper Complaints

Psychologists do not file or encourage the filing of ethics complaints that are frivolous and are intended to harm the respondent rather than to protect the public.

◆ ◆ ◆

Commentary: There is little doubt that the 1981 and 1989 APA ethical principles needed changing. Although they were serviceable and clear in some respects, many of their provisions were ambiguous. In fact, application of this code was challenged by a clinician who was disciplined by his state licensure board. In that 1990 case,[1] the board voted to revoke the psychologist's license to practice for violating the 1981 Ethical Principles of Psychologists. Such action is not atypical: Many state laws regulating psychologists incorporate the APA ethics code. Where this is true, if a licensed psychologist violates

---

[1]White v. North Carolina State Board of Examiners of Practicing Psychologists, 97 N.C. App. 144, 388 S.E. 2d 148 (1990), *review denied*, 326 N.C. 601, 393 S.E. 2d 891 (1990).

APA ethical principles, then he or she is subject to disciplinary action by the relevant state board. The most severe form of discipline is revocation of the license to practice, a sanction with serious economic consequences. Because of the magnitude of the board's decision, the psychologist filed a complaint against the board in state court, claiming that the various enforceable preambles and principles under which he was charged were unconstitutionally vague and did not provide him with proper notice of potential misconduct. Essentially, he alleged that, under the state and federal constitutions, it was fundamentally unfair for the state to deprive him of his right to practice on the basis of standards that were not comprehensible to the reasonably intelligent psychologist.

With regard to the preambles to various principles in the 1981 code, the court agreed. Their language, the court held, failed to inform licensees of what conduct was forbidden. Although it rejected the psychologist's claim that the specific principles under which he was charged were also unconstitutional, the court stated:

> Psychologists ... have a right and fundamental need to be guided by Ethical Codes of Conduct of sufficient clarity and specificity to meet applicable constitutional standards and to adequately apprise practitioners of the boundaries of conduct. While we have concluded that those Prin-

ciples in question meet such standards, suffice it to say that for the most part it is by the slimmest of margins. (White v. North Carolina State Board, 1990)

Such indeterminancy showed the ethics code to be a disservice to organized psychology and its members. Thus, the planned revision was awaited with great and positive anticipation.

The 1992 code was reviewed by a number of respected psychologists with experience in ethics in a special section of an APA journal. See Keith-Spiegel, P. (Ed.). (1994). The 1992 ethics code: Boon or bane? Professional Psychology: Research and Practice, 25, 315–387. Whether from the perspective of science, practice, or public interest, most of the commentators applauded the broadened and specific attention in the new code to important issues. But they also found that, in many respects, the new code lacked clarity, contained qualifying language that may make many provisions difficult to enforce, and may not completely fulfill its mission of protecting the public (see chapter 2). As readers examine the Ethical Principles and address the particular issues represented in this book, they should come to their own conclusions about the usefulness of the new Code of Conduct.

The Canadian Psychological Association has also promulgated an ethics code. It is reproduced in the following pages.

Canadian Code of Ethics for Psychologists

Canadian Psychological Association

PREAMBLE

Structure and Derivation of Code

Structure. Four ethical principles, to be considered and balanced in ethical decision making, are presented. Each principle is followed by a statement of those values which are included in and give definition to the principle. Each values statement is followed by a list of ethical standards which illustrates the application of the specific principle and values to the activities of psychologists. The standards range from minimal behavioural expectations (e.g., Standards I.14, II.34, III.1, IV.24) to more idealized, but achievable, attitudinal and behavioural expectations (e.g., Standards I.16, II.10, III.10, IV.5)....

When Principles Conflict

All four principles are to be taken into account and balanced in ethical decision making. However, there are circumstances in which ethical principles will conflict and it will not be possible to give each principle equal weight.

The complexity of ethical conflicts precludes a firm ordering of the principles. However, the four principles have been ordered according to the weight each generally should be given when they conflict, namely:

Principle I: Respect for the Dignity of Persons. This principle, with its emphasis on moral rights, generally should be given the highest weight, except in circumstances in which there is a clear and imminent danger to the physical safety of any individual.

Principle II: Responsible Caring. This principle generally should be given the second highest weight. Responsible caring requires competence and should be carried out only in ways that respect the dignity of persons.

Principle III: Integrity in Relationships. This principle generally should be given the third highest weight. Psychologists are expected to demonstrate the highest integrity in all of their relationships. However, in rare circumstances, values such as openness and straightforwardness may need to be subordinated to the values contained in the Principles of Respect for the Dignity of Persons and Responsible Caring.

Principle IV: Responsibility to Society. This principle generally should be given the lowest weight of the four principles when it conflicts with one or more of them. Although it is necessary and important to consider responsibility to society in every ethical decision, adherence to this principle must be subject to and guided by Respect for the Dignity of Persons, Responsible Caring, and Integrity in Relationships. When individual welfare appears to conflict with benefits to society, it is often possible to find ways of working for the benefit of society which do not violate respect and responsible caring for individuals. However, if this is not possible, then greater weight must be given to individual welfare.

PRINCIPLE I: RESPECT FOR THE DIGNITY OF PERSONS

Values Statement

In the course of their work as scientists, practitioners, or scientist-practitioners, psychologists come into contact with many different individuals and groups, including: research participants; clients seeking help with personal, family, organizational, industrial or community issues; students; supervisees; employees; colleagues; employers; third-party payers; and, the general public.

In these contacts, psychologists accept as fundamental the principle of respect for the dignity of persons; that is, the belief that each person should be treated primarily as a person or an end in him/herself, not as an object or a means to an end. In so doing, psychologists acknowledge that all persons have a right to have their innate worth as human beings appreciated and that this worth is not enhanced or reduced by their culture, nationality, ethnicity, colour, race, religion, gender, marital status, sexual orientation, physical or mental abilities, age, socio-economic status, and/or any other preference or personal characteristic, condition, or status.

Although psychologists have a responsibility to respect the dignity of all persons with whom they come in contact in their role as psychologists, the nature of their contract with society demands that their greatest responsibility be to those persons directly receiving or involved in the psychologist's activities and, therefore, normally in a more vulnerable position (e.g., research participants, clients, students). This responsibility is almost always greater than their responsibility to those indirectly involved (e.g., employers, third-party payers, the general public).

Adherence to the concept of moral rights is an essential component of respect for the dignity of persons. Rights to privacy, self-determination, personal liberty, and natural justice are of particular importance to psychologists, and they have a responsibility to protect and promote these rights in all of their activities. As such, psychologists have a responsibility to develop and follow procedures for informed consent, confidentiality, fair treatment, and due process that are consistent with those rights.

As individual rights exist within the context of the rights of others and of responsible caring (see Principle II), there may be circumstances in which the possibility of serious detrimental consequences to themselves or others, a diminished capacity to be autonomous, or a court order, might disallow some aspects of the rights to privacy, self-determination,

and personal liberty. Indeed, such circumstances might be serious enough to create a duty to warn others (see Standards I.40 and II.36). However, psychologists still have a responsibility to respect the rights of the person(s) involved to the greatest extent possible under the circumstances, and to do what is necessary and reasonable to reduce the need for future disallowances.

In addition, psychologists recognize that as individual, family, group, or community vulnerabilities increase and/or as the power of persons to control their environment or their lives decreases, psychologists have an increasing responsibility to seek ethical advice and to establish safeguards to protect the rights of the persons involved. For this reason, psychologists consider it their responsibility to increase safeguards to protect and promote the rights of persons involved in their activities proportionate to the degree of dependency and the lack of voluntary initiation. For example, this would mean that there would be more safeguards to protect and promote the rights of fully dependent persons than partially dependent persons, and more safeguards for partially-dependent than independent persons.

Respect for the dignity of persons also includes the concept of equal justice. With respect to psychologists, this concept implies that all persons are entitled to benefit equally from the contributions of psychology and to equal quality in the processes, procedures, and services being conducted by psychologists. Although individual psychologists might specialize and direct their activities to particular populations, psychologists must not exclude persons on a capricious or unjustly discriminatory basis.

Ethical Standards

In adhering to the Principle of Respect for the Dignity of Persons, psychologists would:

General Respect

I.1 Demonstrate appropriate respect for the knowledge, insight, experience, and areas of expertise of others.

I.2 Not engage publicly (e.g., in public statements, presentations, research reports, or with clients) in demeaning descriptions of others, including jokes based on culture, nationality, ethnicity, colour, race, religion, gender, etc., or other remarks which reflect adversely on the dignity of others.

I.3 Use language that conveys respect for the dignity of others (e.g., gender-neutral terms) in all written or verbal communication.

I.4 Abstain from all forms of harassment, including sexual harassment.

General Rights

I.5 Avoid or refuse to participate in practices disrespectful of the legal, civil, or moral rights of others.

I.6 Refuse to advise, train, or supply information to anyone who, in the psychologist's judgement, will use the knowledge or skills to infringe on human rights.

I.7 Make every reasonable effort to ensure that psychological knowledge is not misused, intentionally or unintentionally, to infringe on human rights.

I.8 Respect the right of recipients of service, research participants, employees, supervisees, students, and others, to safeguard their own dignity.

Non-Discrimination

I.9 Not practice, condone, facilitate, or collaborate with any form of unjust discrimination.

I.10 Act to prevent or correct practices that are unjustly discriminatory.

Informed Consent

I.11 Seek as full and active participation as possible from others in decisions which affect them.

I.12 Respect and integrate as much as possible the opinions and wishes of others regarding decisions which affect them.

I.13 Obtain informed consent from all independent and partially dependent persons for any psychological services provided to them except in circumstances of urgent need (e.g., suicidal gesture). In such circumstances, psychologists would proceed with the assent of such persons, but fully informed consent would be obtained as soon as possible. (Also see Standard I.22.)

I.14 Obtain informed consent for all research activities which involve obtrusive measures, invasion into the private lives of research participants, risks to the participant, or any attempt to change the behaviour of research participants.

I.15 Establish and use signed consent forms which specify the dimensions of informed consent

or which acknowledge that such dimensions have been explained and are understood, if such forms are required by law or if such forms are desired by the psychologist, the person(s) giving consent, or the organization for whom the psychologist works.

I.16 Recognize that informed consent is the result of a process of reaching an agreement to work collaboratively, rather than of simply having a consent form signed.

I.17 Provide, in obtaining informed consent, as much information as a reasonable or prudent person, family, group, or community would want to know before making a decision or consenting to an activity. The psychologist would relay this information in language which the persons understand (including providing translation into another language, if necessary) and would take whatever reasonable steps are necessary to assure that the information was, in fact, understood.

I.18 Assure, in the process of obtaining informed consent, that at least the following points are understood: purpose and nature of the activity; mutual responsibilities; likely benefits and risks; alternatives; the likely consequences of non-action; the option to refuse or withdraw at any time, without prejudice; over what period of time the consent applies; and, how to rescind consent if desired.

I.19 Clarify the nature of multiple relationships to all concerned parties before obtaining consent, if providing services to or conducting research with individuals, families, groups, or communities at the request or for the use of third parties. This would include, but not be limited to: the purpose of the service or research; the use that will be made of information collected; and, the limits on confidentiality. Third parties may include schools, courts, government agencies, insurance companies, police, and special funding bodies.

Freedom of Consent

I.20 Take all reasonable steps to ensure that consent is not given under conditions of coercion or undue pressure. (Also see Standard III.31.)

I.21 Not proceed with any research activity, if consent is given under any condition of coercion or undue pressure. (Also see Standard III.31.)

I.22 Take all reasonable steps to confirm or reestablish freedom of consent, if consent for service is given under conditions of duress or conditions of extreme need.

I.23 Respect the right of individuals to discontinue participation or service at any time, and be responsive to non-verbal indications of a desire to discontinue if the individual has difficulty with verbally communicating such a desire (e.g., young children, verbally disabled persons).

Fair Treatment/Due Process

I.24 Work and act in a spirit of fair treatment to others.

I.25 Help to establish and abide by due process or other natural justice procedures for employment, evaluation, adjudication, editorial, and peer review activities.

I.26 Compensate others justly for the use of their time, energy, and intelligence, unless such compensation is refused in advance.

Vulnerabilities

I.27 Seek an independent and adequate ethical review of human rights issues and protections for any research involving vulnerable groups and/or persons of diminished capacity to give informed consent, before making a decision to proceed.

I.28 Not use persons of diminished capacity to give informed consent in research studies, if the research involved might equally well be carried out with persons who have a fuller capacity to give informed consent.

I.29 Carry out informed consent processes with those persons who are legally responsible or appointed to give informed consent on behalf of individuals who are not competent to consent on their own behalf.

I.30 Seek willing and adequately informed participation from any person of diminished capacity to give informed consent, and proceed without this assent only if the service or research activity is considered to be of direct benefit to that person.

I.31 Be particularly cautious in establishing the freedom of consent of any individual who is in a dependent relationship to the psychologist (e.g., student, employee). This may include, but is not limited to, offering that person an alternative activity to fulfil their educational or employment goals, or offering a range of research studies or experience opportunities from which the person can select.

Privacy

I.32 Explore and collect only that information which is germane to the purpose(s) for which consent has been obtained.

I.33 Take care not to infringe, in research or service activities, on the personally or culturally defined private space of individuals or groups unless clear permission is granted to do so.

I.34 Record only that private information necessary for the provision of continuous, coordinated service, or for the goals of the particular research study being conducted, or which is required by law (see Standards IV.15, and IV.16).

I.35 Respect the right of employees, supervisees, students, or psychologists-in-training to reasonable personal privacy.

I.36 Store, handle, and transfer all records, both written and unwritten (e.g., computer files, videotapes), in a way that attends to the needs for privacy and security. This would include having adequate plans for records in circumstances of one's own serious illness or death.

I.37 Take all reasonable steps to ensure that records over which they have control remain personally identifiable only as long as is necessary in the interests of those to whom they refer and/or to the research project for which they were collected, or as required by law, and render anonymous or destory any records under their control that no longer need to be personally identifiable.

Confidentiality

I.38 Be careful not to relay information which they have gained about colleagues, colleagues' clients, students, and members of organizations gained in the process of their activities as psychologists and which the psychologist has reason to believe is considered confidential by those persons, except as required or justified by law (see Standards IV.15 and IV.16).

I.39 Clarify what measures will be taken to protect confidentiality, and what responsibilities family, group, and community members have for the protection of each other's confidentiality, when engaged in services to or research with individuals, families, groups, or communities.

I.40 Share confidential information with others only with the informed consent of those involved, or in a manner that the individuals involved cannot be identified, except as required or justified by law, or in circumstances of actual or possible serious physical harm or death (see Standard II.36).

Extended Responsibility

I.41 Encourage others, if appropriate, to respect the dignity of persons and to expect respect for their own dignity.

I.42 Assume overall responsibility for the scientific and professional activities of their assistants, students, supervisees, and employees with regard to Respect for the Dignity of Persons, all of whom, however, incur similar obligations.

PRINCIPLE II: RESPONSIBLE CARING

Values Statement

A basic ethical expectation of any discipline is that its activities will benefit members of society or, at least, do no harm. Therefore, psychologists demonstrate an active concern for the welfare of any individual, family, group, or community with whom they relate in their role as psychologists. This concern includes both those directly involved and those indirectly involved in their activities. However, as with Principle I, psychologists' greatest responsibility is to protect the welfare of those directly involved in their activities and, therefore, normally in a more vulnerable position (e.g., research participants, clients, students). Their responsibility to those indirectly involved (e.g., employers, third-party payers, the general public) is secondary.

As individuals are usually concerned about their own welfare, obtaining informed consent (see Principle I) is one of the best methods for ensuring that their welfare will be protected. However, it is only when informed consent is combined with the responsible caring of the psychologist that there is considerable ethical protection of the welfare of the person(s) involved.

Responsible caring leads psychologists to "take care" to discern the potential harm and benefits involved, to predict the likelihood of their occurrence, to proceed only if the potential benefits outweigh the potential harms, to develop and use methods that will minimize harms and maximize benefits,

and to take responsibility for correcting any harmful effects that have occurred as a result of their activities.

In order to carry out these steps, psychologists recognize the need for competence and self-knowledge. They consider incompetent action to be unethical per se, as it is unlikely to be of benefit and likely to be harmful. They engage only in those activities in which they have competence, and they perform their activities as competently as possible. They acquire, contribute to, and use the existing knowledge most relevant to the best interests of those concerned. They also engage in self-reflection regarding how their own values, attitudes, experiences, and social context (e.g., culture, ethnicity, colour, religion, gender, sexual orientation, physical and mental ability level, age, and socio-economic status) influence their actions, interpretations, choices, and recommendations. This is done with the intent of increasing the probability that their activities will benefit and not harm the individuals, families, groups and communities to whom they relate in their role as psychologists.

Psychologists define harm and benefit in terms of both physical and psychological dimensions. They are concerned about such factors as feelings of self-worth, fear, humiliation, interpersonal trust, cynicism, self-knowledge and general knowledge, as well as such factors as physical safety, comfort, pain, and injury. They are concerned about immediate, short-term, and long-term effects.

Responsible caring recognizes and acknowledges (e.g., through obtaining informed consent) the ability of individuals, families, groups, and communities to care for themselves and each other. It does not replace or undermine such ability. However, psychologists recognize that as vulnerabilities increase and/or as power to control one's own life decreases, they have an increasing responsibility to protect the well-being of the individual, family, group, or community involved. For this reason, as in Principle I, psychologists consider it their responsibility to increase safeguards proportionate to the degree of dependency and the lack of voluntary initiation on the part of the persons involved. However, for Principle II, the safeguards are for the well-being of persons rather than for the rights of persons.

Psychologists' treatment and use of animals in their research and teaching activities are also a component of responsible caring. Although animals do not have the same rights as persons (e.g., informed consent), they do have the right to be treated humanely and not to be exposed to unnecessary discomfort, pain, or disruption.

Ethical Standards

In adhering to the Principle of Responsible Caring, psychologists would:

General Caring

II.1 Protect and promote the welfare of clients, students, research participants, colleagues, and others.

II.2 Avoid doing harm to clients, students, research participants, colleagues, and others.

II.3 Accept responsibility for the consequences of their actions.

II.4 Refuse to advise, train, or supply information to anyone who, in the psychologist's judgement, will use the knowledge or skills to harm others.

II.5 Make every reasonable effort to ensure that psychological knowledge is not misused, intentionally or unintentionally, to harm others.

Competence and Self-Knowledge

II.6 Offer or carry out (without supervision) only those activities for which they have established their competence to carry them out to the benefit of others.

II.7 Not delegate activities to persons not competent to carry them out to the benefit of others.

II.8 Take immediate steps to obtain consultation or to refer a client to a colleague or other appropriate professional, whichever is more likely to result in providing the client with competent service, if it becomes apparent that a client's problems are beyond their competence.

II.9 Keep themselves up to date with relevant knowledge, research methods, and techniques, through the reading of relevant literature, peer consultation, and continuing education activities, in order that their service or research activities and conclusions will benefit and not harm others.

II.10 Evaluate how their own experiences, attitudes, culture, beliefs, values, social context, individual differences, and stresses influence their interactions with others, and integrate this awareness into all efforts to benefit and not harm others.

II.11 Seek appropriate help and/or discontinue scientific or professional activity for an appropriate period of time, if a physical or psychological condition reduces their ability to benefit and not harm others.

II.12 Engage in self-care activities which help to avoid conditions (e.g., burnout, addictions) which could result in impaired judgement and interfere with their ability to benefit and not harm others.

Risk/Benefit Analysis

II.13 Assess the individuals, families, groups, and communities involved in their activities adequately enough to ensure that they will be able to discern what will benefit and not harm those persons.

II.14 Be sufficiently sensitive to and knowledgeable about individual differences and vulnerabilities to discern what will benefit and not harm persons involved in their activities.

II.15 Carry out pilot studies to determine the effects of all new procedures and techniques which might carry some risks, before considering their use on a broader scale.

II.16 Seek an independent and adequate ethical review of the balance of risks and potential benefits of all research which involves procedures of unknown consequence, or where pain, discomfort, or harm is possible, before making a decision to proceed.

II.17 Not carry out any scientific or professional activity unless the probable benefit is proportionately greater than the risk involved.

Maximize Benefit

II.18 Provide services which are coordinated over time and with other service providers, in order to avoid duplication or working at cross purposes. Such coordination would be promoted by the maintenance of adequate records and communication with other service providers.

II.19 Make themselves aware of the knowledge and skills of other disciplines (e.g., law, medicine) and advise the use of such knowledge and skills, where relevant to the benefit of others.

II.20 Strive to obtain the best possible service for those needing and seeking psychological service.

This includes recommending professionals other than psychologists, if appropriate.

II.21 Monitor and evaluate the effect of their activities, record their findings and, if appropriate, communicate new knowledge to others in the field.

II.22 Debrief research participants in such a way that the participants' knowledge is enhanced and the participants have a sense of contribution to knowledge.

II.23 Perform their teaching duties on the basis of careful preparation, so that their instruction is current and scholarly.

II.24 Act on their obligation to facilitate the professional and scientific development of their students, trainees, employees, and supervisees by assuring that these persons understand the values and ethical prescriptions of the discipline, and by providing or arranging for adequate working conditions, timely evaluations, and constructive consultation and experience opportunities.

II.25 Encourage and assist students in publication of worthy student papers.

Minimize Harm

II.26 Be acutely aware of the power relationship in therapy and, therefore, not encourage or engage in sexual intimacy with therapy clients, neither during therapy, nor for that period of time following therapy during which the power relationship reasonably could be expected to influence the client's personal decision making.

II.27 Be careful not to engage in activities in a way that could place incidentally involved individuals at risk.

II.28 Be acutely aware of the need for discretion in the recording and communication of information, in order that the information not be interpreted or used to the detriment of others. This includes, but is not limited to: not recording information which could lead to misinterpretation and misuse; avoiding conjecture; clearly labelling opinion; and, communicating information in language that can be understood clearly by the particular recipient of the information.

II.29 Give reasonable assistance to secure needed psychological services or activities, if personally unable to meet requests for needed psychological services or activities.

II.30 Maintain appropriate contact, support, and responsibility for caring until a colleague or other professional begins service, if referring a client to a colleague or other professional.

II.31 Give reasonable notice and be reasonably assured that discontinuation will cause no harm to the client, before discontinuing services.

II.32 Screen appropriate research participants and select those not likely to be harmed, if risk or harm to some research participants is possible.

II.33 Act to minimize the impact of their research activities on research participants' personality or their physical or mental integrity.

Offset/Correct Harm

II.34 Terminate an activity when it is clear that the activity is more harmful than beneficial, or when the activity is no longer needed.

II.35 Refuse to help individuals, families, groups, or communities to carry out or submit to activities which, according to current knowledge and/or legal and professional guidelines, would cause serious physical or psychological harm to themselves or others.

II.36 Do everything reasonably possible to stop or offset the consequences of actions by others when these actions are likely to cause serious physical harm or death. This may include reporting to appropriate authorities (e.g., the police) or an intended victim, and would be done even when a confidential relationship is involved. (See Standard I.40)

II.37 Act to stop or offset the consequences of clearly harmful activities being carried out by another psychologist or member of another discipline, when these activities have come to their attention outside of a confidential client relationship with that psychologist or member of another discipline. Depending on the nature of the harmful activities, this may include talking informally with the psychologist or member of the other discipline, obtaining objective information and, if possible, the assurance that the harm will discontinue and be corrected. However, if the harm is serious and/or continues to persist, the situation would be reported to the appropriate regulatory body, authority, and/or committee for action.

II.38 Not place an individual, group, family, or community needing service at a serious disadvantage by offering them no service over an unreasonable period of time in order to fulfill the conditions of a control condition in a research study and, where resources allow, offer such person(s) the service found to be most effective after the research study is completed.

II.39 Debrief research participants in such a way that any harm caused can be discerned, and act to correct any resultant harm.

Care of Animals

II.40 Not use animals in their research unless there is a reasonable expectation that the research will increase understanding of the structures and processes underlying behaviour, or increase understanding of the particular animal species used in the study, or result eventually in benefits to the health and welfare of humans or other animals.

II.41 Use a procedure subjecting animals to pain, stress, or privation only if an alternative procedure is unavailable and the goal is justified by its prospective scientific, educational, or applied value.

II.42 Make every effort to minimize the discomfort, illness, and pain of animals. This would include performing surgical procedures only under appropriate anaesthesia, using techniques to avoid infection and minimize pain during and after surgery and, if disposing of experimental animals is carried out at the termination of the study, doing so in a humane way.

II.43 Use animals in classroom demonstrations only if the instructional objectives cannot be achieved through the use of video-tapes, films, or other methods, and if the type of demonstration is warranted by the anticipated instructional gain.

Extended Responsibility

II.44 Encourage others, if appropriate, to care responsibly.

II.45 Assume overall responsibility for the scientific and professional activities of their assistants, students, supervisees, and employees with regard to the Principle of Responsible Caring, all of whom, however, incur similar obligations.

PRINCIPLE III: INTEGRITY IN RELATIONSHIPS

Values Statement

The relationships formed by psychologists in the course of their work embody explicit and implicit mutual expectations of integrity that are vital to the advancement of scientific knowledge and to the maintenance of public confidence in the discipline of psychology. These expectations include: accuracy and honesty; straight-forwardness and openness; the maximization of objectivity and minimization of bias; and, avoidance of conflicts of interest. Psychologists have a responsibility to meet these expectations and to encourage reciprocity.

In addition to accuracy, honesty, and the obvious prohibitions of fraud or misrepresentation, meeting expectations of integrity is enhanced by self-knowledge and the use of critical analysis. Although it can be argued that science is value-free, scientists are not. Personal values can affect the questions psychologists ask, how they ask those questions, what assumptions they make, their selection of methods, what they observe and what they fail to observe, and how they interpret their data. Psychologists are not expected to be value-free in conducting their activities. However, they are expected to understand how their backgrounds and values interact with their activities, to be open and honest about the influence of such factors, and to be as objective and unbiased as possible under the circumstances.

The values of openness and straightforwardness exist within the context of Respect for the Dignity of Persons (Principle I) and Responsible Caring (Principle II). As such, there will be circumstances in which openness and straightforwardness will need to be tempered. Full disclosure may not be needed or desired by others and, in some circumstances, may be a risk to their dignity or well-being. In such circumstances, however, psychologists have a responsibility to ensure that their decision not to be fully open or straightforward is justified by higher-order values.

Of special concern to psychologists is the use of deception in research, or the use of any technique (e.g., temporary withholding of information) which could be interpreted as deception by research participants or clients. Although research which uses such techniques can lead to knowledge which is beneficial, and service which uses techniques which might be interpreted as deception can lead to beneficial changes for the client, such benefits must be weighed against the individual's right to self-determination and the importance of public and individual trust in psychology. Psychologists have a serious obligation never to use deception in service activities, and to avoid as much as possible the use of deception in research or the use of any technique which could be interpreted as deception in either research or service activities. They also have a serious obligation to consider the need for, the possible consequences of, and their responsibility to correct any resulting mistrust or other harmful effects from the use of such techniques.

As public trust in the discipline of psychology includes trusting that psychologists will act in the best interests of members of the public, situations which present real or potential conflicts of interest are of concern to psychologists. Conflict-of-interest situations can readily motivate psychologists to act in ways which meet their own personal, political, or business interests at the expense of the best interests of members of the public. Although avoidance of all situations which present a conflict of interest is not possible, it is the responsibility of psychologists to avoid as many as possible and, when such situations cannot be avoided, to ensure that the best interests of members of the public are protected.

Integrity in relationships implies that psychologists, as a matter of honesty, have a responsibility to maintain competence in any speciality area for which they declare competence, whether or not they are currently practising in that area. It also requires that psychologists, in as much as they present themselves as members and representatives of a specific discipline, have a responsibility to actively rely on and be guided by that discipline and its guidelines and requirements.

Ethical Standards

In adhering to the Principle of Integrity in Relationships, psychologists would:

Accuracy/Honesty

III.1 Not participate in, condone, or be associated with dishonesty, fraud, or misrepresentation.

III.2 Accurately represent their own and their associates' qualifications, education, experience, competence, and affiliations, in all spoken, written, or printed communications, being careful not to use descriptions or information which could be misinterpreted.

III.3 Carefully protect their own and their associates' credentials from being misrepresented by others, and act quickly to correct any such misrepresentation.

III.4 Maintain competence in their declared area(s) of psychological competence, as well as in their current area(s) of activity. (See Standard II.9.)

III.5 Accurately represent their activities, functions, and likely or actual outcomes of their work, in all spoken, written, or printed communication. This includes, but is not limited to: advertisements of services; course and workshop descriptions; academic grading requirements; and, research reports.

III.6 Ensure that their activities, functions, and likely or actual outcomes of their activities are not misrepresented by others, and act quickly to correct any such misrepresentation.

III.7 Take credit only for the work and ideas that they have actually done or generated, and give credit for work done or ideas contributed by others (including students) in proportion to their contribution.

III.8 Acknowledge the limitations of their knowledge, methods, findings, interventions, and views.

III.9 Not suppress disconfirming evidence of their findings and views, acknowledging alternative hypotheses and explanations.

Objectivity/Lack of Bias

III.10 Evaluate how their personal experiences, attitudes, values, social context, individual differences, and stresses influence their activities and thinking, integrating this awareness into all attempts to be objective and unbiased in their research, service and other activities.

III.11 Take care to communicate as completely and objectively as possible, and to clearly differentiate facts, opinions, theories, hypotheses, and ideas, if communicating their knowledge, findings, and views.

III.12 Present instructional information accurately, avoiding bias in the selection and presentation of information, and publicly acknowledge any personal values or bias which influence the selection and presentation of information.

III.13 Act quickly to clarify any distortion by a sponsor, client, or other persons, of the findings of their research.

Straightforwardness/Openness

III.14 Be clear and straightforward about all information needed to establish informed consent or any other valid written or unwritten agreement (for example: fees; concerns; mutual responsibilities; ethical responsibilities of psychologists; purpose and nature of the relationship; alternatives; likely experiences; possible conflicts; possible outcomes; and, expectations for processing, using, and sharing any information generated).

III.15 Provide suitable information about the results of assessments, evaluations, or research findings to the persons involved, if appropriate and/or if asked. This information would be communicated in understandable language.

III.16 Fully explain reasons for their actions to persons who have been affected by their actions, if appropriate and/or if asked.

III.17 Honour all promises and commitments included in any written or verbal agreement unless serious and unexpected circumstances (e.g., illness) intervene. If such circumstances occur, then the psychologist would make a full and honest explanation to other parties involved.

III.18 Make clear whether they are acting as private citizens, as members of specific organizations or groups, or as representatives of the discipline of psychology, when making statements or when involved in public activities.

III.19 Conduct research in a way that is consistent with a commitment to honest, open inquiry, and to clear communication of any research aims, sponsorship, social context, personal values, or financial interests that may affect or appear to affect their research.

III.20 Submit their research, in some accurate form and within the limits of confidentiality, to independent colleagues with expertise in the research area, for their comments and evaluations.

III.21 Encourage the free exchange of ideas between themselves and their students.

III.22 Make no attempt to conceal the status of a trainee.

Avoidance of Deception

III.23 Not engage in deception in any service activity.

III.24 Not engage in deception in research or the use of techniques which might be interpreted as deception, in research or service activities, if there are alternative procedures available and/or if the negative effects cannot be predicted or offset.

III.25 Not engage in deception in research or the use of techniques which might be interpreted as deception in research or service activities, if it would interfere with the individual's understanding of facts which clearly might influence a decision to give informed consent.

III.26 Use the minimum necessary deception in research or techniques which might be interpreted as deception in research, or service activities.

III.27 Provide research participants, during debriefing, with a clarification of the nature of the study, if deception or the use of techniques which could be interpreted as deception has occurred. In such circumstances, psychologists would seek to remove any misconceptions which might have arisen and to re-establish any trust which might have been lost, assuring the participant during debriefing that the real or apparent deception was neither arbitrary nor capricious. (Also, see Standard II.22.)

III.28 Act to re-establish with clients any trust which might have been lost due to the use of techniques which might be interpreted as deception.

III.29 Seek an independent and adequate ethical review of the risks to public or individual trust and of safeguards to protect such trust for any research which uses deception or techniques which might be interpreted as deception, before making a decision to proceed.

Avoidance of Conflict of Interest

III.30 Not exploit any relationship established as a psychologist to further personal, political, or business interests at the expense of the best interests of their clients, research participants, students, employers, or others. This includes, but is not limited to: soliciting clients of one's employing agency for private practice; taking advantage of trust or dependency to engage in sexual activities or to frighten clients into receiving services; appropriating students' ideas, research or work; using the resources of one's employing institution for purposes not agreed to; securing or accepting significant financial or material benefit for activities which are already awarded by salary or other compensation; and, prejudicing others against a colleague for reasons of personal gain.

III.31 Not offer rewards sufficient to motivate an individual or group to participate in an activity that has possible or known risks to themselves or others. (See Standards I.20; I.21; II.2; and II.44.)

III.32 Avoid dual relationships (e.g., with students, employees, or clients) and other situations which might present a conflict of interest or which might reduce their ability to be objective and unbiased in their determinations of what might be in the best interests of others.

III.33 Inform all parties, if a real or potential conflict of interest arises, of the need to resolve the situation in a manner that is consistent with Respect for the Dignity of Persons (Principle I) and Responsible Caring (Principle II), and take all reasonable steps to resolve the issue in such a manner.

Reliance on the Discipline

III.34 Familiarize themselves with their discipline's rules and regulations, and abide by them, unless abiding by them would be seriously detrimental to the rights or well-being of others as demonstrated in the Principles of Respect for the Dignity of Persons or Responsible Caring. (See Standard IV.16 for guidelines regarding the resolution of such conflicts.)

III.35 Familiarize themselves with and demonstrate a commitment to maintaining the standards of their discipline.

III.36 Seek consultation from colleagues and/or appropriate groups and committees, and give due regard to their advice in arriving at a responsible decision, if faced with difficult situations.

Extended Responsibility

III.37 Encourage others, if appropriate, to relate with integrity.

III.38 Assume overall responsibility for the scientific and professional activities of their assistants, students, supervisees, and employees with regard to the Principle of Integrity in Relationships, all of whom, however, incur similar obligations.

PRINCIPLE IV: RESPONSIBILITY TO SOCIETY

Values Statement

Psychology functions as a discipline within the context of human society. Psychologists, both in their work and as private citizens, have responsibilities to the societies in which they live and work, such as the neighbourhood or city, and to the welfare of all human beings in those societies.

Two of the legitimate expectations of psychology as a science and a profession are that it will increase knowledge and that it will conduct its affairs in such ways that it will promote the welfare of all human beings.

In the context of society, the above expectations imply that scientific freedom will be balanced by scientific responsibility; that is, psychologists will actively increase knowledge only through the use of activities and methods that are consistent with ethical requirements, and be willing to demonstrate that such requirements have been met.

The expectations also imply that psychologists will do whatever they can to ensure that psychological knowledge, when used in the development of social structures and policies, will be used for beneficial purposes, and that the discipline's own structures and policies will support those beneficial purposes. Within the context of this document, social structures and policies which have beneficial purposes are defined as those which more readily support and reflect respect for the dignity of persons, responsible caring, integrity in relationships, and responsibility to society. If psychological knowledge or structures are used against these purposes, psychologists have an ethical responsibility to try to draw attention to and correct the misuse. Although this is a collective responsibility, those psychologists having direct involvement in the structures of the discipline, in social development, and/or in the theoretical or research data base that is being used (e.g., through research, expert testimony, or policy advice) have the greatest responsibility to act. Other psychologists must decide for themselves the most appropriate and beneficial use of their time and talents to help meet this collective responsibility.

In carrying out their work, psychologists acknowledge that many social structures have evolved slowly over time in response to human need, are valued by society, and are primarily beneficial. In such circumstances, psychologists convey respect for these social structures and avoid unwarranted or unnecessary disruption. Suggestions for and action toward changes or enhancement of such structures are carried out only through processes which seek to achieve a consensus within society through democratic means.

On the other hand, if structures or policies seriously ignore or oppose the principles of respect for the dignity of the person, responsible caring, integrity in relationships, or responsibility to society, psychologists involved have a responsibility to be critical and advocate for change to occur as quickly as possible.

In order to be responsible to society and to contribute constructively to its ongoing evolution, psychologists need to be self-reflective about the place of the discipline of psychology in society. They need to engage in even-tempered observation and interpretation of the effects of societal structures and policies, and their process of change, developing the ability of psychologists to increase the beneficial use of psychological knowledge and structures, and avoid their misuse. The discipline needs to be willing to set high standards for its members, to do what it can to assure that such standards are met, and to support its members in their attempts to maintain the standards. Once again, individual psychologists must decide for themselves the most appropriate and beneficial use of their time and talents in helping to meet these collective responsibilities.

Ethical Standards

In adhering to the Principle of Responsibility to Society, psychologists would:

Development of Knowledge

IV.1 Contribute to the discipline of psychology and of society's understanding of itself and human beings generally, through a free pursuit and sharing of knowledge, unless such activity conflicts with other basic ethical requirements.

IV.2 Keep informed of progress in their area(s) of psychological activity, take this progress into account in their work, and try to make their own contributions to this progress.

Beneficial Activities

IV.3 Participate in and contribute to continuing education and the professional and scientific growth of self and colleagues.

IV.4 Assist in the development of those who enter the discipline of psychology by helping them to acquire a full understanding of the ethics, responsibilities, and needed competencies of their chosen area(s), including an understanding of critical analysis and of the variations, uses, and possible misuses of the scientific paradigm.

IV.5 Participate in the process of critical self-evaluation of the discipline's place in society and in the development and implementation of structures and procedures which help the discipline to contribute to beneficial societal functioning and changes.

IV.6 Engage in regular monitoring, assessment, and reporting (e.g., through peer review, and in program reviews, case management reviews, and reports of one's own research) of their ethical practices and safeguards.

IV.7 Help develop, promote, and participate in accountability processes and procedures related to their work.

IV.8 Uphold the discipline's responsibility to society by promoting and maintaining the highest standards of the discipline.

IV.9 Protect the skills, knowledge, and interpretations of psychology from being misused, used incompetently, or made useless (e.g., loss of security of assessment techniques) by others.

IV.10 Contribute to the general welfare of society (e.g., improving accessibility of services, regardless of ability to pay) and/or to the general welfare of their discipline by offering a portion of their time to work for which they receive little or no financial return.

IV.11 Uphold the discipline's responsibility to society by bringing incompetent or unethical behaviour, including misuses of psychological knowledge and techniques, to the attention of appropriate regulatory bodies, authorities, and/or committees, in a manner consistent with the ethical principles of this Code, if informal resolution or correction of the situation is not appropriate or possible.

IV.12 Only enter into agreements or contracts which allow them to act in accordance with the ethical principles and standards of this Code.

Respect for Society

IV.13 Acquire an adequate knowledge of the culture, social structure, and customs of a community before beginning any major work there.

IV.14 Convey respect for and abide by prevailing

community mores, social customs, and cultural expectations in their scientific and professional activities, provided that this does not contravene any of the ethical principles of this Code.

IV.15 Abide by the laws of the society in which they work. If those laws seriously conflict with the ethical principles contained herein, psychologists would do whatever they could to uphold the ethical principles. If upholding the ethical principles could result in serious personal consequences (e.g., jail or physical harm), decision for final action would be considered a matter of personal conscience.

IV.16 Consult with colleagues, if faced with an apparent conflict between keeping a law and following an ethical principle, unless in an emergency, and seek consensus as to the most ethical course of action and the most responsible, knowledgeable, effective, and respectful way to carry it out.

Development of Society

IV.17 Act to change those aspects of the discipline of psychology which detract from beneficial societal changes, where appropriate and possible.

IV.18 Be sensitive to the needs, current issues, and problems of society, if determining research questions to be asked, services to be developed, information to be collected, or the interpretation of results or findings.

IV.19 Be especially careful to keep well informed through relevant reading, peer consultation and continuing education, if their work is related to societal issues.

IV.20 Speak out, in a manner consistent with the four principles of this Code, when they possess expert knowledge that bears on important societal issues being studied or discussed.

IV.21 Provide thorough discussion of the limits of their data, if their work touches on social policy and structure.

IV.22 Make themselves aware of the current social and political climate and of previous and possible future societal misuses of psychological knowledge, and exercise due discretion in communicating psychological information (e.g., research results, theoretical knowledge) in order to discourage any further misuse.

IV.23 Exercise particular care when reporting the results of any work regarding vulnerable groups, en-

suring that results are not likely to be misinterpreted or misused in the development of social policy, attitudes, and practices (e.g., encouraging manipulation of vulnerable persons or reinforcing discrimination against any specific population).

IV.24 Not contribute to nor engage in research or any other activity which promotes or is intended for use in the torture or persons, the development of prohibited weapons, destruction of the environment, or any other act which contravenes international law.

IV.25 Provide the public with any psychological knowledge relevant to the public's informed participation in the shaping of social policies and structures, if involved in public policy issues.

IV.26 Speak out and/or act, in a manner consistent with the four principles of this Code, if the policies, practices or regulations of the social structure within which they work seriously ignore or oppose any of the principles of this Code.

Extended Responsibility

IV.27 Encourage others, if appropriate, to exercise responsibility to society.

IV.28 Assume overall responsibility for the scientific and professional activities of their assistants, students, supervisees, and employees with regard to the Principle of Responsibility to Society, all of whom, however, incur similar obligations.

◆　◆　◆

Commentary: *One function that a code of ethics should serve is to translate moral values, or prima facie duties, into enforceable standards. These duties include nonmaleficence, fidelity, beneficence, justice, and autonomy, and each can be defined in the context of professional conduct.*

Perhaps the bedrock ethical duty required of psychologists is nonmaleficence, captured in the Latin phrase primum non nocere—"above all, do no harm." Fidelity most often refers to the obligations of faithfulness and loyalty inherent in the client–clinician relationship, but it may be extended to mean fidelity toward the scientific roots of one's profession. Beneficence is the most commonsense principle; indeed, the concept of psychology as a "helping profession" is its embodiment. Specifically, it refers to the practitioners' responsibility to benefit those they assess and treat and the obligation of investigators to conduct research with scientific or applied value. Justice refers to psychologists' obligation to treat equitably those who they serve and, perhaps, the superordinate responsibility to respect the worth and dignity of each individual. Finally—but by no means least important—is the principle of autonomy, guaranteeing people the freedom to think, choose, and act so long as their actions do not infringe unduly on the rights of others. These principles are explicated more fully in chapter 3. For an analysis of how these prima facie duties have been represented in the current APA Ethical Principles, see Bersoff, D. N., & Koeppl, P. M. (1993). The relation between ethical codes and moral principles. Ethics and Behavior, 3, 345–357.

It would be useful to compare the APA and Canadian codes for these five prima facie duties. Are the two codes equally respectful of autonomy or does one stress beneficence and paternalism over self-determination more than the other? Which is clearer and easier to interpret and follow? For one view of the two codes, see Sinclair, C. (1996). A comparison of codes of professional conduct and ethics. In L. J. Bass et al. (Eds.), Professional conduct and discipline in psychology (pp. 53–70). Washington, DC: American Psychological Association. This text also reproduces in an Appendix the code of conduct published in 1991 by the Association of State and Provincial Psychology Boards.

Despite the relative newness of the 1992 code, another major review has already begun with the first meeting of the Ethics Code Task Force (ECTF) in October 1997. For a description of its creation and membership, see:

APA Ethics Committee. (1997). Report of the Ethics Committee, 1996. American Psychologist, 52, 897–905.

APA Ethics Committee. (1998). Report of the Ethics Committee, 1997. American Psychologist, 53, 969–980.

The ECTF plans to use both methods described by Pope & Vetter. It should complete its work by 2003.

When readers conclude this text, they may want to revisit the currently enforceable code and suggest to the next revisions committee ways in which the 1992 code can be improved and strengthened to ensure that psychology continues to earn and maintain the public's trust through an ethics document that reflects the profession's moral integrity and its primary mission of promoting human welfare.

The interpretation and enforcement of the Ethical Principles are the responsibility of the APA ethics committee. The structure and work of the committee are governed primarily by the APA bylaws, the Association Rules passed by the Council of Representatives, and the Rules and Procedures developed by the ethics committee itself. The two portions of the bylaws relevant to ethics are Article XI, Section 5, and Article II, Sections 17–19. See Bylaws of the American Psychological Association. (Amended May, 1998.) Washington, DC: American Psychological Association.

Bylaws of the American Psychological Association

American Psychological Association

. . .

[Article XI, Section 5 provides:]

5. The Ethics Committee shall consist of not fewer than eight persons, at least seven of whom shall be Members of the Association, elected from different geographical areas, for terms of not less than three years. Members of the Ethics Committee shall be selected to represent a range of interests characteristic of psychology. The Ethics Committee shall have the power to receive, initiate, and investigate complaints of unethical conduct of Members (to include Fellows), Associate members, and Affiliates; to report on types of cases investigated with specific description of difficult or recalcitrant cases; to dismiss or recommend action on ethical cases investigated; to resolve cases by agreement where appropriate; to formulate rules or principles of ethics for adoption by the Association; to formulate rules and procedures governing the conduct of the ethics or disciplinary process for approval by the Board of Directors acting on behalf of Council; and to interpret, apply, and otherwise administer those rules and procedures.

The work of the Ethics Committee, including information and recommendation on all cases before it, shall be kept confidential, except as provided by the Ethics Committee in rules and procedures approved by the Board of Directors, consistent with the objectives of the Committee and the interest of the Association.

. . .

[Article II, Sections 17–19 provide:]

17. A Member (to include Fellows), Associate member or Affiliate may be dropped from membership or otherwise disciplined for conduct which violates the Ethical Principles of the Association, which tends to injure the Association or to affect adversely its reputation, or which is contrary to or destructive of its objects. Allegations of such conduct shall be submitted to the Ethics Committee.

The Ethics Committee shall formulate rules and procedures governing the conduct of the ethics and disciplinary process. However, such rules and procedures and any changes therein must be approved by the Board of Directors acting on behalf of Council. The Ethics Committee, acting at its own discretion or on direction of the Board of Directors, shall review such rules and procedures periodically and may amend them from time to time, subject to the approval of the Board of Directors, provided, however, that no such amendment shall adversely affect the substantive rights of a Member, Associate member or Affiliate whose conduct is being investigated or against whom formal charges have been filed at the time of amendment.

18. A person who has been dropped from membership pursuant to the rules and procedures of the Ethics Committee may reapply for membership after five years have elapsed from the date of termination of his/her membership. A person who has been permitted to resign under a stipulated agreement may reapply for membership only after the period of time stipulated in the agreement has elapsed, and all other conditions set forth in such agreement have been discharged. In all cases the Member, Associate member or Affiliate must show that he/she is ethically as well as technically qualified for membership. Such reapplications shall be considered first by the Ethics Committee, which shall make recommendation to the Membership Committee.

19. Resignations of Members, Associate members or Affiliates may be accepted only by the Board of Directors. In the ordinary course, the Board of Directors will, in its discretion, refuse to accept a resignation tendered by a Member, Associate member or Affiliate while such Member, Associate member or Affiliate is under the scrutiny of the Ethics Committee . . . .

Commentary: *In 1996, the Ethics Committee clarified the meaning of "under scrutiny":*

> *A member will be considered to be under the scrutiny of the Ethics Committee:*
> *1. When the member is first brought to the Committee's attention as a result of disciplinary or criminal investigations or actions by other bodies, or*
> *2. For other matters, when a complaint or other investigation is not dismissed after an initial review by the Chair [of the*

> *Ethics Committee] and [Staff] Director [of the Committee].*
>
> *. . .*
>
> *The member is no longer under the scrutiny of the Committee when all matters regarding the member that are under the scrutiny of the Committee are closed.* (p. 1314)

See APA Ethics Committee. Policy on barring resignations during ethics investigations. (1996). American Psychologist, 51, 1341.

The policy was modified a year later. Members who are under scrutiny for one or more pending matters may execute an affidavit that would provide for their resignations upon the completion of the pending matters. Upon the effective date of the affidavit, "APA would not exercise jurisdiction over any newly filed ethics complaints against th[ose] member[s] (APA Ethics Committee, 1998, p. 972), although APA would retain jurisdiction in cases of noncooperation in connection with pending cases. See APA Ethics Committee. (1998). Report of the Ethics Committee, 1997. American Psychologist, 53, 969–980.

Rules and Procedures
June 1, 1996

Ethics Committee of the American Psychological Association

OVERVIEW

This brief overview is intended only to help the reader to understand the structure of these Rules and Procedures (Rules). The overview is not binding on the Ethics Committee or participants in the ethics process and is not an independent source of authority.

These Rules are divided into five parts, which are further subdivided by sections and subsections. The table of contents lists the major section headings.

Parts I and II: General Provisions

Part I describes the objectives and authority of the Ethics Committee. Part II states the Committee's general operating rules. These address such areas as confidentiality and disclosures of information concerning ethics cases; maintenance and disposition of Ethics Committee records; the Committee's jurisdiction, including the time limits within which ethics complaints must be filed; requests to reopen a closed case; and descriptions of the various sanctions and directives that may be imposed.

Parts III–V: Processing and Review of Complaints and Other Matters by the Ethics Committee

Membership Matters

The Ethics Committee may review applications or reapplications for membership in APA and may review allegations that membership was obtained based upon false or fraudulent information. These procedures are described in Part III.

Investigations of Unethical Conduct

These Rules describe two types of investigations: show cause proceedings and reviews of alleged unethical conduct. The Committee may choose to deal with a matter according to either procedure and may convert an investigation from one type to another as appropriate. A show cause review is commenced based on an adverse action by another body; a review of alleged unethical conduct is initiated by a complainant or the Committee and charges violation of the Ethics Code.

Show Cause Proceedings

The show cause procedure, addressed in Part IV, can be used when another body—including criminal courts, licensing boards, and state psychological associations—has already taken specified serious adverse action against a member. For example, if a member has been convicted of a felony or equivalent criminal offense; has been expelled or suspended by a state psychological association; or has been decertified, unlicensed, or deregistered or had a certificate, license, or registration revoked or suspended by a state or local board, the Committee may notify the respondent that he or she has 60 days to explain why APA should not expel the respondent from membership on the basis of that prior action. The respondent may show that procedures used were not fair and may argue the merits of the previous action. The Committee recommends to the Board of Directors whether the respondent should be expelled or allowed to resign under stipulated conditions, reprimanded or censured, or

From *American Psychologist, 51*, 529–548. Copyright 1996 by the American Psychological Association. Adapted with permission of the author and publisher.

cleared of the charges. Time limits for initiating show cause cases are stated in Part II, Section 5.3.4.

Complaints Alleging Violation of the Ethics Code

Investigations detailed in Part V include those brought by members and nonmembers of the Association and those initiated by the Ethics Committee (*sua sponte* complaints). Complaints must be submitted within specified time periods or allege serious misconduct for which a waiver of the time limit may be granted. (See Part II, Section 5.) Even with a waiver of the time limit, the Committee may not find violations for behavior that occurred 10 years or more before the complaint was filed.

Complaints are evaluated initially by the Ethics Office Director, or Investigators acting as the Director's designees, regarding jurisdictional issues such as whether the subject of the complaint, the respondent, is a member, whether the complaint form is correctly completed, and whether the time limits for filing have been met. Then the Chair of the Ethics Committee and Director of the Ethics Office or their designees determine whether there are grounds for action to be taken by the Committee (defined in Part V, Subsection 5.1). If necessary, the Chair and Director conduct a preliminary investigation (described in Part V, Section 5.3) to assist in making these threshold determinations. If the Committee has no jurisdiction or if cause for action does not exist, the complaint is dismissed. If the Committee has jurisdiction and cause for action exists, the Director will open a case, issue a specific charge letter, and conduct an investigation. The respondent is afforded an opportunity to comment on all evidence that will be considered by the Committee and upon which the Committee may rely in its review of the complaint. At the conclusion of the investigation, the case is referred to the Committee for review and resolution.

In resolving a case, the Committee may dismiss it; recommend that it be resolved with a reprimand or censure, with or without supplemental directives; recommend to the Board of Directors that the respondent be expelled from membership; or offer the member the option of resigning subject to stipulated conditions and subject to approval by the Board of Directors.

If the Committee recommends any action other than dismissal or stipulated resignation, the respondent has a right to an independent case review and evaluation or, in the case of a recommendation of expulsion, a formal hearing or an independent adjudication. In an independent adjudication following a recommendation of censure or reprimand, the respondent provides a rationale for nonacceptance of the Committee's recommendation, and a three-member panel, selected by the respondent from six members of the Board of Directors' standing Hearing Panel, provides the final adjudication based on the written record. The Director implements the final adjudication, whether based on the panel's decision or the respondent's acceptance of the Committee's recommendation.

A formal hearing is an in-person proceeding before a formal hearing committee, which makes an independent recommendation to the Board of Directors. The respondent may elect to have an independent adjudication instead of a formal hearing. The Board reviews the recommendation of the hearing committee, independent adjudication panel, or, if no hearing was requested, the Ethics Committee, and must adopt that recommendation unless specified defects require the matter to be remanded for further actions.

ADOPTION AND APPLICATION

The revised Rules and Procedures of the Ethics Committee of the American Psychological Association, which are set forth below, were approved by the APA Board of Directors on December 9, 1995, with an effective date of June 1, 1996. The Rules will be applied from that date forward to all complaints and cases pending on the effective date, except, as provided in Part II, Subsection 1.2 of the 1992 Rules, "no amendment shall adversely affect the rights of a member of the Association whose conduct is being investigated by the Ethics Committee or against whom the Ethics Committee has filed formal charges" as of the effective date. In the event that application of the revised Rules and Procedures would adversely affect such rights, the pertinent provisions of the Rules and Procedures in effect at the time the member came under the scrutiny of the Ethics Committee will be applied. Failure by the Committee or APA to follow these Rules and Procedures shall be cause to set aside action taken under these Rules only in the event such failure has resulted in genuine prejudice to the respondent.

PART I. OBJECTIVES AND AUTHORITY OF THE COMMITTEE

1. Objectives

The fundamental objectives of the Ethics Committee (hereinafter the Committee) shall be to maintain ethical conduct by psychologists at the highest professional level, to educate psychologists concerning ethical standards, to endeavor to protect the public against harmful conduct by psychologists, and to aid the Association in achieving its objectives as reflected in its Bylaws.[1]

2. Authority

The Committee is authorized to

2.1 Formulate rules or principles of ethics for adoption by the Association;

2.2 Investigate allegations of unethical conduct of members (to include fellows) and associates (hereinafter members) and, in certain instances, student affiliates and applicants for membership;

2.3 Resolve allegations of unethical conduct and/or recommend such action as is necessary to achieve the objectives of the Association;

2.4 Report on types of complaints investigated with special description of difficult cases;

2.5 Adopt rules and procedures governing the conduct of all the matters within its jurisdiction;

2.6 Take such other actions as are consistent with the Bylaws of the Association, the Association Rules, the Association's Ethics Code, and these Rules and Procedures, and as are necessary and appropriate to achieving the objectives of the Committee;

2.7 Delegate appropriate tasks to subcommittees, ad hoc committees, and task forces of the Ethics Committee; to Committee Associates; or to employees or agents of the Association, as necessary or appropriate. All of these individuals and groups shall in any such event be fully bound by these Rules and Procedures.

PART II. GENERAL OPERATING RULES

1. General Provisions

1.1 APA Documents.[2] The Committee shall base its actions on applicable governmental laws and regulations, the Bylaws of the Association, the Association Rules, the Association's Ethics Code, and these Rules and Procedures.

1.2 Applicable Ethics Code. Conduct is subject to the Ethics Code in effect at the time the conduct occurred. If a course of conduct continued over a period of time during which more than one Ethics Code was in effect, each Ethics Code will be applicable to conduct that occurred during the time period it was in effect.

1.3 Rules and Procedures. The Committee may adopt rules and procedures governing the conduct of all matters within its jurisdiction and may amend such rules from time to time upon a two-thirds vote of the Committee members, provided that no amendment shall adversely affect the rights of a member of the Association whose conduct is being investigated by the Ethics Committee or against whom the Ethics Committee has recommended expulsion, stipulated resignation, voiding membership, censure, or reprimand at the time of amendment. Changes to the Rules and Procedures must be ratified by the Board of Directors acting for the Council of Representatives.

1.4 Compliance With Time Requirements. The APA and the respondent shall use their best efforts to adhere strictly to the time requirements specified in these Rules and Procedures. Failure to do so will

---

[1] The Ethics Committee seeks to protect the public by deterring unethical conduct by psychologists, by taking appropriate action when an ethical violation has been proved according to these Rules and Procedures, and by setting standards to aid psychologists in understanding their ethical obligations. Of course, in no circumstances can or does the Committee or the Association guarantee that unethical behavior will not occur or that members of the public will never be harmed by the actions of individual psychologists.

[2] For a copy of the relevant sections of the current Bylaws and Association Rules, contact the APA Ethics Office.

not prohibit final resolution unless such failure was unduly prejudicial. Upon request, the Director may extend time limits stated in these Rules for submitting statements or responses if there is good cause to do so. In all cases in which a time limit for submitting a response is stated in these Rules and Procedures, the period specified is the number of days allowed for receipt of the response by the Ethics Office.

1.5 Computation of Time. In computing any period of time stated by these Rules, the day of the act, event, or default from which the designated period of time begins to run shall not be included. The last day of the period shall be included unless it is a Saturday, a Sunday, or a legal holiday, in which event the period runs until the end of the next business day.

2. Meetings and Officers

2.1 Frequency and Quorum. The Committee shall meet at reasonable intervals as needed. A quorum at such meetings shall consist of the majority of the elected members of the Committee.

2.2 Selection of Officers. The Chair and Vice Chair shall be elected annually at a duly constituted meeting.

2.3 Authority. The Vice Chair shall have the authority to perform all the duties of the Chair when the latter is unavailable or unable to perform them and shall perform such other tasks as are delegated by the Chair or by these Rules.

2.4 Majority Rule. Except as otherwise noted in these Rules and Procedures, all decisions shall be by majority vote of those elected members present or, in the case of a vote by mail, a majority of those elected members qualified to vote.

2.5 Designation of Responsibilities. The Chief Executive Officer of the Association shall designate a staff member to serve as Director of the Ethics Office. Whenever they appear in these Rules, "Chair," "Vice Chair," "Director," and "President" shall mean these individuals or their designees.

2.6 Attendance. Attendance at the Ethics Committee's deliberation of cases is restricted to elected members of the Committee, Committee Associates, the Director of the Ethics Office, the Ethics Office staff, members of the Board of Directors, Legal Counsel of the Association, and other duly appointed persons authorized by the Committee to assist it in carrying out its functions, except when the Committee, by two-thirds vote, authorizes the presence of other persons.

3. Confidentiality and Notifications

3.1 Requirement of Confidentiality. All information concerning complaints against members shall be confidential, except that the Director may disclose such information when compelled by a valid subpoena, in response to a request from a state or local board or similar entity,[3] when otherwise required by law, or as otherwise provided in these Rules and Procedures. Such information may also be released when the Chair and the Director agree that release of that information is necessary to protect the interests of (a) the complainant or respondent; (b) other investigative or adjudicative bodies; (c) the Association; or (d) members of the public, and release will not unduly interfere with the Association's interest in respecting the legitimate confidentiality interests of participants in the ethics process and its interest in safeguarding the confidentiality of internal peer review deliberation.

3.2 Access by Staff, Legal Counsel, and Other Duly Appointed Persons. Information may be shared with Legal Counsel of the Association, with the Chief Executive Officer of the Association, with staff of the Association's Central Office designated by the Chief Executive Officer to assist the Committee with its work, and with other duly appointed persons authorized by the Committee to assist it in carrying out its functions. Subject to the confidentiality provisions in these Rules, these persons are authorized to use this information for the purposes set out

[3] For purpose of these Rules and Procedures, a reference to state or local boards or similar entities shall include state, local, or provincial licensing boards (whether located in the United States or Canada); state, local, or provincial boards of examiners or education in those cases where the pertinent licensing or certification is secured from such entities; or in states or provinces with no licensing authority, nonstatutory boards established for similar purposes (such as registering bodies).

in these Rules regardless of whether the person providing the information has executed a release.

3.3 Notification in Connection With Investigation or Final Disposition of Investigation. Where these Rules provide for notification of final disposition of a matter, this notification shall include the ethical standard(s)[4] that were judged to have been violated and, if violation is found, the standards not violated, and the sanction (including a statement that directives were given), if any. In show cause proceedings under Part IV, this notification shall describe the type of underlying action (e.g., loss of license) without reference to the underlying behavior. In matters in which membership is voided under Part III, Subsection 3.3, the notification shall indicate that membership was voided because it was obtained on the basis of false or fraudulent information. In any of these matters, the rationale may also be included (a) if the notification is required by these Rules, at the discretion of the Board or Committee; (b) if the notification is not required, at the discretion of the entity or person (i.e., the Board, the Committee, or the Director) authorizing the notification; or (c) as set forth in a stipulation.

3.3.1 Respondent. The Director shall inform the respondent of the final disposition in a matter. This notification shall include the rationale for the Association's actions. As used in these Rules and Procedures, the term *respondent* includes any member, student affiliate, or membership applicant who is under the scrutiny of the Ethics Committee.

3.3.2 Complainant. The Director shall inform the complainant of the final disposition in a matter. The Director may also at any time, as a matter of discretion, provide such information as is necessary to notify the complainant of the status of a case.

3.3.3 Membership. The Director shall report annually to the membership the names of members who have lost membership due to unethical behavior and the ethical standard(s) violated or the type of underlying action for a show cause case or that

membership was voided because it was obtained on the basis of false or fraudulent information. No report to membership shall be made for stipulated resignations in which such a report was not stipulated.

3.3.4 Council of Representatives. The Director shall report annually and in confidence to the Council the names of members who have been allowed to resign under stipulated conditions.

3.3.5 Other Entities. When the Board of Directors, the Committee, or the Director (for stipulated resignations as provided in Part IV, Subsection 12.1.2) determines that further notification is necessary for the protection of the Association or the public or to maintain the standards of the Association, the Director shall communicate the final disposition to those groups and/or individuals so identified. Such notification may be made to (a) affiliated state and regional associations,[5] (b) the American Board of Professional Psychology, (c) state or local boards or similar entities, (d) the Association of State and Provincial Psychology Boards, (e) the Council for the National Register of Health Service Providers in Psychology, and/or (f) other appropriate parties.

3.3.6 Other Parties Informed of the Complaint. The Director may inform such other parties as have been informed of any matter reviewed under these Rules of the final disposition of that matter. Parties with knowledge of a matter may have been informed by the Committee, the Director, the respondent, or the complainant.

3.3.7 Notification in Cases That Have Been Converted. In any cases that have been converted under Part II, Subsections 7.3 or 7.4, the complainant and other persons informed of the complaint shall be notified of final disposition, including the fact that there has been a stipulated resignation, as set forth in Part IV, Subsections 12.1.2 and 12.2.1 and Part V, Subsection 7.6.5.

3.3.8 Disclosure of Fact of Investigation. The Director may disclose to any of the entities enumerated in Subsection 3.3.5 (a)–(f) of this part the fact that an

---

[4] In this document *ethical standard(s)* refers to the ethical standard(s) in the Ethical Principles of Psychologists and Code of Conduct, the ethical principle(s) in the Ethical Principles of Psychologists, or the enforceable provisions of any subsequent ethics code.

[5] For purposes of these Rules and Procedures, a state association shall include territorial, local, or county psychological associations, and in cases of Canadian members of the Association, provincial psychological associations.

individual is under ethical investigation in cases deemed to be serious threats to the public welfare (as determined by a two-thirds vote of the Committee), but only when to do so before final adjudication appears necessary to protect the public.

3.3.9 Notification of Additional Parties at the Request of Respondent. The Director may notify such additional parties of the final disposition as are requested by the respondent.

3.3.10 Notification of Loss of Membership Upon Written Request. The Director shall inform any person who submits a written inquiry concerning a psychologist that a former member has lost membership due to unethical behavior or that an individual's membership was voided because it was obtained on the basis of false or fraudulent information. The notification will not include actions that were already decided or were under the scrutiny of the Committee prior to June 1, 1996, or stipulated resignations unless so stipulated.

3.4 Initiation of Legal Action Constitutes Waiver.
Initiation of a legal action against the Association or any of its agents, officers, directors, employees, or volunteers concerning any matters considered or actions taken by the Ethics Committee or Director shall constitute a waiver by the person initiating such action of any interest in confidentiality recognized in these Rules or other organic documents of the Association with respect to the subject matter of the legal action.

3.5 Communication for Investigation or Other Functions.
Nothing in this section shall prevent the Director from communicating any information (including information from the respondent, complainant, or a witness) to the respondent, complainant, witnesses, or other sources of information to the extent necessary to facilitate the performance of any functions set forth in these Rules and Procedures.

4. Records

4.1 Confidentiality of Ethics Files.
Files of the Committee related to investigation and adjudication of cases shall be confidential, within the limitations of Section 3 of this part, and shall be maintained consistent with these Rules and Procedures.

4.2 Investigation Files.
Investigation records containing personally identifiable information shall be maintained for at least five years after a matter is closed.

4.3 Files Involving Loss of Membership.
In cases in which members have lost membership, records shall be maintained indefinitely, except as provided in Subsection 4.4 of this part.

4.4 Readmission or Death of a Member.
Records concerning members whom the Association has readmitted to membership or determined to be deceased shall be maintained for at least five years after that determination was made.

4.5 Records for Educative Purposes.
Nothing in these Rules and Procedures shall preclude the Committee from maintaining records in a secure place for archival or record keeping purposes, or from using or publishing information concerning ethics matters for educative purposes without identifying individuals involved.

5. Jurisdiction

5.1 Persons.
The Committee has jurisdiction over individual members (to include fellows), associate members, and applicants for membership in the American Psychological Association. The Committee shall also have jurisdiction over student affiliates, but only to the extent that the conduct at issue is not under the direct supervision of the student's educational program or of a training site that is officially approved by the program as part of the student's supervised training.[6]

5.2 Subject Matter.
The Committee has jurisdiction to achieve its objectives and perform those functions for which it is authorized in these Rules and Procedures and other organic documents of the Association.

---

[6] Whether an individual is a member of the Association is determined according to the Bylaws, Association Rules, and other pertinent organic documents of the Association. Under the current rules, nonpayment of dues results in discontinuation of membership only after two consecutive calendar years during which dues to the Association have remained unpaid. For a copy of the relevant sections of the current Bylaws and Association Rules, contact the APA Ethics Office. For purposes of these Rules and Procedures, high school and foreign affiliates are not members of the Association.

5.3 Time Limits for Complaints and Show Cause Notices

5.3.1 Complaints by Members. Except as provided in Subsections 5.3.5 and 5.3.6 of this part, the Committee may consider complaints brought by members of the Association against other members only if the complaint is received less than three years after the alleged conduct either occurred or was discovered by the complainant.

5.3.2 Complaints by Nonmembers and Student Affiliates. Except as provided in Subsections 5.3.5 and 5.3.6 of this part, the Committee may consider complaints brought by nonmembers and student affiliates only if the complaint is received less than five years after the alleged conduct either occurred or was discovered by the complainant.

5.3.3 Sua Sponte Complaints. Except as provided in Subsection 7.4 of this part, the Committee may initiate a *sua sponte* complaint under Part V of these Rules and Procedures only if it does so, or has provided the notice specified in Subsection 5.6.2 of this part, less than 1 year after it discovered the alleged unethical conduct and less than 10 years after the alleged conduct occurred, except that whether or not such periods have expired, the Committee may initiate a *sua sponte* complaint less than 1 year after it discovered that any of the following actions had become final and less than 10 years after the following alleged conduct occurred: (a) a felony conviction, (b) a finding of malpractice by a duly authorized tribunal, (c) expulsion or suspension from a state association for unethical conduct, or (d) revocation, suspension, or surrender of a license or certificate, or deregistration for ethical violations by a state or local board or similar entity, or while ethical proceedings before such board were pending.

5.3.4 Show Cause Notices. The Committee may issue a show cause notice under Part IV of these Rules and Procedures only if it does so, or has provided the notice specified in Subsection 5.6.2 of this part, less than 1 year after the date it discovered that the applicable predicate for use of show cause procedures (i.e., an event described in Part IV, Section 1) had become final and less than 10 years after the alleged conduct occurred, except this latter time limit shall be 20 years in any matter involving an offense against a minor.

5.3.5 Exceptions to Time Limits for Complaints by Members and Nonmembers

5.3.5.1 Threshold Criteria. Any complaint not received within the time limits set forth in this section shall not be considered unless, with respect to complaints subject to Subsections 5.3.1 and 5.3.2 of this part, the Chair and Director (with the vote of the Vice Chair if agreement is not reached by the Chair and Director) determine that each of the following criteria is met:

5.3.5.1.1 The behavior alleged involved one of the following: sexual misconduct; felony conviction; insurance fraud; plagiarism; noncooperation; blatant, intentional misrepresentation; or other behavior likely to cause substantial harm;

5.3.5.1.2 The complaint was received less than 10 years after the alleged conduct occurred.

5.3.5.2 Determination to Supersede Applicable Time Limit. Where the Chair and Director have determined (with the vote of the Vice Chair if agreement is not reached by the Chair and Director) that the threshold criteria in Subsection 5.3.5.1 are met, the applicable limit shall be superseded.

5.3.6 Conduct Outside the Time Limits. The Committee may consider evidence of conduct outside these time limits in connection with the commencement, investigation, review, or disposition of a matter involving conduct that is within the applicable time limits. However, the Committee may impose sanctions only for conduct that occurred within the time limits. In order for a sanction to be imposed for conduct occurring outside the time limits, the Chair and Director must decide to supersede the time limits applicable to that conduct as stated in Subsection 5.3.5 of this part.

5.3.7 Reopened Investigations. In a matter reopened under Part II, Section 6, the investigation shall be considered within the time limits as long as the complaint in the original matter was received, or the original investigation was initiated, in a timely manner or a decision was made to supersede the time limit under Part II, Subsection 5.3.5. The Committee may not proceed with such an investigation, however, if the new evidence is received more than 10 years after the date the alleged unethical behavior occurred (except that this time limit shall be 20 years in any case that was initiated as or converted to a show cause case and involves an offense against a minor).

5.4 Resignation Barred. Except as provided in Subsection 11.4 of this part of these Rules, no one under the scrutiny of the Committee will be allowed to resign from the Association either by letter of resignation, by nonpayment of dues, or otherwise.

5.5 Concurrent Litigation. Civil or criminal litigation involving members shall not bar action by the Committee; the Committee may proceed or may stay the ethics process during the course of litigation. Delay in conducting the investigation by the Committee during the pendency of civil or criminal proceedings shall not constitute waiver of jurisdiction.

5.6 Other Concurrent Disciplinary Proceedings

5.6.1 Concurrent Jurisdiction. Disciplinary proceedings or action by another body or tribunal shall not bar action by the Committee; the Committee may proceed or may stay the ethics process during the course of such proceedings. Delay in conducting the investigation by the Committee during the pendency of such proceedings shall not constitute a waiver of jurisdiction. Where the Committee learns that disciplinary action by another authorized tribunal has been stayed, such stay shall neither require nor preclude action by the Committee. When another body or tribunal has investigated the same allegations and found no merit to the allegations, the Ethics Committee may, in its discretion, decide not to open a matter or, if a matter has already been opened, the Ethics Committee may close the matter.

5.6.2 Nonfinal Disciplinary Action by Another Body. The Chair, Vice Chair, and Director may decide not to open a *sua sponte* or show cause case when a state or local board or similar entity has taken disciplinary action against an Association member if the action is either not final or the member has not completed all directives, probation, or other requirements and if the behavior at issue is not likely to result in expulsion from the Association. If this decision is made, the member will be notified that the matter is under the scrutiny of the Committee, that the member will be monitored until completion of actions required by the state or local board or similar entity, that failure to complete the action may result in further action by the Committee, and that

completion of such requirements may result in the Committee taking no further action.

5.7 Referral and Retention of Jurisdiction. The Committee may at any time refer a matter to another recognized tribunal for appropriate action. If a case is referred to another tribunal, the Committee may retain jurisdiction and consider the matter independently under these Rules and Procedures.

6. Reopening a Closed Case

If significant new evidence of unethical conduct comes to the attention of the Committee after a matter has been closed, the investigation may be reopened and acted upon under regular procedures. If, in the judgment of the Director, such information is furnished, the new evidence shall be submitted to the Committee, which may reopen the investigation if it agrees that the criteria listed below are satisfied. To be considered under this rule, new evidence must meet each of the following criteria:

6.1 The evidence was brought to the attention of the Committee after the investigation was closed;

6.2 The evidence could not with reasonable diligence have been brought to the attention of the Committee before the investigation was closed;

6.3 The evidence was provided to the Committee in a timely manner following its discovery;

6.4 The evidence would probably produce a different result.

7. Choice and Conversion of Procedures

7.1 Choice of Procedures. Where a case might be adjudicated according to the show cause procedures in Part IV of these Rules and Procedures, the Chair and the Director shall determine whether to proceed under Part IV or Part V of these Rules and Procedures.

7.2 Conversion of Show Cause Action to *Sua Sponte* Action. The Chair and the Director may convert a proceeding begun by show cause procedures under Part IV to a *sua sponte* action under Part V. In the event of such conversion, the complaint shall be deemed filed in a timely manner if the show cause proceeding was initiated in a timely fashion.

7.3 Conversion to Show Cause Action. Where the predicates for use of show cause procedures stated in Part IV, Section 1 are present, the Chair and the Director may convert a proceeding begun as a *sua sponte*, member, or nonmember complaint under Part V to a show cause proceeding under Part IV if the predicates are based on some or all of the same underlying conduct as was the basis for the original proceeding. In such event, the show cause proceeding shall be deemed initiated in a timely manner as long as the original proceeding was commenced within the time limits applicable to that proceeding or a decision was made to supersede the time limit under Part II, Subsection 5.3.5.

7.4 Conversion of Action Initiated by a Complainant to a *Sua Sponte* Action. The Chair and the Director may convert a proceeding commenced following a complaint submitted by a member or nonmember (including a proceeding in which the complaint is withdrawn) into a *sua sponte* action under Part V, Subsection 2.2. The action will be deemed filed in a timely manner as long as the member or nonmember complaint was received within the time limits applicable to the initial complaint or a decision was made to supersede the time limit in Part II, Subsection 5.3.5.

8. Correspondence and Documentation

8.1 Use of Correspondence. The Committee shall conduct as much of its business as is practical through correspondence, including telecopied information.

8.2 Personal Response. Although the respondent has the right to consult with an attorney concerning all phases of the ethics process, the respondent must respond to charges and recommendations of the Ethics Committee personally and not through legal counsel or another third party. If the respondent shows good cause as to why he or she cannot respond personally, the Director may waive this requirement.

8.3 Transcription of Audiotapes, Videotapes, and Similar Data Compilations. It shall be the responsibility of the individual or entity submitting to the Committee an audiotape, videotape, or similar data compilation to provide an accurate transcription of the information it contains. The Director may reject any audiotape, videotape, or similar data compilation provided unaccompanied by a transcrip-

tion as required in this subsection unless and until such transcription is provided.

8.4 Service of Documents. For purposes of notice, service shall be made by delivery to the respondent or the respondent's attorney or by mail or common carrier to the respondent or the respondent's attorney at the respondent's or attorney's last known address. Delivery within this rule means handing the correspondence to the respondent or the attorney or leaving it at the respondent's office or place of abode or the attorney's office with a receptionist, secretary, clerk, or other person in charge thereof, or, if there is no one in charge, leaving it in a mailbox or a conspicuous place at that address. Service by mail is complete upon mailing. Where, after good faith efforts, the Committee has been unable to locate the respondent, it may give notice by publishing in a newspaper of general circulation in the respondent's last known place of domicile a notice to contact the Ethics Office concerning an important matter.

8.5 Material From the Public Domain. The Committee may consult authoritative resources from the public domain (e.g., the Directory of the American Psychological Association and the National Register of Health Service Providers in Psychology) without providing this material to the respondent.

9. Failure to Cooperate With Ethics Process

Members are required to cooperate fully and in a timely fashion with the ethics process. Failure to cooperate shall not prevent continuation of any proceedings and itself constitutes a violation of the Ethics Code that may warrant being expelled from the Association.

10. Board of Directors' Standing Hearing Panel

The President of the Association shall appoint members of the Standing Hearing Panel. Standing Hearing Panel members shall serve a three-year renewable term. The Standing Hearing Panel shall consist of at least 30 members at least 5 of whom shall be public members, and the remainder shall be members of the Association in good standing and shall not include any present members of the Ethics Committee.

11. Available Sanctions

On the basis of circumstances that aggravate or mitigate the culpability of the member, including prior sanctions, directives, or educative letters from the Association or state or local boards or similar entities, a sanction more or less severe, respectively, than would be warranted on the basis of the factors set forth below, may be appropriate.

11.1 Reprimand. Reprimand is the appropriate sanction if there has been an ethics violation but the violation was not of a kind likely to cause harm to another person or to cause substantial harm to the profession and was not otherwise of sufficient gravity as to warrant a more severe sanction.

11.2 Censure. Censure is the appropriate sanction if there has been an ethics violation and the violation was of a kind likely to cause harm to another person, but the violation was not of a kind likely to cause substantial harm to another person or to the profession and was not otherwise of sufficient gravity as to warrant a more severe sanction.

11.3 Expulsion. Expulsion from membership is the appropriate sanction if there has been an ethics violation and the violation was of a kind likely to cause substantial harm to another person or the profession or was otherwise of sufficient gravity as to warrant such action.

11.4 Stipulated Resignation. Stipulated resignation may be offered by the Committee as follows:

11.4.1 At the time of the respondent's initial response to the show cause notice, contingent upon execution of an acceptable affidavit admitting responsibility for the violations charged, under Part IV, Subsection 12.1;

11.4.2 Following a Committee finding that the respondent has committed a violation of the Ethics Code or failed to show good cause why he or she should not be expelled, contingent on execution of an acceptable affidavit and approval by the Board of Directors, under Part IV, Subsection 12.2, or Part V, Subsection 7.6.

12. Available Directives

12.1 Cease and Desist Order. Such a directive requires the respondent to cease and desist specified unethical behavior(s).

12.2 Other Corrective Actions. The Committee may require such other corrective actions as may be necessary to remedy a violation, protect the interests of the Association, or protect the public. Such a directive may not include a requirement that the respondent make a monetary payment to the Association or persons injured by the conduct.

12.3 Supervision Requirement. Such a directive requires that the respondent engage in supervision.

12.4 Education, Training, or Tutorial Requirement. Such a directive requires that the respondent engage in education, training, or a tutorial.

12.5 Evaluation and/or Treatment Requirement. Such a directive requires that the respondent be evaluated to determine the possible need for treatment and/or, if dysfunction has been established, obtain treatment appropriate to that dysfunction.

12.6 Probation. Such a directive requires monitoring of the respondent by the Committee to ensure compliance with the Ethics Committee's mandated directives during the period of those directives.

13. Matters Requiring the Concurrence of the Chair of the Committee and Director of the Ethics Office

Whenever matters entrusted by these Rules and Procedures to the Chair and Director require the concurrence of those officers before certain action may be taken, either officer in the event of disagreement may refer the matter to the Vice Chair, who together with the Chair and Director, shall make a final determination by majority vote.

PART III. MEMBERSHIP

1. Applications

1.1 Specific Jurisdiction. The Committee has the authority to investigate the preadmission scientific and professional ethics and conduct of all applicants for membership or student affiliation in the Association and to make recommendations as to whether an individual shall become a member or student affiliate. In addition, the Committee has the authority to consider all applications submitted by individuals who were previously denied admission as a result of unethical behavior and to make recommendations as to whether such an individual shall become a member or student affiliate. The Membership Committee shall transmit all applications on which there is an indication of possible preadmission unethical conduct and all applications from individuals who were previously denied admission as a result of unethical behavior or as a result of a recommendation by the Ethics Committee to the Director of the Ethics Office.

1.2 Procedures for Review. The Director shall transmit to the Committee a copy of the membership application and any other materials pertinent to the case. The Director shall take such steps, including contacting the applicant or other sources of information, as are necessary and appropriate to making a fair determination. Upon review, the Committee may recommend to the Membership Committee that the application be granted or to the Board of Directors that the application be denied. If a recommendation is made to deny the application, the applicant shall be informed of the basis for that recommendation and shall have 30 days to submit a written response for consideration by the Board of Directors.

2. Applications for Readmission

2.1 Specific Jurisdiction. The Ethics Committee has the authority to review and make recommendations concerning all applications for readmission by persons who have lost membership as a result of unethical behavior or whose membership was voided because it was obtained on the basis of false or fraudulent information. The Membership Committee shall transmit all such applications for readmission to the Director of the Ethics Office.

2.2 Elapsed Time for Review. Applications for readmission by members who have lost membership due to unethical behavior (including submission of false or fraudulent information in a membership application) shall be considered by the Committee only after five years have elapsed from the date of that action. Applications for readmission by members who have been permitted to resign shall be considered only after the stipulated period or, where no period has been stipulated, three years have elapsed.

2.3 Procedures for Review. The Director shall transmit to the Committee a summary of the appli-

cation for readmission and the record of the previous case against the former member. In all cases, the ex-member must show that he or she is technically and ethically qualified and has satisfied any conditions upon readmission established by the Board. The Committee shall make one of the following recommendations to the Membership Committee and, as it deems appropriate, shall provide the rationale therefor.

    2.3.1 Readmit. Recommend that the former member be readmitted;

    2.3.2 Deny Readmission. Recommend that readmission be denied;

    2.3.3 Defer Readmission. Recommend that the application for readmission be deferred until certain conditions have been met;

    2.3.4 Investigate Further. Charge the Director to investigate issues specified by the Committee and to place the matter before the Committee at a future date.

3. Allegations That Membership Was Obtained Under False or Fraudulent Pretenses

3.1 Specific Jurisdiction. The Committee has the authority to investigate allegations that membership was obtained on the basis of false or fraudulent information and to take appropriate action. The Membership Committee shall transmit all such allegations to the Director of the Ethics Office.

3.2 Procedures for Review. The respondent will be given notice of the allegations that membership was obtained on the basis of false or fraudulent information, a copy of any evidence relating to these allegations that is submitted to the Committee, and an opportunity to respond in writing. The Director may take any other steps, such as contacting other sources of information, that are considered necessary and appropriate to making a fair determination in the circumstances of the case. The Director shall transmit to the Committee a copy of the membership application and any other materials pertinent to the case.

3.3 Committee's Recommendation. Upon completion of this review, the Committee may recommend to the Board of Directors that it void the election to membership in the Association of any person who obtained membership on the basis of false or fraudulent information.

3.4 Procedures Subsequent to Committee's Recommendation to Void Membership. If the respondent does not accept the Committee's recommendation, the respondent shall, within 30 days of receipt of the recommendation, either submit a written response to the Board of Directors, request a formal hearing in writing, or request an independent adjudication in writing and provide a written rationale for nonacceptance. The respondent's failure to respond within 30 days after notification shall be deemed acceptance of the Committee's recommendation and a waiver of the right to a formal hearing or an independent adjudication. If a written response is submitted, the Ethics Committee shall have 30 days to reply in a written statement to the Board. If a formal hearing is requested, it shall be conducted according to the procedures explained in Part V, Subsections 10.2 through 10.3.4 of these Rules and Procedures. If an independent adjudication is requested, it shall be conducted according to the procedures explained in Part V, Subsections 9.2.2 through 9.2.7 and Subsections 10.3 through 10.3.4.

3.5 Action by the Board of Directors. Within 180 days after receiving the record, the Committee's recommendation, any written response and statement described in Subsection 3.4, above, or any recommendation from a Hearing Committee or Independent Adjudication Panel, the Board of Directors shall vote whether to void the respondent's membership or not.

PART IV. SHOW CAUSE PROCEDURES BASED UPON ACTIONS BY OTHER RECOGNIZED TRIBUNALS

1. Predicates for Use of Show Cause Procedures

1.1 Felony or Equivalent Offense. If a member has been convicted of a felony (including any felony as defined by state/provincial law and any other criminal offense with a possible term of incarceration exceeding one year) and such conviction is not under appeal, the show cause process may be used, if determined by the Chair and the Director to be appropriate.

1.2 Expulsion, Suspension, Unlicensure, Decertification, or Other Actions. If one of the following actions has been taken and is not under appeal, the show cause process may be used, if determined by the Chair and the Director to be appropriate: (a) a member has been expelled or suspended from an affiliated state or regional psychological association; (b) a member has been denied a license, certificate, or registration, has been unlicensed, decertified, or deregistered, has had a license, certificate, or registration revoked or suspended by a state or local board or similar entity, or has voluntarily surrendered a license or certificate of registration as a result of pending allegations. The show cause procedures may also be used if a state or local board or similar entity has taken any of the actions specified in (a) or (b) above and has then in any way stayed or postponed that action.

2. Notice by the Committee and Response by Respondent

The respondent shall be notified by the Director that he or she has been barred from resigning membership in the Association (subject only to the terms of Section 12 of this part) and, on the basis of Part IV of these Rules and Procedures, will be afforded 60 days in which to show good cause as to why he or she should not be expelled from membership in the Association.

3. Showing by Respondent That Prior Proceeding Lacked Due Process

In addition to a response to the substance of the charges under Section 2 of this part, the respondent may seek within the 60-day period to show that the other recognized tribunal did not follow fair procedure. If the Committee finds merit to this contention, it may exercise its discretion under Part II, Subsection 7.2 of these Rules and convert the matter to a *sua sponte* action under Part V, or it may dismiss the complaint.

4. Investigation

The Committee may conduct a further investigation, including seeking additional information from the respondent or others or requesting that the respondent appear in person. Any evidence not obtained directly from the respondent and relied upon by the Committee in connection with its review and recommendation shall first have been provided to the respondent, who shall have been afforded not less than 15 days to respond thereto in writing.

5. Failure to Respond

If the 60-day period expires without receipt of a response, the respondent shall be notified that unless a response is received within 30 days, the Committee members may review the matter and vote by mail. If no response is received, the Committee may vote by mail to take one of the actions specified in Subsection 6 of this part.

6. Review and Recommendation by the Committee Following a Response

Upon receipt of the respondent's response and upon conclusion of any necessary further investigation, or the expiration of 60 days without response, the case shall be reviewed by the Ethics Committee. Members of the Ethics Committee and Ethics Committee Associates may be assigned to review and summarize the case. Members and Associates may also be assigned to participate on a panel to review the case and make a preliminary recommendation prior to review by the full Ethics Committee. Ethics Committee Associates may also attend and participate in the full Committee meetings, but shall not vote on the full Committee's disposition of a case. When review of a case has been completed, the Committee shall vote to take one of the following actions:

6.1 Remand

6.2 Dismiss the Matter

6.3 Recommend One of the Following Actions to the Board of Directors:

6.3.1 Reprimand or Censure, With or Without Directives. The Committee may recommend that the respondent be reprimanded or censured, with or without one or more directives.

6.3.2 Expulsion. The Committee may recommend that the respondent be expelled from the Association; or, the Committee may recommend the sanction of stipulated resignation, under the procedure in Subsection 12.2 of this part.

7. Notification of Respondent

The Director shall notify the respondent of the Committee's recommendation and shall provide the respondent the opportunity to file a written response with the Board of Directors.

8. Respondent's Response to Recommendation

Within 15 days of receipt of notification of the Committee's recommendation, the respondent may file a written response with the Board of Directors. The response should be mailed to the Ethics Office.

9. Committee's Statement

The Ethics Committee shall have 15 days from the time it receives the respondent's written response, or from the time such response was due, to file a written statement, if any. A copy will be provided to the respondent.

10. Respondent's Final Response

Within 15 days of receipt of the Ethics Committee's statement, if any, the respondent may submit to the Director a written response to that statement.

11. Review by the Board of Directors

Within 180 days after receiving the record, the Committee's recommendation, any written response by the respondent, any written statement by the Committee, and any final response from the respondent, the Board of Directors shall vote whether to accept the Committee's recommended sanction, to issue a different sanction, or to dismiss the case. The Board may select a sanction more or less severe than that recommended by the Committee, or it may remand the matter to the Ethics Committee for further consideration.

12. Stipulated Resignation

12.1 Stipulated Resignation With Admission of Violation in Respondent's Initial Response to the Show Cause Notice

12.1.1 Respondent's Offer of Stipulated Resignation With Admission of Violation. In his or her initial response to the Committee's notice to show cause under Section 2 of this part, the respondent may offer to resign membership in the Association with admission of violation. Such an offer must include a statement of intent to execute an affidavit acceptable to the Committee (a) admitting the violation underlying the criminal conviction, expulsion, unlicensure, decertification, or deregistration, and (b) resigning membership in the Association.

12.1.2 Director's Response and Proposed Affidavit of Stipulated Resignation. When the respondent makes such an offer, the Director will forward to the respondent a proposed affidavit of stipulated resignation. Such stipulations shall include the extent to which the stipulated resignation and its basis shall be disclosed and a minimum period of time, after resignation, during which the resigned member shall be ineligible to reapply for membership.

12.1.3 Acceptance by Respondent. Within 30 days of receipt, the respondent may resign membership in the Association by signing and having notarized the proposed affidavit and returning it to the Committee. Resignation shall be effective upon the Committee's timely receipt of the signed notarized affidavit.

12.1.4 Rejection by Respondent. If the member fails to sign, have notarized, and return an acceptable affidavit within 30 days or formally notifies the Committee of rejection of the proposed affidavit, the offer of stipulated resignation shall be deemed rejected. The respondent shall be afforded an additional 30 days within which to supplement his or her response to the Committee's show cause notice. The matter shall then be resolved according to the applicable procedures in this part. All materials submitted by the respondent shall be part of the file to be considered by the Committee and/or the Board of Directors in connection with the case.

12.1.5 Availability of Stipulated Resignation With Admission of Violation. Stipulated resignation with admission of violation is available only at the time and in the manner set forth in this section. Unless stipulated resignation with admission of violation is accomplished at the time and in the manner stated in this section, respondents may not resign while under scrutiny of the Ethics Committee except as stated in Subsection 12.2 of this part.

12.2 Stipulated Resignation After Review and Recommendation by the Committee.
In lieu of the recommendations set forth in Section 6 of this part, with the agreement of the respondent, the Committee may recommend that the respondent be permitted to resign from the Association under stipulations stated by the Committee, according to the following procedure:

12.2.1 Offer of Stipulated Resignation by Committee. When the Committee finds that another body has taken one of the actions specified in Part IV, Section 1 against a member, the Committee may offer, contingent upon approval by the Board of Directors, the respondent the opportunity to resign from the Association under mutually agreed upon stipulations. Such stipulations shall include the extent to which the stipulated resignation and its basis shall be disclosed and a minimum period of time, after resignation, during which the resigned member shall be ineligible to reapply for membership. The Committee may, in its direction, also vote to recommend to the Board and inform the respondent of an alternative sanction chosen from among Subsections 11.1–11.3 of Part II of these Rules in the event the respondent does not accept the offer of stipulated resignation.

12.2.2 Notification of Respondent. In such cases, the respondent shall be notified, in writing, of the Committee's offer of stipulated resignation and that he or she may accept the Committee's offer within 30 days of receipt. The respondent shall also be notified of any alternative recommended sanction.

12.2.3 Acceptance by Respondent. Within 30 days, the respondent may accept the offer of stipulated resignation by signing a notarized affidavit of resignation acceptable to both the respondent and the Committee and forwarding the signed notarized affidavit to the Committee. Such resignation shall become effective only with the approval of the Board, as set forth in this section.

12.2.4 Transmittal to Board of Directors. If the respondent accepts the stipulated resignation, the Committee shall submit a copy of the affidavit of resignation, with the record in the matter and the rationale for recommending stipulated resignation on the terms set forth in the affidavit, to the Board of Directors.

12.2.5 Action by Board of Directors. Within 180 days, the Board of Directors shall take one of the following actions:

12.2.5.1 Acceptance of Stipulated Resignation.

The Board of Directors shall accept the respondent's resignation on the terms stated in the affidavit of resignation, unless it is persuaded that to do so would not be in the best interest of the Association and/or of the public. If the resignation is accepted by the Board, the Director shall so notify the respondent.

12.2.5.2 Reprimand or Censure. The Board may reject the stipulated resignation and impose a lesser sanction (reprimand or censure with or without directives). If the Board selects this option, the respondent shall be so notified and shall have 30 days to submit a written request seeking reconsideration of the Board's decision. If no such request is submitted, the Board's decision shall become final. If a request for reconsideration is submitted, the Board shall choose from the options set forth in Subsection 12.2.5 (including adherence to its prior decision).

12.2.5.3 Remand to the Committee. The Board may choose to reject the affidavit of resignation and remand the matter to the Committee for further consideration. If the Board selects this alternative, the Director shall so notify the respondent and the Committee shall then reconsider the matter.

12.2.6 Rejection of Stipulated Resignation by Respondent. If the respondent fails within 30 days to accept the recommended resolution, or formally notifies the Committee of rejection of the offer of stipulated resignation within the 30-day period, the offer of stipulated resignation shall be deemed rejected. The Committee shall reconsider the matter or, if an alternative recommended sanction has previously been identified by the Committee, such alternative recommended sanction shall automatically become the recommended sanction. The Director shall notify the respondent of the recommendation and of his or her opportunity to file written responses with the Board of Directors, as stated in Section 8 of this part. Sections 8–11 of this part shall also apply.

PART V. COMPLAINTS ALLEGING VIOLATION OF THE ETHICS CODE

1. Initiation of Actions

Ethics proceedings against a member are initiated by the filing of a complaint or, in the case of a *sua sponte* action, by the issuance of a letter notifying the respondent that a *sua sponte* action has been commenced.

2. Complaints

2.1 Complaints Submitted by Members or Non-members.   Complaints may be submitted by members or nonmembers of the Association.

2.2 *Sua Sponte* Action.   When a member appears to have violated the Association's Ethics Code, the Committee may proceed on its own initiative. The Committee may, at any time, exercise its discretion to discontinue a *sua sponte* action. If the Committee does so, the respondent shall be so notified.

2.3 *Sua Sponte* Action Based Upon a Member's Filing of a Capricious or Malicious Complaint. To prevent abuse of the ethics process, the Committee is empowered to bring charges itself against a complainant if the initial complaint is judged by two thirds of Committee members voting to be (a) frivolous and (b) intended to harm the respondent rather than to protect the public. The filing of such a complaint constitutes a violation of the Ethics Code.

2.4 Countercomplaints.   The Committee will not consider a complaint from a respondent member against a complainant member during the course of its investigation and resolution of the initial complaint. Rather, the Committee shall study all sides of the matter leading to the first complaint and consider countercharges only after the initial complaint is finally resolved. The Committee may waive this procedure by a vote of at least two thirds of the voting Committee members and consider both complaints simultaneously.

2.5 Anonymous Complaints.   The Committee shall not act upon anonymous complaints. If material in the public domain is provided anonymously, the Committee may choose to consider such material in connection with a *sua sponte* matter or other complaint or may initiate a *sua sponte* action but only if the respondent has been provided with a copy of the material and afforded an opportunity to respond to the material.

2.6 Complaints Against Nonmembers.   If the complaint does not involve an individual within the jurisdiction of the Committee, the Director shall inform the complainant and may suggest that the complainant contact another agency or association that may have jurisdiction.

2.7 Consecutive Complaint. When a complaint is lodged against a member with respect to whom a case involving similar alleged behavior was previously closed, materials in the prior case may be considered in connection with the new case and may be considered as evidence as long as the Ethics Committee and/or the Board of Directors is informed of the final disposition of the original case.

2.8 Simultaneous Complaints. When more than one complaint is simultaneously pending against the same member, the Committee may choose to combine the cases or to keep them separate. In the event the cases are combined, the Committee shall take reasonable steps to ensure that the legitimate confidentiality interests of any complainant, witness, or respondent are not compromised by combination.

3. Procedures for Filing Complaints

A complaint by a member or nonmember shall be comprised of

3.1 A completed APA Ethics Complaint Form;

3.2 Such releases as are required by the Committee;

3.3 A waiver by the complainant of any right to subpoena from APA or its agents for the purposes of private civil litigation any documents or information concerning the case.[7]

3.4 For purpose of determining time limits, a complaint shall be considered filed with APA as soon as a completed complaint form has been received by the Ethics Office. A deficiency or omission in the preparation of the complaint form may, at the discretion of the Director, be disregarded for purposes of determining compliance with time limits.

4. Preliminary Evaluation of Complaints by the Director

The Director shall review each complaint to determine if jurisdictional criteria are met and if it can be determined whether cause for action exists.

4.1 Lack of Jurisdiction. If jurisdictional criteria

are not satisfied, the matter shall be closed and the complainant so notified.

4.2 Information Insufficient to Determine Jurisdiction

4.2.1 Request for Supplementation of Complaint. If the information is not sufficient to determine whether jurisdictional criteria are met, the Director shall so inform the complainant, who will be given 30 days from receipt of the request to supplement the complaint.

4.2.2 Consequences of Failure to Supplement Complaint. If no response is received from the complainant within 30 days from receipt of the request, the matter may be closed. If at a later date the complainant shows good cause for delay and demonstrates that jurisdictional criteria can be met, the supplemented complaint shall be considered.

4.3 Process With Respect to Superseding Applicable Time Limit

4.3.1 Consideration by Chair and Director. If a complaint otherwise within the jurisdiction of the Ethics Committee appears to have been filed outside the applicable time limit, the Chair and the Director will determine whether the criteria set forth in Part II, Subsection 5.3.5 appear to be satisfied. If they agree that the criteria do not appear to be satisfied, the matter will be closed, unless there are other allegations that are filed in a timely manner, in which case processing of the timely allegations continues under Section 5, below. If they agree that the criteria appear to be satisfied, the Director will contact the respondent according to the procedure in Subsection 4.3.2, below. If they are not in agreement on whether or not those criteria appear to be satisfied, the Vice Chair shall review the matter and cast the deciding vote.

4.3.2 Response by Respondent Where Criteria Appear To Be Satisfied. If a determination is made according to Subsection 4.3.1 above that the criteria of Part II, Subsection 5.3.5 appear to be satisfied, the Director shall notify the respondent and provide the respondent with a copy of the complaint and any other materials the Director deems appropriate. The

---

[7]This waiver is required to help assure participants in the APA ethics process, including complainants, that the process will not be inappropriately used to gain an advantage in other litigation.

respondent shall have 30 days from receipt of these materials to address whether the criteria of Part II, Subsection 5.3.5 are met.

4.3.3 Determination by Chair and Director. If the respondent does not provide a response under Subsection 4.3.2, above, the decision made under Subsection 4.3.1, above, shall become final. In any case in which the respondent provides a response, the Chair and the Director shall consider whether the criteria set forth in Part II, Subsection 5.3.5 are satisfied, based upon any materials provided by the complainant and respondent, and any other information available to the Chair and the Director. If they agree that the criteria are not satisfied, the matter will be closed, unless there are other allegations that are filed in a timely manner, in which case processing of the timely allegations continues under Section 5, below. If they agree that the criteria are satisfied, processing continues under Section 5, below. If they are not in agreement on whether or not those criteria are satisfied, the Vice Chair shall review the matter and cast the deciding vote.

5. Evaluation of Complaints by Chair and Director

All complaints not closed by the Director under Section 4 of this part shall be reviewed by the Chair and the Director to determine whether cause for action by the Ethics Committee exists.

5.1 Cause for Action Defined. Cause for action shall exist when the respondent's alleged actions and/or omissions, if proved, would in the judgment of the decision maker constitute a breach of ethics. For purposes of determining whether cause for action exists, incredible, speculative, and/or internally inconsistent allegations may be disregarded.

5.2 Information Insufficient to Determine Cause for Action

5.2.1 Request for Supplementation of Complaint. If the information is not sufficient to determine whether a case should be opened, the Director may so inform the complainant, who will be given 30 days from receipt of the request to supplement the complaint. The Chair and Director may additionally, or in the alternative, commence a preliminary investigation under Subsection 5.3 of this part.

5.2.2 Consequences of Failure to Supplement Com-

plaint. If no response is received from the complainant within 30 days, the matter may be closed. If at a later date the complainant shows good cause for delay and responds to the request for supplementation, the supplemented complaint shall be considered.

5.3 Preliminary Investigation Due to Insufficient Information. If the Chair and Director agree that they lack sufficient information to determine whether a case should be opened, in either a case initiated by a complainant or in a *sua sponte* action, a preliminary investigation may be initiated.

5.3.1 Notification to Respondent. If a preliminary investigation is opened, the Director shall so inform the respondent in writing. The Director will include a copy of all evidence in the file; a copy of the APA Ethics Code; the Committee's Rules and Procedures; and a statement that information submitted by the respondent shall become a part of the record and can be used if further proceedings ensue.

5.3.2 Time for Respondent Response. The respondent shall have 30 days after receipt of the notification of a preliminary investigation to file an initial response.

5.3.3 Information From Other Sources. Additional information may be requested from the complainant, respondent, or any other appropriate source. The Committee will not rely upon information submitted by such sources unless it has been shared with the respondent and the respondent has been afforded an opportunity to respond thereto.

5.3.4 Action if There Continues to Be Insufficient Information. At the conclusion of the preliminary investigation, if the Director and Chair determine that they still lack evidence sufficient to determine whether cause for action exists, the matter shall be closed.

5.4 Determination of Cause for Action. If the Chair and Director agree that cause for action exists, they shall consider whether to open a formal case under Subsection 5.5, below. If the Chair and Director agree that cause for action does not exist, the matter shall be closed. If the Chair and Director disagree on whether or not there is cause for action by the Committee, the matter shall be reviewed by the Vice Chair, who will cast the deciding vote.

5.5 Decision to Open a Case. In any case in which the determination has been made that cause for action exists, the Chair and Director shall consider whether (a) there is a reasonable basis to believe the alleged violation cannot be proved by a preponderance of the evidence and (b) the allegations would constitute only minor or technical violations that would not warrant further action, have already been adequately addressed in another forum, or are likely to be corrected. If they agree that one or more of the conditions are met, the matter shall be closed. Otherwise, the matter shall be opened as a case.

5.6 Educative Letter. If a matter is closed under Sections 4 or 5 of this part, the Chair and Director may, if appropriate, send an educative letter to the respondent.

5.7 Reconsideration of Decision to Open. A matter not opened under either Subsection 5.4 or 5.5, above, may be considered by the Committee only if it does so in accordance with Part II, Section 6.

5.8 Supplementary or Alternative Action. The Chair and Director may recommend that the complainant refer the complaint to an appropriate state psychological association, state board, regulatory agency, subsidiary body of the Association, or other appropriate entity, or they may make such referral on their own initiative. Such referral does not constitute a waiver of jurisdiction over the complaint provided that the Committee opens a formal case within 24 months from the date of referral.

6. Case Investigation

6.1 Issuance of Charge Letter and Response From Respondent

6.1.1 Charge Letter. If a case is opened, the Director shall so inform the respondent in a charge letter. The charge letter shall contain a concise description of the alleged behaviors at issue and identify the specific section(s) of the Ethics Code that the respondent is alleged to have violated. The Director shall enclose a copy of any completed Ethics Complaint Form and any materials submitted to date by the complainant or on the complainant's behalf that will be included in the record before the Committee; a copy of the APA Ethics Code and the Committee's Rules and Procedures; and a statement that information submitted by the respondent shall become a part of the record, and can be used if further proceedings ensue.

6.1.2 Significance of Charge Letter. A charge letter does not constitute or represent a finding that any unethical behavior has taken place, or that any allegations of the complaint are or are not likely to be found to be true.

6.1.3 Issuance of New Charge Letter to Conform to Evidence Discovered During Investigation. At any time prior to final resolution by the Committee, in order to make the charges conform to the evidence developed during the investigation, the Director and Chair may determine that a new charge letter should be issued setting forth ethical standard(s) and/or describing alleged behaviors different from or in addition to those contained in the initial charge letter. In a *sua sponte* case, the date of issuance shall, for purposes of applicable time limits, be deemed to relate back to the date of the initial letter notifying the respondent that a *sua sponte* action has been initiated. The new charge letter shall in all other respects be treated exactly as an initial charge letter issued according to Subsection 6.1.1 of this part.

6.1.4 Time for Respondent's Response. The respondent shall have 30 days after receipt of the charge letter to file an initial response. Any request to extend the time for responding to the charge letter must be made in writing, within the 30 days, and must show good cause for an extension.

6.1.5 Personal Appearance. The Chair and Director may request the respondent to appear personally before the Committee. The respondent has no right to such an appearance.

6.2 Information From Other Sources. Additional information may be requested from the complainant, respondent, or any other appropriate source.

6.3 Referral to Committee. When, in the sole judgment of the Chair and Director, the investigation is complete, the case will be referred to the Committee for review and resolution. The Director shall notify the complainant and respondent that the matter has been referred to the Committee.

6.4 Documentation Subsequent to Investigation and Prior to Resolution by the Committee. Within 30 days after receipt of notification that the case is being referred to the Ethics Committee for review and resolution, the complainant and respondent may submit any additional information or documentation. Any materials submitted in a timely manner by the complainant or on the complainant's or respondent's behalf will be forwarded to the respondent. Within 15 days from receipt of those materials, the respondent may submit any additional information or documentation. All such materials submitted within these time limitations shall be included in the file to be reviewed by the Ethics Committee. Materials submitted outside of the time limit will not be included in the file materials relative to the ethics case and will not be reviewed by the Ethics Committee.

In the sole discretion of the Director, where good cause for noncompliance with these time limits is shown by the complainant or the respondent, the resolution of the case may be postponed until the next scheduled meeting of the Ethics Committee, and the information or documentation provided outside of the time limit may be included in the file materials to be reviewed by the Committee at that later time. In the sole discretion of the Director, in the event the respondent fails to comply with these time limits, the information or documentation provided outside of the time limits may be included in the file materials to be reviewed by the Committee and the matter maintained for resolution by the Committee as originally scheduled.

7. Review and Resolution by the Committee

The Ethics Committee may assign a member of the Committee or an Ethics Committee Associate to serve as a case monitor. The monitor may provide assistance to assure that an adequate record is prepared for Ethics Committee review and in such other respects as necessary to further the objectives of these Rules and Procedures.

Upon conclusion of the investigation, the case shall be reviewed by the Ethics Committee. Members of the Ethics Committee and Ethics Committee Associates may be assigned to review and summarize the case. Members and Associates may also be assigned to participate on a panel to review and make a preliminary recommendation prior to review by the full Ethics Committee. Ethics Committee Associates may also attend and participate in the full

Ethics Committee meetings, but shall not vote on the full Committee's disposition of a case. When review of a case has been completed, the Ethics Committee shall vote to take one of the following actions described below: remand, dismiss the charges, recommend reprimand or censure, recommend expulsion, or recommend stipulated resignation. In addition to any of these actions, the Committee may vote to issue an educative letter. The Committee may choose to dismiss some charges but find violation and take disciplinary action on the basis of other charges in the charge letter. The respondent shall then be notified of the Committee's action, the ethical standard(s) involved, if any, the rationale for the Committee's decision, any sanction, and any directives.

7.1 Remand. The Committee may remand the matter to the Director for continued investigation or issuance of a new charge letter according to Subsection 6.1.3 of this part.

7.2 Dismiss the Charges

7.2.1 No Violation. The Committee may dismiss a charge if it finds the respondent has not violated the ethical standard as charged.

7.2.2 Violation Would Not Warrant Further Action. The Committee may dismiss the complaint if it concludes that any violation it might find (a) would constitute only a minor or technical violation that would not warrant further action, (b) has already been adequately addressed in another forum, or (c) is likely to be corrected.

7.2.3 Insufficient Evidence. The Committee may dismiss a charge if it finds insufficient evidence to support a finding of an ethics violation.

7.3 Educative Letter. Where the Committee deems it appropriate, the Committee may issue an educative letter, to be shared only with the respondent, concerning the behaviors charged or other matters. An educative letter may be issued whether the Committee dismisses the charges or recommends finding violations.

7.4 Recommend Reprimand or Censure. If the Committee finds that the respondent has violated the Ethics Code, but decides that the nature of the respondent's behavior is such that the matter would be most appropriately resolved without recommending loss of membership, the Committee will recommend reprimand or censure of the respondent, with or without one or more available directives. See Part II, Subsections 11.1, 11.2, and Section 12.

7.5 Recommend Expulsion. The Committee may recommend expulsion if it concludes that there has been an ethics violation, that it was of a kind likely to cause substantial harm to another person or the profession, or that it was otherwise of such gravity as to warrant this action.

7.6 Recommend Stipulated Resignation. In lieu of the other resolutions set forth in this section, with the agreement of the respondent, the Committee may recommend to the Board that the respondent be permitted to resign under stipulations set forth by the Committee, according to the following procedure:

7.6.1 Offer of Stipulated Resignation by the Committee. When the Committee finds that the respondent has committed a violation of the Ethics Code, the Committee may offer to enter into an agreement with the respondent, contingent upon approval by the Board of Directors, that the respondent shall resign from the Association under mutually agreed upon stipulations. Such stipulations shall include the extent to which the stipulated resignation and underlying ethics violation shall be disclosed and a minimum period of time after resignation during which the respondent shall be ineligible to reapply for membership. The Committee may also vote to recommend and inform the member of an alternative sanction chosen from among Subsections 11.1–11.3 of Part II of these Rules in the event the member does not accept the offer of stipulated resignation.

7.6.2 Notification of Respondent. In such cases, the respondent shall be notified, in writing, of the Committee's recommended sanction of stipulated resignation and that he or she may accept the Committee's recommended sanction within 30 days of receipt. The respondent shall also be notified of any alternative recommended sanction.

7.6.3 Acceptance by Respondent. Within 30 days, the respondent may accept the recommended sanction of stipulated resignation by executing a notarized affidavit of resignation acceptable both to the respondent and the Committee and forwarding the executed notarized affidavit to the Committee. Such

resignation shall become effective only with the approval of the Board, as set forth in Subsection 7.6.5 of this part.

7.6.4 Transmittal to Board of Directors. If the respondent accepts the recommended sanction of stipulated resignation, the Committee shall submit a copy of the affidavit of resignation, with the record in the matter and the rationale for recommending stipulated resignation on the terms stated in the affidavit, to the Board of Directors.

7.6.5 Action by Board of Directors. Within 180 days, the Board of Directors shall accept the respondent's resignation on the terms stated in the affidavit of resignation, unless it is persuaded that to do so would not be in the best interest of the Association and/or of the public. If the resignation is accepted by the Board, the Director shall notify the complainant and respondent of the final disposition of the case.

7.6.6 Rejection of Stipulated Resignation by Respondent. If the respondent fails to accept the determination within 30 days, or formally notifies the Committee of rejection of the offer of stipulated resignation within the 30-day period, the offer of stipulated resignation shall be deemed rejected. The Committee shall reconsider the matter or, if an alternative recommended sanction has previously been identified by the Committee, such alternative recommended resolution shall automatically become the recommended sanction according to Subsection 7.4 or 7.5 of this part.

7.6.7 Rejection of Stipulated Resignation by Board. If the Board rejects the affidavit of resignation under Subsection 7.6.5 of this part, the Committee shall so notify the respondent and reconsider the matter.

8. Procedures Subsequent to Dismissal by Committee

The Committee may reconsider a case dismissed under Subsection 7.2 of this part only if it does so in accordance with Part II, Section 6.

9. Procedures Subsequent to Committee Recommendation of Reprimand or Censure

If the Committee proceeds under Subsection 7.4 of this part, the following procedures shall govern:

9.1 Acceptance of Reprimand or Censure. If the

respondent accepts the Committee's recommended sanction and directives, if any, the right of independent adjudication shall be waived, any directives will be implemented by the Director, and the case will remain open until the directives are met. The respondent's failure to respond within 30 days of notification shall be deemed acceptance of the Committee's recommended sanction and directives.

9.2 Independent Adjudication After Recommended Sanction of Reprimand or Censure. The method of adjudication for a recommended sanction of reprimand or censure is an independent adjudication based on the written record by a three-person Independent Adjudication Panel.

9.2.1 Request for Independent Adjudication and Rationale for Nonacceptance. The respondent may exercise his or her right to independent adjudication by furnishing the Committee, within 30 days after notification of the Committee's recommendation, a written request for independent adjudication and rationale for nonacceptance of the recommendation.

9.2.2. Statement by Committee. Within 30 days of receipt of the respondent's rationale for nonacceptance, the Committee may prepare a statement and provide a copy to the respondent. No statement by the Committee is required.

9.2.3 Respondent's Final Response. Within 15 days of receipt of the Ethics Committee's statement, if any, the respondent may submit to the Director a written response to that statement.

9.2.4 Selection of Independent Adjudication Panel

9.2.4.1 Provision of Standing Hearing Panel List. Within 60 days of receipt of the request for an independent adjudication, the Director shall provide the respondent with the names and curricula vitae of six members of the Board of Directors' Standing Hearing Panel, of whom at least one shall be a public member. The proposed panel members need not include any member having a particular speciality or representing a particular geographic location. The Director shall make inquiry and ensure that proposed panel members do not have a conflict of interest as defined by applicable law and appear otherwise able to apply fairly the APA Ethics Code based solely on the record in the particular case.

9.2.4.2 Designation of Panel Members. Within 15 days after receipt of the six-member list, the re-

spondent shall select three of the six to constitute the Independent Adjudication Panel. The Panel shall include not fewer than two members of the Association. Whenever feasible, the respondent's selection will be honored. If at any time prior to conclusion of the adjudication, any panelist cannot serve on the Independent Adjudication Panel for any reason, the respondent shall be notified promptly and afforded the opportunity within 10 days of receipt of notification to replace that individual from among a list of not fewer than four members of the Board of Directors' Standing Hearing Panel. In the event the respondent fails to notify the Director of his or her initial or replacement selections in a timely fashion, the right to do so is waived, and the President of the Association shall select the member(s), whose name(s) shall then be made known to the respondent.

9.2.4.3 Designation of Chair of Independent Adjudication Panel. The President shall designate one of the three Panel members to serve as Chair. The Chair of the Panel shall ensure that the Panel fulfills its obligations according to these Rules and Procedures.

9.2.5 Provision of Case File to Independent Adjudication Panel. Within 15 days of selection of the Independent Adjudication Panel, receipt of the Committee's statement according to Subsection 9.2.2 of this part, if any; receipt of the respondent's final response according to Subsection 9.2.3 of this part, if any; or if no statement or response is received, the expiration of the time period for such statement or response, whichever occurs latest, the Director will provide the case file to the members of the Independent Adjudication Panel. The case file shall include the complaint and all correspondence and evidence submitted to the Ethics Committee, the respondent's rationale for nonacceptance of the Committee's recommendation, the Committee's statement, if any, and the respondent's final response, if any.

9.2.6 Consideration and Vote by Independent Adjudication Panel. Within 60 days of receipt of the case file, the members of the Panel shall confer with each other and, solely on the basis of the documentation provided and deliberations among themselves, shall vote to take one of the following actions:

9.2.6.1 Adopt the Committee's Recommended Sanction and Directives

9.2.6.2 Adopt a Lesser Sanction and/or Less Burdensome Directives

9.2.6.3 Dismiss the Case

9.2.7 Decision of Independent Adjudication Panel. Decisions of the Independent Adjudication Panel will be made by majority vote, and at least two reviewers must agree to written findings, a sanction, if any, and a directive or directives, if any. The Committee bears the burden to prove the charges by a preponderance of the evidence. The panelists' votes and the majority's written decision must be submitted to the Ethics Office within the 60-day period set forth in Subsection 9.2.6 of this part. If no two panelists can agree as to the appropriate outcome or a written decision, the case will be referred back to the Committee for further action.

9.2.8 Finality of Decision by Independent Adjudication Panel. The decision of the Independent Adjudication Panel is unappealable. The decision is binding on the Committee and the respondent except that subsequent to the Panel's decision, the Committee may determine that directives are impractical or unduly burdensome and may choose to reduce or dismiss directives required in the Panel's decision. A decision by the Panel either to impose a sanction and/or directive(s) or to dismiss the case will be implemented by the Director as the final adjudication, unless modified by the Committee.

9.2.9 Notification. The Director shall inform the respondent and complainant, if any, of the final disposition. The respondent shall be provided a copy of the majority's written decision.

10. Procedures Subsequent to Committee Recommendation of Expulsion

If the Committee proceeds under Subsection 7.5 of this part, the following procedures shall govern:

10.1 Acceptance of Recommendation of Expulsion. If the respondent accepts the Committee's recommendation to the Board of Directors that he or she be expelled from membership, the right to a formal hearing shall be waived, and the Committee shall proceed with its recommendation to the Board of Directors according to Subsection 10.3.5 and other subsections of this part. In such event, the recommendation of the Ethics Committee shall be treated as the equivalent of the recommendation of a

Formal Hearing Committee that the respondent be expelled from membership. The respondent's failure to respond within 30 days after notification shall be deemed acceptance of the Committee's recommendation.

10.2 Formal Hearing After Recommendation of Expulsion. The method of adjudication for a recommended sanction of expulsion issued under Subsection 7.5 of this part is a formal hearing before a three-member Hearing Committee. Upon request, the respondent will be provided with a copy of the APA Ethics Office's "Guidelines for Formal Hearings." These guidelines are for guidance and information purposes only and are not binding on the APA, the Ethics Committee, or hearing participants. The proceedings are governed soley by the Rules and Procedures of the Ethics Committee and the Ethical Principles of Psychologists and Code of Conduct. Alternatively, a respondent may request an independent adjudication to be provided according to the procedures described in Subsections 9.2.2 through 9.2.7 of this part of these Rules in place of the Subsections 10.2.2 through 10.2.6. The Independent Adjudication Panel will make a recommendation that will be subject to review by the Board of Directors as described in Subsection 10.3.

10.2.1 Request for Formal Hearing. The respondent may exercise his or her right to a formal hearing by requesting a hearing in writing within 30 days of notification of the Committee's recommendation. Alternatively, the respondent may request an independent adjudication by furnishing the Committee a written request for independent adjudication and a written rationale for nonacceptance of the Committee's recommendation within 30 days after notification of the Committee's recommendation.

10.2.2 Formal Hearing Date and Hearing Committee

10.2.2.1 Establishment of Hearing Date and Provision of Standing Hearing Panel List. Within 60 days after the receipt of the respondent's request for a formal hearing, the Director shall establish the date of the hearing and provide the respondent with the date and the names and curricula vitae of six members of the Board of Directors' Standing Hearing Panel. The six identified members of the Board of Directors' Standing Hearing Panel shall include at least one public member. The proposed panel members need not include any member having a particular specialty or representing a particular geographic location. The Director shall make inquiry and ensure that proposed panel members do not have a conflict of interest as defined by applicable law and appear otherwise able to apply fairly the Ethics Code based solely on the record in the particular case.

10.2.2.2 Designation of Hearing Committee Members. The Hearing Committee shall consist of three individuals, selected from among the six individuals from the Board of Directors' Standing Hearing Panel identified according to Subsection 10.2.2.1 of this part. The Hearing Committee shall include not fewer than two members of the Association. Within 15 days after the receipt of the names and curricula vitae, the respondent shall notify the Director of his or her selections for the Hearing Committee. Whenever feasible, the respondent's selections will be honored. In the event an individual selected by the respondent cannot serve on the Hearing Committee for any reason, the respondent shall be notified and afforded the opportunity within 10 days of receipt of notification to replace that individual from among a list of not fewer than four members of the Board of Directors' Standing Hearing Panel. If the respondent fails to notify the Director of his or her initial or replacement selections in a timely fashion, the right to do so is wavied and the President shall select the Hearing Committee member(s), whose name(s) shall then be made known to the respondent.

10.2.2.3 *Voir Dire* of Designated Hearing Committee Members. At the time the respondent selects the three designated Hearing Committee members, the respondent may submit in writing, to the Director, a request to question designated Hearing Committee members with respect to potential conflict of interest. If the President has chosen the three Hearing Committee members, the respondent shall have 15 days after receipt of their names to submit such a request. Upon receipt of such written request, the Director shall convene by telephone conference call, or otherwise, a formal opportunity for such questioning by the respondent or the respondent's attorney. Legal Counsel for the Association shall preside at such *voir dire*, shall be the sole judge of the pro-

priety and pertinency of questions posed, and shall be the sole judge with respect to the fitness of designated Hearing Committee members to serve. Failure by the respondent to submit a timely request shall constitute a waiver of the privilege to conduct *voir dire*.

10.2.2.4 Designation of Chair of Hearing Committee. The President shall designate one of the three Hearing Committee members to serve as Chair. The Chair of the Hearing Committee and Legal Counsel for the Association shall assure proper observance of these Rules and Procedures at the formal hearing.

10.2.3 Documents and Witnesses

10.2.3.1 Committee. At least 30 days prior to the scheduled date of the formal hearing, the Ethics Committee shall provide the respondent and the Hearing Committee with copies of all documents and other evidence, and the names of all witnesses that may be offered by the Committee in its case in chief.

10.2.3.2 Respondent. At least 15 days prior to the scheduled date of the formal hearing, the respondent shall provide the Ethics Committee and the Hearing Committee with copies of all documents and other evidence, and the names of all witnesses that may be offered by the respondent.

10.2.3.3 Rebuttal Documents and Witnesses. At least 5 days prior to the scheduled date of the formal hearing, the Committee shall provide the respondent and the Hearing Committee with copies of all documents and other evidence, and the names of all witnesses that may be offered in rebuttal.

10.2.3.4 Audiotapes, Videotapes, and Similar Data Compilations. Audiotapes, videotapes, and similar data compilations are admissible at the formal hearing, provided usable copies of such items, together with a transcription thereof, are provided in a timely fashion according to the provisions of this section.

10.2.3.5 Failure to Provide Documents, Other Evidence, and Names of Witnesses in a Timely Fashion in Advance of the Formal Hearing. Failure to provide copies of a document or other evidence or the name of a witness in a timely fashion and consistent with this section and these Rules and Procedures is grounds for excluding such document, other evidence, or witness from evidence at the formal hearing, unless good cause for the omission and a lack of prejudice to the other side can be shown.

10.2.4 *Formal Hearing Procedures*

10.2.4.1 Presiding Officers

10.2.4.1.1 The Chair of the Hearing Committee shall preside at the hearing. The General Counsel of the Association shall designate Legal Counsel to assist the Hearing Committee.

10.2.4.1.2 Legal Counsel for the Hearing Committee shall be present to advise on matters of procedure and admission of evidence and shall represent neither the Ethics Committee nor the respondent at the formal hearing.

10.2.4.2 Legal Representation of the Respondent and Committee

10.2.4.2.1 Respondent. The respondent may choose, at the respondent's own expense, to be represented by a licensed attorney.

10.2.4.2.2 Committee. The General Counsel of the Association may designate Legal Counsel to advise the Ethics Committee. The Chair of the Ethics Committee, the Chair's designee, or Legal Counsel to the Committee presents the Committee's case.

10.2.4.3 Rules of Evidence. Formal rules of evidence shall not apply. All evidence that is relevant and reliable, as determined for the Hearing Committee by Legal Counsel for the Hearing Committee, shall be admissible.

10.2.4.4 Rights of the Respondent and the Committee. Consistent with these Rules and Procedures, the respondent and the Committee shall have the right to present witnesses, documents, and other evidence, to cross-examine witnesses, and to object to the introduction of evidence.

10.2.4.5 Burden of Proof. The Ethics Committee shall bear the burden to prove the charges by a preponderance of the evidence.

10.2.5 *Decision of the Hearing Committee.* The decision shall be by a simple majority vote. Within 30 days of the conclusion of the hearing, the Hearing Committee shall submit in writing to the Board of Directors, through the Director, its decision and rationale for that decision. The Hearing Committee may decide to

10.2.5.1 Adopt the Committee's Recommendation to the Board of Directors

10.2.5.2 Recommend to the Board of Directors a Lesser Sanction With or Without Directives

10.2.5.3 Dismiss the Charges

10.2.6 *Notice to the Respondent and the Ethics Committee.* Within 15 days of receipt of the Hearing Committee's decision, a copy of the decision and the rationale for the decision shall be provided to the respondent and the Ethics Committee. If the Hearing Committee determines that the charges must be dismissed, the Ethics Committee will implement this as the final adjudication.

10.3 Proceedings Before the Board of Directors

10.3.1 *Referral to Board of Directors.* If the Hearing Committee or Independent Adjudication Panel recommends that the respondent be expelled from membership or otherwise disciplined, the matter will be referred to the Board of Directors. The Director shall provide the materials of record to the Board, including a copy of the Hearing Committee's or Independent Adjudication Panel's decision; the respondent's timely response, if any, under Subsection 10.3.2 of this part; the Ethics Committee's timely statement, if any, under Subsection 10.3.3 of this part; the respondent's timely final response, if any, under Subsection 10.3.4 of this part; and the record.

10.3.2 *Respondent's Response.* Within 30 days of receipt of the Hearing Committee's or Independent Adjudication Panel's decision, the respondent may file a written response with the Board of Directors, through the Ethics Office. A copy of the respondent's written response shall be retained by the Chair of the Ethics Committee.

10.3.3 *Ethics Committee's Statement.* Within 15 days of receipt of the respondent's response or the date such response was due, the Ethics Committee may prepare a written statement and provide a copy to the respondent.

10.3.4 *Respondent's Final Response.* Within 15 days of receipt of the Ethics Committee's statement, if any, the respondent may file with the Board of Directors, through the Director, a written response to the Ethics Committee's statement. A copy of this response shall be retained by the Chair of the Ethics Committee.

10.3.5 *Action by the Board of Directors.* Within 180 days of receipt of the recommendation of the

Hearing Committee or Independent Adjudication Panel (or of the Ethics Committee if no subsequent adjudication was held), together with any timely responses thereto and the record, the Board of Directors will consider these materials and will take action as follows:

10.3.5.1 Adopt. The Board of Directors shall adopt the recommendation, unless by majority vote it finds grounds for nonacceptance, as set forth in Subsection 10.3.5.2.

10.3.5.2 Not Adopt After Determining Grounds for Nonacceptance. Only the following shall constitute grounds for nonacceptance of the recommendation by the Board:

10.3.5.2.1 Incorrect Application of Ethical Standard(s). The Ethics Code of the Association was incorrectly applied.

10.3.5.2.2 Erroneous Findings of Fact. The findings of fact were clearly erroneous.

10.3.5.2.3 Procedural Errors. The procedures used were in serious and substantial violation of the Bylaws of the Association and/or these Rules and Procedures.

10.3.5.2.4 Excessive Sanction or Directives. The disciplinary sanction or directives recommended are grossly excessive in light of all the circumstances.

10.3.5.3 Consequences of Nonacceptance. If the Board of Directors finds grounds for nonacceptance, it shall refer the case back to the Ethics Committee. In its discretion, the Ethics Committee may return the matter for reconsideration before a newly constituted Hearing Committee or Independent Adjudication Panel or may continue investigation and/or readjudicate the matter at the Committee level.

10.4 Notification.   If the Board of Directors does not adopt the recommendation, it shall notify the Ethics Committee in writing why the decision was not accepted, citing the applicable ground(s) for nonacceptance under Subsection 10.3.5.2 of this part.

10.5 Reconsideration.   If a reconsideration is instituted, the procedures of relevant subsections of this part shall apply. Unless any of the following is offered by the respondent, none shall be part of the record before the second Hearing Committee or Independent Adjudication Panel: the original Hearing Committee's or Independent Adjudication Panel's re-

port; the respondent's written responses or Ethics Committee's written statements made under Subsection 10.3.2, 10.3.3, and 10.3.4 of this part; and the Board of Directors' rationale for nonacceptance of the original Hearing Committee's or Independent Adjudication Panel's recommendation. If the respondent offers any portion of any of the foregoing documents as evidence in the reconsideration, the Committee may introduce any portion of any or all of them.

◆ ◆ ◆

Commentary: *This most recent set of procedures replaced an earlier version published in 1992. Do you think they are comprehensible to the average APA member? Would you know how to navigate your way through the Ethics Committee if you were the unfortunate recipient of an ethics complaint? It takes about a year to adjudicate a formal complaint. Is the process too lengthy, cumbersome, and expensive, or does it provide the appropriate procedural safeguards for both complainants and respondents? An ad hoc Committee on Ethics Procedures composed of representatives from the ethics committee and APA Board of Directors was given the mission of reviewing and recommending ways to streamline the process. See APA Ethics Committee. (1998). Report of the Ethics Committee, 1997. American Psychologist, 53, 969–980.*

What do you think are the most frequent kinds of cases that the ethics committee is adjudicating currently, in comparison with cases seen a decade ago? For answers and other interesting data, see these articles, in chronological order:

Ethics Committee of the American Psychological Association. (1988). *Trends in ethics cases, common pitfalls, and published resources.* American Psychologist, 43, 564–572.

APA Ethics Committee. (1991). *Report of the Ethics Committee, 1989 and 1990.* American Psychologist, 46, 750–757.

APA Ethics Committee. (1993). *Report of the Ethics Committee, 1991 and 1992.* American Psychologist, 48, 811–820.

APA Ethics Committee. (1994). *Report of the Ethics Committee, 1993.* American Psychologist, 49, 659–666.

APA Ethics Committee. (1995). *Report of the Ethics Committee, 1994.* American Psychologist, 50, 706–713.

APA Ethics Committee. (1996). *Report of the Ethics Committee, 1995.* American Psychologist, 51, 1279–1286.

APA Ethics Committee. (1997). *Report of the Ethics Committee, 1996.* American Psychologist, 52, 897–905.

APA Ethics Committee. (1998). *Report of the Ethics Committee, 1997.* American Psychologist, 53, 969–980.

The 1998 report indicated that from 1985 through 1997, APA terminated the membership of 269 members due to ethical violations—about 20 per year. What do these data imply about the vigor with which the Ethical Principles have been enforced by APA? Keep in mind that from 1956 to 1980 APA dropped from membership only eight psychologists for ethical violations.

I conclude this chapter as it began: with an excerpt from Pope and Vetter's 1992 article. This material provides an introduction to the wide variety of ethical issues that psychologists face as teachers, scholars, and professionals. Many of these issues are addressed later in this book in greater detail.

Ethical Dilemmas Encountered by Members of the American Psychological Association: A National Survey

Kenneth S. Pope and Valerie A. Vetter

METHOD

A cover letter and survey form were developed to invite APA members to provide examples of the ethical dilemmas they faced in their work. . . .

A table of random numbers was used to select 1,319 individuals listed as members or fellows in the APA (1989) membership directory. . . .

RESULTS

Replies were received from 679 psychologists, for a return rate of 51%. . . .

Respondents provided 703 ethically troubling incidents in 23 general categories, as presented in Table 1. Examples of the ethical dilemmas are presented in the Discussion section. . . .

DISCUSSION

The primary purpose of this discussion is to present examples of the critical incidents, highlighting areas and instances in which psychologists find themselves confronting ethical challenges in their day-to-day work. . . .

Confidentiality

The most frequently described dilemmas involved confidentiality. Of these troubling or challenging incidents, 38 involved actual or potential risks to third parties, 23 involved child abuse reporting, 8 involved individuals infected with human immunodeficiency virus (HIV) or suffering from acquired immunodeficiency syndrome (AIDS), 6 involved patients who threatened or had committed violence, and 1 involved elder abuse.

An additional 79 dilemmas reveal that respondents are wrestling with agonizing questions about whether confidential information should be disclosed and, if so, to whom. The following were typical:

> One girl underwent an abortion without the knowledge of her foster parents . . . I fully evaluated her view of the adults' inability to be supportive and agreed but worried about our relationship being damaged if I was discovered to know about the pregnancy and her action.

> A colleague withheld information about a client from the therapist to whom she transferred the case (within the same agency). She did so on the grounds of maintaining client confidentiality. This case raises questions not only about client confidentiality and professional relationships, but about the limits of confidentiality within an agency setting.

> . . .

> One of my clients claimed she was raped; the police did not believe her and refused to follow up (because of her mental history). Another of my cli-

From *American Psychologist, 47,* 397–411. Copyright 1992 by the American Psychological Association. Adapted with permission of the author and publisher.

TABLE 1

Categories of 703 Ethically Troubling Incidents

Category	n	%
Confidentiality	128	18
Blurred, dual, or conflictual relationships	116	17
Payment sources, plans, settings, and methods	97	14
Academic settings, teaching dilemmas, and concerns about training	57	8
Forensic psychology	35	5
Research	29	4
Conduct of colleagues	29	4
Sexual issues	28	4
Assessment	25	4
Questionable or harmful interventions	20	3
Competence	20	3
Ethics (and related) codes and committees	17	2
School psychology	15	2
Publishing	14	2
Helping the financially stricken	13	2
Supervision	13	2
Advertising and (mis)representation	13	2
Industrial–organizational psychology	9	1
Medical issues	5	1
Termination	5	1
Ethnicity	4	1
Treatment records	4	1
Miscellaneous	7	1

ents described how he raped a woman (the same woman).

The remaining 11 incidents involved respondents' concerns about the careless or unintentional disclosure of confidential information: for example, "A psychiatrist who leases me space and does some of my billing is careless about discussing patient names in front of other patients. What should I do about this?"

In 1990, confidentiality accounted for only 2% of the primary category of active cases before the APA ethics committee ("Report of the Ethics Committee," 1991), yet participants in this research reported more struggles with confidentiality than any other category. This illustrates what the creators of the initial APA ethics code emphasized—that there may be a significant discrepancy between the ethical dilemmas encountered by the membership and the complaints received by the ethics committee, and there-

fore revisions to the code should be informed by the former as well as the latter.

Perhaps it is not surprising that confidentiality is the most frequently reported ethical dilemma reported by the membership. Although confidentiality is considered one of the most fundamental principles (Knapp & VandeCreek, 1987), and in some research has been endorsed by psychologists as the most important ethical duty (Crowe, Grogan, Jacobs, Lindsay, & Mark, 1985), national studies of psychologists have found that the most frequent *intentional* violations of formal standards involved confidentiality (Pope & Bajt, 1988) and that more than half of the respondents reported *unintentionally* violating confidentiality (Pope, Tabachnick, & Keith-Spiegel, 1987)....

Although the incidents raise a variety of concerns, they highlight two critical areas.... First, the boundaries of confidentiality when multiple caregivers (including administrators and supervisors) or clients are involved (e.g., clinics, therapy groups, and participants in couple or family therapy) need to be explicitly discussed.

Second, some of the incidents, especially about mandatory child abuse reporting laws, illustrate situations in which some psychologists believe it is better to break the law and act on that belief (Kalichman, Craig, & Follingstad, 1989; Koocher & Keith-Spiegel, 1990; Pope & Bajt, 1988; Pope et al., 1987). Most psychologists are likely to have encountered dilemmas in which following legal requirements seemed clinically and ethically wrong, perhaps placing the client or third parties at needless risk for harm and injustice (Pope & Bajt, 1988).... This issue is in need of careful exploration and vigorous, informed debate....

Blurred, Dual, or Conflictual Relationships

The second most frequently described incidents involved maintaining clear, reasonable, and therapeutic boundaries around the professional relationship with a client. In some cases, respondents were troubled by such instances as serving as both "therapist and supervisor for hours for [patient/supervisee's] MFCC [marriage, family, and child counselor] license" or when "an agency hires one of its own clients." In other cases, respondents found dual relationships to be useful "to provide role modeling, nurturing and a giving quality to therapy"; one respondent, for example, believed that providing therapy to couples with whom he has social relationships and who are members of his small church makes sense because he is "able to see how these people interact in group context." In still other cases, respondents reported that it was sometimes difficult to know what constitutes a dual relationship or conflict of interest; for example, "I have employees/supervisees who were former clients and wonder if this is a dual relationship." Similarly, another respondent felt a conflict between his own romantic attraction to a patient's mother and responsibilities to the child who had developed a positive relationship with him. . . .

Taken as a whole, the incidents suggest, first, that the ethical principles need to define dual relationships more carefully and to note with clarity if and when they are ever therapeutically indicated or acceptable. . . . Research and the professional literature focusing on nonsexual dual relationships underscores the importance and implications of decisions to enter into or refrain from such activities (e.g., Borys & Pope, 1989; Ethics Committee, 1988; Keith-Spiegel & Koocher, 1985; Pope & Vasquez, 1991; Stromberg et al., 1988).

Second, the principles must address clearly and realistically the situations of those who practice in small towns, rural communities, and other remote locales. . . . Forty-one of the dual relationship incidents involved such locales. Many respondents implicitly or explicitly complained that the principles seem to ignore the special conditions in small, self-contained communities. For example,

> I live and maintain a . . . private practice in a rural area. I am also a member of a spiritual community based here. There are very few other therapists in the immediate vicinity who work with transformational, holistic, and feminist principles in the context of good clinical training that "conventional" people can also feel confidence in. Clients often come to me *because* they know me already, because they are not satisfied with the other services available, or be-

cause they want to work with someone who understands their spiritual practice and can incorporate its principles and practices into the process of transformation, healing, and change. The stricture against dual relationships helps me to maintain a high degree of sensitivity to the ethics (and potentials for abuse or confusion) of such situations, but doesn't give me any help in working with the actual circumstances of my practice. . . .

Third, the principles need to distinguish between dual relationships and accidental or incidental extra-therapeutic contacts (e.g., running into a patient at the grocery market or unexpectedly seeing a client at a party) and to address realistically the awkward entanglements into which even the most careful therapist can fall. For example, a therapist sought to file a formal complaint against some very noisy tenants of a neighboring house. When he did so, he was surprised to discover "that his patient was the owner-landlord." As another example, a respondent reported,

> Six months ago a patient I had been working with for 3 years became romantically involved with my best and longest friend. I could write no less than a book on the complications of this fact! I have been getting legal and therapeutic consultations all along, and continue to do so. Currently they are living together and I referred the patient (who was furious that I did this and felt abandoned). I worked with the other psychologist for several months to provide a bridge for the patient. I told my friend soon after I found out that I would have to suspend our contact. I'm currently trying to figure out if we can ever resume our friendship and under what conditions.

The latter example is one of many that demonstrate the extreme lengths to which most psychologists are willing to go to ensure the welfare of their patients.

Although it is impossible to anticipate every pattern of multiple relationship or to account for all the vicissitudes and complexities of life, psychologists need and deserve formal principles that provide lucid, useful, and practical guidance as an aid to professional judgment.

Payment Sources, Plans, Settings, and Methods

The third' most frequently described incidents involved payment providers, plans, settings, or methods. Fifty-six focused on insurance coverage. Inadequate coverage for clients with urgent needs created a cruel ethical dilemma in which therapists felt forced either to breach their responsibilities to clients ("Insurance companies force me to provide inadequate care for patients because of policy limitations and patients' limited financial resources") or to be less than honest with what sometimes seems an adversarial provider of reimbursement ("I'm forced to lie about clients' mental condition to obtain insurance coverage that is due them, while insurance company psychologists are struggling to deny their customers their rightfully due coverage"). As one respondent put it: "I feel caught between providing the best service and being truly ethical." A vast range of troubling issues were described, including billing for no-shows, billing family therapy as if it were individual, distorting a patient's condition so that it qualifies for coverage, signing forms for unlicensed staff, and not collecting copayments.

Fifteen focused on what are typically called managed health plans, such as health maintenance organizations (HMOs) and employee assistance plans (EAPs). Most of the dilemmas, such as those focusing on more general insurance, highlighted (a) the discrepancy between the needs of the client and the services covered, and (b) the tensions between the interests of clients and the interests of those providing, administering, or investing in the managed health plan. The following examples were typical:

> A 7 year old boy was severely sexually abused and severely depressed. I evaluated the case and recommended 6 months treatment. My recommendation was evaluated by a managed health care

agency and approved for 10 sessions by a nonprofessional in spite of the fact that there is no known treatment program that can be performed in 10 sessions on a 7 year old that has demonstrated efficacy.

. . .

> A managed care company discontinued a benefit and told my patient to stop seeing me, then referred her to a therapist they had a lower fee contract with.

Twelve dilemmas focused on payment-related issues in hospital settings; again, the emphasis tended to be on the conflict between the needs of the patient and the financial needs of the hospital.

> Need to meet admission quotas . . . for private hospital. Pressure to develop diagnosis for inpatients in private hospital that would support hospitalization.

> Much of my practice is in a private hospital which is in general very good clinically. However its profit motivation is so very intense that decisions are often made for $ reasons that actively hurt the patients. When patients complain, this is often interpreted as being part of their psychopathology, thus reenacting the dysfunctional families they came from. I don't do this myself and don't permit others to do so in my presence—I try to mitigate the problem—but I can't speak perfectly frankly to my patients and I'm constantly colluding with something that feels marginally unethical.

> I have been concerned about the unnecessary hospitalization of teenagers, extensive and expensive testing (often farmed out to MFCCs or interns on commission), 10 minute visits in hospital at $80 to $100 a visit (also often farmed out on a fee splitting basis) with the teenager leaving hospital when medical insurance runs out and receiv-

ing no further treatment.

. . .

Similarly, in six dilemmas that focused on mental health clinics or centers and two that focused on individuals who paid for someone else's therapy, there was an actual or potential conflict between the interests of the patient and the (generally but not always financial) interests of the party paying for or providing the therapy. . . .

> A woman who is married, but unemployed comes to a psychologist for therapy or counseling. The husband of the woman is paying the bills. After a few sessions, it becomes evident that the patient is planning on leaving or divorcing the husband, who is unaware of this. The psychologist is put in a position of helping the patient to carry through an adverse (to the husband) action, which the husband is unknowingly paying for.

Four dilemmas addressed billing issues with clients who were paying for their own therapy; they tended to involve questions about adjusting fees (e.g., "I worry about the ethics of varying fee scale but feel less concerned than I would if I denied services to those unable to pay the higher rate"). Finally, two focused on gifts or financial advantages offered by clients; for example, a consulting psychologists described how "I have had to deal with a number of offers to get expensive items for me 'wholesale.' (I've resisted because it would compromise the relationship but it *is* tempting)."

. . . [T]he growing influence and prevalence of third-party payment sources, from traditional insurance to HMOs and EAPs, seem to have intensified the need for explicit ethical standards that address more directly, realistically, and helpfully the dilemmas created by these payment sources. . . .

Academic Settings, Teaching Dilemmas, and Concerns About Training

Twenty-five dilemmas focusing on teaching, training, and academia involved concern about lax or unenforced standards. Thirteen mentioned "grade inflation" and the pressures to give "A's, whether or

not deserved. An additional 8 worried about the selection and graduation of unqualified students. Although some were worried about "diploma mills" (termed "a crisis" by one respondent), a majority were concerned about more mainstream programs, as the following examples illustrate:

> . . .
>
> I employ over 600 psychologists. I am disturbed by the fact that those psychologists with marginal ethics and competence were so identified in graduate school and no one did anything about it.
>
> Asked to comment to a search committee about a graduate student whom I feel is "ethically dubious" but has a good publication record and is a top candidate for a job.
>
> I have had students who were clearly emotionally disturbed, yet were completing programs in counseling psychology to become "therapists."

One barrier to addressing the dilemmas associated with unsuitable students seemed to be the threat of lawsuits, mentioned by an additional four respondents.

Three dilemmas mentioned academic discrimination on the basis of race, sex, or physical disability. Another three mentioned psychology graduate programs' failure to offer adequate coursework in the areas of ethics and values, the treatment of minorities, and psychopharmacology. The remaining dilemmas were extremely diverse, including such topics as exploitation of students, teaching group therapy using experimental participation by students, teachers using questions taken from licensing exams and distributing them to students, and misuse of power by professors or administrators.

Forensic Psychology

Some of the respondents' most bitter language (e.g., "whores") was used to describe psychologists who seem willing to present false testimony in court.

> There are psychologists who are "hired"

guns who testify for whoever pays them.

A psychologist in my area is widely known, to clients, psychologists, and the legal community to give whatever testimony is requested in court. He has a very commanding "presence" and it works. He will say anything, adamantly, for pay. Clients/lawyers continue to use him because if the other side uses him, that side will probably win the case (because he's so persuasive, though lying).

Four dilemmas stressed the psychologist's willingness to provide such testimony, and an additional three stressed the attorney's pressures or inducements for this kind of testimony. Yet another four, although making no inferences concerning the psychologist's motivations, expressed concern about testimony that is not founded on the data or established scientific principles (e.g., Huber, 1991).

Another psychologist's report or testimony in a court case goes way beyond what psychology knows or his own data supports. How or whether I should respond.

Overstepping of professional knowledge; e.g., testifying in child abuse cases that the perpetrator is "cured" and that there is *no* chance of rebuse (crystal ball predictions).

An additional eight forensic dilemmas reflected these tendencies to go beyond the data or to respond to lawyers' pressure specifically in child custody disputes (especially to provide custody recommendations based on interviews with only one parent).

Colleagues feel uncomfortable in courtroom settings, making recommendations of one parent over another in a custody dispute when the child clearly has a strong relationship with both. Subjective impressions of patients are used as fact.

An attorney wants me to see one patient and the children in a custody case, but won't refer the case to me if I insist on seeing both parents.

Participating in a system in which false or misleading testimony is rendered confronts psychologists with troubling ethical challenges. However, five dilemmas revealed that, bogus testimony aside, psychologists are concerned that presenting *accurate* data in a forensic setting may have harmful consequences.

I find it difficult to have to testify in court or by way of deposition and to provide sensitive information about a client. Although the client has given permission to provide this information, there are times when there is much discomfort in so doing.

I felt compelled to go against a subpoena from a former client's attorney in her divorce proceedings because I strongly believed my written case notes would be severely detrimental to her case. I explained that to her, and barely avoided contempt charges. . . .

Research

Twelve dilemmas focusing on research mentioned pressures or tendencies to misstate research procedures or findings.

. . .

A particular company . . . has been citing my research conclusions . . . without considering my stated cautions, qualifications, and so forth. That is, my work is cited out of the context of conflicting research and the conclusions are uncritically overgeneralized or overstated. I am concerned that my name or my research may be associated with a kind of deceit.

I am co-investigator on a grant. While walking past the secretary's desk I saw an interim report completed by the PI [principal investigator] to the funding source. The interim report claimed double the number of subjects who had actually entered the protocol.

I have consulted to research projects

at a major university medical school where "random selection" of subjects for drug studies was flagrantly disregarded. I resigned after the first phase.

A colleague frequently distorts the results of poorly conducted collaborative research with students in order to gain recognition and material to present at conferences. He typically works in applied areas with considerable public interest.

Eight dilemmas reflected concern about the rights of research participants.

With some field experiments, it is unclear whether informed consent is needed and, if so, from whom it should be sought.

. . .

Deception that was not disclosed, use of a data videotape in a public presentation without the subject's consent (the subject was in the audience), using a class homework assignment as an experimental manipulation without informing students.

The remainder of the dilemmas involved such diverse topics as mistreatment of animals, established researchers squelching new research, inadequate resources, and the difficulties of conducting research for large organizations in which many employees exert influence over how the research should be conducted.

. . .

Conduct of Colleagues

Four percent of the responses described dilemmas created by disruptive (e.g., competitive) relationships with colleagues or difficulties confronting colleagues engaging in unethical or harmful behavior.

. . .

At what point does "direct knowledge" of purportedly unethical practices become direct knowledge which I must report—is reporting through a client "direct" knowledge? . . .

The toughest situations I and my colleague seem to keep running into (in our small town) are ones involving obvious (to us) ethical infractions by other psychologists or professionals in the area. On 3 or more occasions he and I have personally confronted and taken to local Boards . . . issues which others would rather avoid, deal with lightly, ignore, deny, etc., because of peer pressure in a small community. This has had the combined effect of making me doubt my reality (or experience), making me wonder *why* I have such moral compunctions, making me feel isolated and untrusting of professional peers, etc.
. . .

Research evidence suggests that only about 58% of psychologists believe that to file an ethics complaint against a colleague is itself an unquestionably ethical act (Pope et al., 1987), that about 5% believe that it is never ethical to help a student to file an ethics complaint against another teacher (Tabachnick, Keith-Spiegel, & Pope, 1991), and that only 21% report that they have never simply ignored unethical behavior by colleagues (Tabachnick et al., 1991). In some instances, the "whistleblower" may risk punishing consequences for not remaining silent (Simon, 1978), even when his or her critique is offered in the context of formal peer review, a process supposedly created to bring inappropriate, unethical, or harmful practices to light (Kleinfeld, 1991).

Sexual Issues

Four percent of the dilemmas reflected concerns about sexual issues, particularly the conditions under which sexual involvements are unethical.

Not often, but I have had female clients indicate their interest in romantic involvement with me.

Therapists asking patients to masturbate in front of them.

A student after seeing a client for therapy for a semester terminated the therapy as was planned at the end of the semester, then began a sexual relationship with the client. . . . I think APA should take a stronger stance on this issue.

. . .

My psychological assistant was sexually exploited by her former supervisor and threatened her with not validating her hours for licensure if she didn't service his needs.

Sexual involvement with therapy clients (e.g., Bates & Brodsky, 1989; Committee on Women in Psychology, 1989; Ethics Committee, 1988; Feldman-Summers, 1989; Feldman-Summers & Jones, 1984; Gabbard, 1989; Hare-Mustin, in press; Holroyd & Brodsky, 1977; Pope 1990b; Pope & Vasquez, 1991; Sonne, 1987, 1989; Sonne, Meyer, Borys, & Marshall, 1985; Sonne & Pope, 1991; Stromberg et al., 1988) and with students (e.g., Glaser & Thorpe, 1986; Robinson & Reid, 1985; Pope, Levenson, & Schover, 1979; Pope, Schover, & Levenson, 1980; Tabachnick et al., 1991) has been a difficult issue for the profession to address effectively, as the cited references emphasize and illustrate. Part of the difficulty may be due to surprising historical and related factors (see Brodsky, 1989; Pope 1990a). Part may be due to challenging methodological issues that have been repeatedly emphasized and examined since the earliest research reports; among these enduring methodological issues are "selective memory in retrospective studies, reporting biases, unrepresentative samples, and distortions in data obtained from secondary sources" (Pope, 1990b, p. 477). Part may be due to the incongruity of therapists placing those who come to them for help at risk for significant harm. . . . This incongruity highlights the problems of responding effectively to those therapists who sexually abuse their clients. The profession has a significant responsibility to address in good faith the ethical, methodological, legal, and policy questions about rehabilitation approaches that have shown no evidence of validity through independently conducted, carefully controlled research published in peer-reviewed scientific journals and may place future clients at increased risk for severe harm without

their knowledge or consent (Pope, 1991; Pope & Vetter, 1991; Sonne & Pope, 1991). . . .

In the mid-1980s, the scientific and professional literature began to examine in more detail the clinical, ethical, and policy implications of posttermination relationships (Brodsky, 1988; Brown, 1988; Gabbard & Pope, 1989; Keith-Spiegel & Koocher, 1985; Shopland & VandeCreek, 1991; Vasquez, 1991), and to provide research data regarding the harm to the patient (Pope & Vetter, 1991) and consequences for the therapist (Sell, Gottlieb, & Schoenfeld, 1986) that occurs in cases in which sexual intimacies are initiated only after the termination of therapy. . . .

Assessment

As the following examples illustrate, the most typical dilemmas focusing on assessment tended to involve one of two themes: (a) the availability of tests (or computerized interpretations) to those who may not be adequately trained in testing, and (b) basing conclusions on inadequate data or ignoring important sources of data (e.g., observation, interview, or other contact with the client) or expertise.

Eleven of us cover a 22,000 student population (K–12). When the Binet IV came out, only one person was sent for training. . . . We are often asked to add new tests without appropriate supervision. Test publishers aren't motivated to slow down sales by requiring training to purchase tests. Someone like me needs APA protection via strict access to tests only upon proof of training. It sounds self-serving according to our employer to request appropriate training.

I am often asked by social workers to "interpret" psychological tests which they administer without allowing me to see the client. I refuse to render an opinion without client contact. . . .

Colleagues in the medical profession have the right to order psychological tests from computer companies that give computer generated interpretations. . . .

. . .

Some psychologists will omit subtests from the Wechsler and report verbal and performance IQ scores without indicating that they have omitted subtests. This practice was so common we had to require a copy of the summary sheet to ensure that all tests were administered. . . .

Psychologists use computer-generated test reports as the only report of an evaluation, without integrating the test results with other data.

Questionable or Harmful Interventions

In a concise article, Singer (1980) illuminated the implications of psychology's scientific tradition for providing effective interventions in a safe manner. The importance of attending to this aspect of our work is highlighted by dilemmas reflecting respondents' concern about the efficacy, legitimacy, and safety of treatment approaches, modalities, and conditions.

A patient of mine . . . left town to attend college. Very shortly before departure, she revealed an early history of sexual abuse. The recurrent thoughts and memories were extremely disturbing to her. She refused to seek a new therapist at school. . . . She asked me to talk with her by phone. I am not licensed in that state. Would I be practicing in that state? Is "phone therapy" a reasonable choice? . . . If . . . not, is it abandonment? . . .

Seeing clients in an unprofessional atmosphere—e.g., in the home with pets present in the consultation room.

Colleagues . . . making/receiving 4–5 phone calls during a session.

As a state psychologist working with retarded clients . . . we may not use response cost or any negative reinforcers with our clients. . . . To me failure to enforce real controls is unethical, yet it

is a very strong national movement to use only positive reinforcement. . . .

Competence

About 3% of the dilemmas involved moving into areas without adequate competence or the erosion of competence through time and stress. . . .

In our small town, political community, colleagues are less well trained and often practice beyond their training and competence level.

Some current staff psychologists, trained many years ago, who have not kept their skills and/or knowledge base current and thus, we have a problem with competence.

I often feel exhausted and burned out, but lack supervisory therapy resource for myself. How do I know my own limits?

School Psychology

These dilemmas tended to reflect psychologists' struggles to act in the best interests of students despite pressure from administrators.

A retarded boy in a school district is kept isolated from the rest of his class because of his disruptive behavior. The school district hires me to decrease disruptive behaviors while still keeping him isolated. I feel that he should be integrated. Whose agent am I?

My school district administrator would like me to distort test data to show improvement.

I am employed as a school psychologist in a large school district. . . . I am asked to provide a diagnosis which will qualify the examinee for certain services, even if the test results do not justify that diagnosis. I have not done so, but the frequency with which the request is made is troubling.

As a school psychologist there is often pressure from administrators to place children in programs based on the availability of services rather than the needs of the individual student. . . .

Publishing

Dilemmas in the area of publishing tended to focus on giving publication credit to those who do not deserve it, denying publication credit to those who deserve it, and teachers plagiarizing students' papers for their own articles. As one respondent wrote,

> I am asked to give P.I. status to M.D. colleagues on training grants that I write and manage within a Dept. of Family Medicine at a large medical school.

Helping the Financially Stricken

Respondents expressed concerns about addressing the needs of those who are poor, unemployed, or homeless.

> My concern: not enough educational programs and financial support for those who could help the homeless. . . .
> My fee for psychotherapy makes me unavailable to needy clients, but I cannot afford to do pro bono work. . . . I feel wrong (unethical), even though I refer clients to lower-fee therapists.

Although both the current code and the most recent draft revision address the issue of providing services for little or no financial or other personal gain. No section [of the code] explicitly addresses the ethics of interventions, such as those used by community psychologists or primary preventionists, created specifically to serve the needs of those who are poor, unemployed, or homeless, or who are members of other vulnerable populations (e.g., Pope & Garcia-Peltoniemi, 1991; Pope & Morin, 1991). . . .

Supervision

Dilemmas in this area reflected concerns about supervisors who were negligent or disrespectful.

> Individuals hired and supervised by prominent licensed psychologist, who actually receive little or no supervision.
> Clinical supervisors who work with

students and impose their own orientation onto the students without regard or respect for different orientations and personality styles. . . .

Advertising and (Mis)Representations

Dilemmas in this area reflected concerns about how professionals present themselves and their work to the public in a false, misleading, or questionable manner.

> My clinic wishes to advertise my services in ways which I find offensive and unprofessional.
> Advertising in Yellow Pages stating "Psychological Referral Service" which was nothing more than a number generating referrals for several private practice psychologists.
> The Yellow Pages includes "bogus" listings under "Psychologists."
> A psychological assistant allows herself to be misrepresented as a psychologist. The hospital for whom she works supports her misrepresentation. . . .

Industrial–Organizational

Dilemmas in this area tended to describe ways in which management interfered with the psychologist's duties, especially instances in which psychologists were expected or pressured to break pledges of confidentiality to employees or survey respondents or in which a company breaks a pledge (which the psychologist had conveyed in good faith) to remedy problems identified in an employee survey. One respondent, however, noted what he or she felt to be an interesting conflict of interest: As an organizational psychologist in charge, he or she was responsible for setting his or her own pay.

Termination

About 1% of the dilemmas focused on difficulties terminating and rendering appropriate follow-up. Examples include,

> My greatest "ethical crisis" comes from conceptualizing terminations with clients (who have been victims as children

of ritual sexual abuse) in whose lives I have been "involved" for 5–7 years. . . .

A colleague took a 4 month leave of absence and referred a patient to me (as a "babysitter therapist") for the duration. The patient preferred me and did not wish to return to my colleague, who insisted I should force the patient to do so. I am having ambivalent feelings and wondering what is best for the patient—but also, whether to risk losing the friendship of my colleague.

Ethnicity

Dilemmas that focused on ethnicity included the following:

Many clients when referred to my office show initial shock that I am ethnically different from the mainstream. As a result, more time is needed to establish rapport.

In my academic institution, there are verbal statements and policies around affirmative action for courses and academic development of ethnic minority students and faculty. However, efforts directed toward those goals are constantly sabotaged and dismantled by the administration of the campus, who are psychologists.

. . .

[T]he profession may benefit from a discussion of whether confronting racism and similar forms of discrimination is an ethical responsibility that should be explicitly addressed by the formal code (Brown, 1991).

Treatment Records

About 1% of the dilemmas expressed concerns about what information should go into the record, agency policies of charging for records, providing copies of records to patients who have not paid their bills, and what to do when records are unintentionally destroyed. . . .

References

American Psychological Association. (1989). *Directory of the American Psychological Association*. Washington, DC: Author.

Bates, C. M., & Brodsky, A. M. (1989). *Sex in the therapy hour: A case of professional incest*. New York: Guilford.

Borys, D. S., & Pope, K. S. (1989). Dual relationships between therapist and client: A national study of psychologists, psychiatrists, and social workers. *Professional Psychology: Research and Practice, 20*, 283–293.

Brodsky, A. M. (1988, January). *Is it ever o.k. for a therapist to have a sexual relationship with a former patient?* Paper presented at the meeting of Division 12 (Clinical Psychology), San Diego, CA.

Brodsky, A. M. (1989). Sex between patient and therapist: Psychology's data and response. In G. O. Gabbard (Ed.), *Sexual exploitation in professional relationships* (pp. 15–25). Washington, DC: American Psychiatric Press.

Brown, L. S. (1988). Harmful effects of posttermination sexual and romantic relationships between therapists and their former clients. *Psychotherapy, 25*, 249–255.

Brown, L. S. (1991). Antiracism as an ethical imperative: An example from feminist therapy. *Ethics & Behavior, 1*, 113–128.

Committee on Women in Psychology. (1989). If sex enters into the psychotherapy relationship. *Professional Psychology: Research and Practice, 20*, 112–115.

Crowe, M., Grogan, J., Jacobs, R., Lindsey, C., & Mark, M. (1985). Delineation of the roles of clinical psychology. *Professional Psychology: Research and Practice, 16*, 124–137.

Ethics Committee of the American Psychological Association. (1988). Trends in ethics cases, common pitfalls, and published resources. *American Psychologist, 43*, 564–572.

Feldman-Summers, S. (1989). Sexual contact in fiduciary relationships. In G. O. Gabbard (Ed.), *Sexual exploitation in professional relationships* (pp. 193–209). Washington, DC: American Psychiatric Press.

Feldman-Summers, S., & Jones, G. (1984). Psychological impacts of sexual contact between therapists or other health care professionals and their clients. *Journal of Consulting and Clinical Psychology, 52*, 1054–1061.

Gabbard, G. O. (Eds.). (1989). *Sexual exploitation in professional relationships*. Washington, DC: American Psychiatric Press.

Gabbard, G. O., & Pope, K. S. (1989). Sexual intimacies after termination: Clinical, ethical, and legal aspects. In G. O. Gabbard (Ed.), *Sexual exploitation in professional relationships* (pp. 115–127). Washington, DC: American Psychiatric Press.

Glaser, R. D., & Thorpe, J. S. (1986). Unethical intimacy: A survey of sexual contact and advances between psychology educators and female graduate students. *American Psychologist, 41,* 43–51.

Hare-Mustin, R. T. (in press). Cries and whispers. *Psychotherapy.*

Holroyd, J. C., & Brodsky, A. M. (1977). Psychologists' attitudes and practices regarding erotic and nonerotic physical contact with clients. *American Psychologist, 32,* 843–849.

Huber, P. W. (1991). *Galileo's revenge: Junk science in the courtroom.* New York: Basic Books.

Kalichman, S. C., Craig, M. E., & Follingstad, D. R. (1989). Factors influencing the reporting of father–child sexual abuse: Study of licensed practicing psychologists. *Professional Psychology, 20,* 84–89.

Keith-Spiegel, P., & Koocher, G. P. (1985). *Ethics in psychology.* New York: Random House.

Kleinfeld, N. R. (1991, August 5). Doctor's critique of care stains hospital's bond. *New York Times.* p. A-12.

Knapp, S., & VandeCreek, L. (1987). *Privileged communications in the mental health professions.* New York: Van Nostrand Reinhold.

Koocher, G. P., & Keith-Spiegel, G. P. (1990). *Children, ethics, and the law: Professional issues and cases.* Lincoln: University of Nebraska Press.

Pope, K. S. (1989). Therapist–Patient Sex Syndrome: A guide to assessing damage. In G. O. Gabbard (Ed.), *Sexual exploitation in professional relationships* (pp. 39–55). Washington, DC: American Psychiatric Press.

Pope, K. S. (1990b). Therapist–client sexual involvement: A review of the research. *Clinical Psychology Review, 10,* 477–490.

Pope, K. S. (1991). Rehabilitation plans and expert testimony for therapists who have been sexually involved with a patient. *Independent Practitioner, 11*(3), 31–39.

Pope, K. S., & Bajt, T. R. (1988). When laws and values conflict: A dilemma for psychologists. *American Psychologist, 43,* 828.

Pope, K. S., & Garcia-Peltoniemi, R. E. (1991). Responding to victims of torture: Clinical issues, professional responsibilities, and useful resources. *Professional Psychology: Research and Practice, 22,* 269–276.

Pope, K. S., Levenson, H., & Schover, L. R. (1979). Sexual intimacy in psychology training: Results and implications of a national survey. *American Psychologist, 34,* 682–689.

Pope, K. S., & Morin, S. F. (1991). AIDS and HIV infec-

tion update: New research, ethical responsibilities, evolving legal frameworks, and published resources. In P. A. Keller & S. R. Heyman (Eds.), *Innovations in clinical practice: A sourcebook* (Vol. 10, pp. 443–457). Sarasota, FL: Professional Resource Exchange.

Pope, K. S., Schover, L. R., & Levenson, H. (1980). Sexual intimacies between clinical supervisors and supervisees: Implications for professional standards. *Professional Psychology, 11,* 157–162.

Pope, K. S., Tabachnick, B. G., & Keith-Spiegel, P. (1987). Ethics of practice: The beliefs and behaviors of psychologists as therapists. *American Psychologist, 42,* 993–1006.

Pope, K. S., & Vasquez, M. J. T. (1991). *Ethics in psychotherapy and counseling: A practical guide for psychologists.* San Franciso: Jossey-Bass.

Pope, K. S., & Vetter, V. A. (1991). Prior therapist–patient sexual involvement among patients seen by psychologists. *Psychotherapy, 28,* 429–438.

Report of the Ethics Committee, 1989 and 1990. (1991). *American Psychologist, 46,* 750–757.

Robinson, W. L., & Reid, P. T. (1985). Sexual intimacies in psychology revisited. *Professional Psychology, 16,* 512–520.

Sell, J. M., Gottlieb, M. C., & Schoenfeld, L. (1986). Ethical considerations of social/romantic relationships with present and former clients. *Professional Psychology: Research and Practice, 17,* 504–508.

Shopland, S. N., & VandeCreek, L. (1991). Sex with ex-clients: Theoretical rationales for prohibition. *Ethics & Behavior, 1,* 45–62.

Simon, G. C. (1978). The psychologist as whistle blower: A case study. *Professional Psychology, 9,* 322–340.

Singer, J. L. (1980). The scientific basis of psychotherapeutic practice: A question of values and ethics. *Psychotherapy: Theory, Research and Practice, 17,* 372–383.

Sonne, J. L. (1987). Proscribed sex: Counseling the patient subjected to sexual intimacy by a therapist. *Medical Aspects of Human Sexuality, 16,* 18–23.

Sonne, J. L. (1989). An example of group therapy for victims of therapist–client sexual intimacy. In G. O. Gabbard (Ed.), *Sexual exploitation in professional relationships* (pp. 101–127). Washington, DC: American Psychiatric Press.

Sonne, J., Meyer, C. B., Borys, D., & Marshall, V. (1985). Clients' reaction to sexual intimacy in therapy. *American Journal of Orthopsychiatry, 55,* 183–189.

Sonne, J. L., & Pope, K. S. (1991). Treating victims of therapist–patient sexual involvement. *Psychotherapy, 28,* 174–187.

Stromberg, C. D., Haggarty, D. J., Leibenluft, R. F.,

McMillian, M. H., Mishkin, B., Rubin, B. L., & Trilling, H. R. (1988). *The psychologist's legal handbook.* Washington, DC: Council for the National Register of Health Service Providers in Psychology.

Tabachnick, B. G., Keith-Spiegel, P., & Pope, K. S. (1991). Ethics of teaching: Beliefs and behaviors of psychologists as educators. *American Psychologist, 46,* 506–515.

Vasquez, M. J. T. (1991). Sexual intimacies with clients after termination: Should a prohibition be explicit? *Ethics & Behavior, 1,* 35–44.

Commentary: *For a more general discussion of the types of conduct that lead to ethical scrutiny, see Peterson, C. (1996). Common problem areas and their causes resulting in disciplinary actions. In L. J. Bass et al. (Eds.), Professional conduct and discipline in psychology (pp. 71–89). Washington, DC: American Psychological Association.*

CHAPTER 2

HOW ETHICS ARE APPLIED

Suppose you share offices with a close friend and fellow clinician who, like you, is a member of APA. You discover that this office mate has terminated treatments with a female client after two sessions of behavior therapy and that, soon thereafter, he and she have begun a romantic relationship. What should you do? More, interestingly, what *would* you do? If you are like most colleagues, you would probably be among the nearly one third who would not bring his conduct to the attention of any ethics body.

Assume now that you are a psychotherapist asked to consider whether, in the following situations, the psychologists involved acted ethically:

1. A state requires that an applicant for licensure complete 1,500 hours of postdoctoral experience under supervision before becoming eligible to take the licensure examination. An applicant and a licensed psychologist agree that the psychologist will attest in writing that the applicant has completed the requirement even though the applicant has had only 500 hours of supervised experience.
2. At a social gathering attended by people of many professions, a psychologist is overheard discussing one of her patients by name with two of her friends, a physician and an accountant, neither of whom are involved in the case.
3. A patient who has just begun treatment with you tells you that he terminated his professional relationship with his former therapist because the therapist consistently conducted treatment while under the influence of alcohol.

Is there any question that each of these three incidents describes behavior by psychologists that is clearly unethical? Would it surprise you, then, to discover that APA member psychotherapists do not universally agree that the conduct described in these realistic situations is unethical (Pope, Tabachnik, & Keith-Spiegel, 1987)? What about the finding that over 50% of 60 senior psychologists, all of whom had considerable experience with ethics issues, admitted to intentionally violating a law or a formal ethical principle regulating their professional practice (Pope & Bajt, 1988)?

These vignettes and data (or variants thereof) come from research presented throughout this chapter. They may be properly viewed as examples of deplorable and odious behavior. Then again, one could argue that in some instances, violating an ethical rule or even a state or federal law may evidence the proper exercise of professional discretion.

In any event, it is clear that knowledge of ethical provisions and legal rules does not inevitably lead to perfect conformity with these obligations. Thus, putting aside those few colleagues who meet the definition of sociopathy, what stimulates otherwise moral psychologists to take actions that directly contradict what they know they should do?

In some cases, psychologists may violate ethical principles because those principles are vaguely worded. For example, in some informal research, I asked experienced, licensed clinical psychologists to respond to 75 true–false items concerning ethical behavior. To the items I attached the 1989 APA code of ethics. The directions indicated that respondents could refer to the code at any time to answer the items. Yet, in no instance did any of the test takers answer more than 60% correctly.

One could hypothesize that these surprising results, although from an admittedly unsystematic study, show that the old APA ethics code was simply too ambiguous to guide respondents to the presumptively "correct" answer, and that was my guess. But even if an ethical code were written in perfectly clear language, there are plausible and understandable reasons why, at times, psychologists would deliberately violate ethical rules. One of those may be the psychologist's perception that violating the code will satisfy even higher moral values. Is it appropriate, however, for psychologists to engage in civil disobedience, following in the revered footsteps of Henry David Thoreau and Martin Luther King? Or are psychologists obligated to abide by their association's code of ethics and to seek to change those provisions they find objectionable through an orderly, though slow-moving, democratic process?

In this chapter, I explore such issues, providing a great many vignettes and dilemmas that should provoke discussion and debate and, thus, move the reader beyond merely learning ethical rules and procedural regulations to thinking about the meaning and value of a code of ethics. It is my guess, as well, that readers will leave this chapter with a sense of creative uncertainty. But they should not despair. Ideas for best dealing with this uncertainty follow in chapter 3.

References

Pope, K. S., & Bajt, T. R. (1988). When laws and values conflict: A dilemma for psychologists. *American Psychologist, 43,* 828–829.

Pope, K. S., Tabachnik, B. E., & Keith-Spiegel, P. (1987). Ethics of practice: The beliefs and behaviors of psychologists as therapists. *American Psychologist, 42,* 993–1006.

The Failure of Clinical Psychology Graduate Students to Apply Understood Ethical Principles

J. L. Bernard and Carmen S. Jara

. . . With any ethical violation there are two distinct elements that must be recognized: (a) the extent to which the ethical principle applicable to the situation in question is understandable, and (b) the degree of willingness to do what one understands should be done. Of these, it seems unlikely that a lack of understanding is ordinarily the basis for a violation. . . . Rather, in dealings with educated, highly intelligent professionals, it seems much more likely that the crux of the issue with ethical violations is an unwillingness to conform to the demands of the Ethical Principles . . .

. . . Ethical Principles 7(g)[1] clearly places the responsibility for confronting recognized violations squarely on the members of the profession. To ignore an ethical violation is, then, a violation in itself. In this article we report data on the willingness (or, more appropriately, the lack thereof) of graduate students to honor Principle 7(g) when faced with a hypothetical ethical violation by a fellow student who is also a friend.

METHOD

Questionnaire

Packets were distributed to a nationwide sample of clinical graduate students at APA-approved programs with a request that they be returned to the experimenter anonymously. Each packet consisted of an explanatory cover letter soliciting anonymous cooperation, two scenarios constructed to depict ethical violations, a demographic information sheet that the student could discard if he or she felt that it might compromise confidentiality (none did), a questionnaire on which the student would react to the scenarios, and a stamped envelope for the student to use in returning the packet.

In the first scenario, a clinical graduate student was depicted as being sexually involved with a client from a psychotherapy practicum. In the scenarios in half of the packets, the student therapist was female, and in the other half, male. In the second scenario (again balanced for sex) a clinical graduate student was characterized as a problem drinker/alcoholic who is manifesting poor judgment and erratic behavior in various clinical practica, but thus far concealing it from the clinical faculty. In each case, the reader was asked to assume that he or she had discovered the problem, and that the alleged violator was not only a fellow graduate student, but also a friend. Also, according to the scenarios, not only had the reader discovered the problem, but it had already led to one confrontation with the alleged violator that had not produced results. Two Ethical Principles involved, 2(f) and 6(a) (American Psychological Association, 1981), were then presented verbatim in order to eliminate recall of the principles as a factor in students' deciding how to answer the questionnaire. . . . At this point, the reader was asked two distinct questions. The first, "According to the Ethical Principles, what *should* you do?", was used to assess the degree of understanding that the described behavior constituted an ethical violation requiring some sort of action, and what that action

From *Professional Psychology: Research and Practice, 17,* 313–315. Copyright 1986 by the American Psychological Association. Adapted with permission of the author and publisher.

[1] *Ed. note:* See Standards 8.04 and 8.05 of the APA's current (1992) Ethical Principles.

should be. The second question, "Speaking pragmatically, and recognizing that he [she] is a friend and a fellow graduate student, what do you think you probably *would* do?" was used to assess the reader's willingness to do what he or she had already stated should be done. Each of these questions was followed by five possible responses to the situation. To illustrate, those for the problem-drinking/alcoholism scenario in which the student was male were (a) "Nothing"; (b) "Suggest he get help for this problem"; (c) "Keep trying to get him to stop drinking"; (d) "Tell him that if he doesn't get his drinking under control you will have to mention it to the Director of Clinical Training or his clinical supervisor"; and (e) "Tell the Director of Clinical Training or his clinical supervisor." We anticipated that essentially all students would recognize that each scenario depicted a violation that called for a particular course of action. However, we hypothesized that although most students would state a willingness to implement whatever course of action they felt was indicated, a significant number would admit that they would probably do something less than that. Thus the data to be analyzed was the difference between what the reader said should be done and what he or she would actually do if confronted with the situation described in the scenarios. We hypothesized further that to the extent that this was true, some of the demographic items (e.g., whether the student had had coursework in ethics, or the sex of the student who was violating the principles) might enable us to discriminate between these two groups.

As a manipulation check, these scenarios had earlier been presented to the members of a state ethics committee with a request that they respond only to the question of what should be done. With the sexual scenario there was complete agreement that "Tell the Director of Clinical Training or the student's supervisor" was the appropriate response. With the problem-drinking/alcoholism scenario with a male student, 3 of 5 committee members gave this same reply, whereas 2 chose a response one step less severe ("Tell the student that if he doesn't get his drinking under control you will have to tell the Director of Clinical training or his/her supervisor"). . . .

Subjects

Materials for 10 graduate students were sent, with an explanatory cover letter, to each of 25 clinical directors in APA-approved graduate clinical training programs. . . . In the cover letter we asked the clinic directors to distribute the packets to clinical graduate students, attempting to balance for sex and year in the program. The potential return was 250 questionnaires, and the first mailing resulted in 162 returns. . . . [A] second mailing prompted 8 additional returns, which made a total of 170.

RESULTS

. . . First, we analyzed the data by obtaining percentages of clinical graduate students who stated that they would do the same thing that they had already said they should do, and those who stated that they would do something less than they had already stated they should do. (There were no instances of subjects who said that they would do more than they should.) With the sexual scenario, the split was even: 50% said that they would do what they had already said they should do, and 50% said that they would do less. Applying the binomial expansion to these two groups provides a significant normal approximation to distribution of proportions, $Z(1) = 17.39$, $p < .0001$. With the problem-drinking/alcoholism scenario, 45% of the students said that they would do what they had already stated they should do, and the remaining 55% said that they would do less (again, no one said that they would do more). A comparison of these two groups with the same statistics was also highly significant, $Z(1) = 19.94$, $p < .0001$. . . .

. . . No significant differences were obtained for any demographic or scenario variables.

DISCUSSION

In this study we did not assess whether graduate clinical students would conform to some abstract standard for ethical behavior when confronted with an hypothetical violation. Rather, we first asked the student what should be done, and then whether the student would do that or something else. In this way, each student indicated his or her own understanding of how the Ethical Principle pertinent to each scenario should be applied, and then whether that understanding would result in appropriate behavior. For both scenarios, at least half of the students stated that they would not live up to their own interpretation of what the Ethical Principles required of them as professionals. Most simply put, this amounts to saying, "I know what I should do as an ethical psychologist, but I wouldn't do it."

The fact that no significant differences were obtained between these two groups of students on any of the demographic variables suggests that factors such as how far along the student was in training, whether coursework had been taken in ethics or in substance abuse (most respondents had taken a course on ethics), and so on, had no apparent bearing on willingness to put Ethical Principles into action. This may imply that training in ethics is inadequate, or that a willingness to take action when confronted with an ethical violation that involves a colleague/friend is not something that can be taught. Indeed, one fourth-year student who had had coursework in both ethics and substance abuse stated that for both scenarios he believed that he should "Tell the Director of Clinical Training or the student's supervisor"; yet, to the question "What *would* you do?" he replied "Nothing" both times. It seems that psychologists may be teaching the content of the principles without at the same time adequately communicating the importance of their implementation. . . .

Baldick (1980), using the same type of scenario format as we did, found among a sample of clinical psychology interns that those who had had training in ethics were significantly better at understanding ethical dilemmas than were those who had not. Schwitzgebel and Kirkland (1980) observed that

> Most ethical codes are vaguely formulated and rarely enforced. . . . They provide almost no specific and tangible guidance to either practitioner or scientist. (p. 3)

All of this points to a need for a thorough, formal, and systematic approach to training in ethics so that the student will understand what the principles demand of the profession. Yet, our data indicate that although such training is important, the problem is not simply that the Ethical Principles "are vaguely formulated" or "provide almost no guidance." The subjects in this study seemed to understand the ethics of their chosen profession; they simply chose not to apply them in a hypothetical situation involving a peer/friend.

Clearly, there is a problem among those who are training for the profession (and one that may equally well apply to those already practicing). That problem is not how to communicate the ethical principles to students more effectively, but rather how to motivate them to implement principles that they apparently understand quite well. . . .

References

American Psychological Association. (1981). *Ethical standards of psychologists*. Washington, DC: Author.

Baldick, T. L. (1980). Ethical discrimination ability of intern psychologists: A function of training in ethics. *Professional Psychology, 11*, 276–282.

Schwitzgebel, R. L., & Kirkland, R. (1980). *Law and psychological practice*. New York: Wiley.

◆ ◆ ◆

Commentary: Bernard and his colleagues (1987) replicated the preceding study with a sample of members belonging to Division 12 (Clinical) of APA. See Bernard, J. L, Murphy, M., & Little, M. (1987). The failure of clinical psychologists to apply understood ethical principles. Professional Psychology: Research and Practice, 18, 489–491. The scenarios in this study were the same as in Bernard and Jara's (1986) study except that in the first scenario the therapist was a male doctoral-level clinician, and in the second the therapist was a female doctoral-level clinician. Bernard et al. (1987) reported the following results (pp. 490–491):

> . . . *With the sexual scenario, 63% of clinicians responding said that they would do what they felt they should do, and 37% said that they would do less than they felt they should do. Applying the binomial expansion to these data provides a significant normal approximation to distribution of proportions: Z(1) = 9.08, p < .001. With the problem-drinking/alcoholism scenario, 74% of the clinicians responding said that*

they would do what they had already said they should do, whereas 26% said that they would do less. A comparison of these two groups with the same statistic was also highly significant: Z(1) = 9.96, p < .001. . . .

When clinical graduate students were surveyed in this manner (Bernard & Jara, 1986), about the same results were obtained with each scenario. Approximately half of the students said that they would do less than they knew they should do whether the violation involved alcoholism or sex. This was not the case with clinical psychologists. With the problem-drinking/alcoholism scenario, 25% of the clinicians said that they would do less than their understanding of Ethical Principles demanded of them. However, with the sexual scenario, one third of the clinicians would not live up to their understanding of what should be done. This is even more puzzling when one considers that although the problem-drinking/alcoholism scenario requires that the reader interpret the Ethical Principles as they apply to impaired psychologists, sexual intimacies with patients are flatly described as unethical. . . . [I]t is apparent from this survey that although professionals say that they would behave more responsibly than do graduate students, significant numbers of clinical psychologists simply would not do what they know they should do when confronted with an ethical violation by a colleague. Still, it is perhaps encouraging that the proportion of clinicians who would "do the right thing" is substantially higher than obtained with graduate students. This may reflect an increased awareness among professionals that even though reporting the unethical behavior of a colleague is personally repugnant, it is an ethical obligation and should benefit the profession in the long run.

As with the graduate students (Bernard & Jara, 1986), there were no significant differences, on any demographic variable,

between those clinicians who would do what they felt they should do and those who would not. This suggests that the decision to report the unethical behavior of a colleague is a matter of personal values to a large extent. Yet, it seems that if psychology is to prosper, the ethics of the profession must be taken more seriously by the large numbers of clinicians who are not willing to report the unethical behavior of a colleague. The problem is, then, how our profession can motivate more clinicians to implement the Ethical Principles that they understand quite well.

It may be that a different thrust is needed in the teaching of ethics in graduate programs. It is vitally important that students learn that the function of an ethics committee is to help violators change their unethical behavior, using rehabilitative rather than punitive means whenever possible. It is also important that they come to recognize that their own professional self-interest is protected by their willingness to behave ethically and to report those psychologists who do not. It seems probable, in retrospect, that if more of us had been willing to report those instances of unethical conduct of which we were aware, our malpractice premiums might be lower today. . . .

In a more recent study, graduate students were confronted with items that identified ethical improprieties by their peers, such as breaching confidentiality or becoming romantically involved with clients (entering "dual relationships"). Twenty-five percent of the students indicated that they would do nothing. Only 3% said that they would contact an outside agency. On the other hand, 47% said they would consult other students about the problem, 31% would express concerns directly to the faculty, and 28% would directly confront their unethical colleagues. Interestingly, faculty underestimated the extent to which their students would taken any action. Nevertheless, although students deserve more credit than their teachers give them and, in many instances, "indicate that their feelings of ethical obligation . . . outweigh sentiments of loyalty to problematic peers" (Mearns & Allen, 1991, p. 198), a great deal of impaired performance and unethical behavior remains unattended to.

See Mearns, J., & Allen, G. J. (1991). Graduate students' experiences in dealing with impaired peers, compared with faculty predictions: An exploratory study. Ethics and Behavior, 1, 191–202.

Ethics of Practice: The Beliefs and Behaviors of Psychologists as Therapists

Kenneth S. Pope, Barbara G. Tabachnick, and Patricia Keith-Spiegel

The American Psychological Association (APA) has developed elaborate ethical principles and standards of practice to guide the behavior of its membership. . . . However, we still lack comprehensive, systematically gathered data about the degree to which members believe in or comply with these guidelines. Consequently, such data are not available to inform either the clinical decisions of individual practitioners or the attempts of the APA to revise, refine, and extend formal standards of practice.

No implication is intended that norms are the equivalent of ethical standards. In many situations, the formulation and dissemination of formal standards are intended to increase ethical awareness and to improve the behaviors of a professional association. . . . But those who are charged with developing, disseminating, and enforcing professional codes can function much more effectively if they are aware of the diverse dilemmas confronting the membership and of the membership's varied personal codes and behaviors.

METHOD

Survey Questionnaire

A survey questionnaire, a cover letter, and a return envelope were sent to 1,000 psychologists (500 men and 500 women) randomly selected from the 4,684 members of Division 29 (Psychotherapy) as listed in the 1985 *Directory of the American Psychological Association* (APA, 1985).

The survey questionnaire was divided into three main parts.[1] The first part consisted of a list of 83

behaviors. Participants were asked to rate each of the 83 behaviors in terms of three categories [footnote omitted]. First, to what extent had they engaged in the behavior in their practice? Participants either could indicate that the behavior was *not applicable* to their practice or they could rate the behavior's occurrence in their practice as *never, sometimes, fairly often,* or *very often*. Second, to what extent did they consider the practice ethical? In rating whether each behavior was ethical, participants could use five categories: *unquestionably not, under rare circumstances, don't know/not sure, under any circumstances,* and *unquestionably yes.*

RESULTS

Demographic Characteristics of the Participants and Ratings of the 83 Behaviors

Questionnaires were returned by 456 respondents (45.6%). . . . Table 3 presents the percentage of respondents' ratings for each of the 83 behaviors in terms of occurrence in their own practice and the degree to which they believe the behavior to be ethical. . . .

DISCUSSION

Relationship Between Behavior and Beliefs

The data suggest that the psychologists' behavior was generally in accordance with their ethical beliefs. This inference is based on the fact that for all

From *American Psychologist*, 42, 993–1006. Copyright 1987 by the American Psychological Association. Adapted with permission of the author and publisher. Tables 1, 2, 4, and 6 have been omitted.

[1] Only results from the first part of the study are described in this excerpt.

TABLE 3

Percentage of Psychologists (*N* = 465) Responding in Each Category

	Rating										
	Occurrence in Your Practice?						Ethical?				
Item	1	2	3	4	5ª	NA	1	2	3	4	5ª
1. Becoming social friends with a former client	42.1	45.2	9.2	1.8	1.1	0.7	6.4	51.1	13.4	21.9	6.8
2. Charging a client no fee for therapy	33.3	47.4	15.8	1.1	1.8	2.9	4.6	25.2	14.5	24.8	29.6
3. Providing therapy to one of your friends	70.4	25.2	2.2	0.2	0.7	2.2	47.6	40.1	2.9	4.4	3.7
4. Advertising in newspapers or similar media	72.4	13.2	10.1	2.4	0.4	5.5	12.9	14.7	17.8	33.3	20.6
5. Limiting treatment notes to name, date, and fee	48.2	18.4	13.8	6.6	12.1	1.5	18.6	22.4	21.7	20.8	14.7
6. Filing an ethics complaint against a colleague	61.6	25.2	7.5	0.7	1.1	10.7	2.4	11.8	3.1	22.8	57.9
7. Telling a client you are angry at him or her	9.6	45.0	36.8	5.7	2.2	0.7	3.1	26.8	8.3	35.5	25.4
8. Using a computerized test interpretation service	39.0	21.7	20.8	7.9	7.5	13.2	2.0	9.0	12.9	39.3	34.9
9. Hugging a client	13.4	44.5	29.8	7.7	4.2	0.2	4.6	41.2	8.3	35.5	9.2
10. Terminating therapy if client cannot pay	36.2	36.2	20.0	3.7	2.0	5.3	12.1	27.4	15.4	32.7	11.0
11. Accepting services from a client in lieu of fee	66.9	27.0	3.5	0.2	0.4	7.9	22.6	39.3	14.5	16.0	6.4
12. Seeing a minor client without parental consent	65.8	22.4	5.5	0.2	0.7	14.0	23.5	45.6	13.4	11.6	3.7
13. Having clients take tests (e.g., MMPI) at home	43.9	27.0	16.0	4.8	3.5	10.7	20.2	25.9	19.5	22.1	10.1
14. Altering a diagnosis to meet insurance criteria	36.4	26.5	27.0	5.5	2.6	2.9	37.3	28.9	16.0	14.0	2.0
15. Telling client: "I'm sexually attracted to you."	78.5	16.2	3.5	0.2	0.2	4.8	51.5	33.1	5.5	6.8	2.4
16. Refusing to let clients read their chart notes	33.1	21.3	13.6	5.7	14.9	23.2	14.5	28.3	14.9	21.5	16.0
17. Using a collection agency to collect late fees	48.0	21.9	19.7	5.9	1.8	8.6	5.0	15.1	15.6	35.5	27.4
18. Breaking confidentiality if client is homicidal	15.6	9.6	6.6	24.6	17.3	35.7	1.1	5.0	3.5	18.9	69.1
19. Performing forensic work for a contingency fee	67.3	7.0	6.8	0.9	0.7	42.1	35.5	11.0	29.8	7.0	10.3
20. Using self-disclosure as a therapy technique	5.9	22.1	38.6	19.7	12.9	0.7	2.2	17.1	7.9	43.0	29.2
21. Inviting clients to an office open house	76.3	9.6	5.0	0.7	2.0	19.3	28.9	25.7	23.2	12.1	8.3
22. Accepting a client's gift worth at least $50	72.1	19.1	2.4	0.4	0.0	16.7	34.2	36.2	15.8	8.6	3.3
23. Working when too distressed to be effective	38.8	48.5	10.5	0.4	0.2	5.3	46.7	38.4	8.6	4.4	1.3
24. Accepting only male or female clients	83.8	3.7	2.4	0.2	1.1	18.2	11.0	16.2	18.6	16.9	34.6
25. Not allowing client access to testing report	45.0	23.5	13.6	5.9	6.6	14.3	21.7	32.9	14.0	20.6	8.8
26. Raising the fee during the course of therapy	27.6	23.9	29.4	11.8	5.7	3.5	8.3	15.8	13.2	32.5	28.9
27. Breaking confidentiality if client is suicidal	16.2	24.6	25.0	9.6	19.3	11.8	2.0	10.1	5.5	23.5	57.5
28. Not allowing clients access to raw test data	32.2	10.5	9.0	7.9	30.0	1.8	12.1	12.9	11.2	22.8	36.8

(table continues)

TABLE 3 (*cont.*)

Item	Occurrence in Your Practice?						Ethical?				
	1	2	3	4	5[a]	NA	1	2	3	4	5[a]
29. Allowing a client to run up a large unpaid bill	12.5	44.1	34.4	5.7	1.5	2.9	7.2	35.3	22.8	16.9	16.4
30. Accepting goods (rather than money) as payment	65.1	24.8	6.4	0.2	0.4	12.7	15.8	33.8	21.3	18.2	9.6
31. Usual sexual surrogates with clients	81.8	5.7	1.1	0.7	0.2	33.1	36.2	25.7	23.7	8.6	4.6
32. Breaking confidentiality to report child abuse	25.0	16.2	15.1	8.3	22.6	29.4	1.3	4.4	5.3	20.8	64.9
33. Inviting clients to a party or social event	82.9	13.2	2.2	0.2	0.4	4.6	50.0	34.0	8.1	6.1	1.5
34. Addressing client by his or her first name	2.0	2.6	9.4	20.8	65.1	0	0.7	0.9	2.6	30.7	65.1
35. Crying in the presence of a client	42.5	41.5	12.5	1.8	0.7	4.6	5.9	32.0	14.5	18.4	27.6
36. Earning a salary which is a % of client's fee	46.3	4.4	10.1	3.5	5.3	41.0	12.1	8.1	34.2	16.0	16.4
37. Asking favors (e.g., a ride home) from clients	60.5	35.7	2.4	0	0.2	5.0	27.0	45.2	12.3	10.1	4.4
38. Making custody evaluation without seeing the child	76.8	7.2	1.3	0.2	0.2	36.0	64.0	22.8	5.3	2.4	0.9
39. Accepting a client's decision to commit suicide	73.9	16.4	3.7	0.4	0	15.4	45.2	36.6	8.8	2.9	
40. Refusing to disclose a diagnosis to a client	49.8	30.9	10.1	4.6	2.4	4.2	21.5	43.2	13.2	13.4	6.8
41. Leading nude group therapy or "growth' groups	88.6	2.2	0.9	0.2	0	24.3	59.6	16.4	14.9	3.9	2.9
42. Telling clients of your disappointment in them	46.9	39.0	11.4	1.1	0.4	2.6	19.7	37.1	18.0	15.4	7.9
43. Discussing clients (without names) with friends	22.8	46.3	22.4	5.7	2.0	0.9	32.9	38.6	13.8	9.4	4.6
44. Providing therapy to your student or supervisee	63.8	22.4	6.8	0.9	0.9	12.3	45.8	33.6	6.1	8.8	4.2
45. Giving gifts to those who refer clients to you	78.5	11.4	7.0	1.5	1.1	4.2	47.8	21.7	15.6	10.3	4.2
46. Using a law suit to collect fees from clients	62.7	21.3	10.3	0.2	0.4	15.4	10.1	28.3	19.3	19.7	21.1
47. Becoming sexually involved with a former client	88.2	10.5	0.4	0	0.2	7.5	50.2	34.4	7.2	3.9	3.3
48. Avoiding certain clients for fear of being sued	48.9	30.3	13.4	1.3	0.9	13.8	7.9	23.0	23.7	23.9	19.7
49. Doing custody evaluation without seeing both parents	63.8	16.9	6.6	0.7	0.2	30.5	47.1	31.6	10.7	3.9	2.6
50. Lending money to a client	73.7	23.9	1.5	0	0	4.4	40.6	38.8	10.7	5.9	3.3
51. Providing therapy to one of your employees	79.6	12.9	2.0	0	0.7	15.6	55.0	31.1	6.8	2.9	2.4
52. Having a client address you by your first name	3.5	10.5	21.9	21.9	41.9	0.4	1.3	3.3	7.9	23.5	63.6
53. Sending holiday greeting cards to your clients	61.4	16.2	12.9	3.1	4.8	5.3	10.5	12.9	26.8	20.4	28.5
54. Kissing a client	70.8	23.5	4.4	0.2	0.4	2.2	48.0	36.6	4.6	7.7	2.2
55. Engaging in erotic activity with a client	97.1	2.4	0.2	0	0	3.9	95.0	3.5	0.4	0.4	0.4
56. Giving a gift worth at least $50 to a client	95.0	3.7	0.4	0	0	4.6	69.7	16.0	8.1	2.9	2.6

(*table continues*)

TABLE 3 *(cont.)*

	Rating										
	Occurrence in Your Practice?						Ethical?				
Item	1	2	3	4	5[a]	NA	1	2	3	4	5[a]
57. Accepting a client's invitation to a party	59.6	34.9	4.4	0.2	0.4	2.9	25.7	46.1	10.1	10.7	6.8
58. Engaging in sex with a clinical supervisee	95.0	2.9	0.4	0	0	8.8	85.1	9.0	3.5	1.5	0.2
59. Going to client's special event (e.g., wedding)	23.5	50.7	20.4	3.3	1.5	0.4	5.3	34.0	13.8	28.7	17.5
60. Getting paid to refer clients to someone	98.0	0.4	0.2	0	0	7.2	88.4	7.2	3.3	0	0.2
61. Going into business with a client	95.6	1.5	0.2	0	0.2	9.9	78.5	12.7	5.5	1.1	1.1
62. Engaging in sexual contact with a client	97.8	1.5	0.4	0	0	4.2	96.1	2.6	0.2	0.7	0.2
63. Utilizing involuntary hospitalization	30.5	42.1	16.7	2.4	1.1	17.1	3.1	28.9	8.8	24.3	31.8
64. Selling goods to clients	90.6	5.9	2.0	0	0.4	7.5	71.1	18.4	4.4	2.9	2.0
65. Giving personal advice on radio, t.v., etc.	66.0	18.6	9.2	1.5	0.2	18.6	18.4	28.3	22.1	23.7	6.4
66. Being sexually attracted to a client	9.2	38.8	43.9	5.5	1.3	1.1	11.2	11.0	19.5	19.1	33.3
67. Unintentionally disclosing confidential data	36.0	58.6	3.3	0	0	2.9	75.2	14.3	4.6	1.8	1.8
68. Allowing a client to disrobe	94.5	2.9	1.5	0	0	5.0	81.4	12.1	3.1	1.5	1.3
69. Borrowing money from a client	97.1	1.8	0	0	0	4.4	86.2	10.7	1.1	0.4	0.9
70. Discussing a client (by name) with friends	91.2	7.5	0.4	0.2	0	3.5	94.5	3.5	0.7	0.4	0.4
71. Providing services outside areas of competence	74.8	22.8	1.8	0	0	2.0	80.7	16.9	0.2	0.9	0.7
72. Signing for hours a supervisee has not earned	89.0	7.2	0.9	0	0	9.9	92.5	5.5	0.4	0.4	0.7
73. Treating homosexuality per se as pathological	75.0	12.7	6.4	2.6	1.8	4.4	55.7	12.9	17.3	6.6	5.3
74. Doing therapy while under influence of alcohol	92.8	5.7	0.2	0	0	3.5	89.5	7.7	1.1	0	0.9
75. Engaging in sexual fantasy about a client	27.0	46.3	22.4	2.4	0.7	3.5	18.9	15.1	26.8	13.2	21.9
76. Accepting a gift worth less than $5 from a client	8.6	31.8	45.0	9.4	3.7	0.7	5.0	20.0	16.2	36.4	20.2
77. Offering or accepting a handshake from a client	1.3	3.3	17.5	28.1	48.2	1.1	0.7	1.1	3.3	21.7	71.9
78. Disrobing in the presence of a client	97.8	0.9	0	0.2	0.2	4.6	94.7	3.3	0	0.2	0.7
79. Charging for missed appointments	11.8	15.4	26.3	22.6	22.6	2.4	1.1	6.8	7.2	38.2	45.8
80. Going into business with a former client	83.1	10.1	2.0	0	0.4	15.6	36.8	28.9	17.5	9.0	5.9
81. Directly soliciting a person to be a client	89.3	8.6	0.9	0	0.2	4.4	67.5	22.6	5.7	1.8	1.5
82. Being sexually attracted to a client	9.2	39.5	41.0	6.1	0.9	1.3	9.2	13.4	21.9	18.0	30.0
83. Helping client file complaint re a colleague	52.9	19.4	9.4	1.1	1.1	20.0	6.4	22.6	14.9	29.2	25.2

Note. Rating codes: Occurrence in your practice? 1 = never, 2 = rarely, 3 = sometimes, 4 = fairly often, 5 = very often, NA = not applicable; Ethical? 1 = unquestionably not, 2 = under rare circumstances, 3 = don't know/not sure, 4 = under many circumstances, 5 = unquestionably yes.
[a]Responses 1 through 5 sum to less than 100% due to missing data.

but four items, the frequency with which the respondents reported engaging in a behavior was less than the frequency of instances in which the behavior was ethical in their judgment. Of the four exceptions, three involved confidentiality: "discussing a client (by name) with friends," "discussing clients (without names) with friends," and "unintentionally disclosing confidential data." The fourth exception was "providing services outside areas of competence."

Behaviors That Are Almost Universal

For 7 of the 83 items, at least 90% of the respondents indicated that they engaged in the behavior, at least on rare occasions (see Table 3). Two of these almost universal behaviors involved self-disclosure to the clients: "using self-disclosure as a therapy technique" and "telling a client that you are angry at him or her." Thus, it appears that the more extreme versions of the therapist as "blank screen" are exceedingly rare among psychologists. Similarly, the models of the therapist as a distant, almost stand-offish authority figure—which, like the "blank screen" approach, are derived from the classical psychoanalytic tradition—are infrequently practiced. . . . Finally, only 9.2% of the respondents indicated that they had never been sexually attracted to a client. . . .

Behaviors That Are Rare

One of the most surprising results was that only 1.9% of the respondents reported engaging in sexual contact with a client and that only 2.6% reported engaging in erotic activity (which may or may not involve actual contact) with a client. Previously, there have been three national surveys of sexual intimacies between psychologists and their patients. Holroyd and Brodsky (1977) reported 7.7% respondents "who answered positively any of the questions regarding erotic-contact behaviors or intercourse during treatment." Pope, Levenson, and Schover (1979) found that 7% of the therapists in their survey reported engaging in sexual contact with their clients. Pope et al. (1986) reported that 6.5% of their respondents acknowledged engaging in sexual intimacies with clients.

It is difficult to explain the discrepancy between the current findings and those of the previous three studies. It may be that respondents are now less willing to admit, even on anonymous survey, to a behavior that is a felony in some states, or it may be that these findings are reflective of random sampling error or bias in return rate rather than of a change in behavior.

However, the current findings may indicate an actual decrease in the percentage of psychologists engaging in sexual intimacies with their patients. . . . Clinical strategies developed to help therapists at risk to refrain from sexual contact with their patients may also be contributing to this decline. . . .

Some other items concerning sexual behaviors— such as nudity as part of therapy or using sexual surrogates with clients—also had extremely low rates. Engaging in sex with a clinical supervisee was reported by only 3.4% of the respondents. This figure corresponds closely to the 4.0% in a prior survey of APA Division 29 members who reported engaging in sexual intimacies with their clinical supervisees (Pope et al., 1979).

Dishonesty in helping candidates to become degreed or licensed without the requisite supervised experience is relatively rare; it was reported by 8.1%.

A number of the rare practices concerned financial or business practices, such as borrowing money from a client, selling goods to clients, going into business with a client, or giving a gift worth at least $50 to a client. The most infrequently reported behavior was getting paid to refer clients to someone (0.6%). It is heartening to note that psychologists are not putting their judgment and influence up for sale.

Although over a fourth (26.1%) of the respondents advertise in newspapers and similar media, only 9.7% report directly soliciting a person to be a client. . . .

Few psychologists blatantly breach the confidentiality of their clients. However, 8.1% have discussed a client (by name) with friends.

Doing therapy while under the influence of alcohol is also rare (5.9%).

For the most part, psychologists are careful to interview the child when making a custody evaluation, although 8.9% fail to do so.

A gender-based criterion for admission to treatment is rare. Accepting only male or female clients was reported by 7.4%.

Although rare, some of these practices—such as discussing clients by name with friends or doing therapy while under the influence of alcohol—so clearly undermine the rights and welfare of patients that they need to be addressed much more forcefully and effectively by the profession.

Difficult Judgments

We defined a difficult judgment as one in which at least 20% of the respondents indicated "don't know/ not sure." There were 12 behaviors that posed difficult judgments in terms of whether they were ethical: "performing forensic work for a contingency fee," "accepting goods (rather than money) as payment," "using sexual surrogates with clients," "earning a salary which is a percentage of client fees," "avoiding certain clients for fear of being sued," "sending holiday greeting cards to your clients," "giving personal advice on radio, t.v., etc.," "engaging in sexual fantasy about a client," "being sexually attracted to a client," "limiting treatment notes to name, date, and fee," "inviting clients to an office open house," and "allowing a client to run up a large unpaid bill." It is interesting that one third of these directly concerned financial issues, and one fourth concerned sexual issues. The profession may need to develop practical guidelines in these areas. . . .

CONCLUSION

The lack of comprehensive normative data about the behaviors of psychologists and their relationship to ethical standards leaves psychologists without adequate guidelines to inform their choices (Rosenbaum, 1982). Ethical issues in general may be relatively neglected in the professional literature. For example, Baldick (1980) reviewed 250 psychotherapy and counseling texts and found that only 2.8% discussed ethical issues encountered in professional practice. . . .

The integrity of psychology is contingent to a great degree on the extent to which we—both as a discipline or profession and as individuals—can regulate our own behavior. Our ability to engage in effective and ethical regulation, in turn, is contingent on our willingness to study our own behavior and our beliefs about that behavior.

References

American Psychological Association. (1985). *Directory of the American Psychological Association*. Washington, DC: Author.

Baldick, T. L. (1980). Ethical discrimination ability of intern psychologists: A function of training in ethics. *Professional Psychology, 11*, 276–282.

Holroyd, J. C., & Brodsky, A. M. (1977). Psychologists' attitudes and practices regarding erotic and nonerotic physical contact with patients. *American Psychologist, 32*, 843–849.

Pope, K. S., Keith-Spiegel, P. C., & Tabachnick, B. (1986). Sexual attraction to clients: The human therapist and the (sometimes) inhuman training system. *American Psychologist, 41*, 147–158.

Pope, K. S., Levenson, H., & Schover, L. R. (1979). Sexual intimacy in psychology training: Results and implications of a national survey. *American Psychologist, 34*, 682–689.

Rosenbaum, M. (Ed.). (1982). *Ethics and values in psychotherapy*. New York: Free Press.

Ethical Decision Making and Psychologists' Attitudes Toward Training in Ethics

Alexander J. Tymchuk, Robin Drapkin, Susan Major-Kingsley, Andrea B. Ackerman, Elizabeth W. Coffman, and Maureen S. Baum

Psychologists often face ethical dilemmas without clear decision-making guidelines provided by the profession or by society. Although the American Psychological Association (APA) has established ethical standards, new and sometimes controversial clinical research technologies as well as increased community concern with the protection of individual rights continually pose new and complex ethical dilemmas. . . .

. . . When psychologists cannot refer to a specific standard, they must rely more heavily on their own value systems and on their own interpretations of the "spirit" of the APA standards. Such interpretation may lead to variability in professional decision making. . . .

PURPOSE

The present study had three objectives.[1] The first objective was to determine the extent to which a nationwide sample of clinical psychologists concurred in their responses to a set of hypothetical clinical situations. . . .

METHOD

A two-part questionnaire was developed. . . . The second part consisted of 12 vignettes that described a clinical or research situation in which ethical issues were involved (Table 1). These vignettes were typical of ethical problems faced by psychologists. . . .

The questionnaire was mailed to a random sample of 500 members of the Division of Clinical Psychology listed in the Directory of the APA (1976) [return rate = 23%]. . . . The respondents were asked to agree or disagree with the decision described in each hypothetical situation and to indicate the criteria they considered relevant in determining the appropriateness of the hypothetical decision. These criteria included concerns with (a) the interests of the clients, (b) therapeutic leverage, (c) confidentiality, (d) personal freedom, (e) freedom of expression, (f) individual rights, (g) the interests of the community, (h) public policy, (i) standards of morality, (j) the therapist's judgment, (k) informed consent or agreement, (l) financial issues, and (m) state or federal law. Respondents also were given the opportunity to list additional bases for their decision and to comment on each vignette.

FINDINGS

. . . Table 2 summarizes the percentage of responses to each vignette as well as the criteria used. The vignettes are rank ordered according to degree of consensus (from highest to lowest), with the decision described in each situation. Where there is relatively strong consensus regarding the actions of the hypothethical psychologist, there is also strong agreement regarding the criteria on which the respondents base their judgments. Additionally, relatively weak consensus regarding the hypothetical psycholo-

From *Professional Psychology*, 13, 412–421. Copyright 1982 by the American Psychological Association. Adapted with permission of the author and publisher.

[1] *Ed. note:* Only the first objective is discussed in this excerpt.

TABLE 1

Vignettes of Ethical Issues

Vignette	Decision
1. A psychologist at a cocktail party is having a conversation with a woman whom he has just met. He begins to tell her about a client of his, without mentioning names. He reveals to her a set of situations in which the client has recently found himself involved and which the psychologist finds particularly amusing. The woman appears interested in the psychologist's story, until she has heard enough to cause her to believe he is talking about someone she knows. She says, "Are you talking about . . . ?" to which the psychologist replies, "Yes, you know him too?" And they both laugh. The next day she calls her ex-husband and asks him if what she hears about him is true. He files a complaint against the psychologist with the local ethics committee.	The psychologist showed a lack of regard for protecting the identity of his client.
2. A psychologist with considerable skill in behavioral engineering is asked by a state institution for the retarded to plan and assist in executing a behavioral program on its adolescent ward. The purpose of this program will be to increase self-help and ward maintenance skills such as bathing, grooming, dressing, feeding, etc. The program will work only on positive incentives, with special treats such as candy, outings, dances, etc. being provided as rewards for those who improve their skills in these areas. The psychologist meets with each adolescent on the ward to explain the program and finds that about 25% of the youngsters do not understand what he is talking about. Even with a film designed to explain his procedures, the psychologist is unable to get his message across to these youngsters.	These youngsters should not be included in the behavior modification program even though the director of the institution wants all the adolescents on the ward to participate.
3. A male clinical psychologist regularly saw a female patient in his apartment to which he had given her a key. Sometimes the therapeutic sessions lasted past midnight. Eventually the patient and her husband accused the therapist of improper relations. The therapist explained that the highly unusual arrangements for psychotherapy resulted from the fact that he had lost control of the relationship and that his patient dominated it.	It would be ethical for a psychologist to see a client on this basis as long as the client had consented to such sessions and was benefiting from the therapy.
4. A psychologist gives information on a figure drawing test to a writer for an article in a popular magazine. The test is not copyrighted and does not require professional training for appropriate interpretation. The psychologist is under the impression that the article would be a dignified statement about how such tests are an aid to the psychologist in giving services to the public. The article appears under the headline "Figure Out Your Own Personality," with a blank space for drawing and instructions for scoring, showing examples.	The psychologist did not violate ethical standards in giving such materials for a popular article.
5. A researcher in autism provides intensive behavioral treatment for one half of the children under age 3 who come to her treatment/research facility. The other children are placed in a control group. Children in the first group receive up to 2 years intensive behavioral treatment. It is known that beyond the age of 5 or 6, the benefits of the treatment program decrease significantly.	This researcher should be obliged to offer 2 years of intensive treatment to the control group children once they have remained in that group for 2 years.
6. A client signs a contract for six weeks of a popularized therapy for which she pays the ($3,000) amount in full prior to treatment. She agrees that after two weeks of the therapy she can receive portions of her money back over the next four-week period. After one week, the client decides she does not like the therapy, has lost trust in the therapist, and wants all of her money back.	The psychologist should return all of the client's money, even though the contract specified none to be returned within the first two weeks.

(*table continues*)

TABLE 1 (cont.)

Vignette	Decision
7. Current legal developments suggest that rights to treatment for the involuntarily committed include "nutritionally adequate meals," which suggests that contingent availability of meals as reinforcers is unacceptable even if it is deemed therapeutic. A psychologist complies with this requirement by offering his patients nutritious food by taking all the courses and mixing them together in a blender. This blended together meal is freely available to all patients, but patients desiring separate course servings must pay for them with earned tokens.	There is nothing unethical about what the psychologist has done as long as it can be shown that such a program is therapeutically desirable.
8. The parents of a public school child demand that a psychologist in private practice give them a written report since they paid for psychological testing. The psychologist gives them a copy of his report in which actual test scores are included. The parents take the report to the school psychologist who refers it to the APA.	In giving such a report to the parents, the psychologist is unethical and lacking in good judgment.
9. A specialist in child development acts as a consultant to a toy manufacturer. Her major function is to test the toys in free-play situations. The manufacturer wants to use the results of this testing in his advertising, and he requests permission to use the name of the psychologist in this connection. This is not to be an endorsement of any particular toy but a statement of the fact that the psychologist has tested the toys.	An ethical psychologist would not lend her name to advertisements. If there were research findings concerning the value of the toy, the results could speak for themselves.
10. A psychologist advertises by mail a service which offers to introduce marriageable clients to each other on a personality analysis basis, thereby increasing the prospects of a compatible relationship. The psychologist does not influence the clients to make any decision to marry but merely obtains from them by mail, information he deems relevant. The data are sorted by computer and used as a basis for arranging introductions of interested clients.	The psychologist's behavior is ethical.
11. Over a weekend a psychologist conducts a growth group at which twelve persons attend. Prior to the beginning of the weekend, the psychologist informs the participants that they have the freedom to leave the group at any time. The following week, one of the participants files a complaint with the State Ethics Committee, charging that there was nudity during the experience, for which he was unprepared and in which he felt pressured to participate. He states that the experience was emotionally humiliating and damaging and requests that action be taken against the psychologist.	The psychologist in question acted unethically in failing to provide advance notice of techniques to be used during the group, including the possibility of nudity, even though he informed the prospective participants that they could leave at any time.
12. A client, at the close of one of his therapy sessions with you, mentions that he has a secret plan to kill his roommate and that he has a gun. You have reason to believe he has the potential for violent behavior (that there may be clear and imminent danger) and you wish to spend more therapy time dealing with this issue. Your client states that he will not return next week. Should you tell anyone his "secret?"	As his psychotherapist, you should inform either the police or his roommate.

gist's actions corresponds with less agreement about the relevant criteria. . . .

In the vignettes that had relatively strong consensus, the issues were current and timely. These vignettes incorporated confidentiality issues, moral is-

sues involving the male therapist–female client relationship, and standards for growth groups.

. . . [T]he vignettes with the weakest consensus (where decisions tended to be approximately equally split between agreement and disagreement) focused

TABLE 2

Percentage of Responses to the Vignettes and the Criteria Used

Degree of Consensus	Vignette Number	Description	Response Agree	Disagree	No Response	1	2	3	4	5	6	7	8	9	10	11	12	13
High	1	Failure to protect client identity	98	1	1	87[a]	12	92[a]	14	7	46	14	8	22	55[a]	36	3	14
	3	Ethical with client consent	2	96	2	77[a]	50[a]	7	11	5	13	26	16	65[a]	80[a]	14	3	9
	12	Inform police or roommate	84	9	7	62[a]	8	37	15	10	40	72[a]	30	24	24	19	2	54[a]
	11	Failure to provide advance notice	82	15	3	73[a]	15[a]	4	37	20	43	28	16	32	47	55[a]	3	5
	9	Unethical advertising	73	18	9	3	2	13	13	10	10	33	33	7	14	1	18	3
	10	Ethical to advise dating service	22	70	8	49	6	13	11	5	12	29	16	18	35	18	11	2
Moderate	7	Ethical if therapeutically desirable	26	68	6	66[a]	40	3	36	9	56[a]	18	23	24	36	31	3	31
	2	Exclude patients if fail to understand	33	65	2	64[a]	24	2	26	4	42	37	15	10	22	40	2	15
	4	Ethical to provide information for article	49	43	8	7	3	5	11	18	8	48	20	3	30	3	2	3
	5	Must provide treatment and control group	47	42	10	62[a]	7	1	6	13	31	29	7	24	12	19	7	5
Low	6	Should return therapy prepayment	43	47	10	43	18	2	18	3	34	13	19	19	24	38	34	12
	8	Unethical to provide test scores	47	42	10	62[a]	4	25	16	8	36	13	18	6	45	24	1	16

[a]Indicates % use of criteria greater than 50.

on three basic areas that differed from those of the other vignettes: test scrutiny and interpretation, research activities, and remuneration (fees).

These specific findings support the hypothesis that strong consensus in professional decision making may be related to the availability of standards and the nature of the particular situation. When professional or legal standards exist and when the issues are current and related to the therapist–client relationship, the decision-making process appears to

be facilitated. Psychologists seem to have more difficulty agreeing either on treatment issues that may be closely intertwined with clinical orientation or on issues that are not in the forefront of the discipline, including those related to "business" or "contract" decisions. . . .

References

Directory of the APA. (1976). Washington, DC: American Psychological Association.

Ethical Dilemmas in Psychological Practice: Results of a National Survey

Leonard J. Haas, John L. Malouf, and Neal H. Mayerson

Recent years have been marked by a rise in professional consciousness about ethical and legal responsibilities and by a concurrent rise in public consciousness about legal rights. The result, in part, is a level of concern (and confusion) about proper professional behavior that is unprecedented in all professions and is particularly evident in psychology (Chalk, Frankel, & Chafer, 1980). . . .

The widespread concern about ethical and legal aspects of practice notwithstanding, relatively little is known about the nature of the actual situations that practitioners find ethically, legally, or professionally problematic. Of the few studies addressed to the issue of ethical concerns, researchers in some (e.g., Baldick, 1980) assess subjects' ability to recognize or identify an ethical dilemma. In other surveys (e.g., Tymchuk et al., 1982) researchers assess the extent of respondents' agreement with a particular choice already made for them. In still other surveys (e.g., Jagim, Wittman, & Noll, 1978), researchers assess a limited sample of psychologists. There has been no study to date in which the nature of respondents' choices from among a range of options has been assessed.

In this study we attempt to investigate some of these unknown areas. Practitioners were presented a set of problems that had at least two potentially workable alternative resolutions, and a set of possible reasons for making those choices. In addition, we attempt to assess the perceived utility of various sources of ethics education. With increasing pressure for standardized ethics education in professional psychology training programs, it is vital to know more about the mechanisms through which ethical practitioners acquire what they consider to be valuable ethics training. Answers to questions such as these may help in training of ethically responsible psychologists.

METHOD

Instrument

The questionnaire developed for this study consisted of five sections. . . . The first section concerned demographic and background factors such as age, number of years in practice, and theoretical orientation. In the second section respondents indicated the sources of their training in ethics, number of hours spent in various categories of ethical training (e.g., coursework, discussions with colleagues), and the value of each of these experiences (see Table 2).

The third section contained 10 vignettes, each describing a dilemma of professional ethics. . . . The vignettes were chosen to represent five general categories that are considered to encompass the broad range of professional dilemmas: confidentiality problems, issues of informed consent, loyalty conflicts, exploitation, and whistle-blowing (Haas, 1982). In addition, we selected vignettes that involved a *dilemma*, rather than simply knowledge of the relevant standards: that is, vignettes represented situations in which more than one alternative could be considered acceptable on the basis of recognized ethical principles.

For each vignette, alternative ways to respond were presented: as much as possible, the number of

TABLE 2

Amount and Perceived Utility of Education in Ethics

Source of Education	Hours		Mean Utility[a]	
	M	*n*	Rating	*n*
Discussions with colleagues	79.1	236	4.4	269
Independent reading	31.3	238	4.0	240
Internship supervision	17.1	231	3.8	124
Graduate coursework	11.5	258	4.4	174
Continuing education courses	2.7	233	3.3	26

[a]Mean ratings on a 5-point scale anchored by 1 (*not at all useful*) and 5 (*extremely useful*).

alternatives was restricted and respondents were urged to choose one of them, rather than to "rearrange" the dilemma (e.g., resolving the dilemma by noting that "I would have gotten informed consent beforehand" or making some other shift in the conditions). In several cases it was possible to reduce the behavioral alternatives to two: act or not act. After the alternatives, eight possible reasons for choosing an alternative were presented: upholding the law, upholding the code of ethics, protecting society's interests, protecting client's rights, upholding personal standards, safeguarding the therapy process, financial considerations, and "other." Analysis of these rationales and the categories of moral reasoning that they reflect are presented elsewhere (Haas, Malouf, & Mayerson, 1985). Respondents were asked to indicate their preferred response to each dilemma and the most important reason for making this choice. The vignettes and alternatives are listed in Table 3.

In the fourth session, respondents were asked to rate the frequency with which they had encountered 17 ethical/legal issues in practice (e.g., concern about colleagues' actions, insurance reporting requirements, sexual misconduct) and their rating of the seriousness of each issue (see Table 4). . . .

Procedure

The sample consisted of 600 randomly selected members of Division 29 (Psychotherapy) of the American Psychological Association (APA) chosen from the APA Directory. . . . 500 individuals received questionnaires and 294 individuals returned them, which was a response rate of 59%.

Characteristics of Respondents

Overall, the sample had substantial experience, worked largely in private practice delivering clinical services, and was largely composed of PhD-level practitioners. The sample obtained here is quite similar to the clinician sample described in the APA's national work force survey (Stapp & Fulcher, 1983).

RESULTS

Education in Ethics

Subjects' reports of their education in professional ethics are summarized in Table 2. As the table shows, discussions with colleagues is the most widely reported category of ethics education. Graduate coursework, perhaps not surprisingly, is the fourth-ranked category. Subjects were also asked to rate how useful the various sources of education had been in their understanding, coping with, or preventing ethical dilemmas. The means of these ratings are also reported in Table 2. As shown, all categories were rated above 3, but graduate coursework and collegial discussions were both rated as the most useful. Modal number of hours in formal ethics education (e.g., graduate coursework and continuing education courses) was zero.

Responses to Vignettes of Ethical Dilemmas

In Table 3 we show the percentage of respondents who chose each alternative for each vignette in the order in which they were presented to respondents. As the table shows, highest degrees of consensus regarding the appropriate choice were obtained (in descending order) on issues involving the following: conflict of interest (Vignette 9), mandatory reporting of threatened violence (Vignette 7), a superior's order to refer a client to someone who is considered incompetent (Vignette 1), and confidentiality (Vignettes 5 and 4). The modal responses indicated that subjects favored acting in the client's interest when one's own interests might be better served by another response, reporting threatened violence to the police or the intended victim(s), or both, and the protection of clients' rights to confidentiality.

Lower degrees of consensus were obtained on dilemmas involving the following (in ascending order of consensus): others' use of professional credentials in advertising for a local business (Vignette 3), treatment of problems beyond one's established expertise (Vignette 6), and reporting of potentially counter-therapeutic diagnoses to insurance companies (Vignette 10). Regarding both alleged client–therapist sexual contact (Vignette 2) and alleged client-instigated sexual abuse (Vignette 8), slightly more than a majority of the respondents apparently would *not* report the allegation themselves, but instead would try to encourage the client or a family member of the client to make the report.

Frequency and Seriousness of Ethical Dilemmas Actually Experienced

The 17 areas of potential ethical difficulty presented to subjects are listed, along with the overall ratings for each area of concern, in Table 4. Subjects were asked to rate the frequency with which the issues had presented problems for them during the past year. They were also asked to rate the overall severity of those problems, irrespective of how often they had personally encountered them. Interestingly, in terms of mean frequency ratings, none of the issues were reported as more than *occasionally a concern*. In contrast, 11 of the 17 issues were rated as *fairly serious* or *extremely serious* by more than 50% of the respondents. The two issues that overall seemed to be considered most serious involved confidentiality, or privileged communication, and sexual conduct of colleagues. The two issues rated least serious (e.g.,

---

TABLE 3

Vignettes and Choices Presented in Questionnaire, and Percentage of Respondents Endorsing Each Choice

Vignette	Choice	%
1. You are a therapist in a community mental health center. You are about to move to another state, and must terminate or refer your caseload. Your clinical director tells you to refer a particular individual to a therapist whose ability you do not respect.	Refer the patient.	7
	Refer the patient and indicate your reservations to him.	14
	Refuse to refer the patient to that particular therapist.	79
	Other	1
2. A client of yours tells you that she is still quite upset at her previous therapist for, among other things, making sexual advances toward her. This is the third time you have heard such allegations about this particular therapist.	Discuss the patient's anger but do not discuss the issue of professional standards.	10
	Call the previous therapist and tell him that the behavior you have heard about violates professional ethics.	18
	Tell the patient that she has the right to bring her charge to the ethics committee or the state licensing board.	57
	Call the ethics committee or state licensing board.	14
3. A psychologist whom you have met on occasional meetings but do not know well appears in a TV spot endorsing a local health spa. He says, "As child psychologist I find relaxation important—I go to the Palm Spa to get my head and body together."	Call the psychologist and indicate that you think the ad violates professional standards.	25
	Call the professional standards committee of your psychological association and report the incident.	42
	Do nothing.	33
	Other	0

(table continues)

TABLE 3   (cont.)

Vignette	Choice	%
4. You have been treating a married couple conjointly for about 6 months. The wife arrives early for the session and tells you that she is thinking of leaving her husband as she has been involved with another man. She also asks you not to tell her husband. You have not previously discussed your policy regarding secrets.	Do not agree to keep the secret. Agree to keep the secret. Other	30 65 5
5. The mother of a 12-year-old boy comes to pick him up after his initial appointment with you. She asks you if he is taking drugs. He has in fact revealed to you that he has been sniffing glue.	Tell her what you know. Tell her the information is her son's to reveal or not as he sees fit. Other	25 72 5
6. A man with no previous experience in therapy contacts you and asks for sex therapy. While you understand the general principles of sex therapy, you would not consider it your area of expertise. However, he looks like an interesting prospective client.	Accept him as a client. Accept him as a client only after discussing your qualifications. Do not accept him as a client and refer him to another therapist. Other	5 45 49 1
7. You are treating a Vietnam veteran with a history of impulsive anti-social actions. You and he have established a good therapeutic relationship (his first after 3 previous attempts in therapy). At the end of the session, he disclosed that he is planning to kill his current girlfriend, because she has been dating another man.	Contact his girlfriend and/or the police without informing him. Plan to discuss this further at the next session. Inform him that you must warn his girlfriend and/or the police. Other	8 5 87 1
8. During the course of your treatment of a 45-year-old male who has drinking problems, his wife telephones and tells you that he has been sexually molesting his 7-year-old stepdaughter (her daughter of a previous marriage).	Report the case to the child protection bureau. Encourage her to report the matter to the child protection bureau. Reflect her concern but take no further action. Other	25 60 11 4
9. A client of yours who is a CPA suggests that he prepare your tax return in partial payment for therapy. You have been preparing your own taxes and find it increasingly burdensome.	Accept this offer. Decline his offer. Other	7 93 0
10. You work in the emergency room of a community mental health center located within a general hospital. You are about to admit a man best diagnosed as a paranoid schizophrenic; his insurance will cover the cost of hospitalization. This diagnosis may make it difficult for him to obtain other kinds of insurance (e.g., life insurance) later. You suspect that learning of this will make him resist hospitalization since he cannot afford it without insurance.	Inform him of the risks involved. Do not inform him of the risks; diagnose him as indicated. Do not inform him of the risks; give him a much "milder" diagnosis. Other	50 30 18 1

rated about 2) were media appearances and advertising to obtain referrals.

DISCUSSION

. . . If one defines high agreement as 75% concordance, then there was a high agreement on what to do in only 3 of the 10 vignettes presented. Psychologists in our sample agreed that it would not be ap-

propriate to refer a client to a therapist whom they did not respect, even when requested to do so by their clinical director. They also agreed that it would not be appropriate to trade therapeutic services for other professional services. Last, psychologists are apparently quite aware of their duties to warn in cases of threatened violence of the sexual abuse of children, and they appear willing to act ac-

TABLE 4

Mean Ratings of Frequency With Which Areas of Concern Occur and Their Seriousness

Area of Concern	Frequency[a]	Seriousness[b]
1. Confidentiality or privileged communication	3.09	3.94
2. Providing informed consent to clients	2.54	3.33
3. Rights of minors (e.g., in therapy)	2.43	3.52
4. Conflicting interests (employers vs. clients, clients vs. legal system, etc.)	2.41	3.59
5. Personal use of advertising or other means of generating referrals	1.58	2.46
6. Talk shows, interviews, or other personal media appearances	1.67	2.43
7. Colleagues' sexual conduct	2.08	4.12
8. Appropriateness of other actions of colleagues	2.66	3.69
9. Own sexual impulses or conduct	1.69	3.21
10. Legality of own actions	1.82	3.33
11. Own malpractice liability	1.76	3.37
12. Own competence to deal with particular problem or provide requested service	2.43	3.45
13. Insurance company requests (e.g., for information or diagnoses)	2.77	3.15
14. Civil (involuntary) commitment	1.70	3.54
15. Behavior of employees or supervisees	2.11	3.34
16. Testing (e.g., use of test results, appropriateness of test requested)	2.05	3.17
17. Research (e.g., protection of subjects' privacy, minimizing risk)	1.72	3.17

[a]Scale ranges from 1 (*never a concern*) to 5 (*constantly a concern*).
[b]Scale ranges from 1 (*not at all serious*) to 5 (*extremely serious*).

cordingly, in contrast to the sample surveyed by Jagim et al. (1978). However, in the vignette relating to the sexual abuse of a child, there was a clear difference of opinion as to whether the therapist's most appropriate response should be to report or to suggest that someone else report the allegation. Despite the increasing prevalence of mandatory reporting laws (DeKraii & Sales, 1984), this result shows that uncertainty about this complex ethical/legal issue is still widespread.

Results suggest a number of other areas in which high agreement does not exist, as defined by the 75% agreement criterion. One problematic area is the issue of confidentiality within families or couples. Although a majority of respondents would maintain the confidentiality of a spouse or minor child (as shown in the results for Vignettes 4 and 5), a significant minority (30.5% and 23.6%, respectively) would reveal certain types of information to a spouse or parent. Despite the existence of legal constraints (DeKraii & Sales, 1984), confidentiality

within families is clearly a topic in which much is left to the discretion of the therapist (Margolin, 1982). Clearly, practitioners should be aware of the legal standards and in addition carefully think through the ethical and therapeutic implications of their choices.

Another area of apparent low agreement involves unethical behavior of other professionals. Two vignettes (2 and 3) dealt with this topic, one describing a situation in which a psychologist was alleged to have had sexual relations with clients, the other describing a psychologist who publicly endorsed a health spa. In the first case, approximately 90% felt that some action should be taken, and a significant number felt that the client, rather than the current therapist, should report the previous therapist. In the second case, approximately one third of the respondents felt that they should do nothing about reporting the psychologist who endorsed the health spa, even though such behavior is a clear violation of Principle 4 of the *Ethical Principles* (APA, 1981).[1] One

---

[1]*Ed. note:* See Standard 3.01 of the APA's current (1992) Ethical Principles.

issue that can limit the duty to deal with colleagues' questionable behavior is that of client preferences. It is quite likely that those of our respondents who preferred to let the client report in Vignette 2 held the principle of client control of confidential information to be paramount. This confounding principle was not present in Vignette 3, which suggests that many psychologists find it easier to dismiss as trivial those actions that are not obviously harmful rather than risk being considered vigilantes.

Vignette 6, which concerned a therapist's providing sex therapy despite a lack of specialty training, related to the topic of competence. This vignette highlights another area in which much latitude is given the practitioner by the *Ethical Principles*. Although Principle 23 (APA, 1981)[2] specifies that a therapist be competent to provide the services offered, it is primarily the therapist who determines his or her own competence. In the situation described in the survey, about half of the respondents apparently felt that a knowledge of general principles of sex therapy was not adequate to establish competence in that area, whereas about 45% of respondents would discuss their qualifications with the client and, apparently, let the client determine the therapist's competence. Clients' ability to make such a determination can be seriously questioned.

The final vignette raises the complicated and multifaceted issue of diagnosis. Should a client be informed of his or her diagnosis if this information would possibly be harmful? Should the therapist change the diagnosis to something more "acceptable"? Should the therapist be more concerned about the consequences of the diagnosis itself or about the consequences of decreased trust in professional diagnoses? Half of our respondents would inform a paranoid schizophrenic patient about the risks involved in reporting an accurate diagnosis on an insurance form, whereas 30% would not discuss this with the client but would submit an accurate diagnosis, regardless of the consequences. Eighteen percent would not inform the client but would give a milder diagnosis. This variability highlights the ambiguity in this area, in that all response alternatives can be justified by existing ethical guidelines.

In relation to subjects' reports of the sources and value of their ethics education, results seem to confirm the appropriateness of the APA decision to require the development of formal coursework in ethics. Even though the major reported source of learning, in terms of reported hours, is discussions with colleagues and the number of hours spent studying ethics in graduate school is relatively low, this latter endeavor was as highly valued as the former. Independent reading was reported as the other main source of ethical training. It is also interesting to note that internship (in which many assume that young clinicians get their ethics education) was not rated particularly highly as a source of ethics education. In addition, it is interesting that reading and discussing issues with colleagues (both seemingly intrinsically motivated activities) are extensively used as a means of self-education in ethics by this sample. This may be a result of the increasing intensity of concern with ethical and legal issues, or reflect feelings of inadequate preparation in these areas. It is likely that the majority of our respondents completed their graduate training before ethics courses were common in training programs. Given the apparent interest in ethics training and the relatively low ratings given continuing education courses, it seems that further development and improvement of continuing education courses would be appropriate.

Of the 17 areas of potential ethical difficulty that were presented to respondents, only one—confidentiality or privileged communication—received a mean frequency rating of over 3 (*occasionally a concern*). All the other issues received lower ratings. The concerns least frequently encountered involved personal use of advertising and media appearances.

Although the frequency of these 17 topics was not reported to be extremely high, respondents did consider several of them to be serious. The sexual conduct of colleagues was rated as the most serious of the issues, followed by confidentiality or privileged communication, appropriateness of other actions of colleagues, and conflicting interests (e.g., employers vs. clients). Of the 17 issues, all but two received mean ratings of higher than 3 (*somewhat serious*). The questions regarding personal use of ad-

---

[2] *Ed. note:* See Standard 1.04 of the APA's current (1992) Ethical Principles.

vertising and personal media appearances were rated between 2 (*slightly serious*) and 3 (*somewhat serious*).

One interpretation of these findings is that psychologists consider many issues important but do not encounter problems with them very often. In one sense, this can be considered a positive finding insofar as it may mean that psychologists, at least relatively experienced ones, feel comfortable with the ethical decisions that they make.

IMPLICATIONS

Three major implications stand out. First, psychology as a profession has few generally agreed-on choices of action in several important and difficult areas of professional decision making. The fact that our respondents, all of whom were experienced clinicians, concurred that certain areas of professional decision making were areas of serious concern and that at the same time they failed to reach consensus as a group on these areas may be a troublesome state of affairs or not, depending on how one construes the task of professional ethics education in psychology. If this task is construed to involve the training of professionals in specific *behaviors* that are considered ethical, then our results are troubling. The implication of these results for professional ethics education is that such efforts must focus on teaching psychologists more effectively which are the right behaviors to choose in a variety of professional decision-making situations. On the other hand, if the task of professional ethics education is to inculcate ethical reasoning *processes*, then our results may be somewhat more heartening. As researchers in moral development have shown (Blasi, 1980), the same reasoning processes may lead to quite divergent behavioral outcomes. This is likely to be the case if professional moral decision making is involved. Psychologists who use the same ethical reasoning processes may arrive at quite different conclusions about the proper action. . . .

A second implication of this study is that work to further develop graduate course work in ethics (as required for APA accreditation) should be pursued, perhaps with particular attention to real-world ethical problems involving confidentiality, competence, and colleagues' behavior. In addition, our findings suggest that continuing education courses could be quite appropriate even for the experienced clinician.

A third implication is that particular areas of professional decision making deserve added scrutiny, debate, and consideration. They are competence (e.g., What is it? How do we measure it?), confidentiality (What are the implications of preserving it? of failing to uphold it?), diagnoses (For whom are they being done? What about the issue of stigma?), and whistle-blowing (What is the most appropriate means of reporting? To whom should complaints be addressed?). Some of these are empirical issues and should be dealt with as such. Others deserve added scrutiny and debate by the profession at large.

References

American Psychological Association. (1981). *Ethical principles of psychologists.* Washington, DC: Author.

Baldick, T. (1980). Ethical discrimination ability of intern psychologists: A function of training in ethics. *Professional Psychology, 11,* 276–282.

Blasi, A. (1980). Bridging moral cognition and moral action: A critical review of the literature. *Psychological Bulletin, 88,* 1–45.

Chalk, R., Frankel, M., & Chafer, S. (1980). *AAAS Professional Ethics Project: Professional ethics activities in the scientific and engineering societies.* Washington, DC: American Association for the Advancement of Science.

DeKraii, M. B., & Sales, B. D. (1984). Confidential communications of psychotherapists. *Psychotherapy, 21,* 293–318.

Haas, L. J. (1982). *The teaching of ethics in clinical psychology.* Paper presented at the annual convention of the American Psychological Convention. Washington, DC.

Haas, L. J., Malouf, J. L., & Mayerson, N. H. (1985). *Ethics training, professional characteristics, and ethical "styles" of practicing psychologists.* Paper presented at the annual convention of the American Psychological Association, Los Angeles.

Jagim, R. D., Wittman, W., & Noll, J. (1978). Mental health professionals' attitudes toward confidentiality, privilege, and third-party disclosure. *Professional Psychology, 9,* 458–466.

Margolin, G. (1982). Ethical and legal considerations in marital and family therapy. *American Psychologist, 37,* 788–801.

Stapp, J., & Fulcher, R. (1983). The employment of APA members: 1982. *American Psychologist, 38,* 1298–1320.

Tymchuk, A., Drapkin, R., Major-Kingsley, S., Ackerman, A., Coffman, E., & Baum, M. (1982). Ethical decision making and psychologists' attitudes toward training in ethics. *Professional Psychology, 13,* 412–421.

◆ ◆ ◆

Commentary: As demonstrated by the two excerpts from Tymchuk et al. (1982) and Haas et al. (1986), and by the debate concerning the conflict between law and ethics, there are a number of reasons for the variability that one finds in the application, interpretation, and enforcement of the APA's Ethical Principles. For example, Kimmel (1991) has noted that a "growing body of research suggests that individuals systematically differ in the ways they formulate ethical appraisals of research," traced in part "to the fact that the ethical principles that guide research in the scientific community typically are broadly stated and are all too often ambiguous" (p. 768). In addition, he found that psychologists asked to review the ethical acceptability of hypothetical examples of behavioral research could be differentiated in their judgments largely on the basis of personal characteristics:

> . . . Psychologists who tended to be more approving in their ethical evaluations (thereby suggesting a greater emphasis on research benefits) were those who (a) were men, (b) had held their highest degree for a longer period of time, (c) had received the degree in a basic psychology area (such as social, experimental, or developmental psychology), and (d) were employed in research-oriented contexts. Psychologists who tended to disapprove or reflect conservatism in their judgments (thereby suggesting a greater emphasis on research costs) were those who (a) were women, (b) had held their highest degree for a shorter period of time, (c) had received the degree in an applied psychology area (such as counseling, school, or community psychology), and (d) were employed in service-oriented contexts. (p. 787)

See Kimmel, A. J. (1991). *Predictable biases in the ethical decision making of American psychologists.* American Psychologist, 46, 786–788.

There are other, more systemic reasons why codes of ethics do not always engage the respect and authority sought for them. Using the vignettes developed by Haas and his colleagues, Smith, McGuire, Abbott, and Blau (1991) surveyed a sample of 102 eclectically oriented clinicians practicing either in private or in community mental health agencies in an attempt to assess the clinicians' reasoning in resolving professional ethical conflicts. The sample was predominantly White, female, and non-doctoral (70%). Smith et al.'s results supported the research by Bernard and his colleagues, presented earlier in this chapter, indicating a discrepancy between what clinicians recognize they should do and what they actually are willing to do:

> These findings suggest that clinicians are most likely to act consistently with how they believe they should act when they believe the ethical violation involves one of the relatively clear rules of existing professional codes. This is particularly true when such professional rules of conduct are further supported by legal statutes or precedents (e.g., clear danger and duty to protect; prohibition against sexual contact with clients). On the other hand, existing professional codes and standards are more often utilitarian guidelines, not rules of conduct. Utilitarian principles suggest that what is ethically correct depends on an assessment of the effects of one's behavior on oneself and others. Such situations demand increased judgment by the clinician and result in greater inconsistency between perceived should versus would choices. In such conflict situations, what clinicians indicate that they would do is affected not only by professional or legal codes of conduct, but also by personal values and practical considerations of the situation. . . .

See Smith, T. S., McGuire, J. M., Abbott, D. W., & Blau, B. I. (1991). *Clinical ethical decision making: An investigation of the rationales used to justify doing less than one believes one should.* Professional Psychology: Research and Practice, 22, 235–239.

When Laws and Values Conflict: A Dilemma for Psychologists

Kenneth S. Pope and Theresa Rose Bajt

Edmund Burke (1790/1961) stated the importance of absolute compliance with the law: "One of the first motives to civil society, and which becomes one of its fundamental rules, is, *that no man should be judge in his own cause*" (p. 71). The U.S. Supreme Court, in *Walker v. Birmingham* (1967), underscored this "belief that in the fair administration of justice no man can be judge in his own case, however exalted his station, however righteous his motives, and irrespective of his race, color, politics, or religion" (pp. 1219–1220).

Henry David Thoreau (1849/1960), however, urged that if a law "requires you to be the agent of injustice to another, then, I say, break the law" (p. 242). Even the California Supreme Court seemed to give tacit approval to breaking the law *as long as it is done within the framework of civil disobedience*: "If we were to deny to every person who has engaged in . . . nonviolent civil disobedience . . . the right to enter a licensed profession, we would deprive the community of the services of many highly qualified persons of the highest moral courage" (*Hallinan v. Committee of Bar Examiners of State Bar,* 1966, p. 239).

Neither stance may seem acceptable to psychologists who believe that compliance with a legal or professional obligation would be harmful, unjust, or otherwise wrong. Absolute compliance connotes a "just following orders" mentality all too ready to sacrifice personal values and client welfare to an imperfect system of rules and regulations. Selective noncompliance connotes an association of people who have annointed themselves as somehow above the law, able to pick and choose which legal obligations and recognized standards they will obey.

Civil disobedience itself may be precluded in significant areas of psychology. Coined as a term by Thoreau, civil disobedience as a concept has been developed, defined, and justified as an act involving open and public violation of the law while volunteering to accept the legal penalties. . . . This absolute openness—the lack of any attempt to avoid detection and prosecution—is essential in reaffirming respect for the process of law and accountability. But how can a psychologist, for example, *publicly* refuse to make a mandated report (e.g., regarding child abuse or potential harm to third parties) about a student, client, or subject without betraying the supposedly secret information?

We used an anonymous survey, with a 60% return rate, to explore this dilemma. The questionnaire was mailed to 100 senior psychologists, presumably acknowledged by their peers as knowledgeable and scrupulous regarding professional accountability: 60 current or former members of state ethics committees (50 of whom had served as chairs), 10 current or former members of the American Psychological Association (APA) Ethics Committee, 10 authors of textbooks focusing on legal or ethical aspects of psychology, and 20 diplomates of the American Board of Professional Psychology.

The first question was: "In the most serious, significant, or agonizing instance, if any, what law or formal ethical principle have you broken intentionally in light of a client's welfare or other deeper

From *American Psychologist, 43,* 828–829. Copyright 1988 by the American Psychological Association. Adapted with permission of the author and publisher.

value?" A majority (57%) acknowledged such instances. Of these 34 instances, the following were reported by more than one respondent: 7 (21%) involved refusing to report child abuse, 7 (21%) involved illegally divulging confidential information, 3 (9%) involved engaging in sex with a client, 2 (6%) involved "dual relationships" (no details), and 2 (6%) involved refusing to make legally mandated warnings regarding dangerous clients. It is interesting to note that 48% involve the issue of whether certain information should be kept confidential. It is dismaying to note that 9% involve psychologists' using "client welfare or other deeper value" as a rationale for engaging in sex with a client.

Incidents reported by one respondent each were giving a student an inappropriately high grade to "help" the student, helping a colleague to fake a credential, using one's professional status and expertise to help someone obtain an illegal abortion, committing perjury to keep a client from going to jail, engaging in "insurance fraud" (respondent's phrase) to help the client pay for services, treating a minor without parents' consent, refusing to turn over a former client's records in response to a legitimate request, accepting a very expensive gift from a client, withholding significant information from a patient, refusing to collect insurance copayment, blurring a personal and professional relationship, continuing therapy beyond the point at which it should have ended, and "lied about my experience treating a particular disorder, in order to instill confidence in the patient-to-be."

Exactly half of the respondents consulted someone before taking the action: 68% discussed the incident afterwards. Beneficial results were reported by 91%; ill effects by 44%. Only one psychologist was, as a result of the incident, the object of a formal complaint. Seventy-three percent would, in hindsight, take the same action if the circumstances were the same.

Seventy-seven percent of the respondents believed "that formal legal and ethical standards should ever be violated on the basis of patient welfare or other deeper values." In light of the fact that three fourths of this select sample believed that psychologists should sometimes violate formal legal and ethical standards, and that a majority have actually

done so, it is regrettable that only 18% report that the topic of conflicts between deeply held values and formal legal or ethical obligations was adequately addressed in their education, training, and supervision, and that only 22% believe that the topic is adequately addressed in the professional literature.

Are the aims toward which our laws and formal ethical standards strive ultimately supported or subverted when psychologists intentionally violate explicit legal and ethical standards that conflict with the psychologists' deeply held values? How can psychologists who believe that the authority of the legal and ethical codes is not absolute ensure that their actions are based on sound professional judgment rather than on self-interest, prejudice, rationalization, and the sense that one is "above the law"? Are the integrity, effectiveness, and fairness of our mechanisms of accountability—such as university grievance committees, human subjects review committees, and ethics committees—enriched or eroded when those who sit in judgment on the behavior of others have themselves intentionally broken the rules that they are seeking to enforce? Such dilemmas are in need of open acknowledgment and serious study.

References

Burke, E. (1961). *Reflections on the revolution in France.* Garden City, NY: Doubleday. (Original work published 1790)

Hallinan v. Committee of Bar Examiners of State Bar, 55 Cal. Rptr. 228 (1966).

Thoreau, H. D. (1960). *Walden and civil disobedience.* Boston: Houghton Mifflin. (*Civil disobedience* originally published 1849)

Walker v. City of Birmingham. 388 U.S. 307, 18 L ed 2d 1210 (1967).

◆ ◆ ◆

Commentary: Commenting on Pope & Bajt (1988), Ansell & Ross (1990) argued that because psychologists were not involved in drafting child abuse-reporting statutes, no thought was given to their effect on clinical practice:

> *The ethicist might have assumed that a psychotherapist who suspected a client of*

child abuse might consider a range of options before rushing to report. These options lie within the clinical function to
make a judgment call. To deny therapists
that judgment is a clear usurpation of professional function. Worse, it compels psychologists to turn away from their professional responsibilities to become agents of
the police. . . . (p. 399)

See Ansell & Ross (1990). Reply to Pope and Bajt.
American Psychologist, 45, 399. They also called upon
ethicists to conduct research on the issue. In a response
to Ansell & Ross, Kalichman (1990) affirmed that "as
many as 60% of psychologists have elected not to report
suspected child abuse" (p. 1273), but countered that
"disregarding reporting laws is potentially dangerous for
practitioners as well as their clients" (p. 1273). Kalichman concluded that it was "paradoxical that ethical
psychologists so frequently choose to break the law" (p.
1273). See Kalichman, S. (1991). Reporting laws, confidentiality, and clinical judgment: Reply to Ansell and
Ross. American Psychologist, 45, 1273.

About 25 years ago, I published an article in which
a well-trained psychologist faithfully followed the then
extant version of the APA ethics code, resulting in five
law suits against the psychologist and/or her employing
institution. I attempted to discern the reasons why ethics
codes fail to provide adequate bases for behavior. I hypothesized that they: (a) are written from the profession's point of view, not the client public; (b) are written
too abstractly, merely providing general guides to behavior; (c) may be used to present a misleading picture to
the public of an ethical profession, without its members
necessarily subscribing to the profession's ethical values;
and (d) may be disregarded by the legal system when a
profession's claim to autonomy is in conflict with the
rights of individuals or the public at large. See Bersoff,
D. N. (1975). Professional ethics and legal responsibilities: On the horns of a dilemma. Journal of School
Psychology, 13, 359–376. Based on a reading of the
1992 ethics code in chapter 1, are these still valid hypotheses?

The inclusion of those affected by professionals' conduct in the development and application of ethics codes
remains an idea whose time has not yet come. Recently,
however, Prilletensky and his colleagues reintroduced the
idea in an elegant and organized way. They contrast

what they call the current restrictive framework of defining ethics with their concept of a participatory
framework. In applying ethics under this alternative,
power would be shared equally between professionals
and clients, ethics would deal not only with the micro-
cosmic, individualistic relationship between professional
and client, but also with ethical issues involving social,
cultural, and organizational contexts. For a lengthier
discussion of these issues see:

Prilleltensky, I., Rossiter, A., & Walsh-Bowers, R.
(1996). Preventing harm and promoting ethical discourse in the helping professions: Conceptual, research,
analytical, and action frameworks. Ethics and Behavior, 6, 287–306.

Rossiter, A., Walsh-Bowers, R., & Prilleltensky, I.
(1996). Learning from broken rules: Individualism, bu-
reaucracy, and ethics. Ethics and Behavior, 6, 307–
320.

Walsh-Bowers, R., Rossiter, A., & Prilleltensky, I.
(1996). Ethics and Behavior, 6, 321–336.

In response, Checkland (1996) cautioned that the focus of Prilleltensky et al. may not appropriately "distinguish ethics (as that which is concerned primarily with
questions of right and wrong) from politics (where our
fundamental concern is to contest and clarify the nature
of the collective good and bad)" (p. 343). See Checkland, D. (1996). Individualism, subjectivism, democracy,
and "helping" professions. Ethics and Behavior, 6,
337–343. In a similar vein, see also Kendler, H. H.
(1993). Psychology and the ethics of social policy.
American Psychologist, 48, 1046–1053 (arguing that
psychology is limited in its ability to identify and support social policies or guide human behavior through
ethical principles).

Other authors also have addressed the value of a
code of ethics and criticized the method of its development. Pope and Vetter (1992) (see chapter 1) complained that the revision process that led to the 1992
Code of Conduct was flawed because that code was not
drafted in the same way as the original code, that is,
"guided by contemporary empirical data about the incidents faced by the full range of APA's current membership" (p. 409). They argued that unless a critical incident or empirical approach is used, "the code risks
losing relevance and applicability" (p. 409). See Pope,
K. S., & Vetter, V. A. (1992). Ethical dilemmas encoun-

tered by members of the American Psychological Association: A national survey. American Psychologist, 47, 397–411.

Barlow (1989) has asserted that although "respected, quoted, and esteemed by all," ethics codes "have influence, but little, if any actual authority" (p. 9). He believes that, in addition to often containing contradictory principles, such codes have limited moral authority because they undergo regular revision:

> Sponsoring agencies tend to proceed with regard to special interests and a democratic process of voting to affirm the declarations they compose. By nature the statements can be emended, amended, or revised as the voting body decides. This policy allows for important updating and adjustments called for by technological innovation. But it also allows for amended restatement in response to changes in social policy and moral sentiment.
>
> Moreover, contemporary promulgations are often little more than consensus statements affirming no more than what everyone in the group at that moment agrees upon. The larger, more heterogeneous is the sponsoring body, the more general, simplified, and minimalist is the position taken. A mark is chiseled into the ethical bench, but its reach is usually only as high as the least common denominator. (p. 13)

See Barlow, J. (1989). The practical limits of codes and declarations. In L. P. Bird & J. Barlow (Eds.), Codes of medical ethics, oaths, and prayers: An anthology (pp. 9–14). Richardson, TX: Christian Medical and Dental Society.

Welfel and Lipsitz (1984) were in accord with Barlow's (1989) view:

> In recent years, the profession has shown an increased awareness that even thorough familiarity with the code and powerful sanctions against nonconforming psychologists are insufficient in themselves to guar-

antee ethical practice. For example, a number of authors . . . have pointed out that the ethical codes serve only as general guidelines for practice. They suggest that changes in professional practice happen so quickly that not even regular revision of the standards can address every aspect of current practice. They also contend that many ethically sensitive situations arising in the course of practice are difficult to categorize according to the tenets of the code. In some extreme cases, adherence to one portion of the code even seems to result in violation of another portion. Most importantly, they argue that the purpose of the code was never to provide blueprints that would remove all need for the use of judgment by individual psychologists, but rather, to act as a foundation to assist the psychologist in determining the applicability of the code to his or her unique and often complex situation. (p. 31)

See Welfel, E. R., & Lipsitz, N. E. (1984). The ethical behavior of professional psychologists: A critical analysis of the research. The Counseling Psychologist, 12(3), 31–41.

As chapter 1 indicates, the first APA ethics code was published in 1953 and has been revised or amended eight times since. Although the latest version was adopted in 1992, it too is presently being revised. In light of the comments by Barlow (1989) and Welfel & Lipsitz (1984), does this constant revision so distract from the code's moral authority that it is disobeyed or, at least, ignored?

The other criticism of codes of ethics is that they are often vague and ambiguous. In 1994, the current APA code was reviewed by several authors in a special section of Professional Psychology: Research and Practice. I was asked by its guest editor, Patricia Keith-Spiegel, to act as a discussant. What follows is a relevant excerpt from that review and a response from the current chair of the Ethics Code Task Force and the former chair of the APA Ethics Committee.

Explicit Ambiguity: The 1992 Ethics Code as an Oxymoron

Donald N. Bersoff

. . . Three overarching and related critical themes emerged from the reviewers' articles: (a) The current code, although broader and more explicit, paradoxically, lacks clarity and precision; (b) the code is filled with qualifying language that makes it difficult for those charged with enforcement to find violations; and (c) it is a document designed more to protect psychologists than to protect the public. These criticisms are so pervasive that any future group charged with revising the current code is obligated to respond to them with the utmost seriousness and in good faith. I address each in turn.

PROBLEMS OF VAGUENESS

Dana (1994) faulted the assessment portion of the code for failing to provide "clarity on how to use cultural factors for test interpretations" (p. 352) and suggested that it be supplemented by "guidelines for assessment practice with each" (p. 353) racial and ethnic group. Lakin (1994) disapproved of the code's lack of specific and comprehensive contemplation of major issues is multiperson therapies. Vasquez (1994) found the provision allowing therapists to disclose confidential information gleaned in therapy without the client's consent, Standard 5.05(a), to be "alarmingly vague" (p. 326). Keith-Spiegel (1994) faulted the portion of the new code concerning academia for not speaking "clearly and directly to many of the ethical dilemmas that teaching psychologists face in their everyday lives" (p. 368).

Sonne's (1994) review of the provisions concerning multiple relationships provided a further example of the code's lack of clarity. She cited, in particular, Standard 1.17(c):

> If a psychologist finds that, due to unforeseen factors, a potentially harmful multiple relationship has arisen, the psychologist attempts to resolve it with due regard for the best interests of the affected person and maximal compliance with the Ethics Code. (APA, 1992, p. 1601)

This provision, she said, is so "vague and abstract" (Sonne, 1994, p. 343) that it makes it impossible for the ethical psychologist to satisfy the code and protect the interests of the client. The "limited guidance" (p. 343) of the current code, she complained, "can lead to difficulties for the psychologist desiring to pursue ethical practice and can also aid psychologists interested in rationalizing unethical behavior" (p. 341).

Koocher (1994) and Keith-Spiegel (1994) agreed that Standard 6.04 is also highly problematic. Koocher asserted that this provision, prohibiting psychologists from teaching certain clinical techniques to those who lack required training and expertise, "was not well conceptualized and may lead to considerable confusion" (p. 356) because it fails both to define precisely what the drafters intended and to provide guidance to psychologists as to what constitutes adequate training. Thus, he concluded, "without resolution of such ambiguity, this section . . . will be subject to a wide variation in interpretation by practitioners and enforcement authorities"

(p. 356). Keith-Spiegel (1994), in her characteristically direct way, called Standard 6.04 "extraordinarily unclear," sending "shudders through [her] colleagues" (p. 364).

Similarly, when it comes to forensic services, Perrin and Sales (1994) argued that Standard 7.01, requiring clinicians to "base their forensic work on appropriate knowledge . . . and competence" (APA, 1992, p. 1610), gives "no guidance, even in general terms, . . . as to what comprises appropriate knowledge or competence in forensic psychology" (Perrin & Sales, 1994, p. 376). Furthermore, they criticized the forensic provisions concerning the reporting of assessment findings because they "provide virtually no specific guidance" (p. 379).

Sieber (1994), in her review of the research provisions, was perhaps the most critical commentator. She found the provisions, despite the current code's comprehensive attention to scientific ethics, to be "very confusing" (p. 369) and potentially "seriously misleading to the naive researcher in several respects" (p. 373). She rebuked the drafters for failing to provide any substantive guidance to researchers concerning essential topics such as privacy, confidentiality, deception, debriefing, data sharing, autonomy, research with vulnerable populations such as children and people with mental disabilities, and research in organizations and institutions. . . .

PROBLEMS OF ENFORCEMENT

Perhaps the most pointed criticism of the current code concerns the rampant use of qualifying language throughout. As almost all the reviewers pointed out, the code is full of such lawyer-driven "weasel words" as *reasonable* and *feasible* (see. e.g., Keith-Spiegel, 1994, p. 363; Sieber, 1994, p. 369; Vasquez, 1994, p. 321). For example, as Dana (1994) argued, the injunction in Standard 2.02(b) that testers take "reasonable steps" (APA, 1992, p. 1603) to ensure competence in assessments lacks such specificity that it "leaves interpretation in the hands of assessors who may be naive, uninformed, or unintentionally biased" (p. 352). Perrin and Sales (1994) complained that Standard 7.06, requiring forensic psychologists to be "reasonably familiar with the rules governing their roles" (APA, 1992, p.

1610), is so vague and without definition that "a psychologist might consider that he or she is reasonably familiar with what is required . . . when others would strongly disagree" (Perrin & Sales, 1994, p. 377).

There are, as the commentators viewed them, two major consequences of relying on such easily used but poorly implementable terms as reasonable, feasible, and *with due concern for* in the current code. First, because they provide "no clear indication" (Koocher, 1994, p. 360) of what these terms mean, they undermine the code as an educational document. As Sieber (1994) pointedly noted, exhorting psychologists to have due concern for research participants and to take reasonable measures to honor commitments to them fails to inform interested psychologists, particularly novice researchers, about how to perform ethical experiments and is "analogous to an etiquette book that simply advises readers to be considerate" (p. 369). The enfeeblement of ethical imperatives through attenuating phrases leaves some provisions, to use Keith-Spiegel's (1994) colorful language, "barely breathing" and "limp" (Keith-Spiegel, 1994, p. 363). To the reviewers, then, the new code seems to be suffering from some terminal illness rather than serving as a potent moral force. Or to adopt Payton's (1994) pithy and pointed summary, "the current code has been diluted almost to the point of uselessness" (p. 319).

Second, the lack of precision and its intentional lack of clarity make the code difficult to enforce. Interestingly, the term *loophole* appears in at least four of the critiques (Keith-Spiegel, 1994; Koocher, 1994; Sonne, 1994; Vasquez, 1994). For example, Vasquez (1994) complained that "with the enforceable principles containing so much qualifying language, it potentially allows loopholes for psychologists" (p. 321–322). Sonne (1994) predicted that the use of the words "feasible" and "reasonable" (APA, 1992, p. 1601) in Standard 1.17(a). Multiple Relationships, "may serve as a huge loophole . . . for psychologists who argue that . . . it wasn't 'reasonable' for them to avoid contact outside of the primary professional relationship" (p. 340). Trying to determine whether a dual relationship "reasonably might interfere" (APA, 1992, p. 1601) with the effective and objective functioning of a psychologist "gives the prudent psychologist a Herculean task . . . and the unethical psychologist a sizable loophole" (Sonne, 1994, p. 340). More picturesquely, Keith-Spiegel (1994) perceived these escape clauses as "yawning gap[s] through which many interpretations can flow" (p. 367), leaving their meaning to the whims of individual enforcers of the code.

One wonders, in light of these critiques, whether the current code, if challenged on grounds of vagueness and lack of fair notice to psychologists, would pass constitutional muster any better than did the previous code in *White v. North Carolina State Board of Examiners of Practicing Psychologists* (1990). More important, the code's pervasive use of qualifiers and its deliberate ambiguity raise the question of whether it can be used to enforce anything but the most serious moral and ethical transgressions, behavior that is so egregiously wrong that no code would be necessary to condemn it.

PROBLEMS OF PURPOSE

The lack of precision and the presence of lawyerly qualifiers in the current code have led reviewers to question its true objective. For example, in calling exceptions to protecting client confidentiality (Standard 5.05) "alarmingly vague," Vasquez (1994, p. 326) hypothesized that those exceptions were deliberately included "to protect the psychologist more than the client or patient" (Vasquez, 1994, p. 326). Payton (1994) expressed the same concern: "Previous codes seemed to have been formulated from the perspective of offering protection to the consumers of our discipline. . . . The 1992 revisions appear to be more concerned with offering protection to psychologists first and foremost" (p. 320).

Perhaps the most global critique has been provided by Koocher (1994):

> The . . . "code of conduct" is disappointing. It is largely reflective of the style of lawyers . . . and seems more intended to narrow one's liability than to stir one to the highest plane of ethical functioning. . . . For the next round of revisions the voice of defense and liability lawyers who refocused the new code should be tempered with equal input from advocates of public interest and social responsibility. (p. 361)

. . .

Those who study the current code will observe that there are very few moral absolutes in it. Beyond unequivocally forbidding sexual intimacies with students and supervisees over whom the psychologist has authority or with current therapy patients or those whose treatment ceased before 2 years have passed and absolutely precluding the abandonment of patients, the code contains few, if any other, deontological provisions. It is very much a document full of moral compromise, larded with lawyerly language (some variation of *reasonableness* appears 40 times; *feasible* appears 15 times), that constantly balances the interests of professional and academic psychologists, organizations, and institutions against what are perceived to be the best interests of clients and research participants.

It is fortunate that, as organized psychology begins its second 100 years, the field is, in the main, trusted and valued by the public. One needs to look no further than to those who have populated the White House in the last 30 years, however, to recognize how quickly trust can erode. One means of ensuring that psychologists earn and maintain the public's trust is through an ethics document that reflects our moral integrity and our primary mission of promoting human welfare. In many respects, I believe the current code fails to do this. One can only hope that the next revisions committee, working in the twenty-first century, will place as its highest priority the interests of the one constituency that had no voice in the Council's debate—the vast public psychologists depend on for their income, their data, their status, and their reason for being.

References

American Psychological Association. (1992). Ethical principles of psychologists and code of conduct. *American Psychologist, 47,* 1597–1611.

Dana, R. H. (1994). Testing and assessment ethics for all persons: Beginning and agenda. *Professional Psychology: Research and Practice, 25,* 349–354.

Keith-Spiegel, P. (1994). Teaching psychologists and the new APA ethics code: Do we fit in? *Professional Psychology: Research and Practice, 25,* 362–368.

Koocher, G. P. (1994). The commerce of professional psychology and the new ethics code. *Professional Psychology: Research and Practice, 25,* 355–361.

Lakin, M. (1994). Morality in group and family therapies: Multiperson therapies and the 1992 ethics code. *Professional Psychology: Research and Practice, 25,* 344–348.

Payton, C. R. (1994). Implications of the 1992 ethics code for diverse groups. *Professional Psychology: Research and Practice, 25,* 317–320.

Perrin, G. I., & Sales, B. D. (1994). Forensic standards in the American Psychological Association's new ethics code. *Professional Psychology: Research and Practice, 25,* 376–381.

Sieber, J. E. (1994). Will the new code help researchers to be more ethical? *Professional Psychology: Research and Practice, 25,* 369–375.

Sonne, J. L. (1994). Multiple relationships: Does the new ethics code answer the right questions? *Professional Psychology: Research and Practice, 25,* 336–343.

Vasquez, M. J. T. (1994). Implications of the 1992 ethics code for the practice of individual psychotherapy. *Professional Psychology: Research and Practice, 25,* 321–328.

White v. North Carolina State Board of Examiners of Practicing Psychologists, 97 N.C. App. 144, 388 S.E.2d 148 (1990), *review denied.* 326 N.C. 601, 393 S.E.2d 891 (1990).

◆ ◆ ◆

Commentary: *Given that the most frequent ethical complaints against psychologists involve sexual intimacies with clients, incompetent child custody evaluations, and insurance fraud (see chapter 1), might it not be more effective to draft a seven-word ethics code that simply reads: Thou shalt not lie, cheat, nor steal?*

The Value and Utility of the 1992 Ethics Code

Celia B. Fisher and Jeffrey N. Younggren

. . .

In a series of insightful and provocative articles published as a special section of *Professional Psychology: Research and Practice*, 12 psychologists with expertise in ethics rated the new code with a special emphasis on perceived weaknesses and recommendations for future improvement (Keith-Spiegel, 1994). Although the 1992 ethics code, like any other, has deficiencies and improvement is possible, the purpose of this article is to provide additional perspectives on some of the organizational and conceptual strengths of the new code to help ensure that members of the APA do not misapply previous critiques as rationales for ignoring existing ethical standards.

. . .

One major goal of the code is to educate and guide the ethical decision making of psychologists. Ethical behaviors are generally those that fulfill the fundamental moral obligations to do good, to do no harm, to respect others, and to treat all individuals honestly and fairly.

. . .

A second major goal of the ethics code is to provide a clear statement of the types of behaviors considered ethical violations by the APA. From an educative standpoint, study of the code should help psychologists avoid ethical violations by sensitizing them to potential behaviors that can violate the rights and welfare of individuals with whom they work. In addition, the code should help them avoid these pitfalls before an ethical problem develops. The division of the code into eight topic areas with extensive cross-referencing of specific standards is designed to allow the reader to immediately identify relevant ethical issues when a specific concern arises.

. . .

In addition to helping psychologists avoid ethical violations, the code also is designed to familiarize others with the values and responsibilities held by members of the discipline of psychology and help consumers of psychological services identify when a psychologist has behaved unethically. Bersoff (1994) has described the dilemma faced by the crafters of the current code, who recognized that the older code, with its greater emphasis on aspirational principles, was becoming increasingly difficult to enforce. In addition, it was vulnerable to legal challenges for behavioral vagueness, which deprived psychologists of their right to practice. As Bersoff pointed out, such indeterminacy was seen as a disservice to the APA's membership. Accordingly, the division of enforceable standards from aspirational principles was developed in the hopes that the APA would be more successful in sustaining decisions by the ethics committee in court, thus strengthening both the enforceability and credibility of the APA's ethical guidelines.

One goal of the current format is to clarify the APA's view of what the standard of care, conduct, and practice is for psychologists so that licensing boards and regulatory bodies can effectively use the code for their disciplinary procedures. A second goal is to enable the APA Ethics Committee to fairly and consistently adjudicate ethical complaints against psychologists. In terms of both these goals, the separation of enforceable standards into topic areas with clearly outlined regulations should be an improvement over the former code in assisting both com-

From *Professional Psychology: Research and Practice, 28*, 582–592. Copyright 1997 by the American Psychological Association. Adapted with permission of the author and publisher.

plainants and members of the APA Ethics Committee in identifying those behaviors that are violations of the APA ethics code.

As society has become more legalistic in its response to alleged ethical violations, professional ethics committees can no longer risk adjudicating ethical complaints on the basis of subjective interpretations of broadly worded aspirational principles. Although some might argue that adjudication based on specific ethical standards rather than general principles diminishes the moral foundation on which an ethics committee bases such decisions, in practice the aspirational wording of the principles could make them legally and procedurally unenforceable such that the conceptual goals inherent in the aspirational principles are diluted. In addition, broadly defined "principle"-based decisions are highly vulnerable to overturn on appeal because the complainees can argue that they had no forewarning that specific behaviors were ethical violations and that the extent to which a specific behavior is in violation of a general principle is open to interpretation (Bersoff, 1994). Consequently, efforts to make the standards in the new ethics code simple, behaviorally focused, and representative of unitary concepts (Canter et al., 1994) improve rather than diminish the ability of the APA Ethics Committee to identify when a complainee is in violation of an ethical standard and to successfully sustain that decision on appeal.

Some have argued that the inclusion of qualifying terms such as *reasonable* or *feasible* makes the code less enforceable and places the interests of psychologists over that of consumers (e.g., Vasquez, 1994). Although we agree that this criticism applies in some circumstances, we believe that, overall, these terms can protect psychologists from unwarranted complaints without hindering the ability of

the APA Ethics Committee to find psychologists in violation of specific standards. An ethics code should facilitate the ability of students, research participants, and clients to complain about the services that they have received. Broadly defined aspirational principles should not, however, create unrealistic expectations that any form of consumer dissatisfaction is synonymous with an ethical complaint. Similarly, although qualifying terminology may sometimes regrettably provide a loophole through which a psychologist can escape a deserved ethical sanction, such terminology also allows a psychologist to launch a legitimate defense of his or her actions based on current best practices (as defined by professional guidelines) and documentation of efforts to resolve problems in an ethical manner. The costs and benefits of qualifying terms will most certainly be a point of discussion during the next revision of the ethics code. We believe that an important aspect of that discussion should include the fact that the public is not well served if psychologists restrict their efforts on behalf of those they serve out of fear that they will be unduly vulnerable to accusations of ethical violations.

References

Bersoff, D. (1994). Explicit ambiguity: The 1992 Ethics Code as an oxymoron. *Professional Psychology: Research and Practice, 25,* 382–387.

Canter, M. B., Bennett, B. E., Jones, S. E., & Nagy, T. F. (1994). *Ethics for psychologists: A commentary on the APA Ethics Code.* Washington, DC: American Psychological Association.

Keith-Spiegel, P. (1994). The 1992 ethics code: Boon or bane? *Professional Psychology: Research and Practice, 25,* 315–316.

Vasquez, M. J. T. (1994). Implications of the 1992 ethics code for the practice of individual psychotherapy. *Professional Psychology: Research and Practice, 25,* 321–328.

CHAPTER 3

LEARNING ETHICS

Since the late 1970s, every graduate program training professional psychologists that seeks to be accredited by the APA has been required to offer instruction in ethics and to familiarize students with whatever version of the APA ethics code is current at the time. APA does not accredit programs that train graduate students solely for research positions, but a great many such programs offer similar instruction in ethics, at the very least concentrating on the ethics of experimentation and scholarship. Does this training ensure that those who complete these programs act ethically as professionals? As the data and material presented in chapters 1 and 2 illustrate, this is often not the case.

As we have begun to explore, there are a variety of reasons for psychologists to act in ways that violate the code of ethics. A few miscreants deliberately flout their professional and scientific responsibilities for personal gain—monetary, reputational, and sexual, among others. For example, the psychologist who, without consulting his or her client, rushes to the media with the news that he or she is the therapist of a famous personage just charged with a heinous crime is acting in a purely self-serving and inexcusable manner. Other psychologists violate ethical principles because of imprudence, ignorance, or insensitivity about the ethical consequences of their behavior. For instance, consider the psychologist who calls child protection services after she learns that the parents she is counseling are punishing their 10-year-old child with a rattan cane. When the parents file an ethics complaint, the psychologist responds that she thought she was mandated by law to report child abuse but never realized that the APA ethics code also required her to inform clients of the limits of confidentiality or that failing to do that would damage the development of the therapeutic relationship.

These are relatively simple cases to adjudicate. But there are at least two other kinds of cases that are more complex. In the first case are psychologists who attempt to comply with the rules but, perceiving that they lack the guidance of clearly written, explicit, and precise ethical provisions, rely on their own interpretation of those rules. To illustrate, under the 1992 ethics code, psychologists are supposed to discuss the limits of confidentiality with clients very close to the beginning of a therapeutic relationship, "unless it is not feasible or is contraindicated" (APA, 1992, p. 1606). Suppose now that a patient in the third year of intensive psychoanalysis begins to fall behind in paying for his therapy. For several months the analyst and the patient discuss the patient's failure to pay as part of his resistance to therapy. Finally, however, with the unpaid bills mounting, the analyst and the patient agree to terminate therapy. The analyst then turns over the outstanding account to a collection agency. The client complains that his right to confidentiality was violated when the analyst submitted his name to the collection agency without telling him at any time during treatment that she would do so. In response, the analyst explains that her conduct violated no ethical rule because she believed that any discussion of the limits of confidentiality at the outset of treatment would have interfered with transference issues so crucial to successful psychoanalysis. Thus, in her mind, disclosure was "contraindicated." Lacking specific guidance in this situation by those who drafted the code, the psychologist made a not implausible interpretation of her own.

The most complex situations are those that present ethically sensitive and knowledgeable psychologists with fundamental and profound ethical dilemmas. Psychologists in these cases understand the rules (or the law) but break them because they consider violation to be in the service of higher moral principles. Consider the following case example. A 10th-grade boy is enrolled in research studying violence in adolescents and how it might be prevented through short-term intervention. During an interview portion of the study, the student reveals to the female investigator that he has had many fantasies about harming his next-door neighbor, a slightly older female teenager who refuses to pay him any attention. On further inquiry, the investigator also learns that the student is contemplating the purchase of a gun. The investigator suggests to the student that it would be a good idea to inform his parents of the situation, even though she is aware that he has no history of violent behavior. The student adamantly refuses to inform his parents or to let the investigator do so, warning that he will drop out of the study and treatment if she does not honor his refusal. Believing that preserving confidentiality would, in the long run, be in the student's best interest by not driving him out of needed treatment and would most closely express the psychologists' moral principle of fidelity, the investigator agrees not to tell his parents.

One week later, the psychologist reads in the newspaper that, with a gun bought the day before, her research subject has shot and wounded his teenage neighbor after she ignored him one evening. The parents of the 10th-grade student file a complaint with APA, stating that the psychologist should have informed them of their son's potentially violent and harmful behavior, regardless of his wishes. The psychologist concedes that the code permits disclosure without consent to protect third parties from harm, but she argues that supporting the boy's right to privacy and autonomy and the need to establish trust in therapy outweighed any putative entitlement in the code of ethics to inform his parents.

Although the psychologist's decision in this case may have contributed to a negative outcome, the situation did present her with a genuine ethical dilemma. It would have been perfectly ethical for her to disclose the student's confidences and even to refuse to abide by his demand for secrecy. Nevertheless, she decided that this course of action conflicted with more universal moral principles—the promotion of autonomy and the development of faithfulness to her subject's expressed interests—that were an inherent part of her value system as a psychologist.

All psychologists will be faced with such dilemmas sometime in their careers. They may find that, by necessity or design, the APA code of ethics contains few absolute and explicit prohibitions regarding a particular dilemma. The psychologist who wishes to act ethically in an ethically uncertain world needs to have both a philosophical base from which to make decisions and a method for using that base to build workable options.

In this chapter, I offer some frameworks for recognizing a genuine ethical dilemma, for generating possible solutions to it, and, perhaps for arriving at a reasonable resolution in line with the ethical principles of one's professional association and one's personal value system. However, as the authors of material in this chapter argue, acting ethically is not a compartmentalized function. Instead, ethical behavior results from integrating didactic knowledge, including a thorough familiarity with the APA ethics code; an understanding of problem-solving and decision-making approaches; a clear conception of the philosophical principles (each of which may compete with one another) that underlie the formal code of ethics; and a basically sound character that leads one to respond with maturity, judgment, discretion, wisdom, and prudence.

In the remainder of this book I concentrate on seven central topics that inevitably confront and test the psychology practitioner, researcher, and professor with ethical dilemmas surrounding confidentiality, multiple relationships, assessment, therapeutic interventions, teaching and doing research in an academic institution, serving as an expert witness, and dealing with the commercial and business aspects of psychology. Because this chapter provides the foundation for ethical decision making under each of these topics, I consider it absolutely crucial to understanding and integrating the material in the remaining chapters of the book.

References

American Psychological Association. (1992). Ethical principles of psychologists and code of conduct. *American Psychologist, 47,* 1597–1611.

Problems With Ethics Training by "Osmosis"

Mitchell M. Handelsman

Ethical training by osmosis refers to the practice of allowing ethics to be taught in the context of supervision, in which a sensitivity to issues will seep through during discussions of cases. In this article I argue that relying on such informal methods to teach ethics is a dangerous practice. . . .

The first argument against training in the context of practica concerns the nature and extent of supervision. "It is usually assumed that adequate supervision will always be provided in the clinic or hospital, but this is far from universally true" (Arnhoff & Jenkins, 1969, p. 441). Often, needs and time constraints of the agency take precedence over careful exploration of ethical issues. Competence of supervisors in ethics is also an issue. Dalton (1984) noted that "students' learning is limited by the supervisor's awareness of ethical dilemmas and assumptions; issues not recognized by the supervisor are not recognized or mentioned by students" (p. 186). The "extended supervision" argument, then, may be an instance of transferring responsibility. . . .

Even if one knows that supervisors do an adequate job of exploring ethical issues (this remains, of course, an empirical question) when such issues arise in the course of clinical work, this method does not guarantee that a broad range of ethical issues will arise. In their survey, Tymchuk et al. (1982) found that 58% of doctoral-level psychologists felt "that they were not well informed enough about ethical issues in psychology" (p. 419). One may overcome such a gap in knowledge by exposure to such issues in a formal way, rather than leaving it up to chance. . . .

There is no doubt that important learning takes place in relation to meaningful events, and ethical issues encountered during clinical practice will remain salient. However, to rely on such learning to take place seems to be a dangerous practice. Reconceptualizing ethics and its training is needed in training programs. It is necessary to treat ethical thinking as a skill that must be developed and that is not intimately bound to the process of therapy, testing, and so on. . . .

. . .

Another reason for lack of ethics courses may be that faculty, given their own areas of expertise, are not qualified to teach general ethics courses. A psychotherapist, for example, may not be well qualified to teach about the ethics of deception and informed consent to research. One approach to this problem would be to team-teach the course. In this way, each faculty member would be responsible for covering issues that he or she is (or should be) familiar with. Also, guest lecturers could be recruited from various sources, such as state psychological association ethics committees. This would tap a valuable and underused resource, but might also, because of the contact, facilitate trainees' consultation of such committees in the future. The danger in such an approach is that the course could amount to an appendage to a program for which nobody takes full responsibility. One must take care not to model such an attitude towards ethics.

Ethics courses can be made more stimulating and relevant by being taught with a variety of methods that blend theory and application. Learning can include general ethical concepts (Solomon, 1984), ethical thinking processes (Tymchuk, 1981), values clarification (Abeles, 1980), use of comprehensive

From *Professional Psychology: Research and Practice*, 17, 371–372. Copyright 1986 by the American Psychological Association. Adapted with permission of the author and publisher.

textbooks . . . and exploration of ethical dilemmas. . . .

Just as psychologists have abandoned the apprenticeship model of psychotherapy training and have recognized that courses in therapeutic theory and techniques are desirable and effective, so they need to think of ethical reasoning as a skill that can be taught and studied in much the same way.

References

Abeles, N. (1980). Teaching ethical principles by means of values confrontations. *Psychotherapy: Theory, Research and Practice, 17,* 384–391.

Arnhoff, F. N., & Jenkins, J. W. (1969). Subdoctoral education in psychology: A study of issues and attitudes. *American Psychologist, 24,* 430–443.

Dalton, J. H. (1984). Discussing ethical issues in practicum courses. *Teaching of Psychology, 11,* 186–188.

Handelsman, M. M. (1986). Ethics training at the master's level: A national survey. *Professional Psychology: Research and Practice, 17,* 24–26.

Solomon, R. C. (1984). *Ethics: A brief introduction.* New York: McGraw-Hill.

Tymchuk, A. J. (1981). Ethical decision-making and psychological treatment. *Journal of Psychiatric Treatment and Evaluation, 3,* 507–513.

Tymchuk, A. J., Drapkin, R. S., Major-Kingsley, S., Ackerman, A. B., Coffman, E. W., & Baum, M. S. (1982). Ethical decision making and psychologists' attitudes toward training in ethics. *Professional Psychology, 13,* 412–421.

◆ ◆ ◆

Commentary: *Compare the argument above by Handelsman (1986) to the following, written by Welfel and Lipsitz 2 years earlier:*

> *In spite of the dramatic increase in availability of ethics courses in graduate programs there has been little systematic investigation of the impact of such experiences on students. In fact, there is little information regarding exactly what is being taught in those courses. . . .*
>
> *[The] literature only very weakly supports the interpretation that ethics courses have a positive impact on students. No study has been reported that examines the influence of such training on actual behavior with clients or assesses whether the effects of ethics courses are temporary or permanent. In addition, there are no data to compare whether ethics is best taught in a separate course or integrated into existing courses in the curriculum. Thus, the push to initiate separate ethics courses in graduate programs is based more on the "good hearted assumption" that such courses will have a positive impact than on any scientific data. Given the cost in faculty time and in tuition for such training, systematic research into such courses seems imperative. (p. 37).*

See Welfel, E. R., & Lipsitz, N. E. (1984). The ethical behavior of professional psychologists: A critical analysis of the research. Counseling Psychologist, 12(3), 31–41. *Nevertheless, as Welfel (1992) later noted, since 1979 APA has mandated that all programs accredited by APA include ethics training for graduate students. By 1990, 69% of these programs taught ethics in a separate required course, usually in classes lasting 20 to 30 hours. She concluded that graduate faculties now view ethics training as their responsibility, rather than that of clinical supervisors. See Welfel, E. R. (1992). Psychologists as ethics educator: Successes, failures, and unanswered questions.* Professional Psychology: Research and Practice, 23, 182–189.

Despite the consensus that ethics education in psychology is becoming universal, one author recently

> *found it somewhat surprising that although trainees often are well versed in the ethical principles of the American Psychological Association . . . they usually have very little formal exposure to a number of important professional issues and few day-to-day dealings with ethical dilemmas. (p. 616)*

See Plante, T. G. (1995). Training child clinical predoctoral interns and postdoctoral fellows in ethics and professional issues: An experiential model. Professional Psychology: Research and Practice, 26, 616–619.

Plante's (1995) model seminar is practical and professionally oriented. Other writers exhort trainers to take a very different approach. For example, Pellegrin & Frueh (1994)

> suggest that PhD candidates should receive training in their degree; that is to say, philosophy. Instead of learning only what ethical principles are, PhD candidates should also be well versed in the philosophical issues and debates that are the foundation for the formation of the ethical principles. (p. 970)

See Pellegrin, K. L., & Frueh, B. C. (1994). Why psychologists don't think like philosophers. American Psychologist, 49, 970.

More specifically, Tymchuk et al. (1982) have argued that

> the profession . . . needs to attend more closely to decision-making processes and develop decision-making standards that can be applied to situations as they arise. What may be most useful for the professional are broader and more basic decision-making standards rather than specific rules that attempt to define behavior as "right" or "wrong." Models are needed that incorporate a comprehensive range of ethical considerations in order to assist psychologists in the process of making critical decisions. (p. 420)

See Tymchuk, A. J., Drapkin, R. S., Major-Kingsley, S., Ackerman, A. B., Major, S. M., & Baum, M. S. (1982). Ethical decision making and psychologists' attitudes toward training in ethics. Professional Psychology: Research and Practice, 13, 412–421.

Consider whether the next four excerpts provide the philosophical underpinnings and decision-making models the authors call for in the Commentary.

Integrating Psychology and Philosophy in Teaching a Graduate Course in Ethics

Mark A. Fine and Lawrence P. Ulrich

. . . To explicitly state our position from the outset, we regard the teaching of graduate-level courses in ethics to be a critical and necessary component of graduate training in psychology. It is not sufficient merely to add a short footnote about ethics to the subject matter of various courses. Although this common practice may be helpful in showing how ethical concerns are an integral part of psychological practice, these issues are often addressed in terms of conclusions without sufficient conceptual justification for the positions taken. A separate course is necessary, we believe, because an adequate ethical analysis can occur only when there is a formulation and critical appraisal of the justifications that underlie ethical decisions.

. . . [I]t is important to justify why we feel that it is critically important to include a philosophical component in ethics courses for psychology graduate students. First, philosophers have studied ethics much more thoroughly than have psychologists. Ethics is generally considered the appropriate subject matter of philosophy, insofar as psychologists typically treat ethics as a tool to assist them in conducting their clinical activities, but not as a primary subject matter in itself. Second, as a result of philosophy's greater acquaintance with ethical subject matter, it is better suited to assist when there arise ethical dilemmas that cannot easily be resolved with reference to ethical codes. . . . As Kitchener (1984)

and Eberlein (1987) noted, when such situations arise, one must resort to underlying principles and theories, which are within the expertise of philosophy. Third, a greater understanding of ethical theory may assist psychology as a profession in the continual process of articulating ethical guidelines or codes.

Our model of the ethical decision-making process derives from work by Beauchamp and Walters (1982) and has similarities to a discussion by Kitchener (1984). It consists of four distinct levels. The most general level of ethical reasoning consists of ethical frameworks or theories. We address two of the most commonly articulated frameworks, utilitarianism and deontology. *Utilitarianism*, often associated with John Stuart Mill and Jeremy Bentham, is based on the major principle that an action is ethically appropriate when it leads to the greatest possible balance of good consequences or to the least possible balance of bad consequences in the world as a whole (Beauchamp & Walters, 1982). Thus from a utilitarian perspective, one must carefully evaluate and weigh the relative value of the consequences that are expected to arise from an ethical decision and choose that action that maximizes the ratio of benefits to costs. *Deontology*, initially associated with Immanuel Kant, is based on the major principle (categorical imperative) that one must act to treat every person as an end and never as a

From *Professional Psychology: Research and Practice, 19,* 542–546. Copyright 1988 by the American Psychological Association. Adapted with permission of the author and publisher. Table 1 has been omitted.

means only (Beauchamp & Walters, 1982). This reflects inherent respect for the dignity of all persons. The morality of actions is based on their intrinsic rightness, is independent of the consequences of the behaviors, and thus permits no exceptions to the major principles. . . .[1]

The case of *Tarasoff v. Board of Regents of the University of California* (1976) may help to clarify the meaning of the two ethical frameworks. A utilitarian judgment would involve a careful assessment of the benefits and costs of violating confidentiality and warning potential victims. Because of individual variation in the assessment of benefits and costs, differing conclusions may be reached. In fact, a majority of the justices of the California Supreme Court argued on utilitarian grounds that the potential victim should have been warned, but a minority of the justices, also using utilitarian guidelines, maintained that the greater good arose from not breaking confidentiality in such instances because the integrity of the therapeutic relationship would be enhanced and potentially violent individuals would be more likely to seek and benefit from psychotherapy. A deontological argument would suggest that one should maintain confidentiality in *all* cases because an individual's right to privacy is a moral absolute and should never be violated.

The next level of ethical reasoning represents specific principles derived from the frameworks. Examples of principles (Beauchamp & Walters, 1982) include autonomy (i.e., a person should be free to perform whatever action he or she wishes, regardless of risks or foolishness, provided that it does not impinge on the autonomy of others), beneficence (i.e., one should render positive assistance to others, and abstain from harm, by helping them to further their important and legitimate interests), justice (i.e., one should give to persons what they are owed, what they deserve, or what they can legitimately claim), and paternalism (i.e., one should restrict an individual's action against his or her consent in order to

prevent that individual from self-harm or to secure for that individual a good that he or she might not otherwise achieve). These flow logically from the frameworks; that is, a utilitarian perspective would suggest that one should respect an individual's autonomy, provided that it does not impinge on the autonomy of others, because this maximizes the ratio of benefits to harm. Although deontological perspectives have similar principles, they may take a somewhat different form from those derived from utilitarian perspectives. One such difference is that the purest form of deontological principles permits no exceptions.

The third level in the ethical decision-making process consists of rules. Rules are derived from principles and are general guidelines asserting what ought to be done in a range of particular cases. Ethical codes may be considered rules, insofar as they provide guidelines to assist psychologists in a range of situations.

The final and most particular level in the process consists of judgments, which represent decisions about specific actions of decisions. Kitchener (1984) noted that people make most ethical decisions at this level ("intuitive level") without probing more deeply at the rule, principle, or framework level. We believe that ethical decisions typically are made at the level with which the decision maker feels most comfortable; that is, if individuals feel comfortable with an ethical rule as stated in a code, they are unlikely to probe more deeply to the level of principle or theory. At times, this may lead to questionable decisions, particularly when intuition alone is used as the basis for making ethical decisions. However, some ethical decisions are made routine in such a way that there is no need to probe more deeply because the analysis has been done for similar dilemmas in the past. Maintaining confidentiality, for example, by not revealing that an individual is receiving psychotherapy unless that person grants permission to do so should become a habit and should not require careful analysis for each client. . . .

---

[1] *Ed. note:* Another term often contrasted with *deontology* is *teleology*. Teleological ethical theory holds that actions are judged by the goodness of their consequences. Thus, it is closely akin to utilitarianism.

References

Beauchamp, T., & Walters, L. (Eds.). (1982). *Contemporary issues in bioethics* (2nd ed.). Belmont, CA: Wadsworth.

Eberlein, L. (1987). Introducing ethics to beginning psychologists: A problem-solving approach. *Professional Psychology: Research and Practice, 18,* 353–359.

Kitchener, K. S. (1984). Intuition, critical evaluation and ethics principles: The foundation for ethical decisions in counseling psychology. *The Counseling Psychologist, 12*(3), 43–55.

Tarasoff v. Board of Regents of the University of California, 551 P.2d 334 (Cal. S. Ct. 1976).

Introducing Ethics to Beginning Psychologists: A Problem-Solving Approach

Larry Eberlein

Dr. Phillis Sawyer, a clinical psychologist in private practice, also hosts a popular radio call-in show twice a week. During one program dealing with depression, a male caller wanted to talk about his feelings of inadequacy. Dr. Sawyer indicated that she couldn't discuss his individual case on the radio but suggested that he might want to talk with a psychologist about his concern. She provided a free help number to call and indicated her willingness to provide the names of several qualified psychologists when she went off the air. A few days later, without indicating he had been the caller, Gregory Greenwood made an appointment to see Dr. Sawyer. During the first interview Mr. Greenwood revealed that he had been the caller and had been so impressed with Dr. Sawyer on the radio that he was sure she could help him. Dr. Sawyer decided that she could be of help to him and arranged for a series of sessions. During the second interview Mr. Greenwood revealed that he was taking medication prescribed by Dr. Gendrau, his family physician. Mr. Greenwood asked Dr. Sawyer not to talk with Dr. Gendrau, who had been seeing him every other week for 4 months. Mr. Greenwood explained that Dr. Gendrau had been helpful to Mrs. Greenwood

and their two children, but that he does not like psychologists. He might stop seeing the family if any member were also seeing a psychologist, no matter how well qualified the psychologist was. Dr. Sawyer felt an obligation to talk with Dr. Gendrau, especially to find out about the medication, but did not want to do so without Mr. Greenwood's consent. She was also concerned about seeing Mr. Greenwood without Dr. Gendrau's knowledge, even though it appeared that Dr. Gendrau had been unable to deal with Mr. Greenwood's feelings of inadequacy.

This is the kind of ethical dilemma that was used in a case study approach to the study of ethics by clinical and counseling master's students at the University of Alberta. The course focus was on the process of thinking through the many dimensions of a dilemma with the use of a problem-solving model. . . .

There exist good reasons for Dr. Sawyer to choose any of several different courses of action. Immediate responses, such as "Dr. Sawyer shouldn't have taken this case in the first place," or "She must terminate therapy," or "She must ignore Dr. Gendrau and do what's best for her client," were discouraged in favor of a more careful and balanced consideration of the moral, legal, and ethical elements present in the dilemma. The discussion focused on the short- and long-term consequences of any action

From *Professional Psychology: Research and Practice, 18,* 353–359. Copyright 1987 by the American Psychological Association. Adapted with permission of the author and publisher.

taken and on how each action would affect the dignity of and the responsible caring for all the people involved. Students were encouraged to consult with colleagues to develop and consider many alternative actions by the psychologist with the understanding that in many ethical dilemmas there is no single correct (or perhaps even best) response. This kind of process-oriented, problem-solving approach was very much appreciated by the first-year students; for many, this was the first sustained contact with legal and ethical issues faced by professional psychologists. . . .

THE CURRENT NATURE OF ETHICS EDUCATION

. . .

If we accept the importance of morals and values in ethical decision making, the current nature of ethics education is severely lacking. In the formal courses reviewed by Tymchuk et al. (1979), APA standards were used as the basic text, with additional coverage on research standards, confidentiality, right to treatment, and professional and legal issues. Personal values was the item least frequently discussed: "clarification of values plays no integral part in graduate education" (Tymchuk et al., 1979, p. 1170). Welfel and Lipsitz (1983) said that in addition to simply reviewing a code, many writers feel that "ethics education must broaden its base and include instruction in moral philosophy" (p. 322). Consideration of personal values and the ability to reason on moral issues are considered essential. . . .

THE CORRECT-ANSWER APPROACH

Many of the models examined, even those involving a moral emphasis, focus on the "right" or "best" answer. Bailey (1980), for example, provided a quiz for school counselors. He offered 26 questions, keyed to the official ethical standards of the American Personnel and Guidance Association; one of five responses to each question was the "correct" answer. Casebooks often present real dilemmas and then a judgment as to whether the action was proper (Callis, 1976; Keith-Spiegel & Koocher, 1985). By contrast, the workbook for beginning professionals by Corey, Corey, and Callahan (1979) is more issue oriented, more thought provoking, and less judgmental.

This correct-answer approach is also common in many professional examinations. For example, the Examination of Professional Practice in Psychology is used by many licensing boards. A substantial part of the exam covers "professional conduct, affairs, and ethics; interdisciplinary relations; and knowledge of professional affairs" (Hess, 1977, p. 367). This exam of 150 or more items is graded as being right or wrong. Although forced-choice responses provide data that can be subjected to statistical manipulation, such a format does not always provide the framework and freedom to think about a question in ways that could lead to a more productive resolution of the issue. . . .

Sometimes in the area of professional ethics no response is very satisfying, although more than one may meet the bare requirements of ethical behavior. Members of professional ethics committees usually do not articulate their thought processes or the principles that they apply to a case; the "facts" are reported together with a decision as to whether the situation was seen as unethical behavior (Sanders, 1979). In addition, there are conflicts between code provisions, between the codes of different professional associations, and between codes and the legal requirements of a particular jurisdiction (Bersoff, 1975; Huey, 1986; Mappes, Robb, & Engles, 1985). . . .

On many issues for which there is not a strong consensus and when individual psychologists cannot refer to a specific standard, they fall back on their own value systems and their interpretation of the spirit of the code. There has to be a better approach than trying to apply a limited set of rules to problems of human relationships, a major issue underlying all ethical dilemmas; such an approach must include a value component.

A PROBLEM-SOLVING APPROACH

Problems of human relationship almost always involve some conflict among the values, rights, and responsibilities of the psychologist, the client, related persons, one or more agencies, other professionals, and the community at large. . . . We now realize that values are present in any relationship, and psychologists must confront and deal with attitudes and values within the professional relationship as well as with the respective rights and responsibilities involved.

Frequently, the presence of such conflicting claims presents difficulties for a conscientious psychologist. If we consider Dr. Sawyer's dilemma, the most obvious conflicts involve Gregory Greenwood's autonomy, right to privacy, confidentiality, and self-determination, on the one hand, and the obligation to protect and promote the welfare of the Greenwood family (including Gregory) while maintaining good interprofessional relationships, on the other. Kitchener (1984) discussed two levels of moral thinking: an immediate (intuitive) level and a critical-evaluative level. The "shoulds" and "musts" tend to reflect the intuitive level, the ordinary or perhaps impulsive moral judgments. Upon further reflection and consideration of the conflicting values, rights, and responsibilities, an open-minded psychologist usually will modify or qualify a first response, even though the first response may be ethically acceptable. This is especially true when different ethical guidelines are in conflict. This reflects the critical-evaluative level, which Kitchener described as having three components: rules and codes, ethical principles, and ethical theory. The goal for the University of Alberta course was to challenge students to go beyond a code to the underlying principles, to consider ethical theory when possible, to consult widely, and to maintain flexibility when considering alternatives during the problem-solving process.

Several authors have developed problem-solving models: a common pattern involves the development of alternatives, analysis, choice of action, and evaluation. Several deal directly with ethical concerns. Keith-Spiegel and Koocher (1985, pp. 19–20) offered an eight-step model:

1. Describe the parameters of the situation.
2. Define the potential issues involved.
3. Consult the guidelines, if any, already available that might apply to the resolution of each issue.
4. Evaluate the rights, responsibilities, and welfare of all affected parties.
5. Generate the alternative decisions possible for each issue.
6. Enumerate the consequences of making each decision.
7. Present any evidence that the various consequences or benefits resulting from each decision will actually occur.
8. Make the decision.

Tymchuk (1986) had a useful approach that included seven steps. In the most important step, one determines which alternative to implement by looking at the short-term, ongoing, and long-term consequences and at the psychological, social, and economic costs with a risk–benefit analysis of each alternative.

The problem-solving model recommended by the CPA [Canadian Psychological Association] Committee on Ethics (1986) is reflective of the Tymchuk approach and the following six questions used in the development of the new code (Sinclair et al. 1987):

1. Indicate the individuals and/or groups that need to be considered in arriving at a solution to the dilemma posed by the situation.
2. Take each of the individuals or groups that you feel should be considered, and explain in detail what consideration each is owed and why, particularly in terms of the rights and responsibilities involved.
3. What would be your choice of action, and why would you choose it?
4. What alternative choices of action would you consider, and why did you not choose them?
5. What is the minimal circumstance in the situation that you can conceive of that could lead you to a different choice of action? What would that action be, and why would you choose it?
6. Do you have any further thoughts or comments about this or similar situations? If so, explain.

. . .

Most problem-solving models finish with an evaluation of the action taken. Perhaps the most important omission of such models is the following step that the CPA, Committee on Ethics (1986), included as the seventh and final step:

> Assumption of responsibility for the consequences of the action taken, including correction of negative consequences, if any, or re-engaging in the decision-making process if the ethical issue is not resolved. (p. 6E)

Following a code of conduct does not render a psychologist immune from an ethical complaint or lawsuit. Even more difficult is the choice of action when one is facing an ethical dilemma that is not easy to resolve. There may be conflicts among code provisions or with legal requirements. One example is the lack of competence in some area of practice when there is no other more competent referral source reasonably available. Another is the potential breach of an ethical confidence when one is facing a court subpoena. Such decisions should be well thought out and not taken lightly. The CPA recognizes that final resolution of such dilemmas is a matter of personal conscience, but "psychologists are expected to engage in an ethical decision-making process that is explicit enough to bear public scrutiny" (CPA, Committee on Ethics, 1986, p. 6E).

Psychologists need educational experiences involving a value component that can help them to reach responsible decisions after all consequences have been fully explored. These experiences should help psychologists to develop a structure of ethical or moral decision making that will be useful when they face future dilemmas. . . .

If all psychologists had the same moral value system, a code of conduct would not be necessary, complaints would not be filed, and most lawsuits would be avoided. As it is, there are dramatic value differences, and a code is usually a consensual validation of what *has been* the most recent view of a majority of psychologists ensconced in decision-making roles, often in response to public pressures or specific problematic behavior. Codes are at best incomplete guidelines; ultimately the individual psychologist must decide upon a personal course of action and live with the consequences of that decision.

CONCLUSION

. . .

The reality of the training experience is that students are usually given a copy of a code of ethics, along with the clinic or placement rules, and provided an awareness that consent forms have to be signed and client interviews kept confidential. Few supervisors spend time discussing ethical implications of action taken unless a problem arises. Occasionally an ethical concern might surface, but most of the real issues in the areas of informed consent, confidentiality, and competence are never addressed in the students' classes, seminars, or practicum experiences. Students also are not made aware of the professional issues that they will meet after graduation. Perhaps as psychology continues its professional development outside of university settings, students will need a different exposure to heighten their awareness that there exist more professional dilemmas than are usually recognized and that mere knowledge of a set of guidelines does not a professional make.

Beginning and practicing psychologists all need a comprehensive, more inclusive approach when making decisions that involve ethical issues. Many decisions are easily made and cause no difficulty. In others, the ethical implications are implicit in the action taken but receive no conscious consideration. I recommend that all supervisors in a practicum or institutional setting regularly ask, "What are the ethical issues involved in what we have done or are doing?" I also recommend that regular case conferences be held, not only to discuss the handling of a case, but to discuss the ethical nuances that are involved. I favor a continuing exposure to ethical, problem-solving experiences, but I recognize that the real test comes when principles discussed in the reflective atmosphere of a workshop setting have to be applied in a real-life situation.

References

Bailey, J. A. (1980). School counselors: Test your ethics. *The School Counselor, 27,* 285–293.

Bersoff, D. N. (1975). Professional ethics and legal responsibilities: On the horns of a dilemma. *The Journal of School Psychology, 13*, 359–376.

Callis, R. (1976). *Ethical standards casebook* (2nd ed.). Washington, DC: American Personnel & Guidance Association.

Canadian Psychological Association, Committee on Ethics (1986). Code of ethics. *Highlights, 8*(1), 6E–12E.

Corey, G., Corey, M. S., & Callanan, P. (1979). *Professional and ethical issues in counseling and psychotherapy.* Monterey, CA: Brooks/Cole.

Hess, F. F. (1977). Entry requirements for professional practice of psychology. *American Psychologist, 32*, 365–368.

Huey, W. C. (1986). Ethical concerns in school counseling. *Journal of Counseling and Development, 64*, 321–322.

Keith-Spiegel, P., & Koocher, G. P. (1985). *Ethics in psychology: Professional standards and cases.* New York: Random House.

Kitchener, K. S. (1984). Intuition, critical evaluation and ethical principles: The foundation for ethical decision in counseling psychology. *The Counseling Psychologist, 12*(3), 43–55.

Mappes, D. C., Robb, G. P., & Engels, D. W. (1985). Conflicts between ethics and law in counseling and psychotherapy. *Journal of Counseling and Development, 64*, 246–252.

Sanders, J. R. (1979). Complaints against psychologists adjudicated informally by APA's committee on scientific and professional ethics and conduct. *American Psychologist, 34*, 1139–1144.

Sinclair, C., Poizner, S., Gilmour-Barrett, K., & Randall, D. (1987). The development of a code of ethics for Canadian psychologists. *Canadian Psychology, 28*, 1–8.

Tymchuk, A. J. (1986). Guidelines for ethical decision making. *Canadian Psychology, 27*, 36–43.

Tymchuk, A. J., Drapkin, R. S., Ackerman, A. B., Major, S. M., Coffman, E. W., & Baum, M. S. (1979). Survey of training in ethics in APA-approved clinical psychology programs. *American Psychologist, 34*, 1168–1170.

Van Hoose, W. H. (1980). Ethics and counseling. *Counseling and Human Development, 13*(1), 1–12.

Welfel, E. R., & Lipsitz, N. E. (1983). Wanted: A comprehensive approach to ethics research and education. *Counselor Education and Supervision, 22*, 320–332.

◆ ◆ ◆

Commentary: *Gawthrop and Uhlemann (1992) have provided empirical support for the approaches espoused*

by Eberlein (1987) and by Tymchuk et al. (1982). They presented a vignette containing an ethical dilemma to undergraduate students who were preparing for careers in mental health professions. The treatment group received a 3-hour workshop on ethical decision making using a problem-solving approach. In comparison with two control groups, the treatment group performed significantly better on a rating scale designed to measure quality of the decision-making process. See Gawthrop, J. C., & Uhlemann, M. R. (1992). Effects of the problem-solving approach in ethics training. Professional Psychology: Research and Practice, 23, 38–42. The authors offered the following insights on their study and its implications for teaching students about ethics:

> *The results of this study are consistent with those found in earlier work . . . in that formal exposure to ethics education had a significant positive effect on the dependent variable. In addition, the refinements of the present study made possible several specific conclusions in light of the results.*
>
> *. . . When the brevity of the workshop experience is considered, the strength of the observed treatment effect is notable . . . The results suggest that the problem-solving approach in teaching ethics . . . is effective in fostering quality in ethical decision making and that simply presenting written instructions is not sufficient for eliciting that quality of decision making.*
>
> *It is important to point out that the problem-solving approach . . . was augmented in this study with elements of other ethics teaching models. The workshop goals were to sensitize participants to ethical issues and to maximize the quality of ethical decision making by using reading and discussion of ethical codes and case vignettes, self-generation of ethical dilemmas from experience, and generating and justifying ethical decisions about specific vignettes (Kitchener, 1986). Discussions of ethical dilemmas during the workshops often included an exploration of how values form the basis of codes and decision rationales (Abeles, 1980). The case vignette also*

served to recognize the contribution made by several teaching models (Eberlein, 1987; Fine & Ulrich, 1988; Kitchener, 1984, 1986; McGovern, 1988) with regard to making participant evaluation and accountability an integral part of ethics education.

The present results, in conjunction with findings from earlier studies, permit several suggestions regarding the training of counselors and psychologists in ethical issues. First, it is becoming increasingly clear that the limitations of the informal teaching of ethics need to be accepted (Handelsman, 1986b). The mere provision of ethics information is not sufficient. Rather, the present results support the notion that ethics education be made a formal endeavor in which specific attention is given to the content and process of teaching ethical decision making. Second, the results made it reasonable to suggest that those trainees who do not receive formal exposure to ethics education cannot be assumed to possess the same ethical decision-making skills as trainees who have gone through formal ethics education in which such skills are taught. Third, it seems reasonable to suggest that separate sections of courses or full courses devoted to professional ethics be included in all training programs in the helping professions and that all such courses include the teaching of ethical decision making. Fourth, the results of the present study support the suggestion that educators consider using the problem-

solving approach . . . in teaching ethical decision making. . . .

References

Abeles, N. (1980). Teaching ethical principles by means of value confrontations. *Psychotherapy: Research and Practice, 17,* 384–391.

Eberlein, L. (1987). Introducing ethics to beginning psychologists: A problem-solving approach. *Professional Psychology: Research and Practice, 18,* 353–359.

Fine, M., & Ulrich, L. (1988). Integrating psychology and philosophy in teaching a graduate course in ethics. *Professional Psychology: Research and Practice, 19,* 542–546.

Handelsman, M. (1986b). Problems with ethics training by "osmosis." *Professional Psychology: Research and Practice, 17,* 371–372.

Kitchener, K. (1984). Intuition, critical evaluation and ethical principles: The foundation for ethical decisions in counseling psychology. *Counseling Psychologist, 12*(3), 43–55.

Kitchener, K. (1986). Teaching applied ethics in counselor education: An integration of psychological processes and philosophical analysis. *Journal of Counseling and Development, 64*(5), 306–310.

McGovern, T. (1988). Teaching the ethical principles of psychology. *Teaching of Psychology, 15*(1), 22–26.

Tymchuk, A. J., Drapkin, R. S., Major-Kingsley, S., Ackerman, A. B., Coffman, E. W., & Baum, M. S. (1982). Ethical decision making and psychologists' attitudes toward training in ethics. *Professional Psychology, 13,* 412–421.

In the article excerpted above, Eberlein (1987) referred to the 1986 version of the decision-making model embedded within the Canadian Psychological Association's ethical code (see chapter 1). The model has been reintroduced in the 1991 version of the code and is worth presenting in its entirety.

Canadian Code of Ethics for Psychologists

Canadian Psychological Association

. . . [P]sychologists will be faced with ethical dilemmas which are difficult to resolve. In these circumstances, psychologists are expected to engage in an ethical decision-making process that is explicit enough to bear public scrutiny. In some cases, resolution may be a matter of personal conscience. However, decisions of personal conscience are also expected to be the result of a decision-making process which is based on a reasonably coherent set of ethical principles and which can bear public scrutiny. If the psychologist can demonstrate that every reasonable effort was made to apply the ethical principles of this Code and that resolution of the conflict has had to depend on the personal conscience of the psychologist, such a psychologist would be deemed to have followed this Code.

THE ETHICAL DECISION-MAKING PROCESS

The ethical decision-making process may occur very rapidly, leading to an easy resolution of an ethical issue. This is particularly true of issues for which clear-cut guidelines or standards exist and for which there is no conflict between principles. On the other hand, some ethical issues (particularly those in which ethical principles conflict) are not easily resolved and might require time-consuming deliberation.

The following basic steps typify approaches to ethical decision making:

1. Identification of ethically relevant issues and practices.
2. Development of alternative courses of action.
3. Analysis of likely short-term, ongoing, and long-term risks and benefits of each course of action on the individual(s)/group(s) involved or likely to be affected (e.g., client, client's family or employees, employing institution, students, research participants, colleagues, the discipline, society, self).
4. Choice of course of action after conscientious application of existing principles, values, and standards.
5. Action, with a commitment to assume responsibility for the consequences of the action.
6. Evaluation of the results of the course of action.
7. Assumption of responsibility for consequences of action, including correction of negative consequences, if any, or re-engaging in the decision-making process if the ethical issue is not resolved.

Psychologists engaged in time-consuming deliberation are encouraged and expected to consult with colleagues and/or advisory bodies when such persons can add knowledge and/or objectivity to the decision-making process. Although the decision for action remains with the individual psychologist, the seeking and consideration of such assistance reflects an ethical approach to ethical decision making.

Introduction to the Special Section: Ethics Education—An Agenda for the '90s

Elizabeth Reynolds Welfel and Karen Strohm Kitchener

. . .

Rest [1983] has postulated a model for understanding the components of moral behavior that is useful in organizing the empirical literature on ethics. By contrast, Kitchener's [1984] work is helpful in tying the ethical issues in training to the work of ethics scholars and in providing an ethical rationale for the statements in the Ethical Principles of Psychologists (APA, 1990). . . .

THE COMPONENTS OF MORAL BEHAVIOR

Rest has defined morality as "standards or guidelines that govern human cooperation—in particular, how rights, duties and benefits are allocated" (1983, p. 558). Morality from this perspective provides guidance for how the individual's welfare and intrinsic value is balanced with the welfare of others in the social system. The question he asks is, "What psychological processes are involved in the production of such behavior?" He concludes that the psychological processes can be divided into four components, each of which involves both cognition and affect. In any given circumstance, the failure to act ethically can be traced to a deficiency in one of these four component processes.

The first component of moral behavior, *interpreting the situation as a moral one*, involves the recognition that one's actions affect the welfare of another. This component is sometimes called *moral sensitivity*. For the psychologist, moral sensitivity means the ability to recognize the ethical dimensions of a situation along with its clinical, scholarly, or pragmatic aspects. For example, when a client without insurance asks whether the psychologist will allow her to provide carpentry services in exchange for psychotherapy, the psychologist recognizes that this request is not just pragmatically difficult or possibly symptomatic of the client's difficulties but is also an ethical problem that can affect the welfare of both the client and others.

The second component involves deciding which course of action is just, right, or fair. It concludes deciding what ought to be done in light of sometimes conflicting moral obligations. It is also called *moral reasoning*. In other words, once the ethical issue is recognized, the psychologist must have the capacity to differentiate ethical from unethical choices. This capacity is informed, of course, by one's knowledge of the current code of ethics, the published literature, the philosophical principles underlying the code, and the individual's level of moral reasoning. Sometimes the code of ethics provides adequate guidance; other times, the dilemma is "at the cutting edge of practice" or one ethical principle seems to conflict with another. In cases of the latter, the capacity of the professional to analyze the moral theory underlying the code and use mature moral reasoning greatly affects the definition of what constitutes an ethical choice.

Deciding what one intends to do is the third component of Rest's model, and it involves choosing whether or not to carry out the ethical action in the face of competing values. Here, the psychologist has recognized that a moral issue exists and has identified a morally defensible action. The psychologist

From *Professional Psychology: Research and Practice, 23,* 179–181. Copyright 1992 by the American Psychological Association. Adapted with permission of the author and publisher.

must now decide whether to go forward with the ethical action in spite of possible costs and in light of competing nonmoral values. For example, a faculty member decides that she will confront a colleague about that person's unethical actions with a student despite the awkwardness inherent in that confrontation and the subsequent unpleasantness that may come from it. The psychologist has weighed the ethical values against values such as smooth relations with colleagues and possible professional gain and has selected the ethical value as the value of greatest importance.

The fourth component of the model is the *implementation of the moral action*, or the ability to execute the ethical action despite the costs to self or external pressures to act differently. In essence, this is the ability to be steadfast in doing what is right through a process that may be tedious and isolating. It involves what we often think of as ego strength. In the above example, the psychologist may be threatened by legal action from the colleague she confronts and viewed by other colleagues as causing trouble and jeopardizing the future of the training program. Only if she is able to weather these harsh penalties and not withdraw from the decision to act ethically will the ethical behavior be maintained.

Rest's theory not only provides a framework that allows the empirical literature on ethics training to be organized, it also provides a model for training itself. In other words, it suggests that if psychologists are to train new professionals to act ethically, the profession must be concerned with students' moral sensitivity, their moral reasoning, their ability to sort the moral from the nonmoral issues, and their ego strength. . . .

KITCHENER: PRINCIPLES UNDERLYING ETHICAL STANDARDS

The second model . . . was based on the work of Beauchamp and Childress (1983, 1989) in biomedical ethics and applied to psychology by Kitchener (1984) and Steere (1984). Kitchener has observed that in real life the ethical issues people face often present extremely difficult choices. Initially, individuals rely on their ordinary moral sense (i.e., a person's moral "intuition") in responding to these is-

sues. In some cases, however, one's ordinary moral sense may be misleading or inadequate. When this happens, professionals turn to codes of ethics as the first level of justification when their moral intuitions leave them without clear choices. In this circumstance, psychologists are obligated to evaluate their ethical choices in light of the Ethical Principles of Psychologists (APA, 1990). Ethics codes have their limits, however. For example, they are often conservative, balancing the protection of the consumer against the protection of the professional from outside regulation. Further, they are time limited. Issues that are on the cutting edge of the profession or that arise after the publication of the code are not discussed. In addition, they cannot address every possible ethical issue a professional may encounter.

On the basis of Beauchamp and Childress (1983, 1989), Kitchener (1984) has suggested that the problem stemming from the limitations of professional codes can be addressed by considering more fundamental ethical principles. These principles provide the ethical foundation for professional codes along with a conceptual vocabulary that allows psychologists to analyze ethical issues when codes are silent or do not give clear advice. In psychology, five ethical principles appear most fundamental: benefit others, do no harm, respect others' autonomy, be just or fair, and be faithful. The following defines each principle.

The principle of benefiting others, of accepting a responsibility to do good, underlies the profession. Psychologists are dedicated to promoting the welfare of others, whether in research, teaching, or practice. In fact, benefiting others is one of the primary reasons psychology exists as a profession. When clients contract for services or students enter graduate programs, they are doing so with the expectation that they will profit from our services or tutelage.

The principle of doing no harm, also called nonmaleficence, includes not perpetrating physical or psychological harm on another or engaging in activities that have a high risk of harming others. This principle is fundamental to any helping profession dedicated to promoting the welfare of others, because by engaging in harmful activities the professional would contradict a core concept of the profession.

Similarly, the principle of respecting autonomy underlies the concept of ethical choice. It encompasses the concept of freedom of thought and freedom of action. In the latter case, individuals are at liberty to act in ways that they freely choose as long as their actions do not interfere with similar actions of others. Both concepts imply a reciprocal relationship with others. In other words, if a person wishes his or her choices to be respected by others, then that person must similarly respect the rights and choices others make, even if they appear mistaken. This principle means that the professional position of psychologists does not give psychologists the right to interfere in others' lives just because those persons' decisions seem wrong. The critical factor is the ability of the individual to think and act rationally and with understanding of the consequences of the action. Acting paternalistically (i.e., in violation of the choice of the individual) is ethically justifiable only under special circumstances. (See Beauchamp & Childress, 1989, or Kitchener, 1984, for a more complete discussion.)

The fourth ethical principle is acting fairly or justly. It refers to the fair treatment of an individual when his or her interests must be balanced against the rights and interests of others. For psychology, justice is fundamental because the profession is concerned with the welfare of others. How could others trust psychologists to act in their best interests if they did not believe we would treat them fairly?

Being faithful to commitments, also called fidelity, is the last ethical principle to be considered here. Fidelity includes promise keeping, trustworthiness, and loyalty. Although Beauchamp and Childress suggest that it is derived from the respect due to autonomous persons, Kitchener (1984) has argued that in the helping professions fidelity is at the core of relationships between the professional and client. By virtue of their role, psychologists carry a special ethical obligation to be faithful to promises and commitments and not to deceive or exploit those with whom they work.

References

American Psychological Association. (1990). Ethical principles of psychologists. *American Psychologist, 45,* 390–395.

Beauchamp, T. L., & Childress, J. F. (1983). (2nd ed.). *Principles of biomedical ethics.* Oxford, England: Oxford University Press.

Beauchamp, T. L., & Childress, J. F. (1989). *Principles of biomedical ethics* (3rd ed.). Oxford, England: Oxford University Press.

Kitchener, K. S. (1984). Intuition, critical evaluation and ethical principles: The foundation for ethical decisions in counseling psychology. *The Counseling Psychologist, 12,* 43–56.

Rest, J. R. (1983). Morality. In J. Flavell & E. Markham (Eds.), *Cognitive development* (Vol. IV). P. Mussen (General Ed.). Manual of child psychology (pp. 520–629). New York: Wiley.

Steere, J. (1984). *Ethics in clinical practice.* Cape Town: Oxford University.

◆ ◆ ◆

Commentary: Consider the following cases:

1. *Under immense pressure to be a success, a first-year graduate student with considerable academic potential cheats on a final paper in a required course. Such conduct could justify expulsion. What should the professor do?*

2. *A psychologist tests a 52-year-old resident of an institution for people with mental retardation and finds that the resident's intellectual deficits are not as severe as was previously thought. The psychologist recommends that the resident be moved to a group home in the community, not only making the woman more independent but relieving crowded conditions on the ward where she is institutionalized. The shift will save the state about $10,000. When the psychologist reveals the plan to the resident, she becomes depressed and argues that the institution is her home and she does not want to leave it.*

3. *A psychologist proposes to compare behavioral and pharmacological approaches to the treatment of bulimia. He wants to use a wait-list control group and a placebo group in addition to the two treatment groups.*

Identify the ethical dilemmas facing the professor, the clinical psychologist, and the researcher in each of these vignettes adapted from Kitchener's (1984) article: See Kitchener, K. S. (1984). Intuition, critical evaluation and ethical principles: The foundation for ethical decisions in counseling psychologists. Counseling Psychologist,

12(3), 43–55. What provisions in the APA Code of Conduct would apply in each vignette? For each situation, specify the relevant philosophical ethical principles from those articulated by Welfel and Kitchener in the previous article and those found in the general principles of the code. Using any of the decision-making models you have read about in this chapter, what action would you ultimately take in each of these cases? In completing this exercise, consider the following, also from Kitchener (1984):

> The point has been made that neither the identification of ethical principles nor accepting them as prima facie valid relieves the psychologist from the burden of decision making in ethical dilemmas. A dilemma, after all, is a situation in which there are good reasons to take different courses of action. However, we must still ask: Are there better ways to decide what to do when ethical principles conflict? This question is a very complex one and one which is open for debate among twentieth century ethicists (Abelson & Nielsen, 1967). . . .

> A second approach is to establish by convention a particular ordering of principles for a set of similar issues. (This ordering may rely on an implicit, but unarticulated theory.) Thus, for example, the APA code of ethics has established that not doing harm should take precedence over fidelity in regard to the issue of confidentiality, and over beneficence in the area of research. This approach is problematic because preestablished conventions cannot always anticipate issues that arise. In addition, just as with trying to establish a single principle as absolute, establishing a single ordering of principles as absolute may sometimes lead to bad ethical decisions. For example, if autonomy was always weighed more heavily than beneficence, it would always be unethical to interfere in someone's life against their will. . . .

> While the problems of applying ethical principles in decision making need to be

acknowledged, this does not keep them from being useful or important. By accepting them as prima facie valid, we imply that their relevance always needs to be considered in ethical situations. Because they are at a more general level than ethical rules, they can be applied across many situations when ethical codes remain silent or conflict. . . .

> In addition, they provide a framework and a set of helpful guidelines to use in critical evaluation of our ethical intuitions. What this implies is that our moral insight may be sharpened and our moral intuitions refined and reformulated after careful consideration of our ethical actions in light of ethical principles. Via this kind of feedback process, we may improve as ethical decision makers.

> . . . The principles proposed by Beauchamp and Childress . . . have three advantages. First, they offer us a common vocabulary and a set of prima facie valid principles that ought to be relevant whether we are thinking about ethical problems in vocational counseling or behavioral research. Beauchamp and Childress have observed: "Only by examining moral principles and determining how they apply to cases and how they conflict can we bring some order and coherence to the discussion of these problems" (1979, p. vii).

> Secondly, the principles provide a more general justification for ethical codes and identify areas which ethical codes may need to address. For example, as has been noted, respect for individual autonomy, not harming clients, truthfulness, and justice are minimally addressed by the current APA code. Furthermore, they may illuminate inconsistencies within the code itself.

> Third, when we move to the level of ethical principles we move beyond believing that we have fulfilled our ethical responsibility if we have not broken a specific rule in our professional code. If, as

Drane (1982) and others have argued, the helping professions are involved in ethical issues at their very core, we need to pay attention to more general ethical principles as we evaluate our own ordinary moral judgments as well as those of our colleagues and our profession.

References

Abelson, R., Nielsen, K. (1967). History of ethics. In P. Edwards (Ed.), *The encyclopedia of philosophy* (Vol. 3). New York: Macmillan.

Drane, J. F. (1982). Ethics and psychotherapy: A philosophical perspective. In M. Rosenbaum (Ed.), *Ethics and values in psychotherapy*. New York: Free Press.

The Relation Between Ethical Codes and Moral Principles

Donald N. Bersoff and Peter M. Koeppl

Each of the prima facie duties . . . has been translated in some form in the code (APA, 1992). The duty of nonmaleficence is exemplified throughout the aspirational General Principles and in the enforceable Ethical Standards. In General Principle E (Concern for Others' Welfare), psychologists are importuned to resolve "conflicts and to perform their roles in a responsible fashion that avoids or minimizes harm" (p. 1600) and, more specifically in Principle B (Integrity), to "avoid improper and potentially harmful dual relationships" (p. 1599). Similarly, psychologists are required in enforceable Provision 1.14 to "take reasonable steps to avoid harming [those] with whom they work, and to minimize harm where it is foreseeable and unavoidable" (p. 1601). The concern that psychologists' personal problems may harm clients and research participants (Provision 1.13), the highly cautionary statements about engaging in multiple relationships of any sort (Provision 1.17), and the absolute ban on sexual relations with current and recently terminated therapy clients (Provisions 4.05 and 4.07) because they "are so frequently harmful" (p. 1605) also exemplify the principle. The significant emphasis on nonmaleficence in the code may be explained by the fact that plaintiffs in malpractice actions must prove that injury has occurred as a foreseeable result of the practitioners' actions before they are awarded damages. Thus, a code that attempts to ensure that, at the very least, psychologists do not harm those they serve helps insulate them from litigation.

Fidelity, requiring that psychologists ally themselves with their clients, respect their needs and fundamental rights, and promote a relationship based on veracity and trust, is perhaps (along with nonmaleficence) the most legally salient moral principle. A duty to act in a fiduciary capacity toward those psychologists assess, treat, and study is one that should find robust expression in a code of ethical conduct. The current code (APA, 1992) does not always live up to this hope. Fidelity is best exemplified by the Preamble, which states that the "primary goal" of the code is "the welfare and protection of the individuals and groups with whom psychologists work" (p. 1599). It is represented, among others, in enforceable Provision 1.19, prohibiting the exploitation of research participants, clients, and supervisees, and in Provision 4.09, absolutely forbidding the abandonment of patients. The most obvious application of the fidelity principle, however, is in the obligation to protect the intimate disclosures we obtain in the course of evaluation, treatment, and research. As was true in the debates concerning the adoption of prior APA ethical principles (Bersoff, 1995; Siegel, 1979), how assiduously psychologists are required to protect confidential communications was a source of controversy in the adoption of the current code.

In the original version of the code presented to the Council of Representatives, the central provision read: "Psychologists take reasonable precautions to respect the confidentiality rights of those with whom they work or consult, recognizing that confidentiality may be established by law, institutional rules, or professional or scientific relationships" ("APA's Ethics Code Draft," 1992). Confidentiality is a bedrock value that undergirds a sense of trust and allegiance that must necessarily exist between psychologists and their patients, clients, and research subjects.

From *Ethics and Behavior, 3,* 345–357. Copyright 1993 by Erlbaum. Adapted with permission of the author and publisher.

When we expect and exhort clients to disclose intimate information, they and the public at large should expect that we will protect those communications by taking more than reasonable precautions. Perhaps the greatest contribution of the late Max Siegel, president of the APA in 1983 and a warmly regarded practitioner and trainer, was his constant and compelling arguments in favor of absolute confidentiality in clinical relationships (Siegel, 1979). It would be naive to argue for absolute prohibition of unconsented disclosures given such real-world intrusions as the opinion in *Tarasoff v. Regents of the University of California* (1976), child abuse reporting statutes, and exceptions to privileged communications laws. However, such intrusions do not call for unnecessary dilution of the ethical value of confidentiality.

In an attempt to strengthen the provision, during the debate in Council on the new Code I moved to amend the proposed principle to state: "Psychologists take the utmost care to respect and protect the confidentiality rights of those with whom they work or consult, and disclose confidential information only when compelled by law." The APA attorney hired to consult on this project asserted that the amendment would create undue burdens on practitioners. But the purpose of a code of ethics is to protect the public, not to protect the professionals that are bound by it. Nevertheless, the amendment failed, although some additional wording was added to the original version. Principle 5.02 now states that "Psychologists have a primary obligation and take reasonable precautions to respect . . . confidentiality rights . . ." (p. 1606). This ambivalent protection of clients' private communications does not seem to be an adequate translation of such a central prima facie duty as fidelity.

In contrast, the new code (APA, 1992) appears to endorse the principle of beneficence openly. Just as the predecessor to the current code required that psychologists use their specialized knowledge for the "promotion of human welfare" (APA, 1990, p. 390), the 1992 version encourages psychologists in the Preamble to "improve the condition of both the individual and society" (APA, 1992, p. 1599) and in Principle E to "contribute to the welfare of those with whom they interact professionally" (p. 1600). The duty to act beneficently is also carried forward

in a number of the more specific, enforceable principles in the code. For example, psychologists are responsible for providing "proper training and supervision" to those they teach and oversee so they will learn to apply their services responsibly and competently (Provision 1.22, p. 1602). They are required to "consider" the "best interests" of those legally incapable of giving informed consent (Provision 4.02, p. 1605) and to terminate any professional relationship when the recipient of psychological services "is not benefiting" (Provision 4.09, p. 1606). Scientists are responsible for conducting "research competently and with due concern for the dignity and welfare of the participants" (Provision 6.07, p. 1608).

The principle of justice has also influenced the development of the new code (APA, 1992). For instance, Principle A (Competence) suggests that the competent psychologist be cognizant of the unique needs of distinct groups of people. More explicitly, Principle D (Respect for People's Rights and Dignity) encourages psychologists to "accord appropriate respect to the fundamental rights, dignity, and worth of all people" (p. 1599). Similarly, in enforceable Provision 1.10, psychologists are forbidden in their work from engaging in "unfair discrimination based on age, gender, race, ethnicity, national origin, religion, sexual orientation, disability, socioeconomic status, or any basis proscribed by law" (p. 1601). If they are not competent to work with these diverse groups, psychologists are required to "obtain the training, experience, consultation, or supervision necessary" (Provision 1.08, p. 1601) to do so. The code also prohibits harassing or demeaning behavior toward minority or underrepresented groups, students, and women (see, e.g., Provisions 1.11, 1.12, and 6.03).

Finally, the moral principle of autonomy is also directly addressed in the aspirational components of the code (APA, 1992). Several references endorse the right of users of psychological services to self-determination and free choice. Principle D reminds psychologists to "respect the rights of individuals to privacy, confidentiality, self-determination, and autonomy . . ." (p. 1599). In Principle E, psychologists are advised to be aware of the "real and ascribed differences in power between themselves and others" (p. 1600) and to avoid abusing this potential imbalance.

Whether this essential respect for the integrity

and sovereignty of clients so powerfully and elegantly translated in the aspirational sections of the code (APA, 1992) is reflected in its Ethical Standards is questionable. Certainly, there are many enforceable provisions in which choice, consent, and self-determination are valued. Provision 1.07, for example, requires psychologists to provide "appropriate information before" (p. 1600) psychologists may assess, treat, teach, or gather research data. This general principle is more explicitly reiterated in provisions ensuring that the public is accorded the rights to be sufficiently informed and to consent before one participates in therapy (Provision 4.02) or as a research subject (Provision 6.11). Although, curiously, the code has no specific provision requiring informed consent before one undergoes a psychological evaluation, the code does ensure that clients have the right to an explanation of the results of such an assessment (see Provision 2.09).

Yet, when it comes to autonomy, the code (APA, 1992) is clearly teleological and utilitarian in its approach, consistently balancing autonomy against other interests. This is particularly true when psychologists view autonomy as antagonistic to their perception of their clients' best interests; when they believe there are higher values, such as the safety of the public, that must be satisfied; or when organizational demands conflict with autonomy. For example, we have already noted that confidentiality is not fully protected in the code. But respect for private disclosures is further compromised by Provision 5.05 permitting psychologists to "disclose confidential information without the consent of the individual" (p. 1606) when psychologists consult with their colleagues, seek to protect the patient or third parties from harm, or wish to secure payment for services. Confidentiality may be limited not only by law but by "institutional rules" (Provision 5.02, p. 1606) as well. Similarly, disclosure of assessment results to test takers may be precluded by organizational concerns, by the needs of employers, and in certain forensic evaluations (Provision 2.09). When

children and those adults who are not legally capable of giving informed consent receive therapy, psychologists are only required to "consider such persons' preferences" (Provision 4.02, p. 1605), not to be bound or even guided by those preferences. Despite the beneficent intent of Provision 4.07, absolutely barring sexual intimacies with former therapy patients for 2 years and after that only if several significant factors are considered, the provision can be perceived as relegating clients to the role of passive victims rather than as autonomous, self-determining consenting adults.

One can see from this exposition of a sample of relevant provisions there are very few moral absolutes in the current code (APA, 1992). Beyond unequivocally forbidding sexual intimacies with current therapy patients or those whose treatment ceased within 2 years of termination and absolutely precluding the abandonment of patients, there are few, if any other, deontological provisions in the code. It is very much a document full of moral compromise, larded with the lawyerly language of "reasonableness" and constantly balanced by the interests of professional and academic psychologies, organizations, institutions, and what are perceived to be the best interests of clients and research participants.

References

American Psychological Association. (1990). Ethical principles of psychologists. *American Psychologist, 45,* 390–395.

American Psychological Association. (1992). Ethical principles of psychologists and code of conduct. *American Psychologist, 47,* 1597–1611.

American Psychological Association's ethics code draft. (1992, May). *APA Monitor,* pp. 38–42.

Bersoff, D. N. (1995). *Ethics conflicts in psychology.* Washington, DC: American Psychological Association.

Siegel, M. (1979). Privacy, ethics, and confidentiality. *Professional Psychology: Research and Practice, 10,* 249–258.

Tarasoff v. Regents of the University of California, 17 Cal.3d 425, 551 P.2d 334 (Cal. 1976).

Ethics and the Professional Practice of Psychologists: The Role of Virtues and Principles

Augustus E. Jordan and Naomi M. Meara

Currently, the teaching and practice of ethics in professional psychology tend to focus on the application of ethical principles to situations involving dilemmas. These dilemmas take a variety of forms, but they typically emphasize the competing rights and claims of clients or institutions and the related responsibilities faced by service providers. . . . However, philosophical and practical limitations to this approach have been identified. We review some of these limitations and identify an additional approach to ethical analysis called virtue ethics. Our analysis of virtue ethics suggests that this approach offers a supplement to the application of ethical principles in dilemmas. . . .

We believe that the difference between this focus on what we call *principle ethics* (i.e., approaches that emphasize the use of rational, objective, universal, and impartial principles in the ethical analysis of dilemmas) and *virtue ethics* (i.e., characterized by an emphasis on historical virtues) is significant and could have implications for the professional development and practice of psychologists. For example, ethical systems that emphasize universally or prima facie valid principles tend to become salient in the presence of dilemmatic situations and tend to claim objective independence from the people involved. In contrast, virtue ethics focus on the historically formed character of identifiable persons; such character development provides the basis for professional judgment. In addition, principle ethics typically focus on acts and choices. Through the application of what are taken to be objective, rational standards, rules, or codes, they attempt to answer the question

"What shall I do?" Virtues, on the other hand, emphasize agents or actors. Through the formation of internal qualities, traits, or mature habits, virtue ethics attempt to answer the question "Who shall I be?"

. . .

THE LIMITATIONS OF ETHICAL PRINCIPLES AND DILEMMAS

The form of ethics currently reigning as the "paradigmatic center of moral reflection" (Hauerwas, 1981, p. 114) in medical, psychological, and religious contexts is that of principle ethics. . . . The prevalent pedagogy of this approach is the evaluation of competing prima facie valid principles in the context of significant quandaries or dilemmas (Beauchamp & Childress, 1983). . . .

All in all, however, the primary content or subject matter of these approaches involves dilemmas cast in the form of brief case histories that typically highlight a significant conflict between the perceived rights, demands, duties, or obligations of several individuals or groups, agencies, or institutions. Such an approach has led some to call this type of ethical discourse *quandary ethics* or *decisionism* (McClendon, 1974; Pincoffs, 1971). The methodology is to sort through the principles involved and then evaluate the actions taken by participants in the case or articulate what actions are appropriate on the basis of relevant but competing principles, or both (Beauchamp & Childress, 1983; Callahan, 1988). . . .

However, others have suggested that principle ethics may be too narrow a characterization of what

From *Professional Psychology: Research and Practice, 21,* 107–114. Copyright 1990 by the American Psychological Association. Adapted with permission of the author and publisher. Table 1 has been omitted.

it means to be engaged in ethical discourse (Dykstra, 1981; Kilpatrick, 1986; Pincoffs, 1971) and thus may be professionally limiting (May, 1984). A narrowing of focus on problem solving in an atmosphere of reasoned deliberation could limit the relevant contextual and methodological resources of the professional psychologist. For instance, Kilpatrick (1986) suggested that "even handed, dispassionate discussion of values . . . may habituate students to the notion that moral questions are merely intellectual problems rather than human problems that naturally call up strong emotion" (p. 189). . . . When this happens, case studies risk becoming primarily abstract thought puzzles to be analyzed according to specified rules. Other critical psychological dimensions, such as human pain, pathos, and historical particularity, tend to be underestimated or forgotten. . . .

. . . By definition, ethical principles seek grounding in a universal context freed from individual bias, and yet the definitive nature of quandaries places principles in direct conflict with each other. . . . To solve this dilemma, appeal must be made to a fundamental moral principle supported by one's moral theory (Steininger et al., 1984). However, different solutions may be achieved, depending on whether one is a utilitarian who emphasizes the public good or a deontologist who advocates a duty to "above all, do no harm" (Jonsen, 1977). Even within a given theoretical orientation, there may exist disagreement regarding the relative weight of competing principles. As Drane (1982) reported, "There is no evident way to determine which principles should take precedence over which others. In such painful dilemmas the psychotherapist simply does the best he (or she) can" (p. 37). The empirical result is that universal principles, as well as their overarching theories, come to be applied idiosyncratically. . . .

. . . As professional psychologists migrate with increasing frequency into large industrial and health maintenance organizations, the likelihood of conflicting principles increases. Professionals, the clients whom they serve, and the service organizations that they create risk becoming hostage to the reasoned, principle based, but potentially controversial choices of these organizations (Eyde & Quaintance, 1988; May, 1984).

VIRTUES AND THE HISTORY OF MORAL DISCOURSE

. . .

In contrast to principles, virtues historically have been viewed neither as situation specific nor as universal maxims but rather as character and community specific. Thus they are nurtured habits grown mature in the context of a formative community and a shared set of purpose and assumptions. This process begins in the community of one's childhood and continues throughout life. Professional training and practice introduce new contexts and communities wherein professional virtues can be articulated and nurtured by students and professionals. People socialize one another into a professional culture that they continually construct and shape and from which they seek inspiration and support. As time passes, certain shared assumptions and values are "taken for granted" and form the character of the profession and are part of the individual characters of the professionals. . . .

EMPLOYING VIRTUE ETHICS IN PSYCHOLOGY

. . . Two examples of how specific virtues influence professional practice are offered in this section. The first concerns the use of informed consent in a counseling relationship; the second involves the role of professional virtues in conceptualizing therapeutically relevant constructs such as "genuineness." Although explicitly psychotherapeutic in content, these examples are intended to offer a starting point for more general discussions of potentially relevant virtues for professional psychologists.

Informed Consent

A client's right to informed consent has received increasing attention (Berger, 1982; Burstein, 1987). Respect for the principles of autonomy and beneficence has encouraged therapists to design explicit contracts in response to the rights of clients (Everstine et al., 1980). . . .

There is, however, another layer of ethical concern that is typically overlooked in the midst of such quandaries: Whereas most attention has focused on what information a therapist ought to tell a client, or what information rightly belongs to a client, there is yet a more subtle but equally important ethical issue that concerns *how* the client will be told (May, 1984). As therapists know, how the truth is spoken in therapy is as morally relevant as what truth is spoken.

For example, Everstine et al. (1980) fully illustrated what information ought to be included in an informed consent procedure, but they did not adequately consider the ethical dimension associated with *how* such information is presented. In an effort to address legal and ethical concerns over informed consent, they developed a therapist–client contract that identified clients' legal rights. Issues were explored in depth and clearly delineated. Client autonomy was respected. However, Everstine et al. did not call into question how to present these matters to clients. As they put it, "The form taken by these consent procedures is irrelevant by contrast with the procedure itself. What is important is that specific ground rules be decided upon in advance and endorsed with a signature before the hard work of therapy begins" (p. 832). Such a legalistic procedure, however, may not be in the client's best interests, nor does it adequately reflect the mutual trust and respect or therapist's integrity that are essential for productive therapy. Specifically, at face value, the rights, the contract, and the consent forms provided by Everstine et al. subtly suggest that therapy is first and perhaps foremost a legal transaction of commodities or services. Modern therapy often includes such a transaction, but it is not clear that therapy is best understood, first and foremost, within the limits of such categories. What is more, the forms imply that the client is a passive recipient of these services, for which the client will be billed. Indeed, the client's rights and the therapist's responsibilities are listed in great detail, but little is said of the client's responsibilities, the mutuality of the therapy process, or what "set" such a document provides for the client.

Clearly, Everstine et al. (1980) developed these forms in an environment that presses escalating legal responsibilities on therapists. The prevailing question was, and continues to be, What are therapists legally required to do in order to protect client rights and their own legal culpability? Everstine et al. addressed these issues, and virtue ethics does not deny the importance of the question. But in virtue ethics, such concerns would be seen as an outgrowth of a professional's concern for the integrity of the process and practice of psychotherapy itself and an abiding respect for clients who engage in it. Such concern adds another, equally valid question: Who are therapists required to be in order to competently and credibly inform clients about their rights and responsibilities, as well as concerning the nature and tradition of the practice of psychotherapy? The virtues of prudence and discretion and of fidelity to a particular client with whom the therapist is in a particular relationship are ethically relevant to informed consent. It may be that standardized, legal contracts are necessary and can be presented articulately and sensitively (i.e., professionally) to a depressed client without the need of a lawyer to interpret the contract's legal implications. But this is precisely the point: How professionals present such information is morally relevant without being necessarily rule dependent. The character of the professional is as ethically decisive as the content of the contract.

Genuineness

. . . Rogers (1959; Meador & Rogers, 1984) considered genuineness to be essential to the development of a therapeutic relationship. But apart from a person, how does one define genuineness? For example, to what extent does the therapist reveal personal values, perspectives, and problems to a client or clients (Brammer & Shostrom, 1977)? Such questions have both therapeutic and ethical dimensions that are difficult to differentiate. The therapeutic dimensions usually involve a clinical and empirical evaluation of the effectiveness or curative value of genuineness and related constructs proposed by Rogerians, such as transparency, congruence, realness, and authenticity (Truax & Carkhuff, 1964). Similarly, ethical considerations are typically utilitarian. Genuineness is appropriate insofar as it advances the therapeutic interest of the client and does not violate other relevant ethical principles. The exact parameters and nuances of genuineness that are most effective, however, are difficult to isolate and require continued study.

From the perspective of virtue ethics, genuineness might be approached and defined in a different way. In addition to, and perhaps before, questions concerning the curative value of genuineness in the therapeutic encounter is this question: Is genuineness an essential attribute of being a professional in a therapeutic relationship? Many would argue that genuineness, as articulated by Rogers (1959), is not essential, that it is a technique or approach and not a quality. Some might further argue that as such it can be therapeutically counterproductive. But beyond such theoretical arguments is a fundamental question: Is there a sense in which one expects professionals *to be*, for example, genuine, trustworthy, or competent in a way that is not completely dependent on therapeutic consequences? These questions place our deliberations regarding effectiveness in a wider context that includes astute considerations of what is meant by *professionalism*.

From this second perspective, the virtue-oriented dimensions of genuineness become salient. Genuineness is a complex concept based on a quality of truthfulness. Genuineness includes both a principle-oriented guide to proper action (e.g., tell the truth) and a virtue-oriented characteristic of professionals (e.g., integrity or trustworthiness). But these two admonitions (i.e., "tell the truth" and "be trustworthy") are not necessarily or logically interdependent. . . . [T]he maintenance of trust sometimes demands of trustworthy therapists a certain measured deliberateness with respect to the truth that they speak. "Measured deliberateness" is not a code for subtle and deceptive manipulations but rather is a reference to three additional virtues: discretion, prudence, and humility. Not speaking or speaking with care and discretion can be just as critical to maintaining integrity and trustworthiness of the therapist as speaking out. . . .

Thus the "genuine" therapist is involved in an intricate interaction that balances honesty and subtle therapeutic manipulation. How the therapist manages this interaction is an ethical, as well as a therapeutic, issue. . . . Rather, ethics from a virtue perspective serves to remind us that professional psychology is a discipline with pervasive moral, as well as scientific, dimensions. These moral dimensions are intimately tied to the character of the professional.

BEYOND PRINCIPLE TO CHARACTER

Last, a focus on virtues, in addition to principles, may offer a tentative response to the problem of individual inconsistencies in the use of ethical principles. Specifically, on what criteria do therapists rely when choosing among rationally justifiable alternatives in a dilemma? . . . .

In such situations, the client and the community rely not simply on a therapist's rational, cognitive processing of universal or prima facie valid principles, nor simply on his or her specific technical skills or legal expertise. Principles, technical skills, and legal knowledge are necessary in evaluating a course of action but are not logically sufficient or necessarily primary. What is demanded of professionals is a dimension of character appropriately understood by way of the virtues. Professionals use words such as *maturity, professional judgment, discretion, wisdom,* or *prudence,* which depend for their exercise not so much on rational, objective principles as on a quality of character identified by the virtues. A serious consideration in psychological training and practice of what constitutes virtuous character will not eliminate professional disagreement about what is proper or ethical, but it could result in the development of professionals who are better prepared to make such judgments. Such professionals might more easily identify their bias, more carefully guard against imposing their values on clients, and be more vigilant in separating personal and cultural preferences from the psychological and therapeutic phenomena. . . .

References

Beauchamp, T. L., & Childress, J. F. (1983). *Principles of biomedical ethics.* New York: Oxford University Press.

Berger, M. (1982). Ethics and the therapeutic relationship: Patient rights and therapist responsibilities. In M. Rosenbaum (Ed.), *Ethics and values in psychotherapy* (pp. 67–95). London: Free Press.

Brammer, L., & Shostrom, E. (1977). *Therapeutic psychology: Fundamentals of counseling and psychotherapy.* Englewood Cliffs, NJ: Prentice-Hall.

Burstein, A. G. (1987). The virtue machine. *American Psychologist, 42,* 199–202.

Callahan, J. C. (1988). *Ethical issues in professional life.* New York: Oxford University Press.

Drane, J. (1982). Ethics and psychotherapy: A philosophical perspective. In M. Rosenbaum (Ed.), *Ethics and values in psychotherapy: A guidebook* (pp. 15–50). New York: Free Press.

Dykstra, C. (1981). *Vision and character: A Christian educator's alternative to Kohlberg.* New York: Paulist Press.

Everstine, L., Everstine, D. S., Heymann, G. M., True, R. M., Johnson, H. G., & Seiden, R. H. (1980). Privacy and confidentiality in psychotherapy. *American Psychologist, 35,* 828–840.

Eyde, L. D., & Quaintance, M. K. (1988). Ethical issues and cases in the practice of personnel psychology. *Professional Psychology: Research and Practice, 19,* 148–154.

Hauerwas, S. (1981). *A community of character.* Notre Dame, IN: University of Notre Dame Press.

Jonsen, A. (1977). Do no harm: Axiom of medical ethics. In S. Spicker & T. Engelhardt, Jr. (Eds.), *Philosophical medical ethics: Its nature and significance* (pp. 27–41). Dordrecht, The Netherlands: Reidel.

Kilpatrick, W. K. (1986). Moral character, story-telling and virtue. In R. Knowles & G. McLean (Eds.), *Psychological foundations of moral education and character development* (pp. 183–199). New York: University Press of America.

May, W. F. (1984). The virtues in a professional setting. *Soundings, 67,* 245–266.

McClendon, J. W. (1974). *Biography as theology: How life stories can remake today's theology.* Nashville, TN: Abingdon.

Meador, B., & Rogers, C. (1984). Person-centered therapy. In R. Corsini (Ed.), *Current psychotherapies* (pp. 142–195). Itasca, IL: Peacock Publishers.

Pincoffs, E. (1971). Quandary ethics. *Mind, 80,* 552–571.

Rogers, C. (1959). Client-centered therapy. In S. Arieti (Ed.), *American handbook of psychiatry* (Vol. 3, pp. 183–200). New York: Basic Books.

Steininger, M., Newell, J., & Garcia, L. (1984). *Ethical issues in psychology.* Homewood, IL: Dorsey.

Truax, C., & Carkhuff, R. (1984). The old and the new: Theory and research in counseling and psychotherapy. *Personnel and Guidance Journal, 42,* 860–866.

◆ ◆ ◆

Commentary: *More recently, Meara and her colleagues provided an exegesis on the concept of virtue ethics in a special issue of* The Counseling Psychologist *that is well worth studying. They summarized their views, in relevant part:*

> We have argued that a more complete understanding of professional ethics included, in addition to principle ethics, a cognitive grasp of virtue ethics, and that better ethical practice can be achieved through efforts to develop virtues commensurate with one's professional mission. . . . We have . . . tried to provide a rationale for how integrating principles and virtues can assist professionals in making difficult decisions, setting policies (e.g., revising or interpreting ethics codes), and developing the ethical character of themselves and their professions. We discussed the particular relevance of virtue ethics in enhancing professional competences and sensitivity as well as public trust of professions in a pluralistic, multicultural society. (p. 69)

Meara, N. M., Schmidt, L. D., & Day, J. D. (1996). *Principles and virtues: A foundation for ethical decisions, policies, and character.* The Counseling Psychologist, 24, 4–77.

The Virtue of Principle Ethics

Donald N. Bersoff

. . .

From empirical and practical perspectives, an argument concerning the relative importance of virtue ethics and principle ethics . . . is inconsequential. The complaints brought before and adjudicated by the American Psychological Association's (APA) Ethics Committee almost exclusively involve behavior that the criminal law would call *malum in se*, that is, conduct that is inherently wrong (Dressler, 1987). Among the primary reasons psychologists are sanctioned by the APA Ethics Committee are because they make false or misleading public statements, engage in sexual intimacies with their clients, or defraud insurance companies (APA Ethics Committee, 1994). In that light, psychology need not go through the endless debate, huge expense, and vast expenditure of time involved in developing, implementing, and enforcing a code of ethics, as it has done every decade in the past half century. It could simply borrow the all-encompassing honor code commandment found at our military academies: Thou shalt not lie, cheat, or steal. Debates about ethics codes or the relative merits of virtue and principle ethics are only relevant at the very outer margins of professional or scholarly conduct.

. . .

Principle ethics encompass five prima facie duties—nonmaleficence, fidelity, beneficence, justice, and autonomy (Beauchamp & Childress, 1994; Bersoff & Koeppl, 1993; Ross, 1930). Like the components of virtue ethics, these prima facie duties provide an array of moral choices and can be applied flexibly in relation to the context of a dilemma. There does not seem to be a great deal of difference between these moral principles and the "four virtues," i.e., prudence, integrity, respectfulness, and benevolence, as Meara et al. (1996) define them. Only prudence, which is more categorizable as a means for arriving at an ethical outcome, is sufficiently different from prima facie duties to merit recognition as a separable concept. Integrity is highly similar to fidelity and justice; benevolence is closely congruent to beneficence; and respectfulness is little different from autonomy.

Although Meara et al. deride the resolution of ethical dilemmas as "abstract thought puzzles," judgment, choice, and the resolution of conflict are some of the inevitable, obligatory, and probably unwelcome tasks confronting human beings (Bersoff & Koeppl, 1993; Hogarth, 1987). The most virtuous, principled, and law-abiding psychologists will be faced with difficult dilemmas throughout their careers for which there are no "cookbooks" prescribing a set of expected behaviors or universally acceptable solutions.

Consider the following facts, for example (adapted from Bersoff, 1995). A tenth grader is enrolled in research studying violence in adolescents and how it might be prevented through short-term intervention. During an interview as part of the study, the student reveals that he has had many fantasies about harming his slightly older female next-door neighbor who refuses to pay him any attention. Upon further inquiry, the psychologist learns that he is contemplating buying a gun but that he has no history of violence. The researcher suggests that she inform his parents of the situation. The young man adamantly refuses to let the researcher do so and warns that he will drop out of the study and treatment if she does not honor his refusal.

On what basis could the psychologist resolve this problem? Recent critics agree that the current APA ethics code (1992) would be an informative but uncertain guide (e.g., Bersoff, 1994; Lakin, 1994; Vasquez, 1994). Under the code, the psychologist has significant discretion to disclose the threat (see the following Principles—5.01, Discussing Limits of Confidentiality; 5.02, Maintaining Confidentiality; 5.05, Disclosures; 6.11, Informed Consent to Research), but the code offers no definitive answers.

Would reliance on virtue ethics be more helpful? We can agree that being motivated to do good, possessing vision and discernment, allowing affect to enter into the process of decision making, understanding oneself, and being connected to the moral sense of the community (the characteristics of virtuous agents) are all laudable characteristics of any psychologist. Further, we would hope that the psychologists will act with prudence, integrity, respectfulness, and benevolence. It is difficult for me, however, to see how these virtues will resolve the dilemma. . . .

For example, under the APA ethics code, it would be perfectly ethical for the researcher to disclose the young man's confidences and even to refuse to abide by his demand for secrecy. In fact, it might be prudent (a virtue) for her to do so, particularly because that decision would show respect for predominant community values (a quality of a virtuous agent). Additionally, she could decide that beneficence (a central component of virtue and principle ethics) requires her to protect her research participant from engaging in behavior that will lead him to harming, if not killing another, and subject him to criminal penalties. Conversely, she could decide to promote the self-determination and sense of accountability of her subject while reinforcing her obligation to remain faithful to his expressed interests without harming innocent victims. . . . Thus she could conclude that disclosure would conflict with what she considers to be the more overriding moral principles of autonomy, fidelity, and nonmaleficence, prima facie obligations that are also an inherent part of her value system. In any event, the psychologist must judge the risks and benefits of her value choices and decide which prima facie duties should take precedence in this case. By adopting some over others and by deciding what she should do, she is also deciding who she should be.

CHARACTER AND COMMUNITY

If virtues "are traits of character," and if "[v]irtue ethics calls upon individuals to aspire toward ideals and develop . . . traits of character that enable them to achieve these ideals" (Meara et al., 1996), two problems arise. First, I question whether virtue ethics is teachable. Character traits, although potentially malleable, are developed as a result of genetic endowment and life experiences. It is doubtful whether a course in ethics or even 4 years of professional training in which students are sensitized to ethics will produce a virtuous agent able to employ virtuous ideals. Intensive therapy over many years fails to accomplish this goal. Second, if acting ethically depends on character, I wonder if the outcomes will be too individualized and idiosyncratic. An ethical code and ethical conduct, I would assert, relies on consensual decision making about the integrity of the profession, not the singular vagaries of a psychologist's character.

More problematic for me, however, is the heavy reliance on communitarian values. Meara et al. unabashedly assert that "[v]irtue ethics is rooted in community and relies on a community's wisdom and its moral sense." To their credit, they recognize concomitantly that reliance on community can create ethnocentric, even immoral decisions, but they characterize much of virtue ethics as community based. I see the dangers of a communitarian view as outweighing its benefits. It would be difficult for me to subscribe to a system that led me to act in ways that denied women responsible choices in deciding whether to bear children, that treated those denominated as mentally disabled as incompetent to become involved in decisions regarding their own treatment, that refused to permit the works of Ellison, Salinger, Shakespeare, and Blume in the classrooms of our high schools, that advocated religion in our public institutions, or that perceived single mothers on welfare as the cause of society's violence. These are precisely the views that many communities in the United States hold and act on today.

Meara et al. criticize principles ethics in large part because it holds autonomy and self-determinism in high esteem, because it does not place primacy on religious traditions, and because it depends so highly on rationality. But I value these virtues of principle ethics (Bersoff, 1992) precisely because I want to act with prudence, respect, integrity, and benevolence. If being virtuous means acting paternalistically, irrationally, and on the basis of faith, I prefer principled iniquity.

References

American Psychological Association Ethics Committee. (1994). Report of the Ethics Committee, 1993. *American Psychologist, 49*, 659–666.

Beauchamp, T. L., & Childress, J. F. (1994). *Principles of biomedical ethics* (3rd ed.). New York: Oxford University Press.

Bersoff, D. N. (1992). Autonomy for vulnerable populations: The Supreme Court's reckless disregard for self-determination and social science. *Villanova Law Review, 37*, 1569–1605.

Bersoff, D. N. (1994). Explicit ambiguity: The 1992 ethics code as an oxymoron. *Professional Psychology: Research and Practice, 25*, 382–387.

Bersoff, D. N. (1995). *Ethical conflicts in psychology*. Washington, DC: American Psychological Association.

Bersoff, D. N., & Koeppl, P. M. (1993). The relation between ethical codes and moral principles. *Ethics & Behavior, 3*(3/4), 345–357.

Dressler, J. (1987). *Understanding criminal law*. New York: Matthew Bender.

Hogarth, R. (1987). *Judgment and choice: The psychology of decision* (2nd ed.). New York: Wiley.

Lakin, M. (1994). Morality in group and family therapies: Multiperson therapies and the 1992 ethics code. *Professional Psychology: Research and Practice, 25*, 344–348.

Meara, N. M., Schmidt, L. D., & Day, J. D. (1996). Principles and virtues: A foundation for ethical decisions, policies, and character. *The Counseling Psychologist, 24*, 4–77.

Ross, W. D. (1930). *The right and the good*. Oxford, England: Clarendon.

Vasquez, M. (1994). Implications of the 1992 ethics code for the practice of individual psychotherapy. *Professional Psychology: Research and Practice, 25*, 321–328.

◆ ◆ ◆

Commentary: For other contrasting views see these analyses, in order of their appearance:

Miller, D. J. (1991). The necessity of principles in virtue ethics. Professional Psychology: Research and Practice, *22, 107.*

Jordan, A. E., & Meara, N. M. (1991). The role of virtues and principles in moral collapse: A response to Miller. Professional Psychology: Research and Practice, *22, 107–109.*

CHAPTER 4

CONFIDENTIALITY, PRIVILEGE, AND PRIVACY

Except for the ultimate precept—above all, do no harm—there is probably no ethical value in psychology that is more inculcated than confidentiality. Whether psychologists are engaging in research; assessing children, families, employees, criminal defendants, or others; or providing any of the several forms of psychological intervention—regardless of whether they are employed in private or public settings—they know that they bear responsibility for protecting information disclosed to them in the context of a professional relationship. Yet, there is probably no ethical duty more misunderstood or honored by its breach rather than by its fulfillment.

There is ample evidence that protecting intimate disclosures by patients, clients, and even research subjects is valued in society. Even though the word *privacy* does not appear in the U.S. Constitution, the Supreme Court has recognized it as a fundamental right. In part, the right of privacy means that federal and state governmental agencies are barred from unreasonable gathering, storage, and dissemination of their citizens' private information. Many states have passed even more particularized statutes that regulate the disclosure of psychological information. Some of these laws call for civil or even criminal penalties if psychologists or other professionals breach confidentiality without the informed consent of those they assess, treat, or study. Other states—but not all—have enacted statutes, called privileged communications laws, that permit a client to bar his or her psychologist from testifying about certain matters in legal proceedings. And, of course, medicine and every mental health profession embed in their codes of ethics provisions for protecting confidential communications.

But, to the same degree that this litany of protections evidences the heightened importance of confidentiality and privacy in society, like the ozone layer of the atmosphere, there has been a gradual but constant erosion of these fundamental values. When clients seek reimbursement for psychotherapy from their insurers, they are almost compelled to waive their right to bar dissemination to the reimbursing agency of vital and personal information, such as their diagnosis, prognosis, and aspects of their history. Although privileged communications laws sound protective, they most often contain exceptions permitting psychologists to report child abuse, to testify in civil commitment hearings, and to sue for collection of debts. Thus, when read in their entirety, many privilege laws contain more holes than fabric.

To those who view confidentiality as a preeminent value, the most noteworthy and troubling example of its dilution was the decision made by the California Supreme Court in *Tarasoff v. Regents of the University of California* (1976). This was perhaps the most well-known and notorious case in mental health law, and so, in this chapter, I provide extensive material written about the *Tarasoff* case and its ramifications.

Briefly, California's highest court held that psychotherapists have certain obligations to nonpatient third parties whom they may not know and have never seen when their patients disclose believable and serious threats to harm those third parties. In possibly the most quoted line from *Tarasoff*, the court stated: "The protective privilege ends where the public peril begins" (*Tarasoff v. Regents*, 1976, p. 347). Although poetically alliterative, this mandate had stark and even frightening implications. It clearly put mental health professionals on notice that society did not hold confidentiality in as high esteem as do most psychologists. Speaking through its legal system, society told psychologists—including, as you will see, researchers—as well as mental health professionals in general that fidelity to one's client must recede when it is necessary to protect third parties from harm.

There should be many questions rustling around in the reader's mind about the long- and short-term effects of *Tarasoff*. What are the consequences, for example, of establishing a role for psychologists as protectors of private third parties external to therapy? How does this affect the client–clinician relationship? What additional obligations to the client does *Tarasoff* suggest? If clients are told that not everything they say in therapy is confidential, will they be less honest and trusting? What if the client is not threatening to harm another person by force but by infecting a lover with AIDS? If confidentiality is such a core value to the psychological profession and to those it serves, then why does the rest of society seem to hold that value in lesser esteem than psychologists? Is the protection of intimate disclosures to a therapist more important to the therapist than it is to the client? Is, in fact, the profession making too much of confidentiality as an ethical value? And at this point in my litany, the risk-averse reader should be asking how a conscientious therapist (and researcher) can handle the complex treatment, ethical, and legal problems that arise when faced with a dangerous client.

The material in this chapter raises these questions, debates the issues, and, perhaps, even provides some answers. It also has some didactic goals that should not be ignored, such as understanding the distinctions among privacy, privilege, and confidentiality and gaining an appreciation of the confidentiality provisions in the APA code of ethics. But clearly there are more important lessons to be learned. Perhaps more than any other topic, confidentiality provides a springboard for contemplating the consequences for psychologists torn between their duty and ethical obligations to clients and their responsibilities to the larger society in which they live. A consideration of these dual roles is the overarching purpose of this chapter.

Reference

Tarasoff v. Regents of the University of California, 551 P.2d 334 (Cal. 1976).

Privacy, Confidentiality, and Privilege in Psychotherapeutic Relationships

Michele Smith-Bell and William J. Winslade

. . .

PRIVACY

Concept of Privacy

The concept of privacy embraces the idea of limiting the access of others in certain respects (Gavison, 1980), such as limiting the access of others to one's body or mind, including information about the self contained in dreams, fantasies, thoughts, and beliefs. Privacy in the law is sometimes linked to freedom from intrusion by the state or third persons; it also designates a domain of personal associations, abortion, and bodily integrity. Privacy is important because it preserves and protects individuals as they exercise their freedom to develop their personal identity, choose their values, and shape the course of their lives.

Some legal commentators argue for a constitutional right to privacy, seeing personal information as an integral part of an individual's identity and as crucial to most theories of personhood . . .

Constitutional Right to Privacy

The Supreme Court first recognized a constitutional right to privacy in the case of *Griswold v. Connecticut* (1965), which struck down a Connecticut statute prohibiting use of contraceptives by married couples. The right to privacy was expanded in the case of *Eisenstadt v. Baird* (1972), in which the Supreme Court reversed the defendant's conviction for distributing contraceptives to unmarried persons. In *Roe v.*

Wade (1973), the Court held that criminal abortion laws, which proscribed abortion except for the purpose of saving the life of the mother, are unconstitutional. However, the *Roe* Court limited the right to privacy by stating that "only personal rights that can be deemed 'fundamental' or 'implicit in the concept of ordered liberty' . . . are included in this guarantee of personal privacy."

The constitutional right to privacy was restricted in the subsequent case of *Whalen v. Roe* (1976), in which the Court ruled that a patient does not have a constitutional right to informational privacy of communications or records generated in the course of medical treatment when the records are adequately protected from unauthorized disclosure. A more recent Supreme Court case further limits the constitutional right to privacy. In *Bowers v. Hardwick* (1985), the Court upheld a Georgia state antisodomy statute, and rejected the assertion that the right to privacy includes the fundamental right of homosexuals to engage in sodomy. Few federal appellate courts or state courts have recognized a constitutional right to privacy for the psychotherapeutic relationship . . .

In California (In re Lifschutz, 1970), a psychotherapist claimed that he had a privacy interest in psychotherapeutic communications with his patients; the court held that only the patient has a constitutionally protected privacy interest in preventing the release of psychotherapeutic communications. In another case (*Caesar v. Mountanos*, 1976), a psychotherapist refused to answer questions about one of his patients even after the patient specifically waived the psychotherapeutic privilege. The court held that the nature of communications between a patient and his therapist brings the relationship within the constitutional right of privacy through the psychotherapist–patient privilege. But on appeal, the court held that the right to privacy may be limited when necessary to advance a compelling state interest, such as ascertaining truth in court proceedings; moreover, it was held to be the patient's right to waive or assert the privilege.

The case of *Hawaii Psychiatric Society v. Ariyoshi* (1979) supported a constitutional right to privacy. A federal district court enjoined the State of Hawaii from enforcing a statute that permitted the issuance of administrative inspection warrants to review the mental health records of Medicaid patients. The court held that an individual's decision to seek the aid of a psychiatrist, or to communicate certain personal information to that psychiatrist, fell squarely within the constitutional right to privacy. The court balanced the patient's privacy interest against the state's interest in protecting the Medicaid program from fraud; it found that the state failed to show that the issuance of warrants to inspect the confidential medical records of a psychiatrist was necessary to advance a compelling state interest (Smith, 1980).

. . .

CONFIDENTIALITY

Distinction From Privacy

Privacy and confidentiality are essential features of the psychotherapeutic relationship, despite the limited recognition of the right to privacy in constitutional law. Both are linked to the general notion of limited access and the exclusion of others; sometimes these concepts are used loosely and interchangeably. For example, privacy and confidentiality both stand as polar opposites to what is public and open to everyone. Nevertheless, it is useful to distinguish these concepts in the context of the psychotherapeutic relationship.

When a person enters into a therapeutic relationship, the client relinquishes his or her personal privacy of thoughts, feelings, beliefs, etc., in exchange

for the prospect of therapeutic understanding and assistance. In this respect privacy is an aspect of *individuals*. Once private information has been disclosed to a therapist with an expectation that such information will not ordinarily be disclosed to third parties, it becomes confidential, and one refers to the confidentiality of information in the relationship. Thus, giving a therapist access to private information is necessary by definition for establishing a confidential relationship; and confidentiality is essential. . . .

In some instances, no third parties have access to private information disclosed in confidence to the therapist or even know that the relationship exists at all. Some clients, for example, choose to pay cash for therapy rather than to file an insurance claim (Domb, 1990–1991, citing Sosfin, 1985). Some therapists organize their offices to protect client privacy by the use of separate entrances and exits and of answering machines rather than answering services. The classic image of the exclusive dyadic relationship of the therapist–client, though increasingly rare, is not extinct.

Obstacles to Preservation

Individual and, increasingly, group therapeutic practice often occurs in a larger context of therapist, client, and an array of third parties including family members, employers, insurers, courts, and government agencies. Therapists' general obligation to protect clients' confidential information is overridden by specific obligations to disclose information at the client's request, when the law requires it, or when ethics demands it. For example, a client in a commitment, competency, sanity, or custody proceeding might desire that a therapist testify about disclosures made in therapy. The law might also require disclosures in such contexts even if the client does not consent to them. Legally mandated reporting requirements, such as those concerning child or elder abuse, override confidentiality. Ethics may dictate disclosures in the absence of specific legal authority. Conflicts arise, for example, concerning therapists' obligation to protect third parties threatened by dangerous patients.

The therapeutic consequences of external pressures on the preservation of confidentiality are that therapists may become wary of seeking sensitive information and clients of disclosing it. Even if therapists do not explicitly notify clients of the limits of confidentiality, the style of conducting therapeutic inquiry is influenced by the encroaching shadow of third-party access to information. If therapists inform clients of the limits of confidentiality, clients may then be inhibited in their communication and thereby hamper therapeutic effectiveness. The challenge to policymakers is to balance the need for confidentiality essential to the therapeutic process with the need for access to otherwise confidential information when necessary to protect legitimate public interests.

Patient expectations. Most therapists should be familiar, even if not happy, with the numerous restrictions placed on the right to confidentiality, but studies indicate that patients have greater expectations of privacy and confidentiality (Weiss, 1982). In a 1986 study, a majority of student psychotherapy patients and nonpatients believed that all communications to psychotherapists are confidential; almost all patients wanted to be informed of exceptions to confidentiality; and most reported that they would react negatively to unauthorized breaches of confidentiality that would undermine their right to privacy (VandeCreek, Miars, & Herzog, 1987). . . .

Therapists should, of course, protect confidentiality to the extent permitted by law and required by ethical standards. But in view of clients' sometimes unrealistic expectations about the scope of confidentiality, it is important to clarify its limits at the outset of therapy or at least early on. Therapeutic relationships are often tentative and fragile until a client trusts a therapist. Trust is threatened, if not undermined, if a client feels misled by the therapist, and such a client may withhold information or not cooperate in the therapy in overt or subtle ways—by cancelling sessions, coming late, failing to pay, etc. Misunderstandings about confidentiality may even irrevocably rupture a therapeutic relationship. Thus, it is important for therapists to know and disclose what clients can reasonably expect concerning confidentiality. Its precise boundaries may be difficult to mark out in advance, but at least the general issues should be addressed.

When therapists are confronted with a specific conflict between a client's interest in confidentiality and a third party's claim to access, it is almost always appropriate to explore the conflict with the client first. This advances the therapeutic process because it demonstrates respect for both the client and the integrity of the therapeutic relationship. Clients may choose to authorize disclosure even if not legally required to do so. When a client does not want to permit disclosure, therapists have a duty to seek protection of confidentiality to the extent that the law and ethics allow. In specific situations, therapists may find it helpful to consult ethics committees of their professional organizations, ethics consultants or attorneys, or experienced colleagues who are familiar with confidentiality rules and practices. Demands to disclose confidential information are sometimes excessive; it may be possible for the client or the therapist to negotiate a limited disclosure that satisfies both the client and the third party. In other situations a client may have waived or forfeited the right to confidentiality by, for instance, signing a waiver or revealing private information to a third party; the therapist may then have no choice but to disclose otherwise confidential information. The damage to the therapeutic relationship can be minimized, however, if the client has been adequately informed and educated by the therapist early in the relationship.

PRIVILEGE

Concept of Privilege

The concept of privilege should be distinguished from that of confidentiality. Privilege is an exception to the general rule that the public has a right to relevant evidence in a court proceeding; confidentiality refers more broadly to legal rules and ethical standards that protect an individual from the unauthorized disclosure of information. Confidentiality alone is not enough to support a privilege; without a privilege statute or a common-law rule, a therapist may be charged with contempt of court for refusing a court order to testify about a patient's psychotherapeutic communications. Thus, confidentiality is a professional duty to refrain from speaking about certain matters, while privilege is a relief from the duty to speak in a court proceeding about certain matters (Domb, 1990–1991, citing In re Lifschutz, 1970). . . .

Patient Rights

The patient's right to privacy and confidentiality is partially protected by the doctrine of privileged communications. Confidential information that would otherwise be admissible in a judicial proceeding may be withheld if it is classified as a privileged communication. Privilege thus protects patients' privacy and confidentiality and, in doing so, renders them more disposed to seek mental health services. Privilege generally belongs to the patient, who decides whether it will be exercised or waived. Although the holder of the privilege is the patient, in appropriate circumstances the therapist may invoke the privilege on behalf of the patient, unless that privilege has been waived or the communication in question falls within a statutory exception to the privilege (Brakel, Parry, & Weiner, 1985, citing In re Lifschutz, 1970).

To be considered privileged, communications from a patient to a therapist must meet a number of requirements. First, the communications must be to a licensed or certified therapist as described in the state's privilege statute, or to an assistant of the therapist, depending upon state law. Second, a professional relationship must exist between the patient and the therapist. Third, the communications must be related to the provision of professional services. Fourth, the communications must be confidential; they may not be released by the client to a third party (Smith, 1980).

. . .

Criticism of Privilege

. . .

Privilege laws and the general obligation of confidentiality have become increasingly subject to exceptions and limitations, effectively reduced by inconsistent federal and state rules, and threatened by changes in health-care financing. . . . In addition, privilege statutes afford only limited protection to confidentiality because of the narrowness of their application; in the litigation setting, they are often only applicable to psychiatrists and psychologists,

thereby decreasing their scope and effectiveness (Brakel, Parry, & Weiner, 1985). The scope of psychotherapeutic privilege is also reduced when it is waived, sometimes unwisely, by patients.

Waiver

Patients waive the privilege for psychotherapeutic communications when they file a tort or Workers' Compensation claim for a psychiatric injury, or when litigants otherwise put their mental states at issue. Unlike exception, in which normally privileged information is not privileged in certain situations prescribed by law (as when a defendant to a criminal charge raises his mental state as a defense), waiver requires action or acquiescence from the patient. . . .

References

Bowers v. Hardwick, 478 U.S. 186. (1985).

Brakel, S. J., Parry, J., & Weiner, B. A. (1985). *The mentally disabled and the law* (3rd ed.). Chicago: American Bar Foundation.

Caesar v. Mountanos, 542 F.2d 1064 (9th Cir. 1976), *cert. denied*, 430 U.S. 954. (1977).

Domb, B. (1990–1991). I shot the sheriff, but only my analyst knows: Shrinking the psychotherapist–patient privilege. *Journal of Law and Health, 5*, 209–236.

Eisenstadt v. Baird, 405 U.S. 438. (1972).

Gavison, R. (1980). Privacy and the limits of the law. *Yale Law Journal, 89*, 421–472.

Griswold v. Connecticut, 381 U.S. 479. (1965).

Hawaii Psychiatric Society v. Ariyoshi, 481 F. Supp. 1028. (D. Hawaii, 1979).

In re Lifschutz, 2 Cal. 3d 415, 467 P.2d 557, 85 Cal. Rptr. 829. (1970).

Roe v. Wade, 410 U.S. 113. (1973).

Smith, S. R. (1980). Constitutional privacy in psychotherapy. *George Washington Law Review, 49*, 1–60.

Sosfin, E. S. (1985). The case for a federal psychotherapist–patient privilege that protects patient identity. *Duke Law Journal*, 1217–1244.

VandeCreek, L., Miars, R. D., & Herzog, C. E. (1987). Client anticipations and preferences for confidentiality of records. *Journal of Counseling Psychology, 34*, 62–67.

Weiss, B. D. (1982). Confidentiality expectations of patients, physicians, and medical students. *Journal of the American Medical Association, 247*, 2695–2697.

Whalen v. Roe, 429 U.S. 589. (1976).

◆ ◆ ◆

Commentary: *Max Siegel, President of the APA in 1983, subscribed to the "absolute position that psychologists may not break confidentiality of a patient or client under any circumstances" (p. 269). See Siegel, M. (1979). Privacy, ethics, and confidentiality. Professional Psychology, 10, 249–258. The APA has never adopted that view in its ethical codes.*

Confidentiality is now covered in 11 separate provisions of Section 5 of the 1992 Ethical Principles of Psychologists and Code of Conduct. Standards 5.02 and 5.05 are the major provisions. As in the adoption of the 1981 code, considerable debate took place about the language of the 1992 confidentiality provisions. For example, one member of the Council of Representatives moved that Standard 5.02 should read: "Psychologists take the utmost care to respect and protect the confidentiality rights of those with whom they work or consult, and disclose confidential information only when compelled by law." The motion was defeated by a large margin in favor of this statement: "Psychologists have a primary obligation and take reasonable precautions to respect the confidentiality rights of those with whom they work or consult, recognizing that confidentiality may be established by law, institutional rules, or professional and scientific relationships."

As you read the material that follows, it may be useful to compare Siegel's (1979) view with prevailing sentiments and to ask this: In what ways does the current provision disserve the ethical ideals of self-determination, the independence to decide matters about one's own private interests, and the right to privacy generally, reflected in aspirational Principle D of the 1992 Ethical Principles?

I begin with a general overview and critique of the confidentiality provisions of the 1992 code.

Implications of the 1992 Code for the Practice of Individual Psychotherapy

Melba Vasquez

. . .

All standards listed under Standard 5, Privacy and Confidentiality, described as "potentially applicable to the professional and scientific activities of all psychologists" (APA, 1992, p. 1606), are especially relevant to the practice of individual psychotherapy. . . .

DISCUSSING THE LIMITS OF CONFIDENTIALITY

Standard 5.01 (a), Discussing the Limits of Confidentiality, requires that psychologists discuss the relevant limitations on confidentiality as well as the foreseeable uses of the information generated through their services. . . . Although the standard does not list those limitations on patient confidentiality, with some variations from state to state, those might include but not be limited to: if the patient or client is a danger to self or others; if the patient or client waives rights to privilege or gives consent to disclosure; if the client or patient is ordered for evaluation or treatment by the court; if the patient or client is a minor, and the psychologist reasonably suspects child abuse; if the client or patient is elderly or disabled and the psychologist believes the client or patient is a victim of physical abuse; if the client or patient files suit against the psychologist for breach of a duty; or if the client is involved in court action and either the client releases records or the records are subpoenaed by court order (Texas Psychological Association, 1993b). Essentially, psychologists are required to notify clients that what they tell psychologists may be used against them, in certain circumstances.

Some therapists fear that discussions of limits of confidentiality influence clients' willingness to self-disclose. . . . [Nevertheless], clients have a right to know about limits of confidentiality. Psychologists may wish to continue to work with their state legislatures to limit situations in which confidentiality must be broken. In the meantime, offering a detailed description of the circumstances under which confidentiality can be broken seems to be psychologists' best course of action at the onset of therapy, as a matter of consumer rights for their clients as well as protection for themselves.

Standard 5.01 (b) suggests that the discussion of confidentiality occur at the outset of the relationship, unless this is not feasible or it is contraindicated, and thereafter as new circumstances may warrant. We assume that the authors refer to the situation in which a client begins therapy in crisis, when it would be contraindicated to use time to discuss limitations of confidentiality, and when crisis intervention is the primary need. In addition, the standard allows additional discussion of the limits of confidentiality as such circumstances arise.

> Case example: A client enters therapy to deal with various unresolved issues, including child sexual abuse, which she has never disclosed to anyone. Several months after the therapy begins, she also wishes to address sexual orientation

From *Professional Psychology: Research and Practice, 25,* 321–328. Copyright 1994 by the American Psychological Association. Adapted with permission of the author and publisher.

issues. The client is married, has two children, and realizes that the unhappiness in her marriage stems largely from her feeling that she is not living her true sexual orientation. At this point, despite the fact that the psychologist has routinely described limits of confidentiality, the psychologist informs the client that divorce proceedings regarding child custody might require the psychologist's notes, testimony, or both, and that her sexual orientation issues would therefore not be kept confidential. The psychologist further suggests that the client consult with a local family attorney to determine the community standards and risks regarding child custody issues and sexual orientation in the local judicial system. The psychologist also provides the client and her attorney with resources regarding the research on parenting rights of lesbian parents. The attorney recommends that the client not discuss any issues around sexual orientation with the therapist; it would indeed be a risk to child custody if that information were to be disclosed.

Although it is frustrating and limiting to the process of therapy, the client must know the risks of disclosure of certain kinds of information. If a client or patient enters therapy to deal with divorce, the psychologist must inform the client that in any court proceeding, the therapist's notes may be required by the court. Standard 5.01 (b) allows for discussion of some limits of confidentiality later in the therapy process for those clients who initially do not indicate that unique risks may arise. It is difficult to anticipate all circumstances of limits of confidentiality and to determine how much to discuss verbally or share in writing at the outset of psychotherapy. Therefore, when a particularly relevant issue regarding potential limits of confidentiality surfaces in therapy, it is crucial to discuss and reiterate the limits of confidentiality. . . .

MAINTAINING CONFIDENTIALITY

Standard 5.02, Maintaining Confidentiality, describes the fundamental responsibility of psychologists to respect the confidentiality rights of all those with whom they work and explains that confidentiality may be established by law, institutional rules, and so on. . . .

MINIMIZING INTRUSIONS ON PRIVACY

Standard 5.03, Minimizing Intrusions on Privacy, includes the proscription, in Standard 5.03 (a), to include only information germane to the purpose for which the communication is made in written and oral reports, consultations, and the like. This standard speaks to various situations, including the reporting of requested information to personnel who review the use of managed care and determine continuation of services for clients. Other challenging situations may arise as well.

> Case example: A psychologist receives a written and signed release for all notes and records of a client whom she has not seen for over 3 years. The request comes from a professional information gathering group hired by the attorney of the client. The client is apparently involved in some litigation with a major company. The psychologist attempts to locate the client, who has left town, but cannot determine the city or even the state in which the client currently resides. The client's attorney refuses to provide the location of the client or the reason and nature of the need for the notes and simply reiterates the need for all records. When the therapist expresses hesitation, the information gathering company says they will obtain a subpoena for the records. After consulting with colleagues and her own attorney, the psychologist reluctantly releases the records and a summary of the psychotherapy.

Should the therapist have waited to be subpoenaed to release the information? Is the psychologist at risk in releasing vulnerable information without knowing how the information is to be used? Typically, psychologists are able to discuss the nature of releases of information that clients sign, including a discussion of how the information is to be used. Consulting with knowledgeable colleagues and an attorney knowledgeable of one's state's mental health laws can help determine the best interests of the client as well as of the psychologist. Often summaries of psychotherapy, which focus on information relevant to the situation, suffice for most requests for information. However, in litigation, the client's attorney often wishes to know the full extent of the information in the files, which may include very vulnerable and intimate details. It is particularly challenging to protect intrusions on client privacy in those situations, and this speaks to careful and respectful notekeeping.

Standard 5.03 (b) requires that psychologists discuss confidential information of clients (and others with whom we work) only for appropriate purposes and only with persons clearly concerned with such matters. Despite legal allowances for exchange of information among professionals within agencies, for example, this ethical standard requires a stricter maintenance of confidentiality of client information.

MAINTENANCE OF RECORDS

Standard 5.04, Maintenance of Records, . . . not only requires confidentiality in the storage and disposal of records, but also requires that

> psychologists maintain appropriate confidentiality in creating, storing, accessing, transferring, and disposing of records under their control, whether these are written, automated, or in any other medium. Psychologists maintain and dispose of records in accordance with law and in a manner that permits compliance with the requirements of this Ethics code. (APA, 1992, p. 1606)

What this standard does not address is the length of time that records should be kept. Psychologists must refer to requirements in their respective states; in the absence of state mandates, psychologists are advised to adhere to the APA's (1981) *Specialty Guidelines for the Delivery of Services.* The aspirational *Specialty Guidelines* vary for each discipline. . . . Although requirements for maintenance of records vary from state to state, and aspirational guidelines vary from discipline to discipline, it would be helpful to have some guidance from the current code. A revision of the current code could include recommended time maintenance considered in the best interest of the client.

DISCLOSURES

Standard 5.05, Disclosures, addresses situations in which psychologists are required or permitted to disclose client information. Standard 5.05 (a) suggests that

> psychologists disclose confidential information without the consent of the individual only as mandated by law, or where permitted by law for a valid purpose, such as (1) to provide needed professional services to the patient or the individual or organizational client, (2) to obtain appropriate professional consultations, (3) to protect the patient or client or others from harm, or (4) to obtain payment for services, in which instance disclosure is limited to the minimum that is necessary to achieve the purpose. (APA, 1992, p. 1606)

Some of these exceptions to confidentiality are alarmingly vague and seem designed to protect the psychologist more than the client or patient. It is unclear, for example, what situations are included as a valid purpose in providing "needed professional services to the patient" (APA, 1992, p. 1606). Do they mean sharing information with the staff of an inpatient psychiatric hospital in case of an emergency such as an overdose? In that situation, it seems reasonable to disclose confidential information without client consent. What other disclosures does law permit? Until now, unless the client were of danger to self or others, a release was required to obtain professional consultations, or the client's identity was to be disguised. Standard 5.05 (a) (2) seems to waive that requirement. Release of information has been required to obtain payment for services from third-party payers. Informed consent, obtained at the onset of therapy, was required with regard to the use of collection agencies. Does Standard 5.05 (a) (4) release psychologists from these practices? This standard seems to allow for great leeway in psychologists' judgment. If so, it is recommended that a revision of the current code return to the requirement of releases of information for those practices. Such requirements are more respectful and protective of clients. Some clients prefer to pay for therapy themselves rather than have their diagnosis given to an administrative representative of their insurance company; or they may at least wish to know, in the case of managed care coverage, that utilization review representatives may hear a summary of their therapy and status.

Standard 5.05 (b) permits psychologists to disclose confidential information with the appropriate consent of the patient or client, unless prohibited by law. Appropriate consent assumes that the client will be informed of the nature and potential implications of the consent. I would note that often clients are not fully aware of those implications, and the psychologist should provide such information. The psychologist should document that consent either through a form signed by the client or in a progress note. A related issue is that psychologists may disclose information but may choose not to, even with the client's consent, if the psychologist deems that it is not in the best interest of the client to do so. . . .

CONSULTATIONS

Standard 5.06, regarding consultations, is a new standard that provides direction in maintenance of confidentiality when consulting with colleagues. The first part suggests that

> psychologists do not share confidential information that reasonably could lead to the identification of a patient, client, research participant, or other person or organization with whom they have a confidential relationship unless they have obtained the prior consent of the person or organization or the disclo-

sure cannot be avoided. (APA, 1992, p. 1606)

The qualifier, "unless . . . the disclosure cannot be avoided," is another vague loophole that puts the client unnecessarily at risk and seems designed to protect the psychologist. If the authors meant to say in case of danger to client or others or unless allowed or mandated by law, then that is what should be specified.

The second part of this standard suggests that psychologists "share information only to the extent necessary to achieve the purposes of the consultation" (APA, 1992, p. 1606). . . .

CONFIDENTIAL INFORMATION IN DATABASES

Standard 5.07, Confidential Information in Databases, consists of three parts. Standard 5.07 (a) requires that psychologists use coding or other techniques to avoid the inclusion of personal identifiers of clients when information is entered into databases of systems of records. Those databases can often be accessed by others for whom consent has not been obtained. Standard 5.07 (b) and 5.07 (c) refer to maintaining confidentiality on research protocols, which is addressed . . . [in chapter 8].

Standard 5.08 . . . consists of two sections. The first requires that psychologists do not disclose in their writings, lectures, or other public media, confidential or personally identifiable information concerning their patients, individual or organizational clients, students, research participants, or other recipients of their services that they obtained during the course of their work, unless consent has been obtained in writing, or unless there is other ethical or legal authorization for doing so. It is not quite clear what other ethical or legal authorization to do so might be. It is reasonable to assume that the authors of the code considered other ways in which clients may provide authorization; however, I asked five colleagues for an interpretation, and none were able to suggest any.

The second part of this standard, Standard 5.08 (b), mandates that psychologists ordinarily disguise confidential information so that they are not individually identifiable to others and so that discussions "do not cause harm to subjects who might identify themselves" (APA, 1992, p. 1607). This is an important point because, even if a client provides consent, it behooves the psychologist to protect the privacy of the client as much as possible, as well as to be sensitive to the potential for harm in public discussions of that client.

PRESERVING RECORDS AND DATA

Standard 5.09, Preserving Records and Data, is a new standard and requires that psychologists make plans in advance so that confidentiality of records and data is protected in the event of the psychologist's death, incapacity, or withdrawal from the position or practice. . . . This requirement may be a straightforward one if a psychologist has a partner or shares an office with someone who would reasonably be contacted if one were searching for one's records. However, it is challenging for the psychologist in solo practice to plan how to notify clients about who holds the records after one's death, incapacity, or withdrawal from the position or practice. Some suggest that the psychologist plan for a public announcement of the name of the psychologist who will be holding client records in the local newspaper. Other ethical and lawful strategies will likely be developed during the next few years.

OWNERSHIP OF RECORDS AND DATA

Standard 5.10, Ownership of Records and Data, suggests that, because ownership of records and data is governed by legal principles, psychologists take reasonable and lawful steps to assure that records and data remain available to the extent needed to serve the best interests of patients and others. This principle speaks to ensuring that records and data are kept in appropriate ways to allow for availability to help others. Note keeping is clearly required for psychotherapy, in whatever manner or form allows for the best interest of clients.

WITHHOLDING RECORDS
FOR NONPAYMENT

The last principle under Privacy and Confidentiality, Standard 5.11, Withholding Records for Nonpay-

ment, directs that psychologists may not withhold records that are requested and imminently needed for a patient's treatment solely because payment has not been received, except as otherwise provided by law. This standard allows psychologists to hold the records for lack of payment if the records are not "imminently needed" (APA, 1992, p. 1607); it appears that records could be withheld unless the patient's care would be clearly compromised if records were not provided promptly. This is another unfortunate judgment call. This has traditionally been referred to as "holding records hostage." Are we now allowing that? Most psychologists would likely assume that imminent cases involve those in which the client has had psychotic episodes and/or is of danger to himself or herself or others. Cases that might not be considered imminent include records that would provide clinical impressions, test data, and previous progress in therapy. However, this standard permits enough vagueness so that what is not imminently needed by one psychologist may be so by another. Future revisions of the current code might consider returning to the higher standard of providing records that are requested and keeping this separate from the financial issue; that is, that record withholding not be allowed as a strategy for collection of payment. . . .

Standard 5.05 (a), which deals with disclosures, seems to deter from the general focus on consumer welfare. . . . Typically, our code has established a higher standard of conduct than is required or allowed by law. . . . The vagueness in some of the principles, the overuse of the term *reasonable*, which potentially dilutes the power and enforceability of some of the principles, and some instances in which it is possible that the psychologist's welfare is placed above that of the client, are problematic. In general, however, the current code provides more thoughtful and specific directions for psychologists in the provision of ethical and competent services for clients, as well as self-protection for the psychologist.

References

American Psychological Association (1981). *Specialty guidelines for the delivery of services by clinical psychologists, counseling psychologists, industrial organizational psychologists, and school psychologists.* Washington, DC: Author.

American Psychological Association (1992). Ethical principles of psychologists and code of conduct. *American*

Psychologist, 47, 1597–1611.

Texas Psychological Association (1993b, June). Sample form: Client information on office practice and policy. *The Texas Psychologist, 45,* 11.

Privacy and Confidentiality in Psychotherapy

Louis Everstine, Diana Sullivan Everstine, Gary M. Heymann,
Reiko Homma True, David H. Frey, Harold G. Johnson, and Richard H. Seiden

. . .

OVERVIEW

. . .[T]he issue is not whether guilt properly falls upon a particular therapist who breaches or declines to breach confidentiality; instead, the issue is one of defining the line between proper and improper conduct. Here in truth is a "doctor's dilemma," created by the tension between two powerful forces that radiate from opposite poles: (a) the client, a private citizen who wishes that the right to privacy be respected and (b) society, which wants to be informed about certain acts or intentions on the part of individual citizens. In choosing a path between these adversaries, a therapist can be excused for seeking the intercession of a guiding star. . . .

DUTY TO WARN

Confusion remains about the case of *Tarasoff v. Board of Regents of the University of California*, confusion that was not dispelled by a final decision handed down by the California Supreme Court in July 1976. Many do not know full details of the events that occurred in 1969 in Berkeley which led to the case being brought. . . .

On August 20, 1969, . . . Prosenjit Poddar, who was a voluntary outpatient at Cowell Memorial Hospital [footnote omitted] on the Berkeley campus informed his therapist, a psychologist, that he was planning to kill a young woman. Poddar did not name the woman, but as established later, the psychologist could easily have inferred who she was

[footnote omitted]. The murder was to be carried out when the woman returned to Berkeley from her summer vacation.

Following this session, the psychologist telephoned the campus police to ask them to observe Poddar for possible hospitalization as a person who was "dangerous to himself or others"; he then wrote a letter, containing a formal request for assistance, to the chief of the campus police. The campus officers took Poddar into custody for the purpose of questioning, but later released him when he gave evidence of being "rational." Soon afterward the psychologist's supervisor, Director of the Department of Psychiatry at Cowell Hospital, asked the campus police to return the psychologist's letter, ordered that the letter and therapy notes that had been made in Poddar's case be destroyed, and directed that no further action be taken to hospitalize Poddar. No warning was given either to the intended victim or to her parents. The client, naturally enough, did not resume his therapy.

On October 27, 1969, Prosenjit Poddar killed Tatiana Tarasoff. The victim's parents filed suit against the Board of Regents of the university, several employees of Cowell Hospital, and the chief of the campus police plus four of his officers. A lower court dismissed the suit, the parents appealed, and the California Supreme Court upheld the appeal in 1974 and reaffirmed its decision in 1976. In July 1977, the suit was settled out of court and the Tarasoff family received a substantial award. Without public scrutiny, a bizarre tragedy had been adjudicated in camera, and a far-reaching and intensely value-laden controversy had been stifled by the fiat of legal precedent.

A crucial point of the Supreme Court decision was this: It was not the failure of the psychologist or his supervisor to predict violence that made the case a viable one (the psychologist had clearly decided that his client was dangerous), but the failure of the psychologist and his supervisor to provide an adequate warning of violence either to the intended victim or to her parents.

In a brief amicus curiae filed by CSPA and other professional organizations acting in concert (see Gurevitz, 1977), it was argued that (a) a therapist cannot predict violence with certainty and (b) warning the intended victim would have breached the confidentiality of the therapist–client relationship, thus jeopardizing both the climate of trust that is necessary for therapy to occur and the effectiveness of therapy itself. The Court ignored the first argument because the therapist *had* accurately predicted that a violent act would be committed. The second argument was flatly rejected by the majority[.] . . . And to the contention that the essential nature of psychotherapy is altered by the stated exception to privilege, the Court responded with the view that a therapy relationship, whether effective or not, is of secondary importance to the preservation of life and safety. In its conclusion, the Court affirmed a guiding principle that had weighed heavily in its decision: "The public policy favoring protection of the confidential character of patient–psychotherapist communications must yield to the extent to which disclosure is essential to avert danger to others. The protective privilege ends where the public peril begins" (p. 24) [footnote omitted]. That was the cornerstone of the decision. No psychologist can be immune to the force of this conclusion, and each must ponder its implications.

What is the major impact of *Tarasoff*? In essence, the Court has chosen to make a narrow interpretation of therapist–client privilege, believing that the privilege should be sharply restricted. In deliberating the concept of privilege, the Court took a dim view of the notion that psychotherapy must occur in an atmosphere of secrecy (the canon of sanctum sanctorum). In reaction, Siegel (1976) and others have concluded that by making these value judgments,

the Court has struck yet another blow against individual freedom of conscience and has come down hard on the side of conformity. Still others are willing to accept that the "duty to warn" is, at least for the present time and indefinite future, a legal requirement.

Although a therapist, a person is still a citizen, and he or she must protect and contribute to the common good. As a private citizen, the person of good conscience will not hesitate to warn an intended victim. That, as far as can be determined, is the meaning of *Tarasoff*.

EROSION OF THE PROFESSIONAL TRUST RELATIONSHIP

A hallmark of psychotherapy is the establishment of a relationship of trust between client and therapist, and this relationship must be carefully protected through the course of the therapeutic experience. Yet a gradual and continuous weakening has occurred in the confidentiality privilege, one legal mechanism by which this professional trust relationship is implemented in our social system. . . . [I]t is urgent that we make every effort to reestablish and strengthen the sociolegal nature of the trust relationship that is so central to our professional work. . . .

There is a psychotherapist–client privilege. In California law, *psychotherapist* is defined as a clinical psychologist, a school psychologist, a clinical social worker, or a psychiatrist. This privilege is controlled by the client, is not independently held by the psychotherapist, and *must* be breached by the psychotherapist under six legal conditions: (a) when criminal action is involved; (b) when the information is made an issue in a court action; (c) when the information is obtained for the purpose of rendering an expert's report to a lawyer; (d) when the psychotherapist is acting in a court-appointed capacity; (e) when the psychotherapist believes that the client is a danger to himself, herself, or others and feels that it is necessary to prevent an actual threat of danger from being carried out; and (f) when a client is under the age of 16 and the therapist believes that the client has been the victim of a crime (e.g., incest, rape) and judges such disclosure to be in the client's best interest. . . .

163

CONCLUSIONS AND RECOMMENDATIONS

. . . [W]e have observed a mysterious trend toward legislation that would seriously impair our efforts to strengthen confidentiality. This trend is embodied by the ever more stringent regulations that are being imposed to require the swift and aggressive reporting of an ever widening array of suspected crimes against the person. . . .

. . . We can with confidence put forward the following *prophesies*: (a) More laws will be passed and more court decisions handed down that will mandate respect for privacy and preservation of confidentiality; (b) more laws will be passed and more court decisions handed down which will require that confidentiality be breached and privacy invaded. . . .

References

Gurevitz, H. *Tarasoff*: Protective privilege versus public peril. *American Journal of Psychiatry*, 1977, *134*, 289–292.

Siegel, M. Confidentiality. *Clinical Psychologist* (Newsletter of Division 12 of the American Psychological Association), Fall 1976, pp. 1; 23.

Tarasoff v. Board of Regents of the University of California, Cal. Rptr. 14, No. S.F. 23042 (Cal. Sup. Ct., July 1, 1976) 131.

Commentary: *No judicial decision has had more of an impact on professional psychologists (and, in some respects, on researchers as well) than Tarasoff v. Regents of the University of California (1976). The basic facts of the case are described in the excerpt above by Everstine et al. There were actually two decisions rendered by California's Supreme Court: one in 1974 (Tarasoff I) and another in 1976 (Tarasoff II). The defendants, including Dr. Moore (the psychologist who treated Poddar), Dr. Powelson (the psychiatrist who ran the university hospital clinic where Poddar was in outpatient treatment), and the Regents of the University of California (their employer), asserted that Tatiana Tarasoff's parents had no legal claim against them for the death of their daughter because she was not their patient, but a private third party to whom they owed no professional duty. Nevertheless, a majority of the state supreme court held that the parents could sue the defendants for failure to warn Ms. Tarasoff or others of Poddar's threat. The following statement by the court sent psychological shock waves across the psychotherapy landscape—far beyond the borders of California:*

> *We shall explain that defendant therapists, merely because Tatiana herself was not their patient, cannot escape liability for failing to exercise due care to warn the endangered Tatiana or those who reasonably could have been expected to notify her of her peril. When a doctor or a psychotherapist, in the exercise of his professional skill and knowledge, determines, or should determine, that a warning is essential to avert danger arising from the medical or psychological condition of his patient, he incurs a legal obligation to give that warning. Primarily, the relationship between defendant therapists and Poddar as their patient imposes the described duty to warn.*

See Tarasoff v. Regents of the University of California, 529 P. 2d 553 (Cal. 1974) (Tarasoff I).

Tarasoff I stimulated a plethora of critical analysis. See, for example, Slovenko, R. (1975). Psychotherapy and confidentiality. Cleveland State Law Review, 24, 375–396; Stone, A. (1976). Suing psychotherapists to safeguard society. Harvard Law Review, 90, 358–378. The following article addressed the ethical implications of the decision.

Therapists as Protectors and Policemen: New Roles as a Result of *Tarasoff*?

Donald N. Bersoff

The emphasis on the clinician's duty to disclose threats to potential victims has obscured the concomitant duty of clinicians to disclose to clients the limits of confidentiality. Thus, *Tarasoff* (1974) has relevance in terms of the informed consent doctrine, an emerging rule of law developed in the context of physician–patient malpractice suits. . . . The philosophical underpinning to the informed consent doctrine is that everyone has the right to self-determination and, more specifically, the right to determine what happens to his or her body. As a result, the patient is entitled to all the facts necessary to make an informed, intelligent choice prior to consenting to medical intervention.

Typically, however, the duty to disclose is not absolute. It is tempered by what may be called the materiality rule. Physicians need not disclose risks that are likely to be known to the average patient or are in fact known to the particular patient as a result of past experience. Rather, the extent of disclosure is determined by the materiality of the risk. As defined in a leading case,

> Materiality may be said to be the significance a reasonable person, in what the physician knows or should know is his patient's position, would attach to the disclosed risk or risks in deciding whether to submit or not to submit to surgery or treatment. (*Wilkinson v. Vesey*, 1972, p. 689)

Some of the information falling within the materiality rule and thus necessitating disclosure are inherent and potential hazards of the proposed treatment, alternatives to that treatment, and the results likely if the patient remains untreated.

With this background, the implications of *Tarasoff* with regard to informed consent become self-evident. The possibility that therapists may be under a duty to make known to both the intended victim and police authorities threats to third persons made by their clients would clearly seem to be a material piece of information requiring disclosure to prospective clients. That such information is material to an individual client is manifest in the consequences of disclosure. Certainly, liberty and privacy interests are at stake (Fleming & Maximov, 1974). Communication of violent threats outside the therapeutic relationship may lead to involuntary incarceration because the standard for emergency commitment in most states is "danger to self or others." Knowledge by the putatively potential victim may lead to abrupt disruption of the relationship between client and third party in instances where such disruption would not, in fact, be warranted. The disclosure clearly violates the confidential association between client and clinician. . . .

It is thus evident that clinicians must now reveal to potential clients the limits of confidentiality. To blithely ensure the secrecy of all communications is to engage in blatant misrepresentation of facts that should now be known to all therapists. To fail to disclose these limits is to hold oneself open to liability under the materiality test. In fact, the failure to disclose the limits of confidentiality in the face of a concomitant duty to disclose threats to third parties

From *Professional Psychology*, 7, 267–273. Copyright 1976 by the American Psychological Association. Adapted with permission of the author and publisher.

may be to entrap the client. Clients, believing that the therapeutic relationship is inviolate, may lay bare heretofore unrevealed secrets, including their most violent urges. Therapists, fearful that their clients' verbal expression of aggression may become manifest in overt behavior, aware of the *Tarasoff* decision, and frightened of the threat to their economic security and professional reputation, may too quickly and frequently inform police officials about the possibility of danger to society. The result will be an increase in involuntary civil commitment of therapy clients who would otherwise have not been incarcerated. . . .

THE DUTY OF DISCLOSURE TO THIRD PERSONS

Tarasoff, important in itself for the implications it has with regard to informed consent, is also important in a larger context. Decisions such as *Tarasoff* make it increasingly clear that therapists not only serve their clients but are also agents of the society in which they work. Psychotherapists have long struggled with the problem of conflicting loyalties to their clients and to society. The traditional cant is that the relationship between client and clinician is an especially private one in which confidentiality is entitled to the utmost respect. The primary allegiance the budding practitioner is told, is to the client. Recently, writers such as [Bersoff (in press)] Halleck (1971), Kittrie (1971), Szasz (1963), and Torrey (1974) have surfaced the many ways in which mental health professionals serve the state and the public, often to the detriment of the individual client. . . .

[W]hile the psychologist in *Tarasoff* was employed by a state agency, the effect of the decision is not limited to those practitioners who work in the government-funded institutions. The therapist in *Tarasoff* was held liable, in part, for breach of a state statute concerning privileged communication that governs the behavior of private, as well as institutional, practitioners. Private therapists who might seek refuge in professional codes of ethics as coun-

terweights in a struggle to protect their clients' confidences will fail to find them safe havens. In fact, the *Tarasoff* court quoted Section 9 of the Principles of Medical Ethics of the American Medical Association to further justify its decision. Section 9 reminds physicians that they may not reveal confidences "unless . . . required to do so by law or unless it becomes necessary in order to protect the welfare of the individual or of the community."[1]

. . . As psychiatrists and psychologists become more identified with the law and its enforcement, there is the danger of discouraging people from seeking psychotherapy and of trusting those whom society has taught are the most trustworthy of professionals (excluding clergypersons, perhaps). Therapists may find themselves in insolvable conflicts as they attempt to reconcile their own personal morality and training regarding confidentiality, the vague reminders of their professional codes of ethics that warn of the consequences of violating the moral and legal standards of the community, and the developing legal requirements that demand complex decision making and a balancing between client and public interests. In any event, it is evident that there are ever decreasing guarantees to client–clinician privacy and that the therapeutic relationship is not immune from the scrutiny of society. Such limits must clearly be conveyed to the prospective client because failure to do so can result in both loss of liberty and privacy to the client as well as loss to the clinician of reputation and money damages to unwarned victims.

References

Bersoff, D. N. Coercion and reciprocity in psychotherapy. In C. T. Fischer & S. Brodsky (Eds.), *The Prometheus principle: Informed participation by clients in human services.* New Brunswick: Transaction, in press.

Fleming, J. G., & Maximov, B. The patient or his victim: The therapist's dilemma. *California Law Review*, 1974, *62*, 1025–1068.

Halleck, S. L. *The politics of therapy.* New York: Science House, 1971.

Kittrie, N. N. *The right to be different.* Baltimore, Md.: Johns Hopkins University Press, 1971.

---

[1] *Ed. note:* See also Standards 5.01 and 5.05 of the APA current (1992) Ethical Principles.

Szasz, T. S. *Law, liberty, and psychiatry.* New York: Macmillan, 1963.

Tarasoff v. Regents of University of California, 13 C.3d 177, 529 P.2d 553, 118 Cal. Rptr. 129 (1974).

Torrey, E. F. *The death of psychiatry.* Radnor, Pa.: Chilton, 1974.

Wilkinson v. Vesey, 110 R.I. 606, 295 A.2d 676 (1972).

Commentary: *In a rare move, the California Supreme Court agreed to hear new arguments and reconsidered its opinion in* Tarasoff II.

Tarasoff v. Regents of the University of California (*Tarasoff II*)

. . .We shall explain that defendant therapists cannot escape liability merely because Tatiana herself was not their patient. When a therapist determines, or pursuant to the standards of his profession should determine, that his patient presents a serious danger of violence to another, he incurs an obligation to use reasonable care to protect the intended victim against such danger. The discharge of this duty may require the therapist to take one or more of various steps, depending upon the nature of the case. Thus it may call for him to warn the intended victim or others likely to apprise the victim of the danger, to notify the police, or to take whatever other steps are reasonably necessary under the circumstances. . . .

. . . [W]hen the avoidance of foreseeable harm requires a defendant to control the conduct of another person, or to warn of such conduct, the common law has traditionally imposed liability only if the defendant bears some special relationship to the dangerous person or to the potential victim. Since the relationship between a therapist and his patient satisfies this requirement, we need not here decide whether foreseeability alone is sufficient to create a duty to exercise reasonable care to protect a potential victim of another's conduct.

Although . . . under the common law, as a general rule, one person owed no duty to control the conduct of another . . . nor to warn those endangered by such conduct . . . the courts have carved out an exception to this rule in cases in which the defendant stands in some special relationship to either the person whose conduct needs to be controlled or in a relationship to the foreseeable victim of that conduct. . . . Applying this exception to the present case, we note that a relationship of defendant therapists to either Tatiana or Poddar will suffice to establish a duty of care: as explained in section 315 of the Restatement Second of Torts, a duty of care may arise from either "(a) a special relation . . . between the actor and the third person which imposes a duty upon the actor to control the third person's conduct, or (b) a special relation . . . between the actor and the other which gives to the other a right of protection."

Although plaintiffs' pleadings assert no special relation between Tatiana and defendant therapists, they establish as between Poddar and defendant therapists the special relation that arises between a patient and his doctor or psychotherapist [footnote omitted]. Such a relationship may support affirmative duties for the benefit of third persons. Thus, for example, a hospital must exercise reasonable care to control the behavior of a patient which may endanger other persons [footnote omitted]. A doctor must also warn a patient if the patient's condition or medication renders certain conduct, such as driving a car, dangerous to others [footnote omitted].

Although the California decisions that recognize this duty have involved cases in which the defendant stood in a special relationship *both* to the victim and to the person whose conduct created the danger, we do not think that the duty should logically be constricted to such situations. . . .

In their summary of the relevant rulings Fleming and Maximov conclude that the "case law should dispel any notion that to impose on the therapists a duty to take precautions for the safety of persons threatened by a patient, where due care so requires, is in any way opposed to contemporary ground rules on the duty relationship. On the contrary,

From *Tarasoff v. Regents of the University of California (Tarasoff II)*, 551 P.2d 334 (Cal. 1976). Adapted with permission of the author and publisher.

there now seems to be sufficient authority to support the conclusion that by entering into a doctor–patient relationship the therapist becomes sufficiently involved to assume some responsibility for the safety, not only of the patient himself, but also of any third person whom the doctor knows to be threatened by the patient." (Fleming & Maximov, *The Patient or His Victim: The Therapist's Dilemma* (1974) 62 Cal.L.Rev. 1025, 1030.)

Defendants contend, however, that imposition of a duty to exercise reasonable care to protect third persons is unworkable because therapists cannot accurately predict whether or not a patient will resort to violence. In support of this argument amicus representing the American Psychiatric Association and other professional societies cites numerous articles which indicate that therapists, in the present state of the art, are unable reliably to predict violent acts; their forecasts, amicus claims, tend consistently to overpredict violence, and indeed are more often wrong than right. Since predictions of violence are often erroneous, amicus concludes, the courts should not render rulings that predicate the liability of therapists upon the validity of such predictions.

The role of the psychiatrist, who is indeed a practitioner of medicine, and that of the psychologist who performs an allied function, are like that of the physician who must conform to the standards of the profession and who must often make diagnoses and predictions based upon such evaluations. Thus the judgment of the therapist in diagnosing emotional disorders and in predicting whether a patient presents a serious danger of violence is comparable to the judgment which doctors and professionals must regularly render under accepted rules of responsibility.

We recognize the difficulty that a therapist encounters in attempting to forecast whether a patient presents a serious danger of violence. Obviously we do not require that the therapist, in making that determination, render a perfect performance: the therapist need only exercise "that reasonable degree of skill, knowledge, and care ordinarily possessed and exercised by members of (that professional specialty) under similar circumstances." . . . Within the broad range of reasonable practice and treatment in which professional opinion and judgment may differ, the therapist is free to exercise his or her own best judgment without liability; proof, aided by hindsight, that he or she judged wrongly is insufficient to establish negligence.

In the instant case, however, the pleadings do not raise any question as to failure of defendant therapists to predict that Poddar presented a serious danger of violence. On the contrary, the present complaints allege that defendant therapists did in fact predict that Poddar would kill, but were negligent in failing to warn.

Amicus contends, however, that even when a therapist does in fact predict that a patient poses a serious danger of violence to others, the therapist should be absolved of any responsibility for failing to act to protect the potential victim. In our view, however, once a therapist does in fact determine, or under applicable professional standards reasonably should have determined, that a patient poses a serious danger of violence to others, he bears a duty to exercise reasonable care to protect the foreseeable victim of that danger. While the discharge of this duty of due care will necessarily vary with the facts of each case, in each instance the adequacy of the therapist's conduct must be measured against the traditional negligence standard of the rendition of reasonable care under the circumstances. As explained in Fleming and Maximov, *The Patient or His Victim: The Therapist's Dilemma* (1974) 62 Cal.L.Rev. 1025, 1067: ". . . the ultimate question of resolving the tension between the conflicting interests of patient and potential victim is one of social policy, not professional expertise. . . . In sum, the therapist owes a legal duty not only to his patient, but also to his patient's would-be victim and is subject in both respects to scrutiny by judge and jury." . . .

Defendants . . . argue that free and open communication is essential to psychotherapy. . . . The giving of a warning, defendants contend, constitutes a breach of trust which entails the revelation of confidential communications.

We recognize the public interest in supporting effective treatment of mental illness and in protecting the rights of patients to privacy. . . .

We realize that the open and confidential character of psychotherapeutic dialogue encourages patients to express threats of violence, few of which are ever executed. Certainly a therapist should not be encouraged routinely to reveal such threats: such disclosures could seriously disrupt the patient's relationship with his therapist and with the persons threatened. To the contrary, the therapist's obligations to his patient require that he not disclose a confidence unless such disclosure is necessary to avert danger in others, and even then that he do so discreetly, and in a fashion that would preserve the privacy of his patient to the fullest extent compatible with the prevention of the threatened danger. . . .

The revelation of a communication under the above circumstances is not a breach of trust or a violation of professional ethics: as stated in the Principles of Medical Ethics of the American Medical Association (1957), section 9: "A physician may not reveal the confidence entrusted to him in the course of medical attendance . . . *unless he is required to do so by the law or unless it becomes necessary in order to protect the welfare of the individual or of the community.* (Emphasis added.) We conclude that the public policy favoring protection of the confidential character of patient–psychotherapist communications must yield to the extent to which disclosure is essential to avert danger to others. The protective privilege ends where the public peril begins.

Our current crowded and computerized society compels the interdependence of its members. In this risk-infected society we can hardly tolerate the further exposure to danger that would result from a concealed knowledge of the therapist that his patient was lethal. If the exercise of reasonable care to protect the threatened victim requires the therapist to warn the endangered party or those who can reasonably be expected to notify him, we see no sufficient societal interest that would protect and justify concealment. The containment of such risks lies in the public interest. . . .

MOSK, Justice (concurring and dissenting).

I concur in the result in this instance only because the complaints allege that defendant therapists did in fact predict that Poddar would kill and were therefore negligent in failing to warn of that danger. . . .

I cannot concur, however, in the majority's rule that a therapist may be held liable for failing to predict his patient's tendency to violence if other practi-

tioners, pursuant to the "standards of the profession," would have done so. The question is, what standards? . . .

I would restructure the rule designed by the majority to eliminate all reference to conformity to standards of the profession in predicting violence. If a psychiatrist does in fact predict violence, then a duty to warn arises. The majority's expansion of that rule will take us from the world of reality into the wonderland of clairvoyance.

CLARK, Justice (dissenting).

Until today's majority opinion, both legal and medical authorities have agreed that confidentiality is essential to effectively treat the mentally ill, and that imposing a duty on doctors to disclose patient threats to potential victims would greatly impair treatment. Further, recognizing that effective treatment and society's safety are necessarily intertwined, the Legislature has already decided effective and confidential treatment is preferred over imposition of a duty to warn.

The issue whether effective treatment for the mentally ill should be sacrificed to a system of warnings is, in my opinion, properly one for the Legislature, and we are bound by its judgment. Moreover, even in the absence of clear legislative direction, we must reach the same conclusion because imposing the majority's new duty is certain to result in a net increase in violence. . . .

Overwhelming policy considerations weigh against imposing a duty on psychotherapists to warn a potential victim against harm. While offering virtually no benefit to society, such a duty will frustrate psychiatric treatment, invade fundamental patient rights and increase violence. . . .

Assurance of confidentiality is important for three reasons. . . .

First, without substantial assurance of confidentiality, those requiring treatment will be deterred from seeking assistance. . . .

Second, the guarantee of confidentiality is essential in eliciting the full disclosure necessary for effective treatment.

Third, even if the patient fully discloses his thoughts, assurance that the confidential relationship will not be breached is necessary to maintain his trust in his psychiatrist—the very means by which treatment is effected. . . .

Given the importance of confidentiality to the practice of psychiatry, it becomes clear the duty to warn imposed by the majority will cripple the use and effectiveness of psychiatry. Many people, potentially violent—yet susceptible to treatment—will be deterred from seeking it; those seeking it will be inhibited from making revelations necessary to effective treatment; and, forcing the psychiatrist to violate the patient's trust will destroy the interpersonal relationship by which treatment is effected. . . .

By imposing a duty to warn, the majority contributes to the danger to society of violence by the mentally ill and greatly increases the risk of civil commitment—the total deprivation of liberty—of those who should not be confined. The impairment of treatment and risk of improper commitment resulting from the new duty to warn will not be limited to a few patients but will extend to a large number of the mentally ill. Although under existing psychiatric procedures only a relatively few receiving treatment will ever present a risk of violence, the number making threats is huge, and it is the latter group—not just the former—whose treatment will be impaired and whose risk of commitment will be increased.

Both the legal and psychiatric communities recognize that the process of determining potential violence in a patient is far from exact, being fraught with complexity and uncertainty. . . .

This predictive uncertainty means that the number of disclosures will necessarily be large. As noted above, psychiatric patients are encouraged to discuss all thoughts of violence, and they often express such thoughts. However, unlike this court, the psychiatrist does not enjoy the benefit of overwhelming hindsight in seeing which few, if any, of his patients will ultimately become violent. Now, confronted by the majority's new duty, the psychiatrist must instantaneously calculate potential violence from each pa-

tient on each visit. The difficulties researchers have encountered in accurately predicting violence will be heightened for the practicing psychiatrist dealing for brief periods in his office with heretofore nonviolent patients. And, given the decision not to warn or commit must always be made at the psychiatrist's civil peril, one can expect most doubts will be resolved in favor of the psychiatrist protecting himself.

Neither alternative open to the psychiatrist seeking to protect himself is in the public interest.

◆ ◆ ◆

Commentary: *Max Siegel (1979) made the following comments after* Tarasoff II *was decided:*

> *This was a day in court for the law and not for the mental health professions. If the psychologist had accepted the view of absolute, inviolate confidentiality, he might have been able to keep Poddar in treatment, saved the life of Tatiana Tarasoff, and avoided what was to become the Tarasoff decision. (p. 253)*

Siegel, M. (1979). Privacy, ethics, and confidentiality. Professional Psychology, 10, 249–258.

Other commentators have suggested that a good client–clinician relationship is based on trust rather than on confidentiality. Thus, they argue, if trust is maintained, then the therapeutic relationship may endure even after a mandated breach in confidentiality. See Brosig, C. L., & Kalichman, S. C. (1992). Child abuse reporting decisions: Effects of statutory wording of reporting requirements. Professional Psychology: Research and Practice, 23, 486–492; Watson, H., & Levine, M. (1989). Psychotherapy and mandated reporting of child abuse. American Journal of Orthopsychiatry, 59, 246–256. Some of the materials that follow may help you judge the respective merits of these positions. In any event, Tarasoff II *was the first of a long string of similar cases that soon spread across the United States.*

Protecting Third Parties: A Decade After *Tarasoff*

Mark J. Mills, Greer Sullivan, and Spencer Eth

. . . Two arguments have been proposed to justify the enduring importance of confidentiality. Moral deontologists assert that privacy and absolute control over personal information are among the natural rights of man. They argue that since a breach of confidentiality constitutes an assault on human dignity, it is always wrong. The alternative and more widely held justification for the importance ascribed to confidentiality is based on a utilitarian calculation of effects (an assessment of likely outcomes). This position holds that the consequences of violating confidentiality outweigh the possible benefits. . . .

Another historic tradition in medicine emphasizes the physician's ethical obligation to act beneficently. This responsibility for altruistic service applies not only to patients but to the community as well. Specific public health interventions, such as quarantining contagious patients, have been common in medical practice for hundreds of years. In direct response to the publication of a series of professional articles on the battered child syndrome, every state in the union has adopted laws requiring physicians to report cases of child abuse (28). . . .

We believe that the responsibility to protect patient confidentiality and to protect community welfare forms the foundation of medical ethics. We do not question the fundamental importance of either duty, despite the inherent potential for conflict.

. . . The utilitarian balance seems, then, to shift in favor of confidentiality generally but to permit selected violations when they are justified by the conflicting duty to prevent harm. "It is, indeed, difficult to formulate a moral argument against the position that therapists should act to protect those whom they believe to be endangered, as should all human beings" (36).

We maintain that both medical ethics and legal jurisprudence prefer that confidentiality be preserved whenever possible. Furthermore, there is abundant evidence that in instances where the welfare of society or third parties is seriously threatened, confidentiality should, and indeed must, be breached. . . .

Within a relatively short time a series of cases followed *Tarasoff* both within and outside of California. Perhaps the cases that most concerned psychotherapists were the 1980 *Lipari* decision (7) and the 1983 *Petersen* decision (15). In the first instance an outpatient, evidently disgruntled with his care, threatened to harm others but did not specify whom he would attack or when. The therapist apparently made no intervention, and the patient then purchased a shotgun and fired it in a nightclub, injuring and killing several people. The subsequent court decision extended the duty to protect to apply even in cases where a victim had not been and could not be specifically identified. . . .

The *Petersen* case extends the *Tarasoff* decision the furthest to date. In this case the female plaintiff was awarded monetary damages for injuries incurred as a result of an automobile accident with a patient who had been released from a state mental hospital 5 days previously. The plaintiff claimed that the patient should not have been released and that the psychiatrist should have reported the patient's parole violation. (It was alleged that the psychiatrist knew that the patient had been convicted of murder and rape.) At the time of discharge, the treating psychiatrist had perceived the patient as fully recovered from a drug-induced (phencyclidine) psychosis. Liability was imposed although at the time of discharge the victim was unknown. The violence was unforeseeable, and the patient had not directly threatened anyone... [I]n a situation in which the patient was threatening to no one in particular, the decision appears to demand predictive powers that are completely beyond present-day psychiatry.

... Mills reviewed many of the post-*Tarasoff* court decisions concerning the protection of third parties from potentially violent psychiatric patients (37). Using a normative analysis, Mills concluded that these cases largely turn on the issue of foreseeability. When the courts have imposed liability, the identity of the subsequently injured party was known to the psychotherapist (*Macintosh*) (5) or the victim would reasonably have been expected to be in close proximity to the target of violence, as in the case of a young child (*Hedlund*) (14) or a home in the vicinity of a building burned by arson (*Peck*) (18,38). In addition, threats were specific, the patient's history was overwhelming, and there were breaches of conventional practice, such as failure to obtain the patient's prior medical record (*Jablonski*) (12), (*Peck*) (18,38), or to examine carefully the patient and his or her medical record (*Clark*) (16). When liability has not been imposed, the patient has, at the time of evaluation, been perceived as not being a threat to any individual or group (*Thompson*) (6), (*Leedy*) (8), (*Doyle*) (9), (*Brady*) (13), (*Furr*) (11), even when the patient had a history of violent behavior or alcoholism (*Hasenei*) (10).

... Public policy evolves only as the courts, attempting to achieve justice in each case, make individual decisions. In the majority of states, no cases involving the issue of third-party protection have been brought to the bar. A few states—for example, Pennsylvania and Maryland—have even considered the issue and have decided against following the policy established in *Tarasoff* (39,40). Nevertheless, the evident trend continues toward a policy of a duty to warn for psychotherapists. In states where the issue has not been litigated, the conservative assumption is that the court will find a *Tarasoff*-like duty when the issue arises.

In August 1985, the California legislature adopted the first state statute concerning the psychotherapist's duty to warn and protect third parties. The law states more clearly the circumstances in which the duty is applicable. A psychotherapist is liable only "where the patient has communicated to the psychotherapist a serious threat of physical violence against a reasonably identifiable victim or victims." The statute further directs that the duty to warn and protect shall be discharged by "reasonable efforts to communicate the threat to the victim or victims and to a law enforcement agency" (2)....

Although the new law limits psychotherapists' liability in some cases, it encourages clinicians to respond to a circumstance in a rote way. No mention is made of protecting a third party through clinical interventions.... [T]herapists should be encouraged to approach a situation of potential violence thoughtfully, to use clinical interventions whenever possible to contain the potential violence, and to warn when public policy so counsels (52)....

References

2. California Assembly Bill 1133, McAllister, 1984

5. Macintosh v Milano, 168 NJ 966, 403 A 2d 500 (1979)

6. Thompson v County of Alameda, 27 Cal 3d 741, 614 P 2d 728 (1980). Mental Disability Law Reporter 1980; 4:313–314

7. Lipari v Sears, Roebuck & Co, 497 F Supp 185 (D Neb 1980)

8. Leedy v Hartnett, 510 F Supp 1125 (MD, Pa 1981). Mental Disability Law Reporter 1981; 5:161–162

9. Doyle v United States, 530 F Supp 1278 (CD Cal 1982). Mental Disability Law Reporter 1982; 6: 336–337

10. Hasenei v United States, 541 F Supp 999 (D Md 1982)

11. Furr v Spring Grove State Hospital, 53 Md App 474, 454 A 2d 414 (1983)

12. Jablonski v United States, 712 F 2d 391 (9th Cir 1983)

13. Brady v Hooper, 570 F Supp 1333 (D Colo 1982). Mental Disability Law Reporter 1983; 7:453–454

14. Hedlund v Orange County, 34 Cal 3d 695, 669 P 2d 41 (1983)

15. Petersen v State, 100 Wn2d 421, 671 P 2d 230 (Wash 1983)

16. Clark v State of New York, 99 AD 2d 616, 472 NYS 2d, 170 (1984)

18. Peck v Counseling Service of Addision County, Inc, No 83-062 (Vt Sup Ct June, 1985). Mental and Physical Disability Law Reporter 1985; 9:364–365

28. Heins NL The "battered child" revisited. JAMA 1984; 251:3295–3300.

36. Appelbaum PS: *Tarasoff* and the clinician: problems in fulfilling the duty to protect. American Journal of Psychiatry 1985; 142:425–429.

37. Mills MJ: The so-called duty to warn: the psychotherapeutic duty to protect third parties from patients; violent acts. Behavioral Sciences and the Law 1984; 2: 237–257.

38. Stone AA: Vermont adopts *Tarasoff*: A real barn-burner. Am J Psychiatry 1986; 143:352–355

39. Hopewell v Adibempe, Number GD78-28756, Civil Division, Court of Common Pleas of Allegheny County, Pennsylvania, June 1, 1981

40. Shaw v Glickman, 415 A 2d 625 (Md Ct Spec App 1980)

52. Klein JI, Macbeth JE, Onek JN: Legal Issues in the Private Practice of Psychiatry. Washington, DC, American Psychiatric Press, 1984

◆ ◆ ◆

Commentary: For other useful collections of post-Tarasoff cases, see, for example, Knapp, S., & Vandecreek, L. (1982). Tarasoff: Five years later. Professional Psychology, 13, 511–516; Fulero, S. M. (1988). Tarasoff: 10 years later. Professional Psychology, 19, 184–190. In an Appendix, Fulero provided a compendium of 70 judicial opinions decided between 1974 and 1987 in which the courts applied the Tarasoff "duty to protect" principle. For an even more extensive discussion, see Vandecreek, L., & Knapp, S. A. (1989). Tarasoff and beyond: Legal considerations in the treatment of life-endangering patients. Sarasota, FL: Professional Resource Exchange. Among the more noteworthy cases these sources discuss are (a) Bellah v. Greenson, 141 Cal. Rptr. 92 (Cal. App. 1977)—in which a California appellate court (but not its Supreme Court) held that the duty to protect does not extend to a patient's suicidal threats; (b) Peck v. Counseling Service of Addison County, 499 A.2d 422 (Vt. 1985)—in which the

Vermont Supreme Court extended the duty to a master's-level counselor whose adolescent patient threatened to burn down his father's barn, creating the possibility that the Tarasoff duty may extend to protecting property (or at least damage to property that may also create risk to people); and (c) Hedlund v. Superior Court, 34 Cal.3d 995, 194 Cal. Rptr. 805 (1983)—in which the California Supreme Court held that a foreseeable, innocent bystander who witnesses the violence inflicted by a patient may sue the patient's therapist for negligent infliction of emotional distress in addition to the victim's suit for failure to protect.

Perhaps the dilution of the ethical value of confidentiality exemplified by these cases will ebb as a result of the U.S. Supreme Court's 7–2 decision in Jaffee v. Redmond, 518 U.S. 1 (1996). In holding that the federal rules of evidence require recognition of a psychotherapist–patient privilege in federal cases (all 50 states have some form of this privilege under state law), the Court gave unusually strong support for the principles of fidelity and confidentiality:

> *Effective psychotherapy . . . depends upon an atmosphere of confidence and trust in which the patient is willing to make a frank and complete disclosure of facts, emotions, memories, and fears. . . . [T]he mere possibility of disclosure may impede development of the confidential relationship necessary for successful treatment. . . . (p. 10)*

The Court was not prepared to delineate the boundaries of the privilege nor to create exceptions. But in a footnote ending the majority's opinion, it made a statement that could have an impact on the manner in which psychologists and other professionals deal with the duty to protect cases: "We do not doubt that there are situations in which the privilege must give way, for example, if a serious threat of harm to the patient or to others can be averted only by means of a disclosure by the therapist" (p. 18). Does this broaden or narrow the duties in Tarasoff-like cases? In answering the question the reader should consider the effect of the word "only" in the footnote.

For some insights on the meaning of Jaffee *and its impact on practice see:*

DeBell, C., & Jones, R. D. (1997). *Privileged communication at last? An overview of* Jaffee v. Redmond. Professional Psychology: Research and Practice, 28, 559–566

Glosoff, H. L., Herlihy, S. B., Herlihy, B., & Spence, E. B. (1997). *Privileged communication in the psychologist–clinician relationship.* Professional Psychology: Research and Practice, 28, 573–581.

Knapp, S., & VandeCreek, L. (1997). Jaffee v. Redmond: *The Supreme Court recognizes a psychotherapist–patient privilege in federal courts.* Professional Psychology: Research and Practice, 28, 567–572.

Tarasoff and the Researcher: Does the Duty to Protect Apply in the Research Setting?

Paul S. Appelbaum and Alan Rosenbaum

A field-worker in an epidemiologic survey of psychiatric disorders among a cohort of young men is startled to hear one of her subjects confess a desire to "get even" with his former boss, whom he blames for his current problems. A research psychologist in a longitudinal study of spouse abusers learns from a subject's wife that he is again beating her regularly. A clinician in a controlled trial of psychotherapy explores the roots of a patient-subject's depression, only to uncover homicidal fantasies about his ex-wife.

The above situations are hypothetical, but each example was posed to us by an investigator of an actual research project. These examples represent real concerns among investigators in the behavioral sciences. All of the scenarios present the same dilemma: To what extent are researchers responsible for preventing the occurrence of violent behavior by one of their research subjects? . . .

DOES THE DUTY APPLY IN THE RESEARCH SETTING?

Despite researchers' concerns, we know of no case in which an attempt has been made to apply the duty to protect in the context of a research project. Nonetheless, without analyzing the reasons for its possible applicability, it would be premature to conclude that a court might not apply the duty in the future, given the proper set of circumstances. . . .

Although it might be argued that the duty to protect was formulated in, and applies only to, the clinical setting, and therefore no further consideration need be given to its application to investigators, such a position seems too simplistic. Research and clinical functions are often integrally related, and they are difficult to tease apart (Fried, 1974). Furthermore, they are often conducted by the same persons. Consider, for example, a controlled trial of psychotherapy. The functions of the therapist–researchers, apart from filling out evaluation forms, differ little from those of their nonresearch colleagues and from the researchers' own functions in nonresearch contexts. One cannot simply maintain that duties that are applied to one group are irrelevant to the other. On the other hand, much behavioral science research—for example, social psychological studies of interactions among small groups of undergraduates—takes place in settings so different from the treatment context and is performed by people who may be so different in their training and functions from clinicians that it would be equally misleading to assume that the duty to protect will invariably be applied to investigators. Some basis is needed for distinguishing between research situations in which a duty to protect may be invoked and those in which it is unlikely to be found.

The courts will be attempting here to determine whether there is something intrinsic to clinical relationships themselves that warrants their being deemed "special" for the purpose of invoking a duty to protect, or whether some characteristic of the actors that transcends the clinical setting is determinative. Given the analysis in *Tarasoff* [1974], it would appear that the abilities of psychotherapists with regard to prediction and prevention of violence—not

From *American Psychologist*, 44, 885–894. Copyright 1989 by the American Psychological Association. Adapted with permission of the author and publisher.

the context in which contact with a potentially violent person occurs—will determine whether the relationship is "special enough" for a duty to protect to be invoked. Thus, the courts will need to inquire into the resemblance between the researchers in question and clinicians with regard to these abilities [footnote omitted].

Ability to Predict Violence: Clinical Training

. . . Social and experimental psychologists without clinical training should fall outside the requirements of the duty to protect, as should relatively untrained research assistants who collect data. Thus, one can envision a variety of research situations to which the duty to protect should not apply. Industrial psychologists conducting research on personnel issues in a corporate setting; developmental psychologists examining child behavior in connection with a public health early intervention program; social psychologists, sociologists, or anthropologists examining the behavior of police officers in the field—all should be free of legal obligations (although some ethical duties may apply in given circumstances, as we will discuss later) to protect potential victims of their subjects. Even investigators who have spent many years studying violence—such as social psychologists evaluating the effectiveness of an intervention program to assist police officers in preventing family violence—lack the putative ability to predict dangerousness, based on clinical training, to which the courts have looked as a basis for the special relationship needed to impose a duty.

What if a nonclinician investigator heads a project, but data collection is performed by clinicians, who have direct contact with subjects? According to our analysis, the data collectors themselves may have an obligation to protect endangered persons. Does their nonclinician supervisor bear any responsibilities? The closest parallel here would seem to be a nonclinical administrator of a hospital or clinic. The administrator is held responsible for the formulation of policies that inform clinicians of their obligations and enable them to fulfill their duties. Similarly, nonclinician researchers might be expected to be aware that their data gatherers may have a duty to protect, to make this duty known to them, and

to oversee the formulation of policies for fulfilling the duty.

Ability to Predict Violence: Data Available

. . .

The reliability and validity of data concerning potential violence are dependent, in part, on an interviewer's ability to determine the accuracy of available information, to probe the seriousness of the subject's resolve, and to seek confirmation of alternative explanations of the subject's apparent violent intent. This requires at a minimum that the data be gathered in direct, face-to-face contact between the clinician–investigator and the subject, a *sine qua non* of ordinary clinical settings (Appelbaum, 1984). Such contact will militate in favor of applying a duty to protect. On the other hand, even assuming a general ability to predict violence, the expectation that the data relevant to capacity for violence can be gathered validly without substantial face-to-face contact, such as from a questionnaire completed by the subject or a telephone interview, is untenable. . . .

The scope of the data available is another important factor that may differentiate between clinical and research settings. Clinicians conduct wide-ranging assessments, with the freedom to inquire about all relevant aspects of thought and behavior; such a broad-ranging inquiry is essential for a predictive process that comports with professional, clinical norms (Monahan, 1981). Some research projects may adopt similar methodologies, using multiple clinical indexes or unstructured interviews. They would seem to be susceptible, on the basis of their comparability to the clinical setting, to the imposition of a duty to protect. Many studies, however, focus their data collection exclusively on particular areas of functioning (e.g., depressive symptoms). Researchers in the latter type of project ought not to be held to have a duty to detect a predisposition for violence and to take appropriate protective measures when the data that clinicians would find relevant to that determination ordinarily would not be uncovered in the course of the study.

The cross-sectional versus longitudinal nature of the data available to researchers, a third major factor in the analysis of whether a duty to protect should apply, affects the mental health professional's ability to determine whether there is a reproducible link between a particular constellation of circumstances (e.g., patients' threats) and their violent behavior. These relationships can be measured only over time. In the clinical setting, repeated contact between therapist and patient allows assessment of the seriousness of a patient's threat by comparison with the patient's previous history. Threats repetitively evoked by given circumstances, particularly when they have resulted previously in violence, should be taken more seriously. Conversely, frequent and diffuse threats that are never actualized over time will appropriately be discounted (Appelbaum, 1986). Repeated contact with subjects, therefore, may encourage application of the duty to protect. This process of assessing the stability of causal relationships in subjects' behavior, however, cannot occur in research projects that involve only single encounters between researchers and subjects. Although one cannot rule out the possibility that even in this situation information might be obtained that would be sufficiently alarming that a reasonable person might act on it after a single contact, the courts might well choose not to impose a duty in such cases. . . .

Facilitating the Prediction of Violence

A more difficult set of questions concerns the degree to which researchers might be held to have a duty to alter their methodologies to facilitate assessment of potential violence, and consequent application of a duty to protect. Data gatherers, as noted earlier, will often collect insufficient information to allow reasonable evaluation, by clinical standards, of subjects' potential for violence. . . .

. . . In most research projects, the risk of subject violence is small and, given difficulties in prediction, even with optimal data, the likelihood that researchers will accurately detect such propensities is even smaller. In contrast, the burdens placed on researchers to alter methods or conduct additional evaluations may be so substantial as materially to impede or even prevent the conduct of their research. One would hope that courts would not lightly impose affirmative obligations on the vast proportion of research investigations.

Studies of populations at high risk for violent behavior, however, may present a different balance of interests. A follow-up study of violent criminals may be an example of such a project. Not only is the likelihood increased that someone may be harmed, but the higher base rate of violence makes accurate prediction more probable. Even in research projects addressing groups at low risk for violence, a given subject might present so blatant a threat to third parties that most reasonable mental health professionals would feel impelled at least to extend their evaluations and perhaps to take other actions. It is an open question whether courts would require affirmative steps to be taken to facilitate evaluation of violence potential in these cases.

On ethical grounds alone, though, it may be reasonable for investigators to consider building provisions for the protection of potential victims into their protocols. Professional associations' codes of ethics contain language permitting disclosures to be made to protect third parties in therapeutic and research contexts. . . .

A somewhat different situation may exist in cases in which a researcher, though a nonclinician, actually alters subjects' propensity for engaging in violent behavior, for example, by manipulating their level of anger. Here the researcher, by inducing the potentially dangerous situation, may have both legal . . . and ethical . . . obligations to ensure that no untoward effects ensue.

STATUTORY AND REGULATORY SOURCES OF A DUTY TO PROTECT

In some states, as noted earlier, the duty to protect has been established or modified by statute. This adds another level of complexity to the analysis. The statutes adopted to date invariably frame the duty in terms of a "patient's" or "client's" potential violence. It is unclear, therefore, what effect they might have in nontherapeutic research settings, although they would seem to apply, at a minimum, to research in which treatment is also being received (e.g., a trial of psychotherapy). Courts, which will ultimately interpret the laws, might determine that the statutes were meant to be exclusive and therefore only apply to situations in which treatment is rendered. Alternatively, they may read the statutes as evidence of the legislatures' intent to place responsibility on mental health professionals in general for the protection of endangered persons without attempting to specify all circumstances in which the duty might arise. It seems safe to conclude that at this point the statutes' effects on researchers are unclear. Legal consultation in states with such laws . . . is advisable. . . .

There are some circumstances in which uncertainty about the existence of a duty disappears. When disclosure is statutorily required, as is true in all states for situations involving child abuse (Green, 1980), researchers who fall into one of the categories of professionals designated by the law must report their information to the authorities. . . . It should be noted that this class of statutes requires more in some respects and less in others than the *Tarasoff*-like duty to protect. The statutes exceed the scope of *Tarasoff*, in most cases, by mandating reporting when an act of abuse has occurred, regardless of whether it is likely to recur. On the other hand, they generally do not require action in the absence of past abuse, and the obligation they impose is limited to reporting the situation to state authorities, who take whatever further measures are necessary.

Circumstances exist, however, in which these requirements may be abrogated. In order to facilitate research on certain sensitive topics, particularly substance abuse, Congress has permitted the Secretary of Health and Human Services to issue confidentiality certificates (Public Health Service Act, 1975). These documents authorize researchers to protect subjects' privacy by withholding "the names or other identifying characteristics" of subjects from "any Federal, State, or local civil, criminal, administrative, legislative, or other proceedings" (42 U.S.C. 242[a]). Although court tests are again lacking, the Department of Health and Human Services (DHHS) has interpreted the statute to mean that researchers holding such certificates are exempt from state and local reporting requirements (Lanman, 1980). The certificates are available to "persons engaged in research on mental health, including research on the use and effect of alcohol and other psychoactive drugs," who make proper application to DHHS ("Protection of Identity—Research Subjects," 1979).

The existence of confidentiality certificates raises the question of what impact they may have on a *Tarasoff*-like duty to protect. Again, in the absence of a court test, the answer is uncertain. There are several reasons why issuance of a certificate might not affect researchers' obligations. First, the certificate does not prevent voluntary disclosure by investigators; it only allows researchers to resist compulsion. Thus, researchers retain the capacity to breach subjects' confidentiality if necessary to protect third parties. Arguably, therefore, if a court found that the duty to protect would otherwise apply, the certificate might not change that conclusion. Similarly, because measures to protect potential victims (such as hospitalizing the threatening subject) can often be taken without breaching confidence (Roth & Meisel, 1977), the certificate may be irrelevant for that reason too. . . .

THE DUTY TO PROTECT AND INFORMED CONSENT

Federal regulations, applicable to most research with human subjects, require that subjects be informed of any limitations that may apply to the confidentiality of information they provide ("Protection of Human Subjects," 1981). Should an investigator who anticipates that a duty to protect may apply, potentially requiring the release of information or other measures, inform potential subjects of that fact? Should IRBs [Institutional Review Boards] require this information to be included on consent forms?

Although federal requirements for disclosure to subjects of limits on confidentiality are framed in absolute terms, suggesting that these two questions should always be answered affirmatively, the matter is not that simple. There is, in any study, the risk that information might be disclosed or other steps taken in emergent or extraordinary situations. For example, should a medical emergency occur, information about a subject will be communicated to allow treatment to take place. If research data are subject to release on court order, investigators will have no choice but to reveal them. Some IRBs may require these eventualities to be included in consent disclosures, but most recognize the impossibility of covering all conceivable situations in a form of reasonable length. Some discretion is required. . . .

... Even in most studies in which provisions are made to protect potential victims, the probability that any given subject's communications will have to be revealed is quite small. Evidence suggests that warnings that confidentiality may be imperiled will restrict full participation by research subjects (Singer, 1978). Because little will be gained from such warnings, the balance of advantages and disadvantages will tip against including them routinely. On the other hand, there will be studies (e.g., research on populations with a high incidence of violence) in which the need to take measures protective of potential victims can be foreseen with reasonable probability. In such cases, we would advocate notifying subjects at the time of recruitment. Subjects' right to be informed of the high likelihood that some action will need to be taken seems to us to have precedence in these cases over the interests of researchers in recruiting subjects. It is probable, however, that these disclosures will have negative impact on recruitment, and thus on the conduct of certain research projects, especially those directly examining phenomena related to violence.

The American Psychological Association has articulated a statement regarding the ethical responsibilities of researchers that addresses some of these issues (American Psychological Association, 1982). Of particular relevance to the present discussion is Principle J, which concerns the anonymity of subjects and the confidentiality of data. It states,

> Information obtained about the research participant during the course of an investigation is confidential unless otherwise agreed in advance. When the possibility exists that others may obtain access to such information, this possibility, together with the plans for protecting confidentiality, is explained to the participant as part of the procedure for obtaining informed consent. (p. 70)

In the explication of this principle, Item 6 discusses deliberate disclosure to protect the participant or other from harm, specifically stating that "the protection afforded research participants by the maintenance of confidentiality may be compromised when the investigator discovers information that se-

rious harm threatens the research participant or others" (p. 72). Finally, Principle J imposes on investigators a "special obligation . . . to inform the individual that the information may have to be disclosed" (p. 72). This ethical principle, although emphasizing the desirability of disclosing to potential subjects the risks of breaching confidentiality, is not necessarily in conflict with the analysis presented earlier, which suggested that such disclosures be limited to high-risk situations. . . .

. . .

References

American Psychological Association. (1982). *Ethical principles in the conduct of research with human participants.* Washington, DC: Author.

Appelbaum, P. S. (1984). Hypotheticals, psychiatric testimony, and the death sentence. *Bulletin of the American Academy of Psychiatry and the Law, 12,* 169–177.

Appelbaum, P. S. (1986). Tarasoff and the clinician: Problems in fulfilling the duty to protect. *American Journal of Psychiatry, 142,* 425–429.

Fried, C. (1974). *Medical experimentation: Personal integrity and social policy.* New York: American Elsevier.

Green, A. H. (1980). Child abuse. In D. H. Schetky & E. P. Benedek (Eds.), *Child psychiatry and the law* (pp. 71–88). New York: Brunner–Mazel.

Lanman, R. B. (1980, April 10). Memorandum opinion. Washington, DC: U.S. Department of Health and Human Services.

Monahan, J. (1981). *The clinical prediction of violent behavior.* Rockville, MD: National Institute of Mental Health.

Protection of Identity–Research Subjects, 42 C.F.R. Part 2a (1979).

Protection of Human Subjects, 45 C.F.R. Part 46 (1981).

Public Health Service Act (as amended 1975), 42 U.S.C. 242a(a).

Roth, L. H., & Meisel, A. (1977). Dangerousness, confidentiality, and the duty to warn. *American Journal of Psychiatry, 134,* 508–511.

Singer, E. (1978). Informed consent: Consequences for response rate and response quality in social surveys. *American Sociological Review, 43,* 144–162.

Tarasoff v. Regents of University of California, 13 C.3d 177, 529 P.2d 553, 118 Cal. Rptr. 129 (1974).

◆ ◆ ◆

Commentary: *Because* Tarasoff *was a duty-to-protect case, its rulings left therapists with more options than merely informing the potential victim. One of those options is to civilly commit the client. Although in many cases that may satisfy one's legal obligations under Tarasoff, involuntary hospitalization has its own drawbacks. First, depriving one's clients of liberty over their objections will likely impair the therapeutic relationship. Second, civil commitment necessarily involves breaching confidentiality. Third, commitment usually requires not only a finding of potential danger to self and others, but also the presence of serious mental illness. Many outpatient therapy clients may not fit that criterion. Voluntary admission to a hospital, on the other hand, circumvents these pitfalls.*

Other options include (a) involving the potential victim in therapy (although that would most likely require the potential victim to be closely related in some way to the client); (b) manipulating the social environment, for example, seeing that the client rids himself or herself of deadly weapons; (c) referring the client for psychotropic medication or for an increased dosage if he or she is already being medicated; and (d) obtaining permission from the client to contact the potential victim, a suggestion that eliminates the involuntary disclosure of confidential communications. What follows is a recently published set of recommendations for therapists.

Limiting Therapist Exposure to *Tarasoff* Liability: Guidelines for Risk Containment

John Monahan

. . .

RISK ASSESSMENT

Four tasks form the basis of any professionally adequate risk assessment: The clinician must be educated about what information to gather regarding risk, must gather it, must use this information to estimate risk, and, if the clinician is not the ultimate decision maker, must communicate the information and estimate to those who are responsible for making clinical decisions.

Education

The essence of being a "professional" is having "specialized knowledge" not available to the general public. In this context, specialized knowledge consists of both knowledge of mental disorder in general (e.g., assessment, diagnosis, and treatment) and knowledge of risk assessment in particular. In addition, one should be thoroughly conversant with the laws of the jurisdiction in which one practices regarding the steps to follow when a positive risk assessment is made.

Clinical education. Familiarity with basic concepts in risk assessment (e.g., predictor and criterion variables, true and false positives and negatives, decision rules and base rates) and with key findings of risk assessment research (e.g., past violence as the single best predictor of future violence) is becoming an important aspect of graduate education in psychology, psychiatry, and social work. . . .

It is not enough to learn the basic concepts and classic findings in the field of risk assessment once and consider one's education complete. Research findings evolve and become modified over time, and the conventions of professional practice become more sophisticated. Continuing education in risk assessment through formal programs sponsored by professional or private organizations is one way to keep apprised of developments in the field. Periodically perusing original research journals (e.g., *Law and Human Behavior, Behavioral Sciences and the Law,* the *International Journal of Law and Psychiatry* is another . . .).

Legal education. The standards to which clinicians will be held in making judgments on risk are set largely by state law. In the past, these standards were usually articulated by judges who applied common law tort principles to the context of clinical risk assessment. This is what happened in *Tarasoff* and similar cases in other states. Increasingly, and after intense lobbying by professional mental health organizations, state legislatures are passing statutes to make standards for liability and immunity in this area explicit (Appelbaum, Zonana, Bonnie, & Roth, 1989). These statutes, however, will still require much adjudication to interpret inevitably ambiguous terminology (e.g., what counts as a "serious threat" or a "reasonably identifiable victim" in California's, 1990, statute?). The point here is that there is no national legal standard for what clinicians should do when they assess risk and that it behooves clinicians to know precisely what the legal standards in their own jurisdiction are regarding violence prevention. State mental health professional as-

From *American Psychologist, 48,* 242–250. Copyright 1993 by the American Psychological Association. Adapted with permission of the author and publisher. Appendix has been omitted.

sociations ought to have this information readily available.

Information

Once a clinician knows what information, in general, may be relevant to assessing risk, he or she must take efforts to gather that information in a given case. Most of the *Tarasoff*-like cases on which I have worked have faulted clinicians not for making an inaccurate prediction but for failing to gather information that would have made a reasonable effort at prediction possible. There are generally four sources in which relevant information can be found: in the records of past treatment, in the records of current treatment, from interviewing the patient, and from interviewing significant others. In some criminal contexts (e.g., assessments for suitability for release on parole or from insanity commitment) additional records in the form of police and probation reports, arrest records, and trial transcripts may also be available and should be consulted. But in the civil context, these records are generally not available to clinicians.

Past records. The only cases in which I have been involved that were, in the words of the defense attorneys, "born dead" were those in which the patient had an extensive history of prior violence that was amply documented in reasonably available treatment records, but those records were never requested. In these cases, the clinician has been forced to acknowledge on the witness stand that if he or she had seen the records, preventive action would have been taken.

. . . [A] line has to be drawn as to what constitutes a reasonable effort to obtain records of past treatment. I know of no standard operating procedure on this question. "Records" does not have to mean the entire hospital file; a discharge summary may often suffice. More of a priority might be accorded to requesting the records of patients whose hospitalization was precipitated by a violent incident, or who exhibited violence in the hospital, than to requesting the records of other patients. In the context of long-term hospitalization, of course, there will be more opportunity to obtain records from distant facilities than would be the case for short-term treatment (this opportunity to obtain records is also present for patients with repeated short-term hospitalizations).

Current records. Reading the chart of the current hospitalization when making risk judgments about hospitalized patients is essential. I am continually amazed, however, at how often clinicians peruse the chart as if it were a magazine in a dentist's waiting room. In particular, nursing notes, in which violent acts and threats are often to be found, are frequently glossed over. Yet, I have seen plaintiff's attorneys introduce exhibits consisting of eight-foot-by-four-foot photographic enlargements of pages from nursing notes containing statements such as, "assaulted several other patients without provocation tonight," and "patient threatening to kill spouse as soon as released." These exhibits certainly concentrated the jury's attention.

Inquiries of the patient. Directly asking patients about violent behavior and possible indices of violent behavior (e.g., arrest or hospitalization as "dangerous to others") is surely the easiest and quickest way to obtain this essential information. Open-ended questions such as "What is the most violent thing you have ever done?" or "What is the closest you have ever come to being violent?" may be useful probes, as might "Do you ever worry that you might physically hurt somebody?" The obvious problem, of course, is that patients may lie or distort their history or their current thoughts. This is always a possibility, but often corroborating information will be available from the records (above) or from significant others (below). Quite often, however, patients are remarkably forthcoming about violence. And although there may be reasons to suspect a negative answer in a given case, a positive answer should always be pursued. Unless a question to the patient is ventured, potentially valuable information on risk will not be gained.

Inquiries of significant others. Records are often unavailable, and patients are sometimes not reliable informants. A significant other, usually a family member, is frequently available in the case of inpatient hospitalization, however, either in person (accompanying the patient to treatment or seen later in conjunction with the patient's therapy) or at least by telephone. Asking the significant other about any violent behavior or threats in the event that precipitated hospitalization, or in the past, as well as open-ended questions such as "Are you concerned that X might hurt someone?" with appropriate follow-up questions as to the basis for any expressed concern, may yield useful information.

Estimation

I have elsewhere suggested a clinical model for estimating a patient's risk of violent behavior (Monahan, 1981). Although the mental health professions have yet to demonstrate that the accuracy of their estimations of risk is high in absolute terms it is clearly high relative to chance. . . .

Communication

In the individual practice of psychotherapy, the clinician who gathers information on risk is also the clinician who makes decisions based on this information. But in outpatient treatment agencies and in mental hospitals, a division of labor often exists: One person may do the intake, another may be responsible for patient care, a team of several professionals may provide a variety of assessment and treatment modalities, and one person will have formal responsibility for making or approving discharge decisions. Although this division of labor may be an efficient use of resources, it does raise an issue not present in the solo practitioner context: the communication of relevant information from one mental health professional to another. Here, information must be transferred between or among clinicians, and significant information must be made salient to the person responsible for making the ultimate decisions regarding the patient. . . .

Placing all relevant information in the chart, of course, is the primary way of transferring information among treatment professionals. As long as the person ultimately responsible for making the institutionalization or discharge decision reads the entire file, the information is thereby communicated to the person who needs to know it.

In the real world of professional practice, however, information is not always effectively communicated by simply passing on a chart. The ultimate decision maker may be a harried senior staff member whose signature is often a pro forma endorsement of the recommendations of line staff, based only on a

brief discharge summary. Or the amount of information in the chart, including information from numerous past hospitalizations, may be literally so voluminous that no final decision maker would be expected to read it verbatim. . . .

It is not sufficient to dump undigested information on the desk of the ultimate decision maker and to claim that he or she assumed the risk of liability by taking possession of the file. Rather, information pertinent to risk should explicitly . . . be brought to the attention of the decision maker. Only by making the information salient can one be assured that the decision maker has had the option to make use of it.

From the decision maker's vantage point, the implications of information overload are equally clear. When the transfer or discharge summary prepared by others makes no explicit positive or negative reference to risk, one should directly ask what information relevant to risk is in the chart and should record the answer.

RISK MANAGEMENT

. . .

Planning

Choice of a plan.   For a patient flagged as *high risk*, it is important to explicitly consider preventive action. Such actions usually fall into three categories (see Appelbaum, 1985, p. 426). Following the literature on crime prevention, the first category might be called *incapacitation*, or negating the opportunity for violence in the community by hospitalizing the patient (voluntarily or involuntarily), or if it is hospital violence that is anticipated, negating that opportunity by transferring the patient to a more secure ward until the level of risk is reduced. The second category could be termed *target hardening*, or warning the potential victim when one can be identified, so that the victim can take precautionary measures. The final category might be called *intensified treatment*, in which outpatient status is maintained but sessions are scheduled more frequently, medication is initiated or increased, or joint sessions are held with the patient and others significant to the occurrence of violence, possibly including the potential victim (Wexler, 1981). More creative options may also be possible (Dietz, 1990).

The issue here is not that the clinician must necessarily adopt one of these violence-prevention strategies as part of a risk management plan but that the clinician consciously *consider* such options and make a reasoned and reasonable decision to adopt or not to adopt one of them. If the steps taken to prevent violence are seen as reasonable, the clinician should not be held liable, even if harm occurs.

Second opinions. The problem with choosing a risk management plan, in terms of tort liability, is that because the plan didn't work (or else there would be no law suit), the plaintiff can often retain another mental health professional as an expert witness to say, with the wisdom of hindsight, that any competent clinician would have known that the plan was defective. The more well thought out the preventive measures taken in a case, the more difficulty the plaintiff will have in finding a credible witness who can with integrity make such a claim.

One way for a clinician to immunize himself or herself from this kind of Monday morning quarterbacking is for the clinician to initiate it on Friday afternoon, by consulting with a respected colleague about a difficult case before risk management decisions are made (Rachlin & Schwartz, 1986). Getting a second opinion has two advantages. First, the clinician may learn something. He or she may learn that the consulting colleague does not think that the contemplated actions are reasonable. The clinician may have missed a significant risk or protective risk factor, or may be overreacting to some aspect of the case—we all have blind spots. Or, the planned course of action may be reasonable, but the consultant may have a more creative suggestion.

The second advantage of obtaining a consultation is that it is a concrete way of demonstrating that the clinician took the case seriously and considered a variety of options for violence prevention. If the consultant is an experienced clinician . . . it becomes much more difficult to claim after the fact that "anyone" would have known that the risk management plan was negligent.

There are two clear disadvantages to obtaining consultation, however. The first is that it takes time to familiarize a colleague with a difficult case and to talk through strategy. In many busy practice settings, there is barely enough time to make a reasoned initial decision, much less to review that decision with someone else. The second disadvantage is that in obtaining consultation the clinician may be exposing the chosen consultant to potential liability should the patient commit a violent act (although I emphasize that I know of no cases in which consultants who have not seen the patient have been found to share liability). Perhaps the most equitable ways to obtain consultation are case conferences or grand rounds in which each clinician gets to discuss a difficult case, thereby broadly sharing potential liability with other colleagues, while incurring potential liability from their cases.

Adherence

Without doubt, the single largest category of cases on which I have served as an expert witness have involved patient noncompliance with aftercare recommendations. The typical case is one in which a patient is seriously violent when acutely disordered, is treated in a mental hospital until the disorder is under control, and is discharged with the recommendation to continue treatment as an outpatient. The patient comes to few, if any, appointments and then stops showing up altogether. No one on the hospital staff calls to find out what the problem is or to assess the patient's condition. The patient decompensates over the course of a few weeks or months and, while acutely disordered, kills someone. This situation is even more egregious when the patient is known to have a long history of noncompliance with treatment (typically, with psychotropic medication) and is also known from the record to become disordered when off medication and to become violent when disordered. It does not take the jury long to complete the syllogism and to conclude that the clinician or hospital could and should have avoided the tragedy by pursuing the missed appointments and nonadherence to treatment recommendations.

I know how understaffed many mental health facilities are. It is hard enough to see those people who do show up for aftercare treatment, much less to track down those who do not. Furthermore, unless the former patient satisfies the criteria for civil commitment (or outpatient commitment), there may be little the clinician can legally do to force the patient to comply with treatment recommendations (but see Meichenbaum & Turk, 1987, for an excellent account of *adherence enhancement*). Yet, it is very hard to convince a jury, with the children of the deceased in the front row of the courtroom, that a good faith effort to assure the patient's compliance with treatment was not worth the clinician's time (Klein, 1986).

DOCUMENTATION

It would be an exaggeration to state that in a tort case what is not in the written record does not exist—but not much of an exaggeration. The violent event that gives rise to the suit may occur weeks or months after the patient was last seen. The resolution of the case through settlement or trial will be a minimum of several years from the time of the violent event. Memories fade or become compromised when numerous, or innumerable, other patients are seen in the interval. The record requested by telephone, the questioning of the patient or family member about violence, the hallway conversation with a colleague to communicate information, or the careful consideration of options is unlikely to be retrieved intact from memory; nor would it make much difference if it were. Juries are rightly skeptical of self-interested statements by people who have a lot to lose. "If you did it, why didn't you write it down?" they will reason. "I was busy" is not a credible retort. Unrecorded warnings to a patient's family member that he or she has been threatened with harm are useless when that family member is dead as a result of the threatened violence or is the plaintiff in a suit for damages against the therapist. From the perspective of violence prevention, the suggestions made regarding obtaining and communicating information and developing and monitoring a risk management plan are equally applicable whether or not a record is made. From the perspective of reducing exposure to liability, there is little point in doing any of them unless they are memorialized in ink or on a dated disk (or by a videotaped exit interview; see Poythress, 1990, 1991).

Documenting information received and actions

taken, or "building the record," is an essential exposure-limitation technique. When recording information relevant to risk—for example, a statement from a family member that a patient made a violent threat—one should note three things: the *source* of the information (e.g., the name of the family member), the *content* of the information (e.g., the nature and circumstances of the threat), and the *date* on which the information was obtained or communicated. In addition, when noting an action taken in furtherance of a risk reduction plan (e.g., committing or not committing a patient, warning or not warning a potential victim), it is essential to include a statement, however brief, of the *rationale* for the action. A comment in the chart or discharge summary reading—for example, "Called mother on 6/21. She said that she did not take patient's threats seriously, and that he had always complied with medication in the past"—is worth its weight in gold (perhaps literally) in demonstrating a good faith effort to attend to risk.

POLICY

The time for a clinician to think through difficult issues regarding risk assessment and management is not when a patient makes a threat or misses a follow-up appointment. Rather, general policy choices should be made and reflected upon before the need for them arises in a given case. These policies or guidelines should be committed to writing and should be reviewed by experienced clinicians and lawyers. Staff should be educated in the use of the guidelines, and their compliance should be audited. Finally, forms should be revised to prompt and record the actions contemplated by the policy statement.

Written Guidelines

Memorializing "risk policy" in writing has several virtues (Bennett, Bryant, VandenBos, & Greenwood, 1990). It promotes clarity of thought and thus is conducive to formulating effective procedures, from both the viewpoints of violence prevention and the reduction of exposure to liability. In an organizational context, it allows for consistency of application, so that staff members are not acting at cross purposes ("I thought that it was *your* responsibility to warn the family!"). And it is efficient in the sense that novice clinicians, or clinicians new to the organization, can more quickly be brought up to the level of practitioners experienced in handling potentially violent patients. The guidelines should periodically (e.g., annually) be reviewed, with an eye to revision in light of developments in research, practice, or state law.

The absolutely essential point here is that the guidelines should reflect *the minimal standards necessary for competent professional practice* and not the ideals to which an organization would aspire if it had unlimited resources. . . .

External Review

Experienced clinicians should be the ones to draft risk policy. But the draft should be reviewed by other clinicians from comparable facilities elsewhere (Poythress, 1987). As with securing consultation on difficult cases . . . policy consultation serves two purposes. It allows the drafting clinicians to learn from the experience of others and, thus, to substantively improve the quality of their procedures. If the question of the reasonableness of the policies is later impugned in a tort suit, it is very helpful to announce that they received the blessing of the most relevant slice of the professional community before the events that gave rise to the suit. A leadership role can productively be played by state and local professional organizations in drafting model guidelines in this area. . . . In addition to review by external clinicians, review by house or retained counsel is also essential to make certain that the policies comport with the statutory and case law of the jurisdiction.

Staff Education and Compliance

It is not enough—indeed, it is counterproductive—to draft exemplary guidelines and subject them to clinical and legal review if the guidelines are merely to be filed in some cabinet or entombed in a staff handbook, never to be read. Again, *it is much better to have no policies at all than to have policies that are not followed in actual practice.* . . .

Once the staff have been educated in the use of

the guidelines, their compliance should be the subject of periodic "audits." A senior colleague . . . should review files to see whether the guidelines are being followed in practice, whether, for example, records are requested, information is communicated, and all actions are properly documented. Corrective action—including the revision of unworkable policies—should then be taken.

Useful Forms

The creation of user friendly forms for documenting actions called for by policy guidelines can both prompt and memorialize appropriate inquiries and responses. I have seen many a case saved for defendants by clinicians having simply checked off "no" to a list of intake questions, including the items "violent history" and "violent ideation." Expanding that list to incorporate more items contemplated in the risk-policy statement—for example, fill-in-the-blanks for "records requested from _____" "concerns communicated to _____" and "attempted to follow-up by _____"—would be very useful both in terms of violence prevention and exposure limitations. Forms should facilitate, rather than impede, gathering necessary information, taking appropriate action, and documenting both information and actions. . . .

DAMAGE CONTROL

Risk assessment and risk management involve probabilistic judgments. By definition, these judgments will sometimes be wrong—not wrong in the sense of mistake, but wrong in the sense that low probability events do happen. . . . In the context of being a mental health professional, having a patient kill or severely injure another qualifies as a major life event. I am amazed at how often clinicians panic and take actions that are unwise, unethical, and sometimes illegal. The two most prevalent forms of maladaptive clinician reaction to the stress of patient violence and the fear of liability are tampering with the record and making inculpatory public statements.

Tampering With the Record

In several of the cases on which I have served as an expert witness, a treating clinician has learned of his or her patient's violence from the media and shortly thereafter has gone to the patient's chart and inserted new material tending to support the reasonableness of the decisions that the clinician had made. In each of these cases, to my knowledge, the new material was factually correct. The clinician was not lying about the events that took place, for example, the questioning of family members about the patient's violent history or the attempt to follow up on missed aftercare appointments. But the clinician was lying about the date that these events were recorded: The entries were back-dated to appear as if they had been written before the violent act took place. . . .

. . . [I]t should be clear why tampering with the record is *always* wrong, even when the intent is to make the record more accurately reflect what actually transpired in a case. It may be legally actionable, and it is strategically catastrophic.

If a suit has not been filed, one can argue that the record does not yet constitute evidence and so changing it is not illegal. But once a suit is filed, changing the record can constitute obstruction of justice. If the clinician is asked under oath whether the records—and the dates of entry are part of the records—are accurate and testifies affirmatively and if the late entries come to light, the clinician is guilty of perjury, a criminal offense.

The most likely outcome of tampering with the record . . . is to completely destroy whatever chances one had of winning the case. . . . It is much better to admit that you didn't keep good records and hope that the jury believes you when you tell them what happened than to manufacture good records after the fact at the cost of your own integrity and credibility.

Public Confessions

Therapists often feel responsible when a patient commits suicide. It is at least as traumatic for the therapist when a patient kills an innocent third party. Clinicians are not immune from the hindsight effect: Everything seems clear and determined in retrospect (Wexler & Schopp, 1989). Given the nature of their occupation, clinicians will often want to talk through their feelings of guilt; however, they are strongly advised to resist such public confessional

urges (and might if necessary be advised to go to their own therapist to express their affect in the context of a confidential relationship). Whatever the clinician says can only hurt his or her case if a suit is filed, and, indeed, it may make the filing of a suit more likely. . . .

References

Appelbaum, P. (1985). *Tarasoff* and the clinician: Problems in fulfilling the duty to protect. *American Journal of Psychiatry, 142,* 425–429.

Appelbaum, P., Zonana, H., Bonnie, R., & Roth, L. (1989). Statutory approaches to limiting psychiatrist's liability for their patients' violent acts. *American Journal of Psychiatry, 146,* 821–828.

Bennett, B., Bryant, B., VandenBos, G., & Greenwood, A. (1990). *Professional liability and risk management.* Washington, DC: American Psychological Association.

Dietz, P. (1990). Defenses against dangerous people when arrest and commitment fail. In R. Simon (Ed.), *Review of clinical psychiatry and the law* (Vol. 1, pp. 205–219). Washington, DC: American Psychiatric Press.

Klein, J. (1986). The professional liability crisis: An interview with Joel Klein. *Hospital and Community Psychiatry, 37,* 1012–1016.

Meichenbaum, D., & Turk, D. (1987). *Facilitating treatment adherence: A practitioner's guidebook.* New York: Plenum Press.

Monahan, J. (1981). *The clinical prediction of violent behavior.* Washington, DC: U.S. Government Printing Office.

Poythress, N. (1987). Avoiding negligent release: A risk-management strategy. *Hospital and Community Psychiatry, 38,* 1051–1052.

Poythress, N. (1990). Avoiding negligent release: Contemporary clinical and risk management strategies. *American Journal of Psychiatry, 147,* 994–997.

Poythress, N. (1991). [Letter]. *American Journal of Psychiatry, 148,* 691–692.

Rachlin, S., & Schwartz, H. (1986). Unforeseeable liability for patients' violent acts. *Hospital and Community Psychiatry, 37,* 725–731.

Tarasoff v. Regents of the University of California, 131 Cal. Rptr. 14, 551 P.2d 334 (1976).

Wexler, D. (1981). *Mental health law: Major issues.* New York: Plenum Press.

Wexler, D., & Schopp, R. (1989). How and when to correct for juror hindsight bias in mental health malpractice litigation: Some preliminary observations. *Behavioral Sciences and the Law, 7,* 485–504.

Outpatient Psychotherapy With Dangerous Clients: A Model for Clinical Decision Making

Derek Truscott, Jim Evans, and Sheila Mansell

. . .

INTERVENTION SELECTION

When a client's potential for violence becomes an issue in outpatient psychotherapy, the therapist rarely has the time to ponder the finer points of ethics, legal duty, diagnosis, and other issues. We propose that the client be thought of as occupying one of four cells in a 2 × 2, Violence Risk × Alliance Strength, table. Interventions are then selected to strengthen the therapeutic alliance and reduce the risk of violence as identified by Botkin and Nietzel (1987) and Monahan (1993), thereby "moving" the client to the lower right cell of low violence risk, strong therapeutic alliance. This formulation is presented in Figure 1.

We assert that attending to the degree of violence risk and the strength of the therapeutic alliance is central both to the effective treatment of these clients and to the protection of their potential victims. The therapeutic alliance should be strengthened as much as possible because it is the foundation on which all treatment interventions are built (Whiston & Sexton, 1993); furthermore, if one acts only to prevent a current violent episode without attending to the therapeutic alliance, it may enrage a client and actually increase the risk of violence while simultaneously deterring the client from seeking further psychotherapeutic services for dealing with any future violent impulses (Weinstock, 1988). If the risk of violence is low, the therapist should attempt to strengthen the alliance and to shift the focus of

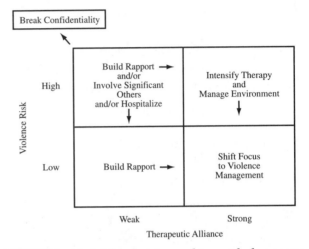

FIGURE 1. Model for decision making with dangerous clients.

therapy to deal more specifically with the violent behavior (as one would with any therapeutic issue).

. . .

CASE ILLUSTRATIONS

The following cases illustrate the application of the model to clients at high risk for violent behavior.

. . .

High Risk, Strong Alliance → Low Risk, Strong Alliance

If the risk of violence is high and the therapeutic alliance is strong, therapy should be intensified and the therapeutic alliance should be used to help the client make his or her environment less lethal, thereby assisting the client to control his or her violent behavior (Roth & Meisel, 1977; Wulsin, Bursztajn, & Gutheil, 1983). Sessions can be scheduled more frequently, medication initiated or increased, weapons removed, or joint sessions held with the client and others who are significant to the occurrence of violence (Monahan, 1993).

Case 1. Mr. B., a 29-year-old welder, was seen following a closed-head injury. In the initial interview, he reported instances of involuntary aggression against a variety of people, including strangers and a playmate of his child, and he requested assistance in dealing with them. Neuropsychological and intelligence test results were within normal limits, as were a computed tomography scan and an electroencephalogram. He complained of blackouts in connection with his violent behavior, but these had never been observed and they appeared to be a dissociative reaction to extreme emotion. At the time, he was taking antiseizure medication with limited effect.

As a child, Mr. B. witnessed his father inflict extreme violence on his mother. As Mr. B. grew older, he became increasingly enraged with his father to the point of threatening to kill him. As an adult, he continued to have nightmares in which he assaulted his father in order to protect his mother. Mr. B.'s wife left him a year after the accident because of his violent behavior toward her.

During therapy, Mr. B. reported being very frightened by his episodes of uncontrolled violence. Anger management training was initiated that focused on his being able to calm himself in interpersonal situations. Shortly after therapy was initiated his mother died and his fiancée miscarried her pregnancy. He reported being increasingly frightened by the feeling that he was likely to harm someone. He and his therapist de-

cided that he should stay in his home, enlist his brother to take away a gun and the knives in his house, and avoid contact with others until he was able to attend a neuropsychiatric consultation. This consultation was arranged on an emergency basis, and a trial of antidepressant medication was initiated, which substantially decreased his violent impulses. Anger management training continued to good effect.

High Risk, Weak Alliance → Low Risk, Strong Alliance

When a client is at high risk for violence and the therapeutic alliance is weak, the therapist should attempt to strengthen the alliance. If an alliance has not yet been established, the therapist should endeavor to behave in an affiliative, autonomy-granting manner and should refrain from responding in a hostile or controlling manner (Henry & Strupp, 1994). If the therapeutic alliance has already been established and is strained by the current situation, the therapist should openly identify and discuss the client's perception of the alliance, listen nonjudgmentally, identify any misperceptions, and make any necessary adjustments to the therapeutic relationship (Safran, Muran, & Samstag, 1994). The strong reactions that the therapist is likely to feel should be used to help understand the client and to help the client understand the reactions that they arouse in others (Gelso & Carter, 1994). Simultaneously, or in sequence, the therapist should work with the client to alter those aspects of the client's physical and interpersonal environment that are promoting or maintaining violence.

Case 2. Mr. V., a 30-year-old laborer, received psychotherapy for the following reasons: to assist him in dealing with seeking a new line of work, despite his being functionally illiterate and physically handicapped; to help him learn how to deal with his constant pain without using medications; and to help him with marital difficulties. His presentation was marked in its extremity; he was very jovial and laughed almost continuously throughout the first interview. He agreed to meet weekly, although he stated that he did not think it necessary.

After missing numerous sessions, Mr. V. asked for an extra session. He presented at this time as very upset. He explained that attempts to improve his relationship with his wife (from whom he was recently separated) had not gone well and that he had been diagnosed as having cancer. He reported feeling very alone with no one to confide in. Additional sessions were scheduled and marital sessions were arranged. Over the next few days, he calmed down, but his marital situation continued to deteriorate, and he cancelled the marital sessions. One and a half weeks (and four sessions) after asking for an extra session, Mr. V. presented on a Friday afternoon as extremely upset. He was very angry and paced around the office. He reported that his wife had taken all of the belongings from their home, including his clothing and every article of furniture. Mr. V. reported that he had felt suicidal the night before but that he now wanted to kill his wife.

The therapist focused on strengthening the therapeutic alliance by clearing his schedule to spend more than 2 hours with Mr. V. and allowing him adequate time to emotionally vent in a nonjudgmental atmosphere. The risk of violence was addressed and the relationship was further strengthened by discussing the rationality of his plan, alternate plans, and ways of reducing other stressors. In the interests of strengthening the alliance further still, and to provide an opportunity to reduce any increase in violence risk, the therapist gave Mr. V. his after-hours telephone number and made an appointment for the following Monday.

On Monday, Mr. V. reported feeling

settled and had decided to sever all ties with his wife. He attended two more sessions over the next two months and reported that he did not desire any further therapy. A year and a half later, he reported that he was doing well and no harm had come to his (now ex-) wife.

High Risk, Weak Alliance → Low Risk, Weak Alliance

If the alliance cannot be strengthened, the factors promoting violence should be eliminated or significantly reduced so that risk is lessened. This risk reduction will often involve including significant others, such as the client's family members or possibly the police in preventive measures; however, a warning to potential victims should not be issued at this stage. A warning may result in needless emotional distress in the potential victim if the violence is prevented, and this psychic injury could even form the basis for a lawsuit against the therapist (Lewis, 1986). The client should be informed of the limits of confidentiality and the steps that will be taken. Civil commitment proceedings should also be considered—even if there is some doubt as to whether or not the client meets the appropriate criteria—ideally by the client on a voluntary basis. Under this circumstance, the therapist would be responsible for following up to ensure that the client had indeed been committed.

Case 3. Mr. K. was never seen in person. He telephoned a receptionist and began a long diatribe about how he had been mistreated by the Compensation Board, the government, and a variety of other institutions. He was intoxicated and, after about 20 min of nonstop talking that grew more and more abusive, threatened to "drive up there and shoot the whole lot of you." The receptionist contacted the Psychology Department for assistance.

A therapist contacted Mr. K. by telephone and assessed the situation as follows: Mr. K. appeared to intend to carry out his threat, he reported having been violent in the past, he had a contentious claim with the Compensation Board that had been ongoing for 4 years, it was unclear whether he had access to a firearm, he appeared to be very much intoxicated, and he had just been notified that he had no further avenues for appeal regarding his claim for compensation. The only positive factor in this assessment was that Mr. K. did not have ready access to his intended victims as he lived in a rural area and did not have a motor vehicle. He also told the therapist, in response to queries as to any social supports, that his brother lived nearby and was a soothing influence. He gave his permission for the therapist to speak to his brother.

The therapist contacted Mr. K.'s brother, who agreed to visit Mr. K. and to try to restrict his alcohol intake and calm him down. When asked, Mr. K.'s brother reported that these episodes occurred with some regularity and that he did not believe that his own life was in danger. He was asked about firearms, and he reported that they had been confiscated by the police a number of years ago under similar circumstances. He phoned back later in the day and reported that Mr. K. was "sleeping it off."

Mr. K. was contacted the following day, was apparently sober, and did not appear to remember having spoken to the therapist. He admitted that he sometimes wanted to harm employees of the Compensation Board, but he stated that he had no intention of doing so at the present time. He was offered psychotherapy in his community and he accepted. He was informed that the police would be notified if he made any more threats and that the receptionists were instructed to do so.

High Risk, Weak Alliance → Break Confidentiality

Only if the therapeutic alliance cannot be strengthened sufficiently enough to implement violence-risk-reducing interventions, or if hospitalization cannot be initiated quickly enough, should potential victims (or their families) and the police be warned, even if there is fear of legal reprisal by the client (Eberlein, 1980). Once confidence is broken, the client's trust in the therapist, and probably in psychotherapy in general, will be lost along with the opportunity for any further therapeutic work. Ideally, permission will be obtained from the client to warn the intended victim(s) or notify the police, thereby circumventing any violation of confidentiality (Fulero, 1988) and loss of trust (Slovenko, 1975). When third parties are involved, only that information necessary to prevent the foreseen violent act should be divulged.

Case 4. Mr. M. telephoned a receptionist and asked to speak with a therapist. After the call was transferred, he proceeded to explain that he had sent his wife and children to a shelter for battered women, that his house had been robbed, and that he was very angry about how he had been treated by the case worker who was handling his Workers' Compensation Board claim. He then issued an ultimatum that he get the money he needed "or else," and he then terminated the telephone call.

Mr. M. telephoned again later that day, and the therapist informed him that he had made enquiries into who would be best able to help him. Mr. M. stated that he would talk to no one else but the therapist and requested a face-to-face meeting. This meeting was arranged and the call was ended. He called again an hour later and asked how things were proceeding. He was much more angry and emotionally upset and spent little time engaged in rational planning. He then issued a veiled threat toward his case worker and hung up. Fifteen minutes later, he called once again and was even more emotional; he stated that he would shoot his case worker and then he hung up.

Mr. M.'s threat was judged to be serious, his history of violence was unknown apart from the implication that he had been violent toward his family, he knew where his intended victim worked, his access to a weapon was unknown, he appeared to be very agitated, he perceived his case worker as the source of his problems, and efforts to dissuade him appeared to be ineffectual in the context of a weak therapeutic alliance.

The therapist informed the police and warned the case worker. Mr. M. was apprehended, and, after two court appearances, he eventually pleaded guilty to criminal charges of uttering a threat to cause death or bodily harm.

References

Botkin, D. J., & Nietzel, M. T. (1987). How therapists manage potentially dangerous clients: Toward a standard of care for psychotherapists. *Professional Psychology: Research and Practice, 18,* 84–85.

Eberlein, L. (1980). Legal duty and confidentiality of psychologists: Tarasoff and Haines. *Canadian Psychology, 21,* 49–58.

Fulero, S. M. (1988). *Tarasoff:* 10 years later. *Professional Psychology, 19,* 184–190.

Gelso, C. J., & Carter, J. A. (1994). Components of the psychotherapy relationship: Their interaction and unfolding during treatment. *Journal of Counseling Psychology, 41,* 296–306.

Henry, W. P., & Strupp, H. H. (1994). The therapeutic alliance as interpersonal process. In A. O. Horvath & L. S. Greenberg (Eds.), *The working alliance: Theory, research, and practice* (pp. 51–84). New York: Wiley.

Lewis, M. B. (1986). Duty to warn versus duty to maintain confidentiality: Conflicting demands on mental health professionals. *Suffolk University Law Review, 20,* 579–615.

Monahan, J. (1993). Limiting therapist exposure to *Tarasoff* liability: Guidelines for risk containment. *American Psychologist, 48,* 242–250.

Roth, L. H., & Meisel, A. (1977). Dangerousness, confidentiality, and the duty to warn. *American Journal of Psychiatry, 134,* 508–511.

Safran, J. D., Muran, J. C., & Samstag, L. W. (1994). Resolving therapeutic alliance ruptures: A task analytic investigation. In A. Horvath & L. S. Greenberg (Eds.), *The working alliance: Theory, research, and practice* (pp. 225–255). New York: Wiley.

Slovenko, R. (1975). Psychotherapy and confidentiality. *Cleveland State Law Review, 24,* 375–391.

Weinstock, R. (1988). Confidentiality and the new duty to protect: The therapist's dilemma. *Hospital and Community Psychiatry, 39,* 607–609.

Whiston, S. C., & Sexton, T. L. (1993). An overview of psychotherapy outcome research: Implications for practice. *Professional Psychology: Research and Practice, 24,* 43–51.

Wulsin, L. R., Bursztajn, H., & Gutheil, T. G. (1983). Unexpected clinical features of the *Tarasoff* decision: The therapeutic alliance and the "duty to warn." *American Journal of Psychiatry, 140,* 601–603.

◆ ◆ ◆

Commentary: In 1978, the Stanford Law Review *published the results of a post-*Tarasoff *survey based on a mailed questionnaire to 1,272 California psychiatrists and psychologists, most of whom were middle-aged males. The survey revealed the following:*

1. *There was only tenuous evidence to suggest that there was an increase in actual warnings by respondents, but when there was, a greater percentage of warnings were made to the potential victim.*
2. *Many respondents reported increased anxiety when their patients raised the subject of dangerousness in therapy; 16% of respondents were more reluctant to probe the topic.*
3. *Many therapists lowered the threshold at which they considered the patient dangerous, triggering warnings to third parties.*

Almost all the respondents in this survey were in private practice. In a study by Beck (1982), who used face-to-face interviews with psychiatrists who worked in institutions that served violent patients, the respondents seemed to deal with the Tarasoff *situation differently. These clinicians were likely to choose civil commitment of the patient rather than issue warnings. Warnings were given only when the violent threat was deemed vague or remote. In many cases, when there was a good therapeutic alliance, the threats were dealt with solely within the therapy itself. See:*

Beck, J. C. (1982). When the patient threatens violence: An empirical study of clinical practice after Tarasoff. American Academy of Psychiatry and Law Bulletin, 10, 189–202.

Wise, T. P. (1978). Where the public peril begins: A survey of psychotherapists to determine the effects of Tarasoff. Stanford Law Review, 31, 165–190; see also

Quinn, K. M. (1984). The impact of Tarasoff on clinical practice. Behavioral Sciences and the Law, 2, 319–329.

In 1984, the Wisconsin Law Review (Givelber, Bowers, & Blitch, 1984), criticizing Wise's (1978, see above) methodology, reported the results of its own survey of 2,875 psychiatrists, psychologists, and social workers located in the eight largest metropolitan population centers in the United States. The most relevant major findings from Givelber et al. were as follows:

1. Almost all mental health professionals had heard of Tarasoff or a case like it: "These data demonstrate that the court and its critics were justified in believing that the . . . decision would be well known and therefore might have a substantial influence on therapeutic practice" (pp. 458–459).

2. About one in four respondents mistakenly believed that the decision applied whenever a client made a threat. The majority recognized that the Tarasoff obligation arises "when a therapist actually believes someone is dangerous and also when a reasonable therapist would believe this" (p. 461).

3. Contrary to the positions taken in the American Psychiatric Association's amicus curiae brief in the California Supreme Court, about 75% of the respondents "felt that they could make a prediction [about future violence] ranging from 'probable' to 'certain'" (p. 463). Only 5% felt that there was no way to predict violent behavior. In addition, a majority of therapists believed that "there are objective professional standards for evaluating dangerousness" (p. 464).

4. A majority of therapists wrongly believed that Tarasoff requires warning the intended victim. Only a small minority understood that the case requires mental health professionals to use reasonable care to protect the intended victim.

5. In the 12 months prior to the survey, an "overwhelming majority" of therapists surveyed had communicated confidential information disclosed in therapy to third parties (although of psychiatrists, social workers, and psychologists, the latter were least

likely to do so). Thus, "while confidentiality may well represent an important ethical and therapeutic value, it is apparently a value which therapists . . . will frequently be forced to compromise" (p. 468).

6. About 50% of the therapists who had communicated with potential victims believed that they "had to violate their own clinical judgment" (p. 470) in doing so.

7. However, a significant majority of therapists considered "responsibility to potential victims to be a professional [or personal] ethical obligation" (p. 475).

8. In addition to producing an increased willingness to notify third parties of their dangerous patients, Tarasoff had "influenced willingness to take notes and to initiate involuntary hospitalization" (p. 478), but it had not lessened willingness to treat dangerous patients.

See Givelber, D. J., Bowers, W. J., & Blitch, C. L. (1984). Tarasoff, myth and reality: An empirical study of private law in action. Wisconsin Law Review, 1984, 443–497.

Using the material concerning the duties generated by Tarasoff and the later cases it spawned, and applying the problem-solving techniques for handling complex ethical dilemmas delineated in chapter 3, how would you handle the following situation?

A woman in her 20s had been involved for almost two years in an abusive relationship. Although the relationship began benignly, once the couple moved in together, over the course of the next year the man inflicted on the woman bruises, a mild concussion, and a broken nose. All injuries were serious enough for the woman to seek treatment in an emergency room. After leaving her husband, the woman now undergoes psychotherapy at a clinic for battered women and presently lives in a safe house connected to the clinic.

Also being seen by the same therapist at the same clinic is another woman who survived an abusive relationship with her husband, albeit only by shooting him during one of his assaults. She was found not guilty of the killing and subsequently sought supportive therapy. After several months of treatment she tells her therapist that she has begun a romantic relationship with a wonderful and kind man. This marvelous man, however, is the same one who had abused the therapist's other battering survivor.

This situation is adapted from a 1994 case vignette: Confidentiality and spouse battering. Ethics and Behavior, *4, 161–162. Think through the issues carefully. They are more complex than you may initially think. For three different analyses, from a noted authority on battered spouses, a lawyer, and an ethicist, respectively, see:*

Walker, L. E. A. (1994). The importance of knowing what you know and don't know. Ethics and Behavior, 4, 162–167.

Bourne, R. (1994). Rocky Brute: A duty to warn? Ethics and Behavior, 4, 167–170.

Ryan, M. A. (1994). Double trouble: "Rocky Brute" and the ethics of confidentiality. Ethics and Behavior, 4, 171–173.

Finally, for an analysis of the therapist's different duties when the client engages in violence impulsively, rather than after disclosure of an articulated plan, see Beck, J. C. (1998). Legal and ethical duties of the clinician treating a patient who is liable to be impulsively violent. Behavioral Sciences and the Law, 16, 375–389.

If It's Not Absolutely Confidential, Will Information Be Disclosed?

David Nowell and Jean Spruill

The latest revision of the ethical principles (APA, 1992) . . . indicat[es] that psychologists should discuss the relevant limitations on confidentiality at the onset of the relationship unless it is not feasible or is contraindicated. In Baird and Rupert's (1987) survey of psychotherapists, only 61% of the respondents reported discussing confidentiality with their clients, and 19% of those reported telling clients that "everything they say in therapy is confidential." Such a statement has been referred to as a "blatant misrepresentation of facts that should be known to all therapists" (Bersoff, 1975, p. 270).

Does telling the client about limits to confidentiality affect the therapeutic relationship or client self-disclosure? . . .

The purpose of the present study was to investigate, in a survey situation, the effect of varying information regarding limits of confidentiality on subjects' anticipated disclosure about a variety of topics. Additionally, the effects of specific inhibition and severity level of the material to be disclosed were investigated. Perhaps psychotherapy clients refrain from divulging sensitive or personal information only in those areas specifically addressed by the therapist in his or her discussion of limits of confidentiality. The typical focus of such discussions concerns the potential to harm oneself or others; therefore, it was predicted that subjects would be less willing to disclose information in the areas specifically addressed in the discussion of the limits of confidentiality than in the areas not specifically discussed. Additionally, it was expected that the subjects would report greater willingness to disclose information considered to be of "low-severity than high-severity" (e.g., symptoms of depression vs. symptoms of psychosis).

METHOD

Subjects

Subjects were 75 undergraduate students enrolled in an introductory psychology course at a large southern university. . . . Approximately 13% of the subjects in this study indicated some prior experience in therapy.

Measure

A questionnaire developed by David Nowell in a preliminary study (Nowell, 1991) was used to assess subjects' anticipated willingness to self-disclose information about several common clinical concerns: depression/anxiety; substance use/abuse; physical/psychological aggression; suicidal thought/behavior; and psychotic thought/behavior. The questionnaire consisted of 2 items of high severity and 2 items of low severity for each of the five areas, along with 25 filler items. Examples of high- and low-severity items in the psychotic thought/behavior category were, respectively, statements such as "hearing voices (that others cannot hear) that command you to perform some act" and "having friends recently tell you that they like you because you are a bit 'odd' or 'eccentric.'"

Procedure

Subjects were randomly assigned to one of three experimental groups. All subjects received a Psychology Clinic Client Awareness Form that gave information about psychological services offered, limits of confidentiality, fees, and appointment cancellation policy. The forms were identical for all subjects except for the information about confidentiality. The absolute confidentiality group was told that all information they disclosed would be held confidential. Subjects in the short-form group were given general information about limits to confidentiality and were told that, in general, information was confidential unless the therapist had reason to believe the client might harm him- or herself or others. Subjects in the long-form group were given information about these exceptions plus detailed information about other specific exceptions to confidentiality, such as the reporting of actual or suspected child abuse, court subpoenas, and so on [footnote omitted].

After reading and signing the Psychology Clinic Client Awareness Form, subjects were given the questionnaire and the following instructions: "Imagine you are seeking psychotherapy and that you have engaged in or experienced each of the behaviors or experiences described in this questionnaire." Subjects then responded to each item of the questionnaire, indicating their degree of willingness to disclose to a therapist information about each of the behaviors or experiences. A 7-point Likert-type scale was used, ranging from *unwillingness to disclose information* (1) to *willingness to disclose information* (7). Subjects were informed that they could discontinue the study at any time without penalty. Subjects were encouraged to contact the experimenters with any questions or concerns they had regarding the study.

[*Ed. note:* The Results section has been omitted. In summary, subjects in the absolute confidentiality condition (*M* = 5.52) were more willing to disclose information than were subjects in the limited confidentiality group (*M* = 4.88). The difference between the means of the short- and long-form (*M* = 5.11) groups was not significant.

Subjects were more willing to disclose information concerning low-severity items than about high-severity items, regardless of content area or group membership; but subjects in the absolute confidentiality group were significantly more willing to disclose information about high-severity items than were subjects in the limited confidentiality group.

With regard to content, subjects were more willing to disclose information about aggressive thoughts than suicidal thoughts and were less willing to disclose information about substance abuse than about depression and thought disorder; but they were more willing to disclose information about depression than about thought disorder.]

. . .

DISCUSSION

. . .

One implication of this study is that clients' understanding of the limits of confidentiality may influence their willingness to self-disclose regarding behaviors or experiences considered serious or extreme. Once informed that there are limits to the confidentiality of the therapeutic relationship, clients may engage in less self-disclosure. However, as indicated by this study and an earlier study comparing levels of information regarding limits of confidentiality (Muehleman et al., 1985), a complete explanation of the limits of confidentiality may not produce more inhibition than would a brief, cursory explanation. Whether they are offered absolute confidentiality or limited confidentiality, subjects in this study anticipated less disclosure about intent to harm others than about other experiences, such as depression. There appears to be an understood taboo against disclosing aggressive behaviors and experiences, independent of the explanation of the limits of the therapist's ability to keep such material confidential.

Caution should be taken in generalizing from the population of this study to the population of interest: psychotherapy clients. What subjects in this study—undergraduate students in an introductory psychology course—did and said may not be predictive of what psychotherapy clients would say or do. Additionally, this was a survey in which subjects were asked to indicate "what they would disclose if in therapy" rather than what they "did disclose in therapy." Studies comparing the experience of clients who have received differential information regarding the limits of confidentiality are needed to address this issue. Concerns held by some clinicians that a discussion with a client about the limits of therapeutic confidentiality will lead to decreased self-disclosure appear to be supported by this and other research (e.g., Woods & McNamara, 1980). However, it should be noted that therapists have an ethical and, in some states, a legal obligation to inform clients of the limits of confidentiality as defined in their state. . . . This research suggests that, contrary to some clinical beliefs, complete, detailed information regarding limits of confidentiality may not lead to greater inhibition of self-disclosure than would a brief, cursory discussion of these limits. As a matter of self-protection for the therapist, and of consumers' rights for the client, offering a detailed description of the circumstances under which confidentiality can be broken may be the therapist's best course of action when establishing a therapy relationship.

References

American Psychological Association. (1992). Ethical principles of psychologists and code of conduct. *American Psychologist, 47,* 1597–1611.

Baird, K. A., & Rupert, P. A. (1987). Clinical management of confidentiality: A survey of psychologists in seven states. *Professional Psychology: Research and Practice, 18,* 347–352.

Bersoff, D. N. (1975). Professional ethics and legal responsibilities: On the horns of a dilemma. *Journal of School Psychology, 13,* 359–376.

Muehleman, T., Pickens, B. K., & Robinson, F. (1985). Informing clients about the limits to confidentiality, risks, and their rights: Is self-disclosure inhibited? *Professional Psychology: Research and Practice, 16,* 385–397.

Nowell, D. D. (1991). *The effects of varying information regarding limits of confidentiality on willingness to self-disclose.* Unpublished master's thesis, University of Alabama, Tuscaloosa.

Woods, K. M., & McNamara, J. R. (1980). Confidentiality Its effect on interviewee behavior. *Professional Psychology, 11,* 714–721.

◆ ◆ ◆

Commentary: *As Nowell and Spruill (1993) stated, Standard 5.01 of the APA's 1992 Code of Conduct mandates that psychologists discuss confidentiality "at the outset of the relationship" unless "it is not feasible or is contraindicated." Standard 4.01 requires therapists to discuss confidentiality with their patients "as early as is feasible." Yet, in surveying 204 midwestern psychologists about what procedures they would follow concerning the mandatory reporting of child abuse, Nicolai and Scott (1994) noted these findings with alarm:*

> *Almost 20% of respondents indicated that they sometimes, rarely, or never provide this information to clients and that more than 5% misleadingly tell clients that everything disclosed in therapy is confidential. We are disturbed by these and other findings and their implications.*
>
> *Without explicit presentation of information regarding confidentiality limits, the novice client may well assume that all disclosures, regardless of content, will be kept confidential. Moreover, clinicians who tell clients that everything they say will be held in confidence are clearly putting clients, as well as themselves, at risk. Legal and ethical guidelines for mental health professionals clearly state that clinicians must breach confidentiality when certain information is disclosed by clients in therapy. (p. 158)*

Nicolai, K. M., & Scott, N. A. (1994). Provision of confidentiality information and its relation to child abuse reporting. Professional Psychology: Research and Practice, 25, *154–160.*

For an article examining public attitudes regarding specific situations in which therapists might reveal confidential information, see Rubanowitz, D. E. (1987). Public attitudes toward psychotherapist–patient confidentiality. Professional Psychology: Research and Practice, 18, *613–618.*

The following articles address two issues that are perhaps more complex than those difficult issues to which the reader has already been exposed. First, I review the extent to which a minor's confidential communications are protected from disclosure. Second, I present views of the potentially conflicting duties and obligations of psychologists who provide services to people infected with HIV or AIDS.

McGuire (1974) asserted that the 1963 APA code of ethics was difficult to understand and apply to the relationship between clinicians and child clients, particularly with regard to confidentiality. Review Standards 1.21, 4.02, and 5.01 of the 1992 Ethical Principles and judge whether they offer any greater clarity or guidance to those who work with children than the 1963 code did.

McGuire also conducted a survey of 45 clinicians and found a growing trend among professionals to act as if minors' confidential disclosures could be accorded the same protection as adults. See McGuire, J. M. (1974). *Confidentiality and the child in psychotherapy.* Professional Psychology, 5, 374–379. Was that trend justified from either a legal or an ethical perspective?

Confidentiality With Minor Clients: Issues and Guidelines for Therapists

Kathryn E. Gustafson and J. Regis McNamara

. . .

LEGAL CONSIDERATIONS IN CONSENT TO TREATMENT

Increasingly, minors are legally allowed to pursue treatment without parental consent. Most jurisdictions allow minors to consent to treatment without parental knowledge in specific situations in which obtaining parental consent may jeopardize the likelihood that the minor will receive that treatment (Wilson, 1978). These specific situations include counseling or medical care for sexual abuse, substance abuse, pregnancy, sexually transmitted diseases, and contraception.

In addition, the law has recognized four general exceptions to the requirement of parent consent for treatment of minors (Plotkin, 1981). The first, the "mature minor" exception, pertains to minors with sufficient maturity to understand the nature and consequences of treatment. The second, "emancipated minor," refers to minors who are legally entitled to the rights and duties of adulthood for reasons that vary from state to state (e.g., a married minor). "Emergency treatment" is the third circumstance in which parental consent is not necessary. It is assumed that parental consent is implied because of the urgency of the situation. The final exception to obtaining parental consent is when treatment is court ordered.

These exceptions, although originally designed to clarify the rights of minors, have actually confused practitioners because the exceptions are vague, vary from state to state, and are open to a great amount of interpretation. Thus Plotkin (1981) recommended that the age at which individuals may give consent to treatment be lowered according to data in the child development literature.

DEVELOPMENTAL CONSIDERATIONS IN CONSENT TO TREATMENT

There is accumulating evidence that minors of certain ages may have obtained sufficient developmental maturity to make well-informed decisions about psychotherapeutic treatment. Grisso and Vierling (1978) reviewed the cognitive developmental literature and concluded that "there is little evidence that minors of age 15 and above as a group are any less competent to provide consent than are adults" (p. 423). Below age 11, however, minors are not capable of voluntary consent because they do not have the necessary intellectual capabilities, and they have a tendency toward deference to authority. Weithorn (1982) concurred that when children acquire formal operational thinking, between ages 11 and 14, they are able to conceptualize abstract possibilities and hypothetical outcomes of multiple courses of action and therefore are competent to provide consent. . . .

Moreover, by age 15, adolescents are capable of comprehending and exercising their rights. In a therapy analogue, information provided about clients' rights improved 15-year-old, but not 9-year-old, boys' recognition of rights violations and their capacity to protect those rights (Belter & Grisso, 1984). The 15-year-olds in this study performed as well on these variables as did the 21-year-old subjects.

Another important component in informed consent is the ability to identify potential risks and benefits of therapy. Kaser-Boyd, Adelman, and Taylor (1985) found that minors with learning and behavior problems were capable of identifying relevant therapy risks and benefits. There was a tendency for minors who were older who had had previous therapeutic experience to identify more risks and benefits and to describe these risks and benefits more abstractly. Younger minors and those without previous therapy experience, however, were able to identify risks and benefits that were relevant and practical to their situation.

There is a growing body of evidence that minors can effectively participate in at least some types of treatment decisions. Minors with learning and related behavior problems reported an interest in, and felt competent to participate in, the psychoeducational decisions that affect them, took the steps necessary to get involved, and then felt satisfied with the results of their involvement (Adelman, Lusk, Alvarez, & Acosta, 1985; Taylor, Adelman, & Kaser-Boyd, 1983, 1985). Older students had a greater desire to participate, had a greater tendency to follow through with their plans, and were rated as more effective in doing so by their parents and teachers (Taylor et al., 1985). In addition, adolescents appear to respond more positively to treatment when involved in treatment planning and evaluation (Janzen & Love, 1977) and when they perceive themselves as having a choice about participation (Bastien & Adelman, 1984).

Messenger and McGuire (1981), investigating the child's conception of confidentiality in the therapeutic relationship, also found that older children (ages 12–15) have a significantly better understanding of confidentiality than do younger children (ages 6–8). Thus it appears that children gradually evolve a concept of confidentiality. . . .

DETERMINING THE BEST INTEREST OF THE CHILD

. . . Several authors believe that minors are entitled to the same rights of confidentiality as are adults (Myers, 1982; Patterson, 1971; Wrenn, 1952). As stated by Myers (1982), "the fact of minority in no fashion lessens the importance of the sanctity of confidential communications" (p. 310). Myers maintained that the therapist's duty of confidentiality is not to the parents but to the child because the child is the client. The American Psychiatric Association's Task Force on Confidentiality of Children's and Adolescents' Clinical Records has recommended in their "Model Law of Confidentiality" that the age at which minors may give consent to release confidential information is 12 years or over (American Psychiatric Association, 1979). . . .

Some authors endorse limited confidentiality with minors. Pardue, Whichard, and Johnson (1970) recommended forewarning minors that their parents or guardians might need to become involved, and minors thus informed of this limitation are then free to choose whether to participate in therapy.

Glenn (1980) and Ross (1966) proposed that the determination of whether confidentiality is necessary with minor clients should be decided on an individual, case-by-case basis. Thompson (1983) maintained that "the therapist should decide how the client's guardian is apt to use the disclosed information before deciding whether or not to release it" (p. 99).

There is a paucity of research on what minors perceive as being in their own best interests in regard to confidentiality in the therapeutic relationship. Kobocow et al. (1983) investigated the effects of varying degrees of assurance of confidentiality on self-disclosure in early adolescents. Subjects were reluctant to admit to behaviors that were not socially sanctioned and appeared not to trust the interviewer, even when confidentiality was ensured. Establishing a trusting relationship may be more important than promises of confidentiality when one is dealing with minors (Koocher, 1976, 1983; Ross, 1966). Messenger and McGuire (1981) also suggested that verbal explanations of confidentiality, although necessary, may not be as important as real-life experiences with a therapist who maintains confidentiality. Thus it does appear that confidentiality is important to the older minor.

PROFESSIONAL ATTITUDES AND BEHAVIORS

There is some variability in professionals' consent and confidentiality practices with minor clients. Many therapists apparently provide psychotherapeutic services to minors without parental consent regardless of whether state statutes allow such action (Apsler, cited in Wilson, 1978; Melton, 1981). When providing services to a minor without parental consent, many clinics and practitioners charge either a nominal fee or no fee at all or base the fee on the adolescent's income. Clinics that do not offer such special payment arrangements for minors may discourage minors from seeking treatment because costs would be too exorbitant or because payment by parental insurance would result in parental notification of treatment.

In regard to confidentiality with minor clients, some clinics limit parental access to the minor's treatment records, whereas others allow unlimited parental access to such information (Melton, 1981). McGuire (1974) assessed community mental health professionals' behaviors regarding confidentiality with minors in therapy. He found that the majority of the mental health professionals supported the position that minors should be extended the same rights of confidentiality as adults. Whether this belief was consistent with agency policy or state law was not assessed. . . .

GUIDELINES FOR THERAPISTS

. . .

Whether confidentiality will be ensured may influence the adolescent's decision to enter psychotherapy. An adolescent not guaranteed confidentiality may decide not to enter therapy or may reluctantly participate without disclosing his or her concerns. Thus as with adult clients, ensuring confidentiality serves the interests of society in that it induces individuals in need of treatment to seek that treatment.

Involving adolescents in treatment planning and assuring confidentiality in the relationship may have therapeutic benefits as well. Minors who construe themselves as active participants in a confidential relationship are more likely to be allied with the therapist and hence less likely to resist therapeutic progress.

Moreover, adolescent involvement in treatment decision making, including what information can be revealed to whom, also provides an important social learning experience. It provides them with experience for future decision making and gives them a sense of being active, responsible participants in their own welfare (Weithorn, 1983).

The degree of confidentiality afforded a minor client should be based on consideration of several factors. First, the therapist should consider the age of the client. . . . The therapist should consider the needs and desires of the child, the concerns of the parents, the particular presenting problem, and relevant state statutes in deciding what degree of confidentiality is appropriate with preadolescent children. Second, because age is only a rough indicator of cognitive functioning, the therapist should make an informal assessment of the minor's cognitive capacity, including factors such as intelligence, Piagetian stage, and Kohlbergian reasoning level. . . .

There are a number of strategies that the clinicians can use to optimize the therapeutic experience while simultaneously upholding the rights of both the minor and the parents:

1. Once the therapist has made a decision regarding the degree of confidentiality believed to be necessary and appropriate, the therapist should schedule a pretreatment family meeting with the parents and the adolescent and explain his or her rationale for this decision. The therapist should develop rapport with all family members, and all family members should demonstrate sufficient understanding of the conditions of treatment, including confidentiality. He or she should then prepare a written professional services agreement . . . fully detailing the conditions and the limits of the confidential relationship. All participating parties—parents, the adolescent, and the therapist—should sign the professional services agreement, and it should become part of the minor's permanent file.

The professional services agreement, as well as open communication and rapport, is likely to discourage parents from demanding information obtained in therapy. In some cases, however, the parents may subsequently demand access to the files. It is unclear whether courts would decide in favor of the parents or uphold the professional service contract. . . .

2. Depending on the nature of the presenting concern and the preferences of the therapist, the parents may be involved in the treatment in different capacities. Indeed, family involvement can be therapeutically beneficial, and it is often the treatment of choice in work with minors. Yet, the adolescent's communications may still remain confidential. Parents are sometimes involved directly in treatment, such as when an improved parent–adolescent relationship is the ultimate therapeutic goal. Maintaining confidentiality does not necessarily interfere with this goal. In some cases, family relationships have deteriorated to a point to preclude immediate, productive family work. Relationship and communication skills enhancement may first be necessary with the therapist and adolescent before it is extended to the parent and adolescent. At other times, parents may be involved indirectly, such as through monitoring the adolescent's behavior at home for change outside of therapy. In cases in which the adolescent has personal concerns, parent involvement may be even more limited. In those cases, the parents should be cautioned that adolescents often develop a strong trusting relationship with the therapist; the adolescent may reveal more intimate information to the therapist than to the parents. The therapist should explore with the parents whether such a relationship between the therapist and their child is likely to be threatening or to provoke jealousy in the parents. A frank, honest discussion of these feelings can be beneficial. . . .

3. Parents should be encouraged to initiate future family meetings if at any time during treatment they have concerns about the therapeutic process. It should be clear to both the parents and the adolescent (as stated in the professional service agreement) that family sessions will not compromise the confidential relationship between the therapist and the minor. It is important to maintain a relationship with the parents while still maintaining confidentiality of the adolescent's private disclosures. This allows the parents to more adequately assess the competence of the therapist and the effectiveness of therapy.

4. Throughout the duration of treatment, the clinician should make an attempt to provide treatment rationales and explanations that are developmentally appropriate for the adolescent. . . .

5. It is imperative that the clinician be familiar with any relevant statutes in his or her state of residence and adopt policies consistent with these statutes. Confidentiality with minors is a subject on which the law is unclear (Herr, Arons, & Wallace, 1983). Some states have adopted inconsistent policies in which minors are allowed to consent to treatment and yet parents have access to minors' treatment records or financial responsibility for any fees incurred. Other states' statutes make no mention of the situation in which parents want access but the minor wants confidentiality.

6. If at any time the therapist is confronted with a situation in which he or she is unclear regarding appropriate professional conduct, he or she should first consult a book on ethics . . . as well as a mental health law text. . . . If there is any uncertainty or concern remaining after such a review, appropriate professional and/or legal consultation should be considered. . . .

References

Adelman, H. S., Lusk, R., Alvarez, V., & Acosta, K. (1985). Competence of minors to understand, evaluate, and communicate about their psychoeducational problems. *Professional Psychology: Research and Practice, 16,* 426–434.

American Psychiatric Association. (1979). Task force on confidentiality of children's and adolescents' clinical records. *American Journal of Psychiatry, 136,* 138–144.

Bastien, R. T., & Adelman, H. S. (1984). Noncompulsory versus legally mandated placement, perceived choice, and response to treatment among adolescents. *Journal of Consulting and Clinical Psychology, 52,* 171–179.

Belter, R. W., & Grisso, T. (1984). Children's recognition of rights violations in counseling. *Professional Psychology: Research and Practice, 15,* 899–910.

Glenn, C. M. (1980). Ethical issues in the practice of child psychotherapy. *Professional Psychology, 11,* 613–619.

Grisso, T., & Vierling, L. (1978). Minors consent to treatment: A developmental perspective. *Professional Psychology, 9,* 412–427.

Herr, S. S., Arons, S., & Wallace, R. E. (1983). *Legal*

rights and mental health care. Lexington, MA: Lexington. .

Janzen, W. B., & Love, W. (1977). Involving adolescents as active participants in their own treatment plans. *Psychological Reports, 41,* 931–934.

Kaser-Boyd, N., Adelman, H., & Taylor, L. (1985). Minors' ability to identify risks and benefits of therapy. *Professional Psychology: Research and Practice, 16,* 411–417.

Kobocow, B., McGuire, J. M., & Blau, B. (1983). The influence of confidentiality conditions on self-disclosure of early adolescents. *Professional Psychology: Research and Practice, 14,* 435–443.

Koocher, G. P. (1976). A bill of rights for children in psychotherapy. In G. P. Koocher (Ed.), *Children's rights and the mental health professions* (pp. 23–32). New York: Wiley.

Koocher, G. P. (1983). Competence to consent: Psychotherapy. In G. B. Melton, G. P. Koocher, & M. J. Saks (Eds.), *Children's competence to consent* (pp. 111–128). New York: Plenum.

McGuire, J. M. (1974). Confidentiality and the child in psychotherapy. *Professional Psychology, 5,* 374–379.

Melton, G. B. (1981). Effects of a state law permitting minors to consent to psychotherapy. *Professional Psychology, 12,* 647–654.

Messenger, C., & McGuire, J. (1981). The child's conception of confidentiality in the therapeutic relationship. *Psychotherapy: Theory, Research & Practice, 18,* 123–130.

Myers, J. E. B. (1982). Legal issues surrounding psychotherapy with minor clients. *Clinical Social Work Journal, 10,* 303–314.

Pardue, J., Whichard, W., & Johnson, E. (1970). Limited confidential information in counseling. *Personnel and Guidance Journal, 49,* 14–20.

Patterson, C. H. (1971). Are ethics different in different settings? *Personnel and Guidance Journal, 50,* 254–259.

Plotkin, R. (1981). When rights collide: Parents, children, and consent to treatment. *Journal of Pediatric Psychology, 6,* 121–130.

Ross, A. O. (1966). Confidentiality in child therapy: A reevaluation. *Mental Hygiene, 50,* 360–366.

Taylor, L., Adelman, H. S., & Kaser-Boyd, N. (1983). Perspective of children regarding their participation in psychoeducational treatment decision making. *Professional Psychology: Research and Practice, 14,* 882–884.

Taylor, L., Adelman, H. S., & Kaser-Boyd, N. (1985). Minors; attitudes and competence toward participation in psychoeducational decisions. *Professional Psychology: Research and Practice, 16,* 226–235.

Thompson, A. (1983). *Ethical concerns in psychotherapy and their legal ramifications.* New York: University Press of America.

Weithorn, L. A. (1982). Developmental factors and competence to make informed treatment decisions. *Child and Youth Services, 5,* 85–100.

Weithorn, L. A. (1983). Involving children in decisions affecting their own welfare: Guidelines for professionals. In G. B. Melton, G. P. Koocher, & M. J. Saks (Eds.), *Children's competence to consent* (pp. 235–260). New York: Plenum.

Wilson, J. (1978). *The rights of adolescents in the mental health system.* Lexington, MA: Heath.

Wrenn, C. G. (1952). The ethics of counseling. *Educational and Psychological Measurement, 12,* 161–177.

Reframing the Confidentiality Dilemma to Work in Children's Best Interests

Linda Taylor and Howard S. Adelman

LIMITS ON CONFIDENTIALITY

. . .

There are times when professionals would prefer to maintain confidences but cannot do so legally or ethically. Examples include instances when clients indicate an intention to harm themselves or someone else and when they have been abused. . . .

In order to adequately inform minors of exceptions to the promise of privacy, therapists must add a statement about exceptions, such as this:

> Although most of what we talk about is private, there are three kinds of problems you might tell me about that we would have to talk about with other people. If I find out that someone has been seriously hurting or abusing you, I would have to tell the police about it. If you tell me you have made a plan to seriously hurt yourself, I would have to let your parents know. If you tell me you have made a plan to seriously hurt someone else, I would have to warn that person. I would not be able to keep these problems just between you and me because the law says I can't. Do you understand that it's OK to talk about most things here but that these are three things we must talk about with other people?

Because youngsters may feel a bit overwhelmed about the exceptions to privacy and the serious problems described, they may simply nod their acquiescence or indicate that they are unsure about how to respond. To soften the impact, therapists may add statements, such as this:

> Fortunately, most of what we talk over is private. If you want to talk about any of the three problems that must be shared with others, we'll also talk about the best way for us to talk about the problem with others. I want to be sure I'm doing the best I can to help you.

. . .

CONFIDENTIALITY AS A LIMITATION ON HELPING

. . .

In its ethical guidelines on confidentiality, the American Psychological Association recognizes that there are instances when information obtained in clinical or counseling relationships should be shared with others. In doing so, the guidelines stress that such sharing should occur "only with persons clearly concerned with the case" (APA, 1981, p. 636).[1] Given that teachers and parents are clearly connected and see themselves as also working in a minor's best interests, some interveners feel it appropriate—even essential—to discuss information with them. In other words, there are times when an intervener sees keeping a specific confidence shared

[1] *Ed. note:* See Standard 5.05 of the APA's current (1992) Ethical Principles.

by a minor client as working against the youngster's best interests and will evaluate the costs of not communicating the information to others as outweighing the potential benefits of maintaining the minor's privacy.

On a practical level, this concern arises whenever parents threaten to withdraw their child because of dissatisfaction about too little access to the information passing between their child and the intervener. It seems clear that the best interests of the child cannot be served if an intervener's unrelenting stance regarding confidentiality results in the child's no longer having access to counseling or to other important resources. In other instances, interveners find that some minors misuse the confidential nature of the counseling relationship by making it secretive and yet another weapon in their conflict with parents and other authority figures, thereby further alienating support systems that the intervener may find are essential links in the helping process.

GUIDELINES FOR RESOLVING THE DILEMMA

Thinking in terms of what would be most beneficial and least damaging to an intervener's efforts to help the client, we have found it best to approach problems related to confidentiality by reframing them. In particular, we have come to focus less on how to avoid breaching confidences and more on how to establish the type of working relationship in which clients take the lead in sharing information when this is indicated. To accomplish this, we stress processes for enhancing youngsters' motivational readiness and empowering them with the ongoing motivation and skills to share information that can help them to solve problems that they are experiencing. In addition, we emphasize steps to minimize the negative consequences of divulging confidences.

Enhancing Motivational Readiness for Sharing

Informing youngsters about reporting requirements can compound negative attitudes toward participating in the intervention (e.g., see Adelman & Taylor, 1985). Thus there may be a need for systematic efforts to enhance motivation to participate. The prob-

lem, of course, is a bit paradoxical: that is, how to elicit sufficient participation to allow the therapist to demonstrate that participation is worthwhile.

One strategy involves demonstrating to the youngster that there is an intrinsic payoff for taking the risk of disclosing very personal thoughts and feelings to the therapist. We start with the assumption, born of experience, that the first sessions with most youngsters allow sufficient access to encourage attendance for a couple of sessions. In other words, we know that skilled therapists use a range of non-threatening activities to help establish enough rapport that most youngsters are willing to return at least for a second session. . . .

Enabling Clients to Share Information

. . . [A] fundamental concern of an intervener in offering a helping relationship is to act in the best interests of the client, as defined by the client, through an informed agreement about ongoing client participation in decision making about means and ends. The ultimate intent is to enable clients to independently pursue their best interests (Swift & Levin, 1987). To accomplish this, intervention focuses on ways to enhance a client's ongoing motivation and skills for autonomous functioning.

In contrast, intervention designed as a socialization process gives primary consideration to the society's best interests. The individual's consent and decision making are not necessarily sought, and empowerment of the individual is pursued only if it is consonant with the socialization agenda (Adelman & Taylor, 1985).

Fortunately, the interests of the individual and the society often are in harmony. However, instances in which confidentiality has been limited by law are indicative of circumstances in which individual and societal interests conflict and society's interests have predominated.

For the most part, clinicians and counselors try to act in the best interests of their clients and look for honest confirmation from clients that they are doing so. Of course, some clients, especially young ones, initially lack the ability to understand and communicate in ways that allow for informed agreements and shared decision making. In such cases, the commitment to empower clients calls for efforts to increase their level of understanding, communication skills, and ability to participate in decision making (Taylor & Adelman, 1986).

All of this has direct implications for the problem of divulging information when the intervener views this as in the client's best interests. In a helping process, the first responsibility of the intervener is to determine whether the client agrees that information should be shared. If the client does not agree, the intervener must be prepared to help the client to explore (in a developmentally appropriate way) the costs and benefits involved (Kaser-Boyd, Adelman, & Taylor, 1985). This may take some time to accomplish, especially insofar as the point is not to convince or seduce but to facilitate comprehension (e.g., understanding of the positive impact that sharing would have on relationships with significant others). In the end, the individual still may not agree, and the ethics of the situation may dictate that the intervener break confidentiality without consent.

If the client sees it in his or her interest to have others informed of certain matters, then discussion shifts to how this will be accomplished. Again, in keeping with a commitment to enabling the client to pursue his or her interests, the client should be in control of what information is shared and, if feasible, should be the one who does the sharing. . . .

Minimizing Negative Consequences of Disclosure

In general, when legal or ethical considerations compel an intervener to divulge confidences, three steps must be taken to minimize the repercussions: (a) an explanation to the client of the reason for disclosure, (b) an exploration of the likely repercussions in and outside of the counseling situation, and (c) a discussion of how to proceed so that negative consequences are minimized and any potential benefits are maximized.

For example, in explaining reasons, one might begin by saying,

> What you have shared today is very important. I know you're not ready to talk about this with your parents, but it is the kind of thing that I told you at the

beginning that I am required to tell them.

Or it might begin an exploration of repercussions for the helping relationship by stating,

> I know that if I do so, you will be upset with me and it will be hard for you to trust me anymore. I feel caught in this situation. I'd like us to be able to work something out to make this all come out as good as we can make it.

With respect to how to proceed, often it is feasible simply to encourage the client to take actions in keeping with his or her best interests or to give consent to allow the counselor to do so:

> This may work best for you if you tell them rather than me. Or, if you don't feel ready to handle this, we both could sit down with your parents while I tell them.

. . .

References

Adelman, H. S., & Taylor, L. (1985). Toward integrating intervention concepts, research, and practice. In S. L. Pfeiffer (Ed.), *Clinical child psychology: An introduction to theory, research, and practice* (pp. 57–92). Orlando, FL: Grune & Stratton.

American Psychological Association. (1981). *Ethical principles of psychologists.* Washington, DC: Author.

Kaser-Boyd, N., Adelman, H. S., & Taylor, L. (1985). Minors' ability to identify risks and benefits of therapy. *Professional Psychology: Research and Practice, 16,* 411–417.

Swift, C., & Levin, G. (1987). Empowerment: An emerging mental health technology. *Journal of Primary Prevention, 8,* 71–94.

Taylor, L., & Adelman, H. S. (1986). Facilitating children's participation in decisions that affect them: From concept to practice. *Journal of Clinical Child Psychology, 15,* 346–351.

◆ ◆ ◆

Commentary: See also Sobocinski, M. R. (1990). *Ethical principles in the counseling of gay and lesbian adolescents: Issues and autonomy, competence, and confidentiality.* Professional Psychology: Research and Practice, 21, 240–247.*This important and controversial article presents a number of vignettes containing ethical dilemmas facing psychologists who work with gay and lesbian youth. Which provisions in the 1992 APA Ethical Principles might be helpful in resolving such dilemmas?*

Balancing the interests of minors and their parents is a difficult task for practitioners and researchers. Because the law considers children to be generally incompetent in making decisions for themselves, whether children are granted the power to make those decisions is determined by constitutional analyses and state law. For psychologists who work in governmental institutions, such as schools or state hospitals, it is very risky to serve minors without parental involvement unless there is an explicit statute permitting it. Psychologists in private institutions—whether in independent practice, nonpublic universities, or mental health clinics—should clearly delineate expectations among themselves, their minor clients, and the minors' parents. For a more complete discussion of legal issues related to assessment, intervention, and research with minors, see Bersoff, D. N., & Hofer, P. (1990). The legal regulation of school psychology. In C. Reynolds & T. Gutkin (Eds.), Handbook of school psychology (2nd ed., pp. 937–961). New York: Wiley.

AIDS: Ethical Implications for Psychological Intervention

Constance F. Morrison

AIDS (acquired immune deficiency syndrome) is perhaps the most frightening disease to be faced in modern times . . .

CONFIDENTIALITY

Record Keeping

. . . Membership in a high-risk group may be considered grounds for cancellation of insurance; testing positive for HIV may result in the loss of one's home or job; and one's friendship with a person who has tested positive may result in one's being shunned socially. Therefore, one should exercise caution in including potentially damaging information with regard to AIDS in records that might end up with insurance companies, with peer-review groups, or in court.

Cohen (1979) recommended that client records include a summary of all contacts with the client and with others concerning the client, regular summaries of progress, documentation of informed consent to treatment, and all psychological test data. On the other hand, Soisson, VandeCreek, and Knapp (1987) suggested that information about illegal behavior, sexual practices, or other sensitive information that may harm the client is rarely appropriate for records. One option available to psychotherapists is the use of dual record keeping, whereby working notes are separate from the client's formal record in order to ensure the confidentiality of potentially damaging information.

Right to Privacy Versus Duty to Warn

Practitioners may find themselves facing an ethical dilemma when their responsibility to maintain the confidentiality of a client's personal information is at odds with their duty to warn. . . . Consider the following scenario based on a case study appearing in the *Hastings Center Report* (Winston, 1987):

> Mr. A requested to see a therapist at a Sexually Transmitted Diseases Clinic after receiving a positive result on the HIV test. He has no symptoms.
>
> The therapist informed Mr. A of the probability of his developing the disease within the next 5 years, the typical course of the disease, and its probable outcome. He then explained to Mr. A that he could infect others through sexual contact, sharing needles, or donating blood. The therapist told Mr. A about "safe sex" and what he could do to protect sexual partners from infection.
>
> At that point Mr. A confided to the therapist that he was bisexual and that he believed he had contracted the virus during one of his homosexual encounters. He went on to say that he had made a decision to discontinue his homosexual activities and had, in fact, recently become engaged. The therapist advised Mr. A to share his diagnosis with his fiancee and again warned him

From *Professional Psychology: Research and Practice, 20,* 166–171. Copyright 1989 by the American Psychological Association. Adapted with permission of the author and publisher.

of the risk of transmitting the virus. Mr. A refused to do so, saying that it would wreck his marriage plans.

This therapist is faced with a conflict between maintaining his client's confidentiality and warning his client's fiancee of a potential threat of harm. Perhaps the first step in dealing with this dilemma is to weigh the risks involved to each party. Informing Mr. A's fiancee about a possible risk to her may, as Mr. A fears, result in a loss of this relationship and thus Mr. A could feel emotionally devastated. It would also place the therapist–client relationship in serious jeopardy. Once this information was given to Mr. A's fiancee, she could disclose it to whomever she chose, which could possibly cause Mr. A further harm. But what of the risks to Mr. A's fiancee if she is not warned of the possible threat to her? There is some question as to the medical risks that she might face. Not all persons who test positive for the HIV are viremic and therefore infectious (Winston, 1987). Although there is substantial evidence that the HIV can be transmitted through heterosexual contact (Chamberland & Dondero, 1987; Redfield et al., 1985), the efficiency of transmission is still in question. Also, the outcome of infection with the HIV is not predictable. At present, 10%–50% of persons with the HIV are expected to develop AIDS. Although there is also the possibility that his fiancee has already been exposed to the virus by Mr. A, Chamberland and Dondero (1987) suggested that repeated unprotected sexual contact with an infected partner over time may increase the likelihood of transmission, and epidemiological evidence suggests that an average of 100 incidents of unprotected vaginal intercourse may be required for male-to-female transmission (Landers, 1988). Therefore, in weighing the risks to each party, the practitioner must also take into consideration the possibility that further unprotected sexual contact will increase the risks of harm to the fiancee.

The therapist in this situation is also bound by legal considerations. If she breaches Mr. A's confidentiality, she may be sued or sanctioned for wrongful disclosure and could be held liable for any personal suffering that he experiences. If the therapist does not inform Mr. A's fiancee and his fiancee does

develop AIDS, the therapist may be liable for failing to warn the fiancee of potential harm. State and case laws concerning confidentiality and duty to warn vary from state to state. For example, in California, the *Tarasoff* decision and the California Civil Code (cited in Weinstock, 1988) make clear the therapist's duty to warn. However, California also recently passed legislation imposing fines or imprisonment or both for willful disclosure of HIV test results without prior written consent (Binder, 1987). . . .

In arguing the importance of maintaining client confidentiality, Landesman (1987) suggested that breaching the client's confidentiality in such a case as the one just described might cause the client immediate harm and may also result in the client's failure to seek help at a later date. It can also discourage others from seeking testing and treatment. Kain (1988) suggested that the role of the psychotherapist in AIDS prevention lies not so much in reporting the behavior but rather in the working through the issues of rejection, abandonment, loneliness, homophobia, and infidelity, which may be restraining a client from informing sexual partners. Winston (1987), on the other hand, argued that failing to warn the fiancee may put her, as well as any children she might bear, at risk. She may also unknowingly transmit the HIV to future sexual partners. In a discussion of the limits of confidentiality with clients who have AIDS or are HIV seropositive, Gray and Harding (1988) recommended more direct methods. They suggested that the therapist directly inform identified sexual partners of the imminent danger when the client is unwilling to do so. In the case of anonymous sexual partners, they suggested that the therapist inform appropriate state health officials and professional or civil authorities. Last, the Council on Ethical and Judicial Affairs of the American Medical Association (1988) suggested that should persuasion fail, the physician should inform appropriate health authorities or the endangered third party.

Obviously, there are no clear or easy answers. In the ideal situation, the therapist would be able, in a relatively short time, to persuade Mr. A to tell his fiancee about the test results. Failing that, the therapist might convince her client to practice safe sex while he continued to consider revealing his HIV status to his fiancee. Last, the therapist should consult with knowledgeable medical and legal advisers and with colleagues before taking any action. If a decision is made to breach the client's confidentiality in order to protect a third party, the client should be informed beforehand (Kerr, 1987). Informing the client first and explaining the legal and ethical bases for the decision may help to minimize the harm to both the client and the therapeutic relationship. Until greater clarity results from either case law or statutes, cases such as these will probably have to be resolved on a case-by-case basis. . . .

Suicide

Another ethical dilemma faced by physicians that psychotherapists may also confront when working with clients who test positive is determining an appropriate response to an intention to commit suicide. In a recent study in New York City, Marzuk et al. (1988) demonstrated a substantially increased risk for suicide among men with AIDS. Men diagnosed with AIDS who are between the ages of 20 and 59 are approximately 36 times more likely to commit suicide than are men in the general population. Issues that must be addressed by the practitioner include consideration of the client's right to commit suicide, the impact of HIV infection on the capacity of the individual to make a rational choice, and the practitioner's legal liability.

Mental health professionals have traditionally accepted an ethical and sometimes legal responsibility to prevent a client's suicide. Preventive measures have ranged all the way from persuasion to involuntary commitment in a psychiatric facility. It has been in the area of what Szasz (1986) termed *coercive interventions*, wherein the client's consent is not obtained and confidentiality is breached, that controversy has developed. Individual psychotherapists and groups such as the Hemlock Society have argued that people have a right to make a rational, competent choice to die, especially in cases of terminal illness or severe, untreatable, debilitating pain (Fujimura, Weis, & Cochran, 1985). On the other hand, some have contended that even in such cases, suicide may be motivated by emotions that are temporary, whereas suicide is permanent (Bursztajn, Gutheil, Warren, & Brodsky, 1986). Central to the

issue is the question of the individual's capacity to rationally and competently choose suicide. In the case of the client with HIV infection, the question of capacity is complicated by the infection itself. Many individuals infected with the HIV show signs of progressive dementia similar to that of Alzheimer's disease (Faulstich, 1987; Volberding & Abrams, 1985). This AIDS-related dementia has been reported to sometimes develop before a definitive diagnosis of AIDS (Ostrow & Gayle, 1986). Central nervous system dysfunction or neuropsychiatric impairment obviously raises questions concerning the client's competency to make a rational choice for suicide, as well as to consent to treatment. Even such staunch advocates of clients' rights as Szasz (1986) justify coercive intervention when there is demonstrable malfunctioning of the brain.

The psychologist must also consider the issue of legal liability. Not only do the Ethical Principles of Psychologists allow a practitioner to breach a client's confidentiality in order to prevent suicide, but in recent reviews, researchers have also found no successful lawsuit against a therapist who breached confidentiality to protect the life of a suicidal client. However, should a practitioner fail to take reasonable action to prevent a suicide, a wrongful death action could be brought against him or her, although the courts are more likely to impose liability in inpatient settings (Kjervik, 1984). Last, although a psychotherapist may view suicide as a rational choice for a client, actually assisting the client to die is clearly defined as a crime, and there would be little question regarding legal liability. . . .

References

Binder, R. L. (1987). AIDS antibody tests on inpatient psychiatric units. *American Journal of Psychiatry, 144*, 176–181.

Bursztajn, H., Gutheil, T. C., Warren, M. J., & Brodsky, A. (1986). Depression, self-love, time, and the "right" to suicide. *General Hospital Psychiatry, 8*, 91–95.

Chamberland, M. E., & Dondero, T. J. (1987). Heterosexually acquired infection with human immunodeficiency virus (HIV). *Annals of Internal Medicine, 107*, 763–766.

Cohen, R. J. (1979). *Malpractice: A guide for mental health professionals*. New York: Free Press.

Council on Ethical and Judicial Affairs of the American

Medical Association (1988). Ethical issues involved in the growing AIDS crisis. *Journal of the American Medical Association, 259,* 1360–1361.

Faulstich, M. E. (1987). Psychiatric aspects of AIDS. *American Journal of Psychiatry, 144,* 551–556.

Fujimura, L. E., Weis, D. M., & Cochran, J. R. (1985). Suicide: Dynamics and implications for counseling. *Journal of Counseling and Development, 63,* 612–615.

Gray, L. A., & Harding, A. K. (1988). Confidentiality limits with clients who have the AIDS virus. *Journal of Counseling and Development, 66,* 219–223.

Kain, C. D. (1988). To breach or not to breach: Is that the question? *Journal of Counseling and Development, 66,* 224–225.

Kerr, C. P. (1987). AIDS and the issue of confidentiality. *Postgraduate Medicine, 81*(8), 95, 98, 101.

Kjervik, D. K. (1984). The psychotherapist's duty to act reasonably to prevent suicide: A proposal to allow reasonable suicide. *Behavioral Sciences and the Law, 2,* 207–219.

Landers, S. (1988). Practitioners and AIDS: Face-to-face with pain. *APA Monitor, 19*(1), 1, 14–15.

Landesman, S. H. (1987). AIDS and a duty to protect: Commentary. *Hastings Center Report, 17*(1), 23.

Marzuk, P. M., Tierney, H., Tardiff, K., Gross, E. M., Morgan, E. B., Hsu, M., & Mann, J. J. (1988). Increased risk of suicide in persons with AIDS. *Journal of the American Medical Association, 259,* 1333–1337.

Ostrow, D. G., & Gayle, T. C. (1986). Psychosocial and ethical issues of AIDS health care programs. *Quality Review Bulletin, 12,* 284–294.

Redfield, R. R., Markham, P. D., Salahuddin, S. Z., Wright, D. C., Sarngadharan, M. G., & Gallo, R. C. (1985). Heterosexually acquired HTLV-III/LAV disease (AIDS-related complex and AIDS): Epidemiological evidence for female-to-male transmission. *Journal of the American Medical Association, 254,* 2094–2096.

Soisson, E. L., VandeCreek, L., & Knapp, S. (1987). Thorough record keeping: A good defense in a litigious era. *Professional Psychology: Research and Practice, 18,* 498–502.

Szasz, T. (1986). The case against suicide prevention. *American Psychologist, 41,* 806–812.

Volberding, P., & Abrams, D. (1985). Clinical care and research in AIDS. *Hasting Center Report, 15*(4), 16–17.

Weinstock, R. (1988). Confidentiality and the new duty to protect: The therapist's dilemma. *Hospital and Community Psychiatry, 39,* 607–609.

Winston, M. (1987). AIDS and a duty to protect: Commentary. *Hastings Center Report, 17*(1), 22–23.

◆ ◆ ◆

Commentary: *Researchers have found a significantly positive relationship between the level of psychologists' homophobia and the likelihood of breaching the confidentiality of individuals diagnosed with AIDS. They warn that personal bias, rather than clinical factors, may affect professional ethical decision making. See McGuire, J., Nieri, D., Abbott, D., Sheridan, K., & Fisher, R. (1995).* Do Tarasoff *principles apply in AIDS-related psychotherapy: Ethical decision making and the role of therapist homophobia and perceived client dangerousness.* Professional Psychology: Research and Practice, 26, *608–611.*

For another helpful article that discusses applying the duty to protect clients who present issues concerning sexually transmitted diseases, see Lamb, D. H., Clark, C., Drumheller, P., Frizzell, K., & Surrey, L. (1989). Applying Tarasoff *to AIDS-related psychotherapy issues.* Professional Psychology: Research and Practice, 20, *37–43.*

In a follow-up study to Lamb et al.'s (1989) conceptual piece, Lamb and other colleagues (1990) empirically investigated the degree to which (a) the dangerousness of a client and (b) the identifiability of their potential victims influenced clinicians to break confidentiality. On the basis of surveys from 241 clinical members of APA, they concluded that both variables were important but that clients' dangerousness appeared to be more relevant than victims' identifiability. Lamb et al. also found that clinicians who had prior contact with AIDS patients in therapy were less likely to disclose confidential information. See Totten, G., Lamb, D. H., & Reeder, G. D. (1990). Tarasoff *and confidentiality in AIDS-related psychotherapy.* Professional Psychology: Research and Practice, 21, *155–160.*

What if an AIDS patient dies during the course of therapy, or a patient dies from any cause? What ethical obligations does the therapist have in such situations? This rarely considered but important confidentiality issue is discussed next, in the context of a much-publicized event.

Until Death Do Us Part: An Exploration Into Confidentiality Following the Death of a Client

Caroline A. Burke

. . . On July 15, 1991, the *New York Times* (Stanley, 1991) printed a front page article that announced the release of over 300 psychotherapy tapes to author Middlebrook, who used them in completing a biography of the deceased poet, Sexton. When Sexton committed suicide in 1974, she left behind something quite different from sentimental photos or a daily diary. It was discovered that Sexton had left "hundreds of spools" (Middlebrook, 1991, p. 401) of psychotherapy audiotapes with her psychiatrist Orne, Sexton's therapist from 1956 to 1964. Sexton's daughter and literary executor, Linda Gray Sexton, authorized a release by Orne of the psychotherapy tapes to the biographer, Middlebrook. In the autumn of 1991, the book was available to the public and was titled *Anne Sexton: A Biography* [footnote omitted]. . . .

The purpose of this article is not to debate the legality or ethics of Orne's release of these tapes. The publicity and controversy surrounding that release have, however, provided occasion to reexamine issues that are raised when psychological records are released after the death of a client. Indeed, given the expressions of concern that other psychologists may now release psychological records of deceased clients—perhaps in situations quite different from Orne's—it is especially important that the implications of release of this information by psychologists be carefully considered. . . .

CONCERN FOR THE PUBLIC
. . .

Could it be that the publication of psychological records after the death of a client reduces the trust other clients may place in their therapist? Many clients already voice questions to their therapists about the limits of confidentiality. Such questions, although disturbing, are by no means the most serious. The unvoiced questions that prospective clients ask themselves about confidentiality before coming for therapy are more serious. These questions we may or may not ever have an opportunity to answer. For example, might individuals who have been involved in infidelities, or who are having serious doubts about commitment to their partner, have reservations about seeking psychotherapy to discuss this issue if they fear that their partner or their children might later come into possession of the psychotherapy record? Or, suppose that a parent is having intense feelings of anger and resentment toward a young child. Will this person be willing to openly discuss with the therapist such feelings, knowing that records of the discussions may later be delivered to the (then adult) child? One can imagine countless other scenarios involving the possibility of "tell all" books, movies, and so on. Certainly, if a potential client is worried about this issue, some peace of mind might be afforded by carefully choosing one's executor or by leaving a letter of instruction. Can we realistically expect anxious clients to confront and overcome such difficulties in addition to all the other internal and external impediments to psychotherapy?

A related issue is the one of informed consent. What should we tell clients about the limits of confidentiality? Should we tell them that after their death, records about their treatment may be released

From *Professional Psychology: Research and Practice, 26*, 278–280. Copyright 1995 by the American Psychological Association. Adapted with permission of the author and publisher.

to their legal representative? What effect might such informed consent have on the treatment process? In my view, the uncertainty of our knowledge calls for caution as well as for research.

CONCERN FOR THE PROFESSION

As a profession, psychology has worked hard to secure the public trust. Does release of psychological records after a patient dies undercut the public's confidence? In the January/February 1992 issue of the magazine *Society*, eight articles were written by legal scholars, psychologists and psychiatrists, and historians on the topic of the release of psychological records by a therapist after a patient dies. Among the facts and issues noted in these articles was one that stated that there may now be fears that the release of information to a biographer might lead to other psychotherapists circulating information to tabloids and talk shows, revealing private information about famous individuals (Lewin, 1991). Is there a way that the profession can reassure clients about confidentiality yet also inform them that their records could be obtained by a legal executor upon their death? As a profession, are we content with the knowledge that the public may become skeptical of matters surrounding confidentiality?

CONCERN FOR THE FUTURE TRAINING OF PSYCHOLOGISTS

Each year, hundreds of students graduate from psychology programs and begin to practice the art of psychotherapy. Each student learns in an ethics in psychology course about the matters of confidentiality and informed consent and the responsibility that is owed to clients regarding their records. When they first practice therapy, what do these neophyte psychologists tell their clients regarding record keeping and confidentiality? Do we now need to teach students to make an addition to the information regarding the limits of confidentiality? Should we advise clients that after their death, records about their treatment may be released to their legal representative? What effect might such informed consent have on the treatment process?

We do not know the answers to the previous questions, although we do know that various types of informed consent forms do have differential effects on potential clients (Handelsman, 1990; Handelsman & Martin, 1992). To my knowledge, there are no current data bearing on the assumptions clients make with regard to confidentiality of treatment records following death.

RECOMMENDATIONS

Although the American Psychological Association's (APA's) Ethical Principles of Psychologists and Code of Conduct has recently been revised (APA, 1992), it seems to me that it omits a clearly written guideline for afterlife issues of clients' records. How are current and future professionals going to handle enquiries into the records by a loved one after a client dies? I believe this needs to be addressed in the next revision of the code. Likewise, I believe that we should seek a consensus as to whether or not this aspect of confidentiality should be a part of the routine informed consent given to the client.

Finally, it is clear that research needs to be conducted in this area. For example, past and current psychotherapy clients could be surveyed to determine whether or not there is client concern surrounding the status of clients' records upon their death. As psychologists, we need to know how to keep the public trust secure and balance matters of both confidentiality and legality in the best interests of our clients.

References

American Psychological Association. (1992). Ethical principles of psychologists and code of conduct. *American Psychologist, 47,* 1597–1611.

Handelsman, M. M. (1990). Do written consent forms influence clients' first impressions of therapists? *Professional Psychology: Research and Practice, 21,* 223–225.

Handelsman, M. M., & Martin, W. L., Jr. (1992). Effects of readability on the impact and recall of written informed consent material. *Professional Psychology: Research and Practice, 23,* 500–503.

Lewin, B. (1991). The Anne Sexton controversy. *Society, 29,* 9–12.

Middlebrook, D. W. (1991). *Anne Sexton: A biography.* New York: Vintage Book, a division of Random House.

Stanley, A. (1991, July 15). Poet told all; therapist provides the record. *The New York Times*, p. A1, C13.

◆ ◆ ◆

Commentary: *As Lakin (1994) asserted, "an . . . important source of ethical ambiguity is the question of whose agent the therapist is" (p. 356). See Lakin, M. (1994). Morality in group and family therapies: Multiperson therapies and the 1992 ethics code.* Professional Psychology: Research and Practice, 25, 344–348. *The following article nicely illustrates this dilemma and provides excellent applications of other issues raised in this chapter.*

Strains on Confidentiality in College-Student Psychotherapy: Entangled Therapeutic Relationships, Incidental Encounters, and Third-Party Inquiries

Bruce S. Sharkin

. . .

The practice of psychotherapy on a college campus appears to be particularly vulnerable to strains on confidentiality. Surveys of ethical dilemmas faced by college therapists conducted by Hayman and Covert (1986) and Malley, Gallagher, and Brown (1992) found that confidentiality issues were reported to be among the most difficult to resolve. According to Malley et al. (1992), there is considerable pressure placed on campus practitioners from administrators, faculty members, and other university-related personnel (who are instrumental in referring students for therapy or psychological evaluation) to reveal confidential information about students, including verification of therapy contact. These requests are often made without the student's knowledge and sometimes occur during informal interactions (e.g., while getting a cup of coffee in the cafeteria). In a recent survey of common referral sources within a university setting including student affairs professionals and faculty members, Sharkin, Scappaticci, and Birky (1994) found that a majority of referral sources expected to have access to confidential information without a student's permission. Thus, although the protection of confidentiality tends to be strictly adhered to by campus therapists (Sherry, Teschendorf, Anderson, & Guzman, 1991), pressures associated with being on a college campus may work against the maintenance of confidentiality (Grayson & Cauley, 1989).

. . .

Like rural communities, college campuses pose unique challenges to the maintenance of confidentiality. In fact, adherence to confidentiality can come at a cost to the campus practitioner's image, credibility, and relationships with other campus personnel. There are three specific types of situations that can result in strains on confidentiality for college campus practitioners: (a) entangled therapeutic relationships (Arnstein, 1972; Grayson, 1986; Spiegel, 1990); (b) incidental or chance encounters with clients, on and off campus (Grayson, 1986; Sharkin & Birky, 1992); and (c) requests for confidential information regarding clients from university-related personnel and parents. Unfortunately, guidelines provided by the Ethical Principles of Psychologists and Code of Conduct (American Psychological Association [APA], 1992) may be difficult to apply to some of the unique problems involved in these situations. Each of these situations will be discussed in the following section.

SOURCES OF STRAINS ON CONFIDENTIALITY

Entangled Therapeutic Relationships

Entangled therapeutic relationships involve clients who are socially or romantically involved with each other seeing the same therapist. This may occur by chance or because of clients referring friends to their own therapist. Standard 4.03 of the Ethical Principles (APA, 1992) provides guidelines for psychologists who agree to provide services to several persons who have a relationship, such as couples or families. But in college therapy, the therapist does not necessarily know from the outset about preexisting relationships (e.g., friends, roommates, etc.) among clients.

Clients may or may not be aware of the fact that people they talk about in therapy are also clients of their own therapist. Even if clients are aware of this and acknowledge this fact to each other, the therapist must be careful not to confirm or disconfirm to one client that someone they refer to in therapy is indeed another client. Instead, therapists are trained to either remain silent or clarify the need to maintain confidentiality if the client asks directly for confirmation. In some cases, the therapist may need to discuss with the clients any potential problems related to sharing the same therapist, with consideration given to the option of referral to another therapist. Therapists must also be careful to keep track of their sources of information so that they do not inadvertently reveal knowledge about one client to another by virtue of contact with the other client.

According to Spiegel (1990), the situation is most problematic when clients discuss other people without being aware that they are also clients of the same therapist and then discover this from someone other than the therapist. Consider the scenario of two roommates experiencing conflict with each other, disclosing that they have been seeing the same therapist. In such a scenario, one or both of the clients may feel betrayed, even though the therapist had behaved in an ethically responsible manner. Ironically then, the preservation of confidentiality can actually have negative consequences for therapy. Grayson (1986) aptly noted that entangled therapeutic relationships can potentially place campus therapists in a kind of no-win situation whereby either the violation or preservation of confidentiality would result in damage to client trust.

As a result of entangled therapeutic relationships, therapists may indirectly obtain information about a client (without his or her knowledge) by virtue of contact with another client, as in the example of two roommates seeing the same therapist. Of course,

it would be inappropriate for the therapist to reveal to one client what has been learned about him or her from another client. The therapist needs to maintain good boundaries and protect the confidentiality of both clients. But information obtained in such an indirect manner may influence the therapist's perceptions of or subsequent behavior with a client. As an example, after learning something about a client (from another client) that the therapist would have expected him or her to share in therapy, the therapist may wonder about the level of trust experienced by the client in the therapy relationship. The therapist may then look for opportunities to explore issues around trust within the therapy relationship.

Entangled relationships may also emerge in group therapy, which is a common therapeutic modality in college-student psychotherapy (Golden, Corazzini, & Grady, 1993). Trying to prevent persons with preexisting relationships from participating in the same therapy group presents a kind of confidentiality Catch-22. To make sure that prospective group members do not know each other beyond a casual acquaintance, identities would have to be revealed and confidentiality breached. In small campus communities, prospective group clients could be asked whether there are specific persons that they could definitely not work with in group therapy. Although information can be obtained during group screenings that may indicate connections between prospective group members (e.g., membership in fraternities, sororities, or other social groups), it is difficult for therapists to avoid having entangled relationships emerge in group therapy. Therefore, therapists need to be prepared to deal with these relationships as they are discovered, typically when the group first meets.

For traditional process-oriented group psychotherapy, therapists tend to discourage group members from having anything beyond casual contact with each other outside of group for the sake of maintaining good boundaries for therapy (Yalom, 1985). Thus, if it is discovered that two members have a relationship that involves extensive contact outside of group, such as with roommates or close friends, it is generally considered best to refer one of them to another group. The general procedure would be to meet with the students individually outside of group, explain why preexisting relationships might compromise the group process, and then make arrangements for the member who joined group last to be transferred to another group. If both joined group at the same time, the therapist might talk with them and see who would be willing to transfer to another group.

In some cases, preexisting relationships might not necessarily be problematic but still need to be explored. Teammates, students who live on the same floor of a residence hall, or members of the same social organization might be able to participate in the same therapy group. When such relationships are discovered, the group therapist should meet with the students individually outside of group and explore with them any inhibitions or discomfort related to their association with each other and being in the same therapy group. If one or both report any discomfort, one of them might be given an option for referral to another group. It is important to point out, however, that even if clients report that they do not have a problem with being in the same group together, the situation should be monitored as group progresses. If any problems are observed, for instance regarding boundary issues, then this needs to be addressed, with consideration of transferring one of the clients to another group.

Incidental Encounters

Incidental encounters are defined as unplanned, extratherapy encounters in public settings, such as a sidewalk or restaurant (Sharkin & Birky, 1992). Such encounters are quite common in the college campus setting, and they may present a challenge to the therapist's efforts to protect the confidentiality of clients (Spiegel, 1990; Weiss, 1975). Standard 1.17 of the Ethical Principles (APA, 1992) admonishes psychologists to avoid dual or social relationships with clients, but incidental encounters typically occur by chance and are very brief.

In a survey of college therapists conducted by Sharkin and Birky (1992), 60% of the respondents reported being concerned about violations of confidentiality during incidental encounters. Grayson (1986) described the therapist's dilemma concerning whether to even greet clients during encounters outside the therapy office. Whereas not responding may be interpreted as being snobbish or rejecting, offering a greeting may indirectly acknowledge to others that a therapy relationship exists. Grayson recommends taking cues from clients as guidance for how to respond; that is, wait to see if and how the client initiates contact.

But perhaps therapists are more concerned than they need to be about incidental encounters with clients. Pulakos (1994) recently conducted a survey of a sample of counseling center clients to get a sense of what incidental encounters are like from the client's perspective. About 60% of the survey respondents had experienced an incidental encounter with their therapist, most of which had involved a brief, passing-on-the-sidewalk type of encounter. Clients reported that their therapists responded in one of three ways: (a) a brief acknowledgment (59%), (b) engagement in conversation (22%), or (c) no response at all (8%). In determining how satisfied clients were with their therapists' responses, Pulakos found that most (79%) wanted the same response if the situation occurred again, but 21% indicated that they would have liked more of a response than was given by the therapist.

The survey of clients by Pulakos (1994) in conjunction with the survey of therapists by Sharkin and Birky (1992) suggests that therapists may be sensitive to consequences of overresponding, whereas clients may be more sensitive to underresponding by their therapists during incidental encounters. It seems reasonable to assume that in most instances a brief acknowledgment on the part of the therapist, such as a simple "hello," will be expected by clients. Depending on the individual client and circumstances of the encounter, brief engagement in conversation might also be acceptable. A greater risk, enacted in client cancellations, may be associated with no acknowledgment or ignoring a client as opposed to offering a greeting during an incidental encounter.

Assuming that involvement with mental health services may represent a form of stigma for some college students, therapists may try to minimize or avoid interaction with clients during incidental encounters. But the denial of the therapy relationship during public encounters may only perpetuate the stigma associated with mental health services. College therapists could perhaps think of incidental encounters as an opportunity to destigmatize psychological services and be more visible on campus. However, it is recommended that therapists consider routinely discussing the prospect of incidental encounters (perhaps within the context of discussing confidentiality) when initiating therapy with clients. By doing so, the therapist can get a sense of what clients expect during such encounters. In general, it is preferable to have an understanding of the client's expectations regarding casual encounters rather than assume that the client will not mind if contact is initiated by the therapist.

Third-Party Inquiries

Faculty members, deans, coaches, physicians, resident assistants, and other university-related personnel are often instrumental in referring students for therapy or psychological evaluation. College psychotherapists frequently get requests for confidential information regarding clients from these referral sources. In most cases these requests are valid and understandable. However, Standard 5.02 of the Ethical Principles (APA, 1992) mandates that therapists not disclose confidential information without the client's permission. This includes an obligation neither to confirm nor deny whether the therapist has had contact with a student. Like most therapy clients, college psychotherapy clients value confidentiality of therapy disclosures and prefer that little information be revealed to others (VandeCreek, Miars, & Herzog, 1987).

Therein lies one of the biggest dilemmas faced by college therapists: By preserving confidentiality, the therapist "protects" the client but may anger or alienate concerned others, especially if they do not understand the need for the therapist to maintain confidentiality. In their survey of common referral sources within a university setting, Sharkin, Scappaticci, and Birky (1994) found that the majority of respondents indicated that, if given a choice, they would like to have access to confidential information without a client's permission. Boswinkel (1987), writing from the perspective of someone who made therapy referrals (as a resident assistant), expressed

her frustrations related to not having access to information about a student's progress in therapy.

By withholding information, then, therapists risk being perceived as arrogant, aloof, evasive, secretive, uncooperative, or unhelpful. Such perceptions can strain relations with other members of the campus community and may contribute to a sense of isolation. This can be especially costly at a time when college therapists are redefining their roles to be more visible in the campus community, for example, through increased outreach and consultation efforts (Stone & Archer, 1990).

Conflicts typically arise when unexpected requests for confidential information are made without the client's permission to release information. A student may be referred for therapy by someone who has an expectation that the student will maintain ongoing therapy contact; at some point the referring person may want verification that the student has indeed maintained such contact. As noted earlier, these requests for verification sometimes occur when the therapist crosses paths on campus with someone who has made a referral.

Many problems can be averted if therapists are able to communicate with referral sources before meeting with the student, so that the nature of confidentiality can be explained and expectations regarding future communications can be addressed. This is especially the case with disciplinary or mandatory referrals (Stone & Lucas, 1994).

When pretherapy communication has not been established with a referral source, the therapist can neither confirm nor deny whether he or she has had contact with a student without the student's permission, and this needs to be explained to the person requesting information. Another possible solution is to routinely request that students give permission to confirm their first appointment with the referral source, which could be incorporated into a written consent form. . . .

Cases involving clients who become disruptive on campus may pose additional challenges. Disruptive or acting-out students typically attract a lot of attention because they place inordinate demands on or otherwise adversely affect the lives of other people on campus (Amanda, 1993; Lamb, 1992), for example, because of disciplinary problems or unusual behavior. Standard 5.05 of the Ethical Principles (APA, 1992) allows for disclosure of confidential information without client consent for the purpose of protecting the client or others from harm. If a client threatens homicide or bodily harm to another person and *Tarasoff* conditions are met (i.e., specific threat, identifiable victim, etc.), then the potential victim or victims, campus police, and the dean of students should be notified. In such cases, the therapist need only identify his or her relationship with the client and the nature and target of the threats.

When a client is assessed to be suicidal, it is generally recommended that the client's permission be obtained to contact his or her parents, who may be able to assist in making hospitalization arrangements. It is also recommended that the dean of students be notified when a client will need to leave campus temporarily or withdraw for a semester or longer because of emotional difficulties. The dean can assist with notifying instructors of the student's absence and with other academic-related matters, such as arranging for make-up exams. In cases in which involuntary hospitalization is necessary, parents and the dean of students should always be notified. Others, including community mental health crisis workers and campus police, may also need to be contacted in order to assist with involuntary hospitalization.

. . .

To balance the needs of individual clients with the needs of the campus community, therapists need to be proactive in providing information to the campus community about their role on campus. Therapists should try to develop close relationships with others on campus, particularly with individuals who are likely to refer students for therapy, such as deans, hall directors, and resident assistants. Indeed, campus therapists could serve as ongoing consultants to such individuals, thereby addressing problems with students before they reach crisis proportions. Also, by working within the campus community in this capacity, therapists can educate others about the limits of disclosure and routinely make arrangements to obtain client consent to speak with concerned third parties. Because of increased political pressure to justify their existence on cam-

puses, campus therapists can no longer afford to isolate themselves because of the issue of confidentiality without proactively seeking to lessen its harmful consequences.

College therapists also need to be able to deal with anxieties and concerns of parents of students who experience emotional or psychological problems. It is not uncommon for parents to contact their son's or daughter's therapist without the student's knowledge or consent. Therapists should not use the issue of confidentiality as an excuse to avoid talking to parents. Although the same general principles regarding the handling of requests for confidential information as discussed earlier hold true for such requests from parents, therapists' communications with parents can be somewhat more challenging, especially when students have conflictual relationships with their parents. Because parents often assume financial responsibility for the student's school expenses, parents may feel entitled to have access to all information relevant to the student's performance at school.

Given the developmental issues of separation and autonomy so common for the college-age population, college therapists may have reservations about communicating with parents. However, as Rockwell (1983) has suggested, therapists need to try to maintain boundaries without alienating parents. Indeed, parents can provide helpful information and may serve as a valuable asset in the course of treatment, particularly in crisis situations. In many instances parents simply provide information or convey their support and appreciation for the therapist's efforts without asking for any information from the therapist.

The nature of communications with parents will partly depend on whether parents are perceived as supportive or antagonistic by the student. Although confidentiality must be maintained regardless of how the student–parent relationship is viewed, how therapists deal with parents will vary, depending on what type of relationship a client has with his or her parents. For example, in student–parent relationships in which direct communication is avoided, parents are likely to call the therapist without the student knowing, potentially placing the therapist in a bind. In other words, parents may convey concerns or information about their son or daughter and then ask the therapist not to tell the student that they have called. Therapists need to pay attention to family dynamics and avoid communications with parents that simply reenact family issues, such as blurred boundaries or indirect communication. It is also important that therapists inform clients whenever there is communication with parents, especially when parents call the therapist without the client's knowledge. Because clients may be told by their parents that they communicated with the therapist, the therapist should acknowledge that communication took place with the reassurance that confidentiality was maintained.

In dealing with parents, there are a few general rules for college therapists to follow. First, therapists should inform parents using general terms that unless a client has given permission, they are not free to disclose any information; however, parents should be invited to share their concerns with the therapist. Second, parents should be told not to share anything with the therapist that they would not want shared with the client in the event the therapist has contact with him or her. This helps the therapist avoid triangulation with the client and his or her parents. Third, when parents raise specific concerns about their son or daughter (e.g., that he or she is depressed), therapists should routinely ask parents whether they have spoken directly to the client about their concerns; if they have not, therapists should find out why. Generally speaking, parents should be encouraged to try to communicate openly about their concerns with their son or daughter. . . .

References

Amanda, G. (1993). The role of the mental health consultant in dealing with disruptive college students. *Journal of College Student Psychotherapy, 8*, 121–137.

American Psychological Association. (1992). Ethical principles of psychologists and code of conduct. *American Psychologist, 47*, 1597–1611.

Arnstein, R. L. (1972). College psychiatry and community psychiatry. *Journal of the American College Health Association, 20*, 257–261.

Boswinkel, J. P. (1987). The college resident assistant and the fine art of referral for psychotherapy. *Journal of College Student Psychotherapy, 1*, 53–62.

Golden, B. R., Corazzini, J. G., & Grady, P. (1993). Cur-

rent practice of group therapy at university counseling centers: A national survey. *Professional Psychology: Research and Practice, 24*, 228–230.

Grayson, P. A. (1986). Mental health confidentiality on the small campus. *Journal of American College Health, 34*, 187–191.

Grayson, P. A., & Cauley, K. (1989). *College psychotherapy.* New York: Guilford Press.

Hayman, P. M., & Covert, J. A. (1986). Ethical dilemmas in college counseling centers. *Journal of Counseling and Development, 64*, 318–320.

Lamb, C. S. (1992). Managing disruptive students: The mental health practitioner as a consultant for faculty and staff. *Journal of College Student Psychotherapy, 7*, 23–39.

Malley, P., Gallagher, R., & Brown, S. (1992). Ethical problems in university and college counseling centers: A Delphi study. *Journal of College Student Development, 33*, 238–244.

Pulakos, J. (1994). Incidental encounters between therapists and clients: The client's perspective. *Professional Psychology: Research and Practice, 25*, 300–303.

Rockwell, W. J. K. (1983). Initial communications with the parents of emotionally disturbed university students. *Journal of American College Health, 23*, 104–109.

Sharkin, B. S., & Birky, I. (1992). Incidental encounters between therapists and their clients. *Professional Psychology: Research and Practice, 23*, 326–328.

Sharkin, B. S., Scappaticci, A. G., & Birky, I. (1994). *Access to confidential information in a university counseling center: A survey of referral sources.* Unpublished manuscript.

Sherry, P., Teschendorf, R., Anderson, S., & Guzman, F. (1991). Ethical beliefs and behaviors of college counseling center professionals. *Journal of College Student Development, 32*, 350–358.

Spiegel, P. B. (1990). Confidentiality endangered under some circumstances without special management. *Psychotherapy, 27*, 636–643.

Stone, G. L., & Archer, J. (1990). College and university counseling centers in the 1990s: Challenges and limits. *The Counseling Psychologist, 18*, 539–607.

Stone, G. L., & Lucas, J. (1994). Disciplinary counseling in higher education: A neglected challenge. *Journal of Counseling and Development, 72* 234–238.

VandeCreek, L., Miars, R. D., & Herzog, C. E. (1987). Client anticipations and preferences for confidentiality of records. *Journal of Counseling Psychology, 34*, 62–67.

Weiss, A. (1975). The effects on the transference of special events occurring during psychoanalysis. *International Journal of Psychoanalysis, 56,* 69–76.

Yalom, I. D. (1985). *The theory and practice of group psychotherapy* (3rd ed.). New York: Basic Books.

◆   ◆   ◆

Commentary: *In a follow-up exploratory study, Sharkin and his colleagues found that, like university faculty, referral sources reacted negatively when they received little or no information about a referred student from the treating therapist. To ameliorate this problem, they suggested the following (p. 181):*

> [P]sychotherapists might benefit from taking active measures to receive from students permission to acknowledge to a referring professor that he or she (the student) attended a session. In the private sector and other settings where psychotherapists are referred clients, similar efforts might be made in recognition of inquiries that might follow a referral. Even a simple brochure handed to all clients could briefly explain that faculty, concerned others, and professional peers sometimes show concern for persons they refer by making inquiries regarding attendance and well-being. The brochure could explain that permission for the therapist to acknowledge client attendance sometimes enhances the work of the office or center.
>
> If the student or prospective client has not yet been seen, the psychotherapist might want to thank the professor or referral person for the referral and then briefly inform the person of the value and necessity of confidentiality and of the need to get permission to respond to specific questions. The conversation might conclude with a promise to get back in touch with the referring person if the student or client is seen and agrees to or requests a release of information.
>
> . . .
>
> *Therapists may be tempted to modulate*

negative emotions by giving information, knowing that short-term perceptions of the psychologist seem unaffected by such breaches of confidentiality. However, long-term consequences may accrue if psychologists fail to maintain ethical positions . . . and they are well-advised to develop the professional capacity to deal with the immediate discomfort of saying no. In doing so, they will continue to serve the client and eventually create an environmental climate where all constituencies respect the need for privacy and confidentiality.

See Birky, I., Sharkin, B. S., Marin, J., & Scappaticci, A. (1998). *Confidentiality after referral: A study of how restrictions on disclosure affect relationships between therapists and referral sources.* Professional Psychology: Research and Practice, 29, 179–182. It would be helpful to explore how these recommendations can be applied in other clinical settings.

Nowhere is the conflict between psychologists' ethical duty to protect client disclosures and the demands of society more salient than in settings where it has been deemed that national security or public safety interests override client interests, such as in correctional facilities, police departments, and the military. For an introduction to the ethical problems that psychologists face in these settings, see, for example,

Archibald, E. M. (1986). *Confidentiality when the police psychologist is evaluator and caregiving practitioner.* In J. T. Reese & H. A. Goldstein (Eds.), Psychological services for law enforcement (pp. 215–217). Washington, DC: Federal Bureau of Investigation, U.S. Department of Justice.

D'Agostino, C. (1986). *Police psychological services: Ethical issues.* In J. T. Reese & H. A. Goldstein (Eds.), Psychological services for law enforcement (pp. 241–247). Washington, DC: Federal Bureau of Investigation, U.S. Department of Justice.

Dietz, P. E. (1986). *The perils of police psychology: 10 strategies for minimizing role conflicts when providing mental health services and consultation to law enforcement agencies.* Behavioral Sciences and the Law, 4, 385–400.

Howe, E. G. (1989). *Confidentiality in the military.* Behavioral Sciences and the Law, 7, 317–337.

Jeffrey, T. B. (1989). *Issues regarding confidentiality for military psychologists.* Military Psychology, 1, 49–56.

Jeffrey, T. B., Rankin, R. J., & Jeffrey, L. K. (1992). In service of two masters: The ethical–legal dilemma faced by military psychologists. Professional Psychology: Research and Practice, 23, 91–95.

Johnson, W. B. (1995). Perennial ethical quandries in military psychology: Toward American Psychological Association–Department of Defense collaboration. Professional Psychology: Research and Practice, 26, 281–287.

Saxton, G. H. (1986). Confidentiality dilemmas for psychologists and psychiatrists in the criminal justice system. American Journal of Forensic Psychology, 4, 25–31.

Weinberger, L. E., & Sreenivasan, S. (1994). Ethical and professional conflicts in correctional psychology. Professional Psychology: Research and Practice, 25, 161–167.

Weiner, B. A. (1986). Confidentiality and the legal issues raised by the psychological evaluations of law enforcement officers. In J. T. Reese & H. A. Goldstein (Eds.), Psychological services for law enforcement (pp. 97–102). Washington, DC: Federal Bureau of Investigation, U.S. Department of Justice.

Zelig, M. (1988). Ethical dilemmas in police psychology. Professional Psychology: Research and Practice, 19, 336–338.

For a treatment of similar issues in organizations, see Shonberg, S. E., & Lee, S. E. (1996). Identifying the real EAP client: Ensuring ethical dilemmas. Ethics and Behavior, 6, 203–212.

Also see generally, Monahan, J. (Ed.). (1980). Who is the client? Washington, DC: American Psychological Association.

CHAPTER 5

MULTIPLE RELATIONSHIPS

When Borys and Pope (1989) surveyed 2,352 psychologists, social workers, and psychiatrists, only about 16 of them considered "engaging in sexual activity with a current client" to be ethical. One of the few absolute prohibitions in the current APA code, as well as in its predecessor, is that barring sexual intimacies with current clients (see Principle 6a, APA, 1990; Standard 4.05, APA, 1992). Yet, the APA Ethics Committee (1998) reported that, in 1997, "the largest single category of unethical behavior in cases that ended in the loss of membership was sexual misconduct" (p. 977).

Accusations that professionals in positions of power have engaged in inappropriate sexual intimacies have evoked publicity and absorbed the public's attention, particularly during the past decade. This notoriety has not been limited to mental health practitioners but has touched senators, governors, presidents, and Supreme Court justices.

Although sexual impropriety between clients and clinicians is the most written about and troubling form of multiple relationship, it is a relatively low probability event. Many other potential forms of multiple relationships are more likely to confront not only the therapist but the researcher, tester, supervisor, and professor as well. For example, what if a carpenter cannot afford to pay for a psychological assessment of his or her child and offers to build some bookshelves in lieu of the psychologist's fee? What if a research subject asks the experimenter for a date? Can faculty members invite their graduate students to their houses for social gatherings? What should the chair of an admissions committee do if a close friend applies to the chair's doctoral program and it is the only one in the area that the friend can afford to attend? What if patients want to give their therapists inexpensive gifts? Can a psychologist supervising a graduate student in a practicum also become the supervisee's therapist? These are potentially knotty problems that are not always easily resolved by explicit prohibitory language in the ethics code.[1]

In this chapter, then, one of the goals is to delineate the wide variety of multiple relationships that can confront psychologists, regardless of the settings in which they work or the roles they perform. With these readings, I also seek to educate readers about the consequences of engaging in multiple relationships and to provide some guidance in avoiding the harm that such relationships can cause.

---

[1] As an example of really low probability events, consider a case brought before the Arizona Board of Psychologist Examiners. It involved a psychologist, also ordained as a minister, who performed an exorcism on a 10-year-old boy and then billed child protective services for his treatment.

But this chapter has more implicit and far-ranging aims. For example, one of the topics the reader considers is the barring of sexual intimacies with former clients. Under Standard 4.07 of the 1992 ethics code, sexual relationships are absolutely forbidden for 2 years after therapy is terminated and, then, after that, only if the therapist can demonstrate that the relationship is not exploitative. The 1992 Ethical Principles was the first of all the ethics codes that APA has promulgated to contain such a provision, and its inclusion was seen as a major advance. Ironically, however, the rule as adopted pleases practically no one (perhaps not even the reluctant majority of the APA Council of Representatives who voted for it as a compromise).

Although the provision barring posttermination sexual relationships for 2 years promotes such moral principles as nonmaleficence, the fact that such relationships are not banned in perpetuity angers those who believe that any possibility of a future nonprofessional relationship will harm therapy and the patient. On the other hand, one could argue that any ban constitutes a form of "ethical imperialism" (Gergen, 1973, p. 910). Because the typical sexual dual relationship involves a male therapist and a female patient, does the ban, in fact, produce a perverse kind of antifeminism, forbidding women to exercise their autonomous right to choose to enter into such a relationship—placing them, therefore, in the role of powerless, passive victims?

Even more broadly, one can ask to what extent a code of ethics should interfere in private relationships. Although one can acknowledge that the profession universally condemns sexual relationships with current and former patients—for all the reasons that the following material advances and the vast majority of psychologists adopt—that does not mean that the issue cannot be debated rationally and in good faith. This chapter, because of its intellectually controversial and emotion-arousing content, lends itself well to a debate, for the larger purposes that such a debate can serve.

References

American Psychological Association. (1990). Ethical principles of psychologists (amended June 2, 1989). *American Psychologist, 45,* 390–395.

American Psychological Association. (1992). Ethical principles of psychologists and code of conduct. *American Psychologist, 47,* 1597–1611.

APA Ethics Committee. (1998). Report of the ethics committee, 1997. *American Psychologist, 53,* 969–980.

Borys, D. S., & Pope, K. S. (1989). Dual relationships between therapist and client: A national study of psychologists, psychiatrists, and social workers. *Professional Psychology: Research and Practice, 20,* 283–293.

Gergen, K. J. (1973). The codification of research ethics: Views of a doubting Thomas. *American Psychologist, 28,* 907–912.

Multiple Relationships: Does the New Ethics Code Answer the Right Questions?

Janet L. Sonne

Since the publication of its first ethics code in 1953, the American Psychological Association (APA) has set forth policy governing dual relationships between psychologists and those with whom they interact. The summary version of the 1953 ethical principles stated that "a cardinal obligation" (APA, 1953b, p. 4) of psychologists is to respect the integrity and protect the welfare of those with whom they work. The standards admonished the psychologist to avoid entering into clinical relationships with people so close that "their welfare might be jeopardized by the dual relationship" (APA, 1953b, p. 4). Yet the ethical issues inherent in dual relationships continue to plague the profession. For example, a recent report of complaints received by the APA Ethics Committee from 1990 through 1992 revealed that about 40% to 50% of all complaints involved dual relationships ("Report of the Ethics Committee," 1993; see also Ethics Committee of the APA, 1988b). Furthermore, involvement in dual relationships was the most frequent cause of termination from APA. The new code has revised and expanded the guidelines regarding dual relationships in an attempt to clarify the ethical issues and the appropriate conduct for psychologists. Even the revised multiple relationships guidelines, however, have generated much discussion and debate among psychologists.

. . .

WHAT ARE MULTIPLE RELATIONSHIPS?

Psychologists can function in any of several professional roles consistent with their education and training, such as researcher, teacher, supervisor, employer, therapist, forensic evaluator, or expert witness. Psychologists can also function in various other roles not directly reflecting their profession as psychologists. These other roles occur within the realms of personal, social, or business relationships (e.g., social acquaintance, friend, sexual partner, family member, business owner, or chief executive officer). The most comprehensive definition of multiple relationships includes those situations in which the psychologist functions in more than one professional relationship, as well as those in which the psychologist functions in a professional role and another definitive and intended role (as opposed to a limited and inconsequential role growing out of and limited to a chance encounter). Multiple relationships may be concurrent or consecutive.

WHEN DO MULTIPLE RELATIONSHIPS CONSTITUTE UNETHICAL CONDUCT?

. . .

The degree to which a multiple relationship may be problematic likely depends on certain dynamics operating within the professional relationship (see, e.g., Borys, 1992; Gabbard & Pope, 1989; Pope, 1994; Pope & Vasquez, 1991). Consider the possible dynamics in the therapist–patient relationship. First, there are relationship-related and individual role-related expectations and responsibilities. Both therapist and client are likely to expect that there is a fiduciary quality to the relationship (see Feldman-Summers, 1989), that is, that the therapist holds the

From *Professional Psychology: Research and Practice, 25,* 336–343. Copyright 1994 by the American Psychological Association. Adapted with permission of the author and publisher.

welfare and best interests of the client foremost. Both therapist and client also are likely to expect that their relationship is initiated and exists for the purpose of assessing and ameliorating the client's difficulties. The professional relationship has clear boundaries around it (see, e.g., Hatcher, 1993). Furthermore, expectations are likely to be held regarding the functions and responsibilities of each person in the relationship. The individual in the client role is expected to come to scheduled sessions, to discuss concerns often of an intimate nature, and to pay an agreed-on fee, among other expectations. The individual in the therapist role is expected to use abilities gained through education and training to assess and treat the problems brought in by the client, to exercise sound professional judgment, to recognize and respond appropriately to transference or countertransference, to maintain confidentiality, to keep records, . . . to present testimony if subpoenaed, and so on.

A second dynamic is the client's emotional involvement with the therapist and the therapeutic process. The client's sense of being cared for, listened to, understood, and helped can lead to a sense of emotional attachment for the client.

The third dynamic is the power differential between therapist and client. Therapists accrue power relative to clients through their professional status and, often, through their gender status (i.e., when the therapist is male and the client is female). Therapists' power is heightened by the depth of personal knowledge about clients. As a natural result of the assessment and treatment process, therapists learn of an individual client's history, psychological profile, strengths and weaknesses, and hopes and fears. In the course of their work, therapists can gain access to information about the clients' developmental problems or traumas, patterns of intimate relationships, sexual habits and fantasies, legal difficulties, use of alcohol and drugs, religious beliefs, and deepest secrets. Clients do not typically have access to such information about the therapist, nor is the client receiving payment (from the therapist or an insurance company) for the process of learning such information. Therapists' power is also heightened by the transference process. Clients who experience a positive, or especially idealizing, transference attri-

bute to therapists exceptional knowledge and personal attributes that dramatically increase the power differential.

A multiple relationship is likely to pose problems or conflicts when a secondary relationship is imposed on a professional relationship in such a manner as to adversely affect the dynamics just described. First, a multiple relationship may result in a failure of relationship-related or role-related expectations or responsibilities. The professional relationship may no longer be fiduciary; the therapist's welfare and best interests may begin to come to the fore and displace or even completely obscure those of the client . . .

. . . [T]he secondary relationship may interfere with expected functions and responsibilities of each person in the professional relationship. . . . The compromise of the disinterest necessary for sound professional judgment can potentially affect the therapist's ability to assess or treat the client appropriately. Furthermore, both client and therapist may experience some confusion over the context of "therapy sessions." . . . Moreover, the client may experience some confusion in his or her internal representation of the therapist. Research indicates that the vividness of the client's internal representation of the therapist and the use of that image to continue therapeutic self-exploration after termination are associated with positive outcome of therapy (Geller, Cooley, & Hartley, 1981–1982; see also Gabbard, 1994). The image of the therapist may be confused or obscured as other role information impinges on the client's experience. Finally, the client's confidentiality may be at risk, particularly if therapeutic discussions are conducted outside the privacy of the office.

With the blurring of the expected functions and responsibilities of the therapist and client comes the breakdown of the boundaries of the professional relationship itself. Therapist and client are likely to experience some slipping between roles. Role slippage may then extend to other roles beyond the original relationships. . . . Gutheil and Gabbard (1993); Pope (1994); Pope, Sonne, and Holroyd (1993); and Strasburger, Jorgenson, and Sutherland (1992) have explored the concept of the "slippery slope" phenomenon, the gradual erosion of the boundaries of the professional relationship from small changes (e.g., sessions during lunch) to the most egregious alterations (e.g., sexual intimacy with a client). In her analysis of data from a large national survey of therapists, Borys (1988) found a positive relationship between certain nonsexual multiple relationships and sexual involvement between therapist and client.

A multiple relationship may also put the client at risk for a perceived—or real—emotional abandonment. As the therapeutic relationship begins to fail with regard to role-related expectations or responsibilities, the client is likely to feel no longer unconditionally cared for and listened to and perhaps will even begin to feel completely misunderstood.

Furthermore, the therapist's interests and needs, as expressed in the secondary relationship, may be fulfilled through the therapist's or the client's conscious or unconscious response to the power differential inherent in the professional relationship. . . . The risk for the client is that the power differential may foster exploitation of the client's vulnerabilities to gratify the therapist's emotional or other needs.

A multiple relationship may be considered unethical when, given a primary professional relationship, another relationship with an individual risks impairment of the psychologist's fulfillment of expectations or responsibilities in the professional relationship, risks exploitation of the individual's diminished power, or risks damage to the client's emotional involvement in the professional relationship. A key factor in the definition of unethical multiple relationships is the concept of *risk*. In our society, most laws and ethical guidelines are intended to prevent undesirable outcomes of behavior—those leading to the emotional or physical harm of individuals. Certain behaviors are assessed to be more likely than not to cause such undesirable outcomes. Thus, laws and guidelines proscribe such behavior, even if in a specific case a behavior did not actually result in the negative consequence. . . . The new code states in the preamble that the psychologist's primary goal is to provide for the welfare and protection of the individuals and groups with whom they work. The psychologist's orientation, then, must be risk-preventive. Conduct that creates undue risk for those who receive psychological services is unethical regardless of

whether it leads to so-called therapeutic gains. Often these supposed "gains" are used in attempts to justify unethical conduct. Those who engage in sexual intimacies (or other unethical multiple relationships with clients), for example, have often claimed that the sexual intimacies were the best or only method by which to gain increased knowledge about a client, to provide emotional support and validation, to create a spontaneous and authentic relationship, to reach an otherwise unreachable client, to help a client with sexual or other specific difficulties, or even to prevent the client from committing suicide (see, e.g., Eyman & Gabbard, 1991; Gabbard, 1989; Pope, 1994; Pope & Bouhoutsos, 1986; Pope et al., 1993; Redlich, 1977). However one may view such claims, multiple relationships that impose on and impair the dynamics of the professional relationship between psychologists and those with whom they work are simply unethical.

References

American Psychological Association. (1953b). *Ethical standards of psychologists: A summary of ethical principles*. Washington, DC: Author.

Borys, D. S. (1988). *Dual relationships between therapist and client: A national survey of clinicians' attitudes and practices*. Unpublished doctoral dissertation, University of California, Los Angeles.

Borys, D. S. (1992). Nonsexual dual relationships. In L. VandeCreek, S. Knapp, & T. L. Jackson (Eds.), *Innovations in clinical practice: A sourcebook* (Vol. 11, pp. 443–454). Sarasota, FL: Professional Resources.

Ethics Committee of the American Psychological Association. (1988b). Trends in ethics cases, common pitfalls, and published resources. *American Psychologist, 43,* 564–572.

Eyman, J. R., & Gabbard, G. O. (1991). Will therapist–patient sex prevent suicide? *Psychiatric Annals, 21,* 669–674.

Feldman-Summers, S. (1989). Sexual contact in fiduciary relationships. In G. O. Gabbard (Ed.), *Sexual exploitation in professional relationships* (pp. 193–209). Washington, DC: American Psychiatric Press.

Gabbard, G. O. (Ed.). (1989). *Sexual exploitation in professional relationships*. Washington, DC: American Psychiatric Association.

Gabbard, G. O. (1994). Reconsidering the American Psychological Association's policy on sex with former patients: Is it justifiable? *Professional Psychology: Research and Practice, 25,* 329–335.

Gabbard, G. O., & Pope, K. (1989). Sexual intimacies after termination: Clinical, ethical, and legal aspects. In G. O. Gabbard (Ed.), *Sexual exploitation in professional relationships* (pp. 115–127). Washington, DC: American Psychiatric Press.

Geller, J. D., Cooley, R. S., & Hartley, D. (1981–1982). Images of the psychotherapist. *Imagination, Cognition, and Personality, 1,* 123–146.

Gutheil, T. G., & Gabbard, G. O. (1993). The concept of boundaries in clinical practice: Theoretical and risk-management dimensions. *American Journal of Psychiatry, 150,* 188–196.

Hatcher, E. R. (1993, June 4). Firm boundaries: No exceptions. *Psychiatric News,* p. 23.

Pope, K. S. (1994). *Sexual involvement with therapists: Patient assessment, subsequent therapy, forensics.* Washington, DC: American Psychological Association.

Pope, K. S., & Bouhoutsos, J. C. (1986). *Sexual intimacy between therapists and patients.* New York: Praeger.

Pope, K. S., Sonne, J. L., & Holroyd, J. (1993). *Sexual feelings in psychotherapy: Explorations for therapists and therapists-in-training.* Washington, DC: American Psychological Association.

Pope, K. S., & Vasquez, M. J. T. (1991). *Ethics in psychotherapy and counseling: A practical guide for psychologists.* San Francisco: Jossey-Bass.

Redlich, F. C. (1977). The ethics of sex therapy. In W. H. Masters, V. E. Johnson, & R. D. Kolodny (Eds.), *Ethical issues in sex therapy* (pp. 143–157). Boston: Little, Brown.

Report of the Ethics Committee, 1991 and 1992. (1993). *American Psychologist, 48,* 811–820.

Strasburger, L. H., Jorgenson, L., & Sutherland, P. (1992). The prevention of psychotherapist misconduct: Avoiding the slippery slope. *American Journal of Psychiatry, 45,* 544–555.

Dual Relationships in Psychotherapy

Kenneth S. Pope

. . .

Dual relationships are relatively easy to define; they are much more difficult for many of us to recognize in our practice. A dual relationship in psychotherapy occurs when the therapist is in another, significantly different relationship with one of his or her patients. Most commonly, the second role is social, financial, or professional.

. . .

Specific examples, more than abstract definitions, may provide us with a useful awareness of how these entanglements occur. The following five fictional scenarios, dismayingly typical of actual practice, were among those created by Keith-Spiegel and Koocher (1985) to illustrate their discussion of dual relationships.

> Jan Job worked as a records clerk for a large community mental-health agency. She was supervised by Helmut Honcho, Ph.D. Jan was experiencing personal problems and asked Dr. Honcho if she could be a client. He agreed. Jan would later bring an ethics complaint against Honcho, charging him with blocking her promotion based on assessments of her as a client rather than as an employee. (p. 270)
>
> Soon after Patty Pal began counseling with Richard Chum, Ed.D., Patty asked Dr. Chum and his wife to spend the weekend at their family beach house. The outing was enjoyable for all parties. During therapy, however, Patty became increasingly reluctant to talk about her problems and insisted that things were going quite well. Other so-cial interactions among the foursome continued to occur on weekends. Chum finally confronted Patty during the therapy with his impression that "nothing was moving." It was at that point that Patty admitted that she was experiencing numerous pressures and problems. But she felt that if she were honest about them in therapy, Chum might choose not to socialize with her and her husband. (p. 271)
>
> Feline Breed, Ph.D., spent much of her time outside her professional role raising pedigree cats. Most of her weekends were devoted to traveling the cat-show circuit. Many of her therapy clients were "cat people" whom she had met through her hobby contacts. The small-talk before and after the therapy sessions was usually devoted to discussion about cats. Interest in purchasing kittens that she raised was often expressed, and she did sell them to clients. In more than one instance, the sale of kittens to clients caused difficulties. Once, for example, the therapy process was not proceeding as the client wished, and the client accused Dr. Breed of "using" him as a way of selling high-priced cats and not really caring about his problems. In another instance, a woman client was upset because Dr. Breed sold her an animal that had never won a single prize. The client assumed that if the therapist raised such defective cats, then the trustworthiness of her

therapy skills should be questioned as well. (p. 286)

Kurt Court, Esq., and Leonard Dump, Ph.D., met at a cocktail party. Mr. Court's law practice was suffering because of his debilitating personal problems. Dr. Dump was about to embark on a bitter divorce proceeding. They hit upon the idea of swapping professional services. Dr. Dump would see Mr. Court as a psychotherapy client, and Mr. Court would represent Dr. Dump in the divorce proceeding. Mr. Court proved to be a difficult and more disturbed client than Dr. Dump had anticipated. Furthermore, Court's representation of Dump was erratic and the likelihood of a favorable outcome looked bleak. Yet Mr. Court brought ethics charges against Dr. Dump. Court charged that the therapy he received was inferior and that Dump spent most of the time expressing anger and berating him for not getting better. (p. 278)

Elmo Brush agreed to paint the house of Peel Schuff, Ph.D., in exchange for psychotherapy for Brush's teenage daughter. Dr. Schuff saw the girl for six sessions and terminated her therapy. Brush complained that his end of the bargain would have brought him $900 in a conventional deal. Thus it was as though he had paid $150 a session for the services of a person who normally charged $50 a session. Dr. Schuff argued that he had satisfactorily resolved the daughter's problems, and the deal was valid because task was traded for task, not dollar for dollar value. (p. 279)

. . .

STRATEGIES OF TOLERATION AND JUSTIFICATION

. . .

Selective Inattention

One of the most prevalent ways in which dual relationships—and many other forms of unethical be-

havior—are made tolerable is through selective inattention. The therapist blocks out sustained, useful awareness of the duality of relationships by splitting the two relationships and refusing to acknowledge that both relationships involve the same patient and have implications for the patient and the patient's treatment.

One indication that selective inattention may have played a role in the development of a dual relationship is the lack of any mention of a second relationship in the treatment notes. . . . The chart contains no mention of the duality of the relationship, no consideration of how the two relationships may be interacting, and no discussion of how the dual relationship may affect the patient's clinical status, prognosis, treatment plan, or response to the treatment plan. . . .

Selective inattention may foster dual relationships in another manner. Often, the colleagues of a therapist who is entering a dual relationship may choose to screen out and remain selectively inattentive to evidence that the therapist is engaging in activities that put the patient at risk for harm. Again, such selective inattention regarding some of our closest colleagues is common to virtually all of us who practice as clinicians. Perhaps he or she is our employer or supervisor or, perhaps, a valuable source of referrals. At times, we may not want to rock the boat and upset the tranquility of a formal organization, such as a clinic, or an informal network of colleagues. And at times, we may experience the "glass house" phenomenon: We may avoid raising ethical issues with others because we are afraid that they will begin raising them with us. Thus, we may enter into a tacit pact with our colleagues: Everyone will ignore everyone else's ethical violations. In such situations, selective inattention becomes an important aspect of the interpersonal or social ecology. . . .

Benefits

A second way in which dual relationships are sometimes justified is that they are beneficial for the patient. . . . The addition of the sexual relationship was said to provide the patient with a more nurturantly human, warmer professional relationship; to provide the patient with a more complete sense of acceptance; to help the patient develop—under the watchful eye of the therapist—a more healthy view of his or her own sexuality and a more varied and completed array of sexual responses; to provide the patient with sexually corrective experiences that would help the patient recover from dysfunction caused by prior sexual trauma; to help the patient overcome a disabling "mind–body" split in which the patient's reactions were overly intellectualized; to provide a way in which the patient could experience and work through "overt transference"; and to provide a safe "bridge" between the therapeutic and nontherapeutic environment (i.e., the patient could "try out" on the therapist what the patient had discovered about sex and intimacy during the early stages of therapy so that the patient could be sure of making it work "in real life").

One difficulty the proponents of this view experienced was that mention of the dual relationship—supposedly a key component of the treatment plan—was often absent from any part of the chart notes or informed consent procedures. Therapists had difficulty explaining why, if they had carefully considered why a dual relationship was the treatment of choice and had implemented it carefully, they had neglected to obtain the patient's informed consent for the procedure and why they failed to note the consideration or use of the treatment strategy in the chart notes.

A second difficulty faced by those who sought to justify their behavior . . . was their difficulty finding substantial research evidence that implementing dual relationship treatment was a safe and effective way to produce positive therapeutic change. . . .

Some therapists acknowledged that there was virtually no research evidence or other systematic data supporting the hypothesis that dual relationships are a safe and effective method to produce therapeutic change. They maintained that their implementation of the dual relationship was on a trial basis, as part of a research or quasi-research effort to obtain just such evidence. However, it was often difficult for these therapists to establish that they had provided adequate procedural safeguards (such as informed consent) to the patients on whom this experimental method was being tested (see Levine, 1988; Pope, 1990a, 1990b).

Prevalence

Therapists may attempt to justify engaging in dual relationships with their patients by asserting that many other therapists engage in the practice. . . . This approach was used in some of the early malpractice trials in which therapists who acknowledged engaging in sexual dual relationships with their patients emphasized that the early surveys of therapist–patient sexual intimacies (e.g., Holroyd & Broadsky, 1977) indicated that around 10% of male therapists reported engaging in sexual relationships with their patients. This 10% figure, according to the defense, represented a sizable minority of the professional community who accepted and endorsed, via their own behavior with patients, the legitimacy of therapist–patient sexual relations.

The reflexive acceptance of the "prevalence" argument may have encouraged or facilitated both sexual and nonsexual dual relationships. The argument itself, however, does not seem to address the issue of whether dual relationships are indeed a safe and effective way to produce beneficial change in the patient. Various behaviors that may be unethical, illegal, or clinically contraindicated may unfortunately be practiced, from time to time, by a sizable minority and sometimes even by a majority of the professional community. . . . The fact that a substantial number of professionals engage in a practice does not, in and of itself, indicate whether the practice is ethical, legal, safe, or effective. . . .

Necessity

Dual relationships may be accepted with virtually no ethical or clinical scrutiny when they are asserted to be necessary. The therapist claims that there was no alternative but to engage in a dual relationship. The therapist using this justification refuses to accept any responsibility for entering a dual relationship; the therapist must simply accept what is determined by forces beyond his or her control. Thus, dual relationships may be termed *inevitable* or *unavoidable*.

Yet the "my hands were tied" and the "what else could I have done?" approach may represent a combination of a failure to explore and create alternative approaches that meet the highest clinical, legal, and ethical standards and a not-too-subtle attempt to evade responsibility. Careful, determined, imaginative attempts to meet the needs of patients without resorting to sexual or nonsexual dual relationships can overcome the rationalization of necessity. . . .

References

Holroyd, J. C., & Brodsky, A. M. (1977). Psychologists' attitudes and practices regarding erotic and nonerotic physical contact with clients. *American Psychologist, 32,* 843–849.

Keith-Spiegel, P., & Koocher, G. P. (1985). *Ethics in psychology.* New York: Random House.

Levine, R. J. (1988). *Ethics and regulation of clinical research* (2nd ed.). New Haven, CT: Yale University Press.

Pope, K. S. (1990a). Therapist–patient sex as sex abuse: Six scientific, professional, and practical dilemmas in addressing victimization and rehabilitation. *Professional Psychology: Research and Practice, 21,* 227–239.

Pope, K. S. (1990b). Therapist–patient sexual involvement: A review of the research. *Clinical Psychology Review, 10,* 477–490.

◆ ◆ ◆

Commentary: For an additional perspective on boundary violations in therapy and a discussion of relevant portions of the codes of ethics of the American Medical and American Psychiatric Associations, as well as that of the APA, see Jorgenson, L. M., Hirsch, A. B., & Wahl, K. M. (1997). Fiduciary duty and boundaries: Acting in the client's best interest. Behavioral Sciences and the Law, 15, 49–62.

Review the following items that may exemplify improper dual relationships. Rate each one on the following scale: 1 = never ethical; 2 = ethical under rare conditions; 3 = ethical under some conditions; 4 = ethical under most conditions; 5 = always ethical.

- *Accepting a gift worth under $10*
- *Accepting a client's invitation to a special occasion*
- *Accepting a service or product as payment for therapy*
- *Becoming friends with a client after termination*
- *Selling a product to a client*
- *Accepting a gift worth over $50*
- *Providing therapy to an employee*
- *Engaging in sexual activity with a client after termination*
- *Disclosing details of current personal stresses to a client*
- *Inviting clients to an office/clinic open house*
- *Employing a client*
- *Going out to eat with a client after a session*
- *Buying goods or services from a client*
- *Engaging in sexual activity with a current client*
- *Inviting clients to a personal party or social event*
- *Providing individual therapy to a relative, friend, or lover of an ongoing client*
- *Providing therapy to a current student or supervisee*
- *Allowing a client to enroll in one's class for a grade*

Readers can compare their results with those of a survey of 1,108 mental health professionals. See Borys, D. B., & Pope, K. S. (1989). Dual relationships between therapist and client: A national study of psychologists, psychiatrists, and social workers. Professional Psychology: Research and Practice, 20, 283–293. Only five behaviors were rated as never ethical by a majority of the respondents. Which are they?

In order of greatest perceived unethicality, the five behaviors are: sex with a current client; selling a product to a client; sex with a client posttermination; inviting clients to a social event; and providing therapy to an employee. No behavior was universally considered unethical. What issues do these data raise?

The Concept of Boundaries in Clinical Practice: Theoretical and Risk-Management Dimensions

Thomas G. Gutheil and Glen O. Gabbard

. . .

ROLE

Role boundaries constitute the essential boundary issue. To conceptualize this entity, one might ask, "Is this what a therapist does?" Although subject to ideological variations, this touchstone question not only identifies the question of clinical role but serves as a useful orienting device for avoiding the pitfalls of the role violations.

> A middle-aged borderline patient, attempting to convey how deeply distressed she felt about her situation, leaped from her chair in the therapist's office and threw herself to her knees at the therapist's feet, clasping his hand in both of her own and crying, "Do you understand how awful it's been for me?" The therapist said gently, "You know, this is really interesting, what's happening here—but it isn't therapy; please go back to your chair." The patient did so, and the incident was explored verbally.

Although such limit setting may appear brusque to some clinicians, it may be the only appropriate response to halt boundary-violating "acting in" (especially of the impulsive or precipitous kind) and to make the behavior available for analysis as part of the therapy.

. . .

> Greenson (22) . . . noted that the rule of absti-

nence was constructed to avoid the gratification of a patient's neurotic and infantile wishes, not to lead to a sterile form of treatment in which all the patient's wishes are frustrated. . . .

TIME

Time is, of course, a boundary, defining the limits of the session itself while providing structure and even containment for many patients, who derive reassurance because they will have to experience the various stresses of reminiscing, reliving, and so forth for a set time only. The beginnings and endings of sessions—starting or stopping late or early—are both susceptible to crossings of this boundary. Such crossings may be subtle or stark.

> A male psychiatrist came in to the hospital to see his female inpatient for marathon sessions at odd times, such as from 2:00 to 6:00 in the morning, rationalizing that this procedure was dictated by scheduling problems. This relationship eventually became overtly sexual.

An interesting prejudice about violating the boundary of time has evolved in sexual misconduct cases, a prejudice deriving from the fact that a clinician interested in having a sexual relationship with a patient might well schedule that patient for the last hour of the day (although, of course, after-work time slots have always been popular). In the fog of uncertainty surrounding sexual misconduct (usually a conflict of credibilities without witnesses), this factor has gleamed with so illusory a brightness that some attorneys seem to presume that because the patient had the last appointment of the day, sexual misconduct occurred! Short of seeing patients straight through the night, this problem does not seem to have a clear solution. Admittedly, however, from a risk-management standpoint, a patient in the midst of an intense erotic transference to the therapist might best be seen, when possible, during high-traffic times when other people (e.g., secretaries, receptionists, and even other patients) are around. . . .

PLACE AND SPACE

The therapist's office or a room on a hospital unit is obviously the locale for almost all therapy; some exceptions are noted in the next section . . .

Some boundary crossings of place can have a constructive effect. As with medication, the timing and dosage are critical.

> After initially agreeing to attend his analysand's wedding, the analyst later declined, reasoning that his presence would be inappropriately distracting. Later, after the death of the analysand's first child, he attended the funeral service. Both his absence at the first occasion and his presence at the second were felt as helpful and supportive by the analysand. They both agreed later that the initial plan to attend the wedding was an error.

A relevant lesson from this example is that boundary violations can be reversed or undone with further consideration and discussion. At times, an apology by the therapist is appropriate and even necessary. . . .

Sorties out of the office usually merit special scrutiny. While home visits were a central component of the community psychiatry movement, the shift in the professional climate is such that the modern clinician is best advised to perform this valuable service with an opposite-sex chaperone and to document the event in some detail.

Sessions during lunch are an extremely common form of boundary violation. This event appears to

be a common way station along the path of increasing boundary crossings culminating in sexual misconduct. Although clinicians often advance the claim that therapy is going on, so, inevitably, is much purely social behavior; it does not *look* like therapy, at least to a jury. Lunch sessions are not uncommonly followed by sessions during dinner, then just dinners, then other dating behavior, eventually including intercourse.

Sessions in cars represent another violation of place. Typically, the clinician gives the patient a ride home under various circumstances. Clinician and patient then park (e.g., in front of the patient's house) and finish up the presumably therapeutic conversation. From a fact finder's viewpoint, many exciting things happen in cars, but therapy is usually not one of them.

The complexity of the matter increases, however, when we consider other therapeutic ideologies. For example, it would not be a boundary violation for a behaviorist, under certain circumstances, to accompany a patient in a car, to an elevator, to an airplane, or even to a public restroom (in the treatment of paruresis, the fear of urinating in a public restroom) as part of the treatment plan for a particular phobia. The existence of a body of professional literature, a clinical rationale, and risk–benefit documentation will be useful in protecting the clinician in such a situation from misconstruction of the therapeutic efforts.

MONEY

Money is a boundary in the sense of defining the business nature of the therapeutic relationship. This is not love, it's work. Indeed, some would argue that the fee received by the therapist is the only appropriate and allowable material gratification to be derived from clinical work (28). Patient and clinician may each have conflicts about this distinction (29), but consultative experience makes clear that trouble begins precisely when the therapist stops thinking of therapy as work.

On the other hand, most clinicians learned their trade by working with indigent patients and feel that some attempt should be made to pay back the debt by seeing some patients for free—a form of "tithing," if you will. Note that this *decision*—to see a patient for free and to discuss that with the patient—is quite different from simply letting the billing lapse or allowing the debt to mount. The latter examples are boundary crossings, perhaps violations. . . .

In rural areas even today, payments to physicians may take the form of barter: when the doctor delivers your child, you pay with two chickens and the new calf. For the dynamic therapist this practice poses some problems, because it blurs the boundary between payment and gift (covered in the next section). The clinician should take a case at a reasonable fee or make a *decision* to see the patient for a low fee (e.g., one dollar) or none. Barter is confusing and probably ill-advised today. Of course, all such decisions require documentation.

GIFTS, SERVICES, AND RELATED MATTERS

> A client became very upset during an interview with her therapist and began to cry. The therapist, proffering a tissue, held out a hand-tooled Florentine leather case in which a pocket pack of tissues had been placed. After the patient had withdrawn a tissue, the therapist impulsively said, "Why don't you keep the case?" In subsequent supervision the therapist came to understand that this "gift" to the patient was an unconscious bribe designed to avert the anger that the therapist sensed just below the surface of the patient's sorrow.

This gift was also a boundary violation, placing unidentified obligations on the patient and constituting a form of impulsive acting in. A related boundary violation is the use of favors or services from the patient for the benefit of the therapist, as Simon's (6) startling vignette illustrates:

> Within a few months of starting . . . psychotherapy, the patient was returning the therapist's library books for him "as a favor." . . . The patient began having trouble paying her treatment bill, so she agreed—at the therapist's

suggestion—to clean the therapist's office once a week in partial payment. . . . The patient also agreed to get the therapist's lunch at a nearby delicatessen before each session. (p. 106)

The obvious exploitive nature of these boundary violations destroys even the semblance of therapy for the patient's benefit. . . .

> A patient in long-term therapy had struggled for years with apparent infertility and eventually, with great difficulty, arranged for adoption of a child. Two years later she unexpectedly conceived and finally gave birth. Her therapist, appreciating the power and meaning of this event, sent congratulatory flowers to the hospital.

In this case, the therapist followed social convention in a way that—though technically a boundary crossing—represented a response appropriate to the real relationship. Offering a tissue to a crying patient and expressing condolences to a bereaved one are similar examples of appropriate responses outside the classic boundaries of the therapeutic relationship.

CLOTHING

Clothing represents a social boundary the transgression of which is usually inappropriate to the therapeutic situation, yet a patient may appropriately be asked to roll up a sleeve to permit measurement of blood pressure. Excessively revealing or frankly seductive clothing worn by the therapist may represent a boundary violation with potentially harmful effects to patients. . . .

Berne (32) noted the technical error of the male clinician who, confronting a patient whose skirt was pulled up high, began to explain to the patient his sexual fantasies in response to this event. Berne suggested instead saying to the patient, "Pull your skirt down." Similar directness of limit setting appears to be suited to the patient who—either from psychosis or the wish to provoke—begins to take off her clothes in the office. As before, the comment, "This behavior is inappropriate, and it isn't therapy; please put your clothes back on," said in a calm voice, is a reasonable response.

LANGUAGE

As part of the otherwise laudable efforts to humanize and demystify psychiatry a few decades back, the use of a patient's first name was very much in vogue. While this may indeed convey greater warmth and closeness, such usage is a two-edged sword. There is always the possibility that patients may experience the use of first names as misrepresenting the professional relationship as a social friendship (28). There may well be instances when using first names is appropriate, but therapists must carefully consider whether they are creating a false sense of intimacy that may subsequently backfire. . . .

. . . Last names also emphasize that this process is work or business, an atmosphere which may promote a valuable mature perspective and minimize acting out. In addition, calling someone by the name used by primary objects may foster transference perceptions of the therapist when they are not desirable, as with a borderline patient prone to forming severe psychotic transferences. For balance, however, recall that use of last names may also sound excessively distant, formal, and aloof. . . .

SELF-DISCLOSURE AND RELATED MATTERS

Few clinicians would argue that the therapist's self-disclosure is always a boundary crossing. . . . [W]hen a therapist begins to indulge in even mild forms of self-disclosure, it is an indication for careful self-scrutiny regarding the motivations for departure from the usual therapeutic stance. . . .

Self-disclosure, however, represents a complex issue. Clearly, therapists may occasionally use a neutral example from their own lives to illustrate a point. Sharing the impact of a borderline patient's behavior on the therapist may also be useful. The therapist's self-revelation, however, of personal fantasies or dreams; of social, sexual, or financial details; of specific vacation plans; or of expected births or deaths in the family is usually burdening the patient with information, whereas it is the patient's fantasies that might best be explored. The issue is somewhat controversial: a number of patients (and, surpris-

ingly, some therapists) believe that the patient is somehow entitled to this kind of information. In any case, it is a boundary violation and as such may be used by the legal system to advance or support a claim of sexual misconduct. The reasoning is that the patient knows so much about the therapist's personal life that they must have been intimate. . . .

Finally, the boundary can be violated from the other side. An example would be the therapist's using data from the therapy session for personal gain, such as insider information on stock trading, huge profits to be made in real estate, and the like.

PHYSICAL CONTACT

. . . [Professionals] working with a patient with AIDS or HIV seropositivity often describe wishing to touch the patient in some benign manner (pat the back, squeeze an arm, pat a hand) in every session. They reason that such patients feel like lepers, and therapeutic touch is called for in these cases. But even such humane interventions must be scrutinized and, indeed, be documented to prevent their misconstruction in today's climate.

From the viewpoint of current risk-management principles, a handshake is about the limit of social physical contact at this time. Of course, a patient who attempts a hug in the last session after 7 years of intense, intensive, and successful therapy should probably not be hurled across the room. However, most hugs from patients should be discouraged in tactful, gentle ways by words, body language, positioning, and so forth. Patients who deliberately or provocatively throw their arms around the therapist despite repeated efforts at discouragement should be stopped. An appropriate response is to step back, catch both wrists in your hands, cross the patient's wrists in front of you, so that the crossed arms form a barrier between bodies, and say firmly, "Therapy is a talking relationship; please sit down so we can discuss your not doing this any more." If the work degenerates into grabbing, consider seriously termination and referral, perhaps to a therapist of a different gender.

What is one to make of the brands of therapy that include physical contact, such as Rolfing? Presumably, the boundary extends to that limited physical contact, and the patient expects it and grants consent; thus, no actual violation occurs. Massage therapists may struggle with similar issues, however. In other ideologies the issue may again be the impact of the appearance of a violation:

> A therapist—who claimed that her school of practice involved hugging her female patient at the beginning and end of every session, without apparent harm—eventually had to terminate therapy with the patient for noncompliance with the therapeutic plan. The enraged patient filed a sexual misconduct claim against the therapist. Despite the evidence showing that this claim was probably false (a specious suit triggered by rage at the therapist), the insurer settled because of the likelihood that a jury would not accept the principle of "hug at the start and hug at the end but no hugs in between." If the claim was indeed false, this is a settlement based on boundary violations alone.

At another level this vignette nicely suggests how nonsexual boundary violations may be harmful to a patient in much the same way that actual sexual misconduct is. Instead of engaging the patient in a mourning process to deal with the resentment and grief about the deprivations of her childhood, the therapist who hugs a patient is often attempting to provide the physical contact normally offered by a parent. The patient then feels entitled to more demonstrations of caring and assumes that if gratification in the form of hugs is available, other wishes will be granted as well. . . . When actual physical contact occurs, the crucial psychotherapeutic distinction between the symbolic and the concrete is lost [(21),]

and the patient may feel that powerful infantile longings within will finally be satisfied. . . .

References

6. Simon RI: Sexual exploitation of patients: how it begins before it happens. Psychiatr Annals 1989; 19:104–122

21. Casement PJ: The meeting of needs in psychoanalysis. Psychoanal Inquiry 1990; 10:325–346.

22. Greenson RR: The Technique of Psychoanalysis, vol 1. New York, International Universities Press, 1967

28. Epstein RS, Simon RI: The exploitation index: an early warning indicator of boundary violations in psychotherapy. Bull Menninger Clin 1990; 54:450–465

29. Krueger DW (ed): The Last Taboo: Money As Symbol and Reality in Psychotherapy and Psychoanalysis. New York, Brunner/Mazel, 1986

32. Berne E: What Do You Say After You Say Hello? The Psychology of Human Destiny. New York, Grove Press, 1972

◆ ◆ ◆

Commentary: "The true base rate of sexual misconduct among psychologists is not known" (p. 455). See Gottlieb, M. (1990). Accusation of sexual misconduct: Assisting in the complaint process. Professional Psychology: Research and Practice, 21, 455–461. In part, that is because of the methodological problems involved in gathering data about sexual intimacies with clients. See, for example, Williams, M. H. (1992). Exploitation and inference: Mapping the damage from therapist–patient sexual involvement. American Psychologist, 47, 412–421; see also Parsons, J. P., & Wincze, John P. (1995). A survey of client–therapist sexual involvement in Rhode Island as reported by subsequent treating therapists. Professional Psychology: Research and Practice, 26, 171–175. Keeping in mind these methodological issues, Pope & Vasquez (1998, next excerpt) compiled the following helpful and intriguing data gathered over the past 2 decades.

Ethics in Psychotherapy and Counseling: A Practical Guide for Psychologists

Kenneth S. Pope and Melba J. Vasquez

					Percentage reporting sex with clients	
Study	**Publication date**	**Discipline**	**Sample size**	**Return rate**	**Male**	**Female**
Holroyd & Brodsky[a]	1977	psychologists	1,000	70%	12.1%	2.6%
K. S. Pope, Levenson, & Schover	1979	psychologists	1,000	48%	12.0%	3.0%
K. S. Pope, Keith-Spiegel, & Tabachnick	1986	psychologists	1,000	58.5%	9.4%	2.5%
Gartrell, Herman, Olarte, Feldstein, & Localio[b]	1986	psychiatrists	5,574	26%	7.1%	3.1%
K. S. Pope, Tabachnick, & Keith-Spiegel[c]	1987	psychologists	1,000	46%	3.6%	0.4%
Akamatsu[d]	1988	psychologists	1,000	39.5%	3.5%	2.3%
Borys & Pope[e]	1989	psychiatrists, psychologists, and social workers	4,800	56.5%	0.9%	0.2%
Bernsen, Tabachnick, & Pope	1994	social workers	1,000	45.3%	3.6%	0.5%

Source: Adapted from Pope, 1994. Copyright 1994 by the American Psychological Association. Adapted with permission of the author and publisher.

Note: This table presents only national surveys that have been published in peer-reviewed scientific and professional journals. Exceptional caution is warranted in comparing the data from these various surveys. For example, the frequently cited percentages of 12.1 and 2.6, reported by Holroyd & Brodsky (1977), exclude same-sex involvements. Moreover, when surveys included separate items to assess posttermination sexual involvement, these data are reported in footnotes to this table. Finally, some published articles did not provide sufficiently detailed data for this table (for example, aggregate percentages); the investigators supplied the data needed for the table.

[a]Although the gender percentages presented in the table for the other studies represent responses to one basic survey item in each survey, the percentages presented for Holroyd & Brodsky's study span several items. The study's senior author confirmed through personal communication that the study's findings were that 12.1 percent of the male and 2.6 percent of the female participants reported having engaged in erotic contact (whether or not it included intercourse) with at least one opposite-sex patient; that about 4 percent of the male and 1 percent of the female participants reported engaging in erotic contact with at least one same-sex patient; and that, in response to a separate survey item, 7.2 percent of the male and 0.6 percent of the female psychologists reported that they had "had intercourse with a patient within three months after terminating therapy" (p. 846; see also Pope, Sonne, & Holroyd, 1993).

[b]"Respondents were asked to specify the number of male and female patients with whom they had been sexually involved" (p. 1127); they were also asked "to restrict their answers to adult patients" (p. 1127).

[c]The survey also included a question about "becoming sexually involved with a former client" (p. 996). Gender percentages about sex with current or former clients did not appear in the article but were provided by an author. Fourteen percent of the male and 8 percent of the female respondents reported sex with a former client.

[d]The original article also noted that 14.2 percent of male and 4.7 percent of female psychologists reported that they had "been involved in an intimate relationship with a former client" (p. 454).

[e]This survey was sent to 1,600 psychiatrists, 1,600 psychologists, and 1,600 social workers. In addition to the data reported in the table, the original article also asked whether respondents had "engaged in sexual activity with a client after termination" (p. 288). Six percent of the male and 2 percent of the female therapists reported engaging in this activity.

◆ ◆ ◆

Commentary: For a summary of data revealing the prevalence of sexual intimacies between psychologists and nonclients, e.g., students, supervisees, advisees, and clients, see Lamb, D. H., & Catanzaro, S. J. (1998). Sexual and nonsexual boundary violations involving psychologists, clients, supervisees, and students: Implications for professional practice. Professional Psychology: Research and Practice, 29, 498–503; Sonne, J. (1994). Multiple relationships: Does the new ethics code answer the right questions? Professional Psychology: Research and Practice, 25, 336–343.

Although in their most recent study Lamb & Catanzaro (1998) indicate that 6% of self-reporting psychologists admit to at least one act of sexual intimacy with a client, Pope & Vasquez (1998) demonstrate that there is a trend toward a lower incidence of these self-reports. What explains this trend? Is it the result of methodological differences in the studies, the increasing trend toward criminalization of sexual activity between therapists and patients (see subsequent material in this chapter), a genuine diminution of this activity, or some other explanation? Parsons & Wincze (1995), discussing data gathered in Rhode Island between 1989 and 1991, noted,

> [O]nly one sexual misconduct case was reported to the . . . Board of Examiners in Psychology during the 3-year period that the survey covers; yet, the survey reported at least 37 incidents [including not only intercourse but genital exposure and erotic hugging] by psychologists during the same time period. (p. 174)

Parson, J. P., & Wincze, John P. (1995). A survey of client–therapist sexual involvement in Rhode Island as reported by subsequent treating therapists. Professional Psychology: Research and Practice, 26, 171–175.

In light of the issues and arguments contained so far in this chapter, readers may profit from discussing the sexually oriented dual-relationship vignettes presented in chapters 2 and 3, as well as the following hypothetical but realistic vignette from Hall, J. E. (1987). Gender-related ethical dilemmas and ethics education. Professional Psychology: Research and Practice, 18, 573–579:

> *A psychologist in a full-time, solo private practice advertises that he limits his practice to marital problems. In 20 years in private practice, he has been successful in solving his clients' marital problems but not in saving his own marriage. Because he works 60–70 hr per week, he is able to avoid focusing on his own problems.*
>
> *His secretary schedules his 5:00 opening with a new client, a 35-year-old married woman, and leaves to catch the 5:00 bus. The client impresses him as someone in need of confirmation of her own worth; after several sessions she admits that she was molested as a child by her father and that her sexual relationship with her husband is both unsatisfactory and coerced. After 3 months pass, the psychologist realizes that he is looking forward to seeing his client each week and is beginning to feel sexually attracted to her. (p. 575)*

Hall (1987) suggested several choices that the male psychologist might make:

1. *Deny attraction to the client as well as "their vulnerability to each other" and continue to see the client in therapy;*
2. *Consult with a colleague and ask for peer supervision on the case;*
3. *Tell the client that it is unethical to have a sexual relationship with her and, therefore, that he must terminate the therapeutic relationship immediately;*
4. *Tell the client that it is unethical to have a sexual relationship with her, and suggest that if they terminate therapy and she initiates treatment with another therapist they could see each other socially after a reasonable period of time; or*
5. *Provide a referral to another therapist, and explain to the client that he cannot help her and that the other therapist is better qualified. He then seeks therapy for himself.*

What boundary violations occurred in this situation? What standards of the 1992 APA Ethical Principles are implicated? Which of these options are in accord with those provisions? Which options are unethical? Which simply reflect poor judgment? See the original article for Hall's own perspectives on each option.

It is noteworthy that Hall did not list an option in which the therapist, after careful evaluation, concludes that the client is not psychotic and is capable of making competent judgments, discusses the issue thoroughly with the client, and decides (with the client's consent) to continue therapy while beginning a social and romantic relationship with her. Are there any conditions under which such an option would be ethical? This response by Pope, Sonne, and Holroyd (1993) represents the professional consensus:

> Under no circumstances should a therapist ever engage in sexual intimacies with a patient. No matter what the situation. No matter who the patient. No matter what the patient has said and done. No matter how the therapist or the patient feels. Therapist–patient sexual intimacies are in all instances wrong and must be avoided. (p. 180)

See Pope, K. S., Sonne, J. L., & Holroyd, J. (1993). Sexual feelings in psychotherapy. Washington, DC: American Psychological Association.

Are there any reasonable counterarguments to this consensus that one can put forth, under the conditions I have described above?

Although there is near unanimity regarding sexual intimacies with current clients, professional opinions do diverge over the propriety of absolutely prohibiting sexual intimacies with former clients. In one survey, Sell, Gottlieb, and Schoenfeld (1986) found that of 54 cases before ethics committees and 48 cases before state licensing boards involving sexual intimacies, not one psychologist was exonerated solely because the adjudicating body agreed that a sufficient amount of time had elapsed between termination of treatment and initiation of a sexual relationship. However, they also found that very few of these bodies had developed guidelines to determine whether sexual relationships between psychologists and former clients would be permissible. Sell et al. urged APA to amend the Ethical Principles to create an absolute ban on sexual intimacies between psychologists and either current or former clients. See Sell, J. M., Gottlieb, M. C., & Schoenfeld, L. (1986). Ethical considerations and social/romantic relationships with present and former clients. Professional Psychology: Research and Practice, 17, 504–508.

In a later survey (Akamatsu, 1988) of 394 members of APA Division 29 (Psychotherapy), 44.7% said that intimate relationships with former clients were highly unethical. However, 31.3% felt that such relationships were neither ethical nor unethical, or even felt them to be ethical to some degree; 23.9% felt that such relationships were only somewhat unethical. The primary factor that respondents stated should be taken into account in determining whether posttherapy intimacy was ethical was time since termination. Other factors included the length and nature of therapy, the mental health of the client, whether therapy would resume, and promotion of the patient's freedom of choice. Interestingly, 14.2% of men and 4.7% of women admitted to intimate relationships with former patients. The average interval between termination and the commencement of the relationship was 15.6 months. See Akamatsu, T. J. (1988). Intimate relationships with former clients: National survey of attitudes and behavior among practitioners. Professional Psychology: Research and Practice, 19, 454–458. Akamatsu then concluded:

> My results strongly suggest that ethical guidelines be established by the APA. However, because of the divergent interpretations possible for current results, it may be that the recommendations . . . for a blanket prohibition of sexual intimacies with clients and former clients is more conservative than the views of many practitioners. Guidelines clearly are necessary, but they should delineate contingencies or circumstances that might be considered in determining the ethics of a particular case. This compromise would probably necessitate the individual handling of each case, but the task would be made considerably easier if guidelines were clear to therapists and their state boards or ethics committees. (p. 457)

As events transpired, Akamatsu's (1988) conjecture that an absolute ban on sex with former clients would not gain consensus turned out to be correct. The 1992 Ethical Principles retains an unconditional prohibition on sexual intimacies with current clients (Standard 4.05), but limits the prohibition to 2 years after termination *for intimacy with former therapy patients. After that, however, the burden is on the psychologist to show that the development of a sexual relationship is a "most unusual circumstance" and that there has been no exploitation of the former client as a result of the relationship, considering all the factors set out in Standard 4.07.*

Is Standard 4.07 sufficiently specific, and does it take into account all of the factors that should be balanced in developing a reasonable rule? Does it go far enough to protect psychotherapy clients, or does even a 2-year ban interfere with autonomous decision making, as long as both parties are adults and there is appropriate disclosure of the risks to the client? Consider the following.

Explicit Ambiguity: The 1992 Ethics Code as an Oxymoron

Donald N. Bersoff

. . .

Gabbard (1994) raised and rebutted "nine arguments frequently set forth as favoring a policy permitting posttermination sexual involvements" (p. 331). He called this permissive policy "premature" (p. 334), however, and urged the APA to permanently bar any sexual intimacies with former therapy clients. In support of his argument, he, as well as many others (Brown, 1988; Gabbard & Pope, 1989; Sell, Gottlieb, & Schoenfeld, 1986; Shopland & VandeCreek, 1991; Vasquez, 1991), provided powerful reasons for such a ban.

There may be excellent reasons for reconsidering the APA's position, and it is worthy of further debate. Certainly, Standard 4.07, as currently written or as it might be revised to bar sexual relations in perpetuity, does reflect such central moral principles as nonmaleficence and beneficence (Beauchamp & Childress, 1989; Bersoff & Koeppl, 1993; Kitchener, 1984). In considering the validity of the current provision or its alternative, however, I suggest that other competing moral or ethical principles be kept in mind. Foremost among those competing principles is autonomy—"forebearing from interfering in the expression of self-determination by those who wish to make decisions for themselves" (Bersoff, 1992, pp. 1569–1570). Society in general and our professional association in particular should be committed to, among other values, respecting each individual's right to choose his or her own fate, even if the choices the individual makes do not serve, in some objective sense, what the majority would consider to be the individual's best interests. . . .

Concern about posttermination sexual intimacies, at least in part, is predicated on the belief that there will always be an unequal relationship between the powerful therapist—usually a man—and the subservient patient—usually a woman (Gabbard, 1994; Vasquez, 1991). Coleman (1988), however, suggested that any permanent bar

> raises fundamental questions about . . . unconscious sexist motivations.
>
> The first such question is the appearance of paternalism. An absolute prohibition means [therapists] are deciding for patients that they will always be incapable of giving informed consent to a sexual relationship with their former therapists. Although such a rule ostensibly applies to both male and female patients, in reality those involved are almost exclusively women. Consequently, an absolute prohibition effectively renders female patients incapable of giving informed consent because they always remain under the influence of their male [therapists]. (p. 48) . . .

That women who were once in therapy will not be able to make an informed, voluntary, and intelligent decision about their sexual partners is precisely the claim proponents make in favor of an absolute ban. There should be more data to support such a hypothesis, however, before it is converted into an ethical rule relegating female clients to the role of

From *Professional Psychology: Research and Practice, 25,* 382–387. Copyright 1994 by the American Psychological Association. Adapted with permission of the author and publisher.

passive victims rather than reinforcing their status as autonomous, self-determining, consenting adults. . . .

References

Beauchamp, T. L., & Childress, J. F. (1989). *Principles of biomedical ethics.* New York: Oxford University Press.

Bersoff, D. N. (1992). Autonomy for vulnerable populations: The Supreme Court's reckless disregard for self-determination and social science. *Villanova Law Review, 37,* 1569–1605.

Bersoff, D. N., & Koeppl, P. M. (1993). The relation between ethical codes and moral principles. *Ethics and Behavior, 3,* 345–357.

Brown, L. S. (1988). Harmful effects of posttermination sexual and romantic relationships between therapists and their former clients. *Psychotherapy, 25,* 249–257.

Coleman, P. (1988). Sex between psychiatrist and former patient: A proposal for a "no harm, no foul" rule. *Oklahoma Law Review, 41,* 1–52.

Gabbard, G. O. (1994). Reconsidering the American Psychological Association's policy on sex with former patients: Is it justifiable? *Professional Psychology: Research and Practice, 25,* 329–335.

Gabbard, G. O., & Pope, K. (1989). Sexual intimacies after termination: Clinical, ethical, and legal aspects. In G. O. Gabbard (Ed.), *Sexual exploitation in professional relationships* (pp. 115–127). Washington, DC: American Psychiatric Press.

Kitchener, K. S. (1984). Intuition, critical evaluation and ethical principles: The foundation for ethical decisions in counseling psychology. *The Counseling Psychologist, 12,* 43–55.

Sell, J. M., Gottlieb, M. C., & Schoenfeld, L. S. (1986). Ethical consideration of social/romantic relationships with present and former clients. *Professional Psychology: Research and Practice, 17,* 504–508.

Shopland, S. N., & VandeCreek, L. (1991). Sex with ex-clients: Theoretical rationales for prohibition. *Ethics and Behavior, 1,* 35–44.

Vasquez, M. (1991). Sexual intimacies with clients after termination: Should a prohibition be explicit? *Ethics and Behavior, 1,* 45–61.

◆ ◆ ◆

Commentary: *Gabbard (1994; cited above) had a different role for statistics:*

> *In the absence of data that would persuasively demonstrate such relationships to be harmless, the prudent course of action would be to proscribe posttermination relationships under the same rationale used to prohibit sex with* current *[emphasis added] patients. When one considers that there are 5 billion people on the planet, the choice of a former patient as a sexual partner must raise serious questions about the judgment and ethics of the psychotherapist. (p. 334)*

Rarely discussed or studied is the instigation of sexual intimacies by clients with their therapists. In a very recent survey of 750 licensed female psychologists (354 of whom responded) the author reported that

> *more than half [53%] . . . have experienced sexual harassment by a patient at some point in their clinical practice. However, the incidence of harassment per therapeutic contact can very roughly be estimated at less than 1 in 5,000 [therapy hours]. The types of harassment reported by psychologists ranged from indirect verbal exchanges, to requests for sex, to threats of sexual assault. (p. 60)*

The most severe incidents occurred with male patients (85%) in outpatient settings (80%), although those who reported the greatest number of incidents worked in state prisons, with sex offenders, or both. See deMayo, R. A. (1997). Patient sexual behavior and sexual harassment: A national survey of female psychologists. Professional Psychology: Research and Practice, 28, 58–62. What implications, if any, can be drawn from these data regarding the assumed power relationship between therapist and client? Does the theory only hold when the therapist is male? Given that women now constitute a majority of new doctoral-level psychologists, are there issues related to the training of clinicians that should be taken into account?

Although most research regarding multiple relationships has focused on sexual activity, a few scholars have looked at nonromantic relationships. Using an adaptation of the Borys & Pope scale (1989, excerpted earlier in this chapter), Baer & Murdock (1995) surveyed 223 APA members (56% female; 96% Caucasian) and found that

> *overall, therapists thought that nonerotic dual-relationship behaviors were ethical in*

only limited circumstances at best. The highest rating of all the presented behaviors was 3.49 [providing therapy to friend of ongoing client], falling in between the scale points of ethical "under some conditions" and "under rare conditions." Therapists judged social and/or financial involvements with their clients as the least ethical of the three classes of nonerotic dual relationships [the other two are incidental, e.g., accepting an inexpensive gift, and dual professional, e.g., allowing client to enroll in one's class]. (p. 143)

Baer, B. E., & Murdock, N. L. (1995). *Nonerotic dual relationships between therapists and clients: The effects of sex, theoretical orientation, and interpersonal boundaries. Ethics and Behavior, 5, 131–145. Given the problems about boundary violations and the findings from the few studies "of nonerotic dual relationships between therapists and clients . . . indicat[ing] that a professionals' (sic) attitude about nonerotic contact is predictive of his or her attitude about and likelihood to have erotic contact with clients (references omitted)"* (Baer & Murdock, 1995, p. 132), *should we be more concerned about nonerotic contacts and about the possible intrapersonal vulnerabilities that lead to them?*

Although prior excerpts reveal the intense debate about romantic liaisons between therapists and former clients, another little studied area is nonerotic relationships with former clients. As a preliminary matter, there is the methodological and ethically relevant issue of defining a former client. If one terminates a professional relationship with a patient for the purpose of developing a social, business, or romantic relationship, is the patient truly a "former patient?" Does the following provide us with a useful definition? "[C]lients for whom there has been a responsible and appropriately documented termination process, who do not anticipate returning to therapy, and who have in no way been led to believe that they are free to return to therapy are . . . former clients" (p. 28). *This definition comes from* Pipes, R. B. (1997). *Nonsexual relationships between psychotherapists and their former clients: Obligations of psychologists. Ethics and Behavior, 7, 27–41. In any event, the following articles are two of the few to study the issue in depth.*

Nonromantic, Nonsexual Posttherapy Relationships Between Psychologists and Former Clients: An Exploratory Study of Critical Incidents

Sharon K. Anderson and Karen S. Kitchener

[*Ed. note:* Using the Critical Incident Technique developed by John Flanagan in the 1950s, the authors identified 8 categories of nonromantic, nonsexual posttherapy relationships gleaned from 63 psychologist–respondents. Respondents were also asked about their perspectives concerning the ethicality of these relationships.]

. . .

PERSONAL OR FRIENDSHIP RELATIONSHIPS

This category included 18 incidents. In these relationships, the therapists and former clients had moved past the position of social acquaintance to a closer or more intimate relationship, and the therapist appeared to be more personally invested in the relationship. It was likely that more of the therapist's personal life was known by the former client. The incidents included in this relationship category reflected either a personal connection between the therapist and former client that had some unique or special quality such that the therapist's private life was accessible to the former client, or a friendship where there was a sense of camaraderie between the therapist and former client. The nine incidents defined as personal relationships spanned a broad range of contexts from the therapist being a neighbor of the former client to the therapist being the parent of a teenager who dated the former client. The following is an example of these incidents:

Former client marries friend of psychologist's spouse. Former client's spouse and therapist's spouse want to socialize together as couples. (personal relationship)

A majority of the participants (seven out of nine) who described these incidents perceived the relationships as ethically problematic. Some of these participants suggested that an equal, normal friendship between a therapist and former client is improbable if not impossible. Other participants shared their belief that a multiple relationship would occur because the therapist–client relationship continues after termination.

One of the two participants who did not see these personal relationships as ethically problematic stated that it was really the former therapist's responsibility to maintain the "appropriate boundary" in the relationship. This person, speaking from the perspective of a former client, went on to provide a rationale for the personal relationship:

> I did, however, make a conscious decision that I would never return to this person as a therapist before developing the friendship [with the therapist's family member] . . . this was hard for me but seemed important.

The other nine incidents in this category described a friendship between the therapist and for-

From *Professional Psychology: Research and Practice*, 27, 59–66. Copyright 1996 by the American Psychological Association. Adapted with the permission of the author and publisher.

mer client. Frequently, the respondents actually used a variation of the word *friend* in their descriptions of the relationships. An example follows:

> A colleague of mine has formed a friendship with a former client (same gender as therapist). I know relatively little of this relationship other than it began after the termination of treatment and the former client approached my colleague about the possibility of having a friendship relationship. It appears to be mutual with clear boundaries. (friendship relationship)

None of the participants who described these relationships saw them as ethically problematic. Their reasons for this perspective included the time lapse since termination, the maturity of both parties, and the discussion by the therapist and former client of the parameters of the new relationship. The following is an example of a response by one of the participants who described a posttherapy incident of friendship:

> Although I had hesitations initially regarding the friendship, I do not see it as ethically problematic because 1) our therapeutic relationship was terminated, 2) it was agreed that if my former client wanted to re-engage in therapy that they would seek a different therapist, and 3) we have discussed in detail and maintain very clear boundaries in our friendship including confidentiality of our previous therapeutic relationship and assuring communication of needs and feelings remains two-way.

SOCIAL INTERACTIONS AND EVENTS

The social interaction and events relationship category also included 18 incidents. Participants described interactions that ranged from a onetime occurrence (e.g., attending the wedding of former clients) to social activities that could have been more ongoing and ranged from casual (e.g., participating in community or neighborhood activities) to

sexual (e.g., participating in "swingers" parties). The circumstantial and intentional subcategories emerged during the sorting process. In the following example, the therapist and former client seemed to have met each other in a social context with little or no prior planning on either person's part.

> Found myself a fellow competitor at a dog show with a former patient. (social interactions and events—circumstantial)

Different from the circumstantial interactions between the therapist and former client, the following example illustrates a type of social activity where the therapist or former client initiated some action to invite contact or ensure interaction with the other in a social context. The former client initiated a majority of these social interactions.

> While coincidentally vacationing in the same resort area, psychologist and family accepted invitation of former client and family to visit at their vacation house along with several other guests. (social interactions and events—intentional)

Six out of the nine participants who described circumstantial social contacts saw these interactions as not ethically problematic. They provided justifications such as the following: the contact was brief and unplanned; confidentiality remained intact; and the psychologist took preventive measures to minimize potential harm in the posttherapy contact. For example, one psychologist who anticipated the possibility of social contact "discussed [with the former client] the potential uncomfortableness of the relationship after discharge."

All of the participants who described incidents of intentional social interactions saw these interactions as ethically problematic. A majority of them shared the belief that the therapist–client relationship continues after termination and that another relationship would create the potential for either exploitation or conflict of role expectations and obligations. The respondent who accepted the invitation to visit the former client at the former client's vacation home shared a slightly different but related reason:

> Clients often idealize their therapist and getting together socially becomes too heavy [a] dose of reality all at once which can be difficult for client, especially when the treatment relationship is over and client may not have a setting to work through this.

BUSINESS OR FINANCIAL RELATIONSHIPS

The common theme in the business or financial category was either (a) exchanging dollars between the therapist and former client for the former client's expertise or assistance or (b) joining areas of expertise that brought in dollars (e.g., hiring a former client, receiving financial assistance or advice from a former client, patronizing the former client's place of business, and having a business together). This category included a total of 12 incidents. The following is an example:

> Psychologist hired a former patient to clean house for psychologist's family on a weekly basis. Was later let go because of poor performance, unreliability. (business or financial relationship)

Seven of the twelve participants saw this type of relationship as ethically problematic. Their reasons for this perspective included the following: dual role issues; negative impact on the former client's internalized image of the therapist; special knowledge about the former client influencing the therapist's objectivity; the power differential; and a limit on the former client's option to return to therapy. The following statements illustrate, from two participants' point of view, the difficulties associated with the business or financial relationships:

> My relationship with the former client as the former therapist causes me to cut this person slack [in two business or financial arrangements]. . . . The former client thrives and appears to benefit greatly, but I'm not always so sure it is

good for me. Also it could cause too much dependency on me.

> I couldn't allow myself to see this person as other than a therapist, to move beyond the role we historically had defined between us. I needed this person to be only a therapist and felt I would be losing that.

Five participants did not see the incidents they described as ethically problematic. These participants identified the following reasons for their perspective: the relationship remained a professional relationship without two-way exchange of personal information, and the boundaries of the business relationship remained clear.

COLLEGIAL OR PROFESSIONAL RELATIONSHIPS

In these 12 incidents, the therapist and former client held positions or took roles potentially equal in power and the relationship was likely to be more externally focused on professional or business issues or problems. An example follows:

> Professor of psychology served as therapist to university colleague (in another department); the two later occasionally worked on university committees together. (collegial or professional relationship)

Nine out of twelve participants said they saw these new relationships as not ethically problematic. Some of the participants argued they could compartmentalize their roles. For example, one participant wrote: "We all have multiple roles. . . . Some degree of compartmentalization is normal in life . . . dual relationships between [the] therapist and client are sensibly managed this way."

The participants who saw the collegial or professional relationship as ethically problematic suggested that the new relationship could produce problems because of dual role conflicts and transference issues. The following is an example of one participant's point of view: "A therapist [might] overlook transferential material as important determinants of relationships long after the 'treatment' aspect has ended."

SUPERVISORY OR EVALUATIVE RELATIONSHIPS

In 10 incidents, the new relationship was more supervisory or evaluative in nature. Typically, the therapist took or held a role that required overseeing or evaluating the former client's performance in a clinical or academic setting. As with the social interactions and events incidents, the raters judged that some of these relationships occurred because of an external factor somewhat out of the control of either the therapist or the former client. The following description is an example of the incidents in this category:

> As an instructor for a psychology course occasionally, it is not uncommon to have students previously seen at the counseling center by myself or others I supervise. (supervisory or evaluative relationship—circumstantial)

There were supervisory or evaluative relationships that occurred by more intentional action by either the therapist or former client. Frequently, the intentional action was a request or invitation. The following is offered as a sample of the eight incidents in the intentional subcategory of supervisory or evaluative relationships:

> I provided clinical supervision to a private agency who employed a counselor–therapist who had been a client of mine before and during the former client's graduate days. (supervisory or evaluative relationship—intentional)

Half of the participants (five) saw these circumstantial and intentional supervisory or evaluative relationships with former clients as ethically problematic because of conflicting role obligations. For example, a participant who was an administrator of an agency completing a job search commented:

> A former client . . . applied for a . . . clinical position . . . [the former client] was fairly pathological and I felt

wouldn't be good for the job . . . I couldn't acknowledge my role due to confidentiality. I was very worried [the former client] would be selected by the search committee.

More specifically, the struggle for these participants revolved around the special knowledge obtained in the therapist–client relationship that influenced or could influence the therapist's ability to be objective toward the former client in his or her new role. A participant wrote that it was hard to "treat the [former client] with the same unbiasness or biasness as other students."

The five participants who saw the supervisory or evaluative relationships as not ethically problematic offered different perspectives. A few believed that the former therapist–client relationship no longer existed. Other participants stated that the therapist–former client relationship "naturally evolved" into a different, but still supportive, relationship. One shared that the therapist–client relationship still existed, but the new supervisory, evaluative relationship was necessary. For example, a participant commented that he or she was the "only psychologist qualified to provide" the therapy to a superior because of the structure of the organization in which the therapist worked.

RELIGIOUS AFFILIATION RELATIONSHIPS

The religious affiliation category included nine incidents. Although the main theme of this category was attending the same church, most of these incidents included another type of interaction, such as working together on church committees, social contact after a service, or support and assistance in another part of the former client's life (e.g., campaigning for a public office). Note the following example:

> A former client family joined the religious institution to which I belonged and where I became an officer. The couple who had seen me in short-term family work around their child's problems became active in the institution and we wound up working together on . . . activities sharing responsibility for

committee work and where they were often in a position of reporting directly to me on committee activities. (religious affiliation relationship)

None of the participants who described these incidents saw the contact or relationship as ethically problematic. Their reasons for this perspective included the following: the therapist–client relationship was over; confidentiality was maintained; the posttherapy relationship was discussed prior to entering it; considerable time had elapsed since termination; and it was unethical to ignore or avoid the former client. More specifically, one participant, who described a posttherapy incident in a religious context, stated:

Given a small community, it is virtually impossible to attend church or social events without contact with present or former clients. . . . The more I practice . . . the more I recognize flexibility is needed with regard to general, social contact with former clients, especially in small communities.

As a note of caution, one participant suggested:

A great deal depends on the individuals involved. There is always a potential for ethical issues to arise when someone has special knowledge of others gained through therapy and then interacts with them in another capacity. This knowledge may take the form of bias, expectations, pushing the others buttons, etc.

COLLEGIAL OR PROFESSIONAL PLUS SOCIAL RELATIONSHIP

The difference between this category and the category of collegial or professional relationships is the presence of social contact in addition to the collegial or professional connection. The social contacts between therapists and former clients took place in a variety of settings (e.g., parties, social involvement in the psychology community, and meeting for lunch). The following is an example:

An ex-patient of mine entered training at the same institute where I was a faculty member. . . . Later, this person too became a faculty member of the same institute. We found ourselves on the same committees, at the same faculty meetings and social events. (collegial or professional plus social relationship)

Similar to those participants who described collegial or professional relationships with former clients, a majority of these participants (six out of seven) did not see these relationships as ethically problematic. Their reasons included length of time since termination, the conscious effort to discuss issues related to the new relationship, and the natural evolution of the new relationship from the therapist–former client relationship. Although these six participants did not see the relationships as ethically problematic, two of them did identify the collegial plus social relationships as being "uncomfortable" for them. For example, one participant commented:

At times [it is] uncomfortable for me (who would like to keep my personal and professional experiences separate) but I see no clear violation of ethical standards. . . . It is extremely important at the outset to discuss potential complications re: overlap of contact with patients in this category.

Four of these seven participants indicated that they worked and lived in small communities and therefore adjusted their behavior because of the greater potential to run into former clients on a frequent, if not regular, basis.

Only one participant saw the collegial plus social relationship as ethically problematic. The therapist felt "uncomfortable" in a study group with a former client and decided not to pursue a coteaching opportunity with the former client because "it would have been impossible for [the former client] and spouse to return to treatment."

WORKPLACE RELATIONSHIPS

In this category, participants described five incidents where the therapist and former client found themselves in the same workplace, either as professional peers or as employees of the same clinical practice. In three incidents, these relationships occurred circumstantially. The following is an example of the incidents that were sorted into the subcategory of circumstantial workplace relationships:

> A psychologist left one job to go to work in another setting where a former client had been recently employed as office help. (workplace relationship— circumstantial)

In the other two workplace incidents, the therapist or former client initiated some purposeful action to bring about the workplace relationship. The following is an example:

> A clinic I work at recently hired a former client's parent as office help (over my objections). This parent was involved in several therapy sessions with the child. Presently, the parent has both computer and file drawer access to our files. (Workplace relationship— intentional)

Four out of the five participants saw these workplace relationships as ethically problematic. Some participants identified the ethical problem of dual role relationships; others indicated a strong concern related to "special knowledge" that the therapist might have about the former client and how this could influence the therapist's objectivity in the new relationship or role. For example, one participant stated it might be difficult "to separate work behavior from the psychological knowledge. . . . Anytime [the] employee was late for work or work behavior was decreasing, it would be difficult to remain unbiased."

. . .

DISCUSSION

Because of the exploratory nature of the study and the small *n*, only tentative implications can be drawn from the data. Four implications are presented. First, some psychologists practicing psychotherapy seem to be dealing with a variety of nonromantic, nonsexual relationships with former clients. In addition, they are dealing with this complex issue with little or no professional guidance from the current APA Ethical Principles and Code of Conduct. At least some of these relationships arise because of circumstances beyond the control of the psychologist or the former client. . . . Clearly, psychologists cannot be held ethically culpable for circumstantial contact with former clients; however, they may be ethically responsible for how they handle those contacts if, in fact, the posttherapy relationship leads to harmful consequences for the former client or if therapeutic gains are reversed as a result of the posttherapy relationship (Kitchener, 1988).

Other contacts reported in this study appeared to be initiated by former clients or therapists. Former clients appeared to initiate contact with their former therapists for a variety of personal reasons as well as for professional ones, such as supervision, whereas the relationships initiated by the therapists appeared to be linked primarily to some kind of business setting. Although in some cases therapists did not believe that these relationships were ethically problematic, the relationships do require further professional dialogue because the therapist does have some responsibility for actively deciding whether to enter into such relationship or not. Psychologists who are presented with the difficult issue of posttherapy contact might benefit from a decision-making model and from guidelines that are both practical and flexible enough to deal with the complexity of issue.

The second implication of the study is related: There seems to be little consensus among psychologists who participated in the study regarding whether or not nonromantic, nonsexual relationships are ethical. . . . [M]any of the participants in this study did not hold to "once a client, always a client." In fact, a majority of participants who described posttherapy relationships saw these relationships as ethical.

The third notable implication of our study was that participants on both sides of the argument about the ethical nature of these relationships identified a number of different therapeutic issues to support their position. For example, participants who saw posttherapy relationships with former clients as unethical suggested that transference issues might not be fully resolved and that contact too soon after termination might reignite issues that were only partially resolved. Furthermore, they noted that clients sometimes carry idealized images of their therapists and that viewing or interacting with their therapists in a real world context might lead clients to reevaluate the positive influence of the therapist. In addition, respondents noted that the former client would not be able to return to therapy with the therapist. Those who did not see the relationship as ethically problematic suggested that therapeutic issues related to termination of services were important considerations. For example, participants suggested that posttherapy relationships were ethical if an appropriate time lapse since termination had occurred. These participants suggested that a time period of 2 to 10 years was sufficient length to then engage in a new relationship with a former client. Others proposed that the posttherapy relationship was ethical if the former client decided not to return to therapy with the former therapist and the posttherapy interaction did not seem to hinder subsequent therapy with different therapists. Furthermore, some participants suggested that the therapeutic issue of confidentiality could be better kept by allowing the relationship or interaction to occur instead of steering clear of it.

The fourth implication of our study is related to the current Ethics Code (APA, 1992). The code makes only one reference to former clients, and (as already noted) it focuses on sexual relationships between therapists and former clients. In future revisions, APA may need to consider whether the code should address nonromantic, nonsexual relationships with former clients (S. E. Jones, personal communi-

cation, April 1993). According to many of the respondents in this study, some of these relationships are potentially harmful, and others may not be. Furthermore, some may be unavoidable; thus, any new ethical standards should be written with clear knowledge of the breadth of the issues and problems involved. . . .

References

American Psychological Association (1992). Ethical principles of psychologists and code of conduct. *American Psychologist, 47,* 1597–1611.

Kitchener, K. S. (1988). Dual role relationships: What makes them so problematic? *Journal of Counseling and Development, 67,* 217–221.

◆　◆　◆

Commentary: In additional analyses of the data, Anderson & Kitchener (1998) noted that the responding psychologists identified four general themes when justifying their decision to enter or not enter posttherapy nonromantic, nonsexual relationships with former clients: the therapeutic contract and its parameters, the dynamics of the therapeutic bond or relationship, social role issues, and the therapist's professional and personal motivation. The themes move respectively, from obvious, overt, and objective issues to hidden, covert, and subject judgment issues. (p. 93).

The authors provide specific questions in each of these domains that the clinician and client should attempt to answer before embarking on a posttherapy relationship. See Anderson, S. K., & Kitchener, K. S. (1998). Nonsexual posttherapy relationships: A conceptual framework to assess ethical risks. Professional Psychology: Research and Practice, 29, 91–99.

Nonsexual Relationships Between Psychotherapists and Their Former Clients: Obligations of Psychologists

Randolph B. Pipes

. . .

OBLIGATIONS TO FORMER CLIENTS

[Based on literature cited in this text,] eight reasons for limiting nonsexual relationships with former clients are briefly described.

First, former clients may need to return to therapy. Becoming entangled in another type of relationship (particularly if the new relationship is significant) following termination almost certainly will interfere with the possibility of resuming therapy with the former therapist. Standard 1.17(b) of the current APA code prohibits the therapist from taking on a professional obligation when a preexisting relationship would create the risk of harm to the client. Thus for example, under the current APA code, a significant posttherapy business relationship virtually ensures that the client cannot return to therapy with the same therapist. That being said, why cannot this dilemma be solved by referring the former client to someone else? This is a reasonable question; reasonable people can disagree about its answer.

Clearly, former therapists do not have a legal obligation to take someone back as a client. Furthermore, therapists become unavailable to former clients for all sorts of reasons (e.g., relocation), so becoming unavailable is not ethically problematic in and of itself. However, because the relationship between therapist and client is often such an integral part of the treatment itself, it seems reasonable to ask therapists to preserve the essential integrity of the therapeutic relationship—that is, to avoid entering into another type of relationship that would preclude the possibility of the therapeutic relationship being reestablished—for a reasonable period of time following termination. . . .

Second, whatever differences there may be among psychologists concerning the advisability of limiting posttherapy contact, it seems reasonable to assert that there are a variety of types of clients who often remain vulnerable following termination. In turn, these clients would seem highly susceptible to exploitation following termination. Furthermore, it should be noted that it is in fact vulnerable clients who may often need additional therapy. . . .

Third, whatever one may believe about the existence or nonexistence of the phenomenon of transference, it seems reasonable to posit that few therapists would deny that some clients have very strong feelings about their former therapists. In turn, the presence of these strong feelings means that even in the absence of a diagnosable mental disorder, the dangers of making poor decisions about another type of relationship with the therapist are self-evident. . . .

Fourth, because former clients may request that psychologists furnish records or even testify in court on their behalf, it is important that therapists maintain their objectivity as much as possible. How can therapists maintain their objectivity if they have, for example, become entangled in joint ownership of a

From *Ethics and Behavior,* 7, 27–41. Copyright 1997 by Erlbaum. Adapted with permission of the author and publisher.

business? Or, can the therapist be objective if the client now works as the secretary for the therapist? Note that this concern about the ongoing obligations of the therapist to the client cannot be satisfied simply by the therapist referring the client to another therapist.

Fifth, there are clear theoretical reasons for assuming that clients should be able to trust that the therapist has no intentions other than to further the welfare of the client. . . . Thus, placing certain types of posttermination relationships "off limits" so to speak, is a way of helping to ensure the welfare of the current client.

Sixth, what are the modeling effects if prospective clients see the psychologist involved in posttherapy relationships with former clients? As an extreme example (but one in which the behaviors are not obviously prohibited under the current APA code), suppose that a therapist uses former clients for his or her attorney, mechanic, stock broker, housekeeper, nanny, tennis partner, and dentist. Although there must certainly be latitude for psychologists working in rural areas, does the situation just described sound like the kind of arrangement the profession is willing to tolerate?

Seventh, what will be the effects on former clients (whether vulnerable or not) who establish posttherapy relationships with their former therapists, only to have the relationship "go bad"? . . . Unfortunately, we do not currently have any data that address the issue of the effects of nonsexual posttermination relationships that end in acrimony or have other deleterious outcomes. Nonetheless, does not such a situation put the former client at much greater risk for losing faith in psychologists, feeling manipulated, and having deep reservations about entering into another psychotherapeutic relationship?

Finally, from a more pragmatic perspective, there are often legal reasons for avoiding posttherapy nonsexual relationships. Because state boards vary in their interpretation of ethical standards, and because legal statutes vary from state to state, it is clear that the safest approach to posttherapy relationships is to use caution and discretion when contemplating entering one . . .

(BEING EXPLICIT ABOUT) OUR OBLIGATIONS TO FORMER CLIENTS

. . . [I]t is worth noting that currently, with the exception of confidentiality and record keeping, there appears to be almost no ethical constraint on the behavior of psychologists with regard to nonsexual relationships with former clients. Looking only at the APA ethics code, one might wonder if psychologists are free to enter into any nonsexual relationship with any former client of their choosing. We have now codified constraints on posttherapy sexual relationships with former clients (APA, 1992). This was done in part because we believed that there was an unreasonable risk to former clients if they immediately entered into a sexual relationship with their former therapist. Should we not also enter into a thoughtful analysis of the risk to former clients of entering into various nonsexual relationships with their former therapist? . . .

There are a number of questions that need to be addressed as psychologists consider their obligations to former clients. For example, if there are to be limits, what should these limits be? Should the focus be on all relationships with former clients or only on those that are exploitative or potentially exploitative? Is it possible to define what is meant by exploitation? What accommodations should be made for rural areas? How can we ensure the protection of minority communities and psychologists from subcultures (Gonsiorek & Brown, 1989; Payton, 1994)? How can the profession be explicit about obligations without prohibiting reasonable interactions such as purchasing a routine item from a business owner? Should obligations vary with different types of therapy (e.g., Gonsiorek & Brown, 1989)? What legal and constitutional issues would be raised by prohibiting certain types of nonsexual posttherapy relationships? Many of these issues were debated with regard to sexual relationships with former clients. Clearly many of the issues have not been resolved (e.g., Bersoff, 1994; Gabbard, 1994). . . .

References

American Psychological Association. (1992). Ethical principles of psychologists and code of conduct. *American Psychologist, 47*, 1597–1611.

Bersoff, D. N. (1994). Explicit ambiguity: The 1992 ethics code as oxymoron. *Professional Psychology: Research and Practice, 25,* 382–387.

Gabbard, G. O. (1994). Reconsidering the American Psychological Association's policy on sex with former patients: Is it justifiable? *Professional Psychology: Research and Practice, 25,* 329–335.

Gonsiorek, J. C., & Brown, L. S. (1989). Post therapy sexual relationships with clients. In G. R. Schoener, J. H. Milgrom, J. C. Gonsiorek, E. T. Luepker, & R. M. Conroe (Eds.), *Psychotherapists' sexual involvement with clients: Intervention and prevention* (pp. 289–301). Minneapolis, MN: Walk-In Counseling Center.

Payton, C. R. (1994). Implications of the 1992 Ethics Code for diverse groups. *Professional Psychology: Research and Practice, 25,* 317–320.

◆ ◆ ◆

Commentary: *Pulakos (1994) found that 59% of clients seen at a university counseling center experienced incidental encounters with their therapists—not a surprising occurrence on a college campus. When asked how their therapists responded to these chance meetings, 8% said their therapists ignored them, 59% said they briefly acknowledged them, and 22% engaged them in conversation. What is interesting is that although 79% felt these respective responses were appropriate, 21% wanted more:*

> *For example, if the therapist had ignored the client, the client wanted a brief acknowledgment or engagement in conversation; if the therapist gave a brief acknowledgement, the client wanted engagement in conversation. In no cases did clients want less than the therapists offered. (p. 301)*

The author thought that the most striking finding was that in only 29% of cases were these encounters discussed in therapy. See Pulakos, J. (1994). Incidental encounters between therapists and clients: The client's perspective. Professional Psychology, 25, 300–303.

This study raises the much broader question of whether psychologists are more concerned about multiple relationships in therapy than are clients. The following material reveals that the issue can be quite controversial.

How Certain Boundaries and Ethics Diminish Therapeutic Effectiveness

Arnold A. Lazarus

. . .

During my internship in the 1950s I was severely reprimanded by one of my supervisors for allegedly stepping out of role (one type of boundary) and thereby potentially undermining my clinical effectiveness. (In many quarters, clearly demarcated client–therapist roles have been very strongly emphasized in recent years.) It had come to my supervisor's attention that at the end of a session I had asked a client to do me the favor of dropping me off at a service station on his way home. My car was being repaired, and I had ascertained that the client would be heading home after the session and that I would not be taking him out of his way. My supervisor contended that therapy had to be a one-way street and that clients should not be called upon to provide anything other than the agreed-upon fees for service. Given my transgression, my supervisor claimed that I had jeopardized the client–therapist relationship. Interestingly, I recall that my rapport with the client in question was enhanced rather than damaged by our informal chat on the way to the service station.

The extent to which some clinicians espouse what I regard as *dehumanizing* boundaries is exemplified by the following incident. During a recent couples therapy session, the husband mentioned that he had undergone a biopsy for a suspected malignancy and would have the result later that week. Our next appointment was 2 weeks away, so I called their home after a few days to ask about the laboratory findings. The husband answered the telephone, reported that all was well, and expressed gratitude at my interest and concern. The wife, a licensed clinical psychologist, had a different reaction. She told a mutual colleague (the person who had referred the couple to me) that she was rather dismayed and put out at what I had done, referring to it as the violation of a professional boundary. A simple act of human decency and concern had been transformed into a clinical assault.

A different boundary issue was raised in the columns of a state journal. A therapist was treating an adolescent and wanted to arrange a meeting with the boy's mother. A busy professional, the mother's schedule was such that the most convenient time was during a lunch break, and she suggested they meet to discuss the matter at a local restaurant. The position taken by various correspondents was that this would not only transgress various boundaries but constitute a dual relationship. I wondered whether meeting in the park, or at the mother's place of work, in a hotel lobby, or in a car would be similarly discounted. Or could the venue indeed be a restaurant if no food but only coffee were ordered? [footnote omitted].

. . . With some clients, anything other than a formal and clearly delimited doctor–patient relationship is inadvisable and is likely to prove counterproductive. With others, an open give-and-take, a sense of camaraderie, and a willingness to step outside the bounds of a sanctioned healer will enhance treatment outcomes. Thus I have partied and socialized with some clients, played tennis with others, taken long walks with some, graciously accepted small gifts, and given presents (usually books) to a fair

From *Ethics and Behavior*, 4, 255–261. Copyright 1994 by Erlbaum. Adapted with permission of the author and publisher.

number. At times, I have learned more at different sides of a tennis net or across a dining room table than might ever have come to light in my consulting room. (Regrettably, from the viewpoint of present-day risk management, in the face of allegations of sexual impropriety, it has been pointed out that such boundary crossings, no matter how innocent, will ipso facto be construed as evidence of sexual misconduct by judges, juries, ethics committees, and state licensing boards.)

Out of the many clients that I have treated, the number with whom I have stepped outside the formal confines of the consulting room is not in the hundreds, but give or take a few dozen. And when I have done so, my motives were not based on capriciousness but arose from reasoned judgments that the treatment objectives would be enhanced. Nevertheless, it is usually inadvisable to disregard strict boundary limits in the presence of severe psychopathology; involving passive–aggressive, histrionic, or manipulative behaviors; borderline personality features; or manifestations of suspiciousness and undue hostility. . . .

Let me not be misunderstood. I am *not* advocating or arguing for a transparent, pliant, casual, or informal therapeutic relationship with everyone. Rather, I am asserting that those therapists who always go by the book and apply predetermined and fixed rules of conduct (specific dos and don'ts) across the board will offend or at the very least fail to help people who might otherwise have benefited from their ministrations.

. . .

I remain totally opposed to any form of disparagement, exploitation, abuse, or harassment, and I am against any form of sexual contact with clients. But outside of these confines, I feel that most other limits and proscriptions are negotiable. But the litigious climate in which we live has made me more cautious in recent years. I would not take certain risks that I gave no thought to in the 1960s. For example, I accepted two clients into my home (at different times). One lived with my family for several weeks, the other for several days. Both were men from out of state who had relocated and were looking for a place to live. Similarly, I would have thought nothing of offering a client our spare bed-

room on a snowy night or furnishing a couple of aspirins if someone asked for them. But like most of my colleagues, I have attended seminars on how to avoid malpractice suits that have made my blood run cold. It is difficult to come away from those lectures without viewing every client as a potential adversary or litigant. Fortunately, the effects tended to wear off after a few days, and I regained my spontaneity. But the ominous undertones remain firmly implanted and are reinforced by passages in books that explain how innocent psychologists can protect themselves against unwarranted lawsuits. . . . Consequently, being more guarded has rendered me a less humane practitioner today than I used to be in the 1960s and 1970s.

. . .

It is, of course, safer and easier to go by the book, to adhere to an inflexible set of rules, than to think for oneself. But practitioners who hide behind rigid boundaries, whose sense of ethics is uncompromising, will, in my opinion, fail to really help many of the clients who are unfortunate enough to consult them. The truly great therapists I have met were not frightened conformists but courageous and enterprising helpers, willing to take calculated risks. If I am to summarize my position in one sentence, I would say that one of the worst professional or ethical violations is that of permitting current risk-management principles to take precedence over humane interventions. By all means drive defensively, but try to practice psychotherapy responsibly—with compassion, benevolence, sensitivity, and caring.

◆　◆　◆

Commentary: *Lazarus's article stimulated an interesting and fiery debate. Although what follows is but a sample of responses, readers are urged to read the more complete versions:*

> Time has demonstrated that many practitioners who fail to acknowledge generally accepted boundaries, regardless of their rationale for breaking the boundary, do not manage their behaviors effectively and eventually violate the client by overstepping a boundary. (p. 265)

Bennett, B. E., Bricklin, P. M., & VandeCreek, L. (1994). *Response to Lazarus's "How Certain Boundaries and Ethics Diminish Therapeutic Effectiveness."* Ethics and Behavior, 4, 263–266.

> The kind of rote, mindless rule-following that Lazarus abhors, and its stultifying interpersonal consequences, are likely to occur primarily where therapists fail to understand the rationale behind and various levels of meaning inherent in therapeutic boundaries and ethics. A therapist who is comfortable with these boundaries, and experiences them as promoting effective, safe treatment, will find [sic] to be allies in the process and to be safeguards that actually allow greater levels of spontaneity and warmth by helping to keep nontherapeutic needs and impulses of the clinician within their proper parameters. (p. 273)

Borys, D. S. (1994). *Maintaining therapeutic boundaries: The motive is therapeutic effectiveness, not defensive practice.* Ethics and Behavior, 4, 267–273.

> A disconcerting aspect of Dr. Lazarus's article is his oversimplification of the complexities inherent in dual roles. When he asserts that he has learned more about his patients from playing tennis with them or eating a meal with them than he has in the consulting room, the reader is left to wonder how he handles such situations. Does he bill his patients for his time when he is playing tennis or eating with them? If not, why is he "working" when he is socializing? Moreover, I wonder how he decides when he is playing tennis if he should try as hard as possible to win or allow the patient to win because of the pa-

> tient's fragile self-esteem. How does the patient react to this unclarity of roles? Does the patient begin to withhold certain material from the therapist for fear that it will damage their friendship? How does the patient know when therapeutic activities are taking place and when the interaction is purely social? (p. 286)

Gabbard, G. O. (1994). *Teetering on the precipice: A commentary on Lazarus's "How Certain Boundaries and Ethics Diminish Therapeutic Effectiveness."* Ethics and Behavior, 4, 283–286.

> Lazarus is right to remind us that following ethical guidelines and risk management procedures must always be done within the context of good clinical judgment. Yet . . . to argue that following such guidelines may even harm patients is not just an unsubstantiated claim, it is irresponsible. (p. 291)

Gottlieb, M. C. (1994). *Ethical decision-making, boundaries, and treatment effectiveness: A reprise.* Ethics and Behavior, 4, 287–293.

> [I]n none of [Lazarus's examples] does he appear to consider the impact on the patient . . . of that very intervention, no matter how benignly intended. The patient's experience may not be benign. (p. 296)

Gutheil, T. G. (1994). *Discussion of Lazarus's "How Certain Boundaries and Ethics Diminish Therapeutic Effectiveness."* Ethics and Behavior, 4, 295–298.

The final comment comes from Laura S. Brown, who broadens the discussion to raise issues of more general ethical, professional, philosophical, and theoretical concern, issues that the reader will recognize from chapters 2 and 3. A longer excerpt from her critique of Lazarus's article appears next.

Concrete Boundaries and the Problem of Literal-Mindedness: A Response to Lazarus

Laura S. Brown

. . .

Coming from the theoretical perspective of feminist therapy, in which empowerment of and respect for the client are core motivating ethical concepts, I would like to argue that Lazarus's article locates the problem incorrectly, and does so in a way that potentially endangers thoughtful dialogues on ethical dilemmas and the problem of creating a frame and boundaries in psychotherapy that not only allow for but nourish the human, compassionate, relational encounter between therapist and client. The location of the problem is not in the development of ethical standards requiring care, circumspection, and the elucidation of boundaries in psychotherapy. Rather, the problem lies in three other places.

This first location of this dilemma is in the failure of mainstream mental health disciplines to appreciate the power dynamics of the psychotherapeutic relationship, not merely at the symbolic level (e.g., transference) but in terms of the real social and political context forming the matrix in which any given psychotherapy relationship situates itself. Abuses in psychotherapy are, from the feminist viewpoint, abuses of the power inherent in the role of the psychotherapist, as enabled by a culture that privileges the powerful players in dominance hierarchies. The second location of the problem is in the difficulties that mental health professionals seem to have with conceiving of our ethics code as a series of decision rules that allow for careful, informed consideration of the meanings of our actions in a manner that allows us to avoid abuses of the power of the psychotherapeutic relationship. Our ethical standards are not a concrete wall hemming us in, forbidding us from human connections. Rather, they are a potential ethical methodology, directions about how to *think* about what constitutes ethical actions so that we can respond freshly to each new situation and person. Yet many therapists who are otherwise powerful abstract thinkers, willing to venture the authority of their hypotheses daily with clients, become submissive and deauthorize themselves when arriving at the threshold of ethical matters. The third aspect of the problem is that ethics are not perceived as core to and integrated into other aspects of clinical practice, such as diagnosis, case conceptualization, and psychotherapy. Instead, for the most part, ethics are treated as an add-on—something to worry about, rebel against, or ignore rather than the core and central component of our epistemologies as psychotherapists. This problem is embedded in how ethics are taught in our training programs. When they are explicitly taught at all, they are either an optional course or one in which few clear connections are made between ethics and everything else that a therapist does.

. . .

For opening this discourse, I appreciate Lazarus's candor and willingness to risk the opprobrium of his colleagues. I can only reiterate my wish that his commentary was less an invitation to comply with sadness and more an explication of how he has made ethical decisions in his work. The promulgation of a decision-based rather than rules-based approach to ethics in psychotherapy benefits from the contributions of every therapist, in the manner in

From *Ethics and Behavior, 4,* 275–281. Copyright 1994 by Erlbaum. Adapted with permission of the author and publisher.

which many of our original ethics codes reflected the lived dilemmas of many psychotherapists. The best possible outcome from this discourse will be that therapists will transform their ethical methodologies and depart from the concrete and legalistic themes that pervade both dominant culture and, increasingly, the cultures of psychotherapy.

◆   ◆   ◆

Commentary: Lazarus was given the opportunity to respond to each of these critiques, which he viewed as ranging from cautionary to downright hostile. It is worth reading his response in full but, as Lazarus notes, "A succinct summary of the major differences between my own views and theirs is that whereas, in terms of 'risk–benefit ratios,' they dwell mostly on potential costs and dangers, I focus on the advantages that may accrue when certain boundaries are transcended" (p. 299). See Lazarus, A. A. (1994). The illusion of the therapist's power and the patient's fragility: My rejoinder. Ethics and Behavior, 4, 299–306.

The issue of sexual intimacy also confronts those who train psychologists. Pope, Levensen, and Schover (1979), in a survey of 481 APA members, found that almost 10% of respondents reported sexual contact as a student with at least one of their educators. By a significant margin, more women (17%) reported such contact in comparison with men (3%). For women, the bulk of their sexual contact was with teachers, whereas for men it was with their clinical supervisors. See Pope, K. S., Levenson, H., & Schover, L. R. (1979). Sexual intimacy in psychology training. American Psychologist, 34, 682–689.

From another perspective, Pope et al. (1979) reported that 12% of psychology teachers, 4% of supervisors, and 3% of administrators disclosed sexual contact with their students (in comparison with about 7% of therapists in the survey who reported such contact with their clients). Only 2% unequivocally endorsed the benefit of educator–trainee sexual relations, 21% thought it might be beneficial, and the remainder indicated that they thought it could not be of benefit.

Based on responses to a questionnaire from 464 female members of the APA's Division 12 (Clinical Psychology), Glaser and Thorpe (1986) found much greater disapproval of sexual intimacy between students and

faculty. Seventeen percent of the women reported having had sexual contact with an educator, which was essentially identical to that reported by Pope et al. However, in comparison with 77% of respondents in the Pope et al. study who believed sexual contact was damaging, Glaser and Thorpe (1986) found that "over 95% of all respondents judged such contact as unethical, coercive, and harmful to the working relationship to a considerable degree" (p. 49), even though at the time of contact most saw no ethical problems or felt coerced or exploited. See Glaser, R. D., & Thorpe, J. S. (1986). Unethical intimacy: A survey of sexual contact and advances between psychology educators and female graduate students. American Psychologist, 41, 43–51.

In the most recent study of sexual intimacies between trainers and students the authors studied 1,000 graduates of clinical and counseling doctoral programs (with a 51% return rate). The results tracked the data found 15 years earlier; 15% of women graduates and 2% of men reported having sexual contact, i.e., intercourse or genital stimulation, with an educator during training. The authors did find that for former female students, a higher proportion of such contact occurred with those who graduated before 1983 but concluded that:

> *Nonetheless, these problematic behaviors still occur with disturbing frequency. . . . Attitudes by student participants toward these experiences appear to become more negative over time, with retroactive opinions that such relationships were coerced and had negative consequences for students. The gender and age composition of these liaisons still reflects a great power differential: The modal relationship is between an older male professor and a younger female graduate student. (Hammer, Olkin, & Taube, 1996, p. 96)*

Even though Standard 1.19 of the 1992 APA Ethical Principles now explicitly prohibits psychologists from engaging in sexual relationships (and other potentially exploitative conduct) with students and supervisees that they evaluate or over whom they have direct authority, Hammer et al. (1996) recommend that "APA . . . take a clearer and more encompassing stand against such relationships and to forbid them outright" (p. 96). See

Hammel, G. A., Olkin, R., & Taube, D. O. (1996). Student–educator sex in clinical and counseling psychology doctoral training. Professional Psychology: Research and Practice, 27, *93–97. Does this mean that a romantic relationship would be precluded between a doctoral student in an organizational psychology program* and a faculty member who specializes in animal behavior and who have no other academic contact? Is this going too far, or are there other values in barring such liaisons? Although sexual intimacy is a troubling issue, other kinds of multiple relationships also occur in training and teaching settings.*

The Ethics of Dual Relationships in Higher Education

Belinda Blevins-Knabe

The ethics of dual relationships between professors and students are unclear and largely unexplored . . .

Several situations involve dual relationships. For example, professors may have a professional colleague, a family member, or a friend who wants to take their class; professors may have a desire to become friends with a member of a class they are currently teaching; professors may want to engage in a business relationship with a member of a current class; professors and their students may be members of the same social organization or church; professors may desire to date their current students; professors may desire to become sexually involved with current students; or professors who are also therapists may have clients who wish to take their courses. All of these situations have a possible conflict of interest, but how do we decide which ones pose a significant threat to the educational process? . . .

The teaching role is rather complex. The professor's role includes teaching, not only in the narrow sense of the specific course material involved, but also in the wider sense of modeling for students how to use authority and knowledge appropriately. Trustworthiness is part of this role. Students often reveal sensitive information to professors, as they might to a therapist or a medical doctor, and they trust professors not to use this information to exploit them. Another component of this role is objective and equitable evaluation of students. In addition, professors should provide equal learning opportunities for all students. If one student has access to a professor's notes or extended tutoring sessions, then all students should have the opportunity for such access. The final component of the professor's role is power. Inherent in the professor–student relationship is the power of the professor over the student. The power comes from two sources; the professor both evaluates the student and is the authority in the subject matter (Paludi, 1990; Zalk et al., 1990). . . . [A] step in determining the ethical risk of a relationship is to use a set of four decision criteria. . . . First, is the professorial role negatively compromised? Here it is necessary to refer back to the components of the professor's role and to remember that more is taught by a professor than course material. Students are also learning about the ethics of dealing with others. Second, is the professor exploiting the student? Two important issues are (a) the extent to which the power of the professor is responsible for establishing the relationship and (b) the extent to which a student can choose not to participate in the relationship. Third, is the professor increasing the likelihood of being exploited? This can happen in situations in which keeping the relationship secret becomes important or in situations in which the student has privileged access to the professor. Fourth, is the professor's behavior interfering with the professional roles of other faculty? At issue here is whether a professor's behavior has gone far enough beyond the appropriate professional boundaries that others must intervene.

Two themes that underlie these criteria need to be made explicit. One is that professors are professionals and as such their behavior should be governed by principles such as those specified by APA. . . . The second theme is based on virtue ethics as

From *Ethics and Behavior,* 2, 151–163. Copyright 1992 by Erlbaum. Adapted with permission of the author and publisher.

discussed by Jordan and Meara (1990). Virtue ethics stresses the importance of the question, "Who shall I be?" In making decisions about dual relationships, professors must ask themselves not only whether their behavior will be influenced, but also whether their professional self-concept will be influenced. The issue for the professor making a decision about a dual relationship is, "Will the integrity of my professorial self be damaged?" . . .

How does [a] sexual dual relationship between a professor and a current student fit with the decision criteria mentioned earlier? Is the professor's role negatively compromised? Yes, every aspect of the professor's role is influenced negatively by such a relationship. Assuming that the professor does not have such a relationship with all class members, the professor has taught other students that favoritism exists and that there are not equal opportunities for all. This means that the professor is discriminating based on gender and sexual preference. Female students receive the message that their sexuality is important in attracting a professor's attention, and male students have learned that in this case they do not have equal status with female students. Their resentment can lead them to trivialize the accomplishments of female students. In addition, male students may receive the message that if you are a man in a position of power it entitles you to sexual privilege (Franklin, Moglen, Zatlin-Boring, & Angress, 1981).

Is the professor exploiting the student or increasing the risk of being exploited? The professor has violated the trust of the student that he as a professional can be counted on not to exploit her. Even if the professor makes every effort to grade the student fairly, there is a perception on the part of others that the student has received unequal treatment. The student herself may question whether she has been treated fairly. The professor has also increased the risk of exploiting the student due to ill feelings once the relationship is over, and he has also increased the risk of being exploited by the student. For many students, these ill feelings can have long-term consequences. Many undergraduate students will be continuing their education and may have to take required classes either from the professor or in the professor's department, and many need letters of recommendation.

Graduate students also run risks, perhaps even greater than those of undergraduates (Schneider, 1987). Graduate students often will remain in the same department as the professor; in fact, that professor may be the only one in their specialty area. Faculty make frequent decisions about the future of graduate students in terms of who will be retained in the program and who will be given funding. Letters of recommendation are critical to getting a professional job. It is important to note that the assumption that older students or graduate students are adults and should be considered as mutually consenting in these relationships ignores the very real power of the professor. Older, more mature students are not immune to the power of the professor, and they risk damaging their careers and self-images both during and after the relationship.

Is the behavior of the professor interfering with the professional roles of other faculty? The answer to this question is likely to be yes. To the extent that the relationship between the professor and the student has become recognized, other faculty members have to spend time deciding how to ensure that all students are being treated fairly. In addition, other faculty members may find that students generalize from the behavior of one faculty member to the rest of the department and expect similar behaviors. Female faculty members may find that the message that women should be treated as sexual objects interferes with their own performance.

. . .

What about nonsexual dual relationships? For example, what if a friend of long standing wishes to take a professor's course? In many ways this relationship poses the same problems as a sexual relationship. This type of relationship can negatively compromise the professional role of the professor. If the professor has a more intimate relationship with the friend than other students, this can interfere with evaluating the student objectively and with treating other students fairly. Other students may feel that it is "not what you know, but who you know" that is important for success. By engaging in this dual relationship, the professor may be increasing the risk of exploiting the student and the risk of being exploited. The friend, who is now a student, may not feel free to say no to social invitations or requests for favors. Alternatively, the friend might try to take advantage of the relationship to gain access to information about tests or special consideration on papers. The professor's behavior may interfere with the roles of other faculty. Other students may generalize that all faculty members show favoritism. Faculty members may find that any evaluation decisions they make about the student are influenced by the fact that the student is a friend of a colleague.

Obviously the cleanest solution to handling the potential problems raised by a dual relationship is to avoid it. In many cases this is possible and desirable given the serious problems raised by dual relationships. There will be occasions, however, when this option presents as many problems as the dual relationship. For example, if the professor is the only one teaching a required course, a close friend may have to take it in order to graduate. Does this mean that the professor is forced to choose between committing a breech of ethics or denying a student entry into a required course?

There are no easy solutions to the question of how to handle a dual relationship that seems un-avoidable. The decision criteria and the themes underlying them, however, can provide ideas about workable solutions. . . .

References

Franklin, P., Moglen, H., Zatlin-Boring, P., & Angress, R. (1981). *Sexual and gender harassment in the academy.* New York: The Modern Language Association of America.

Jordan, A., & Meara, N. (1990). Ethics and the professional practice of psychologists: The role of virtues and principles. *Professional Psychology: Research and Practice, 21,* 107–114.

Paludi, M. (1990). Creating new taboos in the academy: Faculty responsibility in preventing sexual harassment. *Initiatives, 52,* 29–34.

Schneider, B. (1987). Graduate women, sexual harassment, and university policy. *Journal of Higher Education, 58,* 46–65.

Zalk, S., Paludi, M., & Dederich, J. (1990). Women students' assessments of consensual relationships with their professors: Ivory power reconsidered. In E. Cole (Ed.), *Sexual harassment on campus: A legal compendium* (pp. 103–133). Washington, DC: National Association of College and University Attorneys.

Multiple Role Relationships During Internship: Consequences and Recommendations

P. Ann O'Connor Slimp and Barbara K. Burian

. . . Although multiple relationships between trainees and trainers have been addressed by some authors, such relationships that occur specifically during the internship year have largely been left unexplored. Such relationships may confuse interns, influence their professional identities, and prove problematic to the internship site itself. . . .

These guidelines are applied in the following discussion of four specific types of multiple roles that may occur during the internship: sexual, social, therapy, and business relationships. In addition, this discussion is limited to the possible negative impact of dual roles. Although there may be benefits gained from engaging in such relationships, we contend that most often, negative consequences outweigh the advantages, especially for the individuals who possess the least power in these relationships, the interns. . . .

SEXUAL RELATIONSHIPS

Many have recognized that the expectations and obligations of the role of sexual partner diverge greatly from those of supervisor or evaluator (Bartell & Rubin, 1990; Harrar, VandeCreek, & Knapp, 1990; Kitchener, 1988; Kitchener & Harding, 1990). However, staff members and interns may be motivated to engage in "mutually consensual" sexual relationships with each other for a variety of reasons, including natural attraction, gratification of physical, sexual, or emotional needs, the need to please a favored individual or to feel "special," and the need to feel powerful or in control of another person. . . .

The consequences of engaging in such relationships can be numerous and quite serious. First, a staff member engaged in such a relationship may have difficulty in keeping the intern's training interests and needs primary (Pope, Schover, & Levenson, 1980); self-interest and the preservation of the sexual relationship will generally take precedence. As a result, the interns involved may not be expected to complete the same requirements and may not be sufficiently challenged. Second, when engaged in these kinds of dual role relationships, interns may refrain from challenging or disagreeing with staff members or may avoid appropriately exploring various issues in seminars or supervision. For example, an intern who is in a sexual relationship with a member of the training staff may abstain from discussing issues of a sexual or intimate nature (e.g., his or her attraction to clients) for fear of eliciting an undesired reaction by the staff member (Pope, Keith-Spiegel, & Tabachnick, 1986). In addition, the staff member's ability to objectively evaluate the intern's skills is compromised. A supervisor in such a relationship is vulnerable to direct and vicarious liability because of inadequate supervision. Should such a sexual relationship end, the trainee might consequently become, or at least feel like, a target for abuse or unfair negative evaluations.

Furthermore, sexual relationships that are coerced and not "mutually consensual" (e.g., sexual harassment) can have effects on interns ranging from mild discomfort to extreme anxiety and depression that impair the intern's professional or personal functioning (Salisbury, Ginorio, Remick, & Stringer,

1986). An intern may consider or actually leave the internship or the profession or both (Glaser & Thorpe, 1986). Moreover, the current *Ethical Principles of Psychologists and Code of Conduct* (APA, 1992) prohibits psychologists from engaging in sexual harassment, which leaves those who engage in such behavior vulnerable to subsequent ethical and possibly legal consequences.

. . .

The transference phenomenon, in addition to the power differential between interns and staff members (Bernard & Goodyear, 1992; Cormier & Bernard, 1982; Harrar et al., 1990; Kitchener, 1988), compromises an intern's ability to provide true consent for entering into a dual role relationship. Cormier and Bernard (1982) suggested that "it could be argued that because of this, a supervisee is not able to give voluntary consent to participate in *any* form of dual relationships (p. 487, emphasis ours). In addition, Glaser and Thorpe (1986) found that the perception of the degree of coercion involved in such relationships increased with the passage of time and distance from the relationship. This supports Kitchener's (1988) belief that, because trainees are in positions of diminished power, interns' abilities to make knowledgeable and informed decisions that are in their own best interests are compromised.

SOCIAL RELATIONSHIPS

Upon first reflection it may not appear that the role expectations of a professional trainer differ that much from those of a social acquaintance, particularly when one considers friendly collegial interactions that occur during the work day. Those social relationships or interactions can take many forms and can be an important factor in maintaining a congenial work environment and good working relationships with colleagues. Hence, one might conclude that the potential for harm and exploitation in social relationships is much less than in sexual relationships. However, the role expectations and obligations of a friend or social acquaintance do differ from and can conflict with those of a staff member or supervisor. Supervisors are expected not only to evaluate interns but also to recommend interns for future employment. Should a supervisor share a so-

cial relationship with an intern, his or her objective evaluation of the intern's readiness for employment may be influenced. Therefore, even seemingly benign social relationships with positive intentions can still have an adverse effect on the training process (Keith-Spiegel & Koocher, 1985; Kitchener & Harding, 1990). . . .

In addition, Gutheil and Gabbard (1993) observed that sexual relationships with clients usually begin with the crossing of other boundaries such as those involving time, place, and self-disclosure. If this premise is applied to training or supervisory relationships, the boundary crossings involved in social relationships would make it more likely that sexual relationships and other dual role relationships could occur.

THERAPY RELATIONSHIPS

Possible incentives for interns and staff members to engage in therapy relationships with each other are diverse, and such relationships may occur unintentionally. As previously noted, the internship can be a difficult period as trainees, often isolated from their support networks, make the transition to becoming full professionals. When the intense focus on interpersonal relationships and clinical skills is also considered, it is understandable that many interns might benefit from and even need therapy.

Some staff members may feel that they are the most qualified people to provide therapy to interns given their relationships with them (Roberts, Murrell, Thomas, & Claxton, 1982; Stadler, 1986), and an ethical mandate may exist for staff or supervisors to provide such therapy to interns in the event of a crisis (Cormier & Bernard, 1982; Stadler, 1986). In addition, some internship sites (and postdoctoral training institutes), particularly those with psychoanalytic orientations, may require interns to receive therapy as a part of their training. In some graduate programs, it is common for faculty members to serve not only as instructors but also as clinical supervisors . . . Stoltenberg and Delworth (1987) suggested that in such situations students should be given a choice about such arrangements and the implications of these relationships should be openly discussed. If we apply this recommendation to internship sites and postdoctoral training programs regardless of theoretical orientation, then trainees should be allowed choices regarding multiple relationships at their training sites. Opportunities for obtaining therapy from someone with whom they have no other type of relationship should be available to all trainees.

Many have noted the therapy-like aspects of supervision (Newman, 1981; Upchurch, 1985), including the development of transference (Corey, Corey, & Callahan, 1984; Doehrman, 1976; Ethics Committee of the American Psychological Association, 1987). Others maintain that therapy is a proper activity within supervision (Hess, 1980). We agree with Cormier and Bernard (1982) that "this type of dual role relationship probably does occur to some degree in supervision because of the perceived importance of focusing on the supervisee's inter- and intrapersonal dynamics" (p. 487). This may be particularly relevant when one considers the parallel process between the therapy relationship and the supervisory relationship (Doehrman, 1976; McNeill & Worthen, 1989). However, Doehrman (1976) pointed out that the purpose of exploring a trainee's interpersonal and intrapersonal concerns should be confined to assisting the trainee in his or her relationship with the supervisor or client and that it is the supervisor who should take responsibility for providing any needed clarification regarding this relationship dynamic (Bernard & Goodyear, 1992).

Supervisors or staff members who provide therapy to interns place themselves in situations involving a conflict of interest (Stadler, 1986). The role of a staff member is often evaluative. In addition, those responsible for training can significantly influence an intern's future career goals and employment. Supervisors, who have a clear evaluative role with the intern, have the added duty to protect the welfare of the intern's clients (Cormier & Bernard, 1982; Harrar et al., 1990; Wise, Lowery, & Silverglade, 1989). Evaluation, however, is antithetical to the nature and process of therapy and the role of a therapist (Kitchener, 1988). As clients, interns need the same protection of confidentiality that is afforded other clients; they should feel free to explore their thoughts and feelings without fearing that such information

might be used in an evaluative context. Hence, interns who engage in therapy dual role relationships with staff might withhold or censor the information they choose to disclose, and thus both endeavors would suffer. Ethical guidelines (American Association for Counseling and Development, 1988; American College Personnel Association, 1990; APA, 1992) and several authors (Ethics Committee of the APA, 1987; Stadler, 1986; Wise et al., 1989) have suggested that interns who are in need of therapy should be referred to someone with whom they have no other relationship.

BUSINESS RELATIONSHIPS

Although business dual role relationships have typically received rather limited exploration in the literature (see Harrar et al., 1990; Keith-Spiegel & Koocher, 1985; Kitchener & Harding, 1990), we believe that it is not uncommon for interns to be hired as staff members' employees. Examples of this employment might range from house-sitting or babysitting to assisting staff members in research, consultation, or other private practice activities. Reasons for such relationships may include easing one's work load while providing professional and economic opportunities for trainees. However, although the intentions may be partially charitable or educational, the risk of exploitation and the potential for harm do exist.

. . .

As with other types of multiple role relationships, the staff member's ability to objectively evaluate the intern's performance, as a supervisor or employer, is compromised (Kitchener & Harding, 1990). In addition, consider how the intern–staffmember relationships could be affected should a child get hurt, a house burn, or a lucrative consulting contract fall through during the intern's employment. . . .

References

American Association for Counseling and Development. (1988). *Ethical standards.* Alexandria, VA: Author.

American College Personnel Association. (1990). A statement of ethical principles and standards of the American College Personnel Association. *Journal of College Student Development, 31,* 11–16.

American Psychological Association. (1992). Ethical principles of psychologists and code of conduct. *American Psychologist, 47,* 1597–1611.

Bartell, P. A., & Rubin, L. J. (1990). Dangerous liaisons: Sexual intimacies in supervision. *Professional Psychology: Research and Practice, 21,* 442–450.

Bernard, J. M., & Goodyear, R. K. (1992). *Fundamentals of clinical supervision,* Boston: Allyn & Bacon.

Corey, G., Corey, M. S., & Callahan, P. (1984). *Issues and ethics in the helping professions* (2nd ed.). Monterey, CA: Brooks/Cole.

Cormier, L. S., & Bernard, J. M. (1982). Ethical and legal responsibilities of clinical supervisors. *Personnel and Guidance Journal, 60,* 486–491.

Doehrman, M. J. G. (1976). Parallel processes in supervision and psychotherapy. *Bulletin of the Menninger Clinic, 40,* 3–104.

Ethics Committee of the American Psychological Association. (1987). Report of the Ethics Committee: 1986. *American Psychologist, 42,* 730–734.

Glaser, R. D., & Thorpe, J. S. (1986). Unethical intimacy: A survey of sexual contact and advances between psychology educators and female graduate students. *American Psychologist, 41,* 43–51.

Gutheil, T. G., & Gabbard, G. O. (1993). The concept of boundaries in clinical practice. Theoretical and risk-management dimensions. *American Journal of Psychiatry, 150,* 188–196.

Harrar, W. R., VandeCreek, L., & Knapp, S. (1990). Ethical and legal aspects of clinical supervision. *Professional Psychology: Research and Practice, 21,* 37–41.

Herlihy, B., & Corey, G. (1992). *Dual relationships in counseling.* Alexandria, VA: American Association for Counseling and Development.

Hess, A. K. (Ed.). (1980). *Psychotherapy supervision: Theory, research, and practice.* New York: Wiley.

Keith-Spiegel, P., & Koocher, G. P. (1985). *Ethics in psychology.* Hillsdale, NJ: Random House.

Kitchener, K. S. (1988). Dual role relationships. What makes them so problematic? *Journal of Counseling and Development, 67,* 217–221.

Kitchener, K. S., & Harding, S. S. (1990). Dual role relationships. In B. Herlihy & L. B. Golden (Eds.), *Ethical standards casebook* (4th ed.). Alexandria, VA: American Association for Counseling and Development.

McNeill, B. W., & Worthen, V. (1989). The parallel process in psychotherapy supervision. *Professional Psychology: Research and Practice, 20,* 329–333.

Newman, A. S. (1981). Ethical issues in the supervision of psychotherapy. *Professional Psychology, 12,* 690–695.

Pope, K. S., Keith-Spiegel, P., & Tabachnick, B. G. (1986). Sexual attraction to clients: The human therapist and the (sometimes) inhuman training system. *American psychologist, 41,* 147–158.

Pope, K. S., Schover, L. R., & Levenson, H. (1980). Sexual behavior between clinical supervisors and trainees: Implications for professional standards. *Professional Psychology, 11,* 157–162.

Roberts, G. T., Murrell, P. H., Thomas, R. E., & Claxton, C. S. (1982). Ethical concerns for counselor educators. *Counselor Education and Supervision, 22,* 8–14.

Salisbury, J., Ginorio, A. B., Remick, H., & Stringer, D. M. (1986). Counseling victims of sexual harassment. *Psychotherapy, 23,* 316–324.

Stadler, H. A. (1986). To counsel or not to counsel: The ethical dilemma of dual relationships. *Journal of Counseling and Human Services Professions, 6,* 134–140.

Stoltenberg, C. D., & Delworth, U. (1987). *Supervising counselors and therapists: A developmental approach.* San Francisco: Jossey-Bass.

Upchurch, D. W. (1985). Ethical standards and the supervisory process. *Counselor Education and Supervision, 25,* 90–98.

Wise, P. S., Lowery, S., & Silverglade, L. (1989). Personal counseling for counselors in training: Guidelines for supervisors. *Counselor Education and Supervision, 28,* 326–336.

◆ ◆ ◆

Commentary: *For other recent discussions of these issues, see Biaggio, M., Paget, T. L., & Chenoweth, M. S. (1997). A model for ethical management of faculty–student dual relationships.* Professional Psychology: Research and Practice, 28, *184–189; Russell, R. K., & Petrie, T. (1994). Issues in training effective supervisors.* Applied and Preventive Psychology, 3, *27–42.*

The final set of materials in this chapter confronts the issue of how to prevent, punish, or remediate unethical multiple relationships (see Standards 1.13–1.15 and 1.17–1.19) engaged in by psychologists and how to help those who may be injured by such inappropriate conduct.

Avoiding Exploitive Dual Relationships:
A Decision-Making Model

Michael C. Gottlieb

. . . Seven assumptions are required to use the model. First, the model is applicable to all professional relationships in which psychologists engage. . . .

Second, the aspirational goal of striving to avoid all dual relationships . . . is unrealistic in many circumstances. . . . The purpose of the model is to assist colleagues in managing these relationships more sensitively and effectively, when they cannot be avoided.

Third, due to the inherent high risk, all additional relationships with consumers should be evaluated to assess potential harm.

Fourth, the model assumes that not all dual relationships are exploitive per se. It presumes that in some circumstances, dual relationships may be pursued with low risk and may be beneficial; dual relationships must, however, be avoided whenever there is a reason to believe that they may prove harmful.

Fifth, the model is intended to sensitize the psychologist to the relevant issues, and make recommendations for action.

Sixth, the model assumes that the professional's dilemma is the result of contemplating the addition of a second relationship to an existing one. It is not intended for situations where multiple relationships are already in existence.

Seventh, the dimensions below must be assessed from the perspective of the consumer, not from that of the professional. Since the psychologist generally does not have access to the consumer's feelings in these situations, decisions must be made on the most conservative basis to insure consumer welfare.

THE MODEL

The model is based upon the use of three dimensions . . . that are believed to be basic and critical to the ethical decision-making process.

The first dimension is *Power.* It refers to the amount or degree of power which a psychologist may have in relation to a consumer. Power can vary widely. The psychologist who gives a speech at the local PTA on childrearing practices has relatively little power over members of the audience when compared with a therapist's influence over someone in long-term, insight-oriented psychotherapy.

Second, *Duration of the Relationship*, an aspect of power, is important because it is assumed that power increases over time. Power is lower when relationships are brief, such as in a single assessment session for referral, and increases as relationships continue, such as that of a student and teacher.

Third, *Clarity of Termination* refers to the likelihood that the consumer and the psychologist will have further professional contact. Performing a psychological assessment of a job applicant involves an unambiguous termination, with little chance of further contact. On the other hand, some family psychologists assume that their obligation to a family never ends. How does one decide when the professional relationship has been terminated? In this model one must assume that the professional relationship continues, as long as the consumer assumes that it does, regardless of the amount of time elapsed or contact in the interim. When the psychologist does not know the consumer's feelings, the

From *Psychotherapy, 30,* 41–47. Copyright 1993 by Division 29 of the American Psychological Association. Adapted with permission of the author and publisher. Figures 1 and 2 and Cases 1 and 2 have been omitted.

ethical choice is to assume that the consumer always has the right to renew the professional relationship in the future.

Using the Decision-Making Model

When a psychologist is contemplating an additional relationship, the model is to be used as follows.

Step 1. Assess the current relationship according to the three dimensions. From the consumer's perspective, where does the relationship fall on each? How great is the power differential, how long has the relationship lasted, and has it clearly ended? If the relationship falls to the right side on two or three of the dimensions (i.e., higher power, longer duration and no termination), the potential for harm is high, and no other relationship should be contemplated.

For traditional individual psychotherapy, group, marital, and family therapy the case is clear. The power differential is great, the duration of treatment can be long, and termination is not always clear cut. Furthermore, the consumer may presume it their right to return for service at any time in the future.

. . .

If the relationship falls to the left side on the three dimensions (i.e., low power, short duration, and clearly terminated), one may move down to the next level. When the relationship falls at mid-range on the three dimensions, some types of additional relationships may be permissible, and the psychologist may move down to the next level.

Step 2. Examine the contemplated relationship along the three dimensions, as was done for the current relationship. If the contemplated relationship falls to the right side of the dimensions (i.e., it would involve great power over a long time with an uncertain termination), then it should be rejected if the existing relationship also falls to the right. If the proposed relationship falls either in the mid-range or to the left side of the dimensions, it may be permissible, and the psychologist should move down to Step 3. . . .

Another possibility is that the first relationship may fall to the left side on the dimensions, but the contemplated relationship might fall to the right. In this case, the new relationship may be acceptable. For example, a psychologist could consider treating a child in psychotherapy after he gave a speech on children's reactions to divorce which the mother had attended.

Step 3. Examine both relationships for role incompatibility if they fall within the mid-range or to the left side of the dimensions. According to Kitchener (1988) role incompatibility increases as a function of greater differences in expectations of the two roles, greater divergence of the obligations of the two roles, and an increase in the power differential. If the two different roles are highly incompatible, then the contemplated relationship should be refused. For example, a psychologist should not accept an employee as a brief psychotherapy patient. Faculty members should not initiate business relationships with students.

If both relationships fall within the mid-range, or to the left side of the dimensions, and the incompatibility is low, the psychologist might proceed. For example, a faculty member may consider having a student in one of his or her classes work as a research assistant under his or her direction. A psychologist who has treated a man for smoking cessation may consider treating him and his wife for marital problems.

Step 4. Obtain consultation from a colleague. . . . A colleague familiar with the circumstances, the consumer, and the decision-maker is the ideal choice. . . .

Step 5. Discuss the decision with the consumer if the psychologist chooses to proceed with the additional relationship. He or she must review the essence of the decision-making model, its rationale, the pertinent ethical issues, available alternatives, and potential adverse consequences as a matter of informed consent. If the consumer is competent, and chooses to engage in the second relationship, the psychologist may proceed, once the consumer has had adequate time to consider the alternatives. If the consumer is unable to recognize the dilemma or is unwilling to consider the issues before deciding, he or she should be considered at risk, and the contemplated relationship rejected. . . .

References

Kitchener, K. S. (1988). Dual role relationships: What makes them so problematic? *Journal of Counseling and Development, 67,* 217–221.

◆ ◆ ◆

Commentary: See Rodolfa, E., Hall, T., Holms, V., Davena, A., Komatz, D., Antunez, M., & Hall, A. (1994). The management of sexual feelings in therapy. Professional Psychology: Research and Practice, 25, 168–172:

> In 1986, Pope et al. called for the integration of this topic into the resources for teaching counseling and therapy skills. Lerman (1990) provides an annotated bibliography of the 3,000 publications on this topic. There is currently an abundance of material, and models exist for training (Brodsky, 1989; Rodolfa et al., 1990; Vasquez, 1988). It is now up to the training program faculty to decide to integrate this material, for the good of their students, for the good of those who seek our psychological services, and for the good of our profession. It is time to train psychologists to accept and understand their sexual feelings and do no harm.

References

Brodsky, A. (1989). *Sex between patient and therapist: Psychologist's data and response.* In G. G. Gabbard (Ed.), Sexual exploitation in professional relationships (pp. 15–25). Washington, DC: American Psychiatric Press.

Lerman, H. (1990). *Sexual intimacies between psychotherapists and patients: An annotated bibliography of mental health, legal and public media literature and relevant legal cases* (2nd ed.). Washington, DC: American Psychological Association.

Pope, K., Keith-Spiegel, P., & Tabachnik, B. (1986). *Sexual attraction to clients: The human therapist and the (sometimes) inhuman training system.* American Psychologist, 41, 147–158.

Vasquez, M. (1988). *Counselor–client sexual contact implications for ethics training.* Journal of Counseling and Development, 67, 238–241.

APA has also sought to educate members of the public who use psychological services. See, Committee on Women in Psychology, American Psychological Association. (1989). *If sex enters into the psychotherapy relationship.* Professional Psychology: Research and Practice, 20, 112–115.

For other helpful articles on prevention and training (some with discussable vignettes), see:

Anderson, S. K., & Kitchener, K. S. (1998). *Nonsexual posttherapy relationships. A conceptual framework to assess ethical risks.* Professional Psychology: Research and Practice, 29, 91–99.

Biaggio, M., Paget, T. L., & Chenoweth, M. S. (1997). *A model for ethical management of faculty–student dual relationships.* Professional Psychology: Research and Practice, 28, 184–189.

Borys, D. S., & Pope, K. S. (1989). *Dual relationships between therapist and client: A national study of psychologists, psychiatrists, and social workers.* Professional Psychology: Research and Practice, 20, 283–293.

Lamb, D. H., & Catanzaro, S. J. (1998). *Sexual and nonsexual boundary violations involving psychologists, clients, supervisees, and students: Implications for professional practice.* Professional Psychology: Research and Practice, 29, 438–503.

Pope, K. S., Keith–Spiegel, P., & Tabachnik, B. G. (1986). *Sexual attraction to clients: The human therapist and the (sometimes) inhuman training system.* American Psychologist, 41, 147–158.

Slimp, P. A. O., & Burian, B. K. (1994). *Multiple role relationships during internship: Consequences and recommendations.* Professional Psychology: Research and Practice, 25, 39–45.

If education and prevention efforts fail, there are a variety of ways to discipline psychologists and other mental health professionals who violate prohibitions on sexual intimacies and other boundaries with their clients. These include actions by APA and state ethics committees, licensing boards, and plaintiffs bringing malpractice suits. Some insurance companies refuse to cover sexual conduct by therapists with clients under professional liability policies or severely limit what they will pay to damaged plaintiffs. For comprehensive and recent reviews, including an intensive discussion of legal remedies available to clients (e.g., civil actions, administrative complaints to licensing boards, and criminal prohibitions), see Bisbing, S. B., Jorgenson, L. M., & Sutherland, P. K. (1995). Sexual abuse by professionals: A legal guide. *Charlottesville, VA: Michie; Jorgenson, L. M., Hirsch, A. B., & Wahl, K. M. (1997). Fiduciary duty and boundaries: Acting in the client's best interest.* Behavioral Sciences and the Law, 15, 49–62; Jorgenson, L., Randles, R., & Strasburger, L. (1991). The furor over psychotherapist–patient sexual contact: New solutions to an old problem. William and Mary Law Review, 32, 647–732; and Haspel, K. C., Jorgenson, L. M., Wincze, J. P., & Parsons, J. P. (1997). Legislative intervention regarding therapist sexual misconduct: An overview. Professional Psychology: Research and Practice, 28, 63–72.

As of 1997, 15 states (Arizona, California, Colorado, Connecticut, Florida, Georgia, Iowa, Maine, Minnesota, New Hampshire, New Mexico, North Dakota, South Dakota, Texas, and Wisconsin) have made client–therapist sex a criminal activity, continuing to fuel the debate. See Haspel et al. (1997), cited above.

Criminalization of Psychotherapist–Patient Sex

Larry H. Strasburger, Linda Jorgenson, and Rebecca Randles

. . .

ARGUMENTS FOR CRIMINALIZATION

Deterrence

Deterrence is the primary argument in favor of criminalization of psychotherapist–patient sexual activity. A criminal law articulates to everyone the wrongfulness of such behavior. Proponents believe that sexual contact would be restrained by an unmistakable legal message that such behavior is severely damaging and totally unconscionable backed by the threat of a felony conviction and a prison sentence. Controversy exists over the probable effectiveness of this deterrence, but among the categories of exploitative therapists (1, p. 402; 15), those who are naive, uninformed, or undergoing the effects of midlife crisis may well respond to the prospect of punishment.

Retribution

In addition to the utilitarian function of deterrence, retribution is also a primary goal of criminal statutes. . . . This morally justified retaliation constitutes a vindictive justice that metes out suffering to pay back the wrongdoers. One of the strongest arguments for criminalization may now be that sexual exploitation, in the light of the evidence documenting its ill effects on patients, is so outrageous a transgression of societal rules that retribution is called for. Although therapist behavior rooted in the character pathology of impulsive, narcissistic, or sociopathic personalities may not be deterred by criminalization, retribution for such individuals may nonetheless be socially appropriate.

Additional Redress

A criminal statute would augment existing procedures that, for one reason or another, have not functioned effectively. In the past, an exploited victim could obtain redress for sexual exploitation only through complaints to professional societies' ethics committees, complaints to licensing authorities, or lawsuits for civil damages. Each of these routes has presented problems. Ethical procedures are ponderous, often involving long delays and ineffective action from the professional societies, themselves fearful of being sued by therapists. Licensing authorities have often been unresponsive or impotent. A civil lawsuit can be very expensive and may drag on for years. Criminalization, then, provides an additional option for a victim when other avenues fail. Implementing this option, however, may itself be lengthy and be delayed by the motions of a defendant exercising due process rights.

Dealing With Unlicensed Therapists

Although no panacea, criminalization may also provide a practical way to deal with unlicensed therapists and to incapacitate practitioners who continue to practice unregulated after their licenses have been revoked (17). Licensure boards cannot sanction them, and many of them have so few financial resources that a civil suit would be fruitless. A weakness of the criminal process, however, has been demonstrated in Minnesota, where the relatively short sentences imposed on convicted therapists have allowed them to return to practice after brief incarcerations. . . .

Money to Treat Victims

Proponents of criminalization point out that such laws can provide access to money for both prevention and treatment of victims. Minnesota, for example, has used money from federal criminal justice programs to fund educational efforts dealing with the problem (18). Money may be available to help fund ongoing victim treatment in states where public funds are dedicated to assistance of crime victims. Such financial restitution, however, may represent an unkept promise. Although funds for assistance to crime victims do exist in theory, the current austerity of state budgets has led to large cuts in the funding of such programs.

ARGUMENTS AGAINST CRIMINALIZATION

Obscuring the Issue

Paradoxically, criminalization may cause psychotherapist–patient sex to be reported even less. Colleagues may be less willing than they currently are to report an offending psychotherapist if an ethics complaint would lead to criminal charges. This might be the case despite an ethical duty to report (2) and the statutes on mandatory reporting that some states have passed (19). A patient may also be reluctant to complain, appalled at the idea that the psychotherapist would be subject to criminal sanctions. While some complainants want retribution or restitution, others may want help for their impaired therapists. Although some patients may not be aware of it, criminal prosecutions cannot proceed without their testimony, which they can choose to withhold.

Voiding Malpractice Coverage

One of the gravest concerns of victims of therapist exploitation is that criminalization may void malpractice insurance coverage. Although insurers continue to recognize an obligation to defend accused therapists, the trend has been to exclude paying judgments for sexual exploitation. Criminalization provides additional justification for such exclusion, as most policies specifically exclude criminal acts from coverage. Criminalization, then, may eliminate a resource that victims sorely need to finance continuing treatment. There is no victim compensation fund comparable to the therapist's malpractice policy. Although the victim may be able to reach the personal assets of the psychotherapist, these resources are frequently inadequate or nonexistent.

This concern about loss of malpractice coverage may be exaggerated. There are indications that insurers may be required to indemnify such claims even in states which have criminalizing statutes (20). Successful suits are frequently based on assertions of mishandled transference. One appellate opinion has held that in such circumstances, "It is the mishandling of transference, and not the resulting sexual conduct, which gives rise to the alleged malpractice. . . . The sexual acts are an incidental outgrowth of the primary malpractice, not the proximate cause" (21). Some plaintiffs have won lawsuits despite these exclusionary policies by alleging concurrent proximate causes for their injuries—where the injuries have been caused by both the excluded risk (sexual misconduct) and an insured risk (such as wrongful or improper termination of therapy).

Impairment of Civil Actions

Criminalization may make it more difficult for patients to win civil suits for damages. The risk of criminal prosecution certainly will make offending therapists less likely to admit their behavior. The therapist may exercise Fifth Amendment rights. This in effect will prevent the process of discovery by civil and administrative boards until the criminal trial is completed. This could delay not only an award of (money) damages but also restriction or revocation of the therapist's license by the licensing board. Even the simple matter of apology, which some victims find healing, becomes difficult in the face of a possible criminal prosecution. . . .

Inappropriate Catharsis

Victims' advocates observe that pursuit of criminal prosecution provides an anodyne to the shame and feeling of powerlessness experienced by victims of sexual exploitation. Whether this emotional relief is greater than that obtained through a civil lawsuit or action before a licensing board is unclear. Nevertheless, it may be inappropriate to use the blunt instrument of criminal law to palliate and enable victims. . . .

Loss of Control of Process

Many victims of sexual exploitation by psychotherapists feel that they have lost control of their lives, and involvement in criminal prosecution may heighten this feeling. Although some writers believe that a decision to file a criminal complaint helps recover a sense of control, the victim does not control a criminal process and civil process in the same way. Although the victim is free to choose whether or not to come forward with a complaint and a prosecutor cannot proceed if the only witness against the therapist refuses to testify, victims have been concerned that after a complaint is entered the prosecutor's decisions will determine how the case is run.

Unproven Deterrence

Although anecdotal information and common sense suggest that criminalization may act as a deterrent, there is as yet no empirical evidence to demonstrate this premise. In fact, few people even file criminal charges in states where statutes exist. Over 1,600 victims of therapist sexual contact have been seen in the Walk-In Counseling Center in Minneapolis, but Minnesota has prosecuted only nine criminal charges to date.

Absence of Rehabilitation

The absence of a provision for the rehabilitation of offenders is a major omission in the current criminal statutes. Although some sexual exploiters victimize multiple patients, appear to be without conscience, and are probably not treatable, others commit a single offense that may be a response to a situational or life cycle crisis, and these psychotherapists might benefit from treatment and be restored to social productivity. Casting these latter individuals in the role of unredeemable criminals may not be wise social policy.

SPECIAL CONSIDERATIONS

Consent

Some criminal laws, such as those against rape and indecent assault, already apply to therapist sexual misconduct. As a practical matter these laws cover only the most egregious cases, and consent of the victim is an absolute defense (17). Eliminating consent as an issue by defining psychotherapist–patient sexual contact as a specific crime provides a more effective statute. Most statutes criminalizing patient–therapist sex exclude consent as a defense, defining such contact as a crime regardless of the victim's behavior. This strict liability standard means that the only matter to be adjudicated is whether the sexual contact occurred.

Some commentators believe that removing the defense of consent in effect portrays psychotherapy patients as incompetent "presumptive sillies" (23). If this were to occur, the status of patients would clearly be stigmatized. As a practical matter, in our experience victims are not concerned that they will be demeaned through the removal of the issue of consent. Obviously, competent adults are presumed capable of consent and the law is reluctant to remove this presumption. Drawing an analogy between psychotherapy patients and rape victims, as in Masters and Johnson's original proposal, appears to infantilize them by saying that patients are ipso facto unable to consent. This, however, is not the best way to conceptualize the issue.

It is not that the victim cannot consent or that consent is improperly obtained—as through undue influence of transference or lack of information about risks. Consent is irrelevant. The issue is fiduciary breach and abuse of power in the therapeutic relationship. A fiduciary is in a position of special trust, analogous to that of a trustee, involving "a duty to act primarily for another's benefit" and requiring "scrupulous good faith and candor" (24). Trust and confidence are reposed in the therapist on the basis of a perception of social role. Even a sophisticated patient must place himself or herself in a vulnerable, less powerful position vis-à-vis a therapist who has more knowledge, training, and experience of the therapeutic process. It is the duty of the therapist as fiduciary to attend only to the needs of the patient and to do no harm. Sexual contact is countertherapeutic behavior that will harm patients. The consequences of such acts are so socially deleterious that they call for proscription regardless of consent. Attention should focus entirely on the therapist's behavior, not on that of the victim. . . .

False Accusations

For psychotherapists the possibility of having to defend themselves against false accusations of sexual misconduct is terrifying, and false accusations do occur (26). The criminal law, although it exposes the accused therapist to greater jeopardy, provides better protection against false accusations of sexual exploitation than the civil law. The standard of proof in a criminal trial is "beyond reasonable doubt," whereas in a civil trial a jury can find for the plaintiff on "the preponderance of the evidence." In an ambiguous situation a properly instructed criminal court jury should be less likely to enter a judgment against a therapist than a jury in a civil trial. In actuality the difficulty of proving a criminal case beyond reasonable doubt may make prosecutors hesitant to proceed. The vast majority of these cases involve alleged actions in an office in which only two people were present, and the evidence is limited to one person's word against another's. The narrow and specific definition of behavior in a criminal statute, which is necessary to avoid constitutional challenge of the statute on the basis of vagueness, means that a therapist may avoid criminal conviction for acts that could incur civil liability. The criminal law also offers more due process protection to the accused therapist than proceedings before licensure boards, which may allow testimony that would be excluded under strict rules of evidence and which may not be governed by a statute of limitations. . . .

References

1. Schoener G, Milgrom J, Gonsiorek J, et al: Psychotherapists' Sexual Involvement With Clients: Intervention and Prevention. Minneapolis, Walk-In Counseling Center, 1989

2. The Principles of Medical Ethics With Annotations Especially Applicable to Psychiatry. Washington, DC, American Psychiatric Association, 1989

15. Pope K, Bouhoutsos J: Sexual Intimacy Between Therapists and Patients. New York, Praeger, 1986, pp 33–45

17. Jorgenson L, Randles R, Strasburger LH: The furor over psychotherapist–patient sexual contact: new solutions to an old problem. William and Mary Law Review 1991; 32:643–729

18. Sanderson B (ed): It's Never OK: A Handbook for Professionals on Sexual Exploitation by Counsellors and Therapists. St Paul, Minnesota Department of Corrections, 1989

19. Strasburger L, Jorgenson L, Randles R: Mandatory reporting of sexually exploitative psychotherapists. Bull Am Acad Psychiatry Law 1990; 18:379–384

20. Vigilant Insurance Co v Kambly, 114 Mich App 683, 319 NW 2d 382 (1982)

21. St Paul Fire and Marine Insurance Co v Love, 447 NW 2d 5 (Minn Ct App 1989)

23. Leff AA: Unconcionability and the code—the emperor's new clause. University of Pennsylvania Law Review 1967; 115:485–559

24. Black HC: Black's Law Dictionary, 4th ed. St Paul, West Publishing, 1968, p 753

26. Gutheil TG: Borderline personality disorder, boundary violations, and patient–therapist sex: medicolegal pitfalls. Am J Psychiatry 1989; 146:597–602

Remediation for Ethics Violations: Focus on Psychotherapists' Sexual Contact With Clients

Melissa J. Layman and J. Regis McNamara

. . .

In addition to further ethics education and training, punitive actions, informal support options, and practice oversight, mandatory personal therapy has been suggested as an option for rehabilitation of impaired psychologists and ethics offenders (APA, 1992; Burton, 1973; V. Hedges, Ohio Board of Psychology, personal communication, May 1995; Laliotis & Grayson, 1985; Lamb et al., 1987; Pope, 1987; R. Reaves, ASPPB, personal communication, May 1995; Schoener & Gonsiorek, 1988) . . .

[T]here are several reasons against using mandated therapy for ethics violations. First, although personal therapy is highly valued by the field of psychology, psychologists do not appear to be willing to mandate participation for all therapists in training. Second, several problematic issues exist specifically for the therapist in therapy, which may hinder or even prevent the entry of the professional into a therapeutic setting. Third, there is little clear outcome literature suggesting that personal therapy will improve the psychologist or his or her work with clients, let alone remediate violations of ethics. Finally, variables associated with treatment of sex offenders (insofar as those variables are applicable to this population), such as denial and minimization of actions (Brodsky, 1986; Gabbard, 1995; Hanson et al., 1991; Schoener & Gonsiorek, 1988; Schwartz, 1992; Walzer & Miltimore, 1993), and with mandated psychotherapy seem likely to compromise the effectiveness of therapy in a variety of situations.

In addition to these reasons, the issue of viability for rehabilitation must be raised. In a recent survey, 87% of psychologists responded "absolutely yes" or "probably" to the question of whether licensing boards should "be able to require therapists (e.g., who have violated professional standards) to obtain therapy as a condition of their continuing or resuming practice" (Pope & Tabachnick, 1994, p. 254). However, only 34% responded similarly to the question of whether such an intervention would be effective (Pope & Tabachnick, 1994). . . .

Holroyd and Brodsky (1977) discussed the chronic nature of exploitative therapists' problems, stating that "therapists who disregard the sexual boundary once are likely to repeat" (p. 849); this statement appears to hold true today (Pope, 1994). This finding implies that the level of motivation for change in ethics violators is not likely to be sufficient for remediation through personal therapy. In fact, Pope (1994) stated that "It is difficult to find any published evidence . . . that shows any effectiveness of rehabilitation interventions" for sexually offending therapists (p. 43).

Gonsiorek and colleague (Gonsiorek, 1995; Schoener & Gonsiorek, 1988) indicated that success in intervention with ethics violators depends strongly on the type of deficit involved. Of the six categories of sexually exploitative therapists, these researchers described only one group as potentially remediable—the healthy or mildly neurotic therapist, who is often dealing with situational stresses, recognizes the impact of his or her behavior, and seeks help to end it. In further support of this categorization, several researchers have mentioned that the therapist who recognizes his or her problems and commits himself or herself to address them constructively has a good prognosis for change (Brodsky, 1986; Gabbard, 1995; Keith-Spiegel & Koocher, 1985; Vasquez, 1988). Walzer and Miltimore (1993) further noted that a specific emotional, mental, or situational difficulty leading to sexual offending may be handled through treatment; in these cases, one would expect to be able to prevent repeat offenses.

The uninformed or naive therapist who commits ethics violations may be educated or trained further but may not have the ethical instincts or judgment to counsel even after this education (Schoener & Gonsiorek, 1988). Rehabilitation of the severely neurotic therapist may be possible, but it does not carry as good a prognosis because of denial or rationalization of the unethical behavior (Gabbard, 1995; Gonsiorek, 1995; Schoener & Gonsiorek, 1988). In terms of the other of the three categories of therapists—the character disordered—all the above authors stated that these are not candidates for rehabilitation because of their lack of concern over their behavior. Therefore, it seems that ethics violators who can be categorized by the majority of offender categories are not likely to benefit from mandated personal therapy. However, because Schoener and Gonsiorek (1988) did not provide data on the frequency of offenders in each category, it is impossible to determine the proportion of ethics violators that is potentially remediable. Given these difficulties with psychotherapy as remediation, it is not surprising that Schoener (1994) stated, "rehabilitation involves more than just psychotherapy" (p. 15).

SUGGESTIONS FOR ALTERNATIVE METHODS OF REMEDIATION

If mandated personal therapy is not an appropriate treatment for ethics violators, what can be done in the way of remediation for these therapists? . . .

One general suggestion is to carefully identify, monitor, and intervene with therapists at risk for acting on sexual attraction, if possible (Pope, 1987; Schwebel et al., 1994). These therapists may be identified during training or later during their careers by personal characteristics or by the nature of clientele being served, although the chances of accomplishing this scientifically or ethically are low.

Given the low base rate of sexual offending, identification on the basis of possible future offenses would be likely to involve a high number of false positives . . .

Preventative training specifically aimed at sexual misconduct seems to be a topic of current interest (Schwebel et al., 1994). Vasquez (1988) discussed a prevention program that would be implemented during training, where students would be sensitized to ethical issues surrounding sexuality and sexual contact. In this program, knowledge and self-awareness would be emphasized. Vasquez (1988) felt that "most problems . . . are amenable to amelioration in counselors-in-training" (p. 240); this may, in fact, be an excellent time to identify potential offenders. Another important opportunity for identification of ethics violators is during the internship (Lamb et al., 1987). Lamb et al. indicated that the stresses and situation changes present in transition to full-time clinical practice, concurrent with extensive supervision, present a chance to observe, identify, and treat potential unethical behavior. . . .

Unfortunately, both Vasquez's and Lamb et al.'s approaches are limited in that a relatively small number of cases of therapist–client sexual contact occur during graduate training or internships. Variables commonly associated with the sexually exploitative therapist, such as burnout or depression, may not yet play a role in the training therapist's interactions with clients. Moreover, the low base rate of sexual offending makes it difficult to accurately identify future offenders.

Another intervention that may prove useful is educating clients about therapy boundaries (Gottlieb, Vasquez, Applebaum, & Jorgenson, 1993; Strasburger, Jorgenson, & Sutherland, 1992), for example, presenting a sexual misconduct brochure to clients before they enter therapy (Thorn, Shealy, & Briggs, 1993). This brochure would inform the client of the unethical nature of therapist sexual misbehavior as well as the right to file a complaint (Thorn et al., 1993). Given that many therapists have encountered a client who was sexually involved with a previous therapist (Pope, 1993, Stake & Oliver, 1991), a brochure of this type may be a useful resource to clients. In addition, the knowledge that a client is aware of sexual inappropriateness and potential legal action may act as an external source of control for the clinician's actions. Thorn et al. (1993) found that exposure to a brochure did change college students' attitudes about therapist–client sexual contact as well as increase their intention to act assertively if such a situation occurred. Therefore, a sexual misconduct brochure may, in fact, be helpful to an impaired therapist.

. . .

Callanan and O'Connor (1988, p. 11) concluded that "prospects for rehabilitation are minimal and it is doubtful that they [sexually exploitative therapists] should be given the opportunity to ever practice psychotherapy again" (cited in Pope, 1994), a provision echoed by Gabbard (1995) and Gonsiorek (1995), particularly when a character disorder is present. Given the need to protect the public, punitive disciplinary action may be the only current avenue for remediation for the character disordered violators of ethical principles until other interventions can be derived, implemented, and evaluated. Even for those not so deeply affected, the jury is still out on the extent to which remedial therapy or education can be of benefit. Only when well-done evaluation of remediation is undertaken can the jury return to render its verdict.

References

American Psychological Association. (1992). Rules and procedures. *American Psychologist, 47,* 1612–1628.

Brodsky, A. M. (1986). The distressed psychologist: Sexual intimacies and exploitation. In. R. R. Kilburg, P. E. Nathan, & R. W. Thoreson (Eds.), *Professionals in distress: Issues, syndromes, and solutions in psychology* (pp. 153–171). Washington, DC: American Psychological Association.

Burton, A. (1973). The psychotherapist as client. *American Journal of Psychoanalysis, 33,* 94–103.

Callanan, K., & O'Connor, T. (1988). *Staff comments and recommendations regarding the report of the Senate Task Force on Psychotherapist and Patients Sexual Relations.* Sacramento, CA: Board of the Behavioral Science Examiners and Psychology Examining Committee.

Gabbard, G. O. (1995). Psychotherapists who transgress sexual boundaries with patients. In J. C. Gonsiorek (Ed.), *Breach of trust: Sexual exploitation by health care professionals and clergy* (pp. 133–144). Thousand Oaks, CA: Sage.

Gonsiorek, J. C. (1995). Assessment for rehabilitation of exploitative health care professionals and clergy. In J. C. Gonsiorek (Ed.), *Breach of trust: Sexual exploitation by health care professionals and clergy* (pp. 145–162). Thousand Oaks, CA: Sage.

Gottlieb, M. C., Vasquez, M. J. T., Applebaum, P. S., & Jorgenson, L. (1993). Sexual contact between psychotherapists and clients. In J. A. Mindell (Ed.), *Issues in clinical psychology* (pp. 153–182). Dubuque, IA: Brown & Benchmark/Wm. C. Brown.

Hanson, R. K., Cox, B., & Woszcyna, C. (1991). Assessing treatment outcome for sexual offenders. *Annals of Sex Research, 4,* 177–208.

Holroyd, J., & Brodsky, A. (1977). Psychologists' attitudes and practices regarding erotic and non-erotic physical contact with patients. *American Psychologist, 32,* 843–849.

Keith-Spiegel, P., & Koocher, G. P. (1985). *Ethics in psychology: Professional standards and cases.* New York: Random House.

Laliotis, D. A., & Grayson, J. H. (1985). Psychologist heal thyself: What is available for the impaired psychologist? *American Psychologist, 40,* 84–96.

Lamb, D. H., Presser, N. R., Pfost, K. S., Baum, M. C., Jackson, V. R., & Jarvis, P. A. (1987). Confronting professional impairment during the internship: Identification, due process, and remediation. *Professional Psychology: Research and Practice, 18,* 597–603.

Pope, K. S. (1987). Preventing therapist–patient sexual intimacy: Therapy for a therapist at risk. *Professional Psychology: Research and Practice, 18,* 624–628.

Pope, K. S. (1993). Licensing disciplinary actions for psychologists who have been sexually involved with a client. Some information about offenders. *Professional Psychology: Research and Practice, 24,* 374–377.

Pope, K. S. (1994). *Sexual involvement with therapists: Patient assessment, subsequent therapy, forensics.* Washington, DC: American Psychological Association.

Pope, K. S., & Tabachnick, B. G. (1994). Therapists as patients: A national survey of psychologists' experiences, problems, and beliefs. *Professional Psychology: Research and Practice, 25,* 247–258.

Schoener, G. R. (1994, August). *Assessment and rehabilitation of professionals who engage in sexual misconduct.* Paper presented at the annual meeting of the American Psychological Association, Los Angeles, CA.

Schoener, G. R., & Gonsiorek, J. (1988). Assessment and development of rehabilitation plans for counselors who have sexually exploited their clients. *Journal of Counseling and Development, 67,* 227–232.

Schwartz, B. K. (1992). Effective treatment techniques for sex offenders. *Psychiatric Annals, 22,* 315–319.

Schwebel, M., Skorina, J. K., & Schoener, G. (1994). *Assisting impaired psychologists (Rev. ed.): Program devel-*

opment for state psychological associations. Washington, DC: American Psychological Association.

Stake, J. E., & Oliver, J. (1991). Sexual contact and touching between therapist and client: A survey of psychologists' attitudes and behavior. *Professional Psychology: Research and Practice, 22,* 297–307.

Strasburger, L. H., Jorgenson, L., & Sutherland, P. (1992). The prevention of psychotherapist at sexual misconduct: Avoiding the slippery slope. *American Journal of Psychotherapy, 46,* 544–555.

Thorn, B. E., Shealy, R. C., & Briggs, S. D. (1993). Sexual misconduct in psychotherapy: Reactions to a consumer-oriented brochure. *Professional Psychology: Research and Practice, 24,* 75–82.

Vasquez, M. J. T. (1988). Counselor–client sexual contact: Implications for ethics training. *Journal of Counseling and Development, 67,* 238–241.

Walzer, R. S., & Miltimore, S. (1993). Mandated supervision, monitoring, and therapy of disciplined health care professionals. *The Journal of Legal Medicine, 14,* 565–596.

◆ ◆ ◆

Commentary: *Layman & McNamara's (1997) views did not go unchallenged. For example, Gonsiorek (1997) charged that the authors engaged*

> *. . . in a puzzling argument: Since the effectiveness of therapy with therapists is not clearly demonstrated one way or the other, it should be viewed as likely ineffective, despite the fact that the literature on therapy outcomes is generally seen as positive. It seems to me that one would need compelling data, not insufficient data, to suggest that therapists, distinct from the general population, are such a suspect class regarding therapy outcome. I have no disagreement that therapy outcome with therapists is insufficiently researched to draw firm conclusions. I believe, however, that in this situation, the best estimate is that we psychologists are probably most akin to other groups studied. (p. 300)*

Gonsiorek, C. J. (1997). Suggested remediations to "Remediation." Professional Psychology: Research and Practice, 28, *300–303.*

Brown (1997) thought that the arguments for or against remediation of the offending therapist neglected a more fundamental issue:

> *In my clinical and forensic experience with the victims of offending psychotherapists, I have had ample opportunity to observe that, even when the professional has fulfilled all of the requirements of the regulatory agency, has gone into treatment, has gotten supervision, has attended ethics classes, has paid fines, and has lost privileges, the primary and secondary victims are left in a continuing state of distress. Boundary violations in professional psychology occur in the context of relationships between therapists and clients; rehabilitation plans routinely ignore the relationship. Remediation cannot be considered to have occurred if those who we are attempting to heal from the ravages of a boundary violation have never had amends made to them in ways that are meaningful to them; nor will remediation happen if the system in which the boundary violation took place is allowed to continue on as before, creating future risks. (p. 297)*
>
> . . .
>
> *It is extremely common for a direct victim of an offending therapist to state that she simply wishes to have the therapist apologize directly, in person, and with no excuses; to listen to the client's expressions of pain, anger, and betrayal; and to affirm that she, the victim, had no hand in causing the boundary violation. In other words, what is desired is the clear and unequivocal shouldering of personal responsibility by the professional who has done harm. Fines, loss of a therapist's license, and other more usual punishments are frequently quite secondary considerations (aside from the desire for funding of the victim's own future psychotherapy). Yet psychology's regulatory boards and ethics committees persist in imposing the latter and not the former as penalties for gross violations of ethical standards. (p. 298)*

. . .

I believe that as long as we psychologists do not transform our models of remediation to become paradigms of genuine amends, we engage in a massive case of collective denial about solutions to the problem of serious boundary violations. (p. 299)

Brown, L. S. (1997). *Remediation, amends, or denial?* Professional Psychology: Research and Practice, 28, 297–299.

The reader may wish to see Layman & McNamara's (1997) rejoinder to the critiques of their original article by Gonsiorek and Brown: Layman M. J. & McNamara (1997) Remediation revisited. Professional Psychology: Research and Practice, 28, 304–305.

What is your opinion with regard to psychology's response to its members who violate ethical boundaries with clients, students, and trainees? Should these members be treated as criminal perpetrators, as impaired professionals needing treatment, or as requiring remedial ethics training? If they are expelled from APA or delicensed, how will their future conduct be monitored? On the other hand, can the profession afford to have them remain? Perhaps any sanctions are premature at this time. But is it more true that psychology should recognize that the profession "really does not know much at all about boundary violations or violators, that the time for solutions can only come after we have obtained more understanding [and that] it is time for investigation, not for impulsive solutions" (Orr, p. 294)?

Orr, P. (1997). *Psychology impaired?* Professional Psychology: Research and Practice, 28, 293–296.

CHAPTER 6

PSYCHOLOGICAL ASSESSMENT

Assessment, particularly testing, permeates every facet of people's lives. Almost every subset of psychologists uses tests. Researchers use tests to acquire data from those who participate in their studies. Clinical psychologists administer tests for diagnostic purposes and to monitor the course of psychotherapy. School psychologists assess children to determine their eligibility for possible placement in special education programs. Counseling psychologists use vocational, occupational, and interest tests to guide career development and measure problem-solving skills throughout the life span. Forensic psychologists use tests to help courts determine the best placement for children whose parents are divorcing or to assess whether a criminal defendant is competent to stand trial or should be held responsible for an otherwise criminal act. Industrial and organizational psychologists measure skills and job knowledge of those seeking employment or promotion. And, of course, academics often devise their own instruments to assess what their undergraduate and graduate students have learned.

As the nonexhaustive list above illustrates, assessment can take many forms. Each form may have its own ethical implications. For example, when clinicians use intelligence scales, paper-and-pencil personality tests, or projective techniques, issues of privacy and informed consent arise. When psychologists in employment settings use tests, issues of dual loyalties arise: For whom is the psychologist working and to whom does the psychologist owe the primary obligation of fidelity—the test taker or the employer? When school psychologists assess children for special education placement, who is the client—the child, the parent, or the school system that is paying the evaluator? When a researcher gathers data through tests, questions of informed consent and deception become important (see chap. 8, this volume). When forensic clinicians evaluate a criminal defendant, are they working on behalf of the prosecution, the defense, or the court (see chap. 9)? And regardless of the assessor's role, the issue of competence becomes pervasive. Are the tests that are used psychometrically sound, and are the interpretations and judgments that psychologists make from the data valid? Finally, the advent of computerized testing in general and the increased use of so-called honesty or integrity tests in employment in particular open such discussions to a whole new set of issues.

This chapter can only provide an introduction to the complex ethical issues inherent to gathering, storing, interpreting, and disseminating information about test takers that is gleaned from assessment. Such technical issues as validity, reliability, norming, and standardization are addressed here only if they are relevant to ethical and social issues. To gain a broader perspective on both technical and social policy questions, see the two special issues of the *American Psychologist* devoted to testing and edited by Amrine (1965) and by Glaser and Bond (1981). In addition, the National Academy of Sciences has produced two major works evaluating standardized tests in general (Heller, Holtzman, & Messick, 1982; Wigdor & Garner, 1982).

The ethical problems raised in this chapter cannot be fully understood if they are examined outside of their historical, social, and legal contexts. Thus, I urge readers to also examine such classical articles as Cronbach's (1975) and Haney's (1981). For recent reviews of some of the more controversial issues, see Elliot's (1987) book and Helms's (1992) article. I too have contributed to the legal literature on this topic (Bersoff, 1979, 1981, 1982, 1984).

References

Amrine, M. (Ed.). (1965). Testing and public policy [Special issue]. *American Psychologist, 20*(11).

Bersoff, D. N. (1979). Regarding psychologists testily: Legal constraints on psychological testing in the public schools. *Maryland Law Review, 39,* 27–120.

Bersoff, D. N. (1981). Testing and the law. *American Psychologist, 36,* 1047–1056.

Bersoff, D. N. (1982). *Larry P. and PASE:* Judicial report cards on the validity of individual intelligence scales. In T. Kratochwill (Ed.), *Advances in school psychology* (Vol. 2, pp. 61–95). Hillsdale, NJ: Erlbaum.

Bersoff, D. N. (1984). Social and legal influences on test development and usage. In B. Plake (Ed.), *Social and technical issues in testing* (pp. 87–109). Hillsdale, NJ: Erlbaum.

Cronbach, L. J. (1975). Five decades of public controversy over mental testing. *American Psychologist, 30,* 1–14.

Elliot, R. (1987). *Litigating intelligence: IQ tests, special education, and social science in the courtroom.* Dover, MA: Auburn House.

Glaser, R., & Bond, L. (Eds.). (1981). Testing: Concepts, policy, practice, and research [Special issue]. *American Psychologist, 36*(10).

Haney, W. (1981). Validity, vaudeville, and values: A short history of social concerns over standardized testing. *American Psychologist, 36,* 1021–1034.

Heller, K., Holtzman, W., & Messick, S. (Eds.). (1982). *Placing children in special education: A strategy for equity.* Washington, DC: National Academy Press.

Helms, J. (1992). Why is there no study of cultural equivalence in standardized *cognitive* ability testing? *American Psychologist, 47,* 1083–1101.

Wigdor, A. K., & Garner, W. R. (Eds.). (1982). *Ability testing: Uses, consequences, and controversies* (Vols. 1 & 2). Washington, DC: National Academy Press.

Test Validity and the Ethics of Assessment

Samuel Messick

Fifteen years ago or so, in papers dealing with personality measurement and the ethics of assessment, I drew a straightforward but deceptively simple distinction between the psychometric adequacy of a test and the appropriateness of its use (Messick, 1964, 1965). I argued that not only should tests be evaluated in terms of their measurement properties but that testing applications should be evaluated in terms of their potential social consequences. I urged that two questions be explicitly addressed whenever a test is proposed for a specific purpose: First, is the test any good as a measure of the characteristics it is interpreted to assess? Second, should the test be used for the proposed purpose in the proposed way? The first question is a scientific and technical one and may be answered by appraising evidence for the test's psychometric properties, especially construct validity. The second question is an ethical one, and its answer requires a justification of the proposed use in terms of social values. Good answers to the first question are not satisfactory answers to the second. Justification of test use by an appeal to empirical validity is not enough; the potential social consequences of the testing should also be appraised, not only in terms of what it might entail directly as costs and benefits but also in terms of what it makes more likely as possible side effects.

. . .

. . . Values thus appear to be as pervasive and critical for psychological and educational measurement as is testing's acknowledged touchstone, validity. Indeed, "The root remaining of the word 'validity' is the same as that of the word 'value': both derive from a term meaning strength" (Kaplan, 1964, p. 198). . . .

VALIDITY AS EVALUATION OF IMPLICATIONS

. . .

If test validity is the overall degree of justification for test interpretation and use, and if human and social values encroach on both interpretation and use, as they do, then test validity should take account of those value implications in the overall judgment. The concern here, as in most ethical issues, is with evaluating the present and future consequences of interpretation and use (Churchman, 1961). If, as an intrinsic part of the overall validation process, we weigh the actual and potential consequences of our testing practices in light of considerations of what future society might need or desire, then test validity comes to be based on ethical as well as evidential grounds. . . .

References

Churchman, C. W. *Prediction and optimal decision: Philosophical issues of a science of values.* Englewood Cliffs, N.J.: Prentice-Hall, 1961.

Kaplan, A. *The conduct of inquiry: Methodology for behavioral science.* San Francisco: Chandler, 1964.

Messick, S. Personality measurement and college performance. *Proceedings of the 1963 Invitational Conference on Testing Problems.* Princeton, N.J.: Educational Testing Service, 1964.

Messick, S. Personality measurement and the ethics of assessment. *American Psychologist,* 1965, 20, 136–142.

◆ ◆ ◆

Commentary: More recently, Messick (1995) reiterated that validity should be considered a unitary concept

From *American Psychologist, 35,* 1012–1027. Copyright 1980 by the American Psychological Association. Adapted with permission of the author and publisher. Figures 1 and 2 have been omitted.

rather than be fragmented into the traditional tripartite categories of criterion, content, and construct validity. More relevant for our purposes, he asserted that validity is a social as well as a measurement value: "[I]t is fundamental that score validation is an empirical evaluation of the meaning and consequences of measurement" (p. 742). "The consequential aspect," he said, "appraises the value implications of score interpretation as a basis for action as well as the actual and potential consequences of test use" (p. 745) particularly with regard to issues of bias and fairness. Thus, he concluded, "validity and values are one imperative, not two, and test validation implicates both the science and the ethics of assessment, which is why validity has force as a social value" (p. 749). See Messick, S. (1995). Validity of psychological assessment: Validation of inferences from persons' responses and performances as scientific inquiry into score meaning. American Psychologist, 50, 741–749.

Do you think his argument has merit or does considering the consequences of testing as part of validity overburden "an already overburdened concept" (Zimiles, 1996, p. 981) and create "a dangerous intrusion of politics into science" (Lees-Haley, 1996, p. 982)? For the complete responses to Messick's provocative article, see:

Lees-Haley, P. R. (1996). Alice in Validityland, or the dangerous consequences of consequential validity. American Psychologist, 51, 981–983.

Zimiles, H. (1996). Rethinking the validity of psychological assessment. American Psychologist, 51, 980–981.

According to Malgady (1996), "it is estimated that about 40% of the clients in the mental health services system will be members of ethnic minority groups in the year 2000" (p. 73). See Malgady, R. G. (1996). The question of cultural bias in assessment and diagnosis of ethnic minority clients: Let's reject the null hypothesis. Professional Psychology: Research and Practice, 27, 73–77. Malgady also states that it is imperative that those psychologists providing assessment services understand both the technical and social issues concerning testing.

The issue of test fairness is so important that the new version of the 1985 standards for psychological and educational tests, coauthored by APA and currently being completed, will contain an entire chapter on the issue.

In critiquing the APA ethics code with regard to testing ethnic minority clients, the reviewer concluded:

> [I]n my judgment, the 1992 code requires supplementation with guidelines for assessment practice with each visible racial and ethnic group to include (a) examples, vignettes, and case materials; (b) recognition of the current state of research, including the availability of culture-specific and culture-relevant assessment methodologies; and (c) suggestions for a continuing self-examination of racial identity status among all assessors. Noncompliance with or violations of the new code can be responded to with educational and remedial efforts to enhance an understanding of the complex nature of ethical dilemmas stemming from diverse belief systems and expectations. (p. 353)

See Dana, R. H. (1994). Testing and assessment ethics for all persons: Beginning and agenda. Professional Psychology: Research and Practice, 25, 349–354.

On Competence and Ethicality in Psychodiagnostic Assessment

Irving B. Weiner

. . . Knowing what one's tests can do—that is, what psychological functions they describe accurately, what diagnostic conclusions can be inferred from them with what degree of certainty, and what kinds of behavior they can be expected to predict—is the measure of a psychodiagnostician's competence. Acting accordingly—that is, expressing only opinions that are consonant with the current status of validity data—is the measure of his or her ethicality.

Circumstances arise in which competent psychodiagnosticians confront ethical dilemmas that tax their sense of how best to use their knowledge of what tests can do. Perhaps most common in this regard is choosing between a less and a more serious diagnosis when reporting to a third party. The more serious diagnosis may help the person get needed treatment and insurance coverage. The less serious diagnosis may spare the person from an official mental health record that may be used prejudicially against him or her at some later time. Presumably, one could merely weigh the test data, select the diagnosis that fits them best, and let the chips fall where they may. In practice, however, survey data indicate that psychologists often struggle with this kind of situation, especially when the data would justify more than one option, and they differ in the alternatives toward which they lean.

Rarely can competent psychodiagnosticians avoid entirely having to grapple with gray areas of ethicality, especially in matters that have not yet been codified. Two equally ethical practitioners can end up behaving differently in such circumstances. Regrettably, there are also times when competent practitioners exercise poor judgment in the absence of any ethical dilemma. The harried examiner who saves time by signing his or her name to a computer printout and sending it off as a report and the expert psychologist witness who inflates up his or her credentials to lend weight to testimony are being unethical, even though they may be highly competent.

Although it is, therefore, possible in psychodiagnostic work to be competent without being ethical, it is not possible to be ethical without being competent. Competence is prerequisite for ethicality, and psychologists who practice or teach psychodiagnosis without being fully informed concerning what tests can and cannot do are behaving unethically. . . .

◆ ◆ ◆

Commentary: Because assessment may infringe on the test taker's sense of privacy and because it has such serious consequences for both society and the individual, there have been constant calls for either its abolition or its strict regulation. But as Messick warned 30 years ago,

> *absolute rules forbidding the use of . . . tests . . . would be an intolerable limitation both to scientific freedom and to professional freedom. . . . [I]n our consideration of possible ethical bases for self-regulation in assessment, it seems imperative that we*

go beyond ethical absolutism . . . and espouse an "ethics of responsibility," in which pragmatic evaluations of the consequences of alternative actions form the basis for particular ethical decisions. . . . In this sense, then, we need continual assessments of ethics as the basis for an ethics of assessment. (p. 140)

See Messick, S. (1965). *Personality measurement and the ethics of assessment. American Psychologist, 20,* 136–142.

As you read the next group of materials, consider whether there has been too much self-regulation by the profession and too much intrusive involvement in assessment by the federal government and the courts. On the other hand, given the enormous social consequences of testing, has the plethora of professional and legal regulation in the past 30 years been insufficient to deal with the problems?

The Legal Regulation of School Psychology

Donald N. Bersoff and Paul T. Hofer

TESTING AND EVALUATION

Nondiscriminatory Assessment

While every person in the United States probably has been affected in some way by tests, schoolchildren are its most frequent targets. It has been estimated that more than 250 million standardized tests of academic ability, perceptual and motor skills, emotional and social characteristics, and vocational interests and talent are used each year in education (Holman & Docter, 1972). Undoubtedly, test results have been used to admit, advance, and employ, but for the majority of persons scores derived from psychometric instruments serve as exclusionary devices—to segregate, institutionalize, track, and deny access to desired goals. . . .

While criticism of testing by social, political, and psychological commentators arose within the test industry itself, the legal system seriously began to examine the issue of nondiscriminatory assessment only since the mid-1960s. In part, judicial interest in testing may be explained by the Supreme Court's mandate in *Brown v. Board of Education* (1954) that the public schools must be desegregated. Civil rights advocates view educational and psychological tests as tools to hinder integration and, more broadly, as discriminatory instruments, denying the full realization of the constitutional rights of racial and ethnic minorities. As a result, from the mid-1960s to the 1980s there was an explosion of litigation and legislation affecting the administration, interpretation, and use of psychological tests. . . .

. . . In 1975 Congress passed P.L. 94-142 (20 U.S.C. §§ 1401–1461), the Education for All Handicapped Children Act (EAHCA). Two years earlier it had enacted § 504 of the Rehabilitation Act of 1973 (29 U.S.C. § 794). Implementing regulations for the EAHCA were drafted by the Department of Health, Education, and Welfare (now the Department of Education) and for § 504 by what is now the Department of Health and Human Services, both of which took effect in 1977.

P.L. 94-142 is essentially a grant-giving statute providing financial support to state and local education agencies for special education and related services if they meet certain detailed eligibility requirements. P.L. 94-142 and its implementing regulations reaffirmed earlier mandates concerning nondiscriminatory evaluation and fleshed out the meaning of this requirement. Section 300.532 of the regulations states:

> (a) Tests and other evaluation materials:
> (1) Are provided and administered in the child's native language or other mode of communication . . .
> (2) Have been validated for the specific purpose for which they are used; and
> (3) Are administered by trained personnel in conformance with the instructions provided by their producer. . . .

Other provisions also affect psychological and educational assessment. Children with sensory, manual, or speaking impairments are to be given tests that reflect genuine deficits in aptitude or achievement, not those impairments. Further, all assessment is to be comprehensive, multifaceted, and multidisciplinary. Evaluations for placement must be conducted by persons from education, medicine, and psychology who assess children "in all areas related to the suspected disability, including where appropriate, health, vision, hearing, social and emotional status, general intelligence, academic performance, communicative status, and motor abilities." Tests cannot be used which are "merely . . . designed to provide a single general intelligence quotient" nor can one single procedure be "used as the sole criterion for determining an appropriate educational program for a child." In making placement decisions the school is required to "draw upon information from a variety of sources, including aptitude and achievement tests, teacher recommendations, physical condition, social and cultural background and adaptive behavior." Thus, P.L. 94-142 makes it quite clear that assessment and placement decisions are the responsibility not of a school psychologist acting alone, but of a multidisciplinary team. The apparent reasons behind this diffusion of duty are to reduce individual bias and broaden accountability.

To ensure that all these provisions are effectuated, both the statute and the regulations provide mechanisms enabling parents "to present complaints with respect to any matter relating to the identification, evaluation, or educational placement" of their children. The complaints are presented in an impartial administrative hearing in which parents have the right to compel the attendance of, and to cross-examine, witnesses involved in the assessment and programming decisions. The consequence is that psychologists are vulnerable to intense scrutiny of their credentials and performance, including the reliability and validity of the evaluation measures they employ, the interpretations they make from the information gathered, or the recommendations they offer as a result of their evaluation. . . .

With regard to the Rehabilitation Act, a multipurpose law to promote the education, employment, and training of handicapped persons, Congress declared in § 504 that "no otherwise qualified handicapped individual in the United States . . . shall, solely by reason of his handicap, be excluded from participation in, be denied the benefits of, or be subjected to discrimination under any program or activity receiving federal financial assistance." This section thus represents the first federal civil rights law protecting the rights of handicapped persons and reflects a national commitment to end discrimination on the basis of handicap. Unlike P.L. 94-142, the requirements of § 504 are not triggered by receipt of funds under institutions receiving federal financial assistance. Thus, any school system, public or private, receiving federal monies for any program or activity whatsoever is bound by its mandates.

The regulations implementing the broad right-granting language of § 504 were published in 1977. In addition to general principles already established under P.L. 94-142, it sets forth regulations pertaining to the evaluation of children suspected of being handicapped. The language of those provisions, requiring preplacement evaluations, validated tests, multidisciplinary comprehensive assessment, and periodic reevaluations, are almost identical to that which now appears in the implementing regulations to P.L. 94-142. . . .

Reference

Holman, M., & Docter, R. (1972). *Educational and Psychological Testing*. New York: Russell Sage.

◆　◆　◆

Commentary: The Education for All Handicapped Children Act was renamed the Individuals With Disabilities Education Act (IDEA). The Rehabilitation Act of 1973 is applicable to employment settings as well as to schools. Section 84.13 of the act's implementing regulations prohibits the use of employment tests that screen out applicants who are disabled, unless the test is job related and there are no alternative selection devices available that do not screen out such applicants. Even more broadly applicable to employers is the Americans With Disabilities Act (ADA). The ADA covers all employers engaged in interstate commerce that have 15 or more employees, even if these employers receive no federal financial assistance. Like the Rehabilitation Act, it prohibits the use of employment tests with an adverse impact on people who are disabled unless the tests are job related and are consistent with business necessity. On July 26, 1991, the Equal Employment Opportunity Commission published detailed regulations implementing the ADA. See the Federal Register, 56, 35726–35753, 1991. The ADA also restricts the use of medical examinations prior to a contingent offer of employment. The question arises whether psychological testing is defined as "medical" under the Act. The EEOC, rejecting most of the APA's recommendations on the issue, published guidelines stating its interpretation of the regulations. See Equal Employment Opportunity Commission. (1994, May). Enforcement guidance: Preemployment disability-related inquiries and medical examinations under the Americans With Disabilities Act of 1990 (EEOC Notice, 915.002). *Washington, DC: Author; Equal Employment Opportunity Commission. (1995, October).* ADA enforcement guidance: Preemployment disability-related questions and medical examinations. *Washington, DC: Author.*

Novick provided a useful history and summary of existing laws, regulations, and guidelines promulgated by the federal government concerning testing. See Novick, M. R. (1981). Federal guidelines and professional standards. American Psychologist, 36, 1035–1046. The most detailed and relevant of these documents is the Uniform Guidelines on Employee Selection Procedures, published in the 1978 Federal Register (Vol. 43, pp. 38290–38315), and a series of questions and answers designed to clarify and interpret the Uniform Guidelines, published in the 1979 Federal Register (Vol. 44, pp. 11996–12009).

Novick also discussed the work of such organizations as APA, the American Educational Research Association (AERA), and the National Council on Measurement in Education (NCME) in developing professional standards, including the then-current version of the APA, AERA, and NCME Standards for Educational and Psychological Tests (1974), which, for the first time, addressed issues of social importance, such as invasion of privacy and discrimination against women and minorities. But he and others were critical of the 1974 Standards and called for their revision. Not coincidentally, Novick was asked to chair a committee of AERA, APA, and NCME representatives who were to draft new testing standards. The revisions committee completed its work and published the Standards for Educational and Psychological Testing (1985). The tripartite committee specifically noted that the "standards were formulated with the intent of being consistent with" (p. vii) the then-current (1987) APA code of ethics. Are the Standards enforceable under the provisions of Standard 2 of the 1992 Ethical Principles?

Any psychologist involved in the development, administration, scoring, interpretation, or publication of tests should read the Standards for Educational and Psychological Testing thoroughly. However, be aware that they are undergoing major revision under the auspices of the same three organizations that produced the 1985 version. This revision is due to be published in 1999.

AERA, APA, & NCME. (1974). Standards for educational and psychological tests. *Washington, DC: American Psychological Association.*

AERA, APA, & NCME. (1985). Standards for educational and psychological tests. *Washington, DC: American Psychological Association.*

Ethical Issues and Cases in the Practice of Personnel Psychology

Lorraine D. Eyde and Marilyn K. Quaintance

[*Ed. note:* Industrial and organizational psychologists who work in business settings face considerable pressure, both to comply with legal requirements of federal and state civil rights acts and with ethical obligations. At times, the demands of the psychologist's employer may conflict with professional ethics. In this article, the authors present five situations that a psychologist may confront in industry. After reading the vignettes, attempt to discern which ethical principles would be applicable and whether the respective psychologists would be in violation of them.]

. . .

CASE 1: INAPPROPRIATE USE AND INTERPRETATION OF AN ASSESSMENT PROCEDURE

A psychologist administered the California Psychological Inventory (CPI) to assess candidates for promotion to senior management positions within an organization. The CPI results were the only information used by the psychologist in making the promotional decision, and these results were accepted as the "truth" regardless of the situational factors involving the inventory administration process. The psychologist was not familiar with the research evidence suggesting that test and retest CPI profiles differ considerably, depending on specific family or work stresses at the time of administration. No other inventories were administered, and no other evidence (e.g., appropriate performance ratings) was considered. The psychologist used only the CPI because the organizational management wanted to an-

nounce the promotions immediately. The psychologist recommended that a job analysis be performed to link the CPI's constructs to the requirements of the managerial job, but the recommendation was rejected by management because the linkage appeared obvious. The psychologist handled the matter rapidly because the contract to conduct the assessment had tight time requirements.

. . .

CASE 2: LACK OF COMPETENCE IN TEST INTERPRETATION AND MISREPRESENTATION

A personnel psychologist who lacked training in the interpretation of the Minnesota Multiphasic Personality Inventory (MMPI) hired a clinical psychologist to purchase MMPI materials from the test publisher. The clinical psychologist was trained to read and interpret the test records of job applicants for nuclear power plant positions and to determine their emotional fitness for work in one of two power companies. Because of financial pressures, the personnel psychologist discontinued the use of the services of the clinical psychologist. The personnel psychologist continued to purchase the MMPI from the test publisher and did not inform the test publisher that the services of the clinical psychologist had been discontinued. The test publisher's agreement to provide the needed test materials was based on the understanding that consultation by the clinical psychologist, trained in the interpretation of the MMPI, was ongoing. The personnel psychologist also continued to provide the psychological screening service to the

From *Professional Psychology: Research and Practice, 19,* 148–154. Published by the American Psychological Association, 1988. In the public domain.

two power companies without informing these two organizations of the lack of his knowledge of MMPI procedures.

. . .

CASE 3: VIOLATION OF LEGAL STANDARDS AND SUBMISSION TO PERSONAL PRESSURES

A psychologist responsible for administering a test procedure to candidates for hire knows one of the candidates personally as a friend. The psychologist assists the candidate in attaining a good score on the selection instrument by coaching.

. . .

CASE 4: MISLEADING PUBLIC STATEMENTS

Promotional material prepared by a psychologist for a personnel test that she published was misleading in that it suggested that it was the only test of its kind favorably reviewed in a given edition of *Mental Measurements Yearbook*. The promotional literature made no mention of the fact that subsequent editions of the *Yearbook* contained favorable reviews of other instruments that were similar in nature. In addition, the promotional material stated that the *Mental Measurements Yearbook* contains all published psychologist tests; in fact, the *Yearbook* contains only new tests and tests revised since the last edition of the *Yearbook* or tests that have generated 20 or more references since the last *Yearbook* edition.

. . .

CASE 5: LACK OF COMPETENCE IN TEST SELECTION AND INTERPRETATION

A counseling psychologist, who lacked formal training and experience in the use of written examinations for personnel selection and classification, was asked to recommend a test to evaluate competency of teachers in a northeastern state. The psychologist suggested that the Wesman Personnel Classification Test be administered to all practicing teachers to evaluate teacher competency level. The test manual for the Wesman indicated that the examination was a measure of skills in verbal and numerical areas,

but gave no reference to applications of the Wesman to evaluate teacher competency. Although such an application of the Wesman might constitute a legitimate use, there was no research evidence to support it.

In the absence of normative data for teachers, the psychologist recommended a pass–fail score of 70%. This score was established partly for political reasons because that level was "what was expected of school children."

The test manual showed that scores of 70% (28) on the Verbal Wesman are at the 76th percentile for salaried workers and the 73rd percentile for the Air Force Captains. Similarly, scores of 70% (14) on the Numerical Wesman are at the 76th percentile for salaried workers and the 78th percentile for Air Force Captains. However, these same scores of 28 and 14 were considered failing for the examinees.

About half of the teachers, as well as an even larger proportion of school administrators who also took the examination, "failed." The pass rate for minorities was significantly lower than the pass rate for nonminorities. When a summary of the test results appeared in the press, along with a description of the scoring procedures, the state school system experienced a public relations disaster.

◆ ◆ ◆

Commentary: An outgrowth of the 1981 Conference on Testing, Assessment, and Public Policy was the creation of the Test User Qualifications Working Group (TUQWoG)—a subcommittee of the AERA, APA, and NCME Joint Committee on Testing Practices, which devised the 1985 Standards for Testing. TUQWoG's ultimate mission was to develop a model test-user-qualification system, consistent with professional standards and ethical principles. TUQWoG identified seven major factors related to the misuse of tests: (a) failure to conduct a comprehensive assessment, (b) improper test use (such as lack of proper training and use of quality control), (c) ignorance of standard error of measurement, (d) failure to maintain integrity of test results, (e) inaccurate scoring, (f) inappropriate use of norms, and (g) the failure to give proper interpretive information to test takers. See Edye, L. R., Moreland, K. L., & Robertson, G. J. (1988). Test user qualifications: A data-based approach to promoting good test use. Washington,

DC: American Psychological Association, Test User Qualifications Working Group; Moreland, K. L., Eyde, L. D., Robertson, G. J., Primoff, E. S., & Most, R. B. (1995). *Assessment of test user qualifications: A research-based measurement procedure.* American Psychologist, 50, 14–23.

A successor group to TUQWoG—the Test User Training Work Group—has developed a helpful book of

cases that were based on real-life testing situations and designed to raise questions about proper test use and interpretation. See Eyde, L. D., Robertson, G. J., Krug, S. E., Moreland, K. L., Robertson, A. G., Shewan, C. M., Harrison, P. L., Porch, B. E., Hammer, A. L., & Primoff, E. S. (1993). *Responsible test use: Case studies for assessing human behavior. Washington, DC. American Psychological Association.*

Ethical Issues in Testing and Evaluation for Personnel Decisions

Manuel London and Douglas W. Bray

. . .

ETHICAL OBLIGATIONS OF PSYCHOLOGISTS

Organizational staff members who are responsible for formulating and applying evaluation procedures have ethical obligations to their profession, to the people they evaluate, and to their employers. . . .

Psychologists' Obligations to the Profession

Organizations often employ individuals with advanced degrees in personnel-related fields. Psychologists who are members of APA or who are licensed by a state to practice psychology are expected to abide by the standards and principles for ethical practice set forth by APA, regional professional organizations, and/or state statutes. However, nonpsychologists involved in evaluation are not formally responsible for adhering to these standards. Nevertheless, the federal *Uniform Guidelines on Employee Selection Procedures* sets standards for all personnel experts in organizations subject to federal regulations regarding equal employment opportunity. . . . Desirable behaviors for ethical conduct generally include keeping informed of advances in the field, reporting unethical practices, and increasing colleagues' sensitivity to ethical issues.

Maintaining professional competence is necessary for effective application of evaluation techniques. The *Standards for Educational and Psychological Tests* devotes a section to qualifications of test users. Test users must have a general knowledge of measure-ment and validation principles and the limitations of test interpretation as well as an understanding of the literature relevant to the evaluation devices they use. The *Ethical Standards of Psychologists* emphasizes the need for continuing education, being open to new procedures, and remaining abreast of relevant federal, state, and local regulations concerning practice and research. . . .

Psychologists' Obligations to Those Who Are Evaluated

Social and legal influences mandate that career decisions be made with a concern for accuracy and equality in employment opportunity (Division of Industrial and Organizational Psychology, 1975). A concern for the person who is affected by career decisions, however, leads to a number of ethical principles that go beyond improving and maintaining accuracy and ensuring equal employment opportunity. These principles include guarding against invasion of privacy, guaranteeing confidentiality, obtaining employees' and applicants' informed consent before evaluation, respecting employees' right to know, imposing time limitations on data, minimizing false positive and false negative decisions, and treating employees with respect and consideration. . . .

Some organizations routinely provide evaluation results to employees in the hope that knowledge of results will improve performance. Other organizations maintain a policy of secrecy or leave it up to individual supervisors to decide whether to provide feedback. Legislation now guarantees public employ-

From *American Psychologist, 35*, 890–901. Copyright 1980 by the American Psychological Association. Adapted with the permission of the author and publisher.

ees access to this information, and pending legislation, if enacted, will do the same in the private sector. Research on the effects of access on the quality of information and the behavior and attitudes of the employee is necessary. . . .

Another issue pertaining to the confidentiality of evaluations such as recommendations deals with protecting the identity of individuals providing the information. Specifically, should employees have access to recommendations written about them? A similar question was answered by Congress in 1974 when it enacted a law giving students the right to inspect their records (Ewing, 1977). Now students choose whether or not to waive this right before asking someone to complete a recommendation form. Allowing employees to decide whether or not to waive their right to access to recommendations and other information in their personnel files may be a viable solution to employee complaints about confidential information they believe may be used against them. Here, as in other areas, there is a conflict between the rights of the individual and the validity of information obtained. An important research question is whether those named as references will supply negative information if they know the applicant will have access to it.

An especially difficult ethical problem involves maintaining the confidentiality of test results within an organization. Typically, many individuals outside the personnel staff have legitimate access to the information. For instance, a manager who is responsible for filling a position vacancy by promotion from within the company may use information about an employee's job experience and performance. Such information is often used without the knowledge of the employee. This raises the issue of informed consent—that is, of informing candidates about the intended use of test results prior to their taking the test. Tests given by an organization for one purpose are often used later for additional purposes. Thus, a score on an employment test may be used later for selection to a training program, assignment to a specific type of work, or promotion to a higher level. A person has the right to be told every potential use of the test results. This does not mean that the individual has to be informed every time a decision is made. Rather, it simply means that he or she should be aware of the types of decisions that may depend in part on the test results. . . .

Ethical treatment of employees during and after evaluation is another obligation of psychologists. How employees or applicants are treated when they are evaluated can influence the results of the evaluation and their acceptance of the ensuing decision. In general, evaluation procedures should be standardized to guarantee equal treatment and to enable examinees to do their best. . . . Standard procedures should include personal and considerate treatment, a clear explanation of the evaluation process, and direct and honest answers to examinees' questions.

Psychologists' Obligations to the Employer
Ethical obligations to the employer . . . include conveying accurate expectations for evaluation procedures, ensuring high-quality test data, implementing and periodically reviewing the adequacy of decision-making procedures, respecting the employer's proprietary rights, and balancing vested interests of the employer with government regulations, with commitment to the psychology profession, and with the rights of those evaluated for personnel decisions. . . .

Psychologists must attempt to provide high-quality information for personnel decisions, namely, reliable, valid, and fair data. However, psychologists are often unable to use the most rigorous scientific methods to ascertain a test's reliability and validity because of limited resources, time pressure, or other constraints imposed by the employer. . . .

Fairness relates to the absence of discrimination on the basis of race, sex, national origin, or other characteristics not related to the job. The law has responded to this issue in the form of legislation and judicial rulings. In general, a reasonably reliable and valid test that does not exhibit differential validity may still be unfair if it results in a substantially smaller proportion of favorable personnel decisions for one or more protected classes than for the majority group. (A substantially smaller proportion is defined in the *Uniform Guidelines* as less than 80% of the majority group selection rate, but this criterion does not necessarily define unfairness.) Therefore, in addition to determining that an evaluation device is reliable and valid, a psychologist must ascertain that it is free from bias. . . .

Psychologists must respect the proprietary rights of the employer as long as it is possible to maintain standards of ethical practice. Many organizations insist that their selection methods remain confidential, and in some cases they maintain this policy even when under review by government agencies. Companies in a competitive environment that invest heavily in personnel methods may be reluctant to publicize the details of their procedures. Moreover, organizations may fear that information given out about their procedures will lead to difficult questions even if the procedures are perfectly proper. . . . Therefore, psychologists working in industry may be constrained from publishing data regarding test development and validation or other research results sponsored by the employer.

Another ethical issue arises when psychologists are constrained from conducting research because the results may in some way be detrimental to their employer. . . . In such a case, the psychologist must abide by the wishes of the employer, try to persuade the employer otherwise, or change jobs. The ethical issue must be resolved by the psychologist. The issue becomes salient when the psychologist believes that proper practice has been hindered. Indeed, this is the crux of many ethical issues in psychology. Ethical responsibility is a personal and individual issue. Although the situation may be constructed by the employer, the psychologist perceives and interprets the situation and must deal with restrictions that he or she believes contribute to unethical practice. . . .

The potential for conflict among the professional's obligations to the employer, the profession, and employees is perhaps most likely in the area of confidentiality. Management's need to know must be satisfied while keeping promises to employees and applicants that evaluation results will remain confidential and while ensuring that the contents of evaluation devices are not disclosed to the extent that they are invalidated. . . .

SUMMARY AND CONCLUSION

. . .

. . .What was considered ethical several years ago is not necessarily considered ethical today. A grow-

ing concern for human rights has placed career decision-making procedures and associated psychological research and practices in the public domain.

. . .Finally, we must recognize that today's ethical standards are frequently tomorrow's laws. Professional standards are often incorporated into laws and used as the basis for judicial rulings. When published professional standards are insufficient, Congress and the courts do not hesitate to impose their own. Consequently, psychologists must play active roles in lobbying and writing legislation. Recognizing that ethical prescriptions and legal requirements are intertwined and are likely to become more so should be impetus enough for adopting ethical personnel practices and conducting research that will influence legislation.

References

Division of Industrial and Organizational Psychology, American Psychological Association. *Principles for the validation and use of personnel selection procedures.* Dayton, Ohio: Author, 1975.

Ewing, D. W. *Freedom inside the organization: Bringing civil liberties to the workplace.* New York: Dutton, 1977.

◆　◆　◆

Commentary: Although London and Bray did not cite it, in 1979 the U.S. Supreme Court decided a case that raised many of the issues discussed in their article. More important, although the case involved an interpretation of the National Labor Relations Act and the use of tests in employment settings, it had broader ramifications for all psychologists. The case was not only relevant to issues of confidentiality of test results but, in the larger context, it pitted all of APA's ethics code against competing legal obligations (see chap. 2). The case started when 10 employees of a local electric company who applied for promotions failed to achieve acceptable scores on a battery of aptitude tests. Under the terms of a collective bargaining agreement union representatives for the aggrieved employees contested the results and claimed the examination procedure was unfair. They requested that the employer submit the tests, the employees' answer sheets, and other test-related data.

The employer argued that disclosing test data would make the battery useless in the future. Furthermore, the employer refused to disclose test data on any particular individual, claiming a confidential relationship between the employee and the psychologist who administered the test. Union representatives asserted they had the right to see these data.

The dispute was first heard by an administrative law judge (ALJ) who ruled that the employees' test results should be turned over to an industrial psychologist chosen by the union. To protect test security, the ALJ barred union representatives from copying or disclosing questions to employees. Nevertheless, the National Labor Relations Board overruled the ALJ's decision and ordered that the test results and raw data be given directly to union representatives. They had the discretion but were not required to use a psychologist if they needed help in interpreting test results.

That decision was reviewed by a federal appellate tribunal. Over the objections of APA (which had filed a friend of the court brief), the court affirmed the Board's order and ruled that test security would be protected adequately through the Board's banning of test data dis-closure by union officials. The employer countered by claiming that any disclosure of test questions or scores would cause the psychologists involved in the testing to breach their code of ethics. The appellate court rejected that argument, asserting that the APA code of ethics could not stand in the way of union members exercising their rights to collective bargaining.

The employer asked the U.S. Supreme Court to review the lower court's decision. It began its opinion by acknowledging that "psychological aptitude testing is a widely used employee selection and promotion device in both industry and government. Test secrecy is concededly critical to the validity of any such program, and confidentiality of scores is undeniably important to the examinees" (p. 304). The Court held that the National Labor Relations Board's order, enforced by the Court of Appeals, failed to adequately accommodate those concerns. The Board, it said, abused its discretion in ordering the company to turn over the test battery and answer sheets directly to the union. It then addressed the ethical issues.

Detroit Edison Co. v. National Labor Relations Board

. . .

The dispute over Union access to the actual scores received by named employees is in a somewhat different procedural posture. . . . The Company argues that even if the scores were relevant to the Union's grievance (which it vigorously disputes), the Union's need for the information was not sufficiently weighty to require breach of the promise of confidentiality to the examinees, breach of its industrial psychologists' code of professional ethics, and potential embarrassment and harassment of at least some of the examinees. The Board responds that this information does satisfy the appropriate standard of "relevance," . . . and that the Company, having "unilaterally" chosen to make a promise of confidentiality to the examinees, cannot rely on that promise to defend against a request for relevant information. The professional obligations of the Company's psychologists, it argues, must give way to paramount federal law. Finally, it dismisses as speculative the contention that employees with low scores might be embarrassed or harassed.

We may accept for the sake of this discussion the finding that the employee scores were of potential relevance to the Union's grievance, as well as the position of the Board that the federal statutory duty to disclose relevant information cannot be defeated by the ethical standards of a private group. . . . Nevertheless we agree with the Company that its willingness to disclose these scores only upon receipt of consents from the examinees satisfied its statutory obligations under § 8 (a)(5).

The Board's position appears to rest on the proposition that union interests in arguably relevant information must always predominate over all other interests, however legitimate. But such an absolute rule has never been established [footnote omitted], and we decline to adopt such a rule here [footnote omitted]. There are situations in which an employer's conditional offer to disclose may be warranted. This we believe is one.

The sensitivity of any human being to disclosure of information that may be taken to bear on his or her basic competence is sufficiently well known to be an appropriate subject of judicial notice [footnote omitted]. There is nothing in this record to suggest that the Company promised the examinees that their scores would remain confidential in order to further parochial concerns or to frustrate subsequent Union attempts to process employee grievances. And it has not been suggested at any point in this proceeding that the Company's unilateral promise of confidentiality was in itself violative of the terms of the collective-bargaining agreement. Indeed, the Company presented evidence that disclosure of individual scores had in the past resulted in the harassment of some lower scoring examinees who had, as a result, left the Company.

Under these circumstances, any possible impairment of the function of the Union in processing the grievances of employees is more than justified by the interests served in conditioning the disclosure of the test scores upon the consent of the very employees whose grievance is being processed. The burden on the Union in this instance is minimal. The Company's interest in preserving employee confidence in the testing program is well founded.

In light of the sensitive nature of testing information, the minimal burden that compliance with the Company's offer would have placed on the Union,

From *Detroit Edison Co. v. National Labor Relations Board*, 440 U.S. 301 (1979). Adapted with permission of the author and publisher.

and the total absence of evidence that the Company had fabricated concern for employee confidentiality only to frustrate the Union in the discharge of its responsibilities, we are unable to sustain the Board in its conclusion that the Company, in resisting an unconsented-to disclosure of individual test results, violated the statutory obligation to bargain in good faith. . . . Accordingly, we hold that the order requiring the Company unconditionally to disclose the employee scores to the Union was erroneous. . . .

Confidentiality of Industrial Psychological Tests

Larry Eberlein

. . .

IMPLICATIONS FOR PROFESSIONAL PRACTICE

. . . The *Detroit Edison* case involved "in-house" psychologists who were seen to be part of management. Even with the best history of good labor relations, unions approach management with a certain degree of skepticism. Psychologists in such a practice must realize that their job responsibilities will be dictated in part by the collective agreement and can be changed by the collective bargaining process.

In any employment setting, psychologists are involved in deciding where their allegiance lies when inherent conflicts surface. The union's responsibility is to protect the collective rights of its members more than one individual's right. Psychologists must, therefore, clearly indicate the limitations of their role when dealing with union members. Since confidentiality is a privilege reserved to the client, the psychologist would not have breached an ethical duty in providing data to a duly authorized representative of the client. In such an event, however, the employee must consent and understand that he or she is delegating to the union the right to inspect psychological test results.

Consultants face a less severe problem as long as their role is clearly defined at the time a consulting contract is arranged (and is permissible under the labor-management agreements in force). Psychologists may be called on to deviate from their standard practice in some consulting requests and must be prepared to reject a contract as potentially involving conflict of interest or calling for unprofessional conduct. Ethical standards are only guidelines; psychologists should be prepared to deviate from them when substantial reason exists. A legal requirement or court order provides such a reason, and it becomes a matter of conscience whether a psychologist is willing to suffer the consequences of contempt of court or provide the information required by the appropriate legal process. . . .

It is basically clear from the history of this case that psychologists are having difficulty in convincing courts that the nature of psychological test results necessitates protection in all but the most serious cases. . . .

◆ ◆ ◆

Commentary: By far, the overarching point in Detroit Edison *is the Supreme Court's apparent agreement with the National Labor Relations Board that a federal law requiring the disclosure of relevant information cannot be defeated by the ethical standards of a private group like the APA. Thus, the decision in* Detroit Edison *implies that psychologists cannot rely solely on professional ethics and standards to protect them when they are faced with overriding obligations imposed by the law. In what other areas than testing may this conflict create problems for scientists and professionals?*

In any event, Standard 15.7 of the Standards for Testing states as a primary obligation that "test users should protect the security of test materials." Similarly, Standard 2.10 of the current Ethical Principles requires that psychologists "make reasonable efforts to maintain the integrity and security of tests and other assessment techniques consistent with law, contractual obligations, and in a manner that permits compliance with the requirements of this Ethics Code." Detroit Edison shows that there are obvious limits to protecting test security. For example, with the advent of televised trials, consider the position of the psychologist who is compelled by the court to exhibit and discuss the questions, results, and interpretation of such tests as intelligence scales, the Minnesota Multiphasic Personality Inventory, and projective instruments. And, of course, psychologists have no control over the conduct of judges. For example, in a case challenging the validity of the Wechsler and

Stanford-Binet scales—PASE v. Hannon, 506 F. Supp. 831 (N.D. Ill. 1980)—the judge, in evaluating the tests, disclosed all the questions and correct answers to both tests. So even though he held that the tests were not culturally biased, their security had been seriously compromised, if not destroyed. For a more complete discussion of these issues, see Bersoff, D.N. (1982). Larry P. and PASE: Judicial report cards on the validity of individual intelligence tests. In T. Kratochwill (Ed.), Advances in school psychology (Vol. 2, pp. 61–95). Hillsdale, NJ: Erlbaum.

The Release of Psychological Data to Nonexperts: Ethical and Legal Considerations

Daniel Tranel

. . .

A DEFINITION OF RAW PSYCHOLOGICAL DATA

What are raw psychological data? In keeping with the Ethical Principles, and following distinctions proposed by Matarazzo (1990) regarding the nature of psychological assessment and psychological testing, several different types of psychological information can be distinguished:

1. Written reports, in which the psychologist typically summarizes the history, test findings, and other pertinent data, and then presents conclusions, diagnoses, and perhaps recommendations and predictions.
2. Notes, which generally include the handwritten information recorded by a psychologist in the course of interviewing, observing, and testing a client or patient.
3. Scores, typically numerical, which can be raw (e.g., the number of items answered correctly on a test) or standardized (e.g., IQ scores, percentile scores).
4. Test stimuli, which are the actual items used by the psychologist to elicit responses from the client or patient that form the basis for determining levels of cognitive and behavioral function.
5. Responses (i.e., the actual verbal, written, or other responses generated by the client/patient to test stimuli).
6. Test manuals, which typically comprise, in addition to the test stimuli, information regarding

how the test was constructed, its reliability and validity, normative data, appropriate applications, and detailed instructions for administration.

SHARING RAW PSYCHOLOGICAL DATA WITH OTHERS

When a client or patient places his or her mental or emotional condition into litigation, this produces a waiver of privilege, and all pertinent information is "discoverable" by both sides of the case. Given that the privilege has been waived, there is usually no great concern regarding the sharing of written reports and summaries among different parties involved in a case. It is also generally accepted that notes, which are usually not considered to constitute raw data or results, may be shared among different parties in a case. . . .

A much different situation obtains, however, when it comes to the types of information defined in 3 to 6 above (viz., test scores, stimuli, responses, and manuals). The test scores, stimuli, and responses compose what is commonly known as raw psychological data, raw test results, or simply raw data [footnote omitted]. At the center of the problem is the fact that there is a direct conflict between law and ethics when it comes to the release of raw psychological data. The law says one thing ("Provide the data"); the ethics code says the opposite ("Do not provide the data"). Detailed below is a discussion of pertinent issues regarding this problem and a recommended course of action for resolving such a conflict.

From *Professional Psychology: Research and Practice, 25*, 33–38. Copyright 1994 by the American Psychological Association. Adapted with permission of the author and publisher.

PREVENTING MISUSE OF PSYCHOLOGICAL DATA

The new Ethical Principles, which went into effect officially on December 1, 1992, state the following in Ethical Standard 2.02(b):

> Psychologists refrain from misuse of assessment techniques, interventions, results, and interpretations and take reasonable steps to prevent others from misusing the information these techniques provide. This includes refraining from releasing raw test results or raw data to persons, other than to patients or clients as appropriate, who are not qualified to use such information.

It is clear that the APA has taken a position against the release of raw data to unqualified persons. There are two main reasons behind this, both of which pertain directly to several standards explicated in the new Ethical Principles (e.g., Sections 2.02, 2.06, 2.10).

Potential misuse.   Release of raw data creates numerous potentialities for misuse. For example, laypersons lack an appreciation of the context in which psychological test stimuli are administered and may reach erroneous conclusions about the meaning of individual answers. When this occurs, for example, in a courtroom, by lawyers, judges, and jurors, the ramifications of the errors may be great. . . . [A]nalysis of individual items taken out of context can be quite misleading. Add the likelihood that laypersons have limited understanding of how factors such as age, gender, and educational background may play a role in performance on the test, and one is left with a potentially extremely misleading depiction of the plaintiff's abilities.

Raw data may become part of the public domain.   Release of raw data may allow psychological test stimuli to become part of the public domain, the domain of information that is in principle accessible by virtually anyone. This opens up the possibility that test stimuli could be disseminated among the public, perhaps even widely. A potential consequence of this is that future test takers (i.e., persons receiving psychological tests) would not be naive. . . .

Most psychological tests, particularly those used in measurement of intellect, memory, and other aspects of cognition, assume complete or near-complete naivete on the part of the client or patient. (Even in the case of practice effects, which refer to improvements in test performance attributable to prior exposure to the test and not to a change in ability level, it is assumed that all test exposures have occurred under standard, controlled conditions prescribed by the test instructions.) Psychologists cannot risk invalidating tests due to widespread dissemination among the public. It is unreasonable and impractical that psychologists would have to recreate tests on a frequent basis. Thus onus would not be in the best interests of anyone, including psychologists, attorneys, and clients or patients. . . .

The new APA Ethical Principles imply that raw data should only be released to another qualified individual (i.e., someone who is competent to interpret the data). A qualified individual is someone who, by virtue of his or her training and experience, is in a position to appreciate fully the meaning of raw data, including considerations of reliability and validity. In most cases, this will be a licensed psychologist who meets recognized standards of training and experience. In most states, licensure can be taken as evidence that the psychologist has acquired a minimum level of knowledge regarding pertinent issues of reliability and validity, test construction, and psychological appraisal. Licensure also indicates (again, in most states) that the psychologist is responsible for operating in accordance with the Ethical Principles. For the types of raw data typically under consideration in personal injury litigation cases, such as raw test results from neuropsychological and psychological tests, the clearest example of a qualified recipient would be a licensed clinical psychologist or clinical neuropsychologist. . . .

A comment should also be made here regarding the statement in the Ethical Principles that raw test results or raw data may be released to "patients or clients as appropriate." This wording does not imply that raw data should be released directly to clients or patients but rather that it is appropriate for a psychologist to explain and interpret the findings to the client or patient and provide other pertinent feedback. In many circumstances, it would be appropriate for the client or patient to have access to the written report authored by the psychologist. (The client or patient has a legal right to this report in virtually all situations.) But with regard to raw data, including raw test results, it is not advisable in most cases to provide clients or patients with meaningless or misleading test scores, stimuli, and responses. This topic is dealt with directly in Section 2.09 of the Ethical Principles. . . .

A Recommended Course of Action for the Release of Raw Psychological Data

The APA Ethical Principles prohibit the release of raw data to unqualified individuals, and with rare exception, attorneys are not qualified individuals. A viable course of action if an attorney should request raw data from a psychologist (A) would be to advise the attorney to engage the consultation of another psychologist (B), who is qualified, by virtue of licensure, training, and experience, to receive the data. Psychologist A then could send the raw data to Psychologist B (provided the client or patient has given appropriate consent). Psychologist B could then interpret the data to the attorney. Needless to say, Psychologist B must operate under the same rules and standards of ethics and confidentiality as Psychologist A.

By and large, attorneys and judges are reasonably understanding of the dilemma faced by psychologists regarding the sharing of raw data. When given an explanation about why psychologists are restricted from releasing raw data to unqualified persons, attorneys and judges tend to be amenable to the course of action recommended above. This explanation is likely to be more effective, however, if the particular reasons are explained (e.g., that psychologists cannot afford to have test stimuli disseminated in the public domain; that raw data are difficult or impossible for a nonexpert to interpret), rather than simply citing the Ethical Principles that prohibit such release.

There may be instances in which attorneys will be quite insistent on receiving raw data and will go to considerable lengths to secure it. In the well-known series of books by Ziskin and Faust (1988; Faust et al., 1991), the authors recommend strongly that lawyers secure raw data from psychologists in

all cases. Lawyers familiar with this series of books can be expected to make adamant requests for raw data. The principal aim of this strategy, though, is to have an opportunity to scrutinize the psychologist's work product for incorrect scoring, miscalculations, misuse of test manuals, and other errors that might be used by the opposing attorney to impugn the psychologist's competence. Obviously another psychologist would be in a much better position than the attorney to conduct such an analysis; thus, there would appear to be little justification for not following the course of action recommended above (i.e., insisting that the attorney secure the consultation of a qualified expert). In short, there is considerable precedent, legal and professional, for holding to the position that the raw data can only be sent to another qualified individual, and this course of action should be pursued unless there are unusually compelling reasons not to do so.

. . .

TEST MANUALS

An attorney or the court will occasionally request the test manuals on which the psychologist relied to score and interpret psychological tests. The considerations here are much the same as those that pertain to the release of other raw psychological data— test manuals should not be released to unqualified persons. Several portions of the Ethical Principles speak to this issue:

> Psychologists do not promote the use of psychological assessment techniques by unqualified persons. (2.06)
>
> Psychologists make reasonable efforts to maintain the integrity and security of tests and other assessment techniques consistent with law, contractual obligations, and in a manner that permits compliance with the requirements of this Ethics Code. (2.10)

Standard 2.02(b), quoted earlier, also speaks to this issue. Test manuals contain data and information that are part of a specialized discipline (e.g., psychological appraisal, neuropsychological assessment). It is simply not permissible for a layperson (unqualified individual) to attempt to use such information. Use and dissemination of such information by an unqualified person could reduce or vitiate entirely the value of the tests. Many manuals are distributed by reputable test publishers, who require evidence of purchaser qualification (e.g., a license to practice psychology) before selling such manuals. If publishers fail to respect such guidelines and engage in practices that would be considered a violation of law and APA Ethics, this matter should be brought to the attention of the APA. Ziskin and Faust (1988) recommend that lawyers hire an expert consultant to deal with the types of information that are part of test manuals.

. . .

TEST SCORES

. . . [T]est scores, both raw and standardized, constitute yet another domain of psychological information that may be requested for release. When the requestor is a qualified person (i.e., a licensed psychologist), there is no problem in releasing the scores. In fact, in many cases it is actually the scores (rather than the test forms, responses, etc.) in which the requesting psychologist is most interested (e.g., for purposes of comparing performances across time). There are a few other special situations, such as in the determination of disability by social security officials or in a worker's compensation claim, in which it may be permissible to release test scores. These agencies often have employees with special expertise in the interpretation of psychological data (especially IQ scores). Provided the psychologist is confident the test scores will be used appropriately, it is reasonable in these situations to provide requested test scores (assuming the client or patient has given appropriate consent).

For unqualified persons, the matter of releasing test scores should be treated in the same way as the release of other raw psychological data. That is, psychologists should refrain from releasing scores to unqualified individuals, and if asked for such information by attorneys or other nonexperts, psychologists should follow a course of action along the lines elaborated here earlier under the heading *A Recommended Course of Action for the Release of Raw Psychological Data.*

. . .

OTHER CONSIDERATIONS

. . .

. . . [T]he attitude or demeanor of the psychologist can influence substantially the degree of cooperation from members of the legal profession (lawyers, judges, etc.). When an attorney senses that the psychologist is trying to conceal something, or to resist cooperation, the attorney is likely to mount an all-out effort to get everything possible out of the psychologist. By contrast, if the attorney senses that the psychologist is attempting to cooperate fully with the spirit of the proceedings, within the bounds of his or her ethical principles, the attorney is far more likely to go along with the psychologist's recommended course of action. The Ethical Principles do not, in fact, have force of law; thus, it is very much in the best interest of psychologists to solicit cooperation and collegiality from attorneys. . . .

References

American Psychological Association. (1992). Ethical principles of psychologists and code of conduct. *American Psychologist, 47,* 1597–1611.

Faust, D., Ziskin, J., & Hiers, J. B. (1991). *Brain damage claims: Coping with neuropsychological evidence* (Vol. 1–2). Los Angeles: Law and Psychology Press.

Matarazzo, J. D. (1990). Psychological assessment versus psychological testing: Validation from Binet to the school, clinic, and courtroom. *American Psychologist, 45,* 999–1017.

Ziskin, J., & Faust, D. (1988). *Coping with psychiatric and psychological testimony* (4th ed., Vols. 1–3). Marina del Rey, CA: Law and Psychology Press.

◆　◆　◆

Commentary: Tranel raises many significant issues. It would certainly compromise many single-form instruments, such as individually administered intelligence scales, if the questions and the manuals for scoring answers were widely disseminated (although, as I have noted, an Illinois federal judge has already done this). But, is not Tranel's assertion that attorneys and their clients are not qualified to use the information that raw data imparts paternalistic? More fundamentally, is it not just plain wrong when he states that Standard 2.02(b) does not really mean that patients or clients may receive raw data? The least twisted reading of that provision— that psychologists refrain "from releasing raw test results or raw data to persons, other than to patients or clients as appropriate"—states the opposite. The only qualification is the "as appropriate" language, a condition that, unfortunately, is vague and unexplained. But if, in the main, clients can obtain their own raw data, does it not follow that their legal representatives, at the client's request, should also have access to those data? Whatever one's interpretation of the disclosure principles in the Ethical Principles, it is better to anticipate problems rather than to confront them after the fact. What steps can psychologists take at the initiation of an assessment to avoid or minimize the real problems that Tranel has brought to our attention?

Ethical and Professional Considerations in Psychological Assessment

David J. Berndt

. . .

. . . Two different kinds of justifications have been put forth for sharing much, if not all, of the material with the person who is tested. One justification is that assessment instruments may be usefully employed as an adjunctive mode of treatment (e.g., Harrison, 1965; Harrower, 1960). Others (e.g., Ladkin & Levine, 1976) have argued that it is the patient's right to know and that withholding information from the client reinforces the sick role by adding the authority of the psychological battery to the diagnosis.

The current investigation was designed to provide descriptive data about professional and ethical practices of psychologists who administer, interpret, and store the results of psychological assessment. . . .

Respondents were asked a series of questions on how they describe their role to the patient and on how they obtain informed consent. Two open-ended questions concerning a hypothetical consultation from a psychiatrist or colleague asked: "How would you usually introduce your role to the patient?" and "Would you give an example of informed consent?" Typical responses to the question about the role of the tester included some variant of the following: "Dr. _____ has asked me to see you (give you some psychological tests) today, to help you (try and understand yourself)." Nearly all respondents either left it at that or indicated that they considered rapport, willingness to proceed, or the patient's compliance as sufficient. Most also stressed that they attempted to ensure that the patient understood what the testing procedure was, and many stressed that they ex-plored with the patient full understanding of the consultation. A few respondents indicated that they offered to discuss the testing after it was over. In response to more structured questions, 18% of the respondents indicated that they did not attempt to get informed consent for testing, and oral consent was obtained in a 3:1 ratio over written.

The respondents were also asked to respond to a question regarding the feedback process, but they rarely gave written feedback when it was not requested (see Table 1). On the other hand, it was also infrequent for the respondents to refuse to discuss the results. Overall, the respondents tended to agree most with an approach that utilized clinical judgment and took the patient's needs into account. Testing appeared to be frequently used as a supplement to therapy.

The percentage of respondents who indicated how likely they were to go over test results with the subject for each test is listed in Table 2. Comparing the 2 "least likely" points on the 5-point scale for each test, note that results from the Rorschach (41%), Projective Drawings (38%), and the Thematic Apperception Test (34%) are least likely to be shared; there appears to be less concern over sharing results of the IQ instruments (8%) or the Minnesota Multiphasic Personality Inventory (20%). Despite the apparent trend to share results of more objective measures and not go over the more projective measures, more respondents were likely (46%) to share their results of the Rorschach than not share them. . . .

Finally, another set of questions inquired about

TABLE 1

Average Likert Scale Ratings Indicating Feedback Techniques Preferred by Respondents

Response	M	SD
If a patient or research subject asks you what the testing results are, how often do you typically		
Refuse to discuss the results with the person?	1.84	1.23
Ask the patient to have the referral source (e.g., psychiatrist) go over the results?	3.53	1.41
Discuss as little as possible, only talking in vague generalities?	2.10	1.15
Discuss only what the patient can readily understand and use?	3.86	.99
Give full disclosure, avoiding material that would be detrimental in your clinical judgment?	3.23	1.33
Actively share as much of the results as time pemits with the patient, believing testing can be used as a supplement to therapy?	3.47	1.15
Always tell the patient everything because I believe they have a right to know?	2.89	1.35
Make a practice of giving the patient a written report when they ask for such information?	2.67	1.54
Give all the patients you test written feedback even if they don't ask?	1.29	.59

Note. Anchor points on the 5-point Likert Scale were 1 (never) and 5 (always).

---

record-keeping practices. A high percentage (91%) of all respondents had kept a record of old test batteries in which they had the ability to find a particular patient's file. For those who kept old batteries on file, the oldest record ranged from 2 years to 35 years ($M = 12.8$ years). Only 24% maintained they would not release their personal testing files to an outside agency if the agency had the patient's consent, whereas 59% would refuse to supply it to the patient. As far as safety was concerned, 16% admitted to not locking their files, and only 12% used a master code that kept the patient's name coded and in a separate place from the data.

DISCUSSION

. . . Many of the respondents fall into one of two groups. One group enthusiastically advocated sharing most if not all of the information with the patient; as one respondent put it, "using tests as a self-discovery procedure typically results in much growth. . . . I personally feel that using tests in this

---

TABLE 2

Likelihood That Respondents Would Share Specific Assessment Instruments With Their Clients

Instrument	Likert scale				
	1	2	3	4	5
Rorschach	11[a]	30	13	19	27
MMPI	10	10	11	23	46
Projective Drawings	15	23	23	8	31
IQ instruments	4	4	12	35	45
Bender-Gestalt	7	20	18	27	28
Sentence Completion	5	22	24	24	25
Personality Measures	9	16	18	25	32
Thematic Apperception Test	8	26	24	20	22

Note. Likert Scale ranged from 1 (not at all) to 5 (likely). Number of subjects varied among instruments.
MMPI = Minnesota Multiphasic Personality Inventory.
[a]All figures represent percentage of respondents agreeing to points on a 5-point scale (rows sum to 100%).

manner is worth 1–3 months of therapy." A second group of respondents favored sharing some information with the client but had diverse views on how much should be shared. Most felt that as much as could be used by the patient should be shared, but considerable disagreement existed about the fragility of patients. Some advocated sharing only positive results; others opted for consciously experienced phenomena; and others insisted that if it was too troublesome for the patient, they probably would not hear it.

. . . A few indicated that sharing the information was desirable but that institutional constraints, especially lack of time, prevented using tests in this preferred manner. Others commented on the importance of using tests as a supplement to therapy only when one is treating the patient oneself. . . . When the patient is seen in a consultation, coordination with the consultant is important, and patient feedback is sometimes resented. . . .

As for specifics of feedback, respondents rarely gave written feedback, especially if it was not requested; but they usually did not refuse a patient's request to discuss the information. They tended to avoid talking in vague generalities. Rather, they most frequently discussed what the patient could readily understand and use. They also asked the patient to go over the results with the referral source, although as many commented, it depended on the clinical skills of the person who referred the patient. Blind consumerism ("I always tell my patient everything because I believe they have a right to know"), although sometimes advocated, was less frequent than a broader emphasis on clinical judgment used to temper complete disclosure. . . .

The data on how the tester presents the assessor's role indicate a general lack of agreement. Although a majority, but by no means all, of the respondents indicated that they explained to the patient what the testing would be like, several commented that rapport or the willingness to proceed was adequate. In some states, such as Illinois, assessment is considered by the law to be a form of treatment and, hence may be subject to informed consent. Additionally, the ethical standards compel psychologists to see to it that clients understand both the nature and purposes of not only the test results but the tests themselves.

The results on the record-keeping practices also raise some questions. Nearly all of the respondents kept old records on file, and most of them had files dating quite far back. These files were typically stored in locked places; however, only 12% kept the names in a separate code book, apart from the data. Additionally, 76% said they would release such information to an outside agency, with the patient's consent. This implies that the data are stored with the name either attached or linked in some way to the data. . . . Safely locking the data is important, but clearly not sufficient. . . .

References

Harrison, R. Thematic apperceptive methods. In B. Wolman (Ed.), *Handbook of clinical psychology*. New York: McGraw-Hill, 1965.

Harrower, M. Projective counseling—a psychotherapeutic technique. In M. Harrower, P. Vorhaus, M. Roman, & G. Bauman (Eds.), *Creative variations in the projective technique*. Springfield, Ill.: Charles C Thomas, 1960.

Ladkin, J. F., & Levine, L. Interpreting psychological test results to the hospitalized consumer. *Professional Psychology*, 1976, 7, 161–166.

The Ethical Practice of School Psychology: A Rebuttal and Suggested Model

Donald N. Bersoff

. . .

The following is not meant to be an all-encompassing model, but is limited to the process of assessment. It rests on three assumptions:

1. Test responses are a function not only of the characteristics of the organism to whom the test is administered but also of the stimulus properties of the test and the background or environments (e.g., instructions, setting, nature of the experimenter) in which the test is administered (Fiske, 1967; Hamilton, 1970; Murstein, 1965; Sattler & Theye, 1967).

2. Each person perceives the testing situation differently and thus develops an idiosyncratic style or strategy in responding to test material. Without discerning these strategies, the validity of test interpretation is highly attenuated (Fulkerson, 1965).

3. Parents are at least equally capable as the school staff in deciding what is best for their children (Goldman, 1971).

Accepting these assumptions allows the psychologist to include the client in all aspects of the evaluation. In fact, it makes it imperative that he do so if he wants to obtain data that are not obfuscated by mistrust, misunderstanding, and the inhibition of self-disclosure. Because we have not included the client (both the child and his parents) in the assessment transaction it is possible that most of our test data and their subsequent interpretation may be of doubtful veracity. As Jourard (1971) conjectured,

> the millions of psychometric tests mildewing in agency files might be lies told by untrusting clients and patients

to untrustworthy functionaries. If psychologists were serving the interests of bureaucracies, wittingly or unwittingly, in their . . . activities, then it would be quite proper for . . . patients not to trust us; functionaries masquerading as professionals are not to be trusted too far. [p. 2]

If we are to achieve intimate, ethical relationships consonant with the empirical data concerning the interactive nature of test productions, it may be necessary to reconceive of the assessment process as one in which there is mutual disclosure. In a series of papers, Fischer (1970, 1971a, 1971b, 1972, in press-a, in press-b) detailed both the theoretical foundations and the practical expression of just such a relationship in which tester and client become "coevaluators" (Fischer, 1970). Specifically, the following steps are recommended.

1. *Coadvisement.* This is an expansion of the principle of informed consent. The psychologist tells the child and his parents how he functions; informs them of the identity of the referral agent and the purpose for referral; and describes the nature of the assessment devices he will use, the merits and limitations of those devices, what kinds of information will be put in a report, and who might eventually read the report. The psychologist then asks the child to tell how he perceives the purposes of testing and what he feels the consequences of such an evaluation might be. The psychologist secures agreement from the child and his parents to proceed with the

assessment subsequent to full and mutual disclosure concerning the purposes of the evaluation.

2. *Sharing impressions.* Immediately after the administration of the psychometric instruments the psychologist, the child, and his parents engage in a dialogue in which the psychologist gives his interpretation of the child's test behavior as he has just experienced it. By conferring with the child he further attempts to extrapolate from the testing situation to other situations similar to the one represented by the test stimuli. Such a dialogue provides immediate feedback to the child about how others perceive his behavior and enables the assessor to check out hypotheses about how equivalent the test behavior observed is to actual classroom behavior and to develop possible strategies he may use to intervene in the instructional environment (see Fischer, 1970, for an example of how such an interaction might proceed). It also gives the child a chance to disagree with the psychologist's initial interpretations and to offer his perceptions about his own behavior. Rather than assuming that the behavior observed in the testing situation can be extrapolated to all other situations, the psychologist has an opportunity to discover the situations or contexts in which the behavior does occur. Such an approach has been variously called psychosituational (Bersoff, 1971a; Bersoff & Grieger, 1971) or contextual (Fischer, in press-a) assessment, but whatever its title, such a method prevents the child from being mislabeled and interpretations of his behavior from being overgeneralized.

3. *Critique of the written evaluation.* This concludes the sequence of mutually disclosing events. After the evaluation is complete and the psychologist has prepared his report, he shows the child and his parents a copy of the written evaluation. This insures that the report will be recorded so that it is understandable to all concerned. In addition, as Fischer (1970) described,

> This procedure also produces a beneficial side effect: Knowing that his client is going to read his report, the psychologist strives all the more to be true to him, to capture his world as well as words allow, and to avoid overstate-

ments, unintended implications, and loose descriptions [p. 74].

Then, the child and his parents are given the opportunity to clarify the points made, to add further material, and, if there is disagreement between the psychologist and the clients, to provide a dissenting view (in writing if warranted). Finally, the psychologist receives permission to disseminate the report to those whom the child and his parents agree to.

There is no doubt that adopting such an approach requires much rethinking and rebehaving on the part of school psychologists. . . . Admittedly, there may be some difficulty in implementing the approach fully. . . . A comment by Leo Goldman (1971), arguing against psychological secrecy and offering some suggestions for its reduction, may help put the matter in perspective:

> All of this may sound very unappealing to psychologists who would prefer to see themselves as the "good guys" who are there just to help people and make the world a better place. Unfortunately, that just isn't a viable arrangement when one is a member of the staff of a public school serving a community which contains diverse social, ethnic, and political elements. And it certainly is not possible in any pure sense in a setting such as the public schools, where the "clients" are not clients at all but mostly a captive, involuntary audience. We will just have to find a way to work out agreements in each school system . . . so that the professional helpers can do their thing, while the students and their families retain the power to decide *whether* they will be helped, what personal information they will divulge, and what the school may release to anyone. Although this will undoubtedly cramp our style to some extent, it will on the whole make for a healthier social institution than we now have. [p. 11]

The suggestions made in this article for reorienting

assessment will hopefully move us toward making the school a healthier social institution. At the very least we will treat the child and his parents as our equals, with the right to participate in the interpretations and decisions that will directly affect their lives. Certainly, the chances of damaging diagnoses and class placements will be lessened. And those diagnoses and placements that are made will have been a "co-constituted" decision, agreed on by those affected, increasing the probability of greater cooperation in making the changes that *all* have deemed appropriate.

References

Bersoff, D. N. "Current functioning" myth: An overlooked fallacy in psychological assessment. *Journal of Consulting and Clinical Psychology,* 1971, *37,* 391–393. (a)

Bersoff, D. N., & Grieger, R. M. An interview model for the psychosituational assessment of children's behavior. *American Journal of Orthopsychiatry,* 1971, *41,* 483–493.

Fischer, C. T. The testee as co-evaluator. *Journal of Counseling Psychology,* 1970, *17,* 70–76.

Fischer, C. T. Paradigm changes which allow sharing of "results" with the client. In S. L. Brodsky (Chm.), *Shared Results and Open Files With the Client: Professional Responsibility or Effective Involvement.* Symposium presented at the annual meeting of the American Psychological Association, Washington, D.C., September 1971. (a)

Fischer, C. T. Toward the structure of privacy: Implications for psychological assessment. In A. Giorgi, W. F. Fischer, & R. vonEckartsberg (Eds.), *Duquesne studies in phenomenological psychology.* Pittsburgh: Duquesne University Press, 1971. (b)

Fischer, C. T. (1972). Paradigm changes which allow sharing of results. *Professional Psychology, 3,* 364–369.

Fischer, C. T. Contextual approach to assessment. *Journal of Community Mental Health,* in press. (a)

Fischer, C. T. A theme for the child-advocate: Sharable everyday life data of the child-in-the-world. *Journal of Clinical Child Psychology,* in press. (b)

Fiske, D. W. The subject reacts to tests. *American Psychologist,* 1967, *22,* 287–296.

Fulkerson, S. C. Some implications of the new cognitive theory for projective tests. *Journal of Consulting Psychology,* 1965, *29,* 191–197.

Goldman, L. Psychological secrecy and openness in the public schools. In S. L. Brodsky (Chm.), *Shared Results and Open Files With the Client: Professional Responsibility or Effective Involvement.* Symposium presented at the annual meeting of the American Psychological Association, Washington, D.C., September 1971.

Hamilton, J. Stimulus variables in clinical evaluation. *Professional Psychology,* 1970, *1,* 151–153.

Jourard, S. M. Some reflections on a quiet revolution. In S. L. Brodsky (Chm.), *Shared Results and Open Files With the Client: Professional Responsibility or Effective Involvement.* Symposium presented at the annual meeting of the American Psychological Association, Washington, D.C., September 1971.

Murstein, B. I. Assumptions, adaptation level, and projective techniques. In B. I. Murstein (Ed.), *Handbook of projective techniques.* New York: Basic Books, 1965.

Sattler, J. M., & Theye, F. Procedural, situational, and interpersonal variables in individual intelligence testing. *Psychological Bulletin,* 1967, *68,* 347–361.

◆ ◆ ◆

Commentary: In almost all school systems, parental involvement in and consent for psychological or psychoeducational evaluations conducted on children suspected of being, or already labeled as, disabled are controlled by federal law and regulations. In 1975, Congress enacted the Education for All Handicapped Children's Act (Public Law 94-142), now amended as the Individuals With Disabilities in Education Act, and the administrative agency charged with enforcing the act promulgated implementing and detailed regulations. The following, found in Title 34 of the Code of Federal Regulations, (34 C.F.R. § 300.504–505) instructs school systems on the minimum obligations it must fulfill prior to testing:

> (a) Notice. Written notice that meets the requirements of § 300.505 must be given to the parents of a child with a disability a reasonable time before the public agency—
> (1) Proposes to initiate or change the identification, evaluation, or educational placement of the child or the provision of FAPE[1] to the child; or
> (2) Refuses to initiate or change the identi-

---

[1] *Ed. note:* FAPE stands for *free appropriate public education.*

fication, evaluation, or educational placement of the child or the provision of FAPE to the child.

(b) Consent; procedures if a parent refuses consent.

(1) Parental consent must be obtained before—

(i) Conducting a preplacement evaluation; and

(ii) Initial placement of a child with a disability in a program providing special education and related services.

(2) If State law requires parental consent before a child with a disability is evaluated or initially provided special education and related services, State procedures govern the public agency in overriding a parent's refusal to consent.

(3) If there is no State law requiring consent before a child with a disability is evaluated or initially provided special education and related services, the public agency may use the hearing procedures in §§ 300.506–300.508 to determine if the child may be evaluated or initially provided special education and related services without parental consent. If it does so and the hearing officer upholds the agency, the agency may evaluate or initially provide special education and related services to the child without the parent's consent, subject to the parent's rights under §§ 300.510–300.513. . . .

§ 300.505 CONTENT OF NOTICE

(a) The notice under § 300.504 must include—

(1) A full explanation of all of the procedural safeguards available to the parents under § 300.500, §§ 300.502–300.515, and §§ 300.562–300.569;

(2) A description of the action proposed or refused by the agency, an explanation of why the agency proposes or refuses to take the action, and a description of any options the agency considered and the rea-

sons why those options were rejected;

(3) A description of each evaluation procedure, test, record, or report the agency uses as a basis for the proposal or refusal; and

(4) A description of any other factors that are relevant to the agency's proposal or refusal.

(b) The notice must be—

(1) Written in language understandable to the general public; and

(2) Provided in the native language of the parent or other mode of communication used by the parent, unless it is clearly not feasible to do so.

(c) If the native language or other mode of communication of the parent is not a written language, the SEA [state education agency] or LEA [local education agency] shall take steps to ensure—

(1) That the notice is translated orally or by other means to the parent in his or her native language or other mode of communication;

(2) That the parent understands the content of the notice; and

(3) That there is written evidence that the requirements in paragraphs (c)(1) and (2) of this section have been met.

Although these regulations have salutary benefits in that they compel school systems to involve parents in material decisions, the children themselves do not have the right to notice or consent. Given the preceding articles, is this a serious omission or simply recognition that the law gives parents the right to act as children's primary decision makers?

For a more complete explanation of the parental consent and notice rules under Public Law 94-142 and its regulations, see Pryzwansky, W. B., & Bersoff, D. N. (1978). Parental consent for psychological evaluations: Legal, ethical, and practical considerations. Journal of School Psychology, 16, 274–281.

In addition to the Standards for Educational and Psychological Testing, cited earlier in this chapter, another document—one more directly related to practitioners—is General Guidelines for Providers of Psycho-

logical Services, 1987, published in American Psychologist, *42, 712–723. The General Guidelines "are a set of aspirational statements" derived from the APA's 1981 Ethical Principles. Nevertheless, where the guidelines track the Ethical Principles, psychologists "have the same responsibility to uphold these specific General Guidelines as they would the corresponding Ethical Principles" (1987, p. 712).*

Guideline 2.3.7 requires psychologists to "establish and maintain a system that protects the confidentiality of their users' [a term that includes recipients of psychological services] records" (p. 717; also see Standards 2.02(b), 5.04, and 5.10 of the 1992 Ethical Principles). In the commentary following Guideline 2.3.7, APA addresses the right of clients to information contained in their records:

> *Users have the right to information in their agency records and to be informed as to any regulations that govern the release of such information. However, the records are the property of the psychologist or of the facility in which the psychologist works and are, therefore, under the control of the psychologist or of the facility. Users have the right to examine such psychological records. Preferably such examination should be in the presence of a psychologist who judges how best to explain the material in a meaningful and useful manner.*
>
> *In school settings, parents have the legal right to examine such psychological records, preferably in the presence of a psychologist. In the event that a family moves to another school system, the parents have the legal right to examine a copy of such records from the former school in the new*

school setting. In either circumstances, the rationale for allowing parents to examine such records is to assure that parents are not in a disadvantaged position if they choose to challenge a school's decision regarding the child. Disclosure of such psychological information in the records from a former school is conducted under secure conditions: such records have been transmitted to the new school to a psychologist under whose supervision the records may be examined. Psychologists and the institutions in which they work have written policy regarding the storage and access of pupils' records. Parents are informed of the results of a psychological assessment of their child in a form most meaningful and useful to the parents.

> *Raw psychological data (e.g., test protocols, therapy or interview notes, or questionnaire returns) in which a user is identified are ordinarily released only with the written consent of the user or of the user's legal representative, and are released only to a person recognized by the psychologist as competent to interpret the data. Any use made of psychological reports, records, or data for research or training purposes is consistent with this General Guideline. . . . (1987, pp. 717–718)*

Does this guideline comport or conflict with the 1992 Ethical Principles?

More recently, two of APA's governing bodies sought to provide guidance concerning the release of information gleaned from psychological assessments. The first document was approved by the APA Council of Representatives and is thus considered APA policy.

Statement on the Disclosure of Test Data

Committee on Psychological Tests and Assessment, American Psychological Association

PREAMBLE

The issue of disclosure of test data raises a number of concerns for psychologists who develop, validate, and use tests in a variety of settings. The statement that follows was formulated to help psychologists with these issues. Its intent is to be consistent with the *Ethical Principles of Psychologists and Code of Conduct* (APA, 1992; hereinafter referred to as the Ethics Code) and the *Standards for Educational and Psychological Testing* (1985; hereinafter referred to as the Testing Standards).

. . .

GENERAL ISSUES

Test data include an individual's test results, raw test data, records, written/computer-generated reports, global scores or individual scale scores, and test materials such as test protocols, manuals, test items, scoring keys or algorithms, and any other materials considered secure by the test developer or publisher.

. . .

Psychologists should be aware that professional standards and practices as well as legal mandates governing the disclosure of test data often differ substantially depending on the setting, intended purpose, and use of testing. At times, this statement, and APA standards, may conflict with legal mandates, organizational or institutional requirements. When such conflicts arise, psychologists should attempt to identify the relevant issues, make known their commitment to relevant standards, and attempt to resolve them in a way that, to the extent feasible, conforms both to law and professional practice as required by the Ethics Code (APA, 1992), licensing regulations, and other relevant standards.

ACCESS TO TEST DATA

Psychologists, and their employing organizations and institutions, may develop formal procedures and policies to address the retention, review, and release of test data. Psychologists generally discuss limitations on confidentiality or disclosure of test data and test results with test takers, individuals, and organizational clients prior to testing. In this way, psychologists can help to minimize any misunderstanding concerning the release of such confidential and secure test data. . . .

APA's Ethics Code (1992) and *Record Keeping Guidelines* (1993) each contain provisions which address the maintenance and access of confidential psychological records. When appropriate, psychologists should consider that there may be conflict among the confidentiality rights of test takers, contractual obligations with test publishers, and other relevant parties (e.g., third-party payers).

INFORMING THE TEST TAKER OF THE PURPOSE, USE, AND RESULTS OF TESTING

Psychologists usually obtain informed consent from test takers or their legal representatives prior to the testing, except when the nature of the testing does not require such consent (e.g., some types of employment testing, court-ordered assessment). Even when consent is not required, it may be desirable to obtain it. Consent may also be required when an evaluation is requested by an attorney rather than ordered by the court. Informed consent implies the test taker or his/her representative has agreed to the testing after having been informed, prior to testing, of the reasons for testing, the intended use and its range of possible consequences, what testing information will be released, and to whom testing information will be released.

. . .

Following the completion and scoring of the test, psychologists should also provide test takers with explanations of test results when the psychologist's role does not prevent such explanations and when the psychologist has explained possible limitations to this explanation before testing (APA, 1992; Standards 1.07, "Describing the Nature and Results of Psychological Services," and 2.09, "Explaining Assessment Results"). Both the Ethics Code (APA, 1992) and Testing Standards (1985) recognize exceptions to furnishing test results and explanations to clients. Release and explanation of test data may not be required when testing is mandated by law, when testing is conducted as part of an admissions or employment screening process (APA, 1985, Standard 16.1) or, in some organizational consulting, security screening and forensic evaluations (APA, 1992, Standard 2.09, "Explaining Assessment Results"). When appropriate, psychologists inform individuals of these limitations at the outset of testing.

. . . [W]hen test scores or reports are released to test takers or other persons or institutions (e.g., parents, guardians, teachers, human resource departments, legal authorities), psychologists should make reasonable efforts to provide understandable explanations concerning the nature, purposes, and results of the testing (e.g., an explanation of what the scores mean, their confidence intervals, any significant reservations they have about the accuracy or limitations of their interpretations) and how scores will be used.

RELEASING DATA WITH OR WITHOUT THE CONSENT OF THE TEST TAKER

Test data identified by the names of individual test takers are usually not released to any person, third-party payer, or institution without the informed consent of the test taker, the test taker's parent or guardian, or organizational client or legal representatives. Whether such consent is provided or not required (see Section III above), psychologists may still attempt to limit access to test data to only qualified professionals.

. . .

When the client's intention to waive confidentiality is viewed by the psychologist to be contrary to the client's best interest, the psychologist usually discusses the implications of releasing psychological information. The psychologist usually assists the client in limiting disclosure only to information required by the present circumstances and only to other qualified professionals.

. . .

RELEASE OF DATA AND TEST SECURITY

. . .

Disclosure of secure testing materials (e.g., test items, test scoring, or test protocols) to unqualified persons may decrease the test's validity. Availability of test items to an unqualified person can not only render the test invalid for any future use with that individual, but also jeopardizes the security and integrity of the test for other persons who may be exposed to test items and responses. Such release imposes very concrete harm to the general public—loss of effective assessment tools. Because there are a limited number of standardized psychological tests considered appropriate for a given purpose (in some instances only a single instrument), they cannot easily be replaced or substituted if an individual obtains prior knowledge of item content or the security of the test is otherwise compromised.

Development and refinement of items and norms for individual intelligence tests, personality assessment techniques, and achievement tests often require many years of research and considerable effort and expense. Improper disclosure of test items or other test materials also may result in damage to those parties which have developed or have ownership in the test and possibly result in breach of contract claims against psychologists who violate the terms of their test purchase or lease agreements.

RELEASING DATA TO UNQUALIFIED PERSONS

Psychologists usually inform persons or agencies requesting test data of the psychologist's obligations to the Ethics Code (APA, 1992) and professional standards and practices, which includes taking reasonable steps to limit the release of test data to persons qualified to use such information.

Any release of data must conform to the Ethics Code (APA, 1992), which requires psychologists to refrain from misuse of assessment techniques, results, and interpretations and to take reasonable steps to prevent misuse of assessment results by others. Misuse includes releasing test data to unqualified persons. The Testing Standards (1985; Standard 6.6) note that responsibility for test use should only be assumed by and delegated to persons with training and experience necessary to handle these responsibilities in a professional and technically adequate manner. Test users should be knowledgeable about a variety of complex issues, perform a variety of technical activities, and be able to use professional judgment. The primary concern of releasing test data to individuals who are not competent to interpret them, including the limitations of the data, is that the data will be misused, having potentially harmful effects on the client, patient, or others. In addition, untrained and/or unqualified individuals might make harmful and misguided decisions based on a misunderstanding of the test data. The psychologist's responsibilities extend to raw test materials such as responses to test items or recording of observations during assessment that may be contained in test protocols or testing records.

PROTECTING COPYRIGHT INTERESTS WHEN RELEASING DATA

Tests and test protocols are generally protected by the federal copyright laws and usually may not be copied without permission of the copyright holder. Psychologists mandated by law or regulation to provide copies of a test, test manual, or test protocols need to consider copyright laws which may potentially be violated by releasing such materials.

It is prudent for psychologists to be familiar with the terms of their test purchase or lease agreements with test publishers as well as reasonably informed about relevant provisions of the federal copyright laws. Psychologists may wish to consult with test publishers and/or knowledgeable experts to resolve possible conflicts before releasing specific test materials to ensure that the copyright and proprietary interests of the test publisher are not compromised.

CONFORMING TO FEDERAL AND STATE STATUTES AND RULES, REGULATORY MANDATES, AND INSTITUTIONAL/ ORGANIZATIONAL RULES AND REQUIREMENTS

Federal and state statutes, federal/state rules and regulations, and court precedents address disclosure requirements that vary by the setting, use or purpose of testing, and the party requesting disclosure. Court decisions have been largely case specific, that is, decisions based on the specific facts of a case, usually balancing the rights of participants with the degree to which the protected information is considered necessary for resolution of legal issues. There may also be additional constitutional, statutory, or common-law privacy protections governing test disclosure. Therefore, it is advisable for psychologists to become informed about applicable legal constraints governing requests for test information disclosure in their state and in a specific situation.

RELEASING TEST DATA TO THIRD-PARTY PAYERS

Third-party payers (e.g., health insurance organizations, health maintenance organizations) and employers (when self-insured or for other purposes such as disability determination or leave approval) sometimes request test data in determining a client's eligibility for services or reimbursement for a psychologist who has provided testing or assessment services. Psychologists often ask clients or their legal guardians to sign a written release which acknowledges consent for the release of such records to appropriate health insurance organizations. Such records often are released in written form and may include or exclude actual test scores. However, psychologists exert special care concerning release of secure test materials (e.g., protocols, test items) and inform the requesting parties of relevant ethical standards and any contractual obligations which restrict the release of such materials.

RELEASING TEST DATA WHEN THE ORGANIZATION IS THE CLIENT

. . .

Psychologists do retain professional responsibilities to test takers even when the client is an organization. In such circumstances, psychologists working for organizational clients should attempt to anticipate possible competing objectives and clarify with both the organizational client and test takers how such conflicts can be resolved or prevented. In many instances the nature of the psychologist's role within the organization (employee or consultant) and organizational policies will prevent disclosure of test data to individual test takers. In circumstances of legally mandated disclosure of tests or test records in organizational contexts, psychologists should consider attempting to assure appropriate protection of any released tests and test records (e.g., materials in possession of government entities could be subject to disclosure under state or federal freedom of information laws).

The Principles for the Validation and Use of Personnel Selection Procedures (Society for Industrial and Organizational Psychology, 1987) provides more guidance on types of test data and materials deemed appropriate for release within an organization. It cautions that results be reported in language likely to be understood by persons receiving them, and that: (a) scores should not be reported to applicants, incumbents, or managers unless they are explained carefully to make sure they are correctly interpreted; (b) scores should generally not be reported to persons who later may be asked to provide ratings for validation studies; (c) derived scores (e.g., IQs or grade-equivalent scores) should be avoided as they may be easily misinterpreted in employment contexts; and (d) confidential test materials and data, such as selection procedure scores or results of reference checks, should be safeguarded to avoid disclosure, which may harm the individual or undermine the assessments.

ROLE OF PSYCHOLOGISTS IN FORENSIC CONTEXTS

[*Ed. note*: See also chapter 9]
Legal requirements governing disclosure of test data may vary substantially from state to state. Psychologists faced with demands to produce test data are encouraged to secure advice about the governing law(s) in the state where the problem arises as well as federal and local statutes and regulations applicable to specific contexts. Psychologists are also encouraged to refer to ethical and appropriate professional standards, as well as applicable guidelines (e.g., Section 7 of the APA Ethics Code; APA, 1992).
. . .

ROLE OF PSYCHOLOGISTS IN REQUESTING OR OBTAINING SECURE TEST DATA AND TEST MATERIALS

Psychologists who request the release of test data, or who are affiliated (through employment, paid or unpaid consulting relationships, or other related affiliations) with organizations or agencies making such requests, should be aware of applicable ethical and professional standards. Psychologists requesting test data, or who are affiliated with organizations requesting test data, make reasonable attempts to maintain the integrity and security of requested tests and assessments, to protect the confidentiality of clients and test data, and to take reasonable steps to prevent others from misusing test data. Psychologists may assist organizations requesting test data to appropriately restrict the request to test data that are relevant for a specific purpose and to limit access to qualified professionals with a legitimate interest. Psychologists affiliated with organizations and agencies requesting or mandating release of data may also make known their commitment to professional and ethical standards, . . . attempt to inform all parties of appropriate ways to resolve any conflicts in order to ensure conformity to these standards.

OTHER ISSUES

Reprinting of Test Items
In deciding whether to reprint items, psychologists are encouraged to consider the qualifications of the

intended audience, access to the publication by the general public or potential test takers, the intent and use of the publication, the potential for invalidating the assessment technique, and intellectual property/ copyright law. The reprinting or description of individual test items in a publication (e.g., popular press, paper presentation, research article, book, technical report, handout) may jeopardize the integrity and security of many standardized tests.

Psychologists generally obtain permission from the copyright holder prior to reprinting test items. Psychologists may also consider alternatives to providing test items to persons not qualified in assessment by (a) developing similar items having little or no overlap with content in the original test items and (b) using factors, clusters, or content-categories and their descriptions.

Use of Test Items in Teaching and Training

It is advisable for persons in training who use test materials, or who have access to test data, to be directly supervised by a qualified professional. Academic departments and professors should maintain the security of all test materials under conditions that prevent access by unauthorized individuals . . .

When students are administered a test for demonstration purposes, the instructor assures the security and appropriate use of the test. Because exposure to tests in such demonstrations can invalidate

the test for future use with students, simulated test items, film or video demonstrations, or other alternative means are encouraged as alternatives to classroom administration or demonstrations of actual tests, whenever possible.

Retention and Maintenance of Testing Data

The Testing Standards (APA, 1985) state that test protocols and any written reports should be preserved when any test data about a person are retained (Standard 15.9), and data (whether retained on paper, data files, etc.) should be adequately protected from improper disclosure (Standard 16.5). The Ethics Code (APA, 1992) and *Record Keeping Guidelines* (APA, 1993) contain additional information regarding the retention of psychological records. . . .

References

American Psychological Association. (1992). Ethical principles of psychologists and code of conduct. *American Psychologist, 47*, 1597–1611.

American Psychological Association. (1993). *Record keeping guidelines*. Washington, DC: Author.

Society for Industrial and Organizational Psychology. (1987). *Principles for the validation and use of personnel selection procedures* (3rd ed.). Arlington Heights, IL: Author.

Standards for educational and psychological testing. (1985). Washington, DC: American Psychological Association.

Strategies for Private Practitioners Coping With Subpoenas or Compelled Testimony for Client Records or Test Data

Committee on Legal Issues

. . . This document is not intended to establish any standards of care or conduct for practitioners; rather, it addresses the general question, What strategies may be available to psychologists in private practice for responding to subpoenas or compelled court testimony concerning client records, test data, test manuals, test protocols, or other test information?

As a general principle of law, all citizens are required to provide information necessary for deciding issues before a court. From the perspective of the legal system, the more relevant information available to the trier of fact (i.e., judge or jury), the fairer the decision. Statutes, rules of civil and criminal procedure, and rules of evidence have established the procedures for the transmittal of such information. In order to obtain this material, *subpoenas* (legal commands to appear to provide testimony) or *subpoenas duces tecum* (legal commands to appear and bring along specific documents) may be issued. Alternatively, the court may issue a *court order* to provide testimony or produce documents. A subpoena requesting testimony or documents, even if not signed by a judge, requires a timely response, but it may be modified or quashed (i.e., made void or invalid). However, once a court order for testimony or documents is issued and any attempt (made in a timely manner) to have the court vacate or modify its order has been unsuccessful, a psychologist may be held in contempt of court if he or she fails to comply.

The demands of the legal system sometimes conflict with the responsibility of psychologists to maintain the confidentiality of client records. This responsibility arises from tenets of good clinical practice, ethical standards, professional licensing laws, statutes, and other applicable laws. In many contexts, the client material generated in the course of a professional relationship may also fall under an evidentiary privilege, which protects such information from judicial scrutiny. . . . The psychologist has a responsibility to maintain confidentiality and to assert the psychotherapist–patient privilege unless the client has explicitly waived privilege, unless a legally recognized exception to privilege exists, or unless the court orders the psychologist to turn over the client's information. Therapy notes, process notes, client information forms, billing records, and other such information usually may be turned over to the court with an appropriate release by the client or with a court order. Psychological test material presents a more complicated situation because inappropriate disclosure may seriously impair the security and threaten the validity of the test and its value as a measurement tool.

Psychologists have numerous ethical, professional, and legal obligations that touch on the release of client records, test data, and other information in the legal context. Many such obligations may favor disclosure, including, in particular, the general obligation of all citizens to give truthful and complete testimony in courts of law when subpoenaed to do so. But there are often conflicting duties and principles that favor withholding such information. These may include obligations to (a) clients or other individuals who are administered psychological tests (e.g., privileged or confidential communications that may include client responses to test items); (b) the public (e.g., to avoid public dissemination of test items, questions, protocols, or other test information that could adversely affect the integrity and continued validity of tests); (c) test publishers (e.g., contractual obligations between the psychologist and test publishers not to disclose test information; obligations under the copyright laws); and (d) other third parties (e.g., employers). Such obligations may, at times, conflict with one another. Psychologists must identify and seek to reconcile their obligations. . . .

There are specific settings (e.g., educational, institutional, employment) in which the legal or ethical obligations of psychologists as they relate to disclosure of client records or test information present special problems. This document does not purport to address disclosure issues in these special contexts, nor does it attempt to resolve dilemmas faced by psychologists in reconciling legal and ethical obligations.

STRATEGIES FOR DEALING WITH SUBPOENAS

Determine Whether the Request for Information Carries the Force of Law

It must first be determined whether a psychologist has, in fact, received a legally valid demand for disclosure of sensitive test data and client records. If a demand is not legally enforceable for any reason, then the psychologist has no legal obligation to comply with it and may have no legal obligation even to respond. Even a demand that claims to be legally enforceable may not be. For example, the court issuing the subpoena may not have jurisdiction over the psychologist or his or her records (e.g., a subpoena issued in one state may not be legally binding on a psychologist residing and working in a different state). Or, the subpoena may not have been properly served on the psychologist (e.g., some states may require service in person or by certified

mail or that a subpoena for such records be accompanied by a special court order). It is advisable that a psychologist consult with an attorney in making such a determination [footnote deleted]. If the psychologist concludes that the demand is legally valid, then some formal response to the court will be required—either compliance with or opposition to the demand, in whole or in part. A psychologist's obligations in responding to a valid subpoena are not necessarily the same as those under a court order (see section titled *File a Motion to Quash the Subpoena or File a Protective Order* below). The next step, in most cases, will involve contacting the psychologist's client. However, the psychologist may wish to consider grounds for opposing or limiting production of the demanded information before contacting the client so that the client can more fully understand his or her options (see section titled *Possible Grounds for Opposing or Limiting Production of Client Records or Test Data* below).

Contact the Client

The client to whom requested records pertain often has a legally protected interest in preserving the confidentiality of the records. If, therefore, a psychologist receives a subpoena or advance notice that he or she may be required to divulge client records or test data, the psychologist should discuss the implications of the demand with the client (or his or her legal guardian). When appropriate, the psychologist may consult with the client's attorney. This discussion will inform the client which information has been demanded, the purpose of the demand, the entities or individuals to whom the information is to be provided, and the possible scope of further disclosure by those entities or individuals. Following such a discussion, a legally competent client or the client's legal guardian may choose to consent in writing to production of the data. Written consent may avoid future conflicts or legal entanglements with the client over the release of confidential tests or other records pertaining to the client. The client's consent may not, however, resolve the potential confidentiality claims of third parties (such as test publishers) and the obligations of psychologists to withhold test data or protocols. . . .

Negotiate With the Requester

If a client does not consent to release of the requested information, the psychologist (often through counsel) may seek to prevent disclosure through discussions with legal counsel for the requesting party. The psychologist's position in such discussions may be bolstered by legal arguments against disclosure. (Some possible arguments are outlined in the section titled *Possible Grounds for Opposing or Limiting Production of Client Records or Test Data* below.) Such negotiations may explore whether there are ways to achieve the requesting party's objectives without divulging confidential information, for example, through disclosure of nonconfidential materials or submission of an affidavit by the psychologist disclosing nonconfidential information. Negotiation may also be used as a strategy to avoid compelled testimony in court or by deposition. In short, negotiation can be explored as a possible means of avoiding the wholesale release of confidential test or client information—release that may not be in the best interests of the client, the public, or the profession, and that may not even be relevant to the issues before the court. Such an option could be explored in consultation with the psychologist's attorney or the client's attorney.

Seek Guidance From the Court

If, despite such discussions, the requesting party insists that confidential information or test data be produced, the safest course for the psychologist may be to seek a ruling from the court on whether disclosure is required. The simplest way of proceeding, and perhaps the least costly, may be for the psychologist (or his or her attorney) to write a letter to the court, with a copy to the attorneys for both parties, stating that the psychologist wishes to comply with the law but that he or she is ethically obligated not to produce the confidential records or test data or to testify about them unless compelled to do so by the court or with the consent of the client. In writing such a letter, the psychologist (or his or her lawyer) may request that the court consider the psychologist's obligations to protect the interests of the client, the interests of third parties (e.g., test publishers or others), and the interests of the public in preserving the integrity and continued validity of the tests

themselves. This letter may help sensitize the court about the potential adverse effects of dissemination. The letter might also attempt to provide suggestions, such as the following, to the court on ways to minimize the adverse consequences of disclosure if the court is inclined to require production at all:

1. Suggest that, at most, the court direct the psychologist to provide test data only to another appropriately qualified psychologist designated by the court or by the party seeking such information.
2. Suggest that the court limit the use of client records or test data to prevent wide dissemination. For example, the court might order that the information be delivered, be kept under seal, and be used solely for the purposes of the litigation and that all copies of the data be returned to the psychologist under seal after the litigation is terminated. The order might also provide that the requester may not provide the information to any third parties.
3. Suggest that the court limit the categories of information that must be produced. For example, client records may contain confidential information about a third party, such as a spouse, who may have independent interests in maintaining confidentiality, and such data may be of minimal or no relevance to the issues before the court. The court should limit its production order to exclude such information.
4. Suggest that the court determine for itself, through in-camera proceedings (i.e., a nonpublic hearing or a review by the judge in chambers), whether the use of the client records or test data is relevant to the issues before the court or whether it might be insulated from disclosure, in whole or in part, by the therapist–client privilege or another privilege.

File a Motion to Quash the Subpoena or File a Protective Order

If, because of local procedure or other considerations, guidance cannot be sought through the informal means of a letter to the court, it may be necessary to file a motion seeking to be relieved of the obligations imposed by the demand for production of the confidential records. In many jurisdictions, the possible motions include a motion to quash the subpoena, in whole or in part, or a motion for a protective order. Filing such a motion may require the assistance of counsel, representing either the psychologist or the psychologist's client.

Courts are generally more receptive to a motion to quash or a motion for a protective order if it is filed by the client about whom information is sought (who would be defending his or her own interests) rather than by a psychologist who, in essence, would be seeking to protect the rights of the client or other third parties. The psychologist may wish to determine initially whether the client's lawyer is inclined to seek to quash a subpoena or to seek a protective order and, if so, may wish to provide assistance to the client's attorney in this regard. If the client has refused to consent to disclosure of the information, his or her attorney may be willing to take the lead in opposing the subpoena.

A *motion to quash* is a formal application made to a court or judge for purposes of having a subpoena vacated or declared invalid. Grounds may exist for asserting that the subpoena or request for testimony should be quashed, in whole or in part. For example, the information sought may be protected by the therapist–client privilege and therefore may not be subject to discovery, or it may not be relevant to the issues before the court (see section titled *Possible Grounds for Opposing or Limiting Production of Client Records or Test Data* below). This strategy may be used alone or in combination with a motion for a protective order.

A *motion for a protective order* seeks an order or decree from the court that protects against the untoward consequences of disclosing information. A protective order can be tailored to meet the legitimate interests of the client and of third parties such as test publishers and the public. The focus of this strategy first and foremost is to prevent or limit disclosure and the use of sensitive client and test information. The protective order—and the motion— may include any of the elements listed in the preceding section.

PSYCHOLOGISTS' TESTIMONY

If a psychologist is asked to disclose confidential information during questioning at a deposition, he or she may refuse to answer the question only if the information is privileged. If there is a reasonable basis for asserting a privilege, the psychologist may refuse to provide test data or client records until so ordered by the court. A psychologist who refuses to answer questions without a reasonable basis may be penalized by the court, including the obligation to pay the requesting parties' costs and fees in obtaining answers. For these reasons, it is advisable that a psychologist be represented by counsel at the deposition if he or she expects that questions concerning confidential information may be asked. A lawyer may advise the psychologist, on the record, when a question seeks confidential information; such on-the-record advice will help protect the psychologist from the adverse legal consequences of erroneous disclosures or erroneous refusals to disclose.

Similarly, if the request for confidential information arises for the first time during courtroom testimony, the psychologist may assert a privilege and refuse to answer unless directed to do so by the court. The law in this area is somewhat unsettled. Thus, if a psychologist anticipates that confidential materials may be elicited through testimony, it may be advisable for him or her to consult an attorney before testifying.

POSSIBLE GROUNDS FOR OPPOSING OR LIMITING PRODUCTION OF CLIENT RECORDS OR TEST DATA

The following theories may or may not be available under the facts of a particular case and jurisdiction for resisting a demand to produce confidential information, records, or test data . . .

1. The court does not have jurisdiction over the psychologist, the client records, or the test data, or the psychologist did not receive a legally sufficient demand (e.g., improper service) for production of records or test data testimony.
2. The psychologist does not have custody or control of the records or test data that are sought, because, for example, they belong not to the psychologist but to his or her employer.
3. The therapist–client privilege insulates the records or test data from disclosure. The rationale for the privilege, recognized in many states, is

that the openness necessary for effective therapy requires that clients have an expectation that all records of therapy, contents of therapeutic disclosures, and test data will remain confidential. Disclosure would be a serious invasion of the client's privacy. The psychologist is under an ethical obligation to protect the client's reasonable expectations of confidentiality. . . .

4. The information sought is not relevant to the issues before the court, or the scope of the demand for information is over-broad in reaching information not relevant to the issues before the court, including irrelevant information pertaining to third parties such as a spouse.

5. Public dissemination of test information such as manuals, protocols, and so forth may harm the public interest because it may affect responses of future test populations. This effect could result in the loss of valuable assessment tools to the detriment of both the public and the profession of psychology.

6. Test publishers have an interest in the protection of test information, and the psychologist may have a contractual or other legal obligation (e.g., copyright laws) not to disclose such information. Such contractual claims, coupled with concerns about test data devolving into the public domain, may justify issuance of a protective order against dissemination of a test instrument or protocols. . . .

7. Psychologists have an ethical obligation to protect the integrity and security of test information and data and to avoid misuse of assessment techniques and data. Psychologists are also ethically obligated to take reasonable steps to prevent others from misusing such information. In particular, psychologists are ethically obligated to refrain from releasing raw test results or raw data to persons other than the client, as appropriate, who are not qualified to use such information. . . . This prohibition has the force of law in many jurisdictions where state boards of psychology or boards with similar responsibilities have either adopted the APA Ethics Code or a code of ethics with similar provisions.

8. Refer to ethical and legal obligations of psychologists as provided for under ethics codes; professional standards; state, federal, or local laws; or regulatory agencies.

◆ ◆ ◆

Commentary: As of this writing the Ethics Committee is preparing a policy statement to clarify Standard 2.02(b) of the Ethics Code, and to determine who is "qualified" to use raw test data. The statement makes clear that professionals other than psychologists may be considered qualified. According to the statement, if the psychologist who is to provide data determines that the requestor is not qualified,

> *[T]he psychologist can recommend that the information be sent to someone who can make more appropriate use of it, such as another psychologist, or other professionals who have an understanding of statistical measures and data. If the individual requesting the information refuses this process, then the psychologist may be able to take other steps, such as requesting that the person obtain a court order directing the psychologist to release information to that person; requesting that the person sign agreements prohibiting secondary disclosures, and controlling the copying and disposal of the information; requesting a protective order from the court for the information; or requesting that the information be released to a judge. Any one, or more, of such actions may be seen as taking reasonable steps to prevent others from misusing the information. . . . (Draft Policy Statement, March 31, 1997).*

Provisions in other documents also belie Tranel's (1994; see earlier excerpt) assertion that the ethics code precludes giving raw test data to clients who generate them (and their legal representatives or others). See, for example, Ethics Code (see chapter 1)—Standards 2.10; 5.10 (in addition to 2.02(b)); Guidelines for Child Custody Evaluations in Divorce Proceedings (see chapter 9)—Guidelines 9–11; Specialty Guidelines for Forensic Psychologists (see chapter 9)—Guidelines V(A)(2); VI(B); VII(A)(2)(a,b); and most particularly Record Keeping Guidelines (see chapter 10).

Psychologists are justifiably concerned that, at times, disclosure of record-keeping information will be required, despite the protests of the psychologist or client, and may be released to persons unqualified to interpret such records. . . . [N]o record is free from disclosure all of the time, regardless of the wishes of the client or the psychologist.

The following, final section highlights two emerging and vital developments that have raised a number of ethical and legal issues: the use of computerized assessment systems and so-called integrity, or honesty, tests. With regard to the former, many essential articles have appeared in American Psychologist, Professional Psychology, *and* Computers in Human Behavior. *In addition, papers presented at a symposium devoted to computerized testing, sponsored by the Buros Institute, in Nebraska, have appeared in Gutkin, T., & Wise, S. (Eds.). 1991.* The computer and the decision-making process. *Hillsdale, NJ: Erlbaum. The following materials are simply meant to introduce the reader to these important subjects.*

Legal Issues in Computerized Psychological Testing

Donald N. Bersoff and Paul J. Hofer

. . .

PSYCHOLOGY'S RESPONSE TO CPT

. . .

There are several sources of ethical guidelines relevant to computerized psychological testing (CPT). The APA first adopted interim standards of "Automated Test Scoring and Interpretation Practices" more than 20 years ago (APA, 1966). In addition, the 1974 *Standards for Educational and Psychological Tests* (APA, AERA, NCME, 1974), the revised 1985 Standards (APA, 1985), the 1977 *Standards for Providers of Psychological Services* (APA, 1977) and its recently adopted revision, the *General Guidelines for Providers of Psychological Services* (APA, 1987), as well as the 1981 *Specialty Guidelines for the Delivery of Services* (APA, 1981) all contain references to computerized assessment. However, in these latter documents, many CPT issues are subsumed under general standards applicable to all types of testing or psychological practices and the specific implications for CPT may not be clear.

. . .

Many articles addressing the need for standards are appearing in the psychological literature (e.g., Skinner & Pakula, 1986; Matarazzo, 1986, in press; Burke & Normand, 1985; Hofer & Green, 1985). The present authors prepared a document (Hofer & Bersoff, 1983), "Standards for the Administration and Interpretation of Computerized Psychological Testing," for a testing service concerned about the void left by the absence of adequate guidelines.

Given all these sources, many observers have seen the need for organizing the issues unique to CPT under more specific, official, and national standards. The American Psychological Association's Board of Directors in January, 1984, instructed the Committee on Professional Standards and the Committee on Psychological Tests and Assessment to develop guidelines specific to CPT. These guidelines, having gone through several revisions and review by the APA governance, were adopted by the APA Council of Representatives in February, 1986. Importantly, at this point, the guidelines are considered advisory. After they have been tested in the real world, the APA may wish to revise them once again and make them binding standards. For now these guidelines are the clearest statement of the requirements of good practice, and professionals should familiarize themselves with them. Hofer (1985) and Hofer and Green (1985) provide an overview and discussion.

RIGHTS AND RESPONSIBILITIES OF PROFESSIONALS

Should there be any legal challenge to the administration, interpretation, and decisions related to computer-based tests, both the testing service and the test user are likely to be named as defendants. Both may be ultimately liable, either as joint wrongdoers or as individuals each responsible for their own negligence. In such cases, it might appear that clinicians could rely on a defense that they were ignorant of the underlying bases for the interpretations they accepted and passed along to their clients. But, such a defense would be an admission that the clinician violated the APA Ethical Principles and engaged in professional negligence. The *Ethical Principles of Psychologists*, Principle 8(e) (APA, 1981, p.

637) states: "Psychologists offering scoring and interpretation services are able to produce appropriate evidence for the validity of the programs and procedures used in arriving at interpretations."[1]

Conversely, testing services will probably not be able to place the entire blame on the user for injurious decisions resulting from negligent interpretations, and they could be held liable under a number of legal theories. Placing the responsibility for the validity of reports entirely on the user might erode the usefulness of CPT as reviewing the validity of each interpretative statement could be comparable with writing the entire report oneself, and most people use CPT to save time and effort. Actuarial interpretations and statistical predictions of behavior are best made using the power of the computer to summarize empirical relations. Interpretations that can be validated empirically should be. Predictive validation is often legally required when selecting applicants for jobs, and it should be encouraged for other important interpretations, such as treatment recommendations and prognoses. In cases where interpretations are based on empirical findings rather than clinical judgment, and where the clinician has no additional reason to believe the finding is invalid for that test taker, it may be better for practitioners to accept the computerized interpretation without alteration.

These considerations suggest that some division of labor and responsibility between developer and user must be found. The gist of the APA guidelines is: The validity and reliability of the computerized version of a test should be established by the developer, but CPT interpretations should be used only in conjunction with professional review. This rather general principle might be elaborated into a more specific assignment of responsibilities. The developer seems in the best position to assure that the scales and research on which the report is based are not obsolete or otherwise inadequate. Actuarially based interpretations should use the best research and statistical equations. Developers can stay abreast of relevant research, incorporate new findings into the system, and direct practitioners to research that may

assist them in properly using the report. Users can then concentrate on overseeing the context of the testing and evaluating the appropriateness of the norms and validation studies used by the system for interpreting any particular client's scores. They can concentrate on gathering clinical information not used by the CPT system but relevant to clinical decision making. By specializing and working together, developers and users can assure the full advantages of CPT are realized.

For users to meet their responsibilities to review the validity of a CPT report for each test taker, they must have information about the interpretation system. They need to know how interpretations are derived from original item responses. Some of this information is best suited for inclusion in each report, and some can be included in a manual outlining general features of the interpretation system. A major potential conflict in CPT is the tension between users' needs for sufficient information to review reports, and developers' proprietary interest in their algorithms, software, and other business assets.

This conflict is real, but a satisfactory compromise may be available. The APA guidelines call for disclosure of "how interpretations are derived" and information on "the nature of the relationship" between scores and interpretations. Users need not know all the decision rules and algorithms used by the testing service, but they must know enough to review any report they actually use. . . . In cases where interpretations are clinically based, users must have information needed to weigh the credibility of the expert. The names and credentials of these experts could be provided, along with their theoretical rationale. . . .

[*Ed. note:* I have omitted a long section on intellectual property issues—such as copyright, patents, and trade secrets. These problems, although beyond the scope of this text, are extremely important, and readers are referred to the full chapter for their discussion. The issue of copyright for norms and other data related to computerized testing has already been the subject of significant litigation.]

---

[1] *Ed. note:* See Standard 2.08 of the APA's current (1992) Ethical Principles.

THE RIGHTS OF TEST TAKERS

. . .

A major concern about computer-generated reports is that they may not be as individualized as those generated in the conventional manner. Some information, such as demographic characteristics of the examinee, can be included in interpretation programs so that the computer will use more appropriate norms or base rates if they exist and qualify interpretations to take into account the particular test taker's characteristics. But no program can consider all the unique attributes of each individual and in most cases the same programmed decision rules will be applied to all test scores.

The revised *Standards for Educational and Psychological Testing* (APA et al., 1985), clearly indicates that test users are ultimately responsible for their test interpretations, no matter from what format the data are derived. Assessing the validity of interpretations requires that a human being observe the testing situation and decide if conditions are present that could invalidate test results. It is imperative that the final act of decision making be that of a qualified practitioner, consistent with state law, ethical principles, and professional standards, who takes responsibility for overseeing both the process of testing and judging the applicability of the interpretive report for individual examinees.

There must be an interposition of human judgment between the CPT report and decision making to ensure that decisions are made with full sensitivity to all the nuances of test administration and interpretation, and the unique constellation of attributes in each person is evaluated. Relying solely on test developers' computerized conception of the test taker's responses isolated from a clinician's trained observation of the test taker's behavior during the administration of the test, may tend to create bland, impersonal, and nonspecific assessments that fail to capture the test taker's cognitive, affective, and behavioral functioning across a variety of situations. . . .

References

American Psychological Association. (1966). Minutes of the annual meeting of the Council of Representatives. *American Psychologist, 21,* 1141.

American Psychological Association. (1977). *Standards for providers of psychological services.* Washington, DC: Author.

American Psychological Association. (1981). Specialty guidelines for the delivery of services. *American Psychologist, 36,* 640–681.

American Psychological Association. (1985). *Standards for educational and psychological tests.* Washington, DC: Author.

American Psychological Association. (1986). *Guidelines for computerized-based tests and interpretations.* Washington, DC: Author.

American Psychological Association. (1987). *General guidelines for providers of psychological services.* Washington, DC: Author.

American Psychological Association, American Educational Research Association, & National Council of Measurement in Education. (1974). *Standards for educational and psychological tests.* Washington, DC: Author.

Burke, M., & Normand, J. (1985). *Computerized psychological testing: An overview and critique.* Manuscript submitted for publication.

Hofer, P. (1985). Developing standards for computerized psychological testing. *Computers in Human Behavior, 1,* 301–315.

Hofer, P., & Bersoff, D. (1983). *Standards for the administration and interpretation of computerized psychological testing.*

Hofer, P., & Green, B. (1985). The challenge of competence and creativity in computerized psychological testing. *Journal of Counseling and Clinical Psychology, 53,* 826–838.

Matarazzo, J. (1986). Computerized clinical psychological test interpretations: Unvalidated plus all mean and no sigma. *American Psychologist, 41,* 14–24.

Matarazzo, J. (in press). Clinical psychological test interpretation by computer: Hardware outpaces software. *Computers in Human Behavior.*

Skinner, H., & Pakula, A. (1986). Challenge of computers in psychological assessment. *Professional Psychology, 17,* 44–50.

Commentary: Many psychologists are concerned that unqualified and untrained people in other professions will be sold computerized tests and scoring and interpretive services or may otherwise be given access to these. Is this a genuine concern or merely an argument to eliminate competition? For helpful readings on this prob-

lem and other legal and ethical issues, see, for example, these publications:

Eyde, L. D., & Kowal, D. M. (1987). Computerised test interpretation services: Ethical and professional concerns regarding U.S. producers and users. Applied Psychology: An International Review, 36, *401–417.*

Hartman, D. E. (1986). On the use of clinical psychology software: Practical, legal, and ethical concerns. Professional Psychology: Research and Practice, 17, *462–465.*

Zachary, R., & Pope, K. (1984). Legal and ethical issues in the clinical use of computerized testing. In M. D. Schwartz (Ed.), Using computers in clinical practice *(pp. 151–164). New York: Haworth Press.*

Computerized Clinical Psychological Test Interpretations: Unvalidated Plus All Mean and No Sigma

Joseph D. Matarazzo

PSYCHOLOGICAL ASSESSMENT, INVASION OF PRIVACY, AND PROFESSIONAL STANDARDS

I would like to set the stage for my comments by stating a truism that seems to have been forgotten recently in some quarters: The testing by one individual of another human's intellectual, personality, and related characteristics is an invasion of privacy to an extent no less intimate than that involved in an examination carried out on that same individual's person or resources by a physician, attorney, or agent of the Internal Revenue Service.

Alas, there is evidence that sensitivity to these concerns is not uniformly the norm today. In fact, there are alarming signals that the features of a responsible assessment that were first promulgated by Binet and Simon (Matarazzo, 1972) are today being overlooked by for-profit commercial companies and individual psychologist–entrepreneurs who are vigorously touting and over-selling the products of a new computer technology to some ill-prepared and professionally undereducated users who erroneously equate the products of this technology with a full and responsible psychological assessment.

. . . [M]y concern is not with the computer hardware being sold. Along with others in our profession, I believe this new technology, with its seemingly unlimited memory and capacity to store and integrate previously validated relationships, will significantly advance the art and science of assessment.

My intention therefore is not to try to defend the work of today's human clinician nor to deny that computers will one day supplant some types of human clinical judgments. Rather, my concern is with the pages and pages of today's neatly typed, valid-sounding narrative interpretations that are the products, for the most part, of secretly developed disks of software that have not even been offered for scientific evaluation (as has clinical judgment), let alone met even the most rudimentary acceptable tests of science.

. . .

RESPONSIBLE USE OF COMPUTERIZED CLINICAL INTERPRETATIONS REQUIRES MORE THAN A MANUAL

Today's automated and still "canned" clinical psychological interpretations, with almost no exceptions that I have been able to discern, do not offer the plausible interpretations by several well-respected and identified clinicians of the *same* test finding(s); nor, for that matter, do they offer several equally plausible interpretations by a single, publicly identified clinician. Thus, although computerized clinical psychological test interpretations present other problems, an issue that should seriously concern the experienced health service provider–user involves that critical missing element: namely, that the computer rarely delivers several different but equally plausible clinical interpretations. With almost no exceptions, today's software produces only a single, typically very lengthy, clinical narrative. Another danger of this clinical-appearing product is the aura of seeming validity that surrounds its objectively presented, neatly typed page after page of narrative clinical statements.

PSYCHOLOGY BEGINS TO MEET THE CHALLENGE

. . . [T]he proliferation during the past decade of scores of for-profit companies producing hardware and software for yet-to-be validated, computerized clinical psychological interpretations, without safeguards for the consumer or service provider, has presented the profession of psychology with a considerable threat to its integrity. Fortunately, however, developments within our profession since I first communicated my mounting alarm two years ago have begun to ease my anxiety. . . .

. . . [T]he 1985 Council of Representatives was provided a draft of a well-thought-out set of *Guidelines for Computer-Based Tests and Interpretations* that I hope will soon be ratified. These *Guidelines* were prepared jointly by the American Psychological Association's Committee on Professional Standards and its Committee on Psychological Tests and Assessment. Fortunately, these *Guidelines* include a series of detailed and well-reasoned principles by which to initiate and evaluate the needed further development and validation of the clinical and related products of computer software, as well as principles to guide the developer, publisher, and user of these new computer-generated tools.

There have been other equally important recent developments within our discipline. First, Hofer and Bersoff (1983) compiled and promulgated a series of ethical and professional standards for the administration and interpretation of computerized psychological testing tools. Second, a soon-to-be-published issue of the *Journal of Consulting and Clinical Psychology* will be devoted entirely to the problems and promises offered by the new software of clinical psychological interpretations. And third, a relative

avalanche of symposia and paper sessions devoted to a concentrated, critical evaluation of this new computer-assisted, clinical psychological testing industry was presented at the 1984 Annual Meeting of the American Psychological Association in Toronto.

These and related developments will most likely help stimulate the effort in education, training, and research that must be undertaken by our discipline to meet the challenge sparked by the proffering of unvalidated software to unwary users and consumers by large numbers of for-profit companies and their consultants.

References

Hofer, P. J., & Bersoff, D. N. (1983). *Standards for the administration and interpretation of computerized psychological testing.*

Matarazzo, J. D. (1972). *Wechsler's measurement and appraisal of adult intelligence: Fifth and enlarged edition.* New York: Oxford University Press.

◆　◆　◆

Commentary: The Guidelines that Matarazzo referred to were ratified, as he hoped, by the APA's Council of Representatives, and they have been published. See American Psychological Association Committee on Professional Standards and Committee on Psychological Testing and Assessment. (1986). Guidelines for computer-based tests and interpretations. Washington, DC: American Psychological Association.[1]

The Guidelines are advisory in nature and, thus, are not directly enforceable. Among other things, however, they recommend that "computer-generated interpretive reports should be used only in conjunction with professional judgment" (p. 12). It is the psychologist, not the testing company, "who takes responsibility for overseeing both the process of testing and judging the applicability of the interpretive report for individual test takers, consistent with legal, ethical, and professional requirements" (pp. 12–13). Thus, as these Guidelines suggest, psychologists "may need to amend the computer report to take into account their own observations and judgments and

---

[1] These Guidelines have since been rescinded (see later discussion), and, at the time this book was in press, were not available from the APA.

to ensure that the report is comprehensible, free of jargon, and true to the person evaluated" (p. 13).

Unfortunately, a portion of these Guidelines, not relevant here and thus not reprinted herein, cited several provisions from the 1981 APA ethics code that had been criticized by the Federal Trade Commission (see chap. 10). In accordance with a consent agreement between APA and the Federal Trade Commission, those portions of the Guidelines have been rescinded. To avoid further problems, the APA is revising all of the guidelines, and has halted distribution of the current version. The major enforceable ethical principle concerning computerized testing is now found in Standard 2.08 of the 1992 Ethical Principles.

Integrity Tests: Facts and Unresolved Issues

Wayne J. Camara and Dianne L. Schneider

Integrity tests, or honesty tests as they are often referred to, are paper-and-pencil instruments for personnel selection that are used to predict dishonesty or counterproductivity. These tests are composed of items that query job applicants about their attitudes toward theft and inquire about any past thefts. Over the past decade, integrity testing has greatly increased and has become a mainstream selection practice for a wide variety of jobs in which employees have access to cash or merchandise or perform security functions (Goldberg, Grenier, Guion, Sechrest, & Wing, 1991; Guastello & Rieke, 1991; O'Bannon, Goldinger, & Appleby, 1989).

In the past five years, integrity testing has received more scrutiny by the media, policymakers, and the public than has any other class of psychological tests. Much of this increased interest and use of integrity tests followed the passage of the Employee Polygraph Protection Act of 1988. Many of the technical flaws and misuses of polygraphs for employment screening (see Saxe, Dougherty, & Cross, 1985; U.S. Congress, 1983) have, in part, increased skepticism that any psychological instrument can accurately identify individuals who will be dishonest in a specific work environment (Saxe, 1991). Concerns about the reliance on integrity test scores in personnel selection decisions, the potential restriction of opportunities for job applicants, invasion of individuals' privacy, labeling, and basic psychometric issues of validity spurred investigations by Congress and the American Psychological Association (APA). The U.S. Congress Office of Technology Assessment (OTA) completed a two-year study of integrity testing that included several psychologists in advisory and consultant capacities (U.S. Congress, 1990). In addition, a task force of the APA established in conjunction with Division 5 (Division of Evaluation, Measurement, and Statistics) and Division 14 (The Society for Industrial and Organizational Psychology) completed a 20-month study of integrity tests (Goldberg et al., 1991), herein referred to as the APA report. . . .

The APA and OTA studies differed in foci, particularly their intended purposes, evidentiary bases, and conclusions regarding the implications of using integrity tests for employment screening. OTA's report was written to guide Congress in determining what, if any, legislative action on integrity tests was warranted. It focused on public policy issues, such as potential errors in selection decisions, the effect these tests have on labeling, and individuals' reduced employment opportunities—concerns that might generalize to all types of personnel selection processes. In contrast, APA's report was produced by psychologists for psychologists and test users. It targeted scientific and technical issues in integrity testing (e.g., defining the construct; identifying appropriate criteria; and examining the validity, reliability, and utility of the tests) and dealt with policy indirectly, by examining only those issues for which psychology can offer special expertise. . . .

PROFESSIONAL AND PUBLIC POLICY IMPLICATIONS

The continued use of integrity tests for employment screening raises professional and policy issues for psychology. As professionals, psychologists have a

From *American Psychologist, 49*, 112–119. Copyright 1994 by the American Psychological Association. Adapted with permission of the author and publisher. Tables 1 and 2 as well as the Appendix have been omitted.

responsibility to reduce the misuse of integrity tests. Each of the following issues can best be discussed in light of several principles (2.02, 2.05, 2.06, and 2.08) concerning assessment in the *Ethical Principles of Psychologists and Code of Conduct* (APA, 1992).

Two of these principles address a psychologist's responsibility to prevent misuse of assessments and information from assessments by unqualified persons. Principle 2.02 (b) instructs psychologists to refrain from releasing test results or data to persons not qualified to use such information. This presents several dilemmas for the 56% of integrity test publishers who report using no formal screening practices for test users.

Demands for cutting scores by employers and the willingness of test publishers to produce them were cited as a major problem by both APA and OTA. Publishers often appear to have set cutting scores for some tests on purely arbitrary grounds, then created failing and passing categories (Goldberg et al., 1991) based on this scoring dichotomy. Scrivner (1991) pointed out that the integrity testing industry's own association specifies in its guidelines (Association of Personnel Test Publishers [APTP], 1990) that test users should know how a cutting score was derived. Yet, given the complexities of proper procedures to set cutting scores (see Rorer, Hoffman, & Hsieh, 1966), it is unrealistic to impose such responsibilities on the untrained persons who administer integrity tests (Cascio, Alexander, & Barrett, 1988). Similarly, APA's report recommended that standard error of measurement and score ranges be reported but noted that the typical test user may not be qualified to interpret anything more than dichotomous categories (e.g., hire vs. do not hire). When the competence level of test users is not known, test publishers will have difficulty inferring the appropriate amount and level of information that should be provided.

Principle 2.06 (APA, 1992) prohibits psychologists from promoting (e.g., through marketing or sales) the use of tests by unqualified persons. Integrity test publishers might note that test administration is often straightforward and that interpretation requires minimal understanding of categorical (e.g., low-, moderate-, or high-risk categories) or dichotomous data. One might argue that personnel respon-

sible for the administration and use of integrity tests manage other facets of the employment screening process, such as interviews, reference checks, and possibly some cognitive ability tests. Yet, other principles and professional standards (e.g., APA, 1985) suggest that the use of tests and test data require a level of technical knowledge of statistics, measurement, and assessment that many integrity tests users lack. For example, when psychologists serve as test users, they should (a) be familiar with the reliability, validity, standardization, or outcome studies of the techniques (Principle 2.04 [a]); (b) recognize limits to the certainty of predictions made about individuals (Principle 2.04 [b]); (c) consider various test factors and individual characteristics that might limit the accuracy of interpretations, including automated interpretations (Principles 2.04 [c] and 2.05); (d) select scoring and interpretation services on the basis of evidence of the validity and other considerations (Principle 2.08 [b]); and (e) retain responsibility for the interpretation and use of assessments (including automated services; Principle 2.09). Although these principles are relevant for all test users, the *Ethical Principles* can be enforced only with APA members. Similarly, psychologists and all testing professionals responsible for the development, marketing, and sale of assessment products should consider these criteria when determining the qualifications of all test users.

Most integrity tests are classified as *proprietary* by their publishers. The APTP (1990) distinguishes between proprietary and nonproprietary tests [footnote omitted]. Nonproprietary tests are sold to users whom the publisher deems qualified to administer and interpret the test; publishers sell the test, scoring keys, and supporting materials to users possessing the necessary background (e.g., a doctoral degree) or experience (e.g., specialized training). In contrast, proprietary test users purchase a package deal from a publisher, who provides continuous client service. Publishers maintain technical responsibility for norming, scoring, validating, and interpreting tests for the user and providing ongoing psychological expertise to clients (APTP, 1990). Users are responsible for test administration, security of test scores, and final decisions based on the test scores. According to the APTP, "users of proprietary tests are not required to be credentialed by the publisher, although in general the more sophisticated users will make better use of such tests than users who do not have a comprehensive understanding of a test's psychometric properties" (p. 6). However, publishers with minimal or no screening procedures for test purchases and test services cannot evaluate the competence of users or risk of misuse for their services.

A working group of the Joint Committee on Testing Practices (Eyde, Moreland, Robertson, Primoff, & Most, 1988) made no distinctions between proprietary and nonproprietary tests in terms of potential test misuse or in qualifications for test use. Certainly, ensuring that test users are trained appropriately is a common problem in many forms of assessment: clinical, educational, and employment. The *Standards for Educational and Psychological Testing* (APA, 1985) state that "the ultimate responsibility for test use lies with the test user" (p. 41). However, risk of misuse can be reduced if those responsible for the sale of test materials and provision of services take some minimal steps, such as screening test users, requiring organizations that purchase products and services to limit access to only those persons considered competent by the publisher, and requiring test use training for organizations that employ persons who do not satisfy appropriate criteria for test use.

Publishers are justified in making distinctions about the level of competence required for using different types of test data. Few would argue that users who derive a diagnosis and treatment plan for a client using data from multiple scales on a personality test require substantially more expertise and training than users who receive data reported in dichotomous (e.g., hire vs. do not hire) categories on a preemployment assessment report. However, the responsibilities for proper test use (e.g., Eyde et al., 1993) and the importance of decisions based on assessment data may be no less important in employment settings than in clinical practice. Kay (1991) doubted that the unsophisticated test user will ever be competent enough to transform continuous test data into dichotomous selection decisions. He argued that many of the problems attributed to integrity tests result from end users who are largely unqualified to evaluate and interpret test scores. Kay urged publishers to adopt guidelines for the sale and

use of integrity tests, similar to those currently used in qualifying users of other broadband-width personality inventories.

Psychologists are ethically bound (APA, 1992) to consider various test factors (e.g., situational variables, surveillance systems), individual characteristics, and limitations of tests when making recommendations and to ensure the integrity and security of tests and results. However, most users of integrity and employment tests are not psychologists (a situation similar to the administration and interpretation of most large-scale educational testing programs). Personnel managers, security specialists, and supervisors have no such ethical responsibilities and in addition probably lack familiarity with the *Ethical Principles of Psychologists and Code of Conduct* (APA, 1992) and the *Standards for Educational and Psychological Testing* (APA, 1985). Goldberg et al. (1991) acknowledged this problem and called for more concrete, comprehensive training for test users and for screening of potential users. These aspects of psychological testing are generally unregulated in employment settings. Test publishers currently represent the final check in ensuring that only qualified persons administer and interpret tests.

Currently, Massachusetts is the only state that bans integrity tests, although Rhode Island prohibits use of these tests as the sole basis for employment decisions. Both laws went into effect before the studies completed by OTA and APA. Since then, legislation aiming to ban or restrict the use of integrity and other forms of personality tests for preemployment screening has been introduced in at least five other states. However, not one piece of legislation has yet been signed into law. Inquiries about the attitudes and past conduct of applicants and employers have been a major concern of legislators seeking to restrict these tests; however, their misuse by unqualified users has also been cited as a rationale for such legislation (H. A. Fernandez, personal communication, June 18, 1991; Oregon Psychological Association, 1991). . . .

References

American Psychological Association. (1985). *Standards for Educational and Psychological Testing*. Washington, DC: Author.

American Psychological Association. (1992). Ethical principles of psychologists and code of conduct. *American Psychologist, 47,* 1597–1611.

Association of Personnel Test Publishers. (1990). *Model guidelines for pre-employment integrity testing programs.* Washington, DC: Author.

Cascio, W. F., Alexander, R. A., & Barrett, G. V. (1988). Setting cutoff scores: Legal, psychometric, and professional issues and guidelines. *Personnel Psychology, 41,* 1–24.

Employee Polygraph Protection Act of 1988, Sec. 200001 et sec., 29 U.S.C.

Eyde, L. D., Moreland, K. L., Robertson, G. J., Primoff, E. S., & Most, R. B. (1988). *Test user qualifications: A data-based approach to promoting good test use* (Report of the Test User Qualifications Working Group of the Joint Committee on Testing Practices). Washington, DC: American Psychological Association.

Eyde, L. D., Robertson, G. J., Krug, S. E., Moreland, K. L., Robertson, A. G., Shewan, C. M., Harrison, P. L., Porch, B. E., Hammer, A. L., & Primoff, E. S. (1993). *Responsible test use: Case studies for assessing human behavior* (Report of the Joint Committee on Testing Practices). Washington, DC: American Psychological Association.

Goldberg, L. R., Grenier, J. R., Guion, R. M., Sechrest, L. B., & Wing, H. (1991). *Questionnaires used in the prediction of trustworthiness in pre-employment selection decisions: An APA task force report.* Washington, DC: American Psychological Association.

Guastello, S. J., & Rieke, M. L. (1991). A review and critique of honesty test research. *Behavioral Sciences and the Law, 9,* 501–523.

Kay, G. C. (1991). Casting stones at integrity testing, not at integrity tests. *Forensic Reports, 4,* 163–169.

O'Bannon, R. M., Goldinger, L. A., & Appleby, G. S. (1989). *Honesty and integrity testing: A practical guide.* Atlanta: Applied Information Resources.

Oregon Psychological Association. (1991). [From insert distributed with newsletter]. *OPA Newsgram, 10*(8).

Rorer, L. G., Hoffman, P. J., & Hsieh, K. (1966). Utilities as base-rate multipliers in the determination of optimum cutting scores for the discrimination of groups of unequal size and variance. *Journal of Applied Psychology, 50,* 364–368.

Saxe, L. (1991). Lying: Thoughts of an applied social psychologist. *American Psychologist, 46,* 409–415.

Saxe, L., Dougherty, D., & Cross, T. (1985). The validity of polygraph testing: Scientific analysis and public controversy. *American Psychologist, 40,* 355–366.

Scrivner, E. (1991). Integrity testing: A new frontier for psychology. *Forensic Reports, 4,* 75–89.

U.S. Congress, Office of Technology Assessment. (1983). *Scientific validity of polygraph testing* (OTA-TM-H-15). Washington, DC: U.S. Government Printing Office.

U.S. Congress, Office of Technology Assessment. (1990). *The use of integrity tests for pre-employment screening* (OTA-SET-442). Washington, DC: U.S. Government Printing Office.

CHAPTER 7

THERAPY AND OTHER FORMS OF INTERVENTION

Few human relationships so quickly attain the level of intimacy as a working therapeutic relationship. Although in most instances therapists are complete strangers at the beginning of treatment, clients are expected to reveal their innermost and private feelings, thoughts, and behavior to them, and with them, confront the clients' deepest, darkest, and most distasteful sides of themselves. At times, clients may be asked to do this not only in front of their therapists but also in the company of family members or even strangers who make up their therapeutic group.

To compound the problem, in most cases, people enter therapy only after considerable worry and rumination. They are experiencing such symptoms as debilitating feelings or nonproductive, even self-damaging behavior. Although they may want desperately to understand and ameliorate these indicators of distress, it is likely that they do not know much about the process of therapy.

Despite their anxiety, these potential clients are at least facing the prospect voluntarily. However, not all people come to treatment on their own initiative. Some patients—for example, those involuntarily committed to mental hospitals or forced by a court to seek treatment as a condition of probation or parole—may be compelled to see a psychologist. In either case, therapists are likely to encounter clients who, at their initial consultation, are confused, anxious, needy, and vulnerable—and sometimes, downright hostile and negative.

It is almost inevitable, then, that complex ethical issues will arise in settings where therapy and other forms of intervention take place. Preceding chapters have already explored some of these issues. In chapters 4 and 5, I provided materials in which crucial issues concerning confidentiality and multiple relationships, respectively, were debated. In chapter 10, I introduce some of the more ethically sensitive commercial aspects of providing psychological services. In this chapter, I concentrate on several additional issues that are not covered elsewhere in this book.

The previous APA code of ethics (1990) contained no divisible set of ethical principles related directly to therapy. In this regard, the 1992 Ethical Principles offered significant improvement. For example, Standard 4.02 of the 1992 code requires that "psychologists obtain appropriate informed consent to therapy or related procedures" (APA, 1992, p. 1605). As part of this process, psychologists are obliged to inform potential therapy participants "of significant information concerning the procedure" (p. 1605) in some documentable form. Although Standard 4.02 makes it clear that some manner of consent must be obtained from clients, it does not flesh out this requirement in any explicit way. Thus, many authors, reflecting on the 1990 and 1992 codes, have sought to advance their views on how the consent process should take place. Some have even questioned whether consent should be sought at all. Another matter of considerable debate is whether the therapist and the client should enter into a formal written informed-consent contract.

These controversies about the substance and procedure of informed consent to treatment are important in themselves, but they also raise larger, more overarching issues. What does the kind of consent process, if any, say about the nature of the relationship between the professional and the person seeking help? Which of the moral principles discussed in chapter 3 are promoted by consent? Does obtaining consent promote certain values, but endanger others? Can in fact obtaining consent damage—if not destroy—the value of certain forms of therapy?

Single client–therapist issues are complex enough; they become geometrically enlarged when therapists engage in couples, family, or group therapy. Confidentiality issues become paramount, of course, and the materials in this chapter on confidentiality amplify the ideas put forth in chapter 4. Added to this, however, is the complicating fact that family therapy often involves children. Should they have the right to consent to therapy? Do they have independent rights to privacy that should be respected? Should one assume that parents represent their children's interests? When, if ever, should therapists act as children's advocates?

It is essential that this chapter cover these traditional (though yet unresolved, and unsolved) problems. However, the world of psychology is not limited to spoken, face-to-face forms of treatment. For example, psychologists are increasingly involved in behavioral medicine, such as stress and pain management. Moreover, it is impossible to ignore the presently raging debate over the effort of many powerful and influential psychologists to obtain the right for licensed psychologists, given proper training, to prescribe antipsychotic and other psychotropic medications. In addition, some psychologists write self-help texts that become bestsellers, whereas others conduct therapy over the telephone or electronic mail (and probably by fax).

Not only do psychologists engage in different forms of treatment, but they are also confronted with a diversity of clients. Women in general, gays and lesbians, ethnic minorities, those from rural communities, and people with disabilities often confront the responsible psychotherapist (still predominantly men who are White and urban) with a plethora of ethical issues. Finally, ethical problems may even survive the death of the therapist. Consider, for example, what ethical obligations psychologists have toward their patients in contemplation of their own deaths?

These are the issues covered in chapter 7. The challenges they represent clearly show that good therapy is more than technique, empathy, and sound theory.

References

American Psychological Association. (1990). Ethical principles of psychologists (amended June 2, 1989). *American Psychologist, 47,* 390–395.

American Psychological Association. (1992). Ethical principles of psychologists and code of conduct. *American Psychologist, 47,* 1597–1611.

Rights of Clients, Responsibilities of Therapists

Rachel T. Hare-Mustin, Jeanne Marecek, Alexandra G. Kaplan, and Nechama Liss-Levinson

Most psychotherapists formally uphold the ethical principles of their professions. These principles entail a commitment to promote the welfare of clients and to assure their rights. . . .

ETHICAL PRINCIPLES IN THE THERAPY RELATIONSHIP

. . . By assuring clients' rights, therapists can accord their clients equality of status and responsibility for their participation in therapy and, ultimately, for their lives. In addition, assuring clients' rights places corresponding responsibilities on clients (Arbuckle, 1977). Clients are expected to choose wisely, to make use of information provided, and to assume control of their participation in therapy. By helping clients accept their rights and responsibilities, therapists are encouraging healthy functioning and, thus, mental health. Taken together, these responsibilities and rights that follow from the *Ethical Standards* constitute a model for the practice of therapy that can be contrasted with other models. . . .

This model can provide benefits to therapists and to the profession. Assuring clients' rights can make therapists more effective practitioners. Open communication about the methods and goals of therapy can encourage realistic expectations about treatment and outcome. The therapist who is sensitive to the client's rights may be able to minimize therapeutic impasses and unilateral terminations stemming from the client's unspoken dissatisfactions. Finally, assurance of clients' rights can protect the practitioner from criminal or malpractice actions (Roston & Sherrer, 1973). Unless the internal regulation of the profession is visibly effective in protecting clients, professional practice may be open to outside regulation.

Implications for Training

Few therapists are adequately prepared by their training to carry out the *Ethical Standards* in practice. . . . [T]raining should foster an image of clients as powerful, responsible adults and inculcate a sense of responsibility in therapists for clients' rights and dignity. As Kessler (1977) suggested, we must rethink and retool our training programs if our practice of therapy is to be consistent with our ethical principles. . . .

ASSURING THAT CLIENTS MAKE INFORMED CHOICES

. . . .

First, clients need knowledge of procedures, goals, and side effects of therapy. Some of the issues involved in presenting a description of procedures and goals of therapy are discussed in the section below on Establishing a Contract. The issue of whether the client is to be informed of possible side effects of therapy generates more controversy. Information about possible indirect effects is essential if the client is to weigh the benefits and risks of entering treatment (Coyne, 1976; Graziano & Fink, 1973). An example of such an indirect effect is the possibility that progress in individual therapy will disrupt a marital relationship (Hurvitz, 1967). It is only recently that psychologists have turned their attention to the question of indirect effects of therapy

(Strupp & Hadley, 1977). Thus, more research is needed to broaden our knowledge of indirect effects.

An issue that is now receiving much attention is confidentiality and privileged communication in therapy. The extent of confidentiality of communications and records is more limited than many assume. Third-party payers may require the therapist to furnish information that the client would not wish to disclose; such information may be available for later retrieval by others. The *Tarasoff* decision in California established that a therapist must warn a client's intended victim of possible danger (Whiteley & Whiteley, 1977). Confidentiality in group therapy may not be protected under the laws of privileged communication, although many therapists and clients assume that it is (Meyer & Smith, 1977). Some therapies by their nature offer fewer safeguards to confidentiality than others do. For example, . . . [i]n marital therapy, the therapist may provoke disclosures that further harm the marital relationship or that play into the hands of the more powerful partner (Rubin & Mitchell, 1976). Therapists may overlook the need to inform clients that their cases may sometimes be discussed with colleagues, supervisors, or at case conferences. Limitations on confidentiality must be conveyed to prospective clients; guarantees of complete secrecy are tantamount to "blatant misrepresentation of facts that should be known to all therapists" (Bersoff, 1975, p. 270).

Second, clients need information about the qualifications of the therapist to make informed choices about entering therapy. Clients may have uncertainties about the specialties and training of various professionals. As Winborn (1977) suggested, "honest labeling" is necessary if informed choices are to be made. Therapists disagree about the extent of information on skills, qualifications, and training to be presented to the client. However, therapists in training are not the only ones who should inform clients of their status and qualifications. Providing a description of skills and experience and responding to clients' queries safeguard both therapist and client from unrealistic expectations that the client might hold.

Third, clients need to know about alternatives to psychotherapy. It is unusual for therapists to share information on alternative resources with their cli-

ents, yet the *Standards for Providers* state that therapists have a responsibility to inform themselves about the network of human services in their communities and to use this knowledge in making referrals. Because clients' knowledge of the available resources is usually limited, therapists have the responsibility of providing this information. . . .

Issues About Informed Decisions
When should information be presented? . . .
Some therapists (e.g., Winborn, 1977) find that the optimal time for educating clients about therapy is the end of the first interview. However, this may not hold for clients who enter therapy in crisis. For clients who are deeply upset, the therapist may balance the need to offer immediate support and relief against the responsibility to explore whether the client has come to the right place for help. Nonetheless, even if the examination of therapy and its alternatives is postponed for several sessions, it should not be foregone.

How should information about therapy and its alternatives be presented?
The information may be presented orally, in writing, or on audio- or videotape. Certain kinds of information can be presented by a receptionist or intake interviewer. Sometimes therapists may reduce or waive the fee for such an informational session.

The manner of presenting information to clients should be consistent with the ethical principle of informed choice. Biases and inaccurate information are violations of this principle. For example, therapists could be cautious to characterize alternative systems fairly. An ethical dilemma may occur when the therapist has very strong feelings about what course of action is best for a client. In such cases, the therapist may feel obligated to air these feelings to the client, particularly if the client is tending toward a different course of action. Recommending a course of action can be seen as promoting the client's welfare. However, when a course of action is insisted upon by the therapist, the client's right to free choice is diminished.

Are there disadvantages of assuring clients' rights to informed decisions?
A premature or overly enthusiastic discussion of alternatives may convince the client that the therapist does not want him or

her in therapy. Another disadvantage is that some potential clients may choose sources of help other than therapy. For therapists whose livelihoods depend on their clientele, this may be worrisome. However, concerns about losing clients must be viewed in perspective. Many potential clients terminate after the first interview anyway. An open discussion of therapy and its alternatives may lead some of these clients to continue in treatment.

Some psychoanalytic therapists may feel that detailed information about therapy and the therapist weakens the transference relationship (Wolberg, 1967). Other therapists feel that open disclosure promotes the client–therapists relationship.

ESTABLISHING A CONTRACT

. . .

Ethical principles assert that therapists should inform clients about the purpose and nature of therapy and that clients have freedom of choice about their participation. The process of providing information and obtaining agreement through the use of a contract defines the therapeutic relationship as a mutual endeavor to which the therapist contributes knowledge and skill in psychology and to which the client brings specialized personal knowledge and a commitment to work on his or her problems (Adams & Orgel, 1975; Schwitzgebel, 1976; Sulzer, 1962). Developing a contractual agreement is a negotiation between partners.

The purpose of a contract is to clarify the therapeutic relationship. The development of a contract, whether written or verbal, encourages the client and the therapist to specify the goals, expectations, and boundaries of therapy. Specifying both the problem (or diagnosis, if one is made) and the treatment makes the profession more accountable (Schulberg, 1976). In addition, the contract can prevent misunderstandings about the responsibilities, methods, and practical arrangements of therapy. In this regard, contracts can protect both the therapist and the client from disappointment or false expectations.

Most therapy contracts specify some or all of the following: the methods of therapy, its goals, the length and frequency of sessions, the duration of treatment, the cost and the method of payment,

provisions for cancellation and renegotiation of the contract, the extent of each person's responsibility, and the degree of confidentiality. The issues covered by a contract vary according to the therapist's orientation and the inclination of the client. . . . Some therapists emphasize the nature of the relationship; other therapists provide precise specifications of the extent of confidentiality. A contract involving several clients, as in marital and family therapy or group therapy, raises special problems. Likewise, one must be especially sensitive to ethical issues when contracting with a child client, who may not be in a position to give meaningful agreement (Robinson, 1974). The more detailed a contract is, the more frequently it will require renegotiation as the client's circumstances change and the goals of therapy evolve. Periodic reassessment and revision are an integral part of the process of contracting.

The following example of a contract is adapted from a model proposed by the Health Research Group, a Ralph Nader group (Adams & Orgel, 1975):

> I, Alice Bryant, agree to join with Dr. J. Smith each Tuesday from October 4, 1977 to December 6, 1977, at 3:00 p.m. During these 10 45-minute sessions, we will direct our mutual efforts toward 3 goals:
>
> 1. Enabling me to have discussions with my spouse without losing my temper.
>
> 2. Explaining to my satisfaction why I avoid visiting my parents.
>
> 3. Overcoming my fears of meeting new people.
>
> I agree to pay $35 per session for the use of her resources, training, and experience as a therapist. This amount is payable at the time of the session.
>
> If I am not satisfied with the progress made on these goals, I may cancel any future appointments provided I give Dr. Smith 3 days warning of my intention to cancel. In that event, I (am/am not) required to pay for sessions not met. However, if I miss a session with-

out <u>24</u> hrs. forewarning, I (am/am not) financially responsible for that missed session, exceptions to this arrangement being unforeseen and unavoidable accident or illness.

At the end of <u>10</u> sessions, Dr. Smith and I agree to renegotiate this contract. We include the possibility that the stated goals will have changed during the <u>10-session</u> period. I understand that this agreement does not guarantee that I will have attained these goals; however, it does constitute an offer on my part to pay Dr. Smith for access to her resources as a therapist and her acceptance to apply all those resources as a therapist in good faith.

I further stipulate that this agreement become a part of the record which is accessible to both parties at will, but to no other person without my written consent. The therapist will respect my right to maintain the confidentiality of any information communicated by me to the therapist during the course of therapy.

I (give/do not give) my permission to Dr. Smith to audiotape sessions for her review. However, she will not publish, communicate, or otherwise disclose, without my written consent, any such information, which, if disclosed, would injure me in any way.

———————————————
Client's signature

———————————————
Therapist's signature

———————————————
Date

Issues About Contracts
Should the contract specify all techniques?

. . .

Techniques that might be at odds with the client's values should be specified. The client should know whether the therapy will consist of talking, role playing, or body work, if aversive techniques will be used, if he or she is expected to take medication, if others, such as family members, will be involved, and if he or she will be expected to join a group. Therapists who follow up on clients should secure their permission in the contract, even if this might bias future responses. Some practices, such as sexual relations with clients, are unethical and remain so whether or not the client agrees to them. It has been argued that forms of treatment to which some therapists object, such as primal scream or "tickle" therapy, should be permitted if clients freely agree to them with full knowledge of the risks and benefits. The use of contracts cannot protect clients from making decisions that are not in their best interests. However, if there is gross inequity in the bargaining power of the contracting parties so that the client has no real choice or alternative, such a contract may be considered legally unconscionable (Schwitzgebel, 1975, 1976).

What if the therapist has personal or moral problems with the client's goal? . . . Special difficulties can arise in setting goals in therapies that involve more than one person, such as group, marital, or family therapy. . . . Therapists must be cautious about supporting goals for the maintenance of the family unit that override the rights of individuals.

Therapy with children also brings up special considerations. Some therapists who work with children advocate a contract because it encourages self-control and delay of gratification (Croghan & Frutiger, 1977). However, these seem to be goals of the parents and therapist, not goals of the child. The therapist may find it hard to support parental goals that deny the rights of the child client. Certain rights of children may not be waived by their parents (Sehdev, 1976; White House Conference on Children, 1970). It has been suggested that a child who does not have the capacity to give full unpressured agreement to goals and techniques should have an advocate other than the parent or therapist (Koocher, 1976). . . .

How should a therapist respond to a client who does not want a contract? For the therapist who feels strongly about the desirability of specifying the goals and arrangements for therapy, the contract may be such an integral part of the technique that he or she will not work without it. Some clients may reject a contract because they are suspicious that the contract is intended to benefit only the therapist. For those clients as well as others, a contract is such an unusual idea that considerable explanation may be required. However, the explanation must be presented in such a way that the client retains the right to refuse. . . .

References

Adams, S., & Orgel, M. *Through the mental health maze.* Washington, D.C.: Health Research Group, 1975.

Arbuckle, D. S. Consumers make mistakes too: An invited response. *Personnel and Guidance Journal,* 1977, *56,* 219–233.

Bersoff, D. N. Professional ethics and legal responsibilities: On the horns of a dilemma. *Journal of School Psychology,* 1975, *13,* 359–376.

Coyne, J. C. The place of informed consent in ethical dilemmas. *Journal of Consulting and Clinical Psychology,* 1976, *44,* 1015–1016.

Croghan, L. M., & Frutiger, A. D. Contracting with children: A therapeutic tool. *Psychotherapy: Theory, Research and Practice,* 1977, *14,* 32–40.

Graziano, A. M. & Fink, F. S. Second-order effects in mental health treatment. *Journal of Consulting and Clinical Psychology,* 1973, *40,* 356–364.

Hurvitz, N. Marital problems following psychotherapy with one spouse. *Journal of Consulting Psychology,* 1967, *31,* 38–47.

Kessler, J. W. A problem of absorption. *APA Monitor,* March 1977, p. 2.

Koocher, G. P. Civil liberties and aversive conditioning for children. *American Psychologist,* 1976, *31,* 94–95.

Meyer, R. G., & Smith, S. R. A crisis in group therapy. *American Psychologist,* 1977, *32,* 638–662.

Robinson, D. N. Harm, offense, and nuisance: Some first steps in the establishment of an ethics of treatment. *American Psychologist,* 1974, *29,* 233–238.

Roston, R., & Sherrer, C. Malpractice: What's new? *Professional Psychology,* 1973, *4,* 270–276.

Rubin, Z., & Mitchell, C. Couples research as couples counseling: Some unintended effects of studying close relationships. *American Psychologist,* 1976, *31,* 17–25.

Schulberg, H. C. Quality-of-care standards and professional norms. *American Journal of Psychiatry,* 1976, *133,* 1047–1051.

Schwitzgebel, R. K. A contractual model for the protection of the rights of institutionalized mental patients. *American Psychologist,* 1975, *30,* 815–820.

Schwitzgebel, R. K. Treatment contracts and ethical self-determination. *Clinical Psychologist,* 1976, *29*(3), 5–7.

Sehdev, H. S. Patients' rights or patients' neglect: The impact of the patients' rights movement on delivery systems. *American Journal of Orthopsychiatry,* 1976, *46,* 660–668.

Strupp, H. H., & Hadley, S. W. A tripartite model of mental health and therapeutic outcomes: With special reference to negative effects in psychotherapy. *American Psychologist,* 1977, *32,* 187–196.

Sulzer, E. S. Reinforcement and the therapeutic contract. *Journal of Counseling Psychology,* 1962, *9,* 271–276.

White House Conference on Children. *Report to the President.* Washington, D.C.: U.S. Government Printing Office, 1970.

Whiteley, J., & Whiteley, R. California court expands privilege debate. *APA Monitor,* February 1977, pp. 5; 6; 18.

Winborn, B. B. Honest labeling and other procedures for the protection of consumers of counseling. *Personnel and Guidance Journal,* 1977, *56,* 206–209.

Wolberg, L. R. *The technique of psychotherapy* (2nd ed.). New York: Grune & Stratton, 1967.

◆ ◆ ◆

Commentary: *Handelsman and Galvin (1988, next excerpt) studied the effects of consent forms on patients and their therapy. Although these authors have been skeptical about whether such forms protect psychologists against legal liability, they have asserted that the forms "still have a role in facilitating the ethical goals of informed consent: increasing professionals' self-scrutiny, respecting the autonomy of clients, and allowing clients to enhance their welfare by becoming partners with the therapist in their mental health care" (1988, p. 223). In the Appendix to their article, Handelsman and Galvin provided the following form, written for a fourth-grade readability level, that therapists can give their clients to guide an informed decision about whether to enter therapy.*

Facilitating Informed Consent for Outpatient Psychotherapy: A Suggested Written Format

Mitchell M. Handelsman and Michael D. Galvin

When you come for therapy, you are buying a service. Therefore, you need information to make a good decision. Below are some questions you might want to ask. We've talked about some of them. You are entitled to ask me any of these questions, if you want to know. If you don't understand my answers, ask me again.

I. Therapy
   A. How does your kind of therapy work?
   B. What are the possible risks involved? (like divorce, depression)
   C. What percentage of clients improve? In what ways?
   D. What percentage of clients get worse?
   E. What percentage of clients improve or get worse without this therapy?
   F. About how long will it take?
   G. What should I do if I feel therapy isn't working?

II. Alternatives
   A. What other types of therapy or help are there? (like support groups)
   B. How often do they work?
   C. What are the risks of these other approaches?

III. Appointments
   A. How are appointments scheduled?
   B. How long are sessions? Do I have to pay more for longer ones?
   C. How can I reach you in an emergency?
   D. If you are not available, who is there I can talk to?

   E. What happens if the weather is bad, or I'm sick?

IV. Confidentiality
   A. What kind of records do you keep? Who has access to them? (insurance companies, supervisors)
   B. Under what conditions are you allowed to tell others about the things we discuss? (suicidal or homicidal threats, child abuse, court cases, insurance companies, supervisors)
   C. Do other members of my family, or of the group, have access to information?

V. Money
   A. What is your fee?
   B. How do I need to pay? At the session, monthly, etc.?
   C. Do I need to pay for missed sessions?
   D. Do I need to pay for telephone calls or letters?
   E. What are your policies about raising fees? (for example, How many times have you raised them in the past two years?)
   F. If I lose my source of income, can my fee be lowered?
   G. If I do not pay my fee, will you take me to small claims court? Do you use a collection agency or lawyer? Under what circumstances?

VI. General
   A. What is your training and experience? Are you licensed? Supervised? Board certified?
   B. Who do I talk to if I have a complaint about

therapy which we can't work out? (e.g., Supervisor, State Board of Psychologist Examiners, APA ethics committee)

The contract [or brochure, or our conversation] dealt with most of these questions. I will be happy to explain them, and to answer other questions you have. This will help make your decision a good one. You can keep this information. Please read it carefully at home. We will also look this over from time to time.

◆   ◆   ◆

Commentary: In another study, Handelsman and his colleagues found that young adults evaluating a hypothetical male therapist rated him more highly if he used the consent form to evoke discussion in comparison with an identical male therapist who did not use the informed-consent procedure. See Sullivan, T., Martin, W. L., Jr., & Handelsman, M. (1993). Practical benefits of an informed-consent procedure: An empirical investigation. Professional Psychology: Research and Practice, 24, 160–164. They concluded that

> these results provide evidence that an informed-consent procedure, when done well, can be used to provide ethical treatment to clients without risking damage at the beginning of the therapeutic relationship. Indeed, clients may be more favorably disposed to therapists who take the time and effort to provide information. For professional therapists, this consent procedure also seems to enhance impressions of trustworthiness and expertness. (p. 162)

The Responsible Psychotherapist

Thomas A. Widiger and Leonard G. Rorer

[*Ed. note:* These authors' arguments are grounded in the work of H. L. A. Hart (1968), a legal philosopher. Relying on this work, the authors defined four kinds of responsibility: (a) *role responsibility*, or the fulfillment of duties, tasks, or obligations of one's position, office, or title; (b) *causal responsibility*, or causing or producing consequences, results, or outcomes; (c) *capacity responsibility*, or possession of qualities or abilities to govern one's actions; and (d) *liability responsibility*, being held accountable for acts and omissions. *See* Hart, H. L. A. (1968). *Punishment and responsibility: Essays in the philosophy of law.* Oxford, England: Clarendon Press.]

. . .

RECOMMENDED REQUISITES FOR AN ETHICAL PSYCHOTHERAPY

We will argue that the suggestions by those concerned with assuring an ethical psychotherapy (contracts, informed consent, and equal participation in decision making) are often incompatible with the role and causal responsibilities of the therapist and the capacity responsibilities of the therapist and the patient, and that they might have an effect opposite to that intended. The discussion focuses on the use of contracts and informed consent and subsumes the arguments concerned with equal participation in decisions.

Recommended Requisites Vis-à-Vis Role Responsibilities

Therapists are "bound by professional duty to be actively moral and virtuous in all their decisions" (Redlich & Mollica, 1976, p. 125) but "our greatest duty is to our patients or our client and the obligation is to render service" (Foster, 1975, p. 55). It is certainly within the role responsibility of the therapist to be ethical (APA, 1977, 1979), but at times being ethical may be antitherapeutic (Griffith & Griffith, 1978). What is ethical may not be effective, and what is effective may not be ethical (Begelman, 1971). "On the highest level of abstraction is the clash between the individual's right to freedom, autonomy, and personal choice, and the physician's professional duty to heal and cure" (Foster, 1978, p. 71) [footnote omitted].

. . .

The possibility of an inherent incompatibility between ethical and effective therapy derives in part from the fact that the ethical recommendations either do not follow from any theoretical model of psychotherapy or psychopathology or follow from some models but not from others. It follows from these considerations that some therapists may have difficulty in making certain practices congruent with their therapeutic techniques. For example, autonomy and freedom of choice are ethical positions consistent with a democratic ideal. While they are both a goal and a technique of existential psychotherapy consistent with its theoretical model of the person (Bugental, 1965), they are not easily derived from the principles of psychoanalysis or behavior modification. We will consider specifically whether contracts and informed consent are consistent with the role responsibilities of the psychotherapist.

Contracts. Contracts are not inherently or absolutely incompatible with any form of psychotherapy. Indeed, all psychotherapy is conducted under some

From *American Psychologist*, 39, 503–515. Copyright 1984 by the American Psychological Association. Adapted with permission of the author and publisher.

form of implicit or implied contract. The analyst and analysand, for instance, are implicitly under contract to follow certain guidelines of analytic treatment (e.g., not to give specific advice and to free associate, respectively). One could even have a contract that absolved all participants from any responsibilities, though it would probably not be legally acceptable.

A difficulty arises, however, when a contract suitable to one model of therapy is applied to another, incompatible model. The contracts recommended by Atthowe (1975), Hare-Mustin et al. (1979), Schwitzgebel (1975), and Stuart (1975), for instance, are congruent primarily with a behavioral perspective, and it is not coincidental that Atthowe, Schwitzgebel, and Stuart are behaviorally oriented. . . .

It is unclear how contracts specifying goals, length of therapy, and techniques of intervention would work with other models of treatment. Menninger (1958) and Szasz (1965) do use a "contractual model" within a psychoanalytic framework, but their contracts are much different from the specific and explicit contracts of Atthowe, Hare-Mustin, Schwitzgebel, and Stuart. Szasz (1965) leaves open and vague the frequency, duration, and focus of therapy precisely for the purpose of increasing the patient's control. Hare-Mustin et al. (1979) state that if the patient cannot be specific regarding a goal "this challenges the therapist to help translate vague complaints into specific problems" (p. 9). It is likely that an existential, analytic, or client-centered therapist would take issue with the therapeutic value of making such a translation. As Margolin (1982) indicates, in family therapy, "openly stated goals may differ from secret agendas and . . . goals that emerge during the course of therapy may differ from goals stated at the outset" (p. 790). Parker (1976), in his comment on Schwitzgebel (1975), states that in "psychoanalytically oriented psychotherapy . . . such contracts of cure or even contracts outlining the specifics of the treatment process would be wholly inappropriate and, in fact, counterproductive. . . . There is enough built-in resistance to analytic psy-

chotherapy . . . that we should avoid adding more coals to the fire" (p. 258). . . .

Though there are difficulties in making contracts consistent with various models of psychotherapy, there is no difficulty in making them consistent with a business or commercial model, from which they are more appropriately derived. The notion of a formal exchange of goods or services between autonomous participants with free choice is more evident in the purchase of services from professionals such as accountants, carpenters, and painters. A contractual model has been used within the physician–patient relationship, but it has been more of an implied than an explicit contract. . . . "The contractual model is more nearly based upon the notion of a social exchange of goods or services" (Schwitzgebel, 1975, p. 819). Many therapists, who prefer to act like therapists rather than business persons, have complained that patients' rights interfere with their ability to deliver effective treatment (Roth & Meisel, 1977; Stone, 1978; Wise, 1978) and that they are being forced to practice a "defensive psychotherapy" that is less effective and at times impotent (Gurevitz, 1977).

Informed consent.   The APA's (1979) *Ethical Standards* state that "psychologists fully inform consumers as to the purpose and nature" (p. 5) of an intervention.[1] A consent is said to be informed if all risks and possible consequences of the procedure in question, and all alternative procedures, are presented to the patient and the patient has given evidence that the presentation was understood (Meisel, Roth, & Lidz, 1977). However, the instability, distress, confusion, or motivational defensive structure of the psychotherapy patient may make it difficult to disclose all of the relevant information (Morse, 1967). "If disclosure of certain information—especially the risks of treatment—is likely to upset the patient so seriously that he or she will be unable to make a rational decision, then the physician has the 'therapeutic privilege' to withhold such information" (Meisel et al., 1977, p. 286).

Not only do psychotherapists and patients lack the necessary capacities for implementation but in-

---

[1] *Ed. note:* See Standards 1.07 and 4.02 of the APA's current (1992) Ethical Principles.

formed consent is inherently incompatible with many therapeutic techniques. Both deception and covert manipulation are antithetical to informed consent but central to systems, strategic, and "social influence" models of psychotherapy (Gillis, 1979; Haley, 1978; Rabkin, 1977). . . .

There may in fact be a substantial amount of manipulation and social pressure in all forms of psychotherapy (Beutler, 1979; Frank, 1961; Strong, 1978). Margolin (1982) provides illustrations of the difficulty of being both an open and an effective family therapist. Lebensohn (1978), lamenting the deleterious effects of informed consent on analytic techniques, describes a procedure that forewarns the client of possible failure to get better; the possibility of getting worse; the potentially great dependency on, and emotional involvement with, the therapist; the possibility of a resulting divorce or suicide; and that anything said may be used for commitment. "Having properly executed the above form, you may now enter the private consulting room and feel free to tell the psychiatrist anything and everything that comes to mind" (Lebensohn, 1978, p. 36).

The conflict between ethical and effective treatment is illustrated in the paradoxical inconsistency of (a) Coyne's (1976a) and Coyne and Widiger's (1978) advocation of open, equal, and honest participation by the client; and (b) Coyne's (1976b) model of depression and his support of manipulative, strategic techniques.

> [The patient] is assigned to monotonous, nongratifying, and repetitive tasks. . . . Although the patient is not ridiculed or belittled, his task performance is continually criticized as not perfect. This continues . . . until the patient "blows up," refuses to follow orders, or becomes verbally (seldom physically) aggressive. . . . [The staff is] instructed not to give in to the patient's pleadings to be left alone to suffer, not to try to cheer him up, and not to offer sympathy or encouragement. (Coyne, 1976b, p. 38)

This treatment certainly does not follow from an ethical model of mutual participation that grants "the patient the status of a responsible adult" (Coyne & Widiger, 1978, p. 701) with "extensive disclosure" and "an active and responsible role for the patient" (Coyne & Widiger, 1978, p. 707) [footnote omitted].

Recommended Requisites Vis-à-Vis Causal Responsibilities

A major difficulty in establishing legal liability has been the identification of the causal link between the injury and the acts of commission or omission by the therapist (Kennedy, 1975). There is little doubt that some change typically occurs during treatment, but the extent to which a therapist actually causes the results is an unresolved theoretical, empirical, and philosophical question. . . . Given conflicting attributions by different theoretical models combined with the inability to identify single causal effects empirically, it is clearly not possible to obtain agreement on causal responsibility and hence on liability (Rothblatt & Leroy, 1973). . . .

Recommended Requisites Vis-à-Vis Capacity Responsibilities

The APA (1979) *Ethical Standards* state that "psychologists fully inform consumers as to the purpose and nature [of an intervention] . . . and they freely acknowledge that clients, students, or participants in research [and therapy] have freedom of choice with regard to participation" (p. 5). This is a commendable principle, but it may in actuality be beyond the capacities of the patient and the therapist. Therapists may not have the capacity to inform their patients fully, and patients, due to their inherent incapacities or their differential status with respect to the therapist, may not have the capacity to offer a free choice. . . .

Patient capacity. The patient's capacity responsibility is a central issue when one considers contracts or informed consent within psychotherapy (Alexander & Szasz, 1973; Appelbaum & Roth, 1981; Roth, Miesel, & Lidz, 1977). Therapists opposing contracts and informed consent typically express the belief that patients, due to their mental illness or disorder, do not possess the necessary capacities to give an informed consent or to agree to a contract (Moore, 1978). Foster (1975) states that "quite competent patients by any standards" (p. 159) are not likely to understand the complex informed consent forms they sign upon admission to an inpatient unit, because they are too overwhelmed by the issues that brought them to the hospital, and are in a "distraught and distracted state of mind" (p. 159).

Appelbaum, Mirkin, and Bateman (1981) and Olin and Olin (1975) demonstrated in empirical studies that many voluntary mental hospital patients had little idea what they had consented to or what the consent involved. Appelbaum et al. (1981) state that their results "ought to give pause to those who are seeking to extend the ever growing formalization of the relationship, . . . especially those who speak of using a 'contract' " (p. 1175). . . .

. . . Informing the patient of treatment alternatives or risks may be of little value. "All the knowledge in the world will not help a depressed patient make a non-depressed choice. . . . How can the patient make a reasonable choice regarding behavior control when their choosing mechanism is so often the very object of the procedure?" (Neville, 1972, pp. 7–8).

> Mental disease is not an independent variable which is inversely related to the dependent variable of free choice, but is *by definition* inversely related to it. . . . That an act is the product of mental illness logically *implies* lack of intention and, thus, lack of responsibility. (Leifer, 1964, p. 828)

The advocates of the ethical ameliorations, of course, adamantly reject the contention of patient incapacity. Coyne and Widiger (1978) would have it both ways. On the one hand they argue that there is no patient incapacity and that the appearance of it is created when therapists withhold information or describe therapy in intentionally vague terms. However, they simultaneously reject both informed consent and contracts on the basis of therapist and patient incapacities. "Patients often enter therapy in great distress. . . . While the explicitness and accountability of formal contracts may be desirable, many patients would find them threatening at the start of therapy and constraining as therapy progresses" (Coyne & Widiger, 1978, p. 706). . . .

Alexander and Szasz (1973) and Finkel (1980) view the questioning of patient capacity as just another instance of paternalistic violation of liberty and freedom. An intervention is defined to be paternalistic when the therapist acts without the full consent, or against the resistance, of the patient. Dworkin (1972) indicates that paternalism is acceptable when "it preserves and enhances for the individual his ability to rationally consider and carry out his own decisions" (p. 83). This is precisely the goal of most psychotherapies. Dworkin (1972) also points out that those who would restrict the practice of therapists for the protection of the patient are as paternalistic as those who practice therapy, because both assume that patients cannot protect themselves.

The malleable nature of the attribution of capacity responsibility to mental patients is evident in other efforts to promote ethical rights. While patients are attributed the capacity to control their behavior and give consent when the use of contracts and informed consent is at issue, it is precisely the incapacity to control their behavior and give consent that is their defense in many malpractice suits. In the case of malpractice suits patients need not be psychotic to be assumed incapable of protecting, or deciding for, themselves. The judges in *Roy v. Hartogs* (1975) split on this very issue. A dissenting judge held that, because the patient was able to give consent, she was not entitled to claim that she was coerced into sexual relations by the overpowering influence of, or trust in, the therapist.

It appears that attributions of capacity in the patient, when motivated by a desire to protect ethical rights, can result in quite contradictory conclusions. Patients are capable if this entails their right to decision-making power but are incapable if they decided to engage in sexual activities. While Finkel (1980) may attribute complete capacity to the mental patient, thereby questioning involuntary treatment, Davison (1978) attributes incapacity to the mental patient (i.e., homosexuals), thereby questioning voluntary treatment. Both positions are based on an interest in protecting the ethical rights of patients.

Patient capacity and differential status. In discussions of informed consent, the question of capacity responsibility is often conflated with that of differential status or power. . . .

351

"If there is a gross inequity in the bargaining power of the parties to a contract so that the weaker party has no meaningful choice or no real alternatives the contract may be considered legally unconscionable" (Schwitzgebel, 1975, p. 818). What is ethically unconscionable may be even less stringent (Foster, 1975). Schwitzgebel (1975) criticizes informed consent as a protection of a patient's rights precisely for its failure to deal adequately with the patient's disadvantageous, unfavorable position. He does not, however, hold this to be a problem when a contract is used. It is unclear how the presence of a contract changes the status of patients and their unfavorable position (Parker, 1976). Coyne and Widiger (1978), while rejecting the notion of patient incapacity, argue that a patient's unfavorable position relative to a therapist belies a valid contractual relationship. The inconsistencies are clear. Patients have the capacity for participatory decision making but not for contracts (Coyne & Widiger, 1978); patients have the capacity to sign contracts but not to give an informed consent (Schwitzgebel, 1975); and patients have the capacity to give an informed consent (Redlich & Mollica, 1976) [footnote omitted].

Therapist capacity. Finally, we consider whether the ethical recommendations are compatible with the capacity responsibility of the therapist. Contracting for goals, length, means, or effects of therapy implies some capacity to govern or direct the process and outcome of therapy. It is unclear, however, how a therapist can assure a client that treatment will, or will not, affect certain beliefs, behaviors, or other persons. . . . It is unclear that the therapist has the capacity to present the necessary information for an informed consent, because the risks and consequences of the treatment and its alternatives are so vast, indeterminate, and complex that they belie adequate presentation. . . .

CONCLUSIONS

. . .

Part of the role responsibility of a psychotherapist is to be ethical, but resolution of the therapeutic with the ethical involves inherent dilemmas. It is not simply a matter of including contracts and informed consent. Nor is it a matter of abandoning ethical principles. As Jung (1963) observed, "Nothing can spare us the torment of ethical decision" (p. 330).

Our analysis suggests that the torment is greater than has been acknowledged, because it is not possible to have a single set of ethical principles that is consistent with currently extant therapeutic orientations. Ethical principles consistent with some theoretical and philosophical positions will necessarily be inconsistent with others (unless they are vacuous). Therefore, resolution of the ethical with the therapeutic will likely have to be relative to different therapeutic orientations . . . If some relativism is unavoidable, then a possible solution would be to require each therapist to formulate and to have on file with a designated ethics committee a set of ethical principles that would be made available to each prospective client. Each therapist's actions would be judged according to his or her set of ethical principles. Such a relativistic resolution obviously might not be acceptable to those who believe in absolute values and insist on universal standards, but some compromise appears to be necessary. It does not appear that the standards can be both universal and specific. The above proposal has the advantage that it would allow each therapist to formulate a consistent set of ethical guidelines and therapeutic principles.

. . .

References

Alexander, G. J., & Szasz, T. (1973). From contract to status via psychiatry. *Santa Clara Lawyer, 13,* 537–559.

American Psychological Association. (1977). *Standards for providers of psychological services.* Washington, DC: Author.

American Psychological Association. (1979). *Ethical standards of psychologist* (Rev. ed.). Washington, DC: Author.

Appelbaum, P. S., Mirkin, S. A., & Bateman, A. (1981). Empirical assessment of competency to consent to psychiatric hospitalization. *American Journal of Psychiatry, 138,* 1170–1176.

Appelbaum, P. S., & Roth, L. H. (1981). Clinical issues in the assessment of competency. *American Journal of Psychiatry, 138,* 1462–1467.

Atthowe, J. (1975). Legal and ethical accountability in everyday practice. *Behavioral Engineering, 3,* 25–38.

Begelman, D. A. (1971). The ethics of behavioral control and a new mythology. *Psychotherapy: Theory, Research and Practice, 8,* 165–169.

Beutler, L. (1979). Values, beliefs, religion, and the persuasive influence of psychotherapy. *Psychotherapy: Theory, Research and Practice, 16,* 432–440.

Bugental, J. (1965). *The search for authenticity.* New York: Holt, Rinehart & Winston.

Coyne, J. C. (1976a). Comments: The place of informed consent in ethical dilemmas. *Journal of Consulting and Clinical Psychology, 44,* 1015–1016.

Coyne, J. C. (1976b). Toward an interactional description of depression. *Psychiatry, 39,* 29–40.

Coyne, J. C., & Widiger, T. (1978). Toward a participatory model of psychotherapy. *Professional Psychology, 9,* 700–710.

Davison, G. C. (1978). Not can but ought: The treatment of homosexuality. *Journal of Consulting and Clinical Psychology, 46,* 170–172.

Dworkin, G. (1972). Paternalism. *The Monist, 52,* 64–84.

Finkel, N. J. (1980). *Therapy and ethics: The courtship of law and psychology.* New York: Grune & Stratton.

Foster, H. (1975). The conflict and reconciliation of the ethical interests of therapist and patient. *Journal of Psychiatry and Law, 2,* 39–61.

Foster, H. (1978). Informed consent of mental patients. In W. E. Barton & C. Sanborn (Eds.), *Law and the mental health professions.* New York: International Universities Press.

Frank, J. (1961). *Persuasion and healing.* Baltimore, MD: Johns Hopkins University Press.

Gillis, J. S. (1979). *Social influence in psychotherapy.* Jonesboro, TN: Pilgrimage Press.

Griffith, E. J., & Griffith, E. E. (1978). Duty to third parties, dangerousness, and the right to refuse treatment: Problematic concepts for psychiatrist and lawyer. *California Western Law Review, 14,* 241–274.

Gurevitz, H. (1977). *Tarasoff:* Protective privilege versus public peril. *American Journal of Psychiatry, 134,* 289–292.

Haley, J. (1978). *Problem-solving therapy.* San Francisco: Jossey-Bass.

Hare-Mustin, R. T., Maracek, J., Kaplan, A., & Liss-Levinson, N. (1979). Rights of clients, responsibilities of therapists. *American Psychologist, 34,* 3–16.

Jung, C. (1963). *Memories, dreams, reflections.* New York: Pantheon.

Kennedy, C. (1975). Injuries precipitated by psychotherapy: Liability without fault as a basis for recovery. *South Dakota Law Review, 20,* 401–417.

Lebensohn, Z. (1978). Defensive psychiatry or how to treat the mentally ill without being a lawyer. In W. Barton & C. Sanborn (Eds.), *Law and the mental health professionals.* New York: International Universities Press.

Leifer, R. (1964). The psychiatrist and tests of criminal responsibility. *American Psychologist, 19,* 825–830.

Margolin, G. (1982). Ethical and legal considerations in marital and family therapy. *American Psychologist, 37,* 788–801.

Meisel, A., Roth, L., & Lidz, C. (1977). Toward a model of the legal doctrine of informed consent. *American Journal of Psychiatry, 134,* 285–289.

Menninger, K. (1958). *Theory of psychoanalytic technique.* New York: Basic Books.

Moore, R. (1978). Ethics in the practice of psychiatry—Origins, functions, models and enforcement. *American Journal of Psychiatry, 135,* 157–163.

Morse, H. (1967). Psychiatric responsibility and tort liability. *Journal of Forensic Sciences, 12,* 305–358.

Neville, R. (1972, December 17). *Ethical and philosophical issues of behavior control.* Paper presented at the 139th annual meeting of the American Association for the Advancement of Science.

Olin, G., & Olin, H. (1975). Informed consent in voluntary mental hospital admissions. *American Journal of Psychiatry, 132,* 938–941.

Parker, K. (1976). Comment: On a contractual model of treatment. *American Psychologist, 31,* 257–258.

Rabkin, R. (1977). *Strategic psychotherapy.* New York: Basic.

Redlich, F., & Mollica, R. (1976). Overview: Ethical issues in contemporary psychiatry. *American Journal of Psychiatry, 133,* 125–136.

Roth, L., & Meisel, A. (1977). Dangerousness, confidentiality, and the duty to warn. *American Journal of Psychiatry, 134,* 508–511.

Roth, L., Meisel, A., & Lidz, C. (1977). Tests of competency to consent to treatment. *American Journal of Psychiatry, 134,* 279–284.

Rothblatt, H., & Leroy, D. (1973). Avoiding psychiatric malpractice. *California Western Law Review, 9,* 260–272.

Roy v. Hartogs, 381 N.Y.S. 2d 587 (New York, 1975).

Schwitzgebel, R. K. (1975). A contractual model for the protection of the rights of institutionalized mental patients. *American Psychologist, 30,* 815–820.

Stone, A. (1978). Psychiatry and law. In A. M. Nicholi, Jr. (Ed.), *The Harvard guide to modern psychiatry.* Cambridge, MA: Belknap Press.

Strong, S. (1978). Social psychological approach to psychotherapy research. In S. Garfield & A. Bergin

(Eds.), *Handbook of psychotherapy and behavior change: An empirical analysis* (2nd ed.). New York: Wiley.

Stuart, R. B. (1975). *Guide to client–therapist treatment contract.* Champaign, IL: Research Press Co.

Szasz, T. (1965). *The ethics of psychoanalysis.* New York: Basic Books.

Wise, T. P. (1978). Where the public peril begins: A survey of psychotherapists to determine the effects of *Tarasoff. Stanford Law Review, 31,* 165–190.

◆   ◆   ◆

Commentary: *Graca (1985) disagreed that "treatment effectiveness should take precedence over ethical disclosure" (p. 1062):*

> *Leaving the ethical guidelines for obtaining informed consent to individual therapists to determine can only negatively affect the perception of our profession by consumers and members of the legal profession, who are already wary of our ethical fortitude. (pp. 1062–1063)*

What Graca suggested is that psychologists who take Widiger and Rorer's position inform their clients that because of their theoretical orientation, they will not discuss the specific techniques or objectives of therapy. See Graca, J. (1985). Whither informed consent to psychotherapy? American Psychologist, 40, *1062–1063. Would Graca's alternative comport with the informed consent provisions of the 1992 Ethical Principles?*

Whether ethical or not, consent and contractual agreements may be incompatible with some forms of therapy. Perhaps the technique that raises the most ethical questions is paradoxical intention. Paradoxical strategies usually require the client to maintain or intensify a presenting symptom; for example, a therapist encourages an anxious client to act anxiously in an actual situation. For the strategy to work, it is at times necessary for the therapist to distort his or her rationale for using it. Thus, it is claimed, the use of paradoxical intention is unethical. Others respond that the ethical issues are no different in the use of this technique than in any other form of psychotherapy. What ethical principles are involved in the application of paradoxical strategies? For controversial discussions of this topic, see:

Betts, G. R., & Remer, R. (1993). The impact of paradoxical interventions on perceptions of the therapist and ratings

of treatment acceptability. Professional Psychology: Research and Practice, 24, *164–170.*

Brown, J. E., & Slee, P. T. (1986). Paradoxical strategies: The ethics of intervention. Professional Psychology: Research and Practice, 17, *487–491.*

Hunsley, J. (1988). Conceptions and misconceptions about the context of paradoxical therapy. Professional Psychology: Research and Practice, 19, *553–559.*

In a recent survey of 189 randomly selected doctoral-level APA members (63% men; 95% clinicians), only about 60% of the respondents informed all of their therapy clients about limits to confidentiality, and only 56% informed clients of the therapeutic procedures that might be used. Less than one third informed all of their clients about potential risks, alternatives to therapy, and potential length of treatment. When asked why they did not inform clients about confidentiality, almost 38% of respondents stated that the issue was not relevant, almost 10% felt it would have a negative impact on the client or the therapeutic relationship, and almost 8% said that their clients would not understand the information. See Somberg, D. R. Stone, G. L., & Claiborn, D. C. (1993). Informed consent: Therapists' beliefs and practices. Professional Psychology: Research and Practice, 24, *153–159.*

Given the explicit provisions in the 1992 Ethical Principles about informed consent and the importance of self-determination as a fundamental moral principle, is there any justification for therapists to conclude that discussing the limits of confidentiality with clients is irrelevant? Are not the therapists in Somberg et al.'s survey being quite paternalistic? Regardless of diverging answers to these questions, there is consensus that the issue of informed consent with therapy clients remains complex, as Somberg et al. (1993) did acknowledge:

> *The variability among therapists' self-reported practices and beliefs suggests that a singular focus on ethical standards may not be enough. Ethical standards need to be considered within the unique context of the therapist. This context includes the therapist's values, orientation, and work setting. For example, informing clients of the length of therapy would appear to be incongruent within the context of a psycho-*

dynamic orientation or an open-ended therapy setting. This example highlights the difficult task of applying ethical standards and principles to one's particular context. It seems essential that therapists continue to struggle with such ethical dilemmas presented by their unique therapeutic environment.

Some of the reasons given for not informing clients appear to reflect a concern for the welfare of the client. For example, therapists' concern for the negative impact on the client or therapeutic relationship suggests that informed consent is not only an ethical issue but has clinical implications as well. As potential negative effects appear to be of some relevancy for therapists, more research is needed regarding the negative impact of the consent procedures. It seems, however, that attention must also be given to the positive impact of obtaining informed consent. Because much of psychotherapy focuses on increasing a client's sense of control and autonomy, informed-consent procedures have been suggested as a part of the treatment (Haas, 1991). From another perspective, viewing informed consent as a means of sharing power with the client can have clinical significance, especially for those clients who have been previously victimized. For such clients, issues of power and control can be of central concern, issues that also exist in each therapeutic relationship. Such therapeutic implications highlight the notion that informed consent is not simply an ethical issue but needs to be considered from a clinical perspective as well.

Reasons given for not informing clients also indicated that informed consent is not considered relevant or practical by some therapists. Hence, the value placed on in-formed consent becomes a central issue in regard to practice. The value given informed consent can be fostered through ethics education, graduate training, and professional discussion grounded in different and specific practice contexts. (p. 159)
. . .

Reference

Haas, L. J. (1991). Hide and seek or show and tell? Emerging issues of informed consent, Ethics and Behavior, 1, 175–189.

For an intriguing study exploring the effects of in-formed-consent disclosure, including the risks of psychotherapy, on mothers' decisions to pursue psychological treatment for their elementary-school-age children, see Gustafson, K. E., McNamara, J. R., & Jensen, D. A. (1994). Parents' informed consent decisions regarding psychotherapy for their children: Consideration of therapeutic risks and benefits. Professional Psychology: Research and Practice, 25, 16–22.

The debate concerning the right of therapy clients to be informed of material matters as they begin therapy has largely been resolved by the current ethics code. Vasquez (1994) provides a useful summary of the relevant provisions in code Sections 4 and 5, particularly with regard to structuring the therapeutic relationship, securing client consent, and discussing the limits of confidentiality. See Vasquez, M. J. T. (1994). Implications of the 1992 Ethics Code for the Practice of Individual Psychotherapy, Professional Psychology: Research and Practice, 25, 321–328. Although she clearly applauds these new, detailed provisions in her critique, she also comments:

> The vagueness in some of the principles, the overuse of the term reasonable, which potentially dilutes the power and enforceability of some of the principles, and some instances in which it is possible that the psychologist's welfare is placed above that of the client, are problematic. (p. 327)

The Ethical Issue of Competence in Working With the Suicidal Patient

Bruce Bongar

Suicide has been found to be the most frequently encountered emergency situation for mental health professionals (Schein, 1976), with clinicians consistently ranking work with suicidal patients as the most stressful of all clinical endeavors (Deutsch, 1984) . . .

Furthermore, it is apparent from empirical findings that the average professional psychologist involved in direct patient care has greater than a 20% chance of losing a patient to suicide at some time during his or her professional career. . . . Another study (Kleespies, Smith, & Becker, 1990) investigating the incidence, impact, and methods of coping with patient suicide during the training years of psychology graduate students found that one out of six students had experienced a patient's suicide at some time during their training. . . .

. . . The APA's ethical principles mandate that "Psychologists recognize the boundaries of their competence and the limitation of their techniques. They only provide services and only use the techniques for which they are qualified by training and experience" [(APA, 1981,] p. 634).[1] Harrar, Vande-Creek, and Knapp (1990), in discussing the ethical and legal aspects of clinical supervision, pointed out that, direct liability could also occur if the supervisor assigned a task to a trainee whom the supervisor knew or should have known to be inadequately trained to execute it" (Harrar et al., 1990, p. 39).

. . . Because the APA . . . has taken such an unambiguous position on the need for psychologists to manage the problem of suicide competently, it is clear that formal graduate training in the study of suicide is a necessary part of our graduate curriculum for professional practice. . . .

CONFIDENTIALITY AND THE SUICIDAL PATIENT

. . .

In general, ethical considerations require that clinicians provide their clients with complete information about the limits to confidentiality. In addition, they should give careful thought regarding how they would handle various types of requests to release information or breach confidences before the specific situations occur. . . .

My essential advice is to develop a good understanding of the issues involved in breaching confidentiality with suicidal patients before the fact, that is, to have thought out carefully one's policy on breaching confidentiality before being required to implement it, and to seek consultation in any situation of uncertainty.

Simon (1988) pointed out that the competent patient's request for the maintenance of confidentiality must be honored unless the patient is a clear danger to himself or herself or to others. However, the legal duty to warn or inform third parties exists in some jurisdictions only if the danger of physical harm is threatened toward others (Simon, 1988).

Psychologists must understand laws and regulations related to breaching confidentiality when patients are a "danger to self" (VandeCreek & Knapp,

From *Ethics and Behavior, 2,* 75–89. Copyright 1992 by Erlbaum. Adapted with permission of the author and publisher.

[1] *Ed. note:* See Standard 1.04 of the APA's current (1992) Ethical Principles.

1989). Pope, Tabachnick, and Keith-Spiegel (1988) noted that:

> Apparently the argument made by the defense in many of the early "duty to protect" cases (e.g., *Tarasoff v. Regents of the University of California et al.,* 1976), that absolute confidentiality is necessary for psychotherapy, is not persuasive for many psychotherapists: Breaking confidentiality is seen by a large number of practitioners as uniformly good practice in cases of homicidal risk, suicidal risk, and child abuse. (p. 550)

Shneidman (1981) went even further and stated that confidentiality, when a patient has exhibited suicidal behavior, should not be an important issue between psychologists and their patients. He argued forcibly that the main goal of suicidal therapy is to defuse the potentially lethal situation. Thus, to hold to the principle of confidentiality is contradictory to a basic tenet of an ethical psychotherapeutic relationship.

The official policy of the APA states that psychologists have a primary obligation to respect the confidentiality of information obtained from persons in the course of their work and that they may reveal such information to others only with the consent of the person or her or his legal representative, except in those unusual circumstances when not doing so would result in clear danger to the person or to others (Keith-Speigel & Koocher, 1985).

Gutheil (1984) noted that, with patients for whom suicidal issues are predominant, it is important to assess their ability to participate in a therapeutic alliance with the clinician:

> The patient who is collaborative, who sees the issue as a joint problem for both patient and clinician, is in a completely different position from the patient who sees himself as being acted upon.... The distinction between the patient who can cooperate but does not and the patient who is too sick to cooperate may mean the difference between success and failure in the litigation area. (p. 3)

Therefore, at the most basic level, I believe that clinicians have a professional duty to take appropriate affirmative measures to prevent their patients from harming themselves. At times, this may well necessitate communicating with family members about the specifics of a patient's case, attempting to ameliorate toxic family interactions with the patient, or mobilizing support from the family and significant others (Bongar, 1991).

As with all other individual rights recognized by our society, the courts have held that the right to privacy must be balanced against the rights of other individuals and against the public interest (i.e., the legitimate regulatory functions of government) to determine which rights should prevail. As a result of this balancing process, the courts have carved out many exceptions to the general rule of therapeutic confidentiality. The critical point is that the psychologist should inform patients of the exceptions that exist to confidentiality before the patient enters treatment (Bongar, 1991).

Simon (1988) noted that common sense and good judgment can lead to a decision to breach patient confidentiality, specifically where "a patient will probably commit suicide and the act can be stopped only by the psychiatrist's intervention. . . . However, any limitations on the maintenance of confidentiality should be explained to patients from the beginning of any evaluation or treatment" (pp. 60–61).

Furthermore, regarding breaches of confidentiality, Stromberg et al. (1988) noted:

> Ethically, the therapist may be bound to disclose information concerning a patient in an emergency, when disclosure would obviously be best for the patient. Courts have increasingly defined "emergency" narrowly so that it does not cover all breaches of confidentiality which a particular therapist views as appropriate but only those made because the patient's health is seriously and imminently at stake. (p. 14)

Stromberg et al. continued that the scope of the disclosure should be limited to what is necessary for providing appropriate care and that, for example, disclosures made in good faith in seeking a civil commitment of the patient will be largely protected.

Bongar (1991) stated that if a breach of confidentiality is necessary to save the patient's life, the psychologist is bound to take this step. Bongar agreed with Shneidman (1981) that if such a breach of confidentiality is necessary to defuse the lethal situation, the psychologist must act to do so and "not ally herself/himself with death" (p. 348). (For an extended discussion of the complex ethical and legal dilemmas that often emerge when working with suicidal patients, e.g., the issues of rational suicide and euthanasia, the reader is directed to the work of Amchin, Wettstein, & Roth, 1990.) . . .

References

Amchin, J., Wettstein, R. M., & Roth, L. H. (1990). Suicide, ethics and the law. In S. J. Blumenthal & D. J. Kupfer (Eds.), *Suicide over the life cycle: Risk factors, assessment, and treatment of suicidal patients* (pp. 637–664). Washington, DC: American Psychiatric Press.

American Psychological Association. (1981). Ethical principles of psychologists. *American Psychologist, 36,* 633–638.

Bongar, B. (1991). *The suicidal patient: Clinical and legal standards of care.* Washington, DC: American Psychological Association.

Deutsch, C. J. (1984). Self-report sources of stress among psychotherapists. *Professional Psychology: Research and Practice, 15,* 833–845.

Gutheil, T. G. (1984). Malpractice liability in suicide. *Legal Aspects of Psychiatric Practice, 1,* 1–4.

Harrar, W. R., VandeCreek, L., & Knapp, S. (1990). Ethical and legal aspects of clinical supervision. *Professional Psychology, 21*(1), 37–41.

Keith-Spiegel, P., & Koocher, G. P. (1985). *Ethics in psychology.* New York: Random House.

Kleespies, P. M., Smith, M. R., & Becker, B. R. (1990).

Psychology interns as patient suicide survivors: Incidence, impact, and recovery. *Professional Psychology: Research and Practice, 21*(4), 257–263.

Pope, K. S., Tabachnick, B. G., & Keith-Spiegel, P. (1988). Good and poor practices in psychotherapy: National survey of beliefs of psychotherapists. *Professional Psychology: Research and Practice, 19*(5), 547–552.

Schein, H. M. (1976). Obstacles in the education of psychiatric residents. *Omega, 7,* 75–82.

Shneidman, E. S. (1981). Psychotherapy with suicidal patients. *Suicide and Life-Threatening Behavior, 11*(4), 341–348.

Simon, R. I. (1988). *Concise guide to clinical psychiatry and the law.* Washington, DC: American Psychiatric Press.

Stromberg, C. D., Haggarty, D. J., Leibenluft, R. F., McMillan, M. H., Mishkin, B., Rubin, B. L., & Trilling, H. R. (1988). *The psychologist's legal handbook.* Washington, DC: The Council for the National Register of Health Service Providers in Psychology.

VandeCreek, L., & Knapp, S. (1989). *Tarasoff and beyond: Legal and clinical considerations in the treatment of life-endangering patients.* Sarasota, FL: Professional Resource Exchange, Inc.

◆ ◆ ◆

Commentary: *For additional readings on legal, ethical, and competency issues in treating clients who threaten suicide, see, for example:*

Bongar, B. *(1991). The suicidal patient: Clinical and legal standards of care. Washington, DC: American Psychological Association.*

Pope, K. S., & Vasquez, M. J. T. *(1991). Ethics in psychotherapy and counseling (pp. 153–168). San Francisco: Jossey-Bass.*

Bongar and the authors he cites appear to adopt a beneficence-paternalism model in treating suicidal clients. Are there any moral principles or provisions in the 1992 Ethical Principles that would permit a therapist to abide by a client's wish to die?

Ethical and Legal Considerations in Marital and Family Therapy

Gayla Margolin

. . .

RESPONSIBILITY

The therapist's primary responsibilities are to protect the rights and to promote the welfare of his or her clients. The dilemma with multiple clients is that in some situations an intervention that serves one person's best interests may be countertherapeutic to another. Indeed, the very reason that families tend to seek therapy is because they have conflicting goals and interests. . . .

The family therapist must insure that improvement in the status of one family member does not occur at the expense of another family member. This objective is not entirely unique to family therapy. . . . Yet what sets the family therapist apart from the individual therapist is the family therapist's clear commitment to promoting the welfare of each family member. Moreover, through direct involvement with all family members, the family therapist can directly assess how each person's behavior affects other family members. Thus, the family therapist has more responsibility for exercising judgment that takes those other individuals into account.

To work constructively in the face of conflicting family needs, some therapists identify the family system, rather than one or another individual, as "the patient." The family therapist then becomes an advocate of the family system and avoids becoming an agent of any one family member. Assuming that change by one person affects and is affected by other family members, the system advocate ensures that all problem definitions and plans for change are considered in the context of the entire family. . . . If informed of the therapist's role as an advocate of the system, family members generally understand and accept this position, although at certain moments they still solicit the therapist as a personal ally. . . .

There are certain instances in which working as an advocate of the relationship system and changing patterns of interaction is not advised. Weiss and Birchler (1978) point out that a therapeutic alliance based on the ostensible goal of changing the relationship is countertherapeutic if one spouse seeks therapy as a way to exit from the relationship or to ease the burden of announcing a decision to separate. In this case, an emphasis on the relationship is likely to heighten the hope and emotional investment of the rejected individual, with further disappointment and sense of failure as the ultimate result for that person. Similarly, it is misleading to maintain a guise of working on the relationship when the actual objective is to change the behavior of one family member (e.g., to reduce a father's drinking or to increase a child's compliance). If the target individual in those cases is under the mistaken impression that there will be mutual change, she or he may end up feeling deceived by both the therapist and the other family members.

Finally, in addition to clinical considerations, there are legal prescriptions defining when the welfare of an individual takes precedence over relationship issues. The clearest obligation in this regard occurs in the instance of physical abuse among family members. Child abuse reporting laws require thera-

From *American Psychologist*, 37, 788–801. Copyright 1982 by the American Psychological Association. Adapted with permission of the author and publisher.

pists to inform authorities if they suspect that a child has been abused, despite the possible consequences for the therapeutic alliance with other family members. Though the legal prescription for action is not quite as obvious for abuse between marital partners, the primary goal still is to reduce the danger of physical harm. If this objective cannot be realized within the context of conjoint therapy, it is the therapist's ethical responsibility to abdicate the role of relationship advocate and help the threatened person find protection (Margolin, 1979). More generally, it can be concluded that a family therapist's responsibility includes being an advocate of individual family members who cannot accurately represent their own rights and needs or recognize when these are infringed on by another family member. Toward this end, there are certain situations in which an intervention to help an individual extricate from the family takes precedence over the goals of the family as a system. . . .

CONFIDENTIALITY

. . .

How do standard practices of confidentiality translate from the traditional dyadic client–therapist relationship to a therapeutic relationship that includes several family members? There are two divergent positions in this regard. One preference is for the therapist to treat each family member's confidences as though that person were an individual client. That is, information obtained during a private session, during a telephone call, or from written material is not divulged to other family members. Some therapists, in fact, arrange for sessions with individual family members to actively encourage the sharing of "secrets" to better understand what is occurring in the family. The therapist then may work with the individual client in the hope of enabling that person to disclose the same information in the family session. Should that fail to occur, however, the therapist upholds the individual client's confidentiality and remains silent on that issue vis-à-vis other family members.

Other therapists adopt the policy of not keeping secrets from other family members. They explicitly discourage the sharing of any information that might lead to a special alliance with one individual and that excludes the remaining uninformed family members. Contrary to more traditional views of psychotherapy that hold the client–therapist confidence as a crucial factor in the overall effectiveness of therapy, this stance essentially blocks the occurrence of confidences between one family member and the therapist. Therapists who subscribe to this approach generally avoid receiving individual confidences by conducting joint, as opposed to individual, sessions. However, this one safeguard often proves insufficient against the sharing of individual confidences. Unless the client is directly informed of the therapist's policies, the client who seeks to divulge personal information will find a way to do so.

Between these two extreme positions are intermediary steps. Rather than treat all information shared in individual sessions as confidential, the therapist may indicate that (1) in general, confidentiality conditions do not apply, but (2) the client has the right to request that any specific information be kept confidential and the therapist will comply with any such requests. Likewise, it should be recognized that the therapist who does not promise to maintain confidences may, indeed, wish to exercise the option not to divulge certain information. For instance, faced with information that one spouse has had an affair, particularly one that has terminated long since, many therapists find it unnecessary and inadvisable to share such information. In conveying that she or he does not preserve the confidences of individual family members, the therapist should avoid implying that she or he will not conceal anything. Except for legal considerations mentioned previously, it is the therapist's discretion, not his or her responsibility, to divulge confidential information.

One instance that complicates issues of confidentiality is a change in the format of therapy, for example, individual therapy being replaced by marital therapy. How does the therapist handle the information that she or he has obtained during the course of individual therapy? One possibility is to obtain the individual client's permission to use such information, when necessary, in the conjoint sessions. If permission is not granted, however, that information must be kept confidential, a resolution far from desirable for the therapist who prefers not maintaining individual confidences in conjoint therapy. Even if the patient permits the information to be shared, this permission has been granted *after* the information was obtained. Does the client remember all that she or he has confided under the previously assumed condition of confidentiality? Would that person have responded differently in individual therapy if it were known from the outset that such information would be available to the spouse?

As in individual therapy, clients must be informed of the limits of their confidentiality. This is particularly important in family therapy, since the limits of confidentiality, vis-à-vis other family members, essentially are left to the therapist's discretion. Therapists who will not keep confidences must inform clients of this policy before any such information has been received. Otherwise, the client, particularly one who has had previous experience in individual therapy, is likely to presume that the therapist will maintain the confidentiality of his or her statements from other family members. The therapist who does keep individual confidences likewise should inform clients of this policy so that family members do not persist in trying to obtain information about one another through the therapist.

Although both sides of the decision about whether or not to maintain confidentiality are ethically defensible, they carry different clinical implications. In certain situations, maintaining one partner's confidences severely limits the therapist's options with another family member. Consider, for example, the situation in which marital therapy has been initiated by the wife on discovering that her husband had been having an affair. While willing to give the relationship one last try, she is adamant about terminating the marriage if the husband does not end his affair and then remain sexually faithful. Although the husband initially agrees to this condition, several months later he reveals to the therapist that he has resumed the extramarital relationship. Desperate to avoid the possibility of his wife's leaving him, the husband refuses to divulge this information in a conjoint session.

What is the therapist's course of action? If confidentiality has been promised, the therapist may find himself or herself in a position of concealing information that is crucial to the wife's decision about re-maining both in therapy and in the marriage. When the wife learns about the affair, she may believe that the therapist has neglected her welfare in favor of the husband and may even accuse the therapist of keeping her in therapy for personal gain. Even if the therapist were to terminate the case, an explanation is owed to the wife, which is likely to compromise the husband's confidentiality. Even though the therapist might believe that dealing openly with the husband's behavior would have long-range therapeutic benefit, this course of action is not possible without violating the husband's confidentiality.

The therapist who has not promised confidentiality has more options open and thus must carefully consider the therapeutic ramifications of his or her actions. Deciding not to divulge this information about the husband's affair might be justifiable if (1) the wife had made it clear that she did not want to know about the husband's indiscretions, (2) the affair would not interfere with the ongoing therapy, and (3) the affair had ended, so the therapist's action could not be construed as encouraging the husband's behavior. In view of the specifics of this case, however, in which the wife has clearly stated her preference not to be duped into believing her husband is sexually faithful, open discussion of the husband's affair and the wife's ultimatum is indicated. Such discussion is likely to precipitate a relationship crisis, the long-range effects of which cannot be predicted. One or both spouses may receive the information they need, finally, to pronounce the marriage over. Alternatively, the couple may make certain accommodations despite their divergent values regarding fidelity; for example, the husband could terminate his long-term liaison while not committing himself to sexual fidelity, and the wife could abandon her ultimatum regarding sexual faithfulness as long as there are no long-standing affairs.

The most difficult predicament for the therapist would be if she or he failed to convey a policy on confidentiality. In that case, it is possible that the husband and wife would be functioning under different assumptions, for example, the husband assuming confidentiality would be maintained and the wife assuming that there would be no individual secrets in marital therapy. Neither spouse knows the limits of confidentiality nor has made a conscious decision to accept those limits. As with the clinical options available to the other two therapists, any action taken by this therapist is potentially unsatisfactory to at least one spouse. However, this therapist faces the additional risk of misleading one or another partner about the conditions of the therapeutic relationship. . . .

This example . . . illustrates that the therapist's position in terms of confidentiality can have important ramifications for how marital therapy is conducted. By maintaining the confidentiality of individual partners, the therapist is likely to have information that otherwise might not be available. The therapist's options with that information are severely limited, however, and she or he may not find it possible to put the information to therapeutic advantage from a family-system perspective. On the other hand, obtaining permission to discuss conjointly information that either partner chooses to reveal individually poses risks to the spouses (i.e., that there is no safe environment for personal disclosures) and risks to the therapist (i.e., that she or he will not gain access to important information). When this stance is clearly understood, however, individual disclosures to the therapist may simply signal the desire for guidance on how to broach a particularly difficult topic with one's partner. . . .

Confidentiality issues also arise when a therapist has individual sessions with a child. Ethical standards of confidentiality apply to the child as a client just as they do for adult clients. In some states parents have the right to inspect the therapist's records, but they have no legal right to demand that the therapist reveal information to them. The therapist's foremost objective in child therapy is to protect the rights of the child, particularly since the child is less able to understand or guard his or her rights. Yet secondarily the therapist must show sensitivity to the concerns of interested parents, since their help and support is often quite influential in the overall effectiveness of child therapy. Before beginning child therapy sessions, it is important to set up an agreement with both the child and the parents about what, if any, information from the child's sessions will be discussed with the parents. The limits of confidentiality should be determined; for example, can the child specifically request that the parents

not be told certain information? The structure of this feedback also should be determined: for example, How often will the therapist meet with the parents? Will the child be present at those meetings? In setting up these conditions, the therapist may wish to indicate that other family members are not to pressure the child to reveal what has transpired in his or her individual sessions. . . .

PATIENT PRIVILEGE

. . .

For the most part, privilege tends to be ill-defined for the situation in which two or more clients are seen simultaneously in therapy. Since privilege only covers communications that are uttered in confidence, the question arises of whether statements made in the presence of another family member indeed are confidential. The question also arises of whether privilege covers client-to-client communications. Since some states extend privilege to persons who aid in the delivery of personal services and are present during the uttering of confidential information (e.g., nurses, technicians), a liberal interpretation of privilege statutes might show that family members (or group members) are agents of the therapist (Bersoff & Jain, 1980). Lacking definitive legislation on these issues, however, family therapists cannot comfortably assume that existing privilege statutes protect the communications that occur during family therapy. In view of the inconsistencies of current laws, the therapist might wish to have a clear understanding with family members on these issues, for example, obtaining a written agreement that none of the members will call on the therapist to testify in litigation.

INFORMED CONSENT AND THE RIGHT TO REFUSE TREATMENT

The trend for clinicians to include some type of informed consent procedures as standard clinical practice reflects both an orientation toward clients as consumers and a recognition of increasing legal regulation of psychotherapeutic practices. The primary consideration in family therapy is that procedures for informed consent be conducted with all persons who participate in therapy, including those family members who join therapy at a later time. In addition to ethical reasons for taking the time to obtain informed consent from the entire family, this procedure communicates important therapeutic messages: No one family member is the "sick" or "crazy" person. No one person will be "treated" while others simply observe. No one will be excluded from knowledge about what is to transpire.

Recent reviews of informed consent (Everstine et al., 1980; Hare-Mustin et al., 1979) recommend that the following types of information be provided to clients before therapy is formally initiated: (a) an explanation of the procedures and their purpose, (b) the role of the person who is providing therapy and his or her professional qualifications, (c) discomforts or risks reasonably to be expected, (d) benefits reasonably to be expected, (e) alternatives to treatment that might be of similar benefit, (f) a statement that any questions about the procedures will be answered at any time, and (g) a statement that the person can withdraw his or her consent and discontinue participation in therapy or testing at any time.

Each of these guidelines also applies to marriage and family therapy. Guidelines c and d, for example, deserve special attention inasmuch as risks and benefits are different in family than in individual therapy. Since each family member has less control over the eventual outcome of family than of individual therapy, clients should be warned that marital and family therapy may lead to an outcome viewed as undesirable by one or another of the participants, for example, the decision to divorce or compromises in one's power over other family members.

Data on individual versus family therapy are central to Guideline e, particularly for the person torn between wanting to improve marital/family relationships and wanting the sanctuary of an individual therapeutic relationship. According to Gurman and Kniskern's (1978) comprehensive review, though marital therapy may be risky, individual therapy for marital problems is even riskier: Individual therapy for marital problems yields improvement in less than half of its consumers, whereas therapies that involve both partners yield improvement in approximately two thirds of the clients. . . .

It is typical of most families that some members are more eager to participate in therapy than others,

raising the issue . . . of voluntary participation. Obviously, coercion of the reluctant individual by other family members or by the therapist is unethical; however, this does not mean that the therapist cannot strongly encourage a family member to attend at least one session to discover what therapy may offer. Nor does it suggest that the therapist ignore what may be underlying reasons contributing to the person's reluctance, such as feeling threatened. In sorting out whether or not a particular family member will participate in therapy, the therapist should identify the extent to which each person will be expected to participate, for example, whether some persons simply can attend the therapy sessions in the role of observer, learning enough about the therapeutic process so that they do nothing to impede its progress. The therapist also should explain to the reluctant member that if other family members still choose to participate, the family as a whole is likely to change regardless of that individual's lack of participation.

A potential source of coercion surrounding voluntary participation comes from the relatively common therapeutic policy of refusing to see families unless all family members are present. Do other family members go untreated just because one person is unwilling to participate? Does one person's decision to terminate mean that all family members must discontinue contact with the therapist? To avoid the conclusion that one family member denies the others access to therapeutic services, therapists with a strong preference for working with the entire family should inform the family that other therapists do not necessarily share this preference and should have available a list of competent referral sources.

Standards for informed consent are necessary, but the family therapist's conceptual model largely determines the degree of specificity in the information presented. . . . [M]ost therapists can give an overview of the objectives (e.g., better family adjustment) as well as the format of therapy (e.g., how often sessions will be held, approximately how long therapy will last). Full compliance with this guideline can be somewhat difficult, however, particularly for a strategic therapist who mobilizes the oppositional tendencies of family members through paradoxical interventions (Stanton, 1981; Watzlawick, Weakland, & Fisch, 1974). . . .

Moreover, most forms of marital and family therapy involve certain types of manipulation limiting "true" informed consent and free choice about therapy. For example, while not guaranteeing changes . . . , therapists often find it helpful to express optimism about the outcome of therapy in an effort to reduce the family's anxiety, to raise expectancies, and to increase the family's persistent efforts (Jacobson & Margolin, 1979). The therapist also might manipulate coalitions to fortify an intervention. Some therapists, for example, capitalize on parents' concern for their children, that is, "stressing the children's entitlements for a trustworthy climate for growth" (Boszormenyi-Nagy & Ulrich, 1981, p. 183) as therapeutic leverage to evoke collaboration in marital therapy. . . .

Thus, even though clients deserve an accurate portrayal of therapy in informed consent procedures, complete objectivity and openness may not be possible. . . .

Children's Right to Consent

Recently there has been an increasing ground swell of opinion that children should be allowed to exercise the right to consent to psychological treatment. Generally speaking it is the parent or legal guardian who takes responsibility for providing the child's consent to treatment (Morrison, Morrison, & Holdridge-Crane, 1979). Exceptions to this general policy are found in some state statutes that offer teenagers the right to obtain sexual counseling, abortions, or drug counseling. In view of the legal constraints for children, the psychological community needs to address the issue of informed consent with children. The therapist needs to be sensitive to the fact that children constitute a consumer group who require extra protection, since even those parents who are well intentioned do not always know what is best for their children. It has been recommended that there be a child advocate to examine and protect what is in the best interest of the child client, particularly when a child is adamantly opposed to therapy (Morrison et al., 1979) or when the child does not have the capacity to give full unpressured consent (Koocher, 1976).

. . . The rationale for obtaining informed consent from children who will be participating in therapy is at least as compelling as that for participating in research. Since the effectiveness of psychotherapy depends on a trusting relationship between the therapist and client, there is much to be gained by explaining what is to occur and having the child become involved in decisions that will contribute to the therapeutic endeavor (LoCicero, 1976). Describing procedures in simplified language that children can understand and questioning the children about what has been said reveals to both the therapist and parents the extent to which each child comprehends what will occur. Children who lack the experiential background or intellectual sophistication to weigh the risks and benefits of an informed decision should not be pressured to give written informed consent (Levy & Brackbill, 1979). Yet even partial understanding without formal consent is preferable to proceeding with therapy in the absence of any explanation. . . .

THERAPIST VALUES

The impact of the therapist's values, inescapable in any therapeutic change process, can play a particularly weighty role in marital and family therapies. Issues discussed in family therapy elicit very important personal, familial, and societal values regarding preservation of the family system, extramarital relationships, and sex roles. Dealing therapeutically with these values is not easy, particularly when the therapist confronts a conflict in values among different family members and is inclined to reinforce the beliefs and attitudes of one family member over another.

Preservation of the Family

To what extent does a marital or family therapist express personal opinions about whether a couple should separate or divorce? The clearest professional standard on this issue is found in the Professional Code of the American Association for Marriage and Family Therapy (AAMFT), which states, "In all circumstances, the therapist will clearly advise a client that the decision to separate or divorce is the responsibility solely of the client" (AAMFT, 1979). Although appealing in principle, this stance is difficult, if not impossible, to exercise in practice. Certainly one function of marital therapy is to help distressed couples decide whether to stay together. Indeed, most couples who enter marital therapy have considered separation or divorce, and some seek therapy with the express purpose of making that decision. These couples "are primed to be influenced by the therapist and are quite sensitive to the cues which the therapist provides concerning his/her opinions about the relationship" (Jacobson & Margolin, 1979, p. 335).

Though few therapists would deny formulating impressions about whether a couple should remain together, there is substantial variability in how comfortable therapists feel in sharing those opinions. A debate on this issue by Yoell, Stewart, Wolpe, Goldstein, and Speierer (1971) conveys two extreme positions. Wolpe, for one, argues that "frequently the therapist needs to make the decision for the patient." He undertakes such a decision "if the patient is gravely unhappy in her marriage, if every step that could be taken seems to have been taken and has failed. If the prognosis for the relationship in terms of happiness is close to zero, then I accept the responsibility not only to advise the dissolution of the marriage but to help in every practical way to bring it about" (pp. 128–129). The opposite viewpoint is expressed in Stewart's response, indicating "discomfiture about making decisions for a person. The thought constantly pops up—Is this going to be a meaningful decision for the individual if it is made by somebody else?" (p. 129).

Several other therapists endorse an explicit statement of one's opinion to the clients while claiming that the opinion is a personal one rather than a reflection of professional expertise (Gurman & Klein, 1981; Halleck, 1971). Perhaps by making this influence explicit, clients are better able to choose how much they want to be swayed by the therapist's opinions and to sort out their own reactions as distinct from those of the therapist. . . .

Extramarital Affairs

. . .

Does knowledge that one partner is currently engaging in an extramarital affair alter the course of therapy? Therapists who answer "no" to this question often focus on improving the primary relationship, which if successful may cause the other relationship to dwindle in importance. A small number of therapists even encourage one spouse to initiate or continue an affair for the well-being of that individual or perhaps even for the betterment of the relationship. . . .

There are, however, . . . potential drawbacks to advocating extramarital affairs for clients. First, even if the affair is beneficial to one person, the other is bound to suffer. Second, therapy that is directed toward the relationship is unlikely to work if one spouse is splitting his or her attention between two relationships. . . .

The other alternative is to actively discourage extramarital relationships or even to stipulate that extramarital affairs must be ended for therapy to commence (e.g., Ables & Brandsma, 1977; Jacobson & Margolin, 1979). This stance, typically described as strategic rather than moralistic, assumes that the affair would impede both partners' abilities to commit themselves fully to relationship improvement and would result in a halting and frustrating course of therapy. Though widely endorsed, this position represents a *professional value,* rather than an empirically derived conclusion. The therapeutic benefit of this stance is that it often prompts termination of an affair as a demonstration of that spouse's desire to work on the relationship. However, the drawback is that a spouse might carefully conceal information about an affair for fear of being excluded from therapy. . . .

Sex Roles

To what extent does the therapist accept the family's definition of sex role identities as opposed to attempting to influence and modify their attitudes in this regard? Recent attention to this question has led to the conclusion that marital and family therapy often tends to reinforce sex role stereotyping (Gurman & Klein, 1981; Hare-Mustin, 1978). Of the sexist attitudes found to characterize psychotherapy in general (APA Task Force on Sex Bias and Sex-Role Stereotyping, 1975), family therapists are particularly vulnerable to the following biases: (1) assuming that remaining in a marriage would result in better adjustment for a woman; (2) demonstrating less interest in or sensitivity to a woman's career than to a man's career; (3) perpetuating the belief that child rearing and thus the child's problems are solely the responsibility of the mother; (4) exhibiting a double standard for a wife's versus a husband's affair; and (5) deferring to the husband's needs over those of the wife.

How does the therapist respond when family members agree that they want to work toward goals that, in the therapist's viewpoint, represent sexist ideologies? By attempting to remain nonjudgmental about the client's objectives, the therapist may unwittingly reinforce these sexist attitudes. But by attempting to reorient them to an egalitarian viewpoint, the therapist might thwart the family from attaining their goals and alienate those individuals whose socialization is such that they are happy with traditional roles (Hare-Mustin, 1978). . . .

A more difficult dilemma arises when the woman challenges traditional sex roles while the husband seemingly is an intractable sexist. As soon as the therapist even privately identifies the husband's sexism as the problem, that therapist has violated guiding principles in marital therapy—balancing alliances with each partner and seeking to understand each spouse's perspective on an issue. What needs to be sorted out is whether the conflict regarding roles reflects vastly divergent ideological positions or whether the ideological differences are accentuated by relationship issues; that is, the wife's demands threaten the husband, who becomes more rigid in his position, which causes the wife to make more demands, and so on. In this latter situation there are a number of ways to reverse the couple's intensifying polarity so that the therapist can avoid becoming embroiled in an ideological conflict. . . .

. . . Since inattention to gender role issues runs the risk of reinforcing sex role inequalities, it is recommended that family therapists examine therapeutic objectives in light of traditional versus nontraditional values. It also is recommended that therapists examine their own behavior for unwitting comments and questions that may imply that the husband and wife command differential roles and status. . . . Finally, it is recommended that the therapist be aware of his or her personal views about sex roles in order to avoid imposing these views on the family or judging the family from a predetermined perspective of how families should function. . . .

References

Ables, B. S., & Brandsma, J. M. *Therapy for couples*. San Francisco, Calif.: Jossey-Bass, 1977.

American Association for Marriage and Family Therapy. *Code of professional ethics and standards for public information and advertising*. Upland, Calif.: Author, 1979.

American Psychological Association Task Force. Report of the Task Force on Sex Bias and Sex-Role Stereotyping in Psychotherapeutic Practice. *American Psychologist*, 1975, *30*, 1169–1175.

Bersoff, D., & Jain, M. A practical guide to privileged communication for psychologists. In G. Cooke (Ed.), *The role of the forensic psychologist*. Springfield, Ill.: Charles C Thomas, 1980.

Boszormenyi-Nagy, I., & Ulrich, D. N. Contextual family therapy. In A. S. Gurman & D. P. Kniskern (Eds.), *Handbook of family therapy*. New York: Brunner/Mazel, 1981.

Everstine, L., et al. Privacy and confidentiality in psychotherapy. *American Psychologist*, 1980, *35*, 828–840.

Gurman, A. S., & Klein, M. H. Women and behavioral marriage and family therapy: An unconscious male bias? In E. A. Blechman (Ed.), *Contemporary issues in behavior modification with women*. New York: Guilford, 1981.

Gurman, A. S., & Kniskern, D. P. Research on marital and family therapy: Progress, perspective, and prospect. In S. L. Garfield & A. E. Bergin (Eds.), *Handbook of psychotherapy and behavior change: An empirical analysis* (2nd ed.). New York: Wiley, 1978.

Halleck, S. L. *The politics of therapy*. San Francisco, Calif.: Jossey-Bass, 1971.

Hare-Mustin, R. T. A feminist approach to family therapy. *Family Process*, 1978, *17*, 181–194.

Hare-Mustin, R. T., Maracek, J., Kaplan, A. G., & Liss-Levinson, N. Rights of clients, responsibilities of therapists. *American Psychologist*, 1979, *34*, 3–16.

Jacobson, N. S., & Margolin, G. *Marital therapy: Strategies based on social learning and behavior exchange principles*. New York: Brunner/Mazel, 1979.

Koocher, G. P. Civil liberties and aversive conditioning for children. *American Psychologist*, 1976, *31*, 94–95.

Levy, C. M., & Brackbill, Y. Informed consent: Getting the message across to kids. *APA Monitor*, March 1979, pp. 3; 18.

LoCicero, A. The right to know: Telling children the results of clinical evaluations. In R. Koocher (Ed.),

Children's rights and the mental health profession. New York: Wiley, 1976.

Margolin, G. Conjoint marital therapy to enhance anger management and reduce spouse abuse. *American Journal of Family Therapy*, 1979, 7, 13–23.

Morrison, K. L., Morrison, J. K., & Holdridge-Crane, S. The child's right to give informed consent to psychiatric treatment. *Journal of Clinical Child Psychology*, 1979, 8, 43–47.

Stanton, M. D. Strategic approaches to family therapy. In A. S. Gurman & D. P. Kniskern (Eds.), *Handbook of family therapy*. New York: Brunner/Mazel, 1981.

Watzlawick, P., Weakland, J., & Fisch, R. *Change: Principles of problem formation and problem resolution.* New York: Norton, 1974.

Weiss, R. L., & Birchler, G. R. Adults with marital dysfunction. In M. Hersen & A. S. Bellack (Eds.), *Behavior therapy in the psychiatric setting*. Baltimore: Williams & Wilkins, 1978.

Yoell, W., Stewart, D., Wolpe, J., Goldstein, A., & Speierer, G. Marriage, morals and therapeutic goals: A discussion. *Journal of Behavior therapy and Experimental Psychiatry*, 1971, 2, 127–132.

◆ ◆ ◆

Commentary: *One of the criticisms of the pre-1992 ethical codes was that they neglected marriage, family, and group therapy issues. In addition to the more general provisions in the current code, Standard 4.03 (Couple and Family Relationships) was included specifically to address these issues. But as Lakin (1994, next excerpt) points out, that provision "is restricted to admonishing psychologists to ensure that their role is clarified to couples or family members" (p. 344). Lakin's article reviews the relevant provisions while providing an overview of more general ethical issues confronting psychologists who do group and family therapy.*

Morality in Group and Family Therapies: Multiperson Therapies and the 1992 Ethics Code

Martin Lakin

. . .

Even the most carefully conceived ethics codes provide only general guidelines in areas of unavoidably complex ethical judgments. Failure to take contexts of treatment into account amplifies already ambiguous ethical dilemmas. I assert that the ethical challenges of multiperson therapies—specifically, group and family treatments—are considerably more complex than those encountered in the practice of individual therapies. The reasons have to do with the characteristic interactions of those being treated, which turn on the many-to-one relationships with their therapist and with each other. These multiple interactions generate characteristic behavioral patterns and an emotional ambience that differs significantly from that of dyadic psychotherapy. The ethics codes for psychologists, however, tend to reflect the dyadic psychotherapy model.

. . .

ETHICAL CHALLENGES IN GROUP PSYCHOTHERAPY

. . .

Informed Consent

The requirement that the therapy obtain informed consent—an ethical imperative for all psychotherapeutic as well as other health-related treatments—poses particular difficulties for group psychotherapists of all orientations. The new code does present informed consent to therapy guidelines in Standard 4.02, but these mandates are not necessarily operant in group therapy. Similarly, therapists working with groups cannot always define the anticipated course of therapy or answer all of the clients' questions as mandated in the standard on structuring the relationship, Standard 4.01. Group psychotherapists can truly anticipate neither the responses of group members in general nor the particular effects of other group members on specific individual participants. Not being able to guarantee the behavior of group therapy participants, particularly with respect to such almost universal concerns as guarding members' confidentially uttered sentiments and minimizing risk from unwanted confrontations, the therapist cannot, in good conscience, provide the kinds of reassurances that might well be taken for granted.

. . . I believe that many group therapists are relatively unpracticed in thinking about, and in describing for intended participants, what is likely to occur in group interactions beyond generalities involving the hoped for benefits that come from people discussing their problems. To be sure, it is difficult to describe the kinds of peer-focused interactions that take place in therapy groups in ways that seem useful to the help seeker. For instance, participants almost invariably experience intense concerns about receiving acceptance, being respectfully listened to, coping with the presence of or being collusive in cliques within the group, encountering scapegoating, sharing the therapist's attention, and providing as well as receiving emotional support. This all proceeds concurrently and is intermingled with learning how to learn about self and others through the group experience. Obviously, such experiential challenges are markedly different from those of the typical one-to-one therapies in which assured professional attention and exclusivity are the rule. Perhaps most significantly, it is the therapist who largely defines reality in individual psychotherapy, not a consensus of peers, some of whom might be subjectively viewed as irresponsible by comembers.

. . .

Competence to Conduct Group Therapy

Competence (Principle A) is understandably the first principle of ethically responsible practice. For this reason, the fact that many current practitioners of group therapy have simply tacked on group practice to other modalities for which they may have been more adequately trained is worrisome. The new code does mandate psychologists, in Principle A, to recognize the boundaries of their competencies and only provide services and use techniques for which they have been qualified by training and experience, but this appears in the General Principles section and is therefore considered aspirational rather than enforceable. Shortcomings in training may be the reason for limited understanding of group dynamics and for an inability to manage those dynamics, outlined later, that comprise significant pressure factors in therapy groups.

Pressures for cohesion. Although a sense of developing togetherness is vital to therapeutic progress in groups, conformist pressures may have contrary effects. The ethical imperative for therapists should be to encourage acceptance of the diversity that actually characterizes help seekers (and everyone else). One should guard against the temptation to interpret character and symptoms in ideological terms. Examples abound in recent years of group therapies in which problems are consistently interpreted in terms of racial, gender, religious, or political oppression, and different perspectives are discouraged. Because groups, by their nature, tend to pursue ideological unanimity in the interest of cohesion, group therapists face unique ethical challenges. Respect for individual differences requires that therapists avoid overinclusive formulas and overgeneralizing to promote particular ideological agendas.

Pushing for emotional expressiveness. Emotions, particularly negative feelings, are regularly elicited in therapies. Groups are particular effective vehicles for evoking and stimulating such affective responses. The ethical, but also technical, problem is that "getting it all out" as a purgative for some may be aversive for others. Equally serious is the likelihood that feelings may be counterfeited to meet the perceived group norm of "being emotional" (Lakin, 1989, 1991a). Emotional expressiveness becomes a kind of ticket of admission that often disinhibits participants who benefit from it. However, it also sets a false standard when used for judging every participant's state. Although the dynamic of facilitating emotionality is surely one of the most powerful change mechanisms in groups, it can also become a vehicle for cathartic theatrics that do not really reflect real-world or experienced problem states among participants.

Pressures for consensus. Therapeutic groups have deserved reputations as sources of support for distressed persons. However, they unfortunately can also pigeonhole specific individuals or scapegoat them. It is rarely an easy matter for therapists to protect members from these latter possibilities. The move to support an apparently scapegoated member risks the appearance of overprotectiveness, taken as evidence of that individual's psychological frailty, and may have a chilling effect on further intermember communication. It seems that groups characteristically speedily develop a negative consensus about particular participants and move rapidly to provide ostensibly helpful feedback to them. Such collusive reactions, particularly when evidenced by signs of premature feedback, should never pass unchecked by therapist-initiated and orchestrated group inquiry. It is ethically imperative as well as therapeutically important that members become aware of their own parts in group reactions to individual participants. Only on such a basis can feedback become the emotionally corrective experience that it should be (Lakin, 1985, 1989).

Grouping Single Clients

The new code does not directly address a significant ethical issue that few practitioners have shown concern about, namely, grouping one's individual clients or patients and adding group sessions on a regular basis. When I interviewed group therapists who regularly engage in this practice, they seemed perplexed that there could be an ethical issue involved. They protested the clinical advantages, namely, more intimate knowledge of the client or patient and positive complementary effects. They did not see that concurrent treatment by the identical therapist complicates the already complex therapy relationship, that confidentiality must be further eroded, and, perhaps most worrisome of all, that they could have financial incentives in referring to themselves. An effort to address the ethical challenges entailed in such concurrent treatments by the same therapist has been made by Taylor and Gazda (1991). In view of the prevalence of this practice, there should be a systematic inquiry into its ethical dimensions.

MODALITY-LINKED ETHICAL ISSUES IN FAMILY THERAPY

. . .

Informed Consent

Problems of obtaining informed consent for family therapies are of a somewhat different nature in group and in family therapies. Sider (1992) and Margolin (1982) have discussed several of them. Mainly the problems involve the help seekers' inability to picture the benefits, risks, or both of the proposed treatment in personally relevant terms. In the case of family therapy, existential pressures of the family situation make the need for treatment more evident to the intending clients, but not the implied limitations on confidentiality. Most difficult of all will be to explain how the therapist will deal with inevitably abrasive interactions in sessions and how the therapist will provide nonprejudiced guidance for all.

The reader will not be surprised to find that obtaining informed consent is high on the list of ethical issues that characterize family therapy. Specifically, beyond descriptive adequacy, the family therapist faces the following challenges: Who gives consent for the family members? Who in the family wants the therapy, and who is being dragged into it? How capable are potential participants of understanding the processes they are about to be involved in? It should be noted that Standard 4.03, which deals with couple and family relationships, states

that the psychologist attempts to clarify at the outset which of the individuals are patients or clients and the relationship the psychologist will have with each person. This clarification includes the role of the psychologist and the probable uses of the service provided or the information obtained. A second clause of Standard 4.03 states that, when it becomes apparent that conflicting roles are involved, such as the role of witness in a divorce proceeding, the therapist tries to clarify and adjust or withdraw "appropriately" (APA, 1992, p. 1605).

Confidentiality

An almost equally important source of ethical ambiguity is the question of whose agent the therapist is. Does the source of payment determine the course of treatment? How will the therapist react to the natural desire among family members for therapist alliances with themselves against other family members? Will a family therapist's protectiveness foster general improvement or further infantilize specific family members?

In any multiperson therapy the issues of confidentiality surface differently and must be dealt with differently than in traditional dyadic therapy. Does the family therapist undertake to safeguard confidences from all family members? Does the therapist issue a blanket ruling that no confidences may be kept? (It is a fact that legal rulings restricting confidentiality increasingly intrude on hitherto privileged contacts in all forms of psychotherapy.) Clearly, the issues demand clarification and definition before treatment and as it proceeds.

. . .

Therapist Values

The issue of therapist values and their intrusion into psychotherapy practice is not a new ethical concern. (See Standard 1.15 in the new code, which touches on this general issue.) However, the proliferation of family therapy, in particular, brings the question sharply into focus, because sessions can have an immediate impact on interdependent people who go home together and must manage to live together. I have in mind values touching on qualities of the marital and other domestic relationships; questions of fidelity or open marriage; attitudes toward conception, pregnancy, and abortion; gender roles; and discipline practices in the home. Bergin's (1985) survey results suggested that therapists may hold strong opinions regarding these issues; many think that mental health is to a considerable extent dependent on how they are resolved. . . .

GENERAL ISSUES IN MULTIPERSON THERAPY

As already discussed, confidentiality is essential to useful exchanges and to progress in therapy. So all therapists promise what they cannot possibly ensure. . . . It is of more than incidental interest that the leading cause of professional liability claims against family therapy practitioners is violations of confidentiality, according to Engelberg and Symansksy (1989) and Baker and Patterson (1990). Although data are not available on group therapies, similar problems of maintaining confidentiality are experienced. Considerable ambiguity arises from the relative ease of revealing to nonparticipants what transpires in sessions; a special problem of family therapy is individual sessions with family members involving disclosures that may or may not be treated as confidential. Whereas Standard 4.03 implicitly recognizes that couple and family relationships may cause complications for the therapist, it does not address these common dilemmas.

The previous and new ethics codes stress the avoidance of exploitative behaviors by psychotherapists. (See Standards 1.11, 1.15, 1.17, 4.05, 4.06, and 4.07 for ethical standards reflecting this theme in the new code.) Exploitative behaviors by psychotherapists may take different forms in multiperson treatment contexts than in dyadic therapies. For instance, interpersonal confrontations may be stimulated by therapists for therapeutically germane reasons; but they also may be initiated because they transiently ensure group or family members (or therapists themselves) that vital and significant things are happening. The momentary gratification of confrontation as a "spectator sport" is a major source of ethical ambiguity in multiperson therapy. The prototypical ethical problems of multiperson therapies, exclusive of obviously exploitative relationships with clients, are those of excess, for example, in requiring

emotional expressiveness because group members (and therapists) feel gratified when it occurs, regarding it as evidence of depth of feeling, and in promoting confrontations as focal points of group arousal.

In considering the relevance of the new code of ethics to multiperson group and family therapies, it is obvious that I have emphasized the lack of comprehensive coverage of the ethical issues that must confront therapists in those modalities. . . . The insufficiency of the new code is readily apparent if one examines the relationship of Standard 4.03, which I discussed previously, to the conceptions and practices of interdependence and interrelationships in problem families. When family dynamics are salient, it is rarely clear who is the "real" patient or client. It is not easy to avoid conflicting roles in a therapy process that almost certainly elicits them, either. The chances of being able to do so ethically would be furthered by a greater technical understanding of why this should be the case.

Coping ethically with the challenges of multiperson therapies will be aided by establishing more relevant specific principles for describing the intended service (Standard 1.07) and avoiding false or deceptive statements (Standard 3.03). Even greater challenges are to rephrase requirements of confidentiality and to specify its limits in terms of group and family treatments (Standards 5.01 and 5.02). Most challenging of all is to create modality-relevant ethical prescriptions and proscriptions that enable therapists to better understand and to avoid misuses of therapist influence (Standard 1.15). This problem is perhaps most readily grasped with respect to family therapies, in which many theorists and practitioners have acknowledged the fact that therapist values play significant roles in treatment strategies (see Chaney & Piercy, 1988; Haley, 1976; Jensen, Josephson, & Frey, 1989; Kirschner & Kirschner, 1986; Libow, Raskin, & Caust, 1982; McGoldrick, Pearce, & Giordano, 1982).

. . .

In preprofessional and continuing education training, the understanding must be inculcated that the very factors that are most powerfully conducive to emotional and behavioral change in therapy groups and therapy families are also, inevitably, the most ethically risky processes. These factors include cohesiveness, emotional experiencing, and consensual validation, without which these modalities could not provide emotionally corrective experiences. The real ethical challenge is for psychologists to become more fully aware of how these factors may be managed for the good of those being treated, not for the practitioners' gratification. It is essential, from this point of view, that the ethical parameters of group and family practice be reassessed and the ethical consciousness of those involved in teaching, supervising, and practicing these therapeutic modalities be raised.

References

American Psychological Association. (1992). Ethical principles of psychologists and code of conduct. *American Psychologist, 42,* 1597–1611.

Baker, L. C., & Patterson, L. C. (1990). The first to know: A systematic analysis of confidentiality and the therapist's family. *American Journal of Family Therapy, 18,* 295–300.

Bergin, A. E. (1985). Proposed values for guiding and evaluating counseling and psychotherapy. *Counseling and Values, 29,* 99–116.

Chaney, S. E., & Piercy, H. P. (1988). A feminist family behavior therapy checklist. *American Journal of Family Therapy, 16,* 305–318.

Engelberg, S., & Symansky, J. (1989). Ethics and the law. *Family Therapy Networker, 13,* 30–31.

Haley, J. (1976). *Problem-solving therapy.* San Francisco: Jossey-Bass.

Jensen, P. S., Josephson, A. M., & Frey, J. (1989). Informed consent as a framework for treatment: Ethical and therapeutic considerations. *American Journal of Psychotherapy, 43,* 378–386.

Kirschner, D. A., & Kirschner, S. (1986). *Comprehensive family therapy: An integration of systematic and psychodynamic models.* New York: Brunner/Mazel.

Lakin, M. (1985). *The helping group: Therapeutic principles and issues.* Reading, MA: Addison-Wesley.

Lakin, M. (1989). *Ethical issues in the psychotherapies.* New York: Oxford University Press.

Lakin, M. (1991a). *Coping with ethical dilemmas in the psychotherapies.* Elmsford, NY: Pergamon Press (currently marketed by Allyn & Bacon).

Libow, J. A., Raskin, P. A., & Caust, B. L. (1982). Feminist and family systems therapy: Are they reconcilable? *American Journal of Family Therapy, 10,* 3–12.

McGoldrick, M., Pearce, J. K., & Giordano, J. (1982). *Ethnicity and family therapy.* New York: Guilford Press.

Margolin, G. (1982). Ethical and legal consideration in marital and family therapy. *American Psychologist, 37,* 788–801.

Sider, R. C. (1992). Family or individual therapy: The ethics of modality choice. *American Journal of Psychiatry, 11,* 1455–1459.

Taylor, R. E., & Gazda, G. M. (1991). Concurrent individual and group therapy: The ethical issues. *Journal of Group Psychotherapy, Psychodrama and Sociometry, 44,* 51–59.

◆　◆　◆

Commentary: For an exposition of the Ethical Guidelines for Group Counselors *published by a division of the American Counseling Association, see Corey, G., Williams, G. T., & Moline, M. E. (1995). Ethical and legal issues in group counseling.* Ethics and Behavior, *5, 161–183. See also*

Hansen, J. C., Green, S., & Kutner, K. B. (1989). Ethical issues facing school psychologists working with families. Professional School Psychology, 4, 245–255.

Lakin, M. (1986). Ethical challenges of group and dyadic psychotherapies: A comparative approach. Professional Psychology: Research and Practice, 17, 454–461.

Patten, C., Barnett, T., & Houlihan, D. (1991). Ethics in marital and family therapy: A review of the literature. Professional Psychology: Research and Practice, 22, 171–175.

Piercy, F. P., & Sprenkle, D. G. (1983). Ethical, legal, and professional issues in family therapy: A graduate level course. Journal of Marital and Family Therapy, 9, 393–401.

For an informative text on ethical issues related to children in general, see Koocher, G., & Keith-Spiegel, P. (1990). Children, ethics, and the law. *Lincoln: University of Nebraska Press.*

Ethical Issues in Rural Mental Health Practice

David S. Hargrove

. . .

Because the environmental context in which mental health workers practice gives shape to ethical concerns, the unique characteristics of the rural environment are important for a proper understanding of the ethical constraints on practice within its confines. The purpose of this article is to identify potentially troublesome ethical problems associated with work in rural areas and to suggest that their possible resolution may reside in the nature of the rural environment itself. . . .

CHARACTERISTICS OF RURAL AREAS

. . .

Residing and working in smaller communities can increase the level of intensity of human relationships because there are fewer people with whom to relate and share experiences. Social and political relationships tend to be close, they frequently overlap, and monopolistic tendencies often characterize the economic environment. . . .

. . . This pattern of interlocking relationships may well constitute a significant component of the community's power structure. Knowledge of real relationships and those that may be represented in the literature reveals that they are, in fact, much more complex and can have deep historical, social, economic, political, and familial roots.

. . .

POTENTIAL ETHICAL ISSUES

. . .

The first, and perhaps most critical, ethical issue for rural mental health practitioners is the confidentiality of and within the professional relationship with a consumer of professional services. . . .

. . .

Solomon, Hiesberger, and Winer (1981) claimed that strict adherence to the ethical guidelines of APA do not provide sufficiently clear resolutions for some of the difficulties and conflicts faced by the psychologist who practices in a rural area. In addition, they identify at least one potential situation in which the ethical guidelines create a double-bind or no-win situation for rural psychologists and, possibly, for the agency for which he or she works. This situation is a result of APA's mandate of confidentiality of information on the one hand and the psychologist's responsibility to "be aware of the prevailing community standards" when community standards may be less restrictive than professional ethics on the other hand. . . .

The problem becomes paramount when there are adverse interprofessional and/or political consequences to behavior resulting from compliance with the ethical standards. Solomon et al. provide a realistic illustration of a referring physician who expects feedback regarding the referral regardless of whether the proper release documents are completed. When information about the referral is not forthcoming, the physician may well take offense and discontinue referrals to the mental health program. Because the physician is likely to be one of few medical providers in the community and certainly will have strong social and political influence, the consequences of alienating him or her could be great.

Another perspective of this dilemma is the reciprocal expectation of shared information among human service workers. Frequently in rural communities, in an effort to provide adequate continuity of care, many human service workers from a variety of agencies will be involved with the same case. It is not uncommon to have representatives from the welfare department, mental health, vocational rehabilitation, health department, Social Security Administration, and corrections involved with a family at the same time. Typically, one agency will refer to the others in the effort to provide access to comprehensive services. Many rural programs have cooperative staff meetings that include personnel from other agencies to discuss mutual clients. The proper paperwork dealing with confidentiality may or may not be completed, and formal and informal communication about the case among the workers may or may not fall within the constraints of ethical practice. Frequently, it appears that clients assume that the necessary interagency and interprofessional communication will take place. I have known of more than a few clients who are amazed upon learning that they have not been discussed among human service professionals. Furthermore, they greet the explanation that it is for their own protection with amusement because of its seeming incompatibility with prevailing patterns of communication in the community.

The clear dilemma experienced by the human service professional in this situation is that if he or she communicates back to the referring physician that the client did, in fact, follow the referral or if the professional provides any information about the person, a violation in the privilege of confidence occurs. If the mental health staff person does not communicate back to the physician, the physician may be offended and refuse further referrals to the center and possibly may use his or her social and political prestige to the detriment on the local mental health program. This disruption would not only be injurious to the sociopolitical base of the center but would endanger both the quality and continuity of care for other clients in the community. If the mental health staff member shares in community service case conferences without permission from the client, there is a clear violation of ethical standards in that

the client's confidence has been breached. If, on the other hand, the staff member refuses to participate, a valuable community resource is lost, and alienation of the mental health program from other community agencies results. Alienation between human service agencies in a small town is particularly harmful because of the already limited resources. Hollister (1982) pointed out the importance of developing smooth relationships between these agencies in small communities. These realistic situations certainly are not without ethical, legal, and potentially political consequences.

A second problematic ethical issue for rural professional persons concerns the limits of practice. . . . The limit of professional competence is a serious and sensitive matter, and frequently a person's credibility rides on his or her interpretation of these limits. In a rural practice, the generalist model of practice prevails because of the lack of available resources and professionals (Hargrove, 1982b). As a consequence, the rural psychologist is likely to be called on to respond to a broad range of problems and people. If the mental health professional can assist in the identification of a client's clinical problem and refer that person to an appropriately trained specialist for further, more refined diagnosis and intervention, the client may be dealt with properly. Problems result, however, when there is no other local resource for diagnosis or treatment. In fact, there are situations in which the choice is either treatment from the person who is available or no treatment at all. . . .

The most appropriate response to this ethically murky situation is not at all clear. At issue is the definition of professional competence in a given area and the consequences of that definition. When is one deemed professionally competent and by whom? How narrow are the areas of professional competence in which one must be judged competent, and what impact does this have on the professional person who must function as a generalist, by either choice or job requirement?

The third ethical dilemma that is pertinent to the practice of mental health service delivery in rural environments is the multiple levels of relationships between persons who live and work in small com-

munities. [*Ed. note:* The section on multiple relationships is omitted. It is covered in the next excerpt.]
. . .

POTENTIAL RESOLUTION OF ETHICAL DILEMMAS

Resolutions of the ethical dilemmas that confront rural practitioners are as varied and creative as the situations and the persons in them. Frequently, mental health professionals find the solutions to problems in the nature of the environment itself and in a proper understanding of APA's Ethical Principles.

First, the rural practitioner needs to develop an appropriate view of the ethical standards themselves. . . . They have built into their structure and content considerable latitude enabling clinicians to make the best decisions possible under a given set of circumstances. The standards are not a substitute for clinical or ethical judgment on the part of the professional mental health worker. The attitude of the practitioner, including his or her intent, is critically important to arriving at proper courses of action in ethically unclear situations.

Second, the rural practitioner needs to look at the resources of the rural environment for solutions to problems that result from that environment. The rural context of practice may well hold the key to the solution of ethically difficult situations just as it may well create the problems in the first place. For example, in the case of the physician who refers a client to the mental health agency with the expectation that he or she will receive follow-up information, it is highly likely that the mental health clinician will have either a professional or personal (or both) relationship with the physician and will have ample opportunity to explain the situation in great detail. If the mental health worker does not have this sort of relationship with the physician, it is highly likely that a member of the board or another friend of the agency will have such a relationship. When a personal relationship with the physician is developed, a different setting enables issues of confidentiality and transfer of information to be discussed in a positive, collegial relationship. Given this rela-

tionship, matters are worked out in a personal way, which is the bread and butter of rural life.

With regard to the widely attended staff conferences, it is possible to design a release of information form that includes all the persons and/or agencies that attend. Presumably, the purpose of the meeting is the well-being of the client, and the client is aware of all the agencies' involvements and would have no objection to the sharing of information. If the client does object, there may be good reason. At this point, the clinician would have to question the propriety of a particular agency or staff person attending such conferences. If the client chooses not to allow discussion of his or her situation in an interagency case conference, the clinician has the responsibility to inform him or her of the possible consequences of this action so that the client's choice is an informed one.

The limits of clinical competence is a serious, double-edged issue that must be carefully and consistently addressed. It is particularly important in view of the psychotherapy research that affirms that people can, in fact, be harmed by the process of psychotherapy. First, the clinician must determine the nature of the problem for which assistance is being sought. Then, a decision must be made whether he or she is more competent to treat the disorder than are other available agencies or whether the client may benefit more from marginally competent intervention than none at all. If not, then this fact can be explained to the client, and the clinician can provide assistance in finding the closest available help. It is important that the client be involved in an informed decision, which is consistent with the ethical standards.

At this point, the entire agency can be of considerable help if it has a precedent of establishing reciprocal relationships with other mental health providers. Some agencies characteristically develop relationships with surrounding mental health agencies to provide whatever specialized services may be needed, thus expanding its own range of services. In this event, it is necessary for each clinician in either agency to be aware of the resources available in the others. . . .

It is important that rural mental health professionals and agencies recognize and respect the realities that underlie the ethical guidelines that govern professional behavior. Frequently, these realities also are factors that could lead to difficult agency problems unless approached in a careful, judicious manner. It is equally important that rural mental health administrators and clinicians anticipate the types of ethical problems that may arise and plan accordingly. . . .

References

Hargrove, D. S. (1982b). The rural psychologist as generalist: A challenge for professional identity. *Professional Psychology, 13,* 302–308.

Hollister, W. G. (1982). Principles guiding the development of an innovative low-cost, rural mental health program. In P. A. Keller & J. D. Murray (Eds.), *Handbook of rural community mental health* (pp. 86–99). New York: Human Sciences.

Solomon, G., Hiesberger, J., & Winer, J. (1981). Confidentiality issues in rural community mental health. *Journal of Rural Community Psychology, 2,* 17–31.

Dual-Relationship Dilemmas of Rural and Small-Community Psychologists

Janet A. Schank and Thomas M. Skovholt

. . . The issue of ethical dilemmas and decision making is compounded for psychologists working in small communities and rural areas. Prevailing standards in training, ethical codes, and regulations are not so easily applied in rural and small-community practice. Cultural differences, along with what Purtilo and Sorrell (1986) described as the "intricate web of professional–personal roles" (p. 23) in small community life, complicate professional boundary issues. Overlapping relationships are inevitable in rural and other small communities where community involvement lessens suspicion and increases approachability and where "denying help to a potential client because of a preexisting relationship could mean that the person gets no help at all" (Smith & Fitzpatrick, 1995, p. 502).

In a study of the myths and realities of rural practice, Rich (1990) noted that in urban practice both clients and psychologists expect a separation between personal and professional roles. Thus, what constitutes an ethical violation is usually clear. Rich went on to say that in rural practice, personal and professional roles can easily become unintentionally blurred. In these rural settings, prevailing standards and codes of ethics cannot be applied in automatic ways. . . .

Psychologists need to find ways to be accepted into small communities and trusted by the people who form the complex web of rural social stratification. This community acceptance and trust is established through involvement in the community (Horst, 1989). The resultant visibility, along with

role flexibility, leaves the rural psychologist vulnerable to conflicts between personal and professional roles. . . .

Rural and small-community psychologists must balance these personal and professional role conflicts to be accepted in the community. They must also work within the existing community system; establish support networks; and utilize a systems approach to understand local politics, power structure, and the informal communications structure (Jeffrey & Reeve, 1978; Sobel, 1984). Rural psychologists must cope with a "multitude of involvements and levels of involvement" (Hargrove, 1982, p. 22) and with "multiple levels of relationships" (p. 23). Psychologists in rural practice are "subject to a wide range of demands at any given time" (p. 23). Their response affects how the agency is seen by the community, and they must at all times be sensitive to community needs.

Standards may conflict, leaving psychologists to resolve the dilemmas. Each clinical situation brings with it new ethical demands, and rote application of codes is not sufficient (Pope & Vasquez, 1991). As Rich (1990) stated, "Informal expectations and formal rules are more likely to come into conflict with each other in rural practice than they are in urban settings" (p. 33). Yet these urban–rural differences and conflicts have only recently begun to be addressed in professional codes of ethics.

The most recent APA Code of Ethics (American Psychological Association, 1992) has "revised and expanded the guidelines regarding dual relation-

From *Professional Psychology: Research and Practice, 28,* 44–49. Copyright 1997 by the American Psychological Association. Adapted with permission of the author and publisher.

ships" (Sonne, 1994, p. 336). . . . The APA Code of Ethics provides an essential framework; however, it cannot foresee every possible dilemma and situation. In this study rural and small-community psychologists talk about these ethical dilemmas, how various relevant factors are weighed, and how decisions are made when providing psychological services to rural people. [*Ed. note:* In the next section, omitted here, the authors describe a qualitative study in which they interviewed 16 licensed, rural psychologists in Minnesota. They chose to focus on professional boundaries because all of the interviewees raised the issue and all "indicated it was the most frequent and complicated of the dilemmas that they face in daily psychological practice" (p. 46).]

DISCUSSION

. . .

The Reality of Overlapping Social Relationships

Simultaneous or overlapping social relationships occurred in a variety of settings that were identified by all 16 of the psychologists: church, parties and social gatherings, eating out in local restaurants, cultural activities, school events, and volunteer activities. . . .

The psychologists faced dilemmas in terms of boundary issues in deciding whom to see as clients and ended up making those decisions on the basis of three different criteria. Some made the decision on the basis of their own comfort level as to whether they could successfully manage overlapping relationships with particular clients. Others involved prospective clients in that decision-making process. Some psychologists used type and severity of clients' presenting problems as indicators of whether they would enter into overlapping relationships. For example, some were more likely to see clients for advice-giving or problem-solving situations but were unlikely to take on a client with a possible personality disorder when there was even a potential for a dual relationship. An often-mentioned situation was in seeing children as clients who were in school or other activities with a psychologist's own children, a

situation that could not always be predicted or avoided. Several of the psychologists talked about how their spouses' (ministers, attorneys, physicians) professional contacts with people affected decisions about taking those people on as clients. Others found that duality unavoidable.

Most of the psychologists talked directly with their clients about the high likelihood of out-of-therapy contact. They made it clear to clients that they would respect client privacy by waiting to see if clients wanted to acknowledge or greet them. This clarity on the part of psychologists was intended to make the context of dual relationships safer for the clients and, somewhat so, for themselves:

> . . .
>
> It is always establishing boundaries. I live on a very busy street in town and was doing some landscaping and working out in the front yard. One of my clients must have seen me and later said, "Oh, is that where you live? I saw you." I said yes, and she said, "Well, I noticed that the house next to you is for sale. Wouldn't that be cool? You know, my parents are thinking of helping me buy a house." I said, "No, that would not be cool because you are my client—you are not a friend. If you moved in next door to me, it would be extremely uncomfortable. I know what you are saying—I listen to you, I care about you—but friends know about one another. You don't come in, and I sit and tell you about my problems and my life. I don't call you when I am hurting or need a friend for support." . . . She said, "Oh, yeah. I didn't even think about that." And so it's continually having to establish boundaries with a number of clients.

One psychologist had the additional constriction of supervising the other therapists in her agency. Besides coping with dual contexts with her own clients, she also had to deal with knowing about others' clients through supervision.

The Reality of Overlapping Business or Professional Relationships

A related concern, which was identified by 12 of the psychologists, underscored the problematic nature of business or professional contacts with clients and their families. As with overlapping social contacts, rural and small-community psychologists thought through the advisability of such contacts and looked for ethical ways of conducting such relationships. It was often a question of degree of involvement in these overlapping business or professional relationships. For example, psychologists had few conflicts over shopping in a store where a client might be working but would be less comfortable entering into a business partnership that directly involved a client or client's family . . .

Some decisions appeared to be more complex. When alternatives were available, some psychologists avoided contact with clients by shopping and trading exclusively outside of their own communities. Others tried to deal with the ambiguity and confusion that came with overlapping business and therapeutic contacts:

> When you do have business dealings with someone, I find it really hard. I won't bargain with them. Recently someone [who was a former client] worked on my car, and I thought the price was a little high. I trust the guy, but I felt awkward in asking him what the charges were for. If it were someone else, I would have had no problem asking.
>
> For instance, there are people that work for my husband that would come to me. It gets a little sticky because he would be sharing with me. "My employee so and so and such and such," and I'm having to sit there and sort of screen that out.

Several psychologists had overlapping professional roles with medical providers and referral resources:

> We have a nice, isolated building here in a beautiful, quiet place. So professionals many times will come here.

> Now, I have seen a lot of professionals in town [as clients], either for personal counseling or for their children. Then I refer [clients] to [those same professionals] because there is no one else. . . . If you read the rules about dual relationships, that is not allowed.

The most difficult situations were those in which psychologists were providing therapy to colleagues or their families. Those who chose to do so acknowledged the discomfort and potential liabilities of such overlapping relationships but believed that in protecting a client's confidentiality or acting in the client's best interest, one ethical choice overrode the other ethical choice:

> I do consulting at a fair number of group homes. Sometimes I'm in that dilemma where there is someone [working there] that I've seen as a client. In fact, I can think of two instances where I currently was seeing people as clients and subsequently discovered that they had obtained employment at one of the group homes. So I was dealing with them as clients, as well as in a professional relationship in terms of some of the consulting.

The Effects of Overlapping Relationships on Members of the Psychologist's Own Family

One topic identified only once in the literature on dual relationships (Jennings, 1992) was raised by 12 of the 16 people who were interviewed for this study: the effect of overlapping relationships on the family members of rural and small-community psychologists. This issue seemed especially significant and resulted in much questioning and searching for ethical balances on the part of the psychologists. The psychologists who were parents faced having clients or former clients as friends of the psychologists' own children. Psychologists had to weigh which of two competing ethical stances best served their clients' interest. Do they have to accept having clients in their homes as guests of their children, or do they break confidentiality by setting limits on whom their children can have as friends? How, when, and where do they limit their children's social lives and involvement in activities?

> I think there are a lot of variables. If I can avoid a situation, I will. Let's say it is a function like a hockey party. My kids are on the hockey team. The kids want to go, and they want the parents to go. So you are at this function [with clients]. You're not going to say to the kids, "Gee, I can't go to the hockey banquet." So you just go. . . . Sometimes you just kind of live with it. My older kids have friends who have been patients in the past. I prefer that they not come over to our house, but you can't say to your kids, "Don't invite so and so."

. . .

Several psychologists spoke of talking directly to child clients about the fact that some segments of their two lives overlapped. They allowed the child client to be in charge of "who knows what" and helped the client weigh the options in arriving at that decision. Psychologists also talked with their children about how to deal with teasing and questioning, self-disclosure from clients, and inadvertently knowing confidential information about their psychologist parent's work.

Two psychologists brought up the dilemmas they faced when their teenage children ended up dating clients or former clients. Neither compromised their client's confidentiality, but both spoke of the uneasiness and worry that came with knowing things about the former client or about abuse issues in the client's family:

> I think the more difficult situation is interaction that my daughter has had. She is now away at college, but when she was here she would end up dating clients—only to find out and just be absolutely horrified and angry. That is probably the most difficult circumstance that we have been in. The confidentiality piece is really difficult because she

would confront me with, "Is so and so your client?" She is real glad to be done with that.

. . .

Working With More Than One Family Member as Clients or With Others Who Have Friendships With Individual Clients

This was an issue highlighted by 9 of the rural psychologists who were interviewed. Therapy choices may be limited in rural areas and small communities, and there is invariably an intersection of clients with other clients. Although some psychologists practiced in settings where new clients could be referred to other therapists, others did not have such options available. Sometimes psychologists knew in advance that their clients' lives overlapped; other times they discovered the overlap in the course of therapy. Consultation and evaluation requests were another source of such overlap:

> It is very bizarre because I have clients, all of whom seem to know each other and talk about their therapy with each other. I have even had cases where two people who are friends who were in therapy with me separately—one will call and say, "I can't make it, but my friend wants my spot. We talked about it, and is it okay if he comes in at 10:00?"
>
> As a matter of fact, one time I had—I did not know this—I had two new clients starting. They didn't know that the other one was coming here, and they were having affairs with each other's mates. Well, I had to make a choice of whom I was going to see. In that particular case, it worked out fine. But just to let you know—there is tremendous overlapping.

CONCLUSIONS AND IMPLICATIONS

Issues Across Small Communities

Small-community psychologists are not just rural practitioners. They are also professionals who live and work in small communities, often separated by important demographic variables (e.g., age, race, sexual orientation, disability, or geographic location). For example, the American military therapist in Korea, the lesbian psychologist serving that community, the Native American counselor working in that culture, and the deaf practitioner with a deaf clientele are all examples of small-community psychologists who potentially struggle with ethical guidelines developed and enforced by urban psychologists, who are able to live apart from their clients and who can more easily distance themselves from their clients while outside their offices. Although there are some needs that are specific to certain populations, the conversations on appropriate ethical conduct could also include these other communities. By joining together to articulate their concerns, small communities could have more of a voice in contributing to an overall discussion of high-quality ethical practice guidelines.

Examining the Content of Ethical Practice

. . . The needs of both rural and urban clients and the voices of both rural and small-community psychologists need to be heard and respected in an overall consideration of professional ethics. Little research is available on this topic; however, psychologists have recently begun discussing these issues within the context of the APA convention (Barnett, 1995; Gutman, 1995; Leigh, 1995) and other forums.

Safeguards to Minimize Risk

1. Nonsexual overlapping relationships are not a matter of "if" as much as "when" in the daily lives of small-community psychologists (Barnett & Yutrzenka, 1995). Ethical codes or standards are necessary but not sufficient and are tempered by experience and context (Barnett & Yutrzenka, 1995). Although it may seem obvious, knowledge of these codes and of state laws is essential in framing the background for small-community application. Continuing education in ethical issues adds to this framework.

2. Clear expectations and boundaries, whenever possible, strengthen the therapeutic relationship. This is especially important in situations where out-

of-therapy contact cannot be closely controlled. Obtaining informed consent, sticking to time limits, protecting confidentiality (and explaining its limits), and documenting case progress (including being explicit about any overlapping relationships) diminished the risk of misunderstandings between client and psychologist.

3. Ongoing consultation and discussion of cases, especially those involving dual roles, provide a context for psychologists to get additional perspectives and decrease the isolation that sometimes accompanies rural and small-community practice. Each of us has blind spots—trusted colleagues can help us constructively examine them.

4. Self-knowledge and having a life outside of work lessen the chances that we as psychologists will use, even unknowingly, our clients for our own gratification. This also involves what Barnett and Yutrzenka (1995) have recommended in maintaining a constant interpersonal style and authentic presence with clients.

Differences between urban and small-community practice may contribute to the professional isolation of rural and small-community psychologists. More open discussion of the issues lessens the potential danger that rural and small-community psychologists may become isolated. If fear of retribution from professional licensing boards in the helping professions, ethics committees, and professional organizations diminishes the opportunities for frank conversations about the realities of rural and small-community practice, this retreat into professional isolation may lead to individual rural and small-community psychologists becoming the sole arbiters in their practices of ethical decision making.

References

American Psychological Association. (1992). Ethical principles of psychologists and code of conduct. *American Psychologist, 47,* 1597–1611.

Barnett, J. E. (1995, August). Rural practice and ethical issues: An overview. In P. L. Craig (Chair), *Ethical issues in rural practice.* Symposium conducted at the annual convention of the American Psychological Association, New York.

Barnett, J. E., & Yutrzenka, B. A. (1995). Nonsexual dual relationships in professional practice, with special applications to rural and military communities. *Independent Practitioner, 14,* 243–248.

Gutman, V. A. (1995, August). Competencies for ethical practice in psychology and deafness. In V. A. Gutman (Chair), *Ethical issues in a small community: Models for deafness.* Symposium conducted at the 103rd Annual Convention of the American Psychological Association, New York.

Hargrove, D. S. (1982). Mental health needs of rural America. In H. A. Dengerink & H. J. Cross (Eds.), *Training professionals for rural mental health* (pp. 14–26). Lincoln: University of Nebraska Press.

Horst, E. A. (1989). Dual relationships between psychologists and clients in rural and urban areas. *Journal of Rural Community Psychology, 10,* 15–23.

Jeffrey, M. J., & Reeve, R. E. (1978). Community mental health services in rural areas: Some practical issues. *Community Mental Health Journal, 14,* 54–62.

Jennings, F. L. (1992). Ethics of rural practice. *Psychotherapy in Private Practice, 10,* 85–104.

Leigh, I. W. (1995, August). How to live with boundary issues within the deaf community. In V. G. Gutman (Chair), *Ethical issues in a small community: Models for deafness.* Symposium conducted at the 103rd Annual Convention of the American Psychological Association, New York.

Pope, K. S., & Vasquez, M. J. (1991). *Ethics in psychotherapy and counseling.* San Francisco: Jossey-Bass.

Purtilo, R., & Sorrell, J. (1986). The ethical dilemmas of a rural physician. *Hastings Center Report, 16,* 24–28.

Rich, R. O. (1990). The American rural metaphor: Myths and realities in rural practice. *Human Services in the Rural Environment, 14,* 31–34.

Smith, D., & Fitzpatrick, M. (1995). Patient–therapist boundary issues: An integrative review of theory and research. *Professional Psychology: Research and Practice, 26,* 499–506.

Sobel, S. B. (1984). Independent practice in child and adolescent psychotherapy in small communities: Personal, professional, and ethical issues. *Psychotherapy, 21,* 110–117.

Sonne, J. L. (1994). Multiple relationships: Does the new ethics code answer the right questions? *Professional Psychology: Research and Practice, 25,* 336–343.

◆   ◆   ◆

Commentary: *One issue that neither Hargrove nor Schank & Skovhold address is bartering for services, a problem that may confront those who serve rural or poor clients, particularly those enrolled in managed care programs that limit the number of reimbursable visits.*

In 1982, the APA ethics committee approved a policy that proclaimed bartering of services a violation of then Principle 6(a) (Dual Relationships). That policy was modified in the 1992 Ethical Principles. Standard 1.18 now generally discourages bartering, permitting it only if it is not clinically contraindicated and is not exploitative. But Sonne (1994) thinks that even this broadening may be problematic:

> Even if the psychologist were able to make the prediction a priori that bartering posed no ethical concerns, at least three other issues remain. First, bartering for services may, in essence, establish an employment relationship. . . . When such conditions of employment are implicit—the potential for harmful effects in the dynamics of the therapist–client relationship is greater.
>
> Second, the practitioner needs to consider the position of the state licensing board regarding employing a client and bartering. . . .
>
> Third, psychologists need to be aware of the position of the American Professional Agency, whose malpractice insurance policy . . . states, 'This policy does not . . . apply to any claims arising out of any business or venture with any prior or current patient or client of the insured' [citation omitted]. Lack of coverage of such acts seems a clear indication of how potentially destructive they can be. (p. 341)

See Sonne, J. (1994). Multiple relationships: Does the new ethics code answer the right questions? Professional Psychology: Research and Practice, 25, 336–343. In a similar vein, Woody argues that "bartering seems so fraught with risks for both parties that it seems illogical even to consider it as an option" (p. 176). He would use it only as a last resort. See Woody, R. J. (1988). Bartering for psychological services. Professional Psychology: Research and Practice, 29, 174–178.

Are these cautionary notes appropriate or do they support the position in the two prior excerpts that ethics codes, licensing boards, and insurers are too rule-bound, and neglect the realities of rural practice and the provision of services to certain ethnic and "small-community" groups?

Antiracism as an Ethical Imperative: An Example From Feminist Therapy

Laura S. Brown

Feminist therapy has from its inception been a field concerned with the ethics of practice. For feminist therapists, *ethics* is a term that has had broad connotations. Rather than framing ethics as simply being a set of rules or principles describing behaviors to be avoided, feminist therapists have attempted to construe ethical behavior in terms that integrated the process of thinking about ethics into all choices made by therapists about the underlying assumptions of our psychotherapy theory and the politics of our practice. Ethics holds a special place in feminist therapy; it is a unifying vision around which we have joined for the creation of our therapy theories. We have poured into the creation of feminist therapy ethics the best and clearest of our collective thought and the most focused of our work (Rave & Larsen, 1990). Feminist therapists may disagree on many aspects of how to practice, but we tend to converge around the idea that our work must reflect feminist ethical principles of empowerment, care, and the necessity of taking proactive rather than reactive stances (Lerman & Porter, 1990).

Over the two decades of its existence, feminist therapy has focused on a number of different ethical concerns. This article represents a divergence from the mainstream of that thought, which has been concerned primarily with the question of sexuality and sexual and social boundaries in psychotherapy, and instead attends to an issue that is painful and yet fertile with potential for enhancing our understanding of ethics in psychotherapy.

The issue is that of racism in feminist therapy. The questions to be raised here are several. How can we develop an ethic of antiracism within feminist therapy? How can we measure that ethical principle equal in weight to the other ethical concerns that have engaged feminist therapists until now? The issue is painful for many reasons. By raising it, White feminist therapists such as myself acknowledge what our sisters of color have been telling us from almost the beginning. Feminist therapy, as a discipline, and many White feminist therapists as individuals have in the main excluded the realities and living presence of women of color from our work, our theories, and our writing. We must attend to rather than deny or gloss over the discrepancy between our goals as feminists of nonoppressiveness and the realities of being participants in a process of institutionalized oppression. Until recently, antiracism has been neglected as an ethical consideration, in part because this self-confrontation is a difficult one that yields an image at odds with the self-concept of many feminist therapists. When it has been addressed, it has been framed by some White women as a political (as opposed to therapeutic) issue in such a way as to potentially minimize its core importance to matters of feminist therapy theory and practice. It has been seen by some White women as divisive, or inessential to the work and focus of feminist therapy, which may itself be a defensive rationalization for the neglect of the issue. Whatever the reasons, feminist therapy has been mostly a White women's movement in which the unconscious racism with which we were raised has been pervasive, our rhetoric of inclusiveness notwithstanding. . . .

It is important to note at this juncture that al-

From *Ethics and Behavior, 1,* 113–127. Copyright 1991 by Erlbaum. Adapted with permission of the author and publisher.

though the specifics to which I speak are derived from feminist therapy, the issues being raised here are more universal. That is, almost all current schools of psychotherapy are, by virtue of their participation in the dominant culture, inherently racist. The ethical questions raised here for feminist therapists are equally germane for any psychotherapist, and the importance of seeing antiracism as an ethical stance is no less valid outside the realm of feminist therapy practice. Placing my arguments within the context of feminist therapy, a socially and politically conscious school of thought, may help to illustrate the degree of difficulty White therapists of good will face when attempting to address our own racism. . . .

What I have begun to arrive at is a reframing of my understanding of racism as an ethical issue. I have conceptualized the presence of racism in therapy in the common language of feminist therapy ethics. That is, I suggest that we can more easily understand the need to be antiracist as an ethical imperative if we see racism through the lenses of failures of mutuality and lack of respect, violations of boundaries, and imbalances of power, terms that inhere to discussion of feminist therapy ethics in other realms such as sexuality or money.

Let us begin with the problem of failures of mutuality and lack of respect. Many women writers of color have criticized the second wave of the U.S. feminist movement (and by implication feminist therapy) for its overreliance on gender as a category of analysis for understanding women's oppression (Davis, 1983; Hooks, 1981; Lorde, 1980). . . . These women point out that the assumption of a generic woman makes invisible the experiences of women of color as people of color and that it eradicates the differences between living as a White woman versus living as a woman of color in a White racist society in which racism and sexism are intertwined.

In feminist therapy, White feminist therapists who constitute the bulk of the population have tended to share in this form of covert racism; we write and speak of "women's experiences" as if we are referring to all women when in fact our data bases are primarily or exclusively White (Brown, 1990; Kanuha, 1990). Thus, White feminist therapists have tended to annihilate women of color in

our words and actions; we have made their lives invisible, their voices inaudible. We have communicated the meta-message that women of color are unimportant to feminist therapy theory and practice because we have not moved to include them. Such behavior is destructive to mutuality and to the process of empathy and connection; it violates a feminist ethical standard of care (Noddings, 1984). This participation in the process of making women of color invisible does not allow the space to be in "right relationship" (Heyward, 1989, p. 10) where each person is known and attended to deeply by the other. Such participation in the process of institutionalized racism within the helping professions may be especially painful to women of color when it comes from feminist therapists because we have declared ourselves to be attentive to and concerned with oppression (Kanuha, 1990). We are, in effect, telling women of color that the only important oppression is gender based and that their experiences as targets of racism are of lesser or no importance. . . .

A second way to conceptualize racism as a problem of ethics is to construe it as a form of boundary violation. Typically, in feminist therapy (and other) ethical writings, we have thought of boundaries as sexual and physical; these terms have become so interchangeable that when someone is described as having "boundary problems" in her practice, the unspoken assumption is that she has sexually exploited a client. Yet personal boundaries are more than sexual. I propose that a woman's identity, her sense of self in her race and ethnicity, her pride or shame in her roots, and her awareness of her culture are all aspects of the boundary phenomenon and are at risk for violation. . . .

Finally, there is the question of power imbalance. Feminist therapists have a shared ethical commitment toward the development of egalitarian relationships. By this we have meant that we wish to practice in ways that reduce unnecessary asymmetries between the power of client and therapist, that empower the client to self-knowledge and self-value, and that lead to increasing mutuality in the therapist–client relationship while preserving those aspects of the frame of therapy (e.g., not having social or romantic relationships with clients) that are necessary for the well-being of the client.

This is clearly not to say that feminist therapists of color as a group are so weak and needy as to lack power or need special protections; they do not. Rather, it is to point to the ethical problem for White feminist therapists that results when we fail to acknowledge the privilege given us by our skin color and the impact that our Whiteness has on colleagues who are women of color, in other words, the ethical conundrum of oppressive exclusivity that derives from a failure to be antiracist. . . .

References

Brown, L. S. (1990). The meaning of a multicultural perspective for theory-building in feminist therapy. In L. S. Brown & M. P. P. Root (Eds.), *Diversity and complexity in feminist therapy* (pp. 1–22). New York: Haworth.

Davis, A. Y. (1983). *Women, race and class.* New York: Vintage Books.

Heyward, C. (1989). *Touching our strength: The erotic as power and the love of God.* San Francisco: Harper & Row.

Hooks, B. (1981). *Ain't I a woman: Black women and feminism.* Boston: South End Press.

Kanuha, V. (1990). The need for an integrated analysis of oppression in feminist therapy ethics. In H. Lerman & N. Porter (Eds.), *Feminist ethics in psychotherapy* (pp. 24–36). New York: Springer.

Lerman, H., & Porter, N. (1990). The contribution of feminism to ethics in psychotherapy. In H. Lerman & N. Porter (Eds.), *Feminist ethics in psychotherapy* (pp. 5–13). New York: Springer.

Lorde, A. (1980, April). *Age, race, class, and sex: Women redefining difference.* Copeland Colloquium, Amherst College, Amherst, MA.

Noddings, N. (1984). *Caring: A feminine approach to ethics and moral education.* Berkeley: University of California Press.

Rave, E. J., & Larsen, C. C. (1990). Development of the code: The feminist process. In H. Lerman & N. Porter (Eds.), *Feminist ethics in psychotherapy* (pp. 14–23). New York: Springer.

◆ ◆ ◆

Commentary: APA has been reasonably forthcoming in producing documents designed to help therapists deal with such sensitive issues as sexism, racism, and the treatment of gays and lesbians. For example, in 1975, an APA task force on sexism in psychotherapy published: American Psychological Association. (1975). Report of the task force on sex bias and sex-role stereotyping in psychotherapeutic practice. American Psychologist, 30, 1169–1175. Like many other task force reports, this one has not been adopted by the Council of Representatives as APA policy. But it has raised many issues that are still of concern, such as the treatment of lesbians by therapists who are not fully trained or knowledgeable in this area and the problem of sexual attraction between therapist and patient.

The 1975 report recommended, among other things, that APA develop guidelines for nonsexist psychotherapeutic practice. APA appropriate funds for this endeavor, and in 1978, these guidelines were published in the American Psychologist, 33, 1122–1123.

Guidelines for Therapy With Women

Task Force on Sex Bias and Sex Role Stereotyping in Psychotherapeutic Practice

. . .

1. The conduct of therapy should be free of constrictions based on gender-defined roles, and the options explored between client and practitioner should be free of sex role stereotypes.

. . .

2. Psychologists should recognize the reality, variety, and implications of sex-discriminatory practices in society and should facilitate client examination of options in dealing with such practices.

. . .

3. The therapist should be knowledgeable about current empirical findings on sex roles, sexism, and individual differences resulting from the client's gender-defined identity.

. . .

4. The theoretical concepts employed by the therapist should be free of sex bias and sex role stereotypes.

. . .

5. The psychologist should demonstrate acceptance of women as equal to men by using language free of derogatory labels.

. . .

6. The psychologist should avoid establishing the source of personal problems within the client when they are more properly attributable to situational or cultural factors.

. . .

7. The psychologist and a fully informed client mutually should agree upon aspects of the therapy relationship such as treatment modality, time factors, and fee arrangements.

. . .

8. While the importance of the availability of accurate information to a client's family is recognized, the privilege of communication about diagnosis, prognosis, and progress ultimately resides with the client, not with the therapist.

. . .

9. If authoritarian processes are employed as a technique, the therapy should not have the effect of maintaining or reinforcing stereotypic dependency of women.

. . .

10. The client's assertive behaviors should be respected.

. . .

11. The psychologist whose female client is subjected to violence in the form of physical abuse or rape should recognize and acknowledge that the client is the victim of a crime.

. . .

12. The psychologist should recognize and encourage exploration of a woman client's sexuality and should recognize her right to define her own sexual preferences.

. . .

13. The psychologist should not have sexual relations with a woman client nor treat her as a sex object.

. . .

◆ ◆ ◆

Commentary: *In 1984, APA's Division 17 (Counseling Psychology) produced a corollary set of precepts titled "Principles Concerning the Counseling and Psychother-*

apy of Women" that are worth studying (*available from Division 17*). For a recent book on this subject, see Lerman, H., & Porter, N. (Eds.). (1990). *Feminist ethics in psychotherapy. New York: Springer.*

In 1990, a report by the Task Force on Bias in Psychotherapy with Lesbians and Gay Men was approved by the APA Committee on Gay and Lesbian Concerns. In a survey conducted as part of this report, the task force found that the conduct of many therapists assessing and treating these client populations violated existing ethical principles that addressed competence and the welfare of the client. This important report, which has not been adopted as official APA-wide policy, is available from the APA's Committee on Gay and Lesbian Concerns.

Finally, the APA's Board of Ethnic Minority Affairs established a task force in 1988 to help psychologists better understand cultural and ethnic factors when providing psychological services to diverse populations. Guidelines from the board's report, which were subsequently adopted by the Council of Representatives as APA policy, are reprinted next.

Guidelines for Providers of Psychological Services to Ethnic, Linguistic, and Culturally Diverse Populations

American Psychological Association

. . .

GUIDELINES

Preamble: The Guidelines represent general principles that are intended to be aspirational in nature and are designed to provide suggestions to psychologists in working with ethnic, linguistic, and culturally diverse populations.

1. Psychologists educate their clients to the processes of psychological intervention, such as goals and expectations; the scope and, where appropriate, legal limits of confidentiality; and the psychologists' orientations.
   a. Whenever possible, psychologists provide information in writing along with oral explanations.
   b. Whenever possible, the written information is provided in the language understandable to the client.
2. Psychologists are cognizant of relevant research and practice issues as related to the population being served.
   a. Psychologists acknowledge that ethnicity and culture impact on behavior and take those factors into account when working with various ethnic/racial groups.
   b. Psychologists seek out educational and training experiences to enhance their understanding and thereby address the needs of these populations more appropriately and effectively.

These experiences include cultural, social, psychological, political, economic, and historic material specific to the particular ethnic group being served.
   c. Psychologists recognize the limits of their competencies and expertise. Psychologists who do not possess knowledge and training about an ethnic group seek consultation with, and/or make referrals to, appropriate experts as necessary.
   d. Psychologists consider the validity of a given instrument or procedure and interpret resulting data, keeping in mind the cultural and linguistic characteristics of the person being assessed. Psychologists are aware of the test's reference population and possible limitations of such instruments with other populations.
3. Psychologists recognize ethnicity and culture as significant parameters in understanding psychological processes.
   a. Psychologists, regardless of ethnic/racial background, are aware of how their own cultural background/experiences, attitudes, values, and biases influence psychological processes. They make efforts to correct any prejudices and biases.

Illustrative Statement: Psychologists might routinely ask themselves, "Is it appropriate for me to view this client or organization any differently than I would if they were from my own ethnic or cultural group?"

b. Psychologists' practice incorporates an understanding of the client's ethnic and cultural background. This includes the client's familiarity and comfort with the majority culture as well as ways in which the client's culture may add to or improve various aspects of the majority culture and/or of society at large.

Illustrative Statement: The kinds of mainstream social activities in which families participate may offer information about the level and quality of acculturation to American society. It is important to distinguish acculturation from length of stay in the United States and not to assume that these issues are relevant only for new immigrants and refugees.

c. Psychologists help clients increase their awareness of their own cultural values and norms, and they facilitate discovery of ways clients can apply this awareness to their own lives and to society at large.

Illustrative Statement: Psychologists may be able to help parents distinguish between generational conflict and culture gaps when problems arise between them and their children. In the process, psychologists could help both parents and children to appreciate their own distinguishing cultural values.

d. Psychologists seek to help a client determine whether a "problem" stems from racism or bias in others so that the client does not inappropriately personalize problems.

Illustrative Statement: The concept of "healthy paranoia," whereby ethnic minorities may develop defensive behaviors in response to discrimination, illustrates this principle.

e. Psychologists consider not only differential diagnostic issues but also the cultural beliefs and values of the client and his/her community in providing intervention.

Illustrative Statement: There is a disorder among the traditional Navajo called "Moth Madness." Symptoms include seizure-like behaviors. This disorder is believed by the Navajo to be the supernatural result of incestuous thoughts or behaviors. Both differential diagnosis and intervention should take into consideration the traditional values of Moth Madness.

4. Psychologists respect the roles of family members and community structures, hierarchies, values, and beliefs within the client's culture.

a. Psychologists identify resources in the family and the larger community.

b. Clarification of the role of the psychologist and the expectations of the client precedes intervention. Psychologists seek to ensure that both the psychologist and client have a clear understanding of what services and roles are reasonable.

Illustrative Statement: It is not uncommon for an entire American Indian family to come into the clinic to provide support to the person in distress. Many of the healing practices found in American Indian communities are centered in the family and the whole community.

5. Psychologists respect clients' religious and/or spiritual beliefs and values, including attributions and taboos, since they affect world view, psychosocial functioning, and expressions of distress.

a. Part of working in minority communities is to become familiar with indigenous beliefs and practices and to respect them.

Illustrative Statement: Traditional healers (e.g., shamans, curanderos, espiritistas) have an important place in minority communities.

b. Effective psychological intervention may be aided by consultation with and/or inclusion of religious/spiritual leaders/practitioners relevant to the client's cultural and belief systems.

6. Psychologists interact in the language requested by the client and, if this is not feasible, make an appropriate referral.

a. Problems may arise when the linguistic skills of the psychologist do not match the language of the client. In such a case, psychologists refer the client to a mental health professional who is competent to interact in the language of the client. If this is not possible, psychologists offer the client a translator with cultural knowledge and an appropriate professional background. When no translator is available, then a trained paraprofessional from the client's culture is used as a translator/culture broker.

b. If translation is necessary, psychologists do not retain the services of translators/paraprofessionals who may have a dual role with the client, to avoid jeopardizing the validity of evaluation or the effectiveness of intervention.

   c. Psychologists interpret and relate test data in terms understandable and relevant to the needs of those assessed.

7. Psychologists consider the impact of adverse social, environmental, and political factors in assessing problems and designing interventions.

   a. Types of intervention strategies to be used match the client's level of need (e.g., Maslow's hierarchy of needs).

Illustrative Statement: Low income may be associated with such stressors as malnutrition, substandard housing, and poor medical care; and rural residency may mean inaccessibility of services. Clients may resist treatment at government agencies because of previous experience (e.g., refugees' status may be associated with violent treatments by government officials and agencies).

   b. Psychologists work within the cultural setting to improve the welfare of all persons concerned, if there is a conflict between cultural values and human rights.

8. Psychologists attend to, as well as work to eliminate, biases, prejudices, and discriminatory practices.

   a. Psychologists acknowledge relevant discriminatory practices at the social and community level that may be affecting the psychological welfare of the population being served.

Illustrative Statement: Depression may be associated with frustrated attempts to climb the corporate ladder in an organization that is dominated by a top echelon of White men.

   b. Psychologists are cognizant of sociopolitical contexts in conducting evaluations and pro-

viding interventions; they develop sensitivity to issues of oppression, sexism, elitism, and racism.

Illustrative Statement: An upsurge in the public expression of rancor or even violence between two ethnic or cultural groups may increase anxiety baselines in any member of those groups. This baseline of anxiety would interact with prevailing symptomatology. At the organizational level, the community conflict may interfere with open communication among staff.

9. Psychologists working with culturally diverse populations should document culturally and sociopolitically relevant factors in the records. These may include, but are not limited to

   a. number of generations in the country

   b. number of years in the country

   c. fluency in English

   d. extent of family support (or disintegration of family)

   e. community resources

   f. level of education

   g. change in social status as a result of coming to this country (for immigrant or refugee)

   h. intimate relationship with people of different backgrounds

   i. level of stress related to acculturation.

◆ ◆ ◆

Commentary: The APA's 1992 Ethical Principles of Psychologists and Code of Conduct is substantially more specific and sensitive to issues of assessment, intervention, and research with clients and participants of different genders, sexual orientations, and cultural, racial, and ethnic diversity than the 1981 ethics code that it replaced, although Payton (1994, next excerpt), seems a bit more skeptical.

Implications of the 1992 Ethics Code for Diverse Groups

Carolyn R. Payton

The current code of ethics (American Psychological Association [APA], 1992), on initial reading, seems to be an improvement on previous codes of the APA in terms of addressing issues of concern to ethnic minorities and women. A number of the revised regulations appear to reflect a sensitivity to the particular needs and treatment that should be accorded women and minorities. Does the code as a whole, however, live up to its stated primary goal of protecting the welfare of those with whom psychologists work when these individuals and groups are drawn from diverse populations?

. . .

Ethnic minorities, gays, and women have reason to be apprehensive about how psychologists' declaration of respect for the dignity and worth of the individual and the pledge to protect fundamental human rights seem to have been downgraded. The endorsement of this ideal as one that undergirds all activities of the psychological profession normally appears as the lead-in sentence of the Preamble (APA, 1953, 1967, 1977, 1990). The current code yields the prominent position of the opening sentence to the enunciation of psychologists' allegiance to the development of a "valid and reliable body of scientific knowledge based on research" (APA, 1992, p. 1599). . . .

I have no way of knowing the argument for the shift from the stance of 1953, "the worth of a profession is measured by its contribution to the welfare of man" (APA, 1953, p. 1), to the current "psychologists work to develop a valid and reliable body of scientific knowledge based on research" (APA,

1992, p. 1599). What is clear to me is that the latter postulation lacks the "vision thing" so poignantly expressed in the 1953 statement.

. . .

The new code addresses the quandary of whether psychologists are to be governed by standards or principles by including a section for principles and one for ethical standards. The general principles overlap the Preamble in several instances and expand the introductory statements. The principles reassert the primacy of our scientific roots and cite competence as Principle A. Social responsibility is Principle F and the last to be listed.

. . .

Psychologists are urged, in Principle D in the new code, to accord "appropriate respect to the fundamental rights, dignity, and worth of all people" (APA, 1992, p. 1599). Why the qualifier for respect? If I am an avowed racist, am I thus given license to treat African Americans in a disrespectful manner? Is the homophobic psychology professor thus empowered to mistreat the gay or lesbian student?

Throughout the principles there are modifiers that render the edicts meaningless: "Psychologists seek to contribute to the welfare of those with whom they interact professionally" (APA, 1992, p. 1600), psychologists are "encouraged" to be involved in pro bono work, and "psychologists are concerned about the ethical compliance of their colleagues' scientific and professional conduct" (APA, 1992, p. 1599). The statements lack the quality of an obligatory sense of duty to carry out certain actions. If the imperative mood cannot be used in sections setting forth idealistic goals, where would it be appropriate?

I fear that, because of the litigious nature of society and the resulting fear of lawsuits, the current code has been diluted almost to the point of uselessness. It certainly represents a retreat from a forthright proclamation of humanitarian allegiance. This does not bode well for diverse groups. Their progress within the organization can be attributed to the successful appeals of these groups for socially responsible behavior from the membership, buttressed by the profession's articulated humanitarian concerns.

. . .

Notwithstanding the previous comments, this code has significantly strengthened regulations pertaining to human differences in Standards 1.08, 1.09, and 1.10. For the first time, acts of sexual harassment merit their very own standard. In the 1989 revision, the sentences banning such acts are embedded under Principle 7, Professional Relationships. Given the prominence of its current position in the new code, it will be far more difficult to plead ignorance because of an oversight. However, the forcefulness of the proscriptions on harassment is diminished in the Other Harassment standard, Standard 1.12, which brings up the qualifier "knowingly" (APA, 1992, p. 1601), as in psychologists do not knowingly engage in harassment. Try using the argument of ignorance with the Internal Revenue Service to explain your failure to withhold appropriate taxes for the housekeeper or baby-sitter.

I am not clear on whether I should feel heartened or dismayed at the array of characteristics defining diverse groups in the new code. It is obvious that care was taken to ensure that no one could complain about having been excluded. Yet the very need to carefully label all possible human variability speaks to how fragmented humans are. What a state of affairs that I must declare my gayness or gender or blindness to ensure that I will be treated with equity and humaneness.

Overall, it is obvious that much time and effort were exerted to develop these revised procedures for governing the activities of psychologists. After my analysis of the code, I am left with a sense of discomfort. Previous codes seemed to have been for-

mulated from the perspective of offering protection to the consumers of our discipline, and that is as it should be. The 1992 revision appears to be more concerned with offering protection to psychologists first and foremost. It reads as though the final draft was edited by lawyers in the employment of the APA. Removal of the many instances of exceptions to the rule would make the code more enforceable and more reflective of our discipline, which at one time was dedicated to the promotion of human welfare. Diverse groups and all who share their concerns should be alerted to a profound philosophical shift represented by the new code. If, as it seems, psychologists have abandoned their moral tradition of endorsing the primacy of fundamental human rights, progress of diverse groups within the APA may be hampered. The current code may be the beginning steps of moving back to the future.

References

American Psychological Association. (1953). *Ethical standards of psychologists: A summary of ethical principles.* Washington, DC: Author.

American Psychological Association. (1967). *Casebook on ethical standards of psychologists.* Washington, DC: Author.

American Psychological Association. (1977, March). Revised ethical standards of psychologists. *APA Monitor,* pp. 22–23.

American Psychological Association. (1990). Ethical principles of psychologists (Amended June 2, 1989). *American Psychologist, 45,* 390–395.

American Psychological Association. (1992). Ethical principles of psychologists and code of conduct. *American Psychologist, 47,* 1597–1611.

◆ ◆ ◆

Commentary: In the final section of this chapter, I address ethical issues related to more nontraditional forms of therapy. Conventional psychological interventions do not intrude into the client's body. Some psychophysical measurements, like electroencephalography, do involve the corpus of the client but do not "break the skin." Thus, they raise no special legal or ethical issues. But with the development of biofeedback, stress and pain management, and behavioral medicine—as well as psychologists' increasing participation in these fields—pro-

cedures that involve physical interventions, (particularly aversive conditioning) have come under increasing governmental and institutional scrutiny. To forestall inappropriate regulation, APA convened a task force to forge its position on physical interventions by psychologists and to make recommendations for their use. In 1981, the APA issued the document titled Psychologists' Use of Physical Interventions: Task Force Report, in which its task force members unanimously concluded that

> the use of physical interventions by psychologists is within the scope of psychological practice so long as the applications of such interventions are: (1) in the interest of more productive and comprehensive health care delivery; (2) within the scope of the practitioner's competence as determined by formal and appropriately supervised training and experience in the application of the given intervention; and (3) primarily determined by a decision based on consumer welfare. (Unpublished manuscript, p. 14)

The task force then recommended that psychologists, among others who use physical interventions, follow informed-consent procedures—providing clients with knowledge of the purposes, values, risks, and techniques of each particular intervention. It further advised that APA develop guidelines for the ethical use of physical procedures and substances.

This 1981 report was never adopted as APA policy by the Council of Representatives. But the task force envisioned "the development of appropriate training courses to qualify the psychologist to prescribe and utilize prescriptive medication . . . especially of the psychoactive types" (p. 16).

The 1981 report and a similar one published in 1985 were precursors to the current intensive effort toward securing for psychologists the privilege to prescribe certain psychotropic medications, although psychologists first raised the issue over a decade ago. See also, for example, Bascue, L. O., & Zlotowski, M. (1981). Psychologists' attitudes about prescribing medications. Psychological Reports, 48, 645–646.

The most comprehensive report was issued in 1992 by the APA ad hoc Task Force on Psychopharmacology.

Although the APA Council of Representatives has now endorsed a policy favoring the securing of prescription privileges for psychologists, there is no consensus within the membership favoring such privileges. See Gutierrez, P. M., & Silk, K. R. (1998). Prescription privileges for psychologists: A review of the psychological literature. Professional Psychology: Research and Practice, 29, 213–222; Massoth, N. A., McGrath, R. E., Bianchi, C., & Singer, J. (1990). Psychologists' attitudes toward prescription privileges. Professional Psychology: Research and Practice, 21, 147–149. The idea is gathering momentum, however, and has stimulated a number of articles, pro and con. Compare, e.g.,

DeLeon, P. H., Fox, R. E., & Graham, S. R. (1991). Prescription privileges: Psychology's next frontier? American Psychologist, 46, 384–393.

May, W. T., & Belsky, J. (1992). Response to "Prescription privileges: Psychology's next frontier?" or the siren call: Should psychologists medicate? American Psychologist, 47, 427.

For an excellent review of relevant problems related to prescription privileges for psychologists who work with children, see DeMers, S. T. (1994). Legal and ethical issues in school psychologists' participation in psychopharmacological interventions with children. School Psychology Quarterly, 9, 41–52.

Do you think that psychology needs a separate set of guidelines to govern the practice and ethics of administering psychotropic medication? For one suggested set, see Buelow, G. D., & Chafetz, M. D. (1996). Proposed ethical practice guidelines for clinical pharmacopsychology: Sharpening a new focus in psychology. Professional Psychology: Research and Practice, 27, 53–58. What provisions of the APA's Ethical Principles and Code of Conduct are already implicated in the controversy over prescription privileges for psychologists?

Another older but still controversial issue concerns interventions that are "totally self-administered without professional consultation" (Rosen, 1976, p. 139), what Rosen (1976) calls "nonprescription" therapies or, more generically, what Jacobs and Goodman (1989) label as "self-care," e.g., "self-help groups, do-it-yourself therapies, and other self-change efforts that do not involve direct contact with a professional'" (Rosen, 1993, p. 340). See Jacobs, M. K. & Goodman, G. (1989). Psychology and self-help groups: Predictions on a partnership.

American Psychologist, 44, 536–544; Rosen, G. M. (1976); Rosen, G. M. (1993). Self-help or hype? Comments on psychology's failure to advance self-care. The development and use of nonprescription behavior therapies. American Psychologist, 48, 139–141. Rosen (1976) recommended that APA develop a set of standards to clarify the steps necessary to appropriately validate self-help programs. Two years later, in 1978, APA created the Task Force on Self-Help Therapies. Its primary assignment was to evaluate the extent to which the then-current ethical principles could be applied to professional activity relative to self-help therapies and manuals. Analyzing principles related to responsibility, competence, and public statements, the task force concluded that many self-help books were violating the then-extant version of the APA ethics code, particularly because they failed both to fully inform purchasers of the limitations of the techniques that authors were espousing and to meet recognized standards for evaluating therapeutic procedures. However, because some self-help therapies do benefit the public, the task force urged the APA not to create an ethical bar to their promulgation and dissemination in books, in public lectures, or through the media.

Fifteen years later Rosen (1993) was still troubled by the fact that very little had been done to address the significant professional and ethical issues raised by self-help materials, such as books and audio- and video-tapes. In sum, his article

> attempted to demonstrate that self-help programs are experiencing explosive growth; that psychologists are to be credited with a substantial body of research dating back to the 1970s; that this research demonstrates the potential and real effectiveness of self-help programs as well as their limits; that some psychologists have failed to heed the results of their own studies by rushing to market with exaggerated product claims; and that the APA has itself set a poor example for the profession

> and failed to advance clear standards. (Rosen, 1993, p. 344)

To what extent do Rosen's concerns find themselves addressed in the current Ethical Principles? What is the cumulative effect of Standards 1.03, 2.01, 3.02, 3.03, and 3.04 on the use of self-help therapies and manuals?

The APA has always been ambivalent about psychologists giving personal advice through the media. On the one hand, permitting this was seen as potentially harmful to the public and demeaning to the profession if the advice was superficial and misleading. On the other hand, disallowing it precluded highly competent professionals from providing educational and, possibly, preventative information to the public. Until 1981 there was an ethical ban on media services. Standard 3.04 of the 1992 Ethical Principles, however, like its 1981 predecessor, does not prohibit giving advice through media presentations, as long as it is grounded in relevant scientific literature, it conforms to other provisions in the Ethical Principles, and there is no implication that a personal "relationship" has been established. Does this mean that it is still unethical for a psychologist to provide a diagnosis or treatment through the media? What does the 1992 ethics code say, if anything, about asking current or former clients to appear on the radio or television with the psychologist? How would you view such a request?

What if the therapist conducts therapy with already established clients over the telephone or—more problematic perhaps—with a client that he or she has never (or only initially) personally seen? Telephone consultations provide immediacy and accessibility as well as financial savings that in-person therapy may not provide, particularly to clients who may need assurance and support during crises. What are some of the risks of providing such help? (Remember that an important element missing in telephone consultations is the information derived from face-to-face contact.) The authors of the next article provide a helpful analysis of the advantages and disadvantages of therapy by telephone. They also raise the question of how well the current code covers the ethical issues it raises.

Psychotherapy by Telephone: Risks and Benefits for Psychologists and Consumers

Leonard J. Haas, J. G. Benedict, and Joseph C. Kobos

. . . The existing professional standards appear to adequately encompass this variation on conventional face-to-face psychotherapy. In addition, the APA Ethics Committee recently published a statement specifically addressing psychotherapy by telephone (see Appendix A).

In almost all respects, telephone-only treatment raises the same issues that arise in providing ethically sound psychological services of other kinds: the obligation to deliver competent service, the obligation to avoid harm to consumers, the obligation to make explicit financial arrangements, the obligation to avoid deceit in public statements, the obligation to obtain informed consent from consumers of services, and the obligation to protect confidentiality (except under certain, well-known, extenuating circumstances). None of these obligations seem to be altered by the use of the telephone as the means of contact with the consumer.

In certain respects, telephone-only therapy can be seen as an emerging area of practice, which is dealt with by the Ethical Code of Psychologists (APA, 1992) in Standard 1.04C (Boundaries of Competence): "In those emerging areas in which generally recognized standards for preparatory training do not yet exist, psychologists take reasonable steps to ensure the competence of their work and to protect patients, clients and others from harm" (p. 133). In the present context, this means that psychologists may need to clarify for which types of treatment nonverbal information is crucial and exclude such approaches from the telephone-only array of services. Also, this standard may imply (a) that psychologists should take steps to recognize their vulnerability to distraction while providing treatment over the telephone or (b) that techniques for focusing be developed and consistently used to ensure that telephone therapy conversations are productive.

Within the more general framework of clinical obligations and responsibilities, psychologists should take particular care to inform potential clients of the realistic limitations of telephone treatment, as noted previously, and of the existence of alternative methods of obtaining service, if these exist. Consideration of the ethical obligations enumerated in the Ethics Code clarifies specific questions that should be answered before the responsible psychologist participates in a telephone therapy service, whether the service is provided independently or by a third-party business. These questions are listed in Appendix B. As can be seen from Appendix B, these issues are little different from conventional therapy; all of the following must be dealt with by the telephone therapist: the need to establish informed consent, the appropriate advertising of the service, the need to keep adequate records, and the need to make productive contact with other providers.

APPENDIX A

APA Ethics Committee's Statement on Psychotherapy by Telephone

The following statement was published in the October 1995 edition of *APA Monitor* (p. 15). It is a revision of the American Psychological Association Ethics Committee's original statement, which appeared in the July 1994 edition of *American Psychologist* (p. 4).

The Ethics Committee can only enforce and address the relevance of the "Ethical Principles of Psychologists and Code of Conduct" and cannot say whether there may be other APA Guidelines that might provide guidance. The Ethics Code is not specific with regard to telephone therapy or teleconferencing or any electronically provided services as such and has no rules prohibiting such services. Complaints regarding such matters would be addressed on a case-by-case basis.

The nature of the contact is an important variable, and the use of telephone for purposes such as educative information, suicide hotlines, or brief crisis contact and referral are reasonably well established. The use of telephone for the provision of regular ongoing therapy or for diagnosis is not established, nor are such services as teleconferencing, Internet, or similar methods. Standard 1.04c, Boundaries of Competence, indicates that "In those emerging areas in which generally recognized standards for preparatory training do not yet exist, psychologists nevertheless take reasonable steps to ensure the competence of their work and to protect patients, clients, students, research participants, and others from harm."

Many of the enforceable ethical standards are, in fact, relevant to such services, and based on these standards it could be difficult for a psychologist to demonstrate that it is ethical to conduct therapy solely by telephone, teleconferencing, Internet, or similar methods.

Since telephone therapy or similar services are still therapy services, they involve all the general concerns of the sections on Assessment (Standards 2.01–2.10), Therapy (4.01–4.09, especially 4.01, Structuring the Relationship, and 4.02, Informed Consent to Therapy), and Confidentiality (5.01–5.11). Within the General Standards section, standards with particular relevance are 1.03, Professional and Scientific Relationship; 1.04 (a, b, and c), Boundaries of Competence; 1.06, Basis for Scientific and Professional Judgments; 1.07a, Describing the Nature and Results of Psychological Services; 1.14, Avoiding Harm; and 1.25, Fees and Financial Ar-

rangements. Standards under Advertising, particularly 3.01–3.03, are also relevant.

Conducting services by teleconferencing adds the element of visual feedback and appears to be an improvement over voice transmission only. However, the cautions described above are still applicable and most are applicable whether the service is diagnostic only, or diagnostic and therapeutic.

On the other hand, Internet is a methodology without nonverbal cues, and appears to be a more limited medium for the delivery of therapy services than telephone or teleconferencing. Psychologists considering such services must review the characteristics of the services and the service delivery method, and consider the relevant ethical standards and other requirements, such as licensure board rules. As an example of the possible variations, consider confidentiality in a situation in which the services involve two individuals directly exchanging confidential information. The ease with which Internet transmissions may be intercepted would be relevant, and use of encryption might be considered a sufficient action on the part of the psychologist to establish that confidential transmissions were protected. On the other hand, the confidentiality of traditional telephone conversations is rarely questioned. Although they may be tapped, such an occurrence is rare and illegal. However, portable telephones, and cellular phones in particular, can be compromised relatively easily. There may be a variety of state laws or licensure board regulations which may also be relevant, particularly regarding confidentiality. In addition, the Committee has not researched whether a psychologist can be licensed in one state, and yet by telephone, teleconferencing, Internet or similar methods, provide services in states in which the psychologist is not licensed.

APPENDIX B

Questions To Be Dealt With by the Provider of Psychotherapy by Telephone

1. Does this choice of treatment benefit the consumer or should face-to-face treatment be recommended, assuming it is possible to provide?
2. Is it possible to conduct an adequate assessment

of the client's psychological condition? Is the psychologist aware of the limits to diagnoses, judgment, or prediction made by telephone evaluation?

3. Are both therapist and caller (and their respective environments) free of distractions and interference with communication and attention? Has the psychologist taken steps to ensure the privacy and confidentiality of the telephone assessment or treatment?

4. Does the psychologist have the necessary and appropriate training, experience, or temperament to offer services by telephone?

5. Does the psychologist have a system for maintaining client records? What is the plan for maintaining client records if the psychologist leaves the telephone service? Has the psychologist or the company arranged a method for the client to obtain a copy of the records?

6. Does the psychologist know how the telephone counseling service is described to the potential user?

7. What are the corporation's and the psychologist's responsibilities for providing care on the departure of the psychologist?

8. Does the psychologist understand the telephone service's financial arrangements, and have reasonable steps been taken to ensure that these are fair and clearly explained to the potential client?

♦ ♦ ♦

Commentary: Note that the Ethics Committee statement reprinted in Haas et al. (1996) mentions therapy conducted over the Internet. It touches on some of the issues connected with cybertherapy, but not all. Doing therapy over cyberspace is sure to become a major point of contention and deserves extended discussion. For this reason, I have provided the next excerpt.

Ethical and Legal Issues in E-Mail Therapy

Daniel Edward Shapiro and Charles Eric Schulman

Psychologists and psychiatrists recently started using computers to provide therapy to clients at distant locations. Like populist advice givers (e.g., Ann Landers, Miss Manners), electronic-mail (e-mail) clinicians offer brief responses to brief questions. Using e-mail, clients send questions (and credit card information) to clinicians who rapidly respond, reportedly between 48 and 72 hr. The questions and answers are brief, approximately a paragraph in length. To illustrate the problems inherent in using the technology in this way, we explore two representative services, Shrink-Link and Help-Net.

. . .

In February 1995 the following electronic advertisement appeared on the World Wide Web. (The World Wide Web uses a format known as hypertext that allows the user to interact with a main page of text and graphics that are linked to other pages and information by keywords. In this advertisement, when a user highlights the words *15–40 years of clinical experience,* using a computer mouse or other method, the user is shown a page that lists the names and credentials of the professionals on staff.)

> Shrink-Link
> Cyberlink Consulting Inc. Presents:
> Shrink-Link
> Shrink-Link helps people develop informed judgments and choices concerning human behavior. Shrink-Link allows direct E-Mail access to a staff of top clinical psychologists and psychiatrists ready to review and comment on almost any important question or conflict in your life.

Concerned about your fears? About who you are? Trouble at home or work? Got the blues? Questions about medication? Shrink-Link psychotherapists have been addressing questions such as these in private sessions for years. Whether you need general guidance, are on the verge of a crisis, or are looking for competent peer review, Shrink-Link may be able to help. Panelists also include in their responses useful referral information, when appropriate.

Shrink-Link is not a substitute for face-to-face counseling and may not be appropriate for everyone. However, it does focus the attention of a group of highly trained mental health professionals on YOU! The Shrink-Link panel currently includes six psychologists and one psychiatrist, each with 15–40 years of clinical experience. These are the same people who normally charge $100–$200 per 45-or-so minute session!

And through Shrink-Link, you can direct your query to one of eight specialty areas of psychotherapy, such as family issues, drug/alcohol abuse, etc. (The choices are listed on the form page.) Here are a few sample queries (including routings).

The cost for using Shrink-Link is $20 per valid question and response. You can expect to receive a response via E-Mail within 72 hours (often within 24

From *Ethics and Behavior,* 6, 107–124. Copyright 1996 by Erlbaum. Adapted with permission of the author and publisher.

hours). Sound interesting? Compose a query!

Help-Net, another e-mail therapy service, is remarkably similar. The primary difference is in how questions are distributed to the psychologists or psychiatrists. Although both services allow users to browse the names and credentials of professionals on-staff (Help-Net also provides online photographs of therapists that may be enlarged by clicking on them), Shrink-Link does not allow clients to address queries to specific providers; rather, the clients address their questions to a specific category, and Shrink-Link routes the query to an appropriate professional. Help-Net allows three methods of question submission. Clients may send their queries directly to a psychologist or psychiatrist they choose, submit questions by an established list of categories, or submit general questions that will be routed by the service to an appropriate provider. As will be discussed later, this difference does have implications.

In June 1995 the president of the American Psychological Association (APA), Robert Resnick, and several board members asked the Board of Directors of APA to consider the ethics of Internet-facilitated therapy. In July of the same year, the APA Ethics Board considered Internet therapy and provided general guidelines directing therapists using telephone, teleconferencing, or Internet services to consider the applicability of the ethical standards applying to therapy. The Ethics Board was general in its response and did not provide guidelines for each treatment modality. This article attempts to present the relevant ethical issues and offers guidelines for therapists interested in exploring e-mail-facilitated treatment. Finally, an ethics standard is presented for this new modality.

EXAMINING A NEW MEDIUM AND ITS USE

When considering the ethical issues in any new treatment modality, a helpful starting point is an analysis of the relationship established between the professional and the client.

Professional Relationship

The nature of the professional relationship established by e-mail therapists is important because dif-

ferent relationship structures and modes of treatment have different standards of practice. For example, a media psychologist does not incur the same responsibilities for maintaining records as does a clinician treating a patient in traditional face-to-face therapy. . . . Simply put, the structure of the professional relationship dictates the ethical obligations of the treater. . . .

Professional relationships make service delivery safe and predictable for both the treater and the client. When a psychologist and client enter into a defined professional relationship, each has expectations regarding acceptable boundaries and what the costs and benefits of the interaction will be. When traditional therapists establish a professional relationship, they abide by, among others, the General Standards (which cover documentation and billing), Therapy Standards (which include informed consent, structuring relationships, and termination), and Privacy and Confidentiality Standards (which mandate maintaining confidentiality and keeping records). Each of these standards is designed to insure safety and predictability for both parties. The therapist following these standards minimizes ambiguity by overtly discussing them early in treatment. . . .

If a professional relationship exists, or should exist, between e-mail psychologists and clients, the ethical standards applying to treatment could also apply to e-mail clinicians. Does e-mail treatment reach a threshold that establishes a professional relationship? Both the Shrink-Link and Help-Net advertisements note that their services are not a substitute for face-to-face counseling. Is this enough to dispel a client's mistaken expectations? Unfortunately, neither advertisement describes the nature or limits of the e-mail relationship. There is no mention of confidentiality, billing, informed consent, or what the client can hope to gain from the interaction. Even more troublesome, neither service prohibits repeated communications with the same provider. Thus, it is possible that a client could have an e-mail relationship with an identified therapist over a course of years. This sounds to us like therapy.

We understand how these psychologists arrived at these vague advertisements. A thorough discussion of the limits of the relationship might seriously hamper the persuasive power of the advertisements.

The writers of the advertisements clearly took some efforts to overtly state that the service was not psychotherapy while implying that the service would be effective for clients. They may believe that they did not need to be specific regarding the limits of the relationship because they were not doing therapy. They might argue that because no professional relationship was offered, rational users of the service would not assume that a professional relationship would exist. Certainly an argument like this is enhanced for the service, Shrink-Link, that does not allow individuals to select a specific treater. Without knowledge of whom the user is communicating with before getting a response, the user cannot assume that he or she has a professional relationship with any specific individual. The Help-Net service has no such advantage. Because users of the Help-Net service select a particular individual, they may have expectations that they are establishing a relationship with a particular provider.

Regardless of the specific structure used by the service to connect provider to client, the vague state of affairs is inadequate. Because the professionals advertise themselves as psychologists and psychiatrists, and provide no disclaimers indicating that they are practicing something other than psychology or psychiatry, a rational user of the systems could assume that the psychologists and psychiatrists on Help-Net and Shrink-Link practice similar to professionals everywhere else. The most obvious mistakes clients might make are to assume that the communications with the e-mail professionals are confidential and that, as clients, they will not be abandoned.

Although the advertisements state that the communications are not therapy, they do not state what they are. Can the user expect advice, help, or assistance? Although the differences between e-mail communication and psychotherapy might appear obvious to most clinicians, it is not so apparent that all laypersons will immediately understand how the structure and benefits of Shrink-Link and Help-Net differ from those experienced in therapy.

So what standard should e-mail clinicians adopt? One approach to evaluating new services is to compare the service to those that are structured similarly. E-mail therapists hoping to avoid encouraging clients to expect a professional relationship might argue that e-mail-facilitated communication is most similar to media psychology. Under the current ethics code, media psychologists are the only clinicians allowed to practice outside of an established professional relationship. Certainly there are similarities. With both media psychologists and e-mail clinicians, the interaction is typically brief and lacks detailed assessment. In both modalities clinicians respond to a specific problem or question from a client who may be geographically distant. The similarities end there.

Ethical Standard 3.05 prohibits media psychologists from encouraging patients to infer that a personal relationship has been offered. This is not difficult for media psychologists because any communication is part of a larger broadcast. The rational caller or participant understands that there is an additional, larger purpose to the communication. It is not only to help the patient but also to educate or entertain an audience. The caller or participant would not be talking to the treater if it were not part of a larger broadcast.

E-mail-facilitated therapeutic communication has no such additional purpose outside of addressing the problem or question posed by the client. A rational client could assume that the treater is establishing a personal relationship. The owners of Shrink-Link do not prohibit repeat use but have suggested they encourage clients who use the service frequently to seek therapy (Resnick, 1995). Because repeated communications with a paid professional are allowed, the clients of Shrink-Link and Help-Net could infer they have a therapeutic relationship with a trained professional. It is easy to imagine circumstances in which a client who regularly used the service started to develop the same intense feelings and expectations that clients in traditional therapy experience.

. . .

The possibility of a professional relationship being established moves e-mail treatment closer to other modalities, such as telephone therapy. Like clinicians using the telephone, the treater and client may be geographically distant. Telephone treaters are currently held to the same standards as other treaters (American Psychological Association Ethics Committee, 1993). They are obligated to get clients' informed consent prior to treatment, they must discuss confidentiality and fee schedules, and they have the duty to protect clients and potential victims of clients from harm.

. . .

Confidentiality

Neither of the services previously described mentions confidentiality. Help-Net, however, does suggest that the providers will answer all questions "professionally and privately." This is misleading and troublesome. E-mail is not private, and confidentiality is an impossible standard for e-mail treaters to provide. In fact, contrary to many users' expectations, most experts assume e-mail is not secure or confidential. Glossbrenner (1990), an expert in computer communication, wrote "All e-mail messages can be read by people other than their intended recipients, so one must assume that they will be read, even if that isn't actually the case."

. . .

The confidentiality of the message is not the only difficulty. Users of both Help-Net and Shrink-Link e-mail their credit card numbers to pay for the service. American Express recently acknowledged that it stores sorted transaction records and has sold this information to a wide range of organizations (Schwartz, 1992).

. . .

Services such as Shrink-Link and Help-Net may provide hackers with fertile ground. Any hackers with entrepreneurial spirit and organizational skills could use their talents to assemble a list of names of users of Help-Net and Shrink-Link and detailed descriptions of the problems they reported. It is naive to believe that agencies or individuals would be uninterested in paying for this information. Insurance companies might be interested in information that would assist them in denying claims, employers might be interested in learning the names of employees or applicants with substance abuse or mental health histories, and spouses might be interested in the secrets of their partners.

These problems must be considered in light of the claims of one of the services examined here, Help-Net, which suggested that privacy is enjoyed by users of their service. We suspect that their claim

to "answer your questions quickly, professionally, and privately" places them at tremendous legal and ethical risk. Imagine an individual who asks a Help-Net clinician to assist her with her great dislike for her boss only to learn that her boss gained access to this information and found reason to fire her! We suspect that courts, ethics committees, and licensure boards would find these circumstances troubling.

. . .

Until these issues are resolved . . . e-mail treaters . . . must, if they are to remain within the bounds of the ethical standards, warn all users that no e-mail communications are private or confidential. Standard 5.01c also mandates that permission must be secured before electronic recordings of clients are permitted. Although the e-mail clinician is not doing the recording, the professional trying to meet the "spirit" of the standard will also warn users that their communications will very possibly be stored by their network and accessed by others.

In sum, to completely inform a client of the limits of confidentiality, the therapist must disclose, first, that e-mail systems often store e-mail interactions; second, that individuals other than the intended recipient may have relatively easy access to e-mail; third, that personal computers may store the interactions and that these may be readable by anyone else with access to the computer; and, finally, as in all therapy cases, the clinician might need to divulge confidential information if he or she perceives that the client is at risk for imminently harming him- or herself or someone else.

Boundaries of Competence

. . . E-mail-facilitated treaters at both Help-Net and Shrink-Link provide professional advice without the benefit of assessment. Such consultation appears to fly in the face of conventional wisdom. Without assessment, the potential for misdiagnosing a client's problem or missing dramatic pathology seems unusually high. Most therapists have had the experience of recognizing late in the first session, or even in the fifth, that the patient's problem was not at all what it appeared during the first few moments. The e-mail therapists receive what is on the client's mind for only a few seconds. To most therapy clients the first few seconds of treatment are rarely powerful enough to have any effect, but this is precisely what e-mail clinicians offer.

The high potential for misdiagnosis must be considered in light of the client's perceptions of the therapist. Shrink-Link advertises its staff as being "top clinical psychologists and psychiatrists . . . each with 15–40 years of clinical experience . . . the same people who normally charge $100–$200 per 45-or-so minute session." Most of Help-Net's staff claim similar qualifications. The fact that the client could view the therapist as a highly trained and trustworthy professional engaged in a proven modality of treatment, combined with the high probability of misdiagnosing serious problems, is a dangerous and potentially explosive combination. . . .

Standard 1.04c reads:

> In those emerging areas in which generally recognized standards for preparatory training do not yet exist, psychologists nevertheless take reasonable steps to ensure the competence of their work and to protect patients, clients, students, research participants, and others from harm.

With no predictable relationship, no assessment, and lightning-fast diagnosis and intervention, it seems likely that e-mail clients are not well protected. This in itself does not preclude use of e-mail therapy. Rather, it warrants informed consent, as with any other experimental treatment. Clients using e-mail therapy should not only be told, as they are in Help-Net and Shrink-Link, that e-mail-facilitated therapeutic communication is not therapy, but also that it is untested and its efficacy may be uncorrelated with the success of traditional therapies. The client needs to know that the information given them may be entirely useless and not applicable to their total situation. Without such disclaimers the potential damage to clients is high.

The ethics code does not only protect clients. The code was also established to protect the profession. The ethics code provides minimal rules of conduct that compel psychologists to conduct themselves in a way that will not reflect poorly on the profession. E-mail treatment represents a genuine threat to the profession. Services such as Help-Net

and Shrink-Link, if not significantly altered, could result in psychologists being relegated to the status of popular advice columnists. On the other hand, in the best-case scenario, e-mail clinicians could serve as models and advertisements for all psychologists. Clients interacting with them could learn that psychologists do not proffer advice without detailed assessments, do not offer unproven treatments without warning and fully informing clients first, and have access to a scientific literature that may be applied with skill to their problem.

. . .

A Proposed New Ethical Standard

In July 1995 the APA Ethics Board provided a general statement that described the ethics code applicable to therapists using telephone, teleconferencing, and Internet services. In our opinion, although this document offers valuable general guidelines, it suffers from a lack of specificity. The Internet offers a number of different modalities of communication. Each one will require examination on its own merits and potential threats to ethical conduct.

To protect clients and the profession, we offer the following to apply specifically to e-mail treatment:

> Psychologists offering e-mail facilitated therapeutic communication encourage clients to ask general questions that do not refer to a specific individual. Psychologists advertising such services include in advertisements all information necessary for clients to understand (a) the modality is experimental and its usefulness may be unrelated to the success of traditional therapies, (b) the communication is not confidential, (c) no therapist–client professional relationship exists, (d) repeated communications with the same professional are discouraged, and (e) records of the interaction may be stored with no report of such storage available to the client. Psychologists using e-mail to communicate with new clients encourage clients to seek more traditional therapies. Psychologists do not transmit con-

fidential information, including payment information such as credit card data, by e-mail without using encryption programs considered the standard.

Although this standard was written to apply to e-mail treatment specifically, it contains principles that can be applied in developing ethics standards for future modalities. These principles are the following: Psychologists make every effort to (a) provide all information necessary to achieve informed consent with the client, especially when using new structures to deliver services; (b) prevent detrimental reliance on advice given via any modality; and (c) insure the greatest level of privacy and confidentiality practical.

References

American Psychological Association Ethics Committee. (April, 1993). *Telephone, teleconferencing, and Internet services.* Washington, DC: Author.

Glossbrenner, A. (1990). *The complete handbook of personal computer communications: The bible of the online world.* New York: St. Martin's Press.

Resnick, R. (1995, March 27). Shrink-Link & beyond. *The Miami Herald Online Column.*

Schwartz, E. I. (1992, June 8). The rush to keep mum. *Business Week,* p. 33.

◆ ◆ ◆

Commentary: For other perspectives on this issue see three analyses of a vignette involving cybertherapy by an administrator of a risk management company, a practitioner, and a trainer who writes about ethics. It is found at (1996). The forum. Ethics and Behavior, 6, 169–177.

Finally, although it is little discussed, the ethical therapist must contemplate taking appropriate steps to protect clients in case of his or her death or disability. In 1989, Jan Sonne, at the request of the APA ethics committee, produced a paper titled "Therapist Death or Disability: Ethical Responsibilities and Practical Considerations." Some of her recommendations found their way into the 1992 Ethical Principles. Standard 4.08, for example, now requires psychologists to plan for their clients' future care should services be interrupted by the clinician's "illness, death, [or] unavailability." Standard 5.09 requires psychologists to develop plans to protect records and data "in the event of the psychologist's death, incapacity, or withdrawal from the position or practice." For APA policy regarding records in general, see APA Committee on Professional Practice and Standards. (1993). Record keeping guidelines. American Psychologist, 48, 984–986 (reprinted in chapter 10).

CHAPTER 8

ACADEMIA: RESEARCH, TEACHING, AND SUPERVISION

The bricks and mortar of college buildings and the various forms of flora growing on them have long hid conduct of concern to ethicists and those in academia. Researchers, scholars, and supervisors have seemed to be beyond the scrutiny of ethics committees. Academicians, after all, were simply data gatherers, teachers, mentors, and initiators of new theories. They were believed immune to the vagaries of professional practice that often landed their clinical colleagues in trouble, such as setting and collecting fees, mediating the needs of clients and the demands of third-party payors, becoming sexually attracted to patients, or disclosing intimate information gathered in therapy. In fact, there seems to have been no articles in English published on research ethics with human beings before 1951. The first empirical study on this topic was not published until 1967 (McGaha & Korn, 1995).

But science and the public are becoming increasingly aware that donning a white lab coat or a tweed, elbow-patched jacket does not insulate one from unethical behavior. People now know that for over 60 years academic scientists working for the federal government engaged in risky research that proved harmful to participants, who were never fully informed about the nature, costs, and benefits of the studies. It has also been acknowledged that professors sometimes do appropriate students' ideas and works as their own; that teachers and supervisors develop intimate, sometimes sexual, relations with students and trainees; and that some teachers are often unprepared to face their classes (or continue to lecture from the proverbial time-stained notes) and leave students languishing for months before returning examinations or seminar papers. These issues have become so salient that for the first time in nine revisions, the current (1992) set of APA Ethical Principles contains a specific section of standards (Section 6) that address teaching, training, supervision, research, and publishing.

Materials in this chapter introduce the reader to a broadening array of ethical issues within academia, although the bulk of the material is devoted to research. Research is an interesting enterprise from an ethical perspective because its purpose is not necessarily devoted to the betterment of those who participate in it. Psychological assessment and therapeutic interventions are, at the least, processes intended to benefit participants. Alternatively—although not true of all studies—research usually does not contribute to the welfare of participants at all. It is ironic, then, that subjects of research—animals as well as humans—may be the least well treated of all those with whom psychologists interact. The validity of this hypothesis may be supported by examining the controversy over *deception research*—studies in which the participant is either not fully informed or is misinformed about the purpose of the experiment so as not to contaminate the data. I have chosen to make such studies a focus of this chapter. This ethical dilemma is not only of central importance in research; rather, like other issues I highlight in this text, it evokes more universal conflicts that should be considered.

Issues concerning deception are at the surface of conflict between the interests of science and those of the participant in research:

> The respect for privacy rests on the appreciation of human dignity, with its high evaluation of individual self-determination. . . . In this, respect for human dignity and individuality shares an historical comradeship with the freedom of scientific inquiry, which is equally precious to modern liberalism. The tension between these values, so essential to each other in so many profoundly important ways, is one of the antimonies of modern liberalism. The ethical problems with which we are dealing . . . arise from the confrontation of autonomy and privacy by a free intellectual curiosity, enriched by a modern awareness of the depth and complexity of the forces that work in us implemented by the devices of a passionate effort to transform this awareness into scientific knowledge. (Shils, 1959, pp. 120–121)

Similar note of this tension was made by psychologist Ross Stagner (*Problems Concerning Federal Support, 1967*) before a Senate subcommittee concerned with government research:

> Social scientists . . . have a genuine obligation to devise protections for the right of privacy, and to avoid mere psychic voyeurism. At the same time they have a compelling obligation to accumulate data—and meaningful generalizations— about the powerful impulses of loyalty, hostility, fear, and ambition, which shape human history. . . .
>
> . . .
>
> There is an obvious conflict between the need of society to know and the right of the individual to dignity and privacy. (pp. 757–758)

The ambivalence between advancing science and protecting the integrity of the individual is also reflected in the APA's (1982) *Ethical Principles in the Conduct of Research With Human Participants*, now undergoing major revision. For example, Principle D states: "The investigator informs the participants of all aspects of the research that might reasonably be expected to influence willingness to participate" (APA, 1982, p. 32). But, with little pause, it cautions: "Failure to make full disclosure prior to obtaining informed consent requires additional safeguards to protect the welfare and dignity of the research participants" (APA, 1982, p. 32).

Beyond exploring this central conflict in social science research, the material in this chapter covers more mundane but crucial issues: exploitation of graduate students (both academically and socially), authorship issues (including publication credit), clinical supervision, and simply bad teaching. These topics have often been neglected in discussions of ethics. I hope that this compilation of materials reveals the seriousness of such issues and promotes even more extended attention to them.

References

American Psychological Association. (1982). *Ethical principles in the conduct of research with human participants*. Washington, DC: Author.

McGaha, A. C., & Korn, J. H. (1995). The emergence of interest in the ethics of psychological research with humans. *Ethics and Behavior, 5,* 147–159.

Problems Concerning Federal Support of Social Science Research: Hearings on S.836 before the Subcommittee on Government Research of the Senate Committee on Government Operations, 90th Cong., 1st Sess. 757 (1967) (testimony of Ross Stagner).

Shils, E. A. (1959). Social inquiry and the autonomy of the individual. In D. Lerner (Ed.), *The human meaning of the social sciences* (pp. 114–148). New York: Meridian Books.

Science and Ethics in Conducting, Analyzing, and Reporting Psychological Research

Robert Rosenthal

. . .

CONDUCTING PSYCHOLOGICAL RESEARCH

Let us turn first to considerations of research design, procedures employed in a study, and the recruitment of human participants. In evaluating the ethical employment of our participants, we can distinguish issues of safety from more subtle issues of research ethics. Obviously, research that is unsafe for participants is ethically questionable. However, I propose that perfectly safe research in which no participant will be put at risk may also be ethically questionable because of the shortcomings of the design.

Issues of Design

Imagine that a research proposal that comes before an institutional review board proposes the hypothesis that private schools improve children's intellectual functioning more than public schools do. Children from randomly selected private and public schools are to be tested extensively, and the research hypothesis is to be tested by comparing scores earned by students from private versus public schools. The safety of the children to be tested is certainly not an issue, yet it can be argued that this research raises ethical issues because of the inadequacy of its design. The goal of the research is to learn about the causal impact on performance of private versus public schooling, but the design of the research does not permit reasonable causal inference because of the absence of randomization or

even some reasonable attempt to consider plausible rival hypothesis (Cook & Campbell, 1979).

How does the poor quality of the design raise ethical objections to the proposed research? Because students', teachers', and administrators' time will be taken from potentially more beneficial educational experiences. Because the poor quality of the design is likely to lead to unwarranted and inaccurate conclusions that may be damaging to the society that directly or indirectly pays for the research. In addition, allocating time and money to this poor-quality science will serve to keep those finite resources of time and money from better quality science in a world that is undeniably zero-sum.

. . .

Issues of Recruitment

The American Psychological Association's (APA) Committee for the Protection of Human Participants in Research and its new incarnation, the Committee on Standards in Research, and such pioneer scholars of the topic as Herbert Kelman have thoughtfully considered a variety of ethical issues in the selection and recruitment of human participants (APA, 1982; Blanck, Bellack, Rosnow, Rotheram-Borus, & Schooler, 1992; Grisso et al., 1991; Kelman, 1968). Only a few comments need to be made here.

On the basis of several reviews of the literature, my friend and colleague Ralph Rosnow and I have proposed a number of procedures designed to reduce volunteer bias and therefore increase the generality of our research results (Rosenthal & Rosnow,

From *Psychological Science, 5,* 127–133. Copyright 1994 by the American Psychological Society. Adapted with permission of the author and publisher.

1975, 1991; Rosnow & Rosenthal, 1993). Employment of these procedures has led us to think of our human participants as another "granting agency"—which, we believe, they are, since they must decide whether to grant us their time, attention, and cooperation. Part of our treating them as such is to give them information about the long-term benefits of the research. In giving prospective participants this information, we have a special obligation to avoid hyperclaiming.

Hyperclaiming.   Hyperclaiming is telling our prospective participants, our granting agencies, our colleagues, our administrators, and ourselves that our research is likely to achieve goals it is, in fact, unlikely to achieve. Presumably our granting agencies, our colleagues, and our administrators are able to evaluate our claims and hyperclaims fairly well. However, our prospective participants are not; therefore, we should tell them what our research can actually accomplish rather than that it will yield the cure for panic disorder, depression, schizophrenia, or cancer.

Causism.   Closely related to hyperclaiming is the phenomenon of causism. Causism refers to the tendency to imply a causal relationship where none has been established (i.e., where the data do not support it).

. . .

If a perpetrator of causism is unaware of the causism, its presence simply reflects poor scientific training. If the perpetrator is aware of the causism, it reflects blatantly unethical misrepresentation and deception.

Whereas well-trained colleagues can readily differentiate causist language from inferentially more accurate language, potential research participants or policymakers ordinarily cannot. When a description of a proposed research study is couched in causal language, that description represents an unfair recruitment device that is at best inaccurate, when it is employed out of ignorance, and at worst dishonest, when it is employed as hype to increase the participation rates of potential participants. . . .

Bad Science Makes for Bad Ethics

Causism is only one example of bad science. Poor quality of research design, poor quality of data anal-

ysis, and poor quality of reporting of the research all lessen the ethical justification of any type of research project. I believe this judgment applies not only when deception, discomfort, or embarrassment of participants is involved, but for even the most benign research experience for participants. If because of the poor quality of the science no good can come of a research study, how are we to justify the use of participants' time, attention, and effort and the money, space, supplies, and other resources that have been expended on the research project? When we add to the "no good can come of it" argument the inescapable zero-sum nature of time, attention, effort, money, space, supplies, and other resources, it becomes difficult to justify poor-quality research on any ethical basis. For this reason, I believe that institutional review boards must consider the technical scientific competence of the investigators whose proposals they are asked to evaluate. . . .

Poor quality of research makes for poor-quality of education as well. Especially when participation is quasi-coercive, the use of participants is usually justified in part by the fact that they will benefit educationally. But if participants are required to participate in poor-quality research, they are likely to acquire only misconceptions about the nature of science and of psychology. . . .

Costs and Utilities

Payoffs for doing research.   When individual investigators or institutional review boards are confronted with a questionable research proposal, they ordinarily employ a cost-utility analysis in which the costs of doing a study, including possible negative effects on participants, time, money, supplies, effort, and other resources, are evaluated simultaneously against such utilities as benefits to participants, to other people at other times, to science, to the world, or at least to the investigator. The potential benefits of higher quality studies and studies addressing more important topics are greater than the potential benefits of lower quality studies and studies addressing less important topics. Any study with low utility and high cost should not be carried out. Studies in which costs equal utilities are very difficult to decide about.

Payoffs for failing to do research.   However, Rosnow and I have become convinced that this cost-utility model is insufficient because it fails to consider the costs (and utilities) of *not* conducting a particular study (Rosenthal & Rosnow, 1984, 1991; Rosnow, 1990; Rosnow & Rosenthal, 1993).

The failure to conduct a study that could be conducted is as much an act to be evaluated on ethical grounds as is conducting a study. . . . The behavioral researcher whose study may have a good chance of reducing violence or racism or sexism, but who refuses to do the study simply because it involves deception, has not solved an ethical problem but only traded in one for another. The issues are, in principle, the same for the most basic as for the most applied research. In practice, however, it is more difficult to make even rough estimates of the probability of finding . . . the racism reducer for the more basic as compared with the more applied research.

This idea of lost opportunities has been applied with great eloquence by John Kaplan (1988), of the Stanford University Law School. The context of his remarks was the use of animals in research and the efforts of "animal rights" activists to chip away "at our ability to afford animal research. . . . [I]t is impossible to know the costs of experiments not done or research not undertaken. Who speaks for the sick, for those in pain, and for the future?" (p. 839). . . .

DATA ANALYSIS AS AN ETHICAL ARENA

Data Dropping

Ethical issues in the analysis of data range from the very obvious to the very subtle. Probably the most obvious and most serious transgression is the analysis of data that never existed (i.e., that were fabricated). Perhaps more frequent is the dropping of data that contradict the data analyst's theory, prediction, or commitment.

Outlier rejection.   There is a venerable tradition in data analysis of dealing with outliers, or extreme scores, a tradition going back over 200 years (Barnett & Lewis, 1978). Both technical and ethical issues are involved. The technical issues have to do with the best ways of dealing with outliers without reference to the implications for the tenability of the data analyst's theory. The ethical issues have to do with the relationship between the data analyst's theory and the choice of method for dealing with

outliers. For example, there is some evidence to suggest that outliers are more likely to be rejected if they are bad for the data analyst's theory but treated less harshly if they are good for the data analyst's theory (Rosenthal, 1978; Rosenthal & Rubin, 1971). At the very least, when outliers are rejected, that fact should be reported. In addition, it would be useful to report in a footnote the results that would have been obtained had the outliers not been rejected.

Subject selection.   A different type of data dropping is subject selection in which a subset of the data is not included in the analysis. In this case, too, there are technical issues and ethical issues. There may be good technical reasons for setting aside a subset of the data—for example, because the subset's sample size is especially small or because dropping the subset would make the data more comparable to some other research. However, there are also ethical issues, as when just those subsets are dropped that do not support the data analyst's theory. When a subset is dropped, we should be informed of that fact and what the results were for that subset. Similar considerations apply when the results for one or more variables are not reported.

Exploitation Is Beautiful

Many of us have been taught that it is technically improper and perhaps even immoral to analyze and reanalyze our data in many ways (i.e., to snoop around in the data). We were taught to test the prediction with one particular preplanned test and take a result significant at the .05 level as our reward for a life well-lived. Should the results not be significant at the .05 level, we were taught, we should bite our lips bravely, take our medicine, and definitely not look further at our data. Such a further look might turn up results significant at the .05 level, results to which we were not entitled. All this makes for a lovely morality play, and it reminds us of Robert Frost's poem about losing forever the road not taken, but it makes for bad science and for bad ethics.

It makes for bad science because while snooping does affect *p* values, it is likely to turn up something new, interesting, and important (Tukey, 1977). It makes for bad ethics because data are expensive in terms of time, effort, money, and other resources and because the antisnooping dogma is wasteful of time, effort, money, and other resources. If the research was worth doing, the data are worth a thorough analysis, being held up to the light in many different ways so that our research participants, our funding agencies, our science, and society will all get their time and their money's worth. . . .

Meta-Analysis as an Ethical Imperative

Meta-analysis is a set of concepts and procedures employed to summarize quantitatively any domain of research (Glass, McGaw, & Smith, 1981; Rosenthal, 1991). We know from both statistical and empirical research that, compared with traditional reviews of the literature, meta-analytic procedures are more accurate, comprehensive, systematic, and statistically powerful (Cooper & Rosenthal, 1980; Hedges & Olkin, 1985; Mosteller & Bush, 1954). . . .

Retroactive increase of utilities. Meta-analysis allows us to learn more from our data and therefore has a unique ability to increase retroactively the benefits of the studies being summarized. The costs of time, attention, and effort of the human participants employed in the individual studies entering into the meta-analysis are all more justified when their data enter into a meta-analysis. That is because the meta-analysis increases the utility of all the individual studies being summarized. Other costs of individual studies—costs of funding, supplies, space, investigator time and effort, and other resources—are similarly more justified because the utility of individual studies is so increased by the borrowed strength obtained when information from more studies is combined in a sophisticated way.

The failure to employ meta-analytic procedures when they could be used thus has ethical implications because the opportunity to increase the benefits of past individual studies has been foregone. In addition, when public funds or other resources are employed by scientists to prepare reviews of literatures, it is fair to ask whether those resources are being used wisely or ethically. Now that we know how to summarize literatures meta-analytically, it seems hardly justified to review a quantitative literature in the pre-meta-analytic, prequantitative manner. Money that funds a traditional review is not available to fund a meta-analytic review. . . .

REPORTING PSYCHOLOGICAL RESEARCH

Misrepresentation of Findings

Mother nature makes it hard enough to learn her secrets, without the additional difficulty of being misled by the report of findings that were not found or by inferences that are unfounded. Although all misrepresentations of findings are damaging to the progress of our science, some are more obviously unethical than others.

Intentional misrepresentation. The most blatant intentional misrepresentation is the reporting of data that never were (Broad & Wade, 1982). That behavior, if detected, ends (or ought to end) the scientific career of the perpetrator. A somewhat more subtle form of intentional misrepresentation occurs when investigators knowingly allocate to experimental or control conditions those participants whose responses are more likely to support the investigators' hypothesis. Another potential form of intentional misrepresentation occurs when investigators record the participants' responses without being blind to the participants' treatment condition, or when research assistants record the participants' responses knowing both the research hypothesis and the participants' treatment condition. Of course, if the research specifically notes the failure to run blind, there is no misrepresentation, but the design is unwise if it could have been avoided.

Unintentional misrepresentation. Various errors in the process of data collection can lead to unintentional misrepresentations. Recording errors, computational errors, and data analytic errors can all lead to inaccurate results that are inadvertent misrepresentations (Broad & Wade, 1982; Rosenthal, 1966). We would not normally even think of them as constituting ethical issues except for the fact that errors in the data decrease the utility of the research and thereby move the cost-utility ratio (which is used to justify the research on ethical grounds) in the unfavorable direction. . . .

Misrepresentation of Credit

. . .

Problems of authorship. Because so many papers in psychology, and the sciences generally, are multi-authored, it seems inevitable that there will be difficult problems of allocation of authorship credit. Who becomes a coauthor and who becomes a footnote? Among the coauthors, who is assigned first, last, or any other serial position in the listing? Such questions have been discussed in depth, and very general guidelines have been offered (APA, 1981, 1987; see also Costa & Gatz, 1992), but it seems that we could profit from further empirical studies in which authors, editors, referees, students, practitioners, and professors were asked to allocate authorship credit to people performing various functions in a scholarly enterprise.

. . .

Failing to Report or Publish

Sometimes the ethical question is not about the accuracy of what was reported or how credit should be allocated for what was reported, but rather about what was *not* reported and why it was not reported. The two major forms of failure to report, or censoring, are self-censoring and external censoring.

Self-censoring. Some self-censoring is admirable. When a study has been really badly done, it may be a service to the science and to society to simply start over. Some self-censoring is done for admirable motives but seems wasteful of information. For example, some researchers feel they should not cite their own (or other people's) unpublished data because the data have not gone through peer review. I would argue that such data should indeed be cited and employed in meta-analytic computations as long as the data were well collected.

There are also less admirable reasons for self-censoring. Failing to report data that contradict one's earlier research, or one's theory or one's values, is poor science and poor ethics. One can always find or invent reasons why a study that came out unfavorably should not be reported: The subjects were just starting the course; the subjects were about to have an exam; the subjects had just had an exam; the subjects were just finishing the course; and so on. A good general policy—good for science and for its integrity—is to report all results shedding light on the original hypothesis or providing data that might be of use to other investigators.

There is no denying that some results are more thrilling than others. If our new treatment procedure

prevents or cures mental illness or physical illness, that fact may be worth more journal space or space in more prestigious journals than the result that our new treatment procedure does no good whatever. But that less thrilling finding should also be reported and made retrievable by other researchers who may need to know that finding.

External censoring. Both the progress and the slowing of progress in science depend on external censoring. It seems likely that sciences would be more chaotic than they are were it not for the censorship exercised by peers: by editors, by reviewers, and by program committees. All these gatekeepers help to keep the really bad science from clogging the pipelines of mainstream journals.

There are two major bases for external censorship. The first is evaluation of the methodology employed in a research study. I strongly favor such external censorship. If the study is truly terrible, it probably should not be reported.

The second major basis for external censorship is evaluation of the results. In my 35 years in psychology, I have often seen or heard it said of a study that "those results aren't possible" or "those results make no sense." Often when I have looked at such studies, I have agreed that the results are indeed implausible. However, that is a poor basis on which to censor the results. Censoring or suppressing results we do not like or do not believe to have high prior probability is bad science and bad ethics (Rosenthal, 1975, 1994).

CONCLUSION

The purpose of this article has been to discuss some scientific and ethical issues in conducting, analyzing, and reporting psychological research. A central theme has been that the ethical quality of our research is not independent of the scientific quality of our research. Detailing some of the specifics of this general theme has, I hope, served two functions. First, I hope it has comforted the afflicted by showing how we can simultaneously improve the quality of our science and the quality of our ethics. Second, and finally, I hope it has afflicted the comfortable by reminding us that in the matter of improving our science and our ethics, there are miles to go before we sleep.

References

American Psychological Association. (1981). Ethical principles of psychologists. *American Psychologist, 36,* 633–638.

American Psychological Association. (1982). *Ethical principles in the conduct of research with human participants.* Washington, DC: Author.

American Psychological Association. (1987). *Casebook on ethical principles of psychologists.* Washington, DC: Author.

Barnett, V., & Lewis, T. (1978). *Outliers in statistical data.* New York: Wiley.

Blanck, P. D., Bellack, A. S., Rosnow, R. L., Rotheram-Borus, M. J., & Schooler, N. R. (1992). Scientific rewards and conflicts of ethical choices in human subjects research. *American Psychologist, 47,* 959–965.

Broad, W., & Wade, N. (1982). *Betrayers of the truth.* New York: Simon and Schuster.

Cook, T. D., & Campbell, D. T. (1979). *Quasi-experimentation: Design and analysis issues for field settings.* Chicago: Rand McNally.

Cooper, H. M., & Rosenthal, R. (1980). Statistical versus traditional procedures for summarizing research findings. *Psychological Bulletin, 87,* 442–449.

Costa, M. M., & Gatz, M. (1992). Determination of authorship credit in published dissertations. *Psychological Science, 3,* 354–357.

Glass, G. V., McGaw, B., & Smith, M. L. (1981). *Meta-analysis in social research.* Beverly Hills, CA: Sage.

Grisso, T., Baldwin, E., Blanck, P. D., Rotheram-Borus, M. J., Schooler, N. R., & Thompson, T. (1991). Standards in research: APA's mechanism for monitoring the challenges. *American Psychologist, 46,* 758–766.

Hedges, L. V., & Olkin, I. (1985). *Statistical methods for meta-analysis.* New York: Academic Press.

Kaplan, J. (1988). The use of animals in research. *Science, 242,* 839–840.

Kelman, H. C. (1968). *A time to speak: On human values and social research.* San Francisco: Jossey-Bass.

Mosteller, F., & Bush, R. R. (1954). Selected quantitative techniques. In G. Lindzey (Ed.), *Handbook of social psychology: Vol. 1. Theory and method* (pp. 289–334). Cambridge, MA: Addison-Wesley.

Rosenthal, R. (1966). *Experimenter effects in behavioral research.* New York: Appleton-Century-Crofts.

Rosenthal, R. (1975). On balanced presentation of controversy. *American Psychologist, 30,* 937–938.

Rosenthal, R. (1978). How often are our numbers wrong? *American Psychologist, 33,* 1005–1008.

Rosenthal, R. (1991). *Meta-analytic procedures for social research* (rev. ed.). Newbury Park, CA: Sage.

Rosenthal, R. (1994). On being one's own case study: Experimenter effects in behavioral research—30 years later. In W. R. Shadish & S. Fuller (Eds.), *The social psychology of science* (pp. 214–229). New York: Guilford Press.

Rosenthal, R., & Rosnow, R. L. (1975). *The volunteer subject.* New York: Wiley.

Rosenthal, R., & Rosnow, R. L. (1984). Applying Hamlet's question to the ethical conduct of research: A conceptual addendum. *American Psychologist, 39,* 561–563.

Rosenthal, R., & Rosnow, R. L. (1991). *Essentials of behavioral research: Methods and data analysis* (2nd ed.). New York: McGraw-Hill.

Rosenthal, R., & Rubin, D. B. (1971). Pygmalion reaffirmed. In J. D. Elashoff & R. E. Snow, *Pygmalion reconsidered* (pp. 139–155). Worthington, OH: C. A. Jones.

Rosnow, R. L. (1990). Teaching research ethics through role-play and discussion. *Teaching of Psychology, 17,* 179–181.

Rosnow, R. L., & Rosenthal, R. (1993). *Beginning behavioral research: A conceptual primer.* New York: Macmillan.

Tukey, J. W. (1977). *Exploratory data analysis.* Reading, MA: Addison-Wesley.

◆ ◆ ◆

Commentary: Could Rosenthal's litany create the potential for finding almost any piece of research unethical? Would it be appropriate to make methodological flaws an ethical violation if they do not place research participants at risk or harm them? For discussions of these questions, see

Parkinson, S. (1994). Scientific or ethical quality? Psychological Science, 5, 137–138.

Pomerantz, J. R. (1995). On criteria for ethics in science: Commentary on Rosenthal. Psychological Science, 5, 135–136.

One of Rosenthal's more controversial proposals was that institutional review boards (IRBs; see the following two excerpts) evaluate the scientific and technical quality of all research, because bad research, even if it causes no palpable harm to participants, still wastes time, effort, and money. How does the proposal comport with self-determination? Does it inappropriately confuse scientific merit with ethics? *For some cogent comments on his proposal and Rosenthal's thoughtful reply, see:*

Colombo, J. (1995). *Cost, utility, and judgments of institutional review boards.* Psychological Science, 6, 313–319.

Mordock, J. B. (1995). *Institutional review boards in applied settings: Their role in judgments of quality and consumer protection.* Psychological Science, 6, 320–321.

Rosenthal, R. (1995). *Ethical issues in psychological science:*

Risk, consent, and scientific quality. Psychological Science, 6, 322–323.

By the 1950s the discretion of physicians to provide treatment without legally sufficient informed consent was severely curtailed. As the next excerpt reveals, the research of behavioral and medical researchers who proved insensitive to the interests of those they studied would also soon be restricted.

Legal and Ethical Concerns in Research

Donald N. Bersoff

. . .

In 1954 a group of professors from law and the social sciences recorded and studied the deliberations of juries with "bugging devices." The researchers obtained the approval of the judges and the lawyers involved, but neither the jurors nor the litigants were aware that microphones had been concealed in the jury room. In 1963 three medical researchers injected "live cancer cells" into 22 chronically ill patients at a New York hospital with the approval of the institution's director of medicine but without the fully informed consent of those injected. (For a lengthy history and description of these cases see Katz, 1972.) In 1972 the American public was finally told that for 40 years, under the leadership, direction, and guidance of the United States Public Health Service there had been a continuing study of the effect of untreated syphilis in approximately 400 Black males in Alabama. There was no evidence that consent for participation had ever been obtained.

Of overriding influence as far as behavior research is concerned was Stanley Milgram's study of obedience (Milgram, 1963). Central to the startling results achieved was the deception, by the experimenter, of the subjects involved. To briefly recount the design, subjects were told that they would be taking part in a learning experiment. Each subject was assigned to a group of four people, three of whom, unknown to the subject, were Milgram's assistants. One of the assistants was the "learner" in the pseudoexperiment. The subject was to play the role of "teacher" whose function it was to instruct the learner by administering an electric shock when the learner made an error in the memory task. The naive subject was put at a control panel that regulated the shock from mild to extremely intense and painful. The teacher was told to deliver the painful stimulus whenever the learner erred. In reality, no electricity was hooked up to the panel and no learning took place. The subject was deceived concerning the purpose of the experiment. Learners deliberately made mistakes and pretended to feel pain so that the real investigators could determine to what levels subjects would raise the amount of electricity. When subjects hesitated they were urged to continue. Sixty-two percent of over 1,000 subjects obeyed the experimenter's commands fully, raising the intensity level of the painful stimulus to the highest point possible. The experiment achieved notoriety not only because of the results obtained but because of the reactions of the deceived subjects. They expressed shame, revulsion, anxiety, and extreme tension during and after the experiment.

The ethics of conducting the research in the first place was soon debated in the psychological literature (Baumrind, 1964; Milgram, 1964) and eventually led to a reconsideration of the American Psychological Association (APA) Code of Ethics regarding research. That examination stimulated the drafting of a lengthy and separate reformulation of ethical principles concerning research with human beings (APA, 1973). In turn, these principles led to a vigorous discussion in print regarding the efficacy of the newly established Code (Baumrind, 1971; Berscheid, Baron, Dermer, and Libman, 1973; Gergan, 1973; Kellman, 1972; Kerlinger, 1972; Menges, 1973; Resnick and Schwartz, 1973; Waterman, 1974). Whatever the debatable points, the APA—the major organization representing behavioral scientists—had at least established minimal ethical guidelines for the design and implementation of research. Soon it would be the turn of the courts and the government to do the same. . . .

THE STATUTORY RESPONSE: THE FEDERAL GOVERNMENT SPEAKS

. . .

In mid 1974 the U.S. Department of Health, Education and Welfare (DHEW) published regulations regarding the protection of human subjects. These regulations govern the activities of those organizations who receive research funds or are accountable to DHEW. First published in the Federal Register (39 Federal Register 18917, May 30, 1974) and now codified as Federal regulations (45 CFR 46), the rules explicitly declare the Department's policy that "no activity involving human subjects to be supported by DHEW grants or contracts shall be undertaken unless a committee of the organization has reviewed and approved such activity and the organization has submitted to DHEW a certification of such review and approval . . ." (45 CFR 46.102(a)).

[*Ed. note*: The regulations are reprinted in the next excerpt.]

Soon after DHEW published these regulations, Congress passed the National Research Act (Pub. L. 93-348, 88 Stat. 342), Title II of which is called "Protection of Human Subjects of Biomedical and Behavioral Research." Its primary purpose was to establish a National Commission whose major task is to identify basic ethical principles that underlie the conduct of human research. . . .

In developing ethical principles, the Commission is charged with considering ways in which it can be determined if human subjects are needed for planned research, constructing guidelines for the selection of human subjects, and arriving at a definition of informed consent. Another significant aspect of its work is to identify the requirements of informed consent for those persons whose capacity for giving consent is either absent or limited. In this category fall prisoners, institutionalized mental patients, and children. To accomplish this task the Commission is to consider the adequacy of information given to such persons about the research, the risks, discomforts, and anticipated benefits from the research, as well as the competence and freedom of such people to make a choice for or against their involvement.

The concern for "limited capacity" populations was apparently stimulated by a recent decision that held that involuntarily detained mental patients could not give informed and adequate consent to experimental psychosurgery (*Kaimowitz v. Dep't of Mental Health* (1973)). . . . The invalidity of consent was predicated on the inherently coercive atmosphere of an institutional setting where release may depend on cooperation with those suggesting surgery as an alternative to indefinite confinement. The court assumed that the absence of meaningful choice on the part of one who has little bargaining power could vitiate any consent given by one in that position. [1977, *Federal Register*, 42, 26318–26326]

The Commission in its recommendations to the Secretary of DHEW has rejected the rationale of the *Kaimowitz* court. It agreed that institutionalization may lessen the ability of prisoners and mental patients to make uncoerced choices, but asserted that the diminished capacity to consent should not absolutely exclude involuntarily confined persons from the opportunity to benefit from new therapies if those interventions are their best or only hope for recovery from disabling disorders.

The Commission focused on the nature of the institution in which research might be conducted. Although prisons and hospitals may have potential for limiting the capacity of their residents to make "free" choices, the Commission believed it was possible to specify the necessary conditions under which research in closed institutions might continue to be supported by the federal government. With regard to prisons, for example, . . . it recommended that research concerning the possible causes, effects, and processes of incarceration and studies of prisons themselves could be supported provided that they presented no more than minimal risk or inconvenience to the subjects, that the research was performed by competent persons, and that the proposed study was approved by the Institutional Review Boards required by DHEW. With the same proviso, the Commission also agreed that research on innovative and accepted practices that had the intent and reasonable probability of improving the well-being of the individual prisoner might be conducted. Any other research—primarily that which would not have the goal of benefiting the individual prisoner—could only be conducted if the planned research filled an important social and scientific need, if the reasons for involving prisoners (in contrast to "free living" subjects) was compelling, and if there was a high degree of voluntariness on the part of prospective participants and openness on the part of the institution. Criteria of openness would include adequate living conditions, opportunity to effectively redress grievances, separation of research participation from parole considerations, and willingness of the prison to bear public scrutiny.

Thus, the Commission focused on standards of conduct for institutional authorities rather than on the capacity of the potential subject. As an alternative to forbidding all research in closed settings, it recommended research participation by inmates where there is evidence that a relatively free choice is probable. The consequence is at once to respect the autonomy of the individual as well as to stimulate positive change in living conditions in previously coercive institutions. The recommendations are, of course, not perfect. They may be considered paternalistic and protectionistic insofar as the prisoner is only allowed a choice when the institution meets the requirements of openness and voluntariness or when the research has substantial promise of benefit to the subject.

The situation regarding consent becomes even more complex when the potential subjects are children or those involuntarily committed to mental institutions. Unlike prisoners, these populations are not always presumed competent to make decisions. Substitute or proxy consent by a parent or legally appointed representative has been the traditional solution but there are those—including some members of the Commission, its staff, and its consultants—who feel that the use of third persons to consent for others is a basic denial of human dignity. It is this fundamental question of whether, or under what conditions, selected others may consent or refuse to consent to participation in research with which the National Commission for the Protection of Human Subjects is now grappling. . . .

This thicket of regulations, guidelines, codes, and statutes is no doubt confusing. . . . [T]he plethora of rules illustrates the progression from ethical standards, binding on only those researchers who belong to professional organizations but with little legal significance, to judicial decisions, binding on only the litigants involved, to statutes and regulations, binding on all those contemplated by the laws. Already, 90 percent of human medical research is sponsored by the federal government and for many who plan, conduct, or participate in research, ethical constraints are now legal mandates. . . .

References

American Psychological Association. *Ethical principles in the conduct of research with human participants.* Washington, D.C.: Author, 1973.

Baumrind, D. Some thoughts on ethics of research—after reading Milgram's "Behavioral Study of Obedience." *American Psychologist*, 1964, *19*, 421–423.

Baumrind, D. Principles of ethical conduct in the treatment of subjects. *American Psychologist*, 1971, *26*, 887–896.

Berscheid, E., Baron, R. D., Dermer, M., and Libman, S. Anticipating informed consent: An empirical approach. *American Psychologist*, 1973, *28*, 913–925.

Gergan, K. J. The codification of research ethics: Views of a doubting Thomas. *American Psychologist*, 1973, *28*, 907–912.

Katz, J. *Experimentation with human beings.* New York: Russell Sage Foundation, 1972.

Kellman, H. C. The rights of the subject in social research: An analysis in terms of relative power and legitimacy. *American Psychologist*, 1972, *27*, 989–1016.

Kerlinger, F. Draft report of the APA Committee on Ethical Standards in Psychological Research: A critical reaction. *American Psychologist*, 1972, *27*, 894–896.

Menges, R. J. Openness and honesty versus coercion and deception in psychological research. *American Psychologist*, 1973, *28*, 1030–1034.

Milgram, S. Behavioral study of obedience. *Journal of Abnormal and Social Psychology*, 1963, *67*, 371–378.

Milgram, S. Issues in the study of obedience: A reply to Baumrind. *American Psychologist*, 1964, *19*, 848–852.

Resnick, J. H. and Schwartz, T. Ethical standards as an independent variable in psychological research. *American Psychologist*, 1973, *28*, 134–139.

Waterman, S. The civil liberties of the participants in psychological research. *American Psychologist*, 1974, *29*, 470–471.

◆ ◆ ◆

Commentary: *The National Commission for the Protection of Human Subjects has long since completed its work, and the federal regulations described in the preceding excerpt have been refined and recodified. For example, some research is now exempt from scrutiny by Institutional Review Boards (IRBs), whereas other re-*

search may undergo expedited review. Recommendations that the commission had made concerning prisoners have been revised and promulgated as regulations by the Department of Health and Human Services (DHHS), as were regulations for research with children. Interestingly, commission recommendations concerning research with people who have been institutionalized as mentally disabled have never been adopted by DHHS. As Dresser (1996) noted:

> The United States has no specific policy on research involving persons with mental disabilities. . . . Instead, federal law assigns . . . IRBs responsibilities for determining whether protective measures for mentally disabled subjects should be added to the basic provisions governing human experimentation. Yet IRBs lack adequate guidance on fulfilling this responsibility. (p. 67)

In the absence of federal regulations and in the light of fundamental ethical principles, Dresser offered the following recommendations:

1. Adopt informed consent procedures that enhance the autonomy of capable subjects but offer them an opportunity to share decision-making with family or friends;

2. When proxy decision-makers are used for incapable participants, instruct proxies on relevant ethical standards;

3. Exclude those who object, including those incapable of decision-making, unless the research provides an exceptional opportunity for direct benefit;

4. Arrange for genuine representation of the relevant subject population in the planning and ethical review of proposed research. See Dresser, R. (1996). Mentally disabled research subjects: The enduring policy issues. Journal of the American Medical Association, 276, 67–72.

The situation may be changing. In November 1998, the National Bioethics Advisory Commission issued recommended rules for conducting research with participants who are mentally disabled, many of which comport with Prof. Dresser's suggestions.

In the early 1990s a federal agency scrutinized a study by university researchers involving participants diagnosed with schizophrenia. Some participants complained that the researchers failed to sufficiently inform them of the possibility that the withdrawal of their medication—one of the components of the study—could lead to severe relapses. The agency concluded that the researchers failed to secure sufficient consent to this procedure from participants. It did agree, however, with the university IRB that the methodology of the research was scientifically sound. See Office for Protection From Research Risks, Division of Human Subject Protections. (1994). Evaluation of human subject protections in schizophrenia research conducted by the University of California, Los Angeles. *Los Angeles: UCLA.* It is an instructive case study.

Relevant parts of the regulations for research conducted or funded by DHHS with human participants generally and with prisoners and children specifically are included in the following pages.

Policy for Protection of Human Research Subjects

U.S. Department of Health and Human Services

SUBPART A—BASIC HHS POLICY FOR PROTECTION OF HUMAN RESEARCH SUBJECTS

. . .

§ 46.101 To What Does This Policy Apply?

(a) Except as provided in paragraph (b) of this section, this policy applies to all research involving human subjects conducted, supported or otherwise subject to regulation by any federal department or agency which takes appropriate administrative action to make the policy applicable to such research. . . .

(b) Unless otherwise required by department or agency heads, research activities in which the only involvement of human subjects will be in one or more of the following categories are exempt from this policy:

(1) Research conducted in established or commonly accepted educational settings, involving normal educational practices, such as (i) research on regular and special education instructional strategies, or (ii) research on the effectiveness of or the comparison, among instructional techniques, curricula, or classroom management methods.

(2) Research involving the use of educational tests (cognitive, diagnostic, aptitude, achievement), survey procedures, interview procedures or observation of public behavior, unless:

(i) Information obtained is recorded in such a manner that human subjects can be identified, directly or through identifiers linked to the subjects; and (ii) any disclosure of the human subjects' responses outside the research could reasonably place the subjects at risk of criminal or civil liability or be damaging to the subjects' financial standing, employability, or reputation.

(3) Research involving the use of educational tests (cognitive, diagnostic, aptitude, achievement), survey procedures, interview procedures, or observation of public behavior that is not exempt under paragraph (b)(2) of this section, if:

(i) The human subjects are elected or appointed public officials or candidates for public office; or (ii) federal statute(s) require(s) without exception that the confidentiality of the personally identifiable information will be maintained throughout the research and thereafter.

(4) Research, involving the collection or study of existing data, documents, records, pathological specimens, or diagnostic specimens, if these sources are publicly available or if the information is recorded by the investigator in such a manner that subjects cannot be identified, directly or through identifiers linked to the subjects.

(5) Research and demonstration projects which are conducted by or subject to the approval of department or agency heads, and which are designed to study, evaluate, or otherwise examine:

(i) Public benefit or service programs; (ii) procedures for obtaining benefits or services under those programs; (iii) possible changes in or alternatives to those programs or procedures; or (iv) possible changes in methods or levels of payment for benefits or services under those programs. . . .

§ 46.107 IRB Membership.

(a) Each IRB [Institutional Review Board] shall have at least five members, with varying backgrounds to

From 45 C.F.R. Part 46. Basic H.H.S. Policy for Protection of Human Research Subjects. Adapted with permission of the author and publisher.

promote complete and adequate review of research activities commonly conducted by the institution. The IRB shall be sufficiently qualified through the experience and expertise of its members, and the diversity of the members, including consideration of race, gender, and cultural backgrounds and sensitivity to such issues as community attitudes, to promote respect for its advice and counsel in safeguarding the rights and welfare of human subjects. In addition to possessing the professional competence necessary to review specific research activities, the IRB shall be able to ascertain the acceptability of proposed research in terms of institutional commitments and regulations, applicable law, and standards of professional conduct and practice. The IRB shall therefore include persons knowledgeable in these areas. If an IRB regularly reviews research that involves a vulnerable category of subjects, such as children, prisoners, pregnant women, or handicapped or mentally disabled persons, consideration shall be given to the inclusion of one or more individuals who are knowledgeable about and experienced in working with these subjects.

(b) Every nondiscriminatory effort will be made to ensure that no IRB consists entirely of men or entirely of women, including the institution's consideration of qualified persons of both sexes, so long as no selection is made to the IRB on the basis of gender. No IRB may consist entirely of members of one profession.

(c) Each IRB shall include at least one member whose primary concerns are in scientific areas and at least one member whose primary concerns are in nonscientific areas.

(d) Each IRB shall include at least one member who is not otherwise affiliated with the institution and who is not part of the immediate family of a person who is affiliated with the institution.

(e) No IRB may have a member participate in the IRB's initial or continuing review of any project in which the member has a conflicting interest, except to provide information requested by the IRB.

(f) An IRB may, in its discretion, invite individuals with competence in special areas to assist in the review of issues which require expertise beyond or in addition to that available on the IRB. These individuals may not vote with the IRB. . . .

§ 46.110 Expedited Review Procedures for Certain Kinds of Research Involving No More Than Minimal Risk, and for Minor Changes in Approved Research.

(a) The Secretary, HHS, has established, and published as a Notice in the FEDERAL REGISTER, a list of categories of research that may be reviewed by the IRB through an expedited review procedure. The list will be amended, as appropriate after consultation with other departments and agencies, through periodic republication by the Secretary, HHS, in the FEDERAL REGISTER. A copy of the list is available from the Office for Protection From Research Risks, National Institutes of Health, HHS, Bethesda, Maryland 20892.

(b) An IRB may use the expedited review procedure to review either or both of the following:

(1) Some or all of the research appearing on the list and found by the reviewer(s) to involve no more than minimal risk.

(2) Minor changes in previously approved research during the period (of one year or less) for which approval is authorized.

Under an expedited review procedure, the review may be carried out by the IRB chairperson or by one or more experienced reviewers designated by the chairperson from among members of the IRB. In reviewing the research, the reviewers may exercise all of the authorities of the IRB except that the reviewers may not disapprove the research. A research activity may be disapproved only after review in accordance with the non-expedited procedure set forth in § 46.108(b). . . .

§ 46.111 Criteria for IRB Approval of Research

(a) In order to approve research covered by this policy the IRB shall determine that all of the following requirements are satisfied:

(1) Risks to subjects are minimized: (i) By using procedures which are consistent with sound research design and which do not unnecessarily expose subjects to risk, and (ii) whenever appropriate, by using procedures already being performed on the subjects for diagnostic or treatment purposes.

(2) Risks to subjects are reasonable in relation to anticipated benefits, if any, to subjects, and the im-

portance of the knowledge that may reasonably be expected to result. In evaluating risks and benefits, the IRB should consider only those risks and benefits that may result from the research (as distinguished from risks and benefits of therapies subjects would receive even if not participating in the research). The IRB should not consider possible long-range effects of applying knowledge gained in the research (for example, the possible effects of the research on public policy) as among those research risks that fall within the purview of its responsibility.

(3) Selection of subjects is equitable. In making this assessment the IRB should take into account the purposes of the research and the setting in which the research will be conducted and should be particularly cognizant of the special problems of research involving vulnerable populations, such as children, prisoners, pregnant women, mentally disabled persons, or economically or educationally disadvantaged persons.

(4) Informed consent will be sought from each prospective subject or the subject's legally authorized representative, in accordance with, and to the extent required by § 46.116.

(5) Informed consent will be appropriately documented, in accordance with, and to the extent required by § 46.117.

(6) When appropriate, the research plan makes adequate provision for monitoring the data collected to ensure the safety of subjects.

(7) When appropriate, there are adequate provisions to protect the privacy of subjects and to maintain the confidentiality of data.

(b) When some or all of the subjects are likely to be vulnerable to coercion or undue influence, such as children, prisoners, pregnant women, mentally disabled persons, or economically or educationally disadvantaged persons, additional safeguards have been included in the study to protect the rights and welfare of these subjects. . . .

§ 46.116 General Requirements for Informed Consent.

Except as provided elsewhere in this policy, no investigator may involve a human being as a subject in research covered by this policy unless the investigator has obtained the legally effective informed consent of the subject or the subject's legally authorized representative. An investigator shall seek such consent only under circumstances that provide the prospective subject or the representative sufficient opportunity to consider whether or not to participate and that minimize the possibility of coercion or undue influence. The information that is given to the subject or the representative shall be in language understandable to the subject or the representative. No informed consent, whether oral or written, may include any exculpatory language through which the subject or the representative is made to waive or appear to waive any of the subject's legal rights, or releases or appears to release the investigator, the sponsored, the institution or its agents from liability for negligence.

(a) Basic elements of informed consent. Except as provided in paragraph (c) or (d) of this section, in seeking informed consent the following information shall be provided to each subject:

(1) A statement that the study involves research, an explanation of the purposes of the research and the expected duration of the subject's participation, a description of the procedures to be followed, and identification of any procedures which are experimental;

(2) A description of any reasonably foreseeable risks or discomforts to the subject;

(3) A description of any benefits to the subject or to others which may reasonably be expected from the research;

(4) A disclosure of appropriate alternative procedures or courses of treatment, if any, that might be advantageous to the subject;

(5) A statement describing the extent, if any, to which confidentiality of records identifying the subject will be maintained;

(6) For research involving more than minimal risk, an explanation as to whether any compensation and an explanation as to whether any medical treatments are available if injury occurs

and, if so, what they consist of, or where further information may be obtained;

(7) An explanation of whom to contact for answers to pertinent questions about the research and research subjects' rights, and whom to contact in the event of a research-related injury to the subject; and

(8) A statement that participation is voluntary, refusal to participate will involve no penalty or loss of benefits to which the subject is otherwise entitled, and the subject may discontinue participation at any time without penalty or loss of benefits to which the subject is otherwise entitled.

(b) Additional elements of informed consent. When appropriate, one or more of the following elements of information shall also be provided to each subject:

(1) A statement that the particular treatment or procedure may involve risks to the subject (or to the embryo or fetus, if the subject is or may become pregnant) which are currently unforeseeable;

(2) Anticipated circumstances under which the subject's participation may be terminated by the investigator without regard to the subject's consent;

(3) Any additional costs to the subject that may result from participation in the research;

(4) The consequences of a subject's decision to withdraw from the research and procedures for orderly termination of participation by the subject;

(5) A statement that significant new findings developed during the course of the research which may relate to the subject's willingness to continue participation will be provided to the subject; and

(6) The approximate number of subjects involved in the study.

(c) An IRB may approve a consent procedure which does not include, or which alters, some or all of the elements of informed consent set forth above, or waive the requirements to obtain informed consent provided the IRB finds and documents that:

(1) The research or demonstration project is to be conducted by or subject to the approval of state or local government officials and is designed to study, evaluate, or otherwise examine: (i) public benefit or service programs; (ii) procedures for obtaining benefits or services under those programs; (iii) possible changes in or alternatives to those programs or procedures; or (iv) possible changes in methods or levels of payment for benefits or services under those programs; and

(2) The research could not practicably be carried out without the waiver or alteration.

(d) An IRB may approve a consent procedure which does not include, or which alters, some or all of the elements of informed consent set forth in this section, or waive the requirements to obtain informed consent provided the IRB finds and documents that:

(1) The research involves no more than minimal risk to the subjects;

(2) The waiver or alteration will not adversely affect the rights and welfare of the subjects;

(3) The research could not practicably be carried out without the waiver or alteration; and

(4) Whenever appropriate, the subjects will be provided with additional pertinent information after participation.

(e) The informed consent requirements in this policy are not intended to preempt any applicable federal, state, or local laws which require additional information to be disclosed in order for informed consent to be legally effective.

(f) Nothing in this policy is intended to limit the authority of a physician to provide emergency medical care, to the extent the physician is permitted to do so under applicable federal, state, or local law. . . .

SUBPART C—ADDITIONAL PROTECTIONS PERTAINING TO BIOMEDICAL AND BEHAVIORAL RESEARCH INVOLVING PRISONERS AS SUBJECTS

§ 46.302 Purpose.

Inasmuch as prisoners may be under constraints because of their incarceration which could affect their ability to make a truly voluntary and uncoerced decision whether or not to participate as subjects in research, it is the purpose of this subpart to provide additional safeguards for the protection of prisoners involved in activities to which this subpart is applicable. . . .

§ 46.304 Composition of Institutional Review Boards Where Prisoners Are Involved.

In addition to satisfying the requirements in § 46.107 of this part, an Institutional Review Board, carving out responsibilities under this part with respects to research covered by this subpart, shall also meet the following specific requirements:

(a) A majority of the Board (exclusive of prisoner members) shall have no association with the prison(s) involved, apart from their membership on the Board.

(b) At least one member of the Board shall be a prisoner, or a prisoner representative with appropriate background and experience to serve in that capacity, except that where a particular research project is reviewed by more than one Board only one Board need satisfy this requirement.

. . .

§ 46.305 Additional Duties of the Institutional Review Boards Where Prisoners Are Involved.

(a) In addition to all other responsibilities prescribed for Institutional Review Boards under this part, the Board shall review research covered by this subpart and approve such research only if it finds that:

(1) The research under review represents one of the categories of research permissible under § 46.306(a)(2);

(2) Any possible advantages accruing to the prisoner through his or her participation in the research, when compared to the general living conditions, medical care, quality of food, amenities and opportunity for earnings in the prison, are not of such a magnitude that his or her ability to weigh the risks of the research against the value of such advantages in the limited choice environment of the prison is impaired;

(3) The risks involved in the research are commensurate with risks that would be accepted by nonprisoner volunteers;

(4) Procedures for the selection of subjects within the prison are fair to all prisoners and immune from arbitrary intervention by prison authorities or prisoners. Unless the principal investigator provides to the Board justification in writing for following some other procedures, control subjects must be selected randomly from the group of available prisoners who meet the characteristics needed for that particular research project.

(5) The information is presented in language which is understandable to the subject population; [and]

(6) Adequate assurance exists that parole boards will not take into account a prisoner's participation in the research in making decisions regarding parole, and each prisoner is clearly informed in advance that participation in the research will have no effect on his or her parole[.] . . .

§ 46.306 Permitted Research Involving Prisoners.

(a) Biomedical or behavioral research conducted or supported by DHHS may involve prisoners as subjects only if:

(1) The institution responsible for the conduct of the research has certified to the Secretary that the Institutional Review Board has approved the research under § 46.305 of this subpart; and

(2) In the judgment of the Secretary the proposed research involves solely the following:

(i) Study of the possible causes, effects, and processes of incarceration, and of criminal behavior, provided that the study presents no more than minimal risk and no more than inconvenience to the subjects;

(ii) Study of prisons as institutional structures or of prisoners as incarcerated persons, provided that the study presents no more than minimal risk and no more than inconvenience to the subjects;

(iii) Research on concerns particularly affecting prisoners as a class (for example, vaccine trials and other research on hepatitis which is much more prevalent in prisons than elsewhere; and research on social and psychological problems such as alcoholism, drug addiction and sexual assaults) provided that the study may proceed only after the Secretary has consulted with appropriate experts including experts in penology medicine and ethics, and published notice, in the FEDERAL REGISTER, of his intent to approve such research; or

(iv) Research on practices, both innovative and accepted, which have the intent and reasonable probability of improving the health or well-being of the subject. In cases in which those studies require the assignment of prisoners in a manner consistent with protocols approved by the IRB to control groups which may not benefit from the research, the study may proceed only after the Secretary has consulted with appropriate experts, including experts in penology medicine and ethics, and published notice, in the FEDERAL REGISTER, of his intent to approve such research.

(b) Except as provided in paragraph (a) of this section, biomedical or behavioral research conducted or supported by DHHS shall not involve prisoners as subjects.

SUBPART D—ADDITIONAL PROTECTIONS FOR CHILDREN INVOLVED AS SUBJECTS IN RESEARCH

. . .

§ 46.402 Definitions.

The definitions in § 46.102 of Subpart A shall be applicable to this subpart as well. In addition, as used in this subpart:

(a) *Children* are persons who have not attained the legal age for consent to treatments or procedures involved in the research, under the applicable law of the jurisdiction in which the research will be conducted.

(b) *Assent* means a child's affirmative agreement to participate in research. Mere failure to object should not, absent affirmative agreement, be construed as assent.

(c) *Permission* means the agreement of parent(s) or guardian to the participation of their child or ward in research.

(d) *Parent* means a child's biological or adoptive parent.

(e) *Guardian* means an individual who is authorized under applicable State or local law to consent on behalf of a child to general medical care.

§ 46.403 IRB Duties.

In addition to other responsibilities assigned to IRBs under this part, each IRB shall review research covered by this subpart and approve only research which satisfies the conditions of all applicable sections of this subpart.

§ 46.604 Research Not Involving Greater Than Minimal Risk.

HHS will conduct or fund research in which the IRB finds that no greater than minimal risk to children is presented, only if the IRB finds that adequate provisions are made for soliciting the assent of the children and the permission of their parents or guardians, as set forth in § 46.408.

§ 46.405 Research Involving Greater Than Minimal Risk but Presenting the Prospect of Direct Benefit to the Individual Subjects.

HHS will conduct or fund research in which the IRB finds that more than minimal risk to children is presented by an intervention or procedure that holds out the prospect of direct benefit for the individual subject, or by a monitoring procedure that is likely to contribute to the subject's well-being, only if the IRB finds that:

(a) The risk is justified by the anticipated benefit to the subjects;

(b) The relation of the anticipated benefit to the risk is at least as favorable to the subjects as that presented by available alternative approaches; and

(c) Adequate provisions are made for soliciting the assent of the children and permission of their parents or guardians, as set forth in § 46.408.

§ 46.406 Research Involving Greater Than Minimal Risk and No Prospect of Direct Benefit to Individual Subjects, but Likely to Yield Generalizable Knowledge About the Subject's Disorder or Condition.

HHS will conduct or fund research in which the IRB finds that more than minimal risk to children is presented by an intervention or procedure that does not hold out the prospect of direct benefit for the individual subject, or by a monitoring procedure which is not likely to contribute to the well-being of the subject, only if the IRB finds that:

(a) The risk represents a minor increase over minimal risk;

(b) The intervention or procedure presents experiences to subjects that are reasonably commensurate with those inherent in their actual or expected medical, dental, psychological, social, or educational situations;

(c) The intervention or procedure is likely to yield generalizable knowledge about the subjects' disorder or condition which is of vital importance for the understanding or amelioration of the subjects' disorder or condition; and

(d) Adequate provisions are made for soliciting assent of the children and permission of their parents or guardians, as set forth in § 46.408.

§ 46.407 Research Not Otherwise Approvable Which Presents an Opportunity to Understand, Prevent, or Alleviate a Serious Problem Affecting the Health or Welfare of Children.

HHS will conduct or fund research that the IRB does not believe meets the requirements of §46.404, § 46.405, or § 46.406 only if:

(a) The IRB finds that the research presents a reasonable opportunity to further the understanding, prevention, or alleviation of a serious problem affecting the health or welfare of children; and

(b) The Secretary, after consultation with a panel of experts in pertinent disciplines (for example: science, medicine, education, ethics, law) and follow-

ing opportunity for public review and comment, has determined either:

(1) That the research in fact satisfies the conditions of § 46.404, § 46.405, or § 46.406, as applicable, or

(2) The following:

(i) The research presents a reasonable opportunity to further the understanding, prevention, or alleviation of a serious problem affecting the health or welfare of children;

(ii) The research will be conducted in accordance with sound ethical principles;

(iii) Adequate provisions are made for soliciting the assent of children and the permission of their parents or guardians, as set forth in § 46.408.

§ 46.408 Requirements for Permission by Parents or Guardians and for Assent by Children.

(a) In addition to the determinations required under other applicable sections of this subpart, the IRB shall determine that adequate provisions are made for soliciting the assent of the children, when in the judgment of the IRB the children are capable of providing assent. In determining whether children are capable of assenting, the IRB shall take into account the ages, maturity, and psychological state of the children involved. This judgment may be made for all children to be involved in research under a particular protocol, or for each child, as the IRB deems appropriate. If the IRB determines that the capability of some or all of the children is so limited that they cannot reasonably be consulted or that the intervention or procedure involved in the research holds out a prospect of direct benefit that is important to the health or well-being of the children and is available only in the context of the research, the assent of the children is not a necessary condition for proceeding with the research. Even where the IRB determines that the subjects are capable of assenting, the IRB may still waive the assent requirement under circumstances in which consent may be waived in accord with § 46.116 of Subpart A.

(b) In addition to the determinations required under other applicable sections of this subpart, the IRB shall determine, in accordance with and to the extent that consent is required by § 46.116 of Subpart A, that adequate provisions are made for soliciting the permission of each child's parents or guardian. Where parental permission is to be obtained, the IRB may find that the permission of one parent is sufficient for research to be conducted under § 46.404 or § 46.405. Where research is covered by §§ 46.406 and 46.407 and permission is to be obtained from parents, both parents must give their permission unless one parent is deceased, unknown, incompetent, or not reasonably available, or when only one parent has legal responsibility for the care and custody of the child.

(c) In addition to the provisions for waiver contained in § 46.116 of Subpart A, if the IRB determines that a research protocol is designed for conditions or for a subject population for which parental or guardian permission is not a reasonable requirement to protect the subjects (for example, neglected or abused children), it may waive the consent requirements in Subpart A of this part and paragraph (b) of this section, provided an appropriate mechanism for protecting the children who will participate as subjects in the research is substituted, and provided further that the waiver is not inconsistent with Federal, state or local law. The choice of an appropriate mechanism would depend upon the nature and purpose of the activities described in the protocol, the risk and anticipated benefit to the research subjects, and their age, maturity, status, and condition.

(d) Permission by parents or guardians shall be documented in accordance with and to the extent required by § 46.117 of Subpart A.

(e) When the IRB determines that assent is required, it shall also determine whether and how assent must be documented.

§ 46.409 Wards.

(a) Children who are wards of the state or any other agency, institution, or entity can be included in research approved under § 46.406 or § 46.407 only if such research is:

(1) Related to their status as wards, or

(2) Conducted in schools, camps, hospitals, institutions, or similar settings in which the majority of children involved as subjects are not wards.

(b) If the research is approved under paragraph (a) of this section, the IRB shall require appointment of an advocate for each child who is a ward, in addition to any other individual acting on behalf of the child as guardian or in loco parentis. One individual may serve as advocate for more than one child. The advocate shall be an individual who has the background and experience to act in, and agrees to act in, the best interests of the child for the duration of the child's participation in the research and who is not associated in any way (except in the role as advocate or member of the IRB) with the research, the investigator(s), or the guardian organization.

◆ ◆ ◆

Commentary: As the regulations show, IRBs wield significant power in determining whether biomedical and behavioral research will be approved. Although only research conducted or funded by the federal government must receive IRB review, almost all proposed institutional research now undergoes such review. Some critics have alleged that IRB members are overly cautious and are guided more by personal and sociocultural values than by valid assessments of methodological rigor, risk to participants, and benefit to society. For example, in a provocative steady, Ceci, Peters, and Plotkin (1985) found that, when asked to review hypothetical research proposals identical in their proposed treatment of human participants but differing in their sociopolitical sensitivity, IRBs were twice as likely to reject the socially sensitive proposals. Nonsensitive proposals that did not include ethical problems (such as deception or the absence of debriefing) were approved 95% of the time, but comparable, sensitive ones were approved only 40%–50% of the time. On the other hand, researchers asked to judge pairs of deliberately flawed experiments that were identical except for the importance of their subject matter were significantly more likely to overlook methodological problems and to recommend publication when they perceived the topic to be important. Thus, although regulations regarding the protection of human subjects specifically instruct IRBs not to consider the public policy effects of research, these studies show that, in fact, review boards do consider the sociopolitical consequences of the proposed research. See

Ceci, S. J., Peters, D., & Plotkin, J. (1985). *Human subjects review, personal values, and the regulation of social science research.* American Psychologist, 40, 994–1002.

Wilson, T. D., DePaulo, B. M., Mook, D. G., & Klaaren, K. J. (1993). *Scientists' evaluations of research: The biasing effects of the importance of the topic.* Psychological Science, 4, 322–325.

Sieber and Stanley (1988) have provided a useful 4 × 10 matrix for identifying the ethical and professional dimensions of socially sensitive research. They saw four major aspects of scientific activity that engender ethical concerns: (a) formulation of the research question, (b) conduct of research and treatment of research participants, (c) institutional setting in which the research is conducted, and (d) interpretation and application of the findings. They then identified 10 ethical issues in socially sensitive research that may arise in these four areas: (a) the person's interest in controlling boundaries between the self and researcher (privacy), (b) confidentiality and control of data, (c) sound and valid methodology and design, (d) deception, (e) informed consent, (f) justice and equitable treatment (e.g., withholding experimental treatment from one group), (g) scientific freedom, (h) ownership of data, (i) humanistic versus scientific values, and (j) risk–benefit ratio. How would you apply this matrix to a pending decision about whether or not to conduct research on racial differences in intelligence or the patterns of the transmission of AIDS? See Sieber, J. E., & Stanley, B. (1988). Ethical and professional dimensions of socially sensitive research. American Psychologist, 43, 49–55. For a full discussion of these issues see the Special Issue of Ethics and Behavior *(Volume 8, Number 4, 1998) titled, "Protection of Participants in Sensitive Social Research."*

As is the case with AIDS, research that may both benefit society by promoting human welfare and aid public health efforts to control disease may conflict with research participants' right to privacy. For example, as Melton and Gray (1988) have explained,

> *disclosure of participants' status, even if simply as members of a risk group, may result in their being subjected to social stigma and legal sanctions (e.g., quarantine; punishment for engaging in prohibited risky behavior). Thus, participants may have a clear interest in avoiding participa-*

tion and, if they choose to participate, preventing disclosures of data to third parties.

> *At the same time, participants, particularly if they are patients themselves or members of risk groups, have a profound interest in promotion of research on the illness in question. They even have an interest in retention of identifiable data when it might be used for longitudinal research or sharing of data sets crucial to understanding the process of the disease. (p. 60)*

Melton, G. B., & Gray, J. N. (1988) *Ethical dilemmas in AIDS research: Individual privacy and public health.* American Psychologist, 43, 60–64.

Recall that 45 CFR Sec 46.101(b)(4) exempts from IRB review research involving the study of existing data, documents, or records if the researcher copies the information in a way that does not reveal the identity of the subjects. The facility where the data are stored, however, has no concomitant obligation before the researcher studies the data. What if the researcher knows some of the subjects and the records are those of former mental patients? Do federal regulations adequately address this issue? Does the current APA ethics code cover it (see, e.g., Standard 5.07)? For a discussion of this topic and suggested guidelines for conducting archival research, see Taube, D. O., & Burkhardt, S. (1997). Ethical and legal risks associated with archival research. Ethics and Behavior, 7, 59–67.

What if the researcher is surveying responses of adolescents to a childhood depression scale and discovers that three of the respondents report they are actively considering suicide? Does the researcher have any obligation to identify them, notify their parents, or provide clinical services? For a discussion of this problem, see Bersoff D. M., & Bersoff, D. N. (1999). Ethical issues in the collection of self-report data. In A. Stone et al. (Eds.), The science of self-report: Implications for research and practice. Mahwah, NJ: Erlbaum; O'Sullivan, C., & Fisher, C. B. (1997). The effect of confidentiality and reporting procedures on parent–child agreement to participate in adolescent risk research. Applied Developmental Science, 1, 187–199.

To some extent, the disclosure of certain sensitive and confidential data gleaned from participation in government-funded mental health research may now be protected by obtaining a Confidentiality Certificate from the Department of Health and Human Services. The certificate, for which one must apply, protects researchers from the compelled disclosure of identifying information obtained from research subjects by any governmental or civil order. See 42 C.F.R. Part 2a (Protection of Identity–Research Subjects); Hoagland, K. (1994). The Certificate of Confidentiality at the National Institute of Mental Health: Discretionary considerations in its applicability in research on child and adolescent mental disorders. Ethics and Behavior, 4, *123–131.*

For an informative and extended debate concerning the ethical conflict between protecting the confidentiality of research data generally and the tradition of open sharing in science, see the articles presented in the Adversary Forum of the June 1988 issue (Vol. 12) of Law and Human Behavior *(pp. 159–206) and those in the Forum section of* Ethics and Behavior *(Vol. 3, pp. 311–317). The relevant standard in the APA's 1992 Ethical Principles is 6.25 (Sharing Data).*

Standards 6.06–6.26 of the Ethical Principles are not the only guidelines that psychologists can consult concerning research. As the first two articles in this chapter cited, APA has produced the Ethical Principles in the Conduct of Research With Human Participants. *These principles were first published in 1973 and were revised and republished in 1982. They are being extensively revised and a new edition should appear in 1999 as* The Ethics of Research With Human Participants.

When the 1973 edition of Research With Human Participants *was being drafted, Gergen (1973) argued that "until we can provide scientific answers to questions about deception, coercion, informed consent, and so on, strong APA policies seem unwarranted" (p. 908). See Gergen, K. J. (1973). The codification of research ethics: Views of a doubting Thomas.* American Psychologist, 28, *907–912. Since then, researchers have been attempting to answer these question. And this research continues.*

Informed Consent for Psychological Research: Do Subjects Comprehend Consent Forms and Understand Their Legal Rights?

Traci Mann

. . .

According to the American Psychological Association (1992), psychologists must "inform participants of the nature of the research; they [must] inform participants that they are free to participate or to decline to participate or to withdraw from the research; they [must] explain the foreseeable consequences of declining or withdrawing; they [must] inform participants of significant factors that may be expected to influence their willingness to participate" (p. 1608). Research subjects have to understand this information to make an informed decision about whether they wish to participate in an experiment. Research is needed on the critical question of whether subjects in psychology experiments understand the information on consent forms.

Even though it is unknown whether subjects comprehend consent forms, researchers continue to add more information to them. In an analysis of consent form readability, Baker and Taub (1983) found that the average length of consent forms for research in Veterans Administration hospitals doubled over the 7-year time span from 1975 to 1982. They concluded that consent forms increased in length in order to include more information about subject's rights in accordance with federal guidelines. It is unclear, however, if these statements about rights, liability, and confidentiality are understood by research participants. Indeed, the quasi-legal language may cause research subjects to think they have signed a legal document designed to protect researchers.

This experiment compared psychology subjects' comprehension of two consent forms matched for readability level—a long, detailed form and a shorter, less detailed one. In addition, we looked specifically at the effectiveness of consent forms in conveying to subjects their legal rights by comparing subjects who had signed a consent form with subjects who had read an information sheet, but who had not signed a consent form. . . .

The data support three main conclusions. First, longer consent forms that attempt to describe a procedure fully may be comprehended less well than shorter forms that suppress some relevant details. Accordingly, federal regulations that require information to be added to already lengthy consent forms may end up reducing the amount of information subjects receive from consent forms. If a subject is to understand a consent form, the form should be as short and concise as possible.

Second, the 53 subjects who signed consent forms for an MRI scan did so without understanding important aspects of the experiment. Subjects answered only 60% of the specific questions correctly. These questions covered information crucial for deciding whether or not to participate in an experiment (e.g., risks, benefits, procedures). Because a consent is not considered valid unless the information on the consent form is understood (Beauchamp & Childress, 1989), subjects in this experiment did not give a valid consent.

In addition, subjects answered correctly only 50% of the general questions (which covered infor-

From *Psychological Science*, 5, 140–143. Copyright 1994 by the American Psychological Society. Adapted with permission of the author and publisher. Tables 1–3 have been omitted.

mation they had presumably been exposed to in other experiments). Less than half of the subjects understood what the researchers would do for them if they got hurt, or could list even two of the four things their signature on the consent form meant. Only 39% of the subjects knew that the consent form included any information on what to do if one had complaints about an experiment, and only 1 of the 53 subjects was able to state the procedure for registering complaints about experiments. This last problem is particularly serious because institutional review boards (IRBs) use feedback from subjects to determine whether an experiment can be continued safely. If no subjects complain when they are upset or hurt in experiments, IRBs may be led to believe that there are no problems, even when problems exist.

The third conclusion supported by the data is that the very act of signing a consent form caused subjects to believe that they had lost the right to sue the researcher, even for negligence [footnote omitted]. Subjects who signed a consent form thought they had lost their right to sue the experimenter, whereas subjects who read the same information but did not sign a consent form generally did not think they had lost this right.

According to the U.S. Department of Health and Human Services (1983), "No informed consent, whether oral or written, may include any exculpatory language through which the subject is made to waive or appear to waive any of the subject's legal rights, or releases or appears to release the investigator, the sponsor, the institution, or its agents from liability for negligence" (45 CFR §46.115). The consent forms used in this study were not in violation of this code. They stated explicitly that subjects who signed the forms were not giving up any rights to sue. Despite this explicit statement on the consent forms, subjects thought they had given up their rights to sue. To rectify this problem will require more than a statement about rights on a consent form.

This research suggests an argument for the use of oral consent procedures. Simply signing a consent form made subjects think they had lost the very rights the consent form was designed to protect. Perhaps subjects who consent orally but do not sign

a legalistic form will not feel that they have lost their rights. Perhaps subjects simply need to be reminded after signing a consent form that they have not given up any rights by signing it, but have merely consented to go ahead with the research. Future research will examine whether oral procedures and reminders are effective ways to overcome problems in informed consent.

References

American Psychological Association. (1992). Ethical principles of psychologists and code of conduct. *American Psychologist, 47*, 1597–1611.

Baker, M. T., & Taub, H. A. (1983). Readability of informed consent forms for research in a Veterans Administration medical center. *Journal of American Medical Association, 250*, 2646–2648.

Beauchamp, T. L., & Childress, J. F. (1989). *Principles of biomedical ethics*. New York: Oxford University Press.

U.S. Department of Health and Human Services. (1983). Protection of human subjects. *Code of Federal Regulations, 45*, §46.115.

◆　◆　◆

Commentary: Mann asserted that consent is not valid unless the participant understands the information in the consent form. Is it the researcher's ethical obligation to ensure that participants comprehend what the form says, or is the obligation simply limited to a duty to disclose the information? What position does Standard 6.11 of the APA's (1992) Ethical Principles take?

One of the most controversial topics in research is the use of deception, which inevitably requires researchers to dilute, if not completely dispense with, the requirement for informed consent from participants. In many areas of psychology, disclosing to subjects the purposes and procedures of the study would significantly alter the data. Thus, researchers may disguise or misrepresent the nature of the experiment or, in some cases, may not even inform participants that they are the subjects of research. These practices have been both pilloried and justified, but "it is clear that over time deception has become normative practice for research in social psychology" (Adair, Dushenko, & Lindsay, 1985, p. 63).

Two recent studies examined the frequency of deception research over the past 75 years. See Nicks, S. D.

Korn, J. H., & Manieri, T. (1997). *The rise and fall of deception in social psychology and personality research, 1921 to 1994.* Ethics and Behavior, 7, 69–77; Sieber, J. E., Iannuzzo, R., & Rodriguez, B. (1995). *Deception methods in psychology: Have they changed in 23 years?* Ethics and Behavior, 5, 67–85. *Sieber et al. found that*

> *Uses of confederates and other kinds of role deception [used in the 1960s] tended to be replaced by uses of computers and other kinds of bogus devices to provide false impressions to subjects. Research generally requiring deception, prevalent in 1969, tended to be supplemented extensively with research in areas such as socialization, personality, sex differences, environmental psychology, and attribution, where the use of deception is often unnecessary. However, by 1992, the percentage of deception studies conducted in these five areas increased to 37% as compared to 22% in 1986, and the percentage of deception studies conducted in the rest of the areas increased to 55%, as compared to 44% in 1986. (p. 82)*

Nevertheless, Adair et al. found that, for the studies they examined, researchers rarely reported on matters related to ethics, including informed consent and their attempts to debrief participants about the real purposes of the experiment after it was concluded. But they agreed with others that psychological research . . . [should] be guided by neither methodological imperialism, in which the dignity and safety of the subject are disregarded in the interests of science, nor an ethical imperialism, in which research progress is thwarted at every turn by an obsession with individual rights. (p. 70)

See Adair, J. G., Dushenko, T. W., & Lindsay, R. C. L. (1985). Ethical regulations and their impact on research practice. American Psychologist, 40, 59–72.

Yet, Diana Baumrind (1985), perhaps the major critic of this position, has adamantly argued that "the use of intentional deception in the research setting is unethical, imprudent, and unwarranted scientifically" (p. 165) and that "effective debriefing does not nullify the wrong done participants . . . and may not even repair their damaged self-image or ability to trust adult authorities" (p. 172). See Baumrind, D. (1985). Research using intentional deception: Ethical issues revisited. American Psychologist, 40, 165–174. *Two excellent articles on this topic follow.*

Deception Methods in Psychology: Have They Changed in 23 Years?

Joan E. Sieber, Rebecca Iannuzzo, and Beverly Rodriguez

. . .

WHEN IS DECEPTION ETHICALLY OBJECTIONABLE OR HARMFUL?

. . .

Kind of Failure to Inform

Deception in research involves some kind of failure to inform (e.g., there may be no informing, false informing, or consent to possible deception). Some approaches to not informing are less objectionable ethically and less likely to harm subjects than are other approaches. Indeed, ethically sensitive researchers have developed approaches to not informing that are highly respectful of subjects' autonomy; these are the first three approaches described in the following list. One would hope that these approaches are becoming more widely used. The basic kinds of noninforming are as follows:

1. *Informed consent* to participate in one of several specified conditions without knowing which condition will actually occur (as in placebo studies).
2. *Consent to deception,* in which subjects are warned that some deception may occur. They are told what events they will experience if they agree to participate in the study and are debriefed completely about the purpose of the study afterward.
3. *Waiver of right to be informed,* in which subjects waive informing but are not explicitly forewarned of the possibility of deception.
4. *Consent and false informing,* in which subjects believe they are engaging in a truthful informed

consent procedure, but are actually misinformed about some aspect of the nature of the research.
5. *No informing, no consent,* in which subjects do not know that they are participating in research.
6. *Self-deception,* in which the aim of the research is so different from what subjects expect that they behave under incorrect assumptions. For example, in incidental learning experiments, subjects are given a task such as learning pairs of nonsense syllables and are then tested on some attribute of the syllables such as their color.
7. *Deception by a third party,* in which the researcher observes a relationship in which someone deceives someone else; for example, in research on "therapeutic privilege" the researcher would observe physicians lying to patients when the physician believes that the truth would be harmful.

The last four approaches to deception seem more objectionable than the first three—but why? The following are ethical objections (as opposed to actual harms) that seem most pertinent to one or more of these kinds of deception:

1. *Invasion of privacy.* The researcher extracts kinds of information that subjects might not wish to reveal.
2. *No informing.* Subjects are not told what to expect regarding procedures or risks.
3. *No self-determination.* Subjects do not have an opportunity to decide whether to participate in the study.
4. *No debriefing.* The researcher does not explain the deception after the study is completed (and in-

| | **TABLE 1** | | | | | |

Potential Ethical Objections to Kinds of Deception

| | **Potential Ethical Objection** | | | | | |
Kind of Deception	Invades Privacy	No Consent	No Self-Determination	No Debriefing	Researcher Lies	Researcher Conceals
Informed consent	1	1	1	1	1	4
Consent to deception	3	1	1	1	1	4
Waives informing	3	4	1	2	4	4
False informing	4	4	4	2	4	4
No informing[a]	4	4	4	3	4	4
Self-deception	4	3	3	3	2	3
Third-party deception	4	4	4	3	2	4

Note. 1 = never; 2 = possibly; 3 = probably; 4 = always.

deed it may be imprudent for him or her to do so).

5. *Researcher lies.* The researcher actively falsifies or misrepresents pertinent information.

6. *Researcher conceals pertinent information.*

As Table 1 indicates, the last four approaches to deception are indeed more likely to be ethically objectionable than are the first three. These strong forms of deception deny people the right of self-determination. In contrast, the weaker forms of deception provide varying degrees of accurate information and are respectful of autonomy.

. . .

Topic of the Deception

Subjects may be deceived about various kinds of things:

1. They may be given, or be caused to hold, false information about the main purpose of the study.

2. They may be given false information concerning stimulus materials (bogus devices). . . .

3. The use of a confederate may cause them to misunderstand the actual role of some individual (role deception).

4. They may be given false feedback about themselves.

5. They may be given false feedback about another person.

6. They may be kept unaware of being subjects in research.

7. They may be unaware that a study was in progress at the time of manipulation or measurement, or unaware of being measured (e.g., video-taped).

8. Two related studies may be presented as unrelated.

None of these deceptive events is necessarily unethical or harmful; for example, the popular TV show *Candid Camera* employed all of these devices and was not regarded by the public as wrong or harmful. But in conjunction with certain other aspects of deception, these deceptive events may be harmful or unethical.

Debriefing

Finally, the deception and its effects may be undone or not. Debriefing has two possible parts. *Dehoaxing* means explaining what really happened. *Desensitizing* means removing any emotional harm, thus returning the person to at least as good a condition as before the study. Unfortunately, dehoaxing is not always possible, feasible, or harmless, and it is not always obvious what emotional harm remains or how to remove it. . . .

Participant Partners: College Students Weigh the Costs and Benefits of Deceptive Research

Celia B. Fisher and Denise Fyrberg

. . .

According to the American Psychological Association's (APA's) *Ethical Principles of Psychologists and Code of Conduct* (hereinafter, *Ethical Principles*), investigators considering the use of deceptive methodologies have special ethical responsibility to determine (a) that the deceptive techniques are justified by the study's prospective scientific, educational, or applied value and whether equally effective alternative procedures are feasible; (b) whether significant aspects of the research, if known to the participants, would affect their willingness to participate; and (c) that participants are ensured sufficient explanation as soon as possible (APA, 1992, Standards 6.15a, 6.15b, 6.15c). The APA guidelines, therefore, while recognizing that deceptive research practices require special ethical concerns, leave the evaluation of a study's ethical acceptability to the judgment of the individual psychologist about how best to contribute to scientific knowledge and protect human welfare. When an ethical issue is unclear, researchers are encouraged "to resolve the issue through consultation with institutional review boards . . . peer consultations, or other proper mechanisms" (APA, 1992, Standard 6.06c).

In practice, the ethical advice that researchers receive is obtained informally from colleagues and formally through institutional review board (IRB) approval or disapproval of research proposals. Equally important but relatively untapped resources for ethical advice are members of the population who will serve as research participants (Bok, 1978; Gergen, 1973; Loo, 1982; Wilson & Donnerstein, 1976). Although there have been a fair number of empirical studies evaluating participant reactions to deception following debriefing (e.g., Milgram, 1964; Ross, Lepper, & Hubbard, 1975; S. S. Smith & Richardson, 1983), there is a paucity of data on how members of a participant population prospectively evaluate the ethical acceptability of deceptive research practices.

Moral arguments for the need to consider research participants as partners in ethical decision making include respect for persons, beneficence, and nonmaleficence. Veatch (1987), for example, has argued that it is morally unacceptable to consider individuals as "research material" rather than as "persons" who should be treated as human beings with dignity and respect. The principle of respect for personhood includes the recognition that prospective participants are themselves moral agents, with the right to apply a moral judgment to the purpose and procedures of research in which they are asked to participate. A second argument favoring prospective participant perspectives rests on the principle of beneficence (to do good) and assumes that society benefits from scientific research. This position warns of the danger of not using scientifically worthwhile procedures on the erroneous assumption that they would be harmful, when in fact prospective participants perceive them as innocuous (Farr & Seaver, 1975; Sullivan & Deiker, 1973). A third moral argument focuses on the principle of nonmaleficence (to do no harm). According to this position, the participant's point of view, rather than merely professional logic or scientific inference, may be essential to de-

From *American Psychologist, 49,* 417–427. Copyright 1994 by the American Psychological Association. Adapted with permission of the author and publisher. Table 1 has been omitted.

termine the degree of potential distress associated with a particular experimental condition (Farr & Seaver, 1975; Veatch, 1987; Wilson & Donnerstein, 1976). . . .

FACTORS IN THE CONSIDERATION OF THE COST–BENEFIT BALANCE

According to the APA *Ethical Principles*, psychologists design and conduct research "in accordance with recognized standards of scientific competence and ethical research" and "take reasonable steps to implement appropriate protections for the rights and welfare of human participants" (APA, 1992, Standards 6.06a, 6.06d). This dual consideration of scientific standards and human welfare is commonly referred to as the cost–benefit balance, where *cost* refers to the potential risks incurred by the research participant and *benefit* refers to the potential scientific and social value of research [footnote omitted].

Factors to be considered when weighing costs and benefits include the scientific value and validity of the research, the efficacy of alternative procedures, the possibility of experimentally induced harm, the ability to remove such harm through dehoaxing procedures, and the compatibility of deceptive practices with participants' moral values.

Scientific Value and Validity

. . . A study is scientifically valid provided it is designed to yield reliable information according to accepted principles of research practice. Accordingly, in evaluating the potential benefits of research using deceptive procedures, the psychologist must be confident that the design ensures a formal relationship between data and conclusions that can yield scientific facts relevant to the question under study (Rutstein, 1969). The validity of conclusions drawn from a study rests in part on confidence that participants believe the experimental situation to be realistic and take it seriously (Aronson & Carlsmith, 1968; J. Freedman, 1969). In this regard, participant perspectives may be more valuable than professional opinion in prospectively judging the "experimental realism" of a study.

A study may be well designed relative to its hypothesis but be of no value because the hypothesis

itself is trivial (B. Freedman, 1987) or cannot be effectively translated into the body of scientific knowledge or into useful application (Sieber, 1990). Thus, the evaluation of the usefulness of both the experimental hypothesis and potential results of a study to science or society plays an integral role in cost–benefit decisions. . . .

Methodological Alternatives

According to the APA *Ethical Principles*, once having made the decision that deceptive research methods are in accordance with standards of scientific competence, the psychologist must consider alternative procedures before concluding that the methodological requirements of a study make the use of concealment or deception necessary (APA, 1992, Standard 6.15). Implicit in this principle is the position that because acquisition of scientific knowledge about human behavior is itself valuable, methodologies, such as deception, cannot be ruled out if the knowledge cannot be achieved by other means (Kelman, 1967).

. . .

A number of researchers have argued that methodological deception, rather than providing stringent experimental control, leads to participant suspicion and subsequent nonsystematic, uncontrolled responding to experimental procedures (Orne, 1962). This suspicion can lead to role playing on the part of participants who seek to support what they believe to be the experimenter's hypothesis, to present themselves in the most favorable light, or to sabotage the experiment (Fillenbaum, 1966; Masling, 1966). Empirical studies document the influence of participant suspicion on response to deceptive procedures (Fillenbaum & Frey, 1970; Golding & Lichtenstein, 1970; Stricker, Messick, & Jackson, 1969; Toris & DePaulo, 1984). As a result, psychologists have examined whether role playing, naturalistic observation, or self-reports are methodologically equal or superior to the use of deception (Cooper, 1976; Forward, Canter, & Kirsch, 1976; Geller, 1982; Weber & Cook, 1972; Willis & Willis, 1970). Empirical comparisons of alternative methodologies have been equivocal, leading some to argue that the prospects for these alternative procedures are poor (Aronson & Carlsmith, 1968; Miller, 1972) and others to conclude that across all methodologies "subjects tend to act in experimental situations as they act in other public situations, by managing the impressions they convey to others" (Forward et al., 1976, p. 598). Accordingly, one factor influencing the cost–benefit balance of deceptive research is the value placed on deceptive procedures as the best way to contribute to scientific knowledge.

Those who seek to find alternatives to deceptive procedures on moral grounds focus on the fact that by failing to inform the participant of the true nature of the study, deception violates the moral value of respect for persons (Geller, 1982). In making this argument, scholars such as Baumrind (1979) distinguish between *nonintentional deception*, in which failure to fully inform cannot be avoided because of the complexity of the information, and *intentional deception*, which is the withholding of information in order to obtain participation that the subject might otherwise decline. On this basis, some have suggested that during the consent stage psychologists using deceptive procedures forewarn participants that deception might be used and that they may experience some form of the experimental manipulation (Geller, 1982; Sieber, 1982).

Forewarning, however, although addressing ethical concerns, raises methodological issues challenging the scientific validity of data collection. For example, forewarning prospective participants about certain elements of the study may create demand characteristics or participant hypothesizing similar to that ascribed to intentionally deceptive procedures and may threaten random sampling by discouraging participation (Resnick & Schwartz, 1973). In this regard, prospective data on the impact of forewarning on decisions to participate in research can provide important information about this methodological alternative.

Psychological Discomfort in Response to Planned Procedures

According to the APA *Ethical Principles*, psychologists take reasonable steps to avoid harming research participants, minimize harm where it is foreseeable and unavoidable, and never deceive research participants about significant aspects that would affect their willingness to participate, such as physical risks, dis-

comfort, or unpleasant emotional experiences (APA, 1992, General Principle G; Standards 1.14, 6.15b). When participant discomfort does arise in the course of an investigation, the psychologist must provide the participant sufficient explanation and desensitization as soon as possible following the experiment (APA, 1992, Standards 6.15c, 6.18a).

. . .

Participant reactions to experimental procedures may be underestimated or overestimated by psychologists (Gergen, 1973; Sullivan & Deiker, 1973). For example, Wilson and Donnerstein (1976) found cases in which the general public's reaction to naturalistic nonreactive research procedures was negative with respect to ethical acceptability and scientific justification as well as individual reactions to participation. On the other hand, Sullivan and Deiker found that undergraduates rated deceptive research practices as less unethical, more justified, and more attractive to volunteers than did psychologists. Along similar lines, Farr and Seaver (1975) were surprised to find that students would not be reluctant to fill out questionnaires about such seemingly personal issues as suicidal ideation and heterosexual–homosexual orientation and did not see such procedures as an invasion of privacy.

Participant Reactions to Dehoaxing

In weighing the welfare and rights of research participants against the scientific value of the deceptive research design, an investigator may determine that the research entails a risk of producing psychological discomfort. Further evaluation of the experimental risk depends on expectations regarding participant reactions to debriefing. Among the elements necessary for successful dehoaxing are these: (a) The participant must believe the investigator when informed of the deception, (b) debriefing should not in and of itself lead to psychological discomfort, and (c) the experimenter must be aware of any negative reactions so that he or she may successfully desensitize the participant (APA, 1973; Mills, 1976; Sieber, 1983b).

Research on the efficacy of debriefing procedures has produced equivocal results. Some studies indicate that a majority of participants experience no harm from participation in deceptive research following dehoaxing (Holmes, 1976a, 1976b; Holmes & Bennett, 1974; Milgram, 1964; S. S. Smith & Richardson, 1983). Other studies find self-reports of harm and increased suspiciousness (Fillenbaum, 1966; Keisner, 1971; Ring, Wallston, & Corey, 1970; S. S. Smith & Richardson, 1983). Several scholars have questioned the adequacy of self-report data following the experience of being deceived, suggesting that cognitive dissonance, distrust of the investigator, masochistic obedience, deferential compliance, and embarrassment, among other mechanisms, may reduce honest responding on the part of the participant (Baumrind, 1985; Rubin, 1985; C. P. Smith, 1981). In the absence of information from prospective participants, investigators considering the use of deceptive procedures must rely on their own a priori judgments concerning the potential cost or benefits that debriefing will provide.

Metaethical Positions

Moral discussions involving deception include consequential philosophies, most notably *act-utilitarianism* and *rule-utilitarianism*, and nonconsequential positions, most notably the deontological perspective. Scholars taking an act-utilitarian position argue that the immediate consequences of conducting the study, rather than universal moral principles, should govern ethical decision making in deceptive research. For example, Baron (1981) proposed that because deceptive research practices are necessary to accomplish beneficial scientific ends, they are ethical when accompanied by the scrutiny of an IRB, limited consent procedures, and thorough debriefing. The weighing of costs and benefits recommended in the APA ethical guidelines can be interpreted as an example of this metaethical position because according to Standards 6.15, deceptive research procedures are ethically acceptable if they have the potential to produce significant scientific benefits and do not cause discomfort that would affect a participant's willingness to participate.

In contrast, the rule-utilitarian applies a consequential argument resulting in the nonrelativistic position that deception in research is never acceptable (Baumrind, 1985). From this metaethical position, truth telling and promise keeping are necessary to promote an ordered and coherent environment in which individuals are held fully accountable for the consequences of their actions (Baumrind, 1990). Accordingly, a violation of trust is particularly immoral in a fiduciary relationship, such as that of a psychologist to a research participant, which is based on the perceived trustworthiness of the fiduciary (Baumrind, 1985; Cupples & Gochnauer, 1985; Holder, 1982).

The deontological argument rests on the nonconsequential Kantian position that we must not treat an individual as a means to an end. From this moral perspective, psychologists should never conduct studies that either violate an individual's autonomy, and thus personhood, or cause harm to an individual (Goldstein, 1981). Consistent with such an approach, Kelman (1972) argued that the experimenter–subject relationship must be considered a real relationship "in which we have responsibility toward the subject as another human being whose dignity we must preserve" (p. 5).

Most of the discussion surrounding the morality of deception has focused on the ethical ideologies of the investigator. Of equal importance, but less scholarly attention, is the compatibility of deceptive research practices with the moral values of the research participant. . . . [*Ed. note:* The authors describe a study designed to gather information on how prospective participants evaluate deception research. Forty-five male and 45 female undergraduates were randomly assigned to read and answer questions about one of three studies selected from the *Journal of Personality and Social Psychology* exemplifying deceptive procedures. The following is a summary of major results:

1. Most students judged the deception studies to be scientifically valuable and valid and the use of deception important even when alternative methodologies were available.

2. A majority believed that individuals would be less willing to participate if they were forewarned that the study might include deception, supporting those who argue that forewarning narrows the subject population, thereby reducing the generalizability of results.

3. The vast majority of students thought that participants would believe the researcher when they

were told of the deception; but about 50% thought that they would also be embarrassed by debriefing revelations, and most of these thought they would not reveal these feelings to the researcher.

4. In the main, students thought that the societal benefits of the studies were greater than the cost to participants. Most took an "act-utilitarian" position, stating that the decision to conduct deception research should rest on a consideration of the social, scientific, or personal benefits of the study; the minimization or alleviation of harm; or full debriefing after the experiment. Only 6 of the 90 participants viewed deception as wrong under any conditions.]

The moral ideologies reflected in the responses of the majority of students are consistent with the APA *Ethical Principles* (1992) emphasis on cost–benefit analysis of deceptive research designs. Most of the students believed that deceptive research was justifiable if the study had the potential to produce scientific or societal benefits or if harm was minimal or alleviated during debriefing. Many of the students operating within a nonconsequential framework saw avoidance of harm rather than deception as the major moral imperative for the conduct of psychological research. Thus, the moral positions reflected in the responses of the students we surveyed did not indicate that they found deception per se to be inconsistent with their own moral principles.

THE CHALLENGE OF INVESTIGATOR–PARTICIPANT PARTNERSHIPS

Majority Rule

When using prospective participant surveys in ethical evaluations of deceptive research, investigators and ethics review committees need to consider the emphasis given to majority versus minority opinions (Wilson & Donnerstein, 1976). . . .

. . . [I]individual psychologists and IRB members must struggle . . . with the question of whether a particular deceptive procedure can be justified if a substantial, or even small, minority of prospective participants believe the costs of participation outweigh potential social benefits. For example, from

40% to 87% of our respondents thought participants would be embarrassed or annoyed to learn that they had been deceived, and as many as 27% of the students . . . thought the costs to participants outweighed societal benefits of the deceptive methodology. As Wilson and Donnerstein pointed out, even one extremely upset research participant can weigh heavily on a researcher's conscience and create a potentially devastating professional and legal problem.

One way to empirically approach this problem is to utilize prospective participant surveys to establish baseline responses to research designs that do not use deception or experimentally induced participant discomfort and then to use these baselines as a way of judging meaningful substantive differences in majority–minority ratios in responding to specific deceptive designs. A second empirical approach is to use the prospective participant survey procedure to ascertain individual characteristics predictive of those who might be negatively impacted by the study. The results of such a survey should not, however, be used to screen out prospective participants because this would inequitably exclude them from our base of scientific understanding (see Rawls, 1971, on the moral value of justice). Rather, knowledge of individual differences in response to descriptions of deceptive procedures can be applied to the design of individually tailored informed consent and debriefing procedures (Fisher & Rosendahl, 1990).

Description Versus Prescription

. . . We do not propose that empirical information on the reactions of prospective participants to research designs be a deciding criterion for ethics approval or disapproval of deceptive research. Empirical information can assist but not substitute for ethical decisions by individual psychologists and their IRBs on the basis of the moral values of beneficence, respect, and justice. Using prospective participant opinions in ethical decision making will help realize these moral principles by contributing to the design and approval of research that protects the participant's welfare and treats participants with the respect due all persons as moral agents in their own right.

References

American Psychological Association, Committee on Ethical Standards in Psychological Research. (1973). *Ethical principles in the conduct of research with human participants*. Washington, DC: Author.

American Psychological Association. (1992). Ethical principles of psychologists and code of conduct. *American Psychologist, 47,* 1597–1611.

Aronson, E., & Carlsmith, J. M. (1968). Experimentation in social psychology. In G. Lindzey & E. Aronson (Eds.), *The handbook of social psychology* (Vol. 2, pp. 1–79). Reading, MA: Addison-Wesley.

Baron, R. A. (1981). The "Costs of deception" revisited: An openly optimistic rejoinder. *IRB: A Review of Human Subjects Research, 3,* 8–10.

Baumrind, D. (1979). IRBs and social science research: The costs of deception. *IRB: A Review of Human Subjects Research, 1,* 1–4.

Baumrind, D. (1985). Research using intentional deception: Ethical issues revisited. *American Psychologist, 40,* 165–174.

Baumrind, D. (1990). Doing good well. In C. B. Fisher & W. W. Tryon (Eds.), *Ethics in applied developmental psychology: Emerging issues in an emerging field* (pp. 17–28). Norwood, NJ: Ablex.

Bok, S. (1978). *Lying: Moral choice in public and private life*. New York: Pantheon.

Cooper, J. (1976). Deception and role playing: On telling the good guys from the bad guys. *American Psychologist, 31,* 605–610.

Cupples, B., & Gochnauer, M. (1985). The investigator's duty not to deceive. *IRB: A Review of Human Subjects Research, 7,* 1–6.

Farr, J. L., & Seaver, W. B., (1975). Stress and discomfort in psychological research: Subject perceptions of experimental procedures. *American Psychologist, 30,* 770–773.

Fillenbaum, S. (1966). Prior deception and subsequent experimental performance: The "faithful" subject. *Journal of Personality and Social Psychology, 4,* 532–537.

Fillenbaum, S., & Frey, R. (1970). More on the "faithful" subject. *Journal of Personality and Social Psychology, 38,* 43–51.

Fisher, C. B., & Rosendahl, S. A., (1990). Psychological risks and remedies of research participation. In C. B. Fisher & W. W. Tryon (Eds.), *Ethics in applied developmental psychology: Emerging issues in an emerging field* (pp. 43–60). Norwood, NJ: Ablex.

Forward, J., Canter, R., & Kirsch, N. (1976). Role-enactment and deception methodologies: Alternative paradigms. *American Psychologist, 31,* 595–604.

Freedman, B. (1987). Scientific value and validity as ethical requirements for research: A proposed explication. *IRB: A Review of Human Subjects Research, 9,* 7–10.

Freedman, J. (1969). Role playing: Psychology by consensus. *Journal of Personality and Social Psychology, 13,* 107–114.

Geller, D. M. (1982). Alternatives to deception: Why, what, and how? In J. E. Sieber (Ed.), *The ethics of social research: Surveys and experiments* (pp. 40–55). New York: Springer-Verlag.

Gergen, K. J. (1973). The codification of research ethics: Views of a doubting Thomas. *American Psychologist, 8,* 907–912.

Golding, S. L., & Lichtenstein, E. (1970). Confession of awareness and prior knowledge of deception as a function of interview set and approval motivation. *Journal of Personality and Social Psychology, 14,* 213–223.

Goldstein, R. (1981). On deceptive rejoinders about deceptive research: A reply to Baron. *IRB: A Review of Human Subjects Research, 3,* 5–6.

Holder, A. R. (1982). Do researchers and subjects have a fiduciary relationship? *IRB: A Review of Human Subjects Research, 4,* 6–7.

Holmes, D. S. (1976a). Debriefing after psychological experiments: 1. Effectiveness of postdeception dehoaxing. *American Psychologist, 31,* 858–867.

Holmes, D. S. (1976b). Debriefing after psychological experiments: 2. Effectiveness of postdeception desensitizing. *American Psychologist, 31,* 868–875.

Holmes, D. S., & Bennett, D. H. (1974). Experiments to answer questions raised by the use of deception in psychological research: 1. Role playing as an alternative to deception; 2. Effectiveness of debriefing after a deception; 3. Effect of informed consent on deception. *Journal of Personality and Social Psychology, 29,* 348–367.

Keisner, R. (1971). *Debriefing and responsiveness to overt experimenter expectancy cues*. Unpublished manuscript, Long Island University, NY.

Kelman, H. C. (1967). Human use of human subjects: The problem of deception in social psychological experiments. *Psychological Bulletin, 27,* 1–11.

Kelman, H. C. (1972). The rights of the subject in social research: An analysis in terms of relative power and legitimacy. *American Psychologist, 27,* 1–11.

Loo, C. M. (1982). Vulnerable populations: Case studies in crowding research. In J. E. Sieber (Ed.), *The ethics of social research: Surveys and experiments* (pp. 105–129). New York: Springer-Verlag.

Masling, J. (1966). Role-related behavior of the subject and psychologist and its effects upon psychological data. *Nebraska Symposium on Motivation, 14,* 67–103.

Milgram, S. (1964). Issues in the study of obedience: A reply to Baumrind. *American Psychologist, 19*, 848–852.

Miller, A. G. (1972). Role-playing, an alternative to deception: A review of the evidence. *American Psychologist, 27*, 623–636.

Mills, J. (1976). A procedure for explaining experiments involving deception. *Personality and Social Psychology Bulletin, 2*, 3–13.

Orne, M. T. (1962). On the social psychology of the psychological experiment: With particular reference to demand characteristics and their implications. *American Psychologist, 17*, 776–783.

Rawls, J. (1971). *A theory of justice.* Cambridge, MA: Harvard University Press.

Resnick, J. H., & Schwartz, T. (1973). Ethical standards as an independent variable in psychological research. *American Psychologist, 28*, 134–139.

Ring, K., Wallston, K., & Corey, M. (1970). Mode of debriefing as a factor affecting subjective reaction to a Milgram-type obedience experiment: An ethical inquiry. *Journal of Representative Research in Social Psychology, 1*, 67–88.

Ross, L., Lepper, M. R., & Hubbard, M. (1975). Perseverance in self-perception and social perception: Biased attributional processes in the debriefing paradigm. *Journal of Personality and Social Psychology, 32*, 880–892.

Rubin, Z. (1985). Deceiving ourselves about deception: Comment on Smith and Richardson's "Amelioration of deception and harm in psychological research." *Journal of Personality and Social Psychology, 48*, 252–253.

Rutstein, D. D. (1969). The ethical design of human experiments. In P. Freund (Ed.), *Experimentation with human subjects* (pp. 383–401). New York: Braziller Daedulus Library.

Sieber, J. E. (1982). Kinds of deception and the wrongs they may involve. *IRB: A Review of Human Subjects Research, 4*, 1–5.

Sieber, J. E. (1983b). The nature and limits of debriefing. *IRB: A Review of Human Subjects Research, 5*, 1–4.

Sieber, J. E. (1990). How to be ethical in applied developmental psychology: Examples from research on adolescent drinking behavior. In C. B. Fisher & W. W. Tryon (Eds.), *Ethics in applied development psychology: Emerging issues in an emerging field* (pp. 61–78). Norwood, NJ: Ablex.

Smith, C. P. (1981). How (un)acceptable is research involving deception? *IRB: A Review of Human Subjects Research, 3*, 1–4.

Smith, S. S., & Richardson, D. (1983). Amelioration of deception and harm in psychological research. *Journal of Personality and Social Psychology, 44*, 1075–1082.

Stricker, L. J., Messick, S., & Jackson, D. N. (1969). Evaluating deception in psychological research. *Psychological Bulletin, 71*, 343–351.

Sullivan, D. S., & Deiker, T. E. (1973). Subject–experimenter perceptions of ethical issues in human research. *American Psychologist, 28*, 587–591.

Toris, C., & DePaulo, B. M. (1984). Effects of actual deception and suspiciousness of deception on interpersonal perceptions. *Journal of Personality and Social Psychology, 47*, 1063–1073.

Veatch, R. M. (1987). *The patient as partner.* Bloomington: Indiana University Press.

Weber, S. J., & Cook, T. D. (1972). Subject effects in laboratory research: An examination of subject roles, demand characteristics, and valid inference. *Psychological Bulletin, 77*, 273–295.

Willis, R., & Willis, Y. (1970). Role playing versus deception: An experimental comparison. *Journal of Personality and Social Psychology, 16*, 472–477.

Wilson, D. W., & Donnerstein, W. (1976). Legal and ethical aspects of nonreactive social psychological research: An excursion into the public mind. *American Psychologist, 31*, 765–773.

◆ ◆ ◆

Commentary: For other perspectives on the views of research subjects regarding deception, see:

Aguinis, H., & Handelsman, M. M. (1997). Ethical issues in the use of the bogus pipeline. Journal of Applied Social Psychology, 27, *557–573. [Ed. Note: The bogus pipeline is a set of procedures that leads participants to believe the researchers have a sophisticated, infallible lie detector to evaluate participants' responses.]*

Soliday, E., & Stanton, A. L. (1995). Deceived versus nondeceived participant's perceptions of scientific and applied psychology. Ethics and Behavior, 5, *87–104.*

Taylor, K. M., & Sheppard, J. A. (1996). Probing suspicion among participants in deception research. American Psychologist, 51, *886–887.*

For a renewal of the debate over whether psychology ought to ban deception outright, compare:

Ortmann, A., & Hertwig, R. (1997). Is deception acceptable? American Psychologist, 52, *746–747; and*

Ortmann, A., & Hertwig, R. (1998). The question remains: Is deception acceptable? American Psychologist, 53, *806–807.*

Broder, A. (1998). Deception can be acceptable. American Psychologist, 53, 805–806;

Kimmel, A. J. (1998). In defense of deception. American Psychologist, 53, 803–805; and

Korn, J. H. (1998). The reality of deception. American Psychologist, 53, 805.

If research participants will, indeed, be embarrassed to find during debriefing that they were deceived, then can any deception research pass muster under Standard 6.15(b) of the APA's 1992 Ethical Principles, which forbids psychologists from ever deceiving "research participants about significant aspects that would affect their willingness to participate, such as physical risks, discomfort, or unpleasant emotional experiences?"

In light of the preceding material, it would be helpful to review the 1992 Ethical Principles that address con-sent and deception in psychological research (see Standards 6.11, 6.12, and 6.15). Which side of the "scientist versus humanist" ledger do these provisions fall on? Do they address Baumrind's concerns? If you were contemplating doing research that involved deception, would these standards be an adequate guide to help you avoid ethical pitfalls?

Designing and conducting psychotherapy research presents special ethical problems, particularly because scientific rigor may conflict with clinical care. A prime example is the controlled clinical trial in which some groups may receive placebo treatment or no treatment at all. The brief excerpt below provides an introduction to the ethical dilemmas that arise when conducting clinical trials.

Informed Consent and Deception in Psychotherapy Research: An Ethical Analysis

Richard T. Lindsey

. . .

One the most problematic of ethical dilemmas . . . is the use of "placebos" in counseling and clinical research. Placebos, by definition, are inert and not expected or designed to do anything really helpful for the subject. By contrast, when people enter treatment and develop a contact with a therapist/ agency, it is with the understanding they will receive an active treatment designed to help them. If clients are given a placebo in place of the active treatment they seek, that contract is violated. In addition, if and when clients discover that they have received a placebo rather than the active treatment they sought, they may feel angered and betrayed by a profession committed to their betterment. As a result, their autonomous choice is violated by using inaccurate and insufficient information. The principle of nonmaleficence is also violated because the possibility of deterioration in the absence of psychotherapy cannot be eliminated. Finally, the principle of beneficence is violated, for they may be no better after "treatment" than before. These ethical violations would be all the more severe in cases where effective alternative forms of treatment were available (O'Leary & Borkovec, 1978). These arguments could hold for no-treatment control groups as well.

It is important to point out that there do seem to be alternative designs available that could be used in place of placebos and no-treatment control groups. For example, O'Leary and Borkovec (1978) argue that since placebo conditions are difficult to create, researchers ought to compare a treatment of interest with an alternative treatment which also appears to be effective for a problem.

As long as two treatments are equated for duration of contact time and other nonspecific variables, and as long as independent assessments . . . indicate equivalent generation of expectancy for improvement through the treatment trial, such a design provides control for some of the usual factors addressed by placebo conditions. (p. 826)

Also, by replacing control groups with comparison groups, as O'Leary and Borkovec have argued ought to be done for placebo groups, we avoid the ethical problem of leaving some clients without treatment who stand in need of it.

The one exception to this procedure would be in situations where resources are scarce, such that the relatively large number of clients needing treatment exceed the available psychotherapists. In such a situation, to randomly assign some to no-treatment control groups would be ethically acceptable (Stricker, 1982).

By using comparison groups, the assignment of clients to the various treatment groups becomes important. It would seem that randomization is the wisest choice, with each client being informed that s/he will be randomly assigned to one of a number of treatments, each of which is viewed as potentially capable of being helpful (Stricker, 1982; O'Leary & Borkovec, 1978). The clients could then make an informed choice (O'Leary & Borkovec, 1978) as to whether they would be willing to be randomly assigned or not. At the conclusion of the study, if one particular method proved to be the more effective treatment, then it could be offered to members of the other treatment groups if they still needed assistance (Stricker, 1982). . . .

References

O'Leary, K. D., & Borkovec, T. D. (1978). Conceptual, methodological, and ethical problems of placebo groups in psychotherapy research. *American Psychologist, 33,* 821–830.

Stricker, G. (1982). Ethical issues in psychotherapy research. In M. Rosenbaum (Ed.), *Ethics and values in psychotherapy: A guidebook.* New York: Free Press, pp. 403–424.

◆　◆　◆

Commentary: For a general discussion of the fundamental principles of research in practice, see Bersoff, D. M., & Bersoff, D. N. (1999). Ethical perspectives in clinical research. In P. C. Kendall, J. M. Butcher, & G. N. Holmbeck (Eds.), Handbook of research methods in clinical psychology (pp. 31–53). New York: Wiley. For a more extensive exploration of ethical problems in conducting not only controlled clinical trials but also collaborative research among several institutional sites, see Imber, S. D., Glanz, L. M., Elkin, E., Sotsky, S. M., Boyer, J. L., & Leber, W. R. (1986). Ethical issues in psychotherapy research. American Psychologist, 41, 137–146. They describe a multisite collaborative investigation in which a clinical trials design was used to evaluate the effectiveness and safety of two forms of brief psychotherapy for depression (cognitive–behavioral therapy and interpersonal therapy) in comparison with the administration of imipramine (psychopharmacological medication) and a placebo-controlled condition. What ethical problems are raised by such a protocol? What are the potential conflicts among the demands of science, the traditional reliance on professional judgment, and the ultimate responsibility for patient welfare? In what ways are these problems exacerbated by the fact that, in the Imber et al. example, the patients were depressed? Read the entire article for a helpful discussion of these rarely analyzed questions.

In contemplating these issues it may be well to keep in mind philosopher Hans Jonas's provocative statement:

> *Let us not forget that progress is an optional goal, not an unconditional commit-*

ment, and that its tempo in particular, compulsive as it may become, has nothing sacred about it. Let us also remember that a slower progress in the conquest of disease would not threaten society, grievous as it is to those who have to deplore that their particular disease is not yet conquered, but that society would indeed be threatened by the erosion of those moral values whose loss, possibly caused by too ruthless a pursuit of scientific progress, would make its most dazzling triumphs not worth having. (p. 28)

Jonas, H. (1970). Philosophical reflections on experimenting with human subjects. In P. Freund (Ed.), Experimentation with human subjects (pp. 1–31). New York: Braziller.

In 1979, Mirvis and Seashore complained that the APA's then-current (1977) ethics documents

> *evolved largely from clinical and counseling practice, from research with unorganized subjects, and from a preoccupation with collegial relationships; they do not adequately address the issues that arise in the context of organizational settings.* (p. 778)

See Mirvis, P. H., & Seashore, S. E. (1979). Being ethical in organizational research. American Psychologist, 34, 766–780. Has the situation improved? What provisions, other than Standard 8.03 in the 1992 Ethical Principles, guide the researcher who must deal "with a social system composed of people who have positions in a hierarchy and who, in their collective identity as an organization, also have relationships with supporters, consumers, government, unions, and other public institutions" (Mirvis & Seashore, 1979, p. 766)? For readers who will face this issue, Mirvis and Seashore have provided a helpful discussion of strategies of addressing ethical dilemmas in organizational research.

McConnell and Kerbs (1993) have offered this reminder:

> *Successful research with human subjects depends on the cooperation of potential subjects and the organizations which they are affiliated with as clients, staff, or ad-*

ministrators. Maintaining viable subject pools requires that researchers be viewed positively by both subjects and nonresearch professionals who are involved in the research process. This is accomplished by adherence to human-subject requirements, including providing appropriate feedback in a timely way. (p. 269).

See McConnell, W. A., & Kerbs, J. J. (1993). Providing feedback in research with human subjects. Professional Psychology: Research and Practice, 24, *266–270. Yet, they and others have complained that subjects (both those included in the experiment and those screened out by preexperimental procedures), institutions in which the research is conducted, and funding agencies often do not receive information about the results of research. Only a few have viewed this as an ethical issue. In addition to McConnell and Kerbs (1993), see*

Gurman, E. B. (1994). Debriefing for all concerned: Ethical treatment of human subjects. Psychological Science, 5, *139.*

Sieber, J. E., & Saks, M. J. (1989). A census of subject pool characteristics and policies. American Psychologist, 44, *1053–1061.*

Interested readers have certainly become aware that experimentation with human participants is not the only kind of research that has engendered controversy. As Galvin and Herzog (1992) have noted, "The use of animals as subjects in behavioral and biomedical research has become a major issue with social, political, philosophical, and psychological ramifications" (p. 263). See Galvin, S. L., & Herzog, H. A. (1992). The ethical judgment of animal research. Ethics and Behavior, 2, *263–286. Because of these ramifications as well as pressure from animal activists, like human research, animal research conducted at universities is scrutinized by review boards called* Institutional Animal Care and Use Committees. *In addition to the provisions in the 1992 Ethical Principles, the APA has developed its own policies concerning animal research (reprinted next).*

Guidelines for Ethical Conduct in the Care and Use of Animals

American Psychological Association

. . .

The following guidelines were developed by the American Psychological Association (APA) for use by psychologists working with nonhuman animals. They are based on and are in conformity with Section 6.20 of the *Ethical Principles of Psychologists and Code of Conduct* of APA. In the ordinary course of events, the acquisition, care, housing, use, and disposition of animals should be in compliance with applicable federal, state, local, and institutional laws and regulations and with international conventions to which the United States is a party. APA members working outside the United States are to follow all applicable laws and regulations of the country in which they conduct research.

. . .

I. JUSTIFICATION OF THE RESEARCH

A. Research should be undertaken with a clear scientific purpose. There should be a reasonable expectation that the research will a) increase knowledge of the processes underlying the evolution, development, maintenance, alteration, control, or biological significance of behavior; b) determine the replicability and generality of prior research; c) increase understanding of the species under study; d) provide results that benefit the health or welfare of humans or other animals.

B. The scientific purpose of the research should be of sufficient potential significance to justify the use of animals. Psychologists should act on the assumption that procedures that would produce pain in humans will also do so in other animals.

C. The species chosen for study should be best suited to answer the question(s) posed. The psychologist should always consider the possibility of using other species, nonanimal alternatives, or procedures that minimize the number of animals in research, and should be familiar with the appropriate literature.

D. Research on animals may not be conducted until the protocol has been reviewed by an appropriate animal care committee, for example, an institutional animal care and use committee (IACUC), to ensure that the procedures are appropriate and humane.

E. The psychologists should monitor the research and the animals' welfare throughout the course of an investigation to ensure continued justification for the research.

II. PERSONNEL

A. Psychologists should ensure that personnel involved in their research with animals be familiar with these guidelines.

B. Animal use procedures must conform with federal regulations regarding personnel, supervision, record keeping, and veterinary care [footnote omitted].

C. Behavior is both the focus of study of many experiments and a primary source of information about an animal's health and well-being. It is therefore necessary that psychologists and their assistants be informed about the behavioral characteristics of their animal subjects, so as to be aware of normal, species-specific behaviors and unusual behaviors that could forewarn of health problems.

D. Psychologists should ensure that all individuals who use animals under their supervision receive explicit instruction in experimental methods and in the care, maintenance, and handling of the species being studied. Responsibilities and activities of all individuals dealing with animals should be consistent with their respective competencies, training, and experience in either the laboratory or the field setting.

III. CARE AND HOUSING OF ANIMALS

The concept of "psychological well-being" of animals is of current concern and debate and is included in Federal Regulations (United States Department of Agriculture [USDA], 1991). As a scientific and professional organization, APA recognizes the complexities of determining psychological well-being. Procedures appropriate for a particular species may be inappropriate for others. Hence, APA does not presently stipulate specific guidelies regarding the maintenance of psychological well-being of research animals. Psychologist familiar with the species should be best qualified professionally to judge measures such as enrichment to maintain or improve psychological well-being of those species.

A. The facilities housing animals should meet or exceed current regulations and guidelines (USDA, 1990, 1991) and are required to be inspected twice a year (USDA, 1989).

B. All procedures carried out on animals are to be reviewed by a local animal care committee to ensure that the procedures are appropriate and humane. The committee should have representation from within the institution and from the local community. In the event that it is not possible to constitute an appropriate local animal care committee, psychologists are encouraged to seek advice from a corresponding committee of a cooperative institution.

C. Responsibilities for the conditions under which animals are kept, both within and outside of the context of active experimentation or teaching, rest with the psychologist under the supervision of the animal care committee (where required by federal regulations) and with individuals appointed by the institution to oversee animal care. Animals are to be provided with humane care and healthful conditions during their stay in the facility. In addition to the federal requirements to provide for the psychological well-being of nonhuman primates used in research, psychologists are encouraged to consider enriching the environments of their laboratory animals and should keep abreast of literature on well-being and enrichment for the species with which they work.

IV. ACQUISITION OF ANIMALS

A. Animals not bred in the psychologist's facility are to be acquired lawfully. The USDA and local ordinances should be consulted for information regarding regulations and approved suppliers.

B. Psychologists should make every effort to ensure that those responsible for transporting the animals to the facility provide adequate food, water, ventilation, space, and impose no unnecessary stress on the animals.

C. Animals taken from the wild should be trapped in a humane manner and in accordance with applicable federal, state, and local regulations.

D. Endangered species or taxa should be used only with full attention to required permits and ethical concerns. . . .

V. EXPERIMENTAL PROCEDURES

Humane consideration for the well-being of the animal should be incorporated into the design and conduct of all procedures involving animals, while keeping in mind the primary goal of experimental procedures—the acquisition of sound, replicable data. The conduct of all procedures is governed by Guideline I.

A. Behavioral studies that involve no aversive stimulation to, or overt sign of distress from, the animal are acceptable. These include observational and other noninvasive forms of data collection.

B. When alternative behavioral procedures are available, those that minimize discomfort to the animal should be used. When using aversive conditions, psychologists should adjust the parameters of stimulation to levels that appear minimal, though compatible with the aims of the research. Psychologists are encouraged to test painful stimuli on themselves, whenever reasonable. Whenever consistent with the goals of the research, consideration should be given to providing the animals with control of the potentially aversive stimulation.

C. Procedures in which the animal is anesthetized and insensitive to pain throughout the procedure and is euthanized before regaining consciousness are generally acceptable.

D. Procedures involving more than momentary or slight aversive stimulation, which is not relieved by medication or other acceptable methods, should be undertaken only when the objectives of the research cannot be achieved by other methods.

E. Experimental procedures that require prolonged aversive conditions or produce tissue damage or metabolic disturbances require greater justification and surveillance. These include prolonged exposure to extreme environmental conditions, experimentally induced prey killing, or infliction of physical trauma or tissue damage. An animal observed to be in a state of severe distress or chronic pain that cannot be alleviated and is not essential to the purposes of the research should be euthanized immediately.

F. Procedures that use restraint must conform to federal regulations and guidelines.

G. Procedures involving the use of paralytic agents without reduction in pain sensation require particular prudence and humane concern. Use of muscle relaxants or paralytics alone during surgery, without general anesthesia, is unacceptable and should be avoided.

H. Surgical procedures, because of their invasive nature, require close supervision and attention to humane considerations by the psychologist. Aseptic (methods that minimize risks of infection) techniques must be used on laboratory animals whenever possible.

  1. All surgical procedures and anesthetization should be conducted under the direct supervision of a person who is competent in the use of the procedures.
  2. If the surgical procedure is likely to cause greater discomfort than that attending anesthetization, and unless

there is specific justification for acting otherwise, animals should be maintained under anesthesia until the procedure is ended.
  3. Sound postoperative monitoring and care, which may include the use of analgesics and antibiotics, should be provided to minimize discomfort and to prevent infection and other untoward consequences of the procedure.
  4. Animals cannot be subjected to successive surgical procedures unless these are required by the nature of the research, the nature of the surgery, or for the well-being of the animal. Multiple surgeries on the same animal must receive special approval from the animal care committee.

I. When the use of an animal is no longer required by an experimental protocol or procedure, in order to minimize the number of animals used in research, alternative uses of the animal should be considered. Such uses should be compatible with the goals of research and the welfare of the animal. Care should be taken that such an action does not expose the animal to multiple surgeries.

J. The return of wild-caught animals to the field can carry substantial risks, both to the formerly captive animals and to the ecosystem. Animals reared in the laboratory should not be released because, in most cases, they cannot survive or they may survive by disrupting the natural ecology.

K. When euthanasia appears to be the appropriate alternative, either as a requirement of the research or because it constitutes the most humane form of disposition of an animal at the conclusion of the research:

  1. Euthanasia shall be accomplished in a humane manner, appropriate for the species, and in such a way as to ensure immediate death, and in accordance with procedures outlined in the latest version of the "American Veterinary Medical Association (AVMA) Panel on Euthanasia." [footnote omitted].
  2. Disposal of euthanized animals

should be accomplished in a manner that is in accord with all relevant legislation, consistent with health, environmental, and aesthetic concerns, and approved by the animal care committee. No animal shall be discarded until its death is verified.

VI. FIELD RESEARCH

Field research, because of its potential to damage sensitive ecosystems and ethologies, should be subject to animal care committee approval. Field research, if strictly observational, may not require animal care committee approval (USDA, 1989, p. 36126).

A. Psychologists conducting field research should disturb their populations as little as possible —consistent with the goals of the research. Every effort should be made to minimize potential harmful effects of the study on the population and on other plant and animal species in the area.

B. Research conducted in populated areas should be done with respect for the property and privacy of the inhabitants of the area.

C. Particular justification is required for the study of endangered species. Such research on endangered species should not be conducted unless animal care committee approval has been obtained and all requisite permits are obtained (see IVD).

VII. EDUCATIONAL USE OF ANIMALS

Laboratory exercises as well as classroom demonstrations involving live animals can be valuable as instructional aids. APA has adopted separate guidelines for the educational use of animals in precollege education, including the use of animals in science fairs and demonstrations. For a copy of APA's "Ethical Guidelines for the Teaching of Psychology in the Secondary Schools," write to: High School Teacher Affiliate Program, Education Directorate, APA, 750 First St., NE, Washington, DC 20002-4242.

A. Psychologists are encouraged to include instruction and discussion of the ethics and values of animal research in all courses that involve or discuss the use of animals.

B. Animals may be used for educational purposes only after review by a committee appropriate to the institution.

C. Some procedures that can be justified for research purposes may not be justified for educational purposes. Consideration should be given to the possibility of using nonanimal alternatives.

References

U.S. Department of Agriculture. (1989, August 21). Animal welfare; Final rules. *Federal Register.*

U.S. Department of Agriculture. (1990, July 16). Animal welfare; Guinea pigs, hamsters, and rabbits. *Federal Register.*

U.S. Department of Agriculture. (1991, February 15). Animal welfare; Standards; Final rule. *Federal Register.*

◆　◆　◆

Commentary: *The federal regulations referenced in the APA's Animal Guidelines concerning the well-being of primates and dogs were printed in the* Federal Register, *56, 6425–6505 (February 15, 1991), and they also appeared in the* Code of Federal Regulations *(Animal Welfare Standards, 9 C.F.R. Part 3). However, in 1993 a federal court ordered the United States Department of Agriculture (USDA) to rewrite these regulations. In overturning the 1991 regulations, the court said that they did not provide the minimum standards that Congress had intended under the Animal Welfare Act. However, the court of appeals later reversed this decision, allowing the USDA regulations to stand. These developments have made it difficult for researchers constructing animal facilities to conform their conduct to the law and ethical demands.*

Obviously, there have been strong reactions to many of the restrictions on animal research advocated by those who identify themselves as protectors of animals rights. For some critiques of the animal rights movement, see for example

King, F. A. (1991). Animal research: Our obligation to educate. In M. A. Novak & A. J. Petto (Eds.), Through the looking glass: Issues of psychological well-being in captive nonhuman primates (pp. 212–230). Washington, DC: American Psychological Association.

Lansdell, H. (1993). The three Rs: A restrictive and refutable rigmarole. Ethics and Behavior, 3, 177–185.

Volume 7, No. 2 (1997) of Ethics and Behavior *is entirely devoted to articles on ethical issues in the use of animals in research. The entire special issue is worth reading, but especially relevant is: Orlans, F. B. (1997). Ethical decision-making about animal experiments.* Ethics and Behavior, *7, 163–171. The APA Committee on Animal Research Ethics has prepared a video titled, "Guidelines for the Use of Animals in Behavioral Projects in Schools." It is available from the APA Science Directorate.*

The most notorious case in the annals of animal activism concerned psychologist Edward Taub and his laboratory monkeys, whose nerves he cut in an experiment at the Institute for Behavioral Research in Maryland. For an extensive and reasonably balance discussion of that case, see Fraser, C. (1993, April 19). The raid at Silver Spring. The New Yorker, 66–74, 76–84. Partly in response to violent disruptions by those opposed to biomedical and behavioral research using animal subjects, Congress in 1992 passed the Animal Enterprise Protection Act, amending the U.S. Criminal Code (18 U.S.C. § 43). It provides, in relevant part:

SEC. 2. ANIMAL ENTERPRISE TERRORISM

(a) In General.—Title 18, United States Code, is amended by inserting after section 42 the following:. . .

§ 43. Animal Enterprise Terrorism

"*(a) Offense.—Whoever—*

"*(1) travels in interstate or foreign commerce, or uses or causes to be used the mail or any facility in interstate or foreign commerce, for the purpose of causing physical disruption to the functioning of an animal enterprise; and*

"*(2) intentionally causes physical disruption to the functioning of an animal enterprise by intentionally stealing, damaging, or causing the loss of, any property (including animals or records) used by the animal enterprise, and thereby causes economic damage exceeding $10,000 to that enterprise, or conspires to do so; shall be fined under this title or imprisoned not more than one year, or both.*

"*(b) Aggravated Offense.—*

"*(1) Serious Bodily Injury.—Whoever in the course of a violation of subsection (a) causes serious bodily injury to another individual shall be fined under this title or imprisoned not more than 10 years, or both.*

"*(2) Death.—Whoever in the course of a violation of subsection (a) causes the death of an individual shall be fined under this title and imprisoned for life or for any term of years.*

"*(c) Restitution.—An order of restitution under section 3663 of this title with respect to a violation of this section may also include restitution—*

"*(1) for the reasonable cost of repeating any experimentation that was interrupted or invalidated as a result of the offense; and*

"*(2) the loss of food production or farm income reasonably attributable to the offense.*

According to Stanley, Sieber, and Melton (1986; reprinted next), one of the ironies of research ethics is that policies and standards that support the development of ethical principles in research are sometimes formulated without empirical data to sustain their validity. Stanley et al. recommend that future researchers investigate such topics as the comprehension of consent information, reaction to informed consent procedures, and decision making by research subjects. Among the most important under-researched areas is the competency of vulnerable populations to consent.

Empirical Studies of Ethical Issues in Research: A Research Agenda

Barbara Stanley, Joan E. Sieber, and Gary B. Melton

. . .

COMPETENCY OF RESEARCH PARTICIPANTS

Competency to give an informed consent recently has been the subject of empirical studies. A major difficulty with conducting research on competency lies in the lack of a uniform standard of competency (Meisel, Roth, & Lidz, 1977; Roth, Meisel, & Lidz, 1977). Three populations are most often identified as having questionable competency: (a) mentally disabled persons, (b) cognitively impaired elderly persons, and (c) children.

Mentally Disabled Persons

The empirical evidence that is available with respect to severely disordered persons presents a somewhat mixed picture. One conclusion that can be safely drawn with respect to psychiatric patients is that they do no better than medical patients in the consent process. The evidence that they are less able to give consent is somewhat equivocal and to a certain extent depends on the definition of competency that is used. With respect to comprehension of consent information, a few studies have assessed psychiatric patients' ability to understand consent information (Appelbaum, Mirkin, & Bateman, 1981; Grossman & Summers, 1980; Roth et al., 1982; Soskis & Jaffe, 1979). In general, psychiatric patients do not have a very high level of understanding of consent information. However, when studies of medical patients are compared with studies of psychiatric patients, their

understanding seems nearly equal (Grossman & Summers, 1980; Soskis & Jaffe, 1979). For example, one study found that schizophrenic patients understood only about 50% of the material on a consent form that was read to them (Grossman & Summers, 1980). However, in a direct comparison of psychiatric and medical patients, schizophrenic patients were found to be more aware of the risks and side effects of their medication than were medical patients (Soskis, 1978). On the other hand, medical patients were better informed about the name and dosage of their medication, as well as their diagnosis. Psychiatric patients' poor knowledge of their diagnosis may have been partly the result of a general reluctance by hospital staff to tell patients that they have schizophrenia.

Related to the comprehension level of psychiatric patients are studies that have examined their literacy skills. Although acutely hospitalized psychiatric patients' comprehension of consent information seems to be equal to that of medical patients, research indicates that reading comprehension scores of chronic patients are only at the fifth-grade level (Berg & Hammit, 1980; Coles, Roth, & Pollack, 1978). Thus, hospital documents should be simplified for psychiatric patients (Berg & Hammit, 1980), as some have suggested they be for medical patients. . . .

Overall, the empirical research on informed consent shows that psychiatric patients do have some impairment in their abilities. However, the research also shows that in some respects they do not differ from medical patients. As a result, further studies

From *American Psychologist, 7*, 735–741. Copyright 1987 by the American Psychological Association. Adapted with permission of the author and publisher.

that use comparison groups, particularly medical patients, are necessary to draw conclusions about the competency of mentally disordered persons as a group to consent to research.

Cognitively Impaired Elderly Persons

Studies of the elderly have shown some impairment in their ability to comprehend consent information (Stanley, Guido, Stanley, & Shortell, 1984). Impaired recall of consent information has been noted in elderly persons who have poor verbal skills (Taub, 1980). However, it appears that the overall quality of decision making is not affected by age, although comprehension and recall may be (Stanley et al., 1984). In other words, elderly people typically reach decisions regarding agreement to proposed procedures that are similar to those of younger people.

Children

As with the other groups, the competence of minors to consent to research probably is often underestimated. A large body of research has developed about children's competence in making personal decisions, including consent to treatment (see generally Melton, 1984; Melton, Koocher, & Saks, 1983). Generally, such studies show that even elementary school children commonly are able to express a preference and, indeed, to make the same decision that average adults make (Weithorn & Campbell, 1982). By age 14, for most decisions, minors are as competent as adults to understand and weigh the risks and benefits of the available alternatives.

Few studies have examined minors' competence to consent to research. However, the studies that are available are consistent with the general findings about minors' decision making (Keith-Spiegel, 1983; Keith-Spiegel & Maas, 1981; Lewis, Lewis, & Ifekwunigue, 1978). . . .

References

Appelbaum, P. S., Mirkin, S., & Bateman, A. (1981). Competency to consent to psychiatric hospitalization: An empirical assessment. *American Journal of Psychiatry, 138*, 1170–1176.

Berg, A., & Hammit, K. B. (1980). Assessing the psychiatric patient's ability to meet the literacy demands of hospitalization. *Hospital and Community Psychiatry, 31*, 266–268.

Coles, G., Roth, L., & Pollack, L. (1978). Literacy skills of long-term hospitalized mental patients. *Hospital and Community Psychiatry, 29*, 512–516.

Grossman, L., & Summers, F. (1980). A study of the capacity of schizophrenic patients to give informed consent. *Hospital and Community Psychiatry, 31*, 205–207.

Keith-Spiegel, P. (1983). Children and consent to participate in research. In G. B. Melton, G. P. Koocher, & M. J. Saks (Eds.), *Children's competence to consent* (pp. 179–211). New York: Plenum Press.

Keith-Spiegel, P., & Maas, T. (1981, August). *Consent to research: Are there developmental differences?* Paper presented at the meeting of the American Psychological Association, Los Angeles, CA.

Lewis, C. E., Lewis, M. A., & Ifekwunigue, M. (1978). Informed consent by children and participation in an influenza vaccine trial. *American Journal of Public Health, 68*, 1079–1082.

Meisel, A., Roth, L., & Lidz, C. (1977). Towards a model of the legal doctrine of informed consent. *American Journal of Psychiatry, 134*, 285–289.

Melton, G. B. (1984). Developmental psychology and the law: The state of the art. *Journal of Family Law, 22*, 445–482.

Melton, G. B., Koocher, G. P., & Saks, M. J. (Eds.). (1983). *Children's competence to consent.* New York: Plenum.

Roth, L. H., Lidz, C. W., Meisel, A., Soloff, P. H., Kaufmen, K., Spiker, D. G., & Foster, F. G. (1982). Competency to decide about treatment or research: An overview of some empirical data. *International Journal of Law and Psychiatry, 5*, 29–50.

Roth, L. H., Meisel, A., & Lidz, C. W. (1977). Tests of competency to consent to treatment. *American Journal of Psychiatry, 134*, 279–284.

Soskis, D. A. (1978). Schizophrenic and medical inpatients as informed drug consumers. *Archives of General Psychiatry, 35*, 645–647.

Soskis, D. A., & Jaffe, R. L. (1979). Communicating with patients about antipsychotic drugs. *Comprehensive Psychiatry, 20*, 126–131.

Stanley, B., Guido, J., Stanley, M., & Shortell, D. (1984). The elderly patient and informed consent. *Journal of the American Medical Association, 252*, 1302–1306.

Taub, H. A. (1980). Informed consent, memory, and age. *The Gerontologist, 20*, 686–690.

Weithorn, L. A., & Campbell, S. B. (1982). The competency of children and adolescents to make informed treatment decisions. *Child Development, 53*, 1589–1598.

◆　◆　◆

Commentary: For more recent studies on the ability of those persons hospitalized as mentally ill to consent, see:

Appelbaum, P. S., & Grisso, T. (1995). *The MacArthur Treatment Competency Study I: Mental illness and competence to consent to treatment.* Law and Human Behavior, 19, 105–126.

Grisso, T., & Appelbaum, P. S. (1995). *The MacArthur Treatment Competence Study III: Abilities of patients to consent to psychiatric and medical treatments.* Law and Human Behavior, 19, 149–174.

Grisso, T., Appelbaum, P. S., Mulvey, E. P., & Fletcher, K. (1995). *The MacArthur Treatment Study II: Measures of abilities related to competence to consent to treatment.* Law and Human Behavior, 19, 127–148.

For a view that the policies and measures advocated in these studies are too paternalistic, see Kirk, T., & Bersoff, D. N. (1996). How many procedural safeguards does it take to get a psychiatrist to leave the lightbulb unchanged? A due process analysis of the MacArthur Treatment Competency Study. Psychology, Public Policy, and the Law, 2, 45–72.

For a series of articles on significant issues related to research with children, see:

Brooks-Gunn, J., & Rotheram-Borus, M. J. (1994). *Rights of privacy in research: Adolescents versus parents.* Ethics and Behavior, 4, 109–121.

Fisher, C. B. (1994). *Reporting and referring research participants: Ethical challenges for investigators studying children and youth.* Ethics and Behavior, 4, 87–95.

Liss, M. B. (1994). *Child abuse: Is there a mandate for researchers to report?* Ethics and Behavior, 4, 133–146.

Scott-Jones, D. (1994). *Ethical issues in reporting and referring in research with low-income minority children.* Ethics and Behavior, 4, 97–108.

For somewhat differing viewpoints on the responsibility, generally, of investigators studying risky behaviors in risky populations, see:

Bersoff, D. M., & Bersoff, D. N. 91998). *Ethical issues in the collection of self-report data. In A. Stone et al. (Eds.),* The science of self-report: Implications for research and practice. Mahwah, NJ: Erlbaum.

Scarr, S. (1994). *Ethical problems in research on risky behaviors and risky populations.* Ethics and Behavior, 4, 147–155.

Although it has been phased out, the APA Committee on Standards in Research issued periodic reports that are still worth reading. See, for example,

Rosnow, R. L., Rotheram-Borus, M. J., Ceci, S. J., Blanck, P. D., & Koocher, G. P. (1993). *The institutional review board as a mirror of scientific and ethical standards.* American Psychologist, 48, 821–826.

Blanck, P. D., Bellak, A. S., Rosnow, R. L., Rotheram-Borus, M. J., & Schooler, N. R. (1992). *Scientific rewards and conflicts of ethical choices in human subjects research.* American Psychologist, 47, 959–965.

Grisso, T., Baldwin, E., Blanck, P. D., Rotheram-Borus, M. J., Schooler, N., & Thompson, T. (1991). *Standards in research: APA's mechanism for monitoring the challenges.* American Psychologist, 46, 758–766.

There are also many well-regarded texts that address the issues introduced in this chapter in a more detailed and comprehensive way. The following are just a few examples:

Boruch, R. F., & Cecil, J. S. (1983). *Solutions to ethical and legal problems in social research: Quantitative studies in social relations.* San Diego, CA: Academic Press.

Elliott, D., & Stern, J. E. (Eds.). (1997). *Research ethics: A reader.* Hanover, NH: University Press of New England.

Kimmel, A. J. (1988). *Ethics and values in applied social research.* Newbury Park, CA: Sage.

Levine, R. J. (1988). *Ethics and regulation of clinical research (2nd ed.).* New Haven, CT: Yale University Press.

Miller, D. J., & Hersen, M. (1992). *Research fraud in the behavioral and biomedical sciences.* New York: Wiley.

Sieber, J. E. (1992). *Planning ethically responsible research: A guide for students and internal review boards.* Newbury Park, CA: Sage.

For timely news, updates, and resources regarding scientific ethics, see Professional Ethics Report published by the American Association for the Advancement of Science.

Certain behaviors in carrying out research may also lead to legal liability as well as scrutiny by ethics bodies. For a review of civil and criminal penalties, see:

Kuzma, S. M. (1992). *Criminal liability for misconduct in scientific research.* University of Michigan Journal of Law Reform, 25, 357–421.

Sise, C. B. (1991). Scientific misconduct in academia: A survey and analysis of applicable law. *San Diego Law Review, 28,* 401–428.

Of interest is that both articles begin with a discussion of the case of Stephen Bruening, a psychologist, who was indicted and pled guilty to two counts of false grant statements, a federal crime.

I end this section of the chapter with a thoughtful critique of the provisions affecting research in the APA's 1992 Ethical Principles.

Will the New Code Help Researchers to Be More Ethical?

Joan E. Sieber

. . .

JUST BE ETHICAL

The code seems to assume that researchers already possess the knowledge and judgment to behave ethically, for in many instances it simply exhorts the reader to exercise such judgment. It fails to address the problem that many who will undertake research lack the required knowledge or judgment to behave ethically. For example, the code states, in Standard 6.06 (d), that "psychologists take reasonable steps to implement appropriate protections" (APA, 1992, p. 1608). What is reasonable? This requirement is neither enforceable nor educational. If the code seeks to educate, it should tell the reader where to find information on assessing and minimizing risk in given kinds of research. Similarly, the code exhorts the reader, in Standard 6.07 (a), to have "due concern" (p. 1608) for the dignity and welfare of participants and, in Standard 6.19, to take "reasonable measures" (p. 1609) to honor commitments to participants. This is analogous to an etiquette book that simply advises readers to be considerate. Etiquette books are useful when they tell readers exactly how to be considerate in situations in which social disasters readily occur. Analogously, the APA ethics code must either tell its readers how to be ethical in those contexts in which researchers are likely to go astray or direct them to the appropriate sources.

. . .

Codes as Useful Educational Tools

. . . [E]thical issues vary with context, and psychological research occurs in diverse contexts. Ethical issues also vary with the times, and the past decade has brought many new issues to the fore. For example, in community-based AIDS research on gay populations, researchers accustomed to unilaterally designing research were forced by the gay community to involve members of their well-educated research population in the research planning process (e.g., Melton, Levine, Koocher, Rosenthal, & Thompson, 1988). Such idiosyncratic problems and solutions comprise the content of contemporary discussions of the ethics of research on humans, yet they are not mentioned specifically in the APA code.

The framers of the code were not oblivious to these idiosyncratic problems. Indeed, Standard 6.07 (d) states that, "as part of the process of development and implementation of research projects, psychologists consult those with expertise concerning any special population under investigation or most likely to be affected" (APA, 1992, p. 1608). In addition, Principle C: Professional and Scientific Responsibility (in the General Principles) states that psychologists adapt their methods to the needs of different populations. Yet how does the inexperienced researcher get from Principle C, or even from consultation with a mentor, to a sophisticated understanding of the needs of the population to be studied, and from there to effective research practice? Few students or researchers are fortunate enough to be able to learn such ethnographic sophistication under the personal tutelage of an expert. Most do not even recognize what it is that they need to know. What do researchers need to know, and how can they acquire the needed knowledge? They cannot acquire these things from the

From *Professional Psychology: Research and Practice, 25,* 369–375. Copyright 1994 by the American Psychological Association. Adapted with permission of the author and publisher.

code. In addition, in most cases, they cannot acquire these things from their institutional review board either.

Basic ethical principles, however, such as respecting the needs and feelings of one's research population and achieving good ends at minimal risk, are universally applicable. Accomplishment of these varies by situation. The researcher must understand the specific needs, politics, and social norms of the setting. This includes the subjects, the gatekeepers, and other legitimate and self-appointed stakeholders who have the power to make or break the research and to exploit or respect the subjects. . . .

REDUCING THE CONFUSION BY PROVIDING PERTINENT BIBLIOGRAPHIES

Psychologists need to be informed, specifically, that the code is not an adequate guide to the ethical conduct of research but only a set of very general rules that must be supplemented with ethical and methodological guidelines appropriate to one's specific area of research. This disclaimer should be prominently located in the code, just before Standard 6.06. It should mention issues that the researcher should know about, and it should direct the reader to a pertinent annotated bibliography.

The following four broad ethical issues are exceedingly complex and idiosyncratic to the context, and they receive virtually no attention in the code: lack of autonomy, research in organizations or institutions, research on marginal populations, and issues of privacy and confidentiality. The nature and importance of these issues should be addressed in the code, and the reader should be directed to pertinent information.

. . .

Psychologists should be directed by the ethics code to the literatures on ethical issues in these particularly problematic research contexts as well as to ethical issues in research in general. The APA should develop and continually update an annotated bibliography of books and articles dealing with ethical issues in each relevant area of research. Such a bibliography could be developed largely out of existing bibliographic material and should include materials in addition to those that have been adopted or endorsed by professional psychological organizations. . . .

The availability of such an on-line bibliography with full-text retrieval capabilities would encourage the responsible researcher to peruse the ethical literature in his or her field. It would encourage enterprising scholars to contribute periodic reviews of selected parts of this literature. In addition, it would provide an important resource for scholarship and empirical study of ethical issues that arise in psychological research. This, in turn, would enhance the effectiveness of the ethical code and simplify the role of those who develop successive revisions of it.

IMPROVING THE CODE

As the preceding remarks suggest, I find the 1992 code for researchers to be adequate if regarded as a minimal, enforceable code and not as a tool for educating psychologists about the ethical conduct of research. However, it may be seriously misleading to the naive researcher in several respects.

Some statements in the code invite the naive reader to assume that there are no issues where, in fact, serious issues may arise. Other statements suggest that there are no solutions to complex problems (e.g., problems of confidentiality), although precise solutions exist. Some statements, in the hands of an unsophisticated review board, could cause undue restriction of research activities. And the advice to researchers to rely on the institutional review board misplaces responsibility for ethical conduct of research. In many cases, the researcher must supply the review board with appropriate literature on ethical standards in a particular kind of research before the board can wisely govern the researcher. The code should facilitate this two-way process rather than imply that the process is one-way.

The following are specific areas in which the code needs to be improved:

Compliance With Federal Law and Regulations (Standard 6.08)

Many inexperienced researchers are unaware of the extent to which psychological research is governed by the Federal Regulations of Human Research. Somehow the code should make researchers aware of the existence of those regulations and of the National Institutes of Health Office for Protection From Research Risk and their relationship to institutional review boards. In some context, perhaps in conjunction with the annotated bibliography suggested herein, the reader should also be made aware of the many regional workshops on research ethics that are partially sponsored by the Office for Protection From Research Risk.

Research Ethics Review Boards

Standard 6.06 (c) implies that institutional review boards and animal care committees are wise and well-informed bodies. Some are not. Worse, some members may have been pressured into service, and some may have sought membership because they had axes to grind. The code should emphasize the importance of seeking understanding and resolution of issues from the literature, as well as from available experts and review boards. For example, back issues of the journal *IRB: A Review of Human Subjects Research* are a far richer source of assistance than are most institutional review board members. Moreover, when a source, such as an article in *IRB*, offers a discussion that is pertinent to one's chosen research method, and when one suspects that one's review board may question the method, this discussion (with references) should be included in the protocol submitted to the review board.

Animal researchers, especially those who study species rarely found in animal laboratories, should be advised to become scholars of the literature on the care and ecology of those species in the research environment. Standards for laboratory animal care often overlook the special needs of some species. To illustrate, the National Science Foundation has sponsored inquiry into the humane care of diverse animal species and found that some wild species do not thrive under conditions generally specified for animal care. . . .

Children

Although much psychological research is done with children, the code is curiously silent on this topic. Parents, institutions, and society at large are sensitive to what is done with children in research. De-

velopmental psychologists recognize many kinds of risks inherent in research on children and adolescents; moreover, these risks vary with each developmental stage. For example, in middle childhood, excessive concerns about physical privacy arise and are replaced by informational privacy concerns in adolescence (Melton, 1991). In fact, type of risk and maturity interact in a variety of ways; see Sieber (1992a) for discussion of risk from a developmental perspective.

The Federal Regulations devote considerable attention to the ethics of research on children, and much has been written by psychologists, ethicists, and legal scholars on this topic. Standard 6.10, however, would seem to imply that one could conduct anonymous surveys with children on any topic or station oneself on the school playground and systematically observe children without permission from parents or the school or the assent of the children. Perhaps the framers of the code consider this issue to be covered under Standard 6.08, which addresses requiring compliance with laws; Standard 6.09, which addresses obtaining institutional approval; or Standard 6.12, which addresses dispensing with informed consent. Others might not get that impression, however. As a former chair of an institutional review board, I can think of many such cases. The code should also point to the emerging literatures on conditions under which parental permission is required and under which a court or other appropriate guardian may act *in loco parentis*.

Inducements to Participants

Standard 6.14 (b) states that "psychologists do not offer excessive or inappropriate financial or other inducements to obtain research participants, particularly when it might tend to coerce participation" (APA, 1992, p. 1609). This section will cause problems for those who study marginal populations such as drug addicts if it is taken literally by their institutional review board. Drug addicts may have no intrinsic interest in participating in research and will participate only if induced by enough money to buy more drugs. Most homeless persons will participate only if offered money or food in return. In short, those marginal populations will only participate if given money, and many advocates for poor and marginal populations argue that they should receive significant financial incentives if their participation is desired by scientists. Arguably such inducements are coercive, but they can cause no risk greater than the risk that exists in the daily lives of those individuals, and, on balance, they can bring about more good than harm to the participants and to society at large. This risk–benefit argument needs to be stated in Standard 6.14 (b).

Deception

Although I agree, generally, with the spirit of Standard 6.15, I am troubled by several aspects of it. First, the term *deception* implies many kinds of activities, some innocent and harmless and other wrongful or harmful; it could mean that the investigator lies, uses mental reservations, lets people deceive themselves, uses deceptive equipment in the research setting, plays a false role, conceals, observes a third party deceiving someone in naturalistic observation, or simply fails to tell the whole story. Deception research might proceed without the consent of subjects, with false informing, with the consent of subjects to be deceived, or with the consent of subjects to participate in a study whose purpose can be revealed or explained only later. Deception research can involve something as innocent as offering people a cookie and seeing whether they will help someone who has just dropped a book, or as nasty as leaving some money on a table and seeing whether people will steal it. Moreover, the induction to do good or harm can vary from being minimal to being very powerful. In short, the term *deception* is a red herring (see Sieber, 1983a, 1983b for a taxonomy of deception and its risks). It tempts institutional review boards and others to think very simplistically about the ethics of psychological research. Yet there are important phenomena such as conformity behavior that cannot be studied without using some form of deception.

Second, debriefing, although generally very desirable, can be unnecessary and even harmful, as explained by Holmes (1976). It must be done in such a way that subjects are left in good emotional condition. If this is impossible, perhaps the research

should not be done, or perhaps debriefing should not be done. What of children or adults who are mildly tempted to take something that is not theirs, or to tell a white lie? Should they be debriefed? Is this not a case in which the research is harmless, but the debriefing is harmful? These issues are examined in *Ethical Principles in the Conduct of Research With Human Participants* (APA, Board of Professional Affairs, Committee on Professional Standards, 1982) and in Sieber (1983b).

Third, there are many ways to do research, including deception research. One needs to examine the kinds of deception research and their consequences and decide which is the most ethical, if indeed the deception is scientifically necessary. . . .

Providing Participants With Information About the Study

The code, in Standard 6.18, requires that

> (a) Psychologists provide a prompt opportunity for participants to obtain appropriate information about the nature, results, and conclusions of the research, and psychologists attempt to correct any misconceptions that participants may have. (b) If scientific or humane values justify delaying or withholding this information, psychologists take reasonable measures to reduce the risk of harm. (APA, 1992, p. 1609)

Providing results and conclusions is generally a great idea, and indeed some research is important enough to be of interest to the participants and is completed quickly enough that they still remember having participated by the time results are available. This is rarely the case, however. Moreover, locating the participants and transmitting this information is often impossible. A more timely and informative piece of information might be a brief, appropriately worded summary of the literature and the rationale on which the research is based. Rarely are the results of a single study more meaty or useful than what was already known about the topic. Also, this information can be handed out to participants at the time of their participation, when it would be most relevant to satisfying their curiosity and needs.

Sharing Data

The code, in Standard 6.25, requires that

> after research results are published, psychologists do not withhold the data on which their conclusions are based from other competent professionals who seek to verify the substantive claims through reanalysis *and who intend to use such data only for the purpose, provided that the confidentiality of the participants can be protected and unless legal rights concerning proprietary data preclude their release* [italics added]. (APA, 1992, p. 1610)

The National Academy of Sciences, in *Sharing Research Data* (Fienberg, Martin, & Straf, 1985), and Sieber (1992b), in *Sharing Social Research Data*, list many purposes for which data can and should be shared, for example, verifying data, conducting methodological research, teaching, reanalyzing by other methods, testing of other hypotheses, building on with additional data sets, extending with newly gathered data, and so on. Moreover, the National Science Foundation and the National Institute of Justice now require grantees to document and share their data and not to restrict the scientific uses to which others might apply those data.

The meaning of Standard 6.25, however, is unclear. It is probably intended to mean that the APA would censure only those who withhold their data from those who seek to verify the findings. However, given the general unwillingness of psychologists to provide their data for any purpose (see, e.g., Sieber, 1992b, Chapters 1 and 8), Standard 6.25 is likely to be used as an excuse for prohibiting other uses of shared data and for refusing to share data with persons who wish to use it for legitimate purposes such as testing new hypotheses, teaching data analysis, or building on it with related new data.

Privacy and Confidentiality

Perhaps the most glaring omission from the code is discussion of issues of privacy and confidentiality as they pertain to research. As research topics become ever more sensitive, it is even more important that psychologists have a correct understanding of issues of privacy and confidentiality. The nature of privacy (Laufer & Wolfe, 1977), especially in social research (Sieber, 1992a, Chapter 5), and solutions to problems of privacy and confidentiality have been discussed extensively. Some clear and specific discussion of these problems and solutions should appear in the code, and an annotated bibliography of this literature should be made available by APA on-line and in hard copy.

References

American Psychological Association, Board of Professional Affairs, Committee on Professional Standards. (1982). *Ethical principles in the conduct of research with human participants*. Washington, DC: Author.

American Psychological Association. (1992). Ethical principles of psychologists and code of conduct. *American Psychologist, 47*, 1597–1611.

Fienberg, S., Martin, M., & Straf, M. (1985). *Sharing research data*. Washington, DC: National Academy Press.

Holmes, D. (1976). Debriefing after psychological experiments: Effectiveness of post experimental desensitizing. *American Psychologist, 32*, 868–875.

Laufer, R., & Wolfe, M. (1977). Privacy as a concept and a social issue: A multidimensional developmental theory. *Journal of Social Issues, 33*, 44–87.

Melton, G. (1991). Respecting boundaries: Minors, privacy and behavioral research. In B. Stanley & J. E. Sieber (Eds.), *The ethics of research on children and adolescents*. Newbury Park, CA: Sage.

Melton, G. B., Levine, R. J., Koocher, G. P., Rosenthal, R., & Thompson, W. C. (1988). Community consultation in socially sensitive research: Lessons from clinical trials on treatment for AIDS. *American Psychologist, 43*, 573–581.

Sieber, J. E. (1983a). Deception in social research: II. Factors influencing the magnitude of potential for harm or wrong. *IRB: A Review of Human Subjects Research, 5*, 1–3, 12.

Sieber, J. E. (1983b). Deception in social research: III. The nature and limits of debriefing. *IRB: A Review of Human Subjects Research, 5*, 1–2, 4.

Sieber, J. E. (1992a). *Planning ethically responsible research: A guide for students and internal review boards*. Applied Social Research Methods Series. Newbury Park, CA: Sage.

Sieber, J. (1992b). *Sharing social research data*. Newbury Park, CA: Sage.

Ethical Issues in the Supervision of Student Research: A Study of Critical Incidents

Rodney K. Goodyear, Clyde A. Crego, and Michael W. Johnston

[*Ed. note:* In this study, 57 well-published and experienced professional psychologists were asked to describe, in free-response form, up to three instances of ethical problems related to student–faculty research collaboration. Respondents reported 114 critical incidents. The results are summarized by category in Table 1. Under the heading "Applicable APA Ethical Principles," provide the appropriate standards in the 1992 Ethical Principles. Then continue with the authors' consideration of each of the categories.]

Kitchener (1984) suggested five broad principles as being especially important bases for ethical behavior: doing no harm, benefiting others, respecting others' autonomy, being fair, and acting faithfully in relationships. These "higher level norms" are broader and more basic than APA's Ethical Principles. For that reason, they are used as criteria for considering the ethically problematic aspects of each of the following categories.

Incompetent supervision. Psychologists recognize that, because of the risk of harm to clients, it is unethical to practice outside their areas of competence when they provide client services. This same principle should extend to the research supervisor, though this application of it has received scant discussion in the literature. Although the critical incidents addressed only the supervisor's methodological competence, another area of competence that is important in research supervision is that of subject matter.

Subject matter competence seems to arise most often as an issue in the supervision of dissertation or thesis research. The ethical tension is between that of respecting the student's autonomy, on the one hand, and that of being able to benefit the student and act faithfully, on the other. In fact, it seems possible to array the ways in which faculty have responded to this matter along a continuum. At one end of the continuum are faculty who would allow each student whom they supervise to follow his or her own interests, regardless of faculty knowledge of that area. Often these seem to be faculty who believe that conducting "independent" research means that the student is to have complete freedom in topic choice. On the other end of the continuum are faculty who define specific areas of expertise for themselves and refuse to supervise any student research that does not fall into one of these areas.

Neither of these extreme solutions is wholly satisfactory. The second approach, however, probably offers the better balance of the competing ethical principles as long as students have the freedom within a program to pair with the faculty member whose interests are closest to their own: Students who feel coerced into research on a topic of little interest to them lose perceived autonomy and may suffer harm (e.g., in their attitudes toward research, in the quality of their work).

The second issue of competence concerns the research supervisor's mastery of research methodology and statistics. Competence, of course, exists on a continuum, and few people are as competent as they could be. However, in the words of one respondent, "Ultimately the authors of articles must assume sole responsibility for all aspects of their scholarly product and their interpretations. It is insufficient to sim-

TABLE 1

Ethical Problems in Faculty Supervision of Student Research

Category	Examples of Critical Incidents	Applicable APA Ethical Principles
Incompetent supervision	(a) Faculty member knows so little about statistics that he refers his students to consultants or other faculty for even the most basic information; (b) Data analysis for a thesis conducted by a statistician without the student's or advisor's knowledge of the statistics being used.	
Inadequate supervision	(a) The faculty advisor to a senior honors thesis was only peripherally involved in the student's research, did not read her thesis draft, and was unavailable prior to the day of her defense meeting. The resulting paper was awful and the student was humiliated. (b) A faculty member participated little in a thesis project and provided minimal supervision. Just before the defense, the faculty member berated the student for the topic as well as the obtained results. (c) Dissertation chair sets inadequate standards for student performance, fails to have the student follow-through on suggestions made by the dissertation committee, and argues that "no one is going to read it anyway."	
Supervision abandonment	(a) "I have seen students dropped in the middle of research projects either because the faculty weren't interested, had moved away, or some other reason." (b) "Three years ago, I was, as an intern, part of a research team that conducted a large treatment outcome study. None of the several papers we outlined have yet been done—and despite my repeated offers to assist in writing/analyzing/editing, I am told my help is not needed." (c) Faculty member gets research teams together, makes them do a great deal of work, says she will write it up, then doesn't.	
Intrusion of supervisor values	(a) Faculty member refused to chair her advisee's dissertation because she was an atheist and the student wanted to study a religious issue; (b) Faculty member insisted her student employ a radical feminist perspective in his dissertation study of campus date rape even though the student did not find the perspective useful.	
Abusive supervision	(a) A student's advisor verbally and emotionally abused her, leading to her hatred of research, self-doubt, and thought of leaving the program. (b) To gain access to needed data, a student was required to join a research team, do work she was not interested in—and to be ridiculed as incompetent in front of the group (her contribution, which ultimately resulted in a publication with the faculty member, was minimized and ridiculed). (c) Professor took student off as coauthor after she confronted his sexual harassment behavior.	
Exploitive supervision	(a) Professor requires graduate assistants to assist in the teaching of his courses. They are afraid to confront him for fear of reprisals. (b) Professor consistently exploited a student's time and regularly insisted that she work on a research project during a time she was scheduled to be in class with another professor.	

(tables continues)

TABLE 1 (*cont.*)		

Category	Examples of Critical Incidents	Applicable APA Ethical Principles
Dual relationships	(a) Dissertation advisor and student were involved romantically, but the relationship went sour, they broke up, and he gave her a hard time on her dissertation research and written document. (b) A professor provided research assistantships and authorships to a student who was in a sexual relationship with him.	
Encouragement to fraud	(a) Faculty member urged students to skew a report of data analyses that failed to support his preferred theory. (b) Student was an RA for a faculty member, doing house-to-house survey: Faculty member told the student to make up data if no one was home.	
Authorship issues		
1. Plagiarism	(a) A GA essentially ghost wrote several chapters of a faculty member's book, but received no credit. (b) A professor published the ideas of one of his students without crediting her. (c) Student wrote a critique of a book; it then was published with the professor who assigned the task as the sole author.	
2. Failure to give (expected) credit	(a) Student and faculty member collaborate on a project; unbeknownst to the student, the faculty member submitted it for convention presentation. (b) A PI wrote up the results of a study and submitted it for publication without inviting the RA (who had been substantially involved) to coauthor. (c) The senior author dropped the 3rd author from authorship on page proofs without notifying 2nd or 3rd authors—who found out after publication.	
3. Giving unwarranted credit	(a) I have observed faculty giving students authorship for activities that likely do not fall under the rubric of authorship. (b) A student conducted a thesis, relying primarily on faculty other than his advisor for guidance and support—then in a nice gesture, gave his advisor second authorship of a resulting article (though uncomfortable, the advisor consented). (c) Faculty member and student are sole collaborators on an article. But when galleys arrive, faculty member adds spouse as third author.	

ply say 'Because the statistician said so.'" There does seem to be a point at which the supervisor's lack of expertise impairs his or her ability to benefit the supervisee or to act faithfully in that relationship; conceivably, it also could cause actual harm to the supervisee.

It might be that a hallmark of research supervisors who could be considered to practice outside their methodological competence is their unwillingness to master new models and procedures along with the students they are supervising (by, for example, joining the student for meetings with the statis-

tical consultant for tutoring in unfamiliar procedures). Fortunately, by tradition there is a committee to whom thesis and dissertation students answer. This can moderate many, though not all, effects of incompetent supervision.

Inadequate supervision. It is possible, of course, for a research supervisor to be competent but still leave students to fend for themselves, with neither the support nor the skills they will need for truly successful completion of their research project. There is no way of knowing what percentage of research supervisors provide consistently inadequate supervision. But it is likely that even the most conscientious of us occasionally is guilty of a less serious version of this type of behavior: providing students with tardy responses to or inadequate critiques of their work (see, e.g., Magoon & Holland, 1984). Of Kitchener's (1984) ethical principles, the one that seems to apply most to inadequate research supervision is that of acting faithfully, although the principles of being fair, benefiting others, and doing no harm apply as well.

Supervision abandonment. Occasionally, a supervisor will fail to fulfill an implicit or explicit contract with the student to see a research project through to completion. The supervisor has not acted faithfully or provided benefit to these supervisees. In fact, she or he actually may cause them some degree of harm (e.g., in graduation delays, in time invested that could have been used more profitably elsewhere).

There seem to be two qualitatively different manifestations of this ethical problem category. In one version, the students participate in a research project, often as members of a research group. They may have done a great deal of work, but the supervising faculty member fails to follow through with his or her promised efforts, and the project is not completed. Because of the power differential or because the faculty member has physical possession of the data, research supervisees are unable to reap the expected (and deserved) rewards of their efforts.

A second type of abandonment occurs when the faculty member leaves the student midway through his or her thesis or dissertation. Although faculty occasionally will do this when they take a sabbatical, this seems to occur more often when faculty move to another university. The degree to which this is a breach of ethical principles (especially those of faithfulness and doing no harm) is moderated by such factors as the stage of the student's research and the extent to which he or she has been given prior information about the likelihood of the supervisor leaving.

It is important to recognize, too, that because research supervision typically occurs in an institutional context, institutional policies and norms have a great deal to do with how research supervision is handled if a faculty member leaves that setting. Some universities, for example, will provide the travel costs and

even some stipend to a departing faculty member in order to see a dissertation through to completion. But if the situation will not permit the department faculty member to continue as the student's primary research supervisor, he or she should be active in helping to arrange the student's transition to another faculty supervisor (just as a psychologist would arrange a client's referral under parallel circumstances).

Intrusion of the supervisor's values. Certainly most people have beliefs about what is important to study and the perspective or perspectives from which that should be done. Research supervision can be no less value free than psychotherapy. There is, though, a fine line between merely sharing those values and actively imposing them on students, a behavior that violates the principles of autonomy and fairness. It is possible to provide reasonable protection to students from this problem by ensuring that the students (a) are clear about strongly held values of faculty members, and (b) have freedom within their training program not to work with faculty members whose guiding values would prove problematic to them.

Abusive and exploitive supervision. Although abusive and exploitive supervision share some similar characteristics, the raters judged that they were sufficiently different to merit separate clustering. The difference seemed to be one of the supervisor's intent: Whereas with exploitive supervision the research supervisor subjects the supervisee to inconvenience for some selfish end, in abusive supervision the supervisor's motive seems to be punishment of the supervisee for some real or imagined "shortcoming." In either case, the offending supervisor is likely to have violated the principles of fairness and of doing no harm.

Dual relationships. Dual relationships apparently constitute a problem in research supervision just as in other areas of psychological practice. Goodyear and Sinnett (1984) have noted that people who choose the same occupation tend to share common values and beliefs, and that such similarities can provide the basis for the mutual attraction that sometimes occurs between faculty and students. Moreover, in contrast to therapist–client relationships, faculty and students interact in multiple contexts and therefore experience fewer boundary constraints on their behaviors. In fact, as Tabachnick et al. (1991) have observed, "sometimes, what with so many social and other types of activities available to both students and faculty on and off campus, boundary blurring seems practically built into the academic system" (p. 514).

The salient issue, though, is one of protecting the student from exploitation, for the power differential is such that the student is at greater risk in these relationships than the faculty member—no matter how well intentioned the involved parties might be. Certainly the critical incidents summarized in Table 1 concerning romantic attachments and research supervision illustrate that concerns about these risks are grounded in reality. The principles of faithfulness and of doing no harm are at issue in these cases.

Encouragement to fraud.   Encouraging students to engage in such fraudulent research activity as faking data or results seems especially reprehensible. To the extent that these efforts are "successful," science is tainted and students are exposed to unfortunate role models who have failed to behave faithfully. As important, though, is the fact that students are placed at risk of harm by such behaviors. One respondent recounted the substantial lengths to which a psychologist, now herself a faculty member, had to go to clear her reputation following an incident of data falsification by her faculty collaborator on a project in which she was involved as a student.

Authorship issues.   Finally, there is the important and often-troublesome matter of authorship credit: Who should be an author and in what order? This matter often emerges as a basis of disputes between or among well-intentioned people who have honest disagreements about authorship. A number of the reported incidents were of this type. It was difficult, however, to identify ethical principles that would justify these situations as being ethically problematic.

It was possible, though, to identify three subcategories of authorship problem that were ethically problematic. The first two of these subcategories involve supervisee exploitation, with consequent harm to the supervisee and a breach of faithfulness on the part of the supervisor. These subcategories differ, though, in that with the first category, plagiarism, the person from whom the ideas of work was taken

may either be unaware of the infraction or actually have colluded in it. Although in the second category, failure to give credit, one or more persons who expected author credit did not receive it.

Some of the more contentious problems arise in determining what authorship, if any, a faculty member can take on an article developed from a dissertation. This, in turn, seems grounded in assumptions about what a dissertation is or should be: If it literally is independent research in which the student has formulated the problem, developed the design, gathered data, and conducted analyses with relative independence, the authorship certainly is the student's. Some faculty apparently believe this is how all dissertations are to be developed. One respondent asked, for example, "Is it ever appropriate for an advisor to coauthor an article based on a student's dissertation?"

In practice, few dissertations would meet such a rigorous standard of independence. This is so because students approach their dissertations with differing levels of preparation and therefore faculty often must assume substantial roles in the conceptualization and execution of the projects. Moreover, students often participate in larger research projects, from which they obtain real benefits.

One element in the debate about what level of authorship, if any, a faculty member should have on dissertation-based articles likely derives from psychology's failure to adopt uniform guidelines for the research preparation of students. Compare this situation, for example, with the practitioner training that students receive in professional psychology programs. For this training, students participate in a series of practica and internship experiences; APA accreditation guidelines provide some general consistency across training programs for these experiences. No such uniformity exists, however, in the research training of students, even in those programs that espouse a scientist–practitioner model. . . . Thus, whereas a dissertation is for some students akin to an internship in research, for many others it is more akin to a first practicum. That is, whereas some students have multiple experiences in conducting research prior to undertaking a dissertation, for too many it is their first research project. In the latter case, it is difficult for the faculty supervisor to avoid making major contributions to the project, thereby earning eventual authorship.

Another cause of authorship uncertainties seems to come from the common use of the implicit metaphor of authorship as a type of currency to purchase resources. Researchers often offer junior authorship as compensation for any of a variety of possible contributions that might be made to a research project, from conducting literature searches to providing access to existing databases. But this metaphor can become a source of problems for the many students who engage in supervised research as graduate assistants and are receiving real currency as compensation. The results of several critical incidents have suggested that the question in many such cases is whether receiving a paycheck adequately compensates for research participation. Perhaps the alternative question is, Does receiving both a paycheck and a junior authorship constitute "double-dipping." (Faculty, of course, receive both salary and authorship for their contributions with no such questions being raised.) In the absence of clear norms for these matters, the best way of handling such issues probably is to have the ground rules for research participation clear to all parties at the outset of a project.

In contrast to the possible "theft" involved in the first two of these authorship subcategories, the third subcategory involves unwarranted gifts of credit. A real difficulty in this case is that the psychologist may operate with the best of motives. He or she may, for example, wish to help promote the career of a mentee. In this way, the supervisor actually is adhering to the principle of benefiting another. A possible difficulty, though, is that if others are involved as coauthors on the basis of having made real contributions to the project, their benefits are "diluted" with the inclusion of the noncontributor (i.e., generally, the greater the number of authors, the less the perceived contribution of each). This raises both the principle of fairness and that of doing no harm. . . .

References

Goodyear, R. K., & Sinnett, E. R. (1984). Current and emerging ethical issues of counseling psychologists. *The Counseling Psychologist, 12,* 87–93.

Kitchener, K. S. (1984). Intuition, critical evaluation, and ethical principles: The foundation for ethical decisions in counseling psychology. *The Counseling Psychologist, 12,* 43–45.

Magoon, T. M., & Holland, J. L. (1984). Research training and supervision. In S. D. Brown & R. W. Lent (Eds.), *Handbook of counseling psychology* (pp. 682–715). New York: Wiley.

Tabachnick, B. G., Keith-Spiegel, P., & Pope, K. S. (1991). Ethics of teaching: Beliefs and behaviors of psychologists as educators. *American Psychologist, 46,* 506–515.

◆ ◆ ◆

Commentary: For a more extended discussion of the assignment of publication credit in student–faculty collaborations, see Costa, M. M., & Gatz, M. (1992). Determination of authorship credit in publishing dissertations. Psychological Science, 3, 354–357. Using vignettes distributed to all students and faculty at seven geographically diverse doctoral-level psychology departments, Costa and Gatz found that students were given more credit by faculty on published dissertations than on nondegree research but that second authorship credit by the faculty member for dissertations was almost automatic. Contrary to expectations, students were more generous to advisors than advisors were to themselves, with senior faculty giving greater credit to graduate students than did junior faculty. Another helpful resource is Fine, M. A., & Kurdek, L. A. (1993). Reflections on determining authorship credit and authorship order on faculty–student collaborations. American Psychologist, 48, 1141–1147. This article was particularly educational because it contained four realistically based but hypothetical cases involving authorship credit, suggested ethical principles to guide decision making, proposed some decision rules, and then applied these principles and rules to the four cases. Readers may not agree with the outcomes, but these cases will surely provoke useful discussion. For three published comments on Fine & Kurdek, see the Comment section of 1994 American Psychologist, 49, 1094–1096. For a study, also using vignettes, that correlates gender and differences in the appraisal of authorship credit, see Rose, M. R., & Fischer, K. (1998). Do authorship policies impact student's judgments of perceived wrongdoing? Ethics and Behavior, 8, 59–79.

Although guidelines for authorship credit appear in the fourth edition of the Publication Manual of the American Psychological Association *(1994), an enforceable provision concerning assignment of publication credit is now found in Section 6.23 of the 1992 Ethical Principles. Other relevant standards are 6.21 (Reporting of Results), 6.22 (Plagiarism), 6.24 (Duplicate Publication of Data), and 6.25 (Sharing Data). For a rare discussion of ethical issues related to the peer review of manuscripts submitted for publication, see Rogers, R. (1992). Investigating psychology's taboo: The ethics of editing.* Ethics and Behavior, 2, *253–261.*

The conduct, reporting, and publishing of research are not the only arenas within the academic environment that engender ethical concerns. Yet, with the exception of the problem of multiple relationships between faculty and students (see chap. 5), few writers have paid attention to a host of ethical dilemmas that may arise in the university. There is beginning to be some literature on the ethics of supervision. See, for example,

Bernard, J., & Goodyear, R. K. (1992). Fundamentals of clinical supervision. Boston: Allyn and Bacon.

Russell, R. K., & Petrie, I. (1994). Issues in training effective supervisors. Applied and Preventive Psychology, 3, 27– 42.

Vasquez, M. T. (1992). Psychologist as clinical supervisor: Promoting ethical practice. Professional Psychology: Research and Practice, 23, 196–202.

Other issues have yet to be addressed in any comprehensive way. The following excerpt represents a step toward filling this void.

Ethics in Academia: Students' Views of Professors' Actions

Patricia C. Keith-Spiegel, Barbara G. Tabachnick, and Melanie Allen

. . . When ethical issues are presented as they apply to academic settings, they largely fall into four circumscribed areas: sexual harassment, rights of "subject-pool" participants, teaching values to students, and scientific misconduct. The general ethical obligations of teaching psychologists—especially those involving responsibilities toward students—have been largely neglected, confined to a spate of articles and book chapters (e.g., Blevins-Knabe, 1992; Goodstein, 1981; Hogan & Kimmel, 1992; Keith-Spiegel & Koocher, 1985; Matthews, 1991). . . .

. . . However, a better understanding of how students view their professors as "ethical beings" could help guide our roles as models and exemplars as well as educators. Knowledge of students' views of the conduct of professors may also uncover areas of misunderstanding between the two groups.

METHOD

Sample
An urban, West Coast (Los Angeles) sample of 200 undergraduate students and a Midwest (rural Indiana) sample of 282 undergraduate students attending large, comprehensive universities completed a questionnaire requesting ratings of professors' behaviors. . . .

Questionnaire
Fifty-nine items in the questionnaire were adapted from the form used in a study of psychology department faculty (Tabachnick et al., 1991). An additional 48 items were culled from incidents contrib-

uted by students responding to a request to supply what they saw to be ethical problems that they had experienced with their professors. Students were asked to rate the 107 faculty behaviors in terms of how ethical they considered the behavior to be. General definitions of unethical behavior (exploitation, causing harm, poor judgment, disrespect, etc.) were offered to assist student respondents with their decision making. Students rated each behavior on the following 5-point scale: *It would not be an unethical act/nothing wrong with this (1), it would be poor manners or "tacky' but not unethical (2), it would be unethical under rare circumstances (3), it would be unethical under many circumstances (4), it would be unethical under virtually all circumstances (5), and don't know* (DK). . . .

RESULTS

. . .

Table 2 shows the percentages of respondents' ratings of ethicality for each of the 107 behaviors.

. . .

Comparisons Between Students and Professors
Fifty-one of the items (the first 51 items in Table 2) either were identical on this survey to those used in the companion article (Tabachnick et al., 1991) or had only minor changes in wording to accommodate student respondents. Responses were highly correlated, $r(49) = -.81$, $p < .011$. (The negative correla-

From *Ethics and Behavior, 3,* 149–162. Copyright 1993 by Erlbaum. Adapted with permission of the author and publisher. Tables 1, 3, and 4 have been omitted.

tion was produced by opposite coding of the response scales.)

These items could not be compared statistically because of differences in response scales. However, six items showed differences of at least one scale unit (after teacher ratings were reflected to make directions comparable) between students and professors.

Disagreement was strongest for "teaching full-time and holding down another job for at least 20 hours a week." Students were more accepting of moonlighting on the part of faculty. Their mean rating was well within the range of ethical judgments. The average faculty rating indicated a judgment between "ethical under rare circumstances" and "don't know/not sure."

Ratings for "requiring students to use electric shock on rats" were also discrepant. Students found the practice to be "unethical under rare circumstances" whereas teachers judged it between "unquestionably not ethical" and "ethical under rare circumstances." Students were also more accepting of "teaching in a nonobjective or incomplete manner," according ratings between "unethical under rare circumstances" and "unethical under many circumstances." Teachers accorded the behavior a rating between "unquestionably not ethical" and "ethical under rare circumstances."

Students considered "accepting an invitation to a student's party" to be "poor manners or 'tacky' but not unethical" on the average, whereas teachers produced an average rating of "don't know/not sure."

"Using university funds or resources to write a 'popular' psychology book for personal profit" was the only item considered less ethical by students than teachers by at least one category. Students considered creating a popular book with school funds to be unethical under many circumstances. Faculty responses were more equivocal, indicating a response of "don't know/not sure."

DISCUSSION

Rather than adversaries, it appears that professors have allies in their students when it comes to expectations of appropriate ethical behavior. When comparisons were possible with the earlier survey of teaching psychologists, students were generally less condemnatory than teaching psychologists were toward themselves.

We would not have been surprised to discover some differences between freshmen and upper division students, but none was discovered. Students apparently enter college with already-set notions of appropriate and inappropriate behavior expected of their teachers, and these do not alter as they mature. We would not have been surprised with differences between ratings made by students living in a huge, diverse, metropolitan city and students in a small, rural, Midwest town: However, there were almost no differences.

We found intriguing patterns in the students' views of the most egregious acts that professors might commit. Defining *egregious* as any action receiving 80% or more ratings of unethical under many or most circumstances, 16 meet the criteria. Practices that could be described as "unfair" because they hinder or bias open competition among students or violate a presumed class contract account for the majority of the acts that students judge to be the most unethical. These are "ignoring strong evidence of cheating," "using a grading procedure that does not adequately measure what students have learned," "allowing how much a student is liked to influence grading," "including false or misleading harmful information in a student's letter of recommendation," "giving every student an A regardless of the quality of their work," "giving a very difficult exam during the third week of school in an attempt to encourage some students to drop the course," "changing the criteria for successful completion of the class in the middle of the semester," and "including material on an exam that was not covered in the lectures or assigned reading." Students appear to be very sensitive to ridicule, embarrassment, or other emotionally upsetting experiences. Five of the eight survey behaviors reflecting these themes were ranked among the most unethical: "insulting or ridiculing a student in the student's presence," "running a film that might offend or emotionally upset some students without prior warning," "requiring students to disclose highly personal information in a group discussion class," "telling a student during a class discussion, 'That was a stupid comment,'" and sex-

TABLE 2

Percentage of Students Responding in Each Category (N = 482)

Item	Rating[a]					
	1	2	3	4	5	DK
1. Using university funds or resources to write a "popular" psychology book for personal profit (e.g., *How to Be Your Own Best Friend*).	5.4	11.2	9.5	28.8	43.6	1.5
2. Ignoring strong evidence of student's cheating.	1.0	3.5	4.8	31.7	58.7	0.2
3. Giving easy courses to ensure popularity with students.	3.9	13.3	14.9	39.0	28.6	0.2
4. Giving academic credit instead of salary for student assistants to perform work for the professor because there are no funds available to hire students.	47.3	17.0	17.2	11.4	4.1	2.9
5. Teaching full-time and holding down another job for at least 20 hours a week.	62.4	16.0	13.3	6.0	1.2	1.0
6. Dating a student.	10.8	25.7	11.8	34.0	17.4	0.2
7. Asking small favors (such as a ride home) from students.	30.9	36.7	18.7	9.8	3.9	0.0
8. Hugging a student.	31.7	22.8	23.4	17.2	4.8	0.0
9. Requiring students to use electric shock on rats.	5.8	6.4	23.4	32.4	29.7	2.3
10. Accepting a student's expensive gift.	16.6	22.0	21.6	24.3	15.4	0.2
11. Teaching classes when too distressed to be effective.	8.3	23.4	30.3	26.1	8.1	3.7
12. Becoming sexually involved with a student.	6.2	14.7	8.3	28.4	42.1	0.2
13. Lending money to a student.	27.2	16.8	25.5	21.2	8.7	0.6
14. Accepting a student's invitation to a party.	38.8	19.1	19.7	17.2	4.6	0.6
15. Selling goods (such as a car or books) to a student.	48.5	20.5	18.0	8.1	3.3	1.5
16. Being sexually attracted to a student.	36.7	27.4	12.9	14.7	7.7	0.6
17. Teaching material that they haven't really mastered or know very much about themselves.	8.1	12.7	16.0	33.6	29.0	0.6
18. Teaching that homosexuality is a mental sickness.	8.9	7.5	9.5	21.8	50.0	2.3
19. Accepting a student's inexpensive gift (i.e., worth less than $5).	57.3	16.0	15.8	6.6	3.9	0.4
20. Teaching a class without being adequately prepared that day.	4.1	38.8	21.4	25.1	10.2	0.4
21. Making deliberate or repeated sexual comments, gestures, or physical contact toward a student that are unwanted by the student.	0.6	2.1	0.8	5.8	90.7	0.0
22. Teaching while under the influence of alcohol.	0.6	1.5	2.3	5.8	89.8	0.0
23. Choosing a particular textbook for a class primarily because the publisher would pay them a "bonus" to do it.	2.1	9.3	11.2	29.3	47.7	0.4
24. Helping a student file a complaint against another professor.	33.2	19.9	25.1	14.3	6.0	1.5
25. Teaching that certain races are intellectually inferior.	0.8	1.7	3.3	10.0	83.8	0.4
26. Encouraging students to volunteer to participate in their research projects as "subjects."	50.6	12.9	20.1	11.2	3.5	1.7
27. Having students be research participants as part of a course requirement (with no alternative way of satisfying the class requirement).	14.3	12.9	21.4	27.8	22.2	1.5
28. Using a grading procedure that does not adequately measure what students have learned.	0.6	4.1	14.1	35.3	44.8	1.0
29. Teaching content in a nonobjective or incomplete manner.	0.8	6.2	15.8	42.3	32.4	2.5
30. Teaching while under the influence of alcohol, cocaine, or some other illegal drug.	0.4	1.0	1.0	3.9	93.6	0.0
31. Refusing to write a letter of recommendation for a particular student because he or she doesn't like that student.	10.2	12.0	14.7	24.3	38.0	0.8
32. Choosing a textbook because the publisher would give the department some free films and software to do it.	11.8	16.4	21.2	33.2	16.2	1.2
33. Allowing how much a student is liked to influence what grade the student gets.	0.6	1.7	7.1	25.5	64.7	0.4
34. Using profanity in class during lectures.	18.0	36.7	17.2	19.3	7.9	0.8
35. Allowing students to drop a class for reasons not officially approved of by the university.	14.7	13.1	36.1	28.0	7.7	0.4
36. Engaging in sexual relationships with other faculty members in the same department.	55.4	25.3	9.1	5.6	3.9	0.6

(table continues)

TABLE 2 *(cont.)*

Item	Rating[a]					
	1	**2**	**3**	**4**	**5**	**DK**
37. Inadequately supervising teaching assistants.	3.7	14.9	28.4	36.7	13.9	2.3
38. Using university funds or resources to create a scholarly textbook.	33.8	10.0	21.2	18.5	13.7	2.9
39. Telling a student "I'm sexually attracted to you."	1.5	18.7	7.9	24.1	47.7	0.2
40. Intentionally leaving out something very important that would help the student when writing a letter of recommendation.	0.0	6.4	7.7	27.8	57.9	0.2
41. Including false or misleading information that hurt the student's chances when writing a letter of recommendation for a student.	0.4	1.7	3.1	14.3	80.3	0.2
42. Grading on a strict curve regardless of class performance level.	8.1	11.4	23.0	35.3	21.4	0.8
43. Using films and videos to fill class time without regard for their educational value to students.	2.5	7.5	19.1	45.0	25.7	0.2
44. Teaching ethics and values to students.	55.8	10.0	16.4	11.4	4.8	1.7
45. Failing to periodically update class lecture notes.	3.3	17.0	26.6	36.3	15.8	1.0
46. Assigning unpaid students to carry out work for the professors that has little educational value for the students.	2.3	8.9	17.4	38.0	32.0	1.5
47. Privately tutoring students in the department for a fee.	20.5	15.4	16.4	23.0	22.4	2.3
48. Taking advantage of a student's offer such as getting wholesale prices at a parent's store.	17.6	25.1	17.8	19.1	19.3	1.0
49. Criticizing all theoretical approaches except those the professor personally prefers.	1.5	9.1	15.8	32.6	39.6	1.5
50. Using cocaine or other illegal drugs in their personal (nonteaching) life.	12.0	17.4	12.2	20.3	37.1	0.8
51. Insulting or ridiculing a student in the student's presence.	1.0	6.0	5.6	23.7	63.5	0.2
52. Encouraging competition among students	36.1	14.5	24.7	17.2	6.8	0.6
53. Ignoring unethical behavior committed by their colleagues.	1.9	8.9	19.7	39.6	28.6	1.2
54. Becoming sexually involved with a student after the class is over and the grades have been assigned.	39.2	24.1	13.5	12.7	9.5	1.0
55. Picking their favorite students to do projects with them.	11.6	17.4	23.2	29.5	18.3	0.0
56. Being absent from class often due to illness.	49.0	22.8	16.2	8.1	3.3	0.6
57. Being absent from class often to travel to professional workshops and conventions.	20.3	28.6	19.7	21.6	9.5	0.2
58. Giving only multiple choice exams as the basis for the course grade.	56.6	16.8	18.0	5.2	2.3	1.0
59. Giving only essay exams and assigning written projects (i.e., no multiple choice exams).	42.5	14.3	19.5	14.9	7.3	1.5
60. Assigning three thick textbooks for a three-unit course.	15.1	21.2	19.1	26.3	16.6	1.7
61. Giving "pop" (unannounced) quizzes.	45.9	19.9	17.8	10.2	5.8	0.4
62. Spending 25–30 hours during the week doing writing and research in their offices or laboratories.	65.4	8.7	13.3	7.1	3.1	2.5
63. Agreeing to write a recommendation letter for a student, but not getting it in until 2 weeks past the deadline.	1.0	15.0	7.3	25.1	50.8	0.0
64. Lecturing only from material taken directly from the textbook.	39.2	25.3	18.0	13.9	3.3	0.2
65. Flirting with students.	4.1	24.3	11.2	29.7	30.3	0.4
66. Humiliating a student for falling asleep in class.	7.1	23.0	25.1	25.3	19.5	0.0
67. Giving an F on a term paper because it was a week late.	30.5	15.1	24.5	17.4	11.4	1.0
68. Not allowing any student to enter the room the instant the "hour" starts.	4.8	17.8	12.0	31.3	33.6	0.4
69. Giving every student an A regardless of the quality of their work.	2.7	2.9	5.8	19.5	68.7	0.4
70. Refusing to let students take makeup exams.	6.4	6.8	24.5	33.8	28.2	0.2
71. Giving only one or two As in each class.	8.5	7.5	17.4	31.7	33.6	1.2
72. Giving 15 hours worth of homework a week for a three-unit class.	10.0	13.5	17.8	33.4	24.3	1.0
73. Giving a very difficult exam during the third week of school in an attempt to encourage some students to drop the course.	1.0	5.4	10.2	35.7	47.7	0.0
74. Setting up a course so that students are encouraged to share aspects of their very personal life in class.	21.2	14.9	26.1	24.7	12.2	0.8
75. Refusing to write a letter of recommendation for a student because he or she doesn't know the student well enough.	48.8	16.4	20.7	9.8	4.4	0.0
76. Assigning reading that is difficult to get to (e.g., articles in journals that cannot be taken home from the library).	5.8	21.4	22.8	35.9	13.9	0.2

(table continues)

TABLE 2 (*cont.*)

Item	Rating[a]					
	1	**2**	**3**	**4**	**5**	**DK**
77. Requiring students to read materials (text, articles, etc.) that the professor acknowledges are "not very good."	8.3	16.4	22.0	36.1	16.0	1.2
78. Taking a "royalty" percentage payment on a collection of previously published readings that the professor puts together himself or herself, and requires students to purchase at the bookstore or a copy store.	10.4	12.7	18.7	28.4	26.8	3.1
79. Not getting exams graded and handed back until 4 weeks after the exam was given.	0.8	19.3	10.4	35.7	33.2	0.6
80. Changing the criteria for successful completion of a class in the middle of the semester (e.g., adding an extra term paper or saying that something was going to count more and changing to it counting less).	1.0	6.0	15.6	31.7	45.2	0.4
81. Announcing exam grades of each student, by name, in front of the class.	0.4	8.1	7.1	23.4	61.0	0.0
82. Running a film that might offend or emotionally upset some students without prior warning.	1.0	9.3	9.3	39.0	41.3	0.0
83. Including material on the test that was not covered in the lectures or assigned reading.	0.4	2.7	5.4	18.7	72.8	0.0
84. Changing the expected format of a test on the day of the test.	1.2	6.4	6.6	28.4	57.3	0.0
85. Accepting current students as psychotherapy clients in a professor's private practice.	11.8	12.2	19.9	25.3	25.9	4.8
86. Ridiculing or discounting the opinion of another professor in a student's presence.	1.9	15.6	16.8	31.3	33.2	1.2
87. Requiring students to disclose highly personal information in a group discussion class (i.e., the student who remains silent or "closed up" is graded down for that).	0.8	2.9	7.5	26.3	61.6	0.8
88. Advising a student not to take a certain professor's class.	7.9	13.7	25.5	30.3	22.4	0.2
89. Giving a student advice in areas in which the professor is not really qualified to offer guidance.	5.8	12.4	25.9	38.6	16.8	0.4
90. Talking to students (in private) about a student's personal problems.	46.3	14.5	19.5	14.1	5.2	0.4
91. Talking to students (in private) about their own personal problems.	18.7	23.0	14.9	24.7	17.6	1.0
92. Telling a student that he or she has problems and should go to the counseling center.	38.2	18.3	24.3	13.3	5.4	0.6
93. Telling a student during a class discussion "That was a stupid comment."	0.8	7.7	7.7	23.7	60.2	0.0
94. Requiring students to watch a film on how to do surgical brain implant techniques on monkeys.	13.1	15.4	21.0	23.9	24.1	2.7
95. Never learning any of the students' names in a class of 30 students.	6.4	37.8	11.4	22.6	21.6	0.2
96. Teaching in jeans and a sweatshirt.	64.3	23.9	5.6	3.9	2.1	0.2
97. Inability to control class (e.g., too-talkative students who dominate class time are not curtailed).	1.7	16.8	18.0	35.3	27.6	0.6
98. Always letting class out 15 minutes early.	43.6	21.0	21.6	10.6	3.3	0.0
99. Requiring students to visit a "locked ward" (most disturbed) patients in a mental hospital.	10.0	11.2	21.2	29.3	26.8	1.7
100. Being more friendly to some students than to others.	9.5	26.1	19.5	27.2	17.4	0.2
101. Telling "off-color" stories or jokes in class.	12.2	22.2	11.8	20.5	32.0	1.2
102. Writing comments on tests or assignments that are illegible.	8.1	42.7	14.1	17.4	17.0	0.6
103. Handing back term projects with a grade, but no other marks on it or indication as to why the grade was assigned.	6.4	23.0	16.4	33.2	20.1	0.8
104. Allowing only students who have English as their second language to use a dictionary during lecture.[b]	12.7	8.9	20.3	26.6	27.6	1.5
105. Offering students no opportunities for "extra credit."	27.6	18.5	23.4	17.4	12.4	0.6
106. Taking points off for assignments handed in late.	68.3	10.6	15.1	5.0	0.8	0.2
107. Grading handwritten papers lower than papers that are typed or done on a computer.	18.5	22.6	24.3	19.5	14.3	0.8

[a]Students rated each behavior on the following 5-point scale: *would not be an unethical act/nothing wrong with this* (1), *would be poor manners or "tacky" but not unethical* (2), *it would be unethical under rare circumstances* (3), *it would be unethical under many circumstances* (4), *it would be unethical under virtually all circumstances* (5), and *don't know* (DK). [b]Row does not sum to 100% because of missing data.

ual harassment. Three items involved the infliction of direct emotionally upsetting experiences on students: "flirting with students," "telling a student 'I'm sexually attracted to you,'" and "humiliating a student for falling asleep in class." Rounding out the list of acts judged as the most unethical are, "teaching while under the influence of alcohol, cocaine, or some other illegal drug" and "teaching that certain races are intellectually inferior."

Some issues that are often informally debated among professors are not generally perceived as ethical problems for students. Defining less troublesome items as those receiving more than 60% of the ratings in the "would not be an unethical act/nothing wrong with this" or "would be poor manners or 'tacky,' but not unethical" category, such items include the following, "giving only multiple choice exams as the basis for the course grade," "lecturing only from material taken directly from the textbook," "giving academic credit instead of salaries to student assistants," "always letting class out 15 minutes early," "engaging in sexual relationships with other faculty members in the same department," and moonlighting.

Although these baseline data provide a portrait in very broad strokes, they provide some insights into how students view the ethical obligations of teaching psychologists. Students, being the consumers of the services of teaching psychologists, deserve to be heard and better understood.

References

Blevins-Knabe, B. (1992). The ethics of dual relationship in higher education. *Ethics & Behavior, 2,* 151–163.

Goodstein, L. D. (1981). Ethics are for academics too! *Professional Psychology, 12,* 191–193.

Hogan, P. M., & Kimmel, A. J. (1992). Ethical teaching of psychology: One department's attempts at self-regulation. *Teaching of Psychology, 19,* 205–210.

Keith-Spiegel, P., & Koocher, G. P. (1985). *Ethics in psychology: Standards and cases.* New York: McGraw-Hill.

Matthews, J. (1991). The teaching of ethics and the ethics of teaching. *Teaching of Psychology, 18,* 80–85.

Tabachnick, B. G., Keith-Spiegel, P., & Pope, K. S. (1991). Ethics of teaching: Beliefs and behaviors of psychologists as educators. *American Psychologist, 46,* 506–515.

◆ ◆ ◆

Commentary: The APA's 1992 Ethical Principles address some heretofore neglected issues in academia, including the design and description of educational programs and the accurate and objective evaluation of students and supervisees (see Standards 6.01 to 6.05). But is the new code too intrusive? For example, should an inaccurate description of a doctoral program become an ethical issue? The code also prohibits faculty members from "personally demeaning" students. What if a teacher writes this on a student's paper or states it in class?: "This is the worst review of the literature I have ever seen. Don't you know where the library is?" Should this lead to an ethics complaint? Although there is probably a consensus that making fools of individuals in the classroom is not good practice, does making it an ethical issue create an atmosphere in which professors' freedom to speak is unduly chilled? For a discussion of the 1992 Ethical Principles relative to academia, see Keith-Spiegel, P. (1994). Teaching psychologists and the new APA ethics code: Do we fit in? Professional Psychology: Research and Practice, 25, 362–368.

She concludes:

> The new ethics code is certainly not without attractive features, but it does not speak clearly and directly to many of the ethical dilemmas that teaching psychologists face in their everyday lives. In some instances the new code poses ominous threats, as when unidentified material may not be taught to students [see Standard 6.04], or the responsibility for minimizing harm that could befall students [is] placed on the shoulders of the teaching psychologists. . . .
>
> The values that teachers in institutions of higher education hold—ideals so dear that they would willingly sacrifice their own welfare to uphold them—are given little weight in the new code. (p. 368)

Perceiving other's disappointment in the 1992 code concerning academic ethics, Keith-Spiegel and her colleagues developed The Ethics of Teaching: A Casebook, *sponsored by APA's Division of the Teaching of*

Psychology. The book is a compilation of 164 cases with commentary. It is available from the Department of Psychology at Ball State University for a modest fee. The Ethics Committee was responsive, however, to the concerns of academics regarding Standard 6.04 (Limitations on Teaching). In a policy statement approved in 1994 and published in APA Ethics Committee (1995). Report of the Ethics Committee, 1994. American Psychologist, 50, 706–713, it said:

> *Standard 6.04 . . . prohibits teaching the use of techniques that require specialized training to individuals who lack the appropriate training or credentials. Teaching about such techniques, as in an undergraduate course, is not prohibited. The standard also does not prohibit teaching a technique that individuals may apply in their own therapeutic programs, such as self-hypnosis. Similarly, teaching the use of specialized techniques to graduate students who are part of an integrated program of study and whose work will be supervised, is not prohibited. However, the student must have the necessary prerequisites to be in the program/course. (p. 713)*

For an intriguing article that discusses a rarely acknowledged but significant problem, see Friedrich, J., & Douglass, D. (1998). Ethics and the persuasive enterprise of teaching psychology. American Psychologist, 53, 549–562.

CHAPTER 9

FORENSIC SETTINGS

The American legal system is complex. One of the complicating factors is that there are two parallel sets of courts: one national network of federal courts and 51 sets of separate state courts (including the District of Columbia). Furthermore, within each there is a criminal justice system and a civil justice system. State courts also have a hybrid criminal–civil system that deals with matters affecting juveniles. Forensic psychologists are called on to provide these systems and divisions within them with useful expert information that, it is hoped, will lead to more informed decisions by judges and juries about human behavior.

A "forensic psychologist refers to any psychologist, experimental or clinical, who specializes in producing or communicating psychological research or assessment information intended for application to legal issues" (Grisso, 1987, p. 831; see also Committee on Ethical Guidelines for Forensic Psychologists, 1991). In the criminal system, a forensic psychologist's traditional role may include evaluating criminal defendants (a) to determine whether they are competent to stand trial, (b) to determine what their mental state was at the time of the crime, or (c) to help the judge or the jury determine the proper sentence, including, in capital cases, whether the defendant should suffer the death penalty. In the civil system, a forensic psychologist may testify about the mental capacity and propensity for violence of someone that the state wishes to involuntary hospitalize (civilly commit) and then offer recommendations for appropriate inpatient treatment. In the juvenile system, the forensic psychologist may offer an opinion, after an assessment, about whether a minor should be tried in juvenile court or waived for trial to an adult court (e.g., when the minor has allegedly been involved in a serious crime, particularly a violent one). Finally, a more academically oriented psychologist may consult with a party in litigation about legal tactics, jury selection, or the influence of pretrial publicity on jury objectivity.

Many of these, as well as other, functions are performed by psychologists who identify themselves as *forensic specialists*. They may belong to Division 41 (American Psychology–Law Society) of the American Psychological Association, or they may have been awarded a diploma by the American Board of Forensic Psychology—signifying that they meet certain educational, experiential, and evaluative criteria identifying them as having forensic expertise. They usually are employed by state-run institutions, but they are also found in community mental health centers and in independent practice (Grisso, 1987). These psychologists, primarily clinicians, spend a great deal of time in the courtroom and are frequent visitors to the witness stand.

It would be a mistake, however, to believe that only those psychologists who identify themselves as *forensic mental health professionals* will find themselves involved with the law.

Every psychologist—whether clinician, scientist, or academician—is a potential expert witness, and each must be prepared to interact with the legal system. For example, clinicians who see children or families may be called to testify in divorce, child custody, or abuse litigation. A therapist whose client is in a serious automobile accident and claims to have been traumatized by it may be called to testify by the plaintiff–client or by the defendant about the client's mental or emotional condition before the accident. A neuropsychologist may be asked to give an opinion about the capacity of an elderly client to make a will or the extent of brain injury suffered by a worker in an industrial accident. An industrial psychologist who has developed a preemployment screening test claimed to discriminate against, for example, people with disabilities, may be compelled to explain how the instrument was constructed and validated. An academician conducting studies on adolescent gang violence or on other socially sensitive issues may be ordered by a judge to reveal otherwise confidential data concerning some or all of the participants in those studies. Likewise, a researcher who specializes in perception may be called by the defense in a criminal matter to inform a jury about the vagaries of eyewitness identification. Finally, psychologists, whatever their training, may wish to inform legislative or regulatory bodies about pending enactments or to lobby for a certain measure.

The psychologist's part in each of these scenarios is guided by ethical considerations. Although lawyers are obligated to champion their clients' causes through zealous and unbridled representation, different ethical imperatives may guide the behavior of psychologists who enter the hallowed halls of the law. This chapter examines the ethical dimensions of three major questions that face forensic psychologists: (a) Should an expert witness be an advocate or an objective teacher? (b) When performing psychological services at the behest of the court, who is the psychologist's ultimate client? and (c) Are there forensic functions that an ethical psychologist should refuse to perform?

References

Committee on Ethical Guidelines for Forensic Psychologists. (1991). Specialty guidelines for forensic psychologists. *Law and Human Behavior, 15,* 655–665.

Grisso, T. (1987). The economic and scientific future of forensic psychological assessment. *American Psychologist, 42,* 831–839.

Use and Then Prove, or Prove and Then Use? Some Thoughts on the Ethics of Mental Health Professionals' Courtroom Involvement

David Faust

. . .

The psychology–law interface obviously involves two systems or institutions in which, however, psychology and law are not equal partners. Rather, in the legal arena, psychology is subsumed under law. It is not the judge who enters the clinician's office and lies down on the couch but the psychologist who enters his or her honor's home field. The legal system dominates in determining not only whether participation occurs but, when allowing it, the rules and procedures under which it takes place.

The court's authority, however, is incomplete. Most important, the potential psychologist–expert usually is not compelled to participate but rather does so voluntarily. For example, although the judge may allow testimony on the likelihood of future violent behavior, a psychologist asked to assist in the determination can refuse the request. The choice to not participate when one could paves the way for the expression of personal or professional (i.e., internal) standards and eases or alleviates the pressure to defer to the court's external standards. Usually, one can make the choice of nonparticipation without violating the rules of the dominant authority structure or without creating legal jeopardy. In contrast, if the law required professionals to serve as expert witnesses whether they wanted to or not, and one's own standards dictated noninvolvement, this would create an immediate legal conflict and put one at risk for official sanction. Of course, one can still live by personal standards under such circumstances, but it is more difficult to do so, and the balance of pluses and minuses may shift dramatically.

Obviously, the court's standards, which are external to the psychologist, and the psychologist's internal or professional standards may clash. At opposing ends of the spectrum are psychologists who always follow external standards and those who always follow internal standards, and in between are various possible combinations. . . .

◆ ◆ ◆

Commentary: *Faust posits that law and psychology operate under two different systems. In what ways is this true, particularly with regard to their respective searches for the "truth" and their tolerance for indecision? Given these differences, one "basic concern is that the ethical standards of the psychologist can be jeopardized in the courtroom setting because of the psychologist's failure to recognize that the basic tenets of the legal system and the science of psychology are often at odds" (pp. 764–765). Anderten, P., Staulcup, V., & Grisso, T. (1980). On being ethical in legal places. Professional Psychology, 11, 764–773.*

From *Ethics and Behavior, 3,* 359–380. Copyright 1993 by Erlbaum. Adapted with permission of the author and publisher.

Reclaiming the Integrity of Science in Expert Witnessing

Bruce D. Sales and Daniel W. Shuman

. . .

Critics complain that many experts who testify abandon their scientific integrity[v] and that the legal system stimulates this result. . . .

Given the importance of expert testimony and the pool of competent attorneys and scientists, what explains the perceived problems with expert witnessing? An important reason lies in the inherent conflicts between the goals of attorneys and the goals of scientists/experts (Champagne, Shuman, & Whitaker, 1991 . . .). Because the legal system is an adversarial system and science is not, the goals of the attorneys and the goals of the scientist/experts differ. Attorneys need partisan experts to persuade the trier of fact (judge or jury), which weighs in favor of the selection of the most articulate, understandable, presentable, and persuasive expert rather than the best scientist. Even when there are good scientists who fit the bill, attorneys have a strong incentive to choose the person whose presentation and interpretation of the data are most sympathetic to the attorney's cause. As Champagne et al. (1991) noted in their empirical study of the use of experts, "lawyers seemingly want articulate, partisan experts with integrity" (p. 387).

Science, on the other hand, demands that scientists focus only on scientific knowledge without the influence—whether subtle or explicit—of the attorney's goals. Of equal concern is that the attorneys respond to current cases, which causes them to pressure experts to reach firm conclusions on the witness stand, even if the science on the issue and the scientific enterprise are tentative and iterative in nature or if the scientific information is available. . . .

Although the law has attempted to address some of these problems (e.g., through the rules of evidence and the cases interpreting them), its solutions have neither quieted the legal debate nor provided helpful guidance to the dilemmas scientists experience as expert witnesses. . . . Thus, to the extent that scientists have placed their hopes for a resolution of this dilemma on the legal system, they have been disappointed. Perhaps the law should not be expected to be overly concerned about the needs of science given that it is not the law's focus; the law focuses on the resolution of disputes between parties.

Prior discussions of these problems by scientists are not terribly helpful. . . . The intervention of a rule or principled analysis could provide a systematic approach to generating insights and guidelines for solutions. To the extent that ethics governs all scientific and professional behavior—which it does—it is only appropriate that it becomes the first metric against which to judge the expert witnessing of scientists and professionals.

. . . [B]ecause psychologists have a well-developed system of ethics that bears on their activities (see, e.g., Section 8.01 of the "Ethical Principles of Psychologists and Code of Conduct," American Psychological Association [APA], 1992, referred to hereinafter as ethics code), an ethical analysis of expert testimony by psychologists is informative. . . .

References

American Psychological Association. (1992). *Ethical principles of psychologists and code of conduct*. Washington, DC: Author.

Champagne, A., Shuman, D. W., & Whitaker, E. (1991). The use of expert witnesses in American courts. *Judicature, 31*, 375–392.

Mental Health Professionals and the Courts: The Ethics of Expertise

Stephen L. Golding

. . .

. . . [I]n the ideal, mental health expertise enters the courtroom in the following steps:

1. An area of expertise, which is beyond the ordinary knowledge and understanding of the trier of fact, is accepted as one which will assist the trier of fact in understanding evidence or determining a fact at issue.
2. An expert in that area is qualified by the trial judge after hearing evidence that the individual is an expert, by virtue of "knowledge, skill, experience, training, or education."
3. The evidence upon which the expert will rely must be judged to be "trustworthy" or "reliable" (i.e., of a type "reasonably relied upon") by experts in the area of expertise. Furthermore, the nature of the evidence and the opinion must be judged to be more probative than it is prejudicial, confusing, misleading, or redundant with other evidence.

SUMMARY CRITIQUE OF MENTAL HEALTH EXPERTISE

It comes as no surprise, of course, that the ideal and the real are frequently at variance with one another. Controversy has surrounded the role of mental health expertise in the courtroom for several centuries. . . . While an exhaustive catalogue of the controversial issues would be quite long, a set of central issues will first be outlined and then discussed under the major section headings which follow.

Moral Advocacy Versus Expertise

While some nihilists argue that mental health expertise simply does not exist or should be banned completely from the courtroom, the more cogent argument has been that such expertise as does exist is quite limited, and that the *real* role of the forensic expert in the courtroom has been that of moral advocate. . . . That is, the problem with forensic expertise is identified with a hidden moral agenda in which the moral controversies underlying the ascription of responsibility and blame-worthiness are played out through the roles of the experts.

The Qualification of Experts

In principle, a trial judge accepts an individual as a qualified expert only after a thorough hearing as to the person's training, knowledge, and experience with respect to a circumscribed area of expertise. In practice, judges rarely exercise this discretionary authority. The resulting problem is the level of expertise available to courts varies widely with many generically trained mental health professionals giving "expert opinions" on complex forensic mental health questions. The court is thereby misled into believing that it is hearing opinions based upon the most current scholarship, research, and experience in the area.

Prejudicial Versus Probative Aspects of Expertise

While judges have the discretionary authority to limit expert evidence, when relevant, on the basis of the balance between its prejudicial versus probative

From *International Journal of Law and Psychiatry, 13,* 281–307. Copyright 1990 by Pergamon Press. Adapted with permission of the author and publisher.

effects, they are rarely asked to evaluate this issue. As a consequence, it has become common practice for both defense and prosecution to (mis)use their experts to introduce evidence that would otherwise be inadmissible, obfuscatory, or prejudicial. A related claim is that the "aura of science" which surrounds expert testimony leads to undue weight being given to the expert's opinions and inferences. Furthermore, since these opinions themselves are frequently seen as "invading the province of the trier of fact," experts are seen as inappropriately influencing the legal system.

Expertise Is Distorted in an Adversarial System

The fundamental structure of evidence production in an adversarial system is seen as incompatible with the basic tenets of expert knowledge systems which are grounded in the scientific methods of evidence appraisal. . . .

Expertise Is for Hire

This claim is expressed most stridently as experts are "whores for hire." The more reasoned critiques question whether the combination of economic forces and a strongly structured adversarial system produces the most useful and probative expert testimony. Thus, the combination of "doctor shopping," inadequate qualification of experts, vaguely defined boundaries of expertise, and adversarial as opposed to court-appointed experts may deprive the court of the most probative expertise available. . . .

Commentary: *One hundred years ago, an author writing an expert testimony quoted this from an unidentified trial lawyer's closing statement: "Gentlemen of the jury," the attorney began, "there are three kinds of liars—the common liar, the damned liar, and the scientific expert" (p. 169). See Foster, W. L. (1897). Expert testimony— Prevalent complaints and proposed remedies.* Harvard Law Review, 11, *169–186.*

There is some evidence that lawyers do frequently coach experts; that experts are generally receptive to this process; and as a result, that these "hired guns"

vary their testimony to suit the needs of the side by which they have been retained. See, for example,

Champagne, A., Shuman, D. W., & Whitaker, E. (1991). The use of expert witnesses in American courts. Judicature, 31, *375–392.*

Homant, R. J., & Kennedy, D. B. (1987). Subjective factors in clinicians' judgments of insanity: A comparison of a hypothetical and an actual case. Professional Psychology: Research and Practice, 18, *439–446.*

Otto, R. K. (1989). Bias and expert testimony of mental health professionals in adversarial proceedings: A preliminary investigation. Behavioral Sciences and the Law, 7, *267–273.*

For a general review of biases to which forensic clinicians are subject, see Bersoff, D. N. (1992). Judicial deference to nonlegal decision-makers: Imposing simplistic solutions on problems of cognitive complexity in mental disability law. Southern Methodist Law Review, 46, *327–370.*

Given these problems, Shuman & Greenberg (1998) complain that the courts have not used ethical codes and guidelines developed by professional associations like APA to reject the admissibility of unreliable testimony. They advocate that, "the judiciary carefully consider the relevant professional ethical norms and the reasoning underlying them" (p. 7). See Shuman, D. W., & Greenberg, S. A. (1998, Winter). The role of ethical norms in the admissibility of expert testimony. The Judges Journal, 37, *4–9, 42–43.*

If there is one category of cases that most frequently evokes the accusation of "hired gun," it is in the assessment of children during custody disputes between two divorcing parents. It is here that the confluence of incompetence, multiple relationships, role conflicts, and biased advocacy is most rampant. Unless these disputes are settled amicably, there are always going to be parents who feel aggrieved by the decision. Rightly or wrongly, such disgruntled parents are increasingly filing ethics complaints against accessors.

As Karras & Berry (1985) acknowledged, the child custody "evaluator is frequently confronted with ethical pitfalls, such as . . . overstepping the boundary of research-supportable recommendations for custody arrangements [and failing to] . . . avoid the adversarial evaluator role" (p. 83). See Karras, D., & Berry, K. K. (1985). Custody evaluations: A critical review. Professional Psychology: Research and Practice, 16, 76–85. *Similarly, Brodzinsky (1993) warned psychologists "to guard against external pressure from lawyers and the court" and "the false assumption that testing inherently imbues the forensic evaluation with a scientific foundation and thus a greater degree of objectivity" (p. 218). See Brodzinsky, D. (1993). On the use and misuse of psychological testing in child custody evaluations. Pro-*fessional Psychology: Research and Practice, 24, *213–219. The views of these and other authors have great merit. Nevertheless, there was consensus that an institutional response by APA to the ethical issues raised by child custody evaluations was necessary to reduce the number of ethical complaints by parents and to educate its members. Thus, the APA developed the following document, which is now APA policy.*

Guidelines for Child Custody Evaluations in Divorce Proceedings

American Psychological Association

INTRODUCTION

Decisions regarding child custody and other parenting arrangements occur within several different legal contexts, including parental divorce, guardianship, neglect or abuse proceedings, and termination of parental rights. The following guidelines were developed for psychologists conducting child custody evaluations, specifically within the context of parental divorce. These guidelines build upon the American Psychological Association's *Ethical Principles of Psychologists and Code of Conduct* (APA, 1992) and are aspirational in intent. *As guidelines, they are not intended to be either mandatory or exhaustive. The goal of the guidelines is to promote proficiency in using psychological expertise in conducting child custody evaluations.*

Parental divorce requires a restructuring of parental rights and responsibilities in relation to children. If the parents can agree to a restructuring arrangement, which they do in the overwhelming proportion (90%) of divorce custody cases (Melton, Petrila, Poythress, & Slobogin, 1987), there is no dispute for the court to decide. However, if the parents are unable to reach such an agreement, the court must help to determine the relative allocation of decision-making authority and physical contact each parent will have with the child. The courts typically apply a "best interest of the child" standard in determining this restructuring of rights and responsibilities.

Psychologists provide an important service to children and the courts by providing competent, objective, impartial information in assessing the best interests of the child; by demonstrating a clear sense of direction and purpose in conducting a child custody evaluation; by performing their roles ethically; and by clarifying to all involved the nature and scope of the evaluation. The Ethics Committee of the American Psychological Association has noted that psychologists' involvement in custody disputes has at times raised questions in regard to the misuse of psychologists' influence, sometimes resulting in complaints against psychologists being brought to the attention of the APA Ethics Committee (APA Ethics Committee, 1985; Hall & Hare-Mustin, 1983; Keith-Spiegel & Koocher, 1985; Mills, 1984) and raising questions in the legal and forensic literature (Grisso, 1986; Melton et al., 1987; Mnookin, 1975; Ochroch, 1982; Okpaku, 1976; Weithorn, 1987).

Particular competencies and knowledge are required for child custody evaluations to provide adequate and appropriate psychological services to the court. Child custody evaluation in the context of parental divorce can be an extremely demanding task. For competing parents the stakes are high as they participate in a process fraught with tension and anxiety. The stress on the psychologist/evaluator can become great. Tension surrounding child custody evaluation can become further heightened when there are accusations of child abuse, neglect, and/or family violence.

Psychology is in a position to make significant contributions to child custody decisions. Psychologi-

From *American Psychologist*, 49, 677–680. Copyright 1994 by the American Psychological Association. Adapted with permission of the author and publisher.

These guidelines were drafted by the Committee on Professional Practice and Standards, a committee of the Board of Professional Affairs, with input from the Committee of Children, Youth, and Families. They were adopted by the Council of Representatives of the American Psychological Association in February 1994.

cal data and expertise, gained through a child custody evaluation, can provide an additional source of information and an additional perspective not otherwise readily available to the court on what appears to be in a child's best interest, and thus can increase the fairness of the determination the court must make.

GUIDELINES FOR CHILD CUSTODY EVALUATIONS IN DIVORCE PROCEEDINGS

I. Orienting Guidelines: Purpose of a Child Custody Evaluation

1. The primary purpose of the evaluation is to assess the best psychological interests of the child. The primary consideration in a child custody evaluation is to assess the individual and family factors that affect the best psychological interests of the child. More specific questions may be raised by the court.

2. The child's interests and well-being are paramount. In a child custody evaluation, the child's interests and well-being are paramount. Parents competing for custody, as well as others, may have legitimate concerns, but the child's best interests must prevail.

3. The focus of the evaluation is on parenting capacity, the psychological and developmental needs of the child, and the resulting fit. In considering psychological factors affecting the best interests of the child, the psychologist focuses on the parenting capacity of the prospective custodians in conjunction with the psychological and developmental needs of each involved child. This involves (a) an assessment of the adults' capacities for parenting, including whatever knowledge, attributes, skills, and abilities, or lack thereof, are present; (b) an assessment of the psychological functioning and developmental needs of each child and of the wishes of each child where appropriate; and (c) an assessment of the functional ability of each parent to meet these needs, including an evaluation of the interaction between each adult and child.

The values of the parents relevant to parenting, ability to plan for the child's future needs, capacity to provide a stable and loving home, and any potential for inappropriate behavior or misconduct that might negatively influence the child also are considered. Psychopathology may be relevant to such an assessment, insofar as it has impact on the child or the ability to parent, but it is not the primary focus.

II. General Guidelines: Preparing for a Child Custody Evaluation

4. The role of the psychologist is that of a professional expert who strives to maintain an objective, impartial stance. The role of the psychologist is as a professional expert. The psychologist does not act as a judge, who makes the ultimate decision applying the law to all relevant evidence. Neither does the psychologist act as an advocating attorney, who strives to present his or her client's best possible case. The psychologist, in a balanced, impartial manner, informs and advises the court and the prospective custodians of the child of the relevant psychological factors pertaining to the custody issue. The psychologist should be impartial regardless of whether he or she is retained by the court or by a party to the proceedings. If either the psychologist or the client cannot accept this neutral role, the psychologist should consider withdrawing from the case. If not permitted to withdraw, in such circumstances, the psychologist acknowledges past roles and other factors that could affect impartiality.

5. The psychologist gains specialized competence. A. A psychologist contemplating performing child custody evaluations is aware that special competencies and knowledge are required for the undertaking of such evaluations. Competence in performing psychological assessments of children, adults, and families is necessary but not sufficient. Education, training, experience, and/or supervision in the areas of child and family development, child and family psychopathology, and the impact of divorce on children help to prepare the psychologist to participate competently in child custody evaluations. The psychologist also strives to become familiar with applicable legal standards and procedures, including laws governing divorce and custody adjudications in his or her state or jurisdiction.

B. The psychologist uses current knowledge of scientific and professional developments, consistent with accepted clinical and scientific standards, in selecting data collection methods and procedures. The

Standards for Educational and Psychological Testing (APA, 1985) are adhered to in the use of psychological tests and other assessment tools.

C. In the course of conducting child custody evaluations, allegations of child abuse, neglect, family violence, or other issues may occur that are not necessarily within the scope of a particular evaluator's expertise. If this is so, the psychologist seeks additional consultation, supervision, and/or specialized knowledge, training, or experience in child abuse, neglect, and family violence to address these complex issues. The psychologist is familiar with the laws of his or her state addressing child abuse, neglect, and family violence and acts accordingly.

6. The psychologist is aware of personal and societal biases and engages in nondiscriminatory practice. The psychologist engaging in child custody evaluations is aware of how biases regarding age, gender, race, ethnicity, national origin, religion, sexual orientation, disability, language, culture, and socioeconomic status may interfere with an objective evaluation and recommendations. The psychologist recognizes and strives to overcome any such biases or withdraws from the evaluation.

7. The psychologist avoids multiple relationships. Psychologists generally avoid conducting a child custody evaluation in a case in which the psychologist served in a therapeutic role for the child or his or her immediate family or has had other involvement that may compromise the psychologist's objectivity. This should not, however, preclude the psychologist from testifying in the case as a fact witness concerning treatment of the child. In addition, during the course of a child custody evaluation, a psychologist does not accept any of the involved participants in the evaluation as a therapy client. Therapeutic contact with the child or involved participants following a child custody evaluation is undertaken with caution.

A psychologist asked to testify regarding a therapy client who is involved in a child custody case is aware of the limitations and possible biases inherent in such a role and the possible impact on the ongoing therapeutic relationship. Although the court may require the psychologist to testify as a fact witness regarding factual information he or she became aware of in a professional relationship with a client,

that psychologist should generally decline the role of an expert witness who gives a professional opinion regarding custody and visitation issues (see Ethical Standard 7.03) unless so ordered by the court.

III. Procedural Guidelines: Conducting a Child Custody Evaluation

8. The scope of the evaluation is determined by the evaluator, based on the nature of the referral question. The scope of the custody-related evaluation is determined by the nature of the question or issue raised by the referring person or the court, or is inherent in the situation. Although comprehensive child custody evaluations generally require an evaluation of all parents or guardians and children, as well as observations of interactions between them, the scope of the assessment in a particular case may be limited to evaluating the parental capacity of one parent without attempting to compare the parents or to make recommendations. Likewise, the scope may be limited to evaluating the child. Or a psychologist may be asked to critique the assumptions and methodology of the assessment of another mental health professional. A psychologist also might serve as an expert witness in the area of child development, providing expertise to the court without relating it specifically to the parties involved in a case.

9. The psychologist obtains informed consent from all adult participants and, as appropriate, informs child participants. In undertaking child custody evaluations, the psychologist ensures that each adult participant is aware of (a) the purpose, nature, and method of the evaluation; (b) who has requested the psychologist's services; and (c) who will be paying the fees. The psychologist informs adult participants about the nature of the assessment instruments and techniques and informs those participants about the possible disposition of the data collected. The psychologist provides this information, as appropriate, to children, to the extent that they are able to understand.

10. The psychologist informs participants about the limits of confidentiality and the disclosure of information. A psychologist conducting a child custody evaluation ensures that the participants, including children to the extent feasible, are aware of the limits of confidentiality characterizing the professional relationship with the psychologist. The psychologist informs participants that in consenting to the evaluation, they are consenting to disclosure of the evaluation's findings in the context of the forthcoming litigation and in any other proceedings deemed necessary by the courts. A psychologist obtains a waiver of confidentiality from all adult participants or from their authorized legal representatives.

11. The psychologist uses multiple methods of data gathering. The psychologist strives to use the most appropriate methods available for addressing the questions raised in a specific child custody evaluation and generally uses multiple methods of data gathering, including, but not limited to, clinical interviews, observation, and/or psychological assessments. Important facts and opinions are documented from at least two sources whenever their reliability is questionable. The psychologist, for example, may review potentially relevant reports (e.g., from schools, health care providers, child care providers, agencies, and institutions). Psychologists may also interview extended family, friends, and other individuals on occasions when the information is likely to be useful. If information is gathered from third parties that is significant and may be used as a basis for conclusions, psychologists corroborate it by at least one other source wherever possible and appropriate and document this in the report.

12. The psychologist neither overinterprets nor inappropriately interprets clinical or assessment data. The psychologist refrains from drawing conclusions not adequately supported by the data. The psychologist interprets any data from interviews or tests, as well as any questions of data reliability and validity, cautiously and conservatively, seeking convergent validity. The psychologist strives to acknowledge to the court any limitations in methods or data used.

13. The psychologist does not give any opinion regarding the psychological functioning of any individual who has not been personally evaluated. This guideline, however, does not preclude the psychologist from reporting what an evaluated individual (such as the parent or child) has stated or from addressing theoretical issues of hypothetical questions, so long as the limited basis of the information is noted.

14. Recommendations, if any, are based on what is in the best psychological interests of the child. Although the profession has not reached consensus about whether psychologists ought to make recommendations about the final custody determination to the courts, psychologists are obligated to be aware of the arguments on both sides of this issue and to be able to explain the logic of their position concerning their own practice.

If the psychologist does choose to make custody recommendations, these recommendations should be derived from sound psychological data and must be based on the best interests of the child in the particular case. Recommendations are based on articulated assumptions, data, interpretations, and inferences based upon established professional and scientific standards. Psychologists guard against relying on their own biases or unsupported beliefs in rendering opinions in particular cases.

15. The psychologist clarifies financial arrangements. Financial arrangements are clarified and agreed upon prior to commencing a child custody evaluation. When billing for a child custody evaluation, the psychologist does not misrepresent his or her services for reimbursement purposes.

16. The psychologist maintains written records. All records obtained in the process of conducting a child custody evaluation are properly maintained and filed in accord with the APA *Record Keeping Guidelines* (APA, 1993) and relevant statutory guidelines.

All raw data and interview information are recorded with an eye toward their possible review by other psychologists or the court, where legally permitted. Upon request, appropriate reports are made available to the court.

References

American Psychological Association. (1985). *Standards for educational and psychological testing.* Washington, DC: Author.

American Psychological Association. (1992). Ethical principles of psychologists and code of conduct. *American Psychologist, 47,* 1597–1611.

American Psychological Association. (1993). *Record keeping guidelines.* Washington, DC: Author.

American Psychological Association: Ethics Committee.

(1985). *Annual report of the American Psychological Association Ethics Committee*. Washington, DC: Author.

Grisso, T. (1986). *Evaluating competencies: Forensic assessments and instruments*. New York: Plenum.

Hall, J. E., & Hare-Mustin, R. T. (1983). Sanctions and the diversity of ethical complaints against psychologists. *American Psychologist, 38,* 714–729.

Keith-Spiegel, P., & Koocher, G. P. (1985). *Ethics in psychology*. New York: Random House.

Melton, G. B., Petrila, J., Poythress, N. G., & Slobogin, C. (1987). *Psychological evaluations for the courts: A handbook for mental health professionals and lawyers*. New York: Guilford Press.

Mills, D. H. (1984). Ethics education and adjudication within psychology. *American Psychologist, 39,* 669–675.

Mnookin, R. H. (1975). Child-custody adjudication: Judicial functions in the face of indeterminacy. *Law and Contemporary Problems, 39,* 226–293.

Ochroch, R. (1982, August). *Ethical pitfalls in child custody evaluations*. Paper presented at the 90th Annual Convention of the American Psychological Association, Washington, DC.

Okpaku, S. (1976). Psychology: Impediment or aid in child custody cases? *Rutgers Law Review, 29,* 1117–1153.

Weithorn, L. A. (Ed.). (1987). *Psychology and child custody determinations: Knowledge, roles, and expertise*. Lincoln: University of Nebraska Press.

◆　◆　◆

Commentary: *On the Psylaw ListServ, David Thompson asked his colleagues to give their opinions to the following interesting question, which I am borrowing and adapting with his kind permission:*

Psychologist A is appointed by the court to conduct a custody evaluation of both parents and their two children. She evaluates the entire family by testing and observing parent–child interactions. She then files a report containing custody, placement, and visitation recommendations. The attorney for the parent who was not recommended to have custody retains Psychologist B. This psychologist reviews A's report, interviews only the parent who hired her, and submits a report recommending that custody be granted to this parent, differing with Psychologist A. Referring to the APA ethics code (particularly Section 7—Forensic Activities), the child custody guidelines, and the Specialty Guidelines for Forensic Psychologists (reprinted later in this chapter), identify the major ethical issues raised in this situation. In particular, has Psychologist B violated the precepts of these three documents by making a custody determination after evaluating only one member of the family? If A believes B has acted unethically, does she have an obligation to contact B and express her concern? If so, when is contact appropriate (i.e., before, during, or after the custody hearing)? Or, does Psychologist B actually have enough information for judgment, given that she has had access to Psychologist A's report and recommendations?

Although the issue of biased advocacy most often surfaces in the context of testimony by professional psychologists—as in child custody cases and other litigation (e.g., the presence of insanity in a criminal defendant, the emotional damage of victims of sexual or physical abuse, the extent of disability in a child needing special education, or the validity of employment tests)—it has become perhaps an even more significant issue for researchers. The controversy has been most heated in cases involving eyewitness identification of a criminal defendant.

The Experimental Psychologist in Court:
The Ethics of Expert Testimony

Michael McCloskey, Howard Egeth, and Judith McKenna

. . . The psychologist who is asked to serve as an expert witness faces several difficult ethical questions, first in deciding whether to testify and then, if this decision is in the affirmative, in considering what duties and responsibilities inhere in the expert witness role. These issues were the topic of a conference held at Johns Hopkins University. . . .

THE ETHICAL QUESTIONS

Advocate or Educator?

The experimental psychologist who testifies as an expert witness is virtually always hired by the attorneys for one side in a case. Because attorneys' ethics require them to be zealous advocates for their clients, they often want the psychologist to discuss in expert testimony only those points for which the available psychological research supports their client's position. Psychologists who offer different testimony depending on who has hired them act at least to some extent as advocates; psychologists whose testimony does not differ according to employer act as impartial educators of the jury.

In some unusual circumstances the roles of advocate and impartial educator may coincide (i.e., on all relevant points the available research may clearly support the contentions of the side hiring the expert). Usually, however, the roles are in conflict (Fersch, 1980). Consider the psychologist who is hired by the defense in a criminal case to testify about research on eyewitness performance. In the role of advocate for the defense, the psychologist

would emphasize in expert testimony only those perceptual and memorial factors that suggest that the identification(s) in the case at hand may have been inaccurate (e.g., brief exposure, stress experienced by the eyewitness). In contrast, the psychologist adopting the role of impartial educator would also discuss factors suggesting that the eyewitness identification of the defendant may have been accurate (e.g., good lighting, short retention interval). Current practice in this sort of expert testimony is probably closer to advocacy than to impartial education (e.g., Loftus, 1979, 1980, . . . ; Loftus & Monahan, 1980).

Most conference participants agreed that the most desirable role for the expert is that of impartial educator, and some held that this is the only ethically defensible position. It is clear that the law defines the role of the expert as that of an impartial educator called to assist the trier of fact. A scientist is called upon to assist the jury to understand the evidence or determine a fact in issue (see, e.g., Federal Rules of Evidence, Rule 702, 1975, p. 80). Therefore, it was argued, the psychologist has the ethical responsibility to present a complete and unbiased picture of the psychological research relevant to the case at hand.

Many conference participants disagreed, however, contending that the educator role is difficult if not impossible to maintain, both because of pressures toward advocacy from the attorneys who hire the expert, and because of a strong tendency to identify with the side for which one is working. Hence, they suggested, the psychologist should accept the realities of working within an adversary system, and seek to be a responsible advocate, presenting one side of an issue without distorting or misrepresenting the available psychological research.

The discussions at the conference also made clear that additional ethical problems arise once a stance has been taken on the basic advocate/educator issue. The psychologist who decides that some degree of advocacy is ethically acceptable must consider how to draw the line between using research to argue one side of an issue fairly, and distorting and misrepresenting the available research.

The psychologist who decides that the role of impartial educator is the only ethically acceptable one also faces difficult problems. An attorney may fail to accept or even to understand the psychologist's desire to be even-handed in expert testimony. Thus, the psychologist who wishes to act as an impartial educator may be faced with a choice between accommodating the attorney's desire for a one-sided presentation, or not being called to testify. . . .

Effects of Expert Testimony

Expert psychological testimony is offered to assist jurors in understanding or evaluating other evidence in a case. However, whenever an experimental psychologist gives expert testimony, there is the possibility that the testimony will affect the jury in some unanticipated and undesirable way. Jurors may misinterpret, overgeneralize, or misapply the information presented by the psychologist, and so may come to unwarranted conclusions. Further concerns expressed in rules of evidence and appellate decisions regarding expert testimony include the possibility that expert testimony may confuse the issues in a case, or that the expert's opinions may be accorded undue weight by the jury.

The risk of deleterious effects is especially evident in light of the fact that the expert witness does not offer to the jury an exhaustive and uninterpreted recitation of research results. Rather, the expert typically states conclusions based upon the available research, often without discussing the studies that form the basis for this conclusion. For example, an expert on eyewitness psychology might state that

cross-race identifications (e.g., Black witness, White defendant) are less reliable than within-race identifications. Expert testimony in this form carries the risk that jurors may accept the expert's statements as scientific fact, when in fact these statements are often better characterized as tentative conclusions drawn on the basis of limited and perhaps inconsistent evidence. . . .

. . .

Bases for Statements

. . .

The issue of bases for statements made in expert testimony generated more discussion—and more disagreement—than any other issue considered at the conference. The discussions made clear that the issue subsumes two distinct questions: (1) how well supported should a statement be?; and (2) how much support do available data provide for the sorts of statements experimental psychologists commonly make in expert testimony?

On the first issue two quite distinct positions were apparent in the discussions. Proponents of the "best available evidence" position held that it is appropriate for a psychologist to state in expert testimony conclusions based on the best available evidence, even if these conclusions must be very tentative. In support of this position it was argued that the judicial system cannot withhold decisions on cases until psychologists have a complete understanding of cognition and social psychology; decisions must be made on the basis of information currently available. Thus, if as the result of psychological research some information relevant to an issue under adjudication is available, psychologists have the right, and perhaps even the ethical obligation, to provide the judicial system with this information.

In contrast, proponents of the "well-established knowledge" position asserted that while absolute certainty about the validity of a statement is not necessary, a conclusion should be scientifically well established before it is offered in expert testimony. In support of this position it was argued that matters at the frontiers of a science—matters that are poorly understood or vigorously debated within the discipline—are not appropriate subjects for expert testimony. In the first place, it may be argued that for issues on which the available research yields no clear conclusions, the expert's judgment has no greater claim to validity than that of the layperson. In addition, if a conclusion is stated in an appropriately tentative fashion (e.g., witness confidence may sometimes be a good indicator and sometimes a poor indicator of witness accuracy, but the circumstances in which it is a good or poor indicator are not understood) it may be of little use to the jury, but if the conclusion is asserted without indication of its tentative nature the jury may inappropriately accept it as scientific fact. . . .

References

Federal Rules of Evidence for United States Courts and Magistrates. (1975). St. Paul, Minnesota: West Publishing Company.

Fersch, E. A., Jr. (1980). Ethical issues for psychologists in court settings. In J. Monahan (Ed.), *Who is the client? The ethics of psychological intervention in the criminal justice system*. Washington, DC: American Psychological Association.

Loftus, E. F. (1979). *Eyewitness testimony*. Cambridge, Massachusetts: Harvard University Press.

Loftus, E. F. (1980). Impact of expert psychological testimony on the unreliability of eyewitness identification. *Journal of Applied Psychology, 65,* 9–15.

Loftus, E. F., & Monahan, J. (1980). Trial by data: Psychological research as legal evidence. *American Psychologist, 35,* 270–283.

Experimental Psychologist as Advocate or Impartial Educator

Elizabeth F. Loftus

. . .

The view that psychologists may serve as advocates, presenting only the beneficial side of the case, begins with the argument that the trial is an adversary process in which each side has the right to make the best possible case. As participants in this process, experts may limit their testimony to points that support the arguments of one side, leaving the opposing attorneys the task of presenting evidence and arguments favoring their position. The opposition can resort to vigorous cross-examination to bring out weaknesses in the testimony offered by the other side. . . .

Rivlin (1973) went so far as to suggest that we acknowledge the development of a "forensic social science" rather than pretend to be balanced, objective, free of personal biases, and acting as if we are offering all sides of the case so that people can judge for themselves. If left to Rivlin's design, a psychologist would simply prepare a position paper for or against a particular proposition. The position would be clearly stated, and the evidence that supports one side of the argument would be brought together. The job of critiquing the case that has been presented and of detailing the counterevidence would be left to a scholar working for the opposition. One advantage of a forensic social science is that it would reduce the hypocrisy of pseudo-objectivity and hidden biases that now pervade the so-called scientifically balanced approach. If used properly, Rivlin argues, forensic social science can sharpen public issues and make social scientific research more relevant to real policy questions than it

has ever been in the past. This is probably an extreme version of the advocacy side of the issue. Yet even while advocating the forensic social science approach, Rivlin is careful to point out that there must be some rules. We still just guard against misrepresentation of facts or findings of studies cited. Moreover, she claims, the evidence has to be available for examination by the advocates on the other side, and by the judge and jury.

. . .

Now consider an opposing point of view. All witnesses take an oath before they take the stand, and that oath is to tell "the truth, the whole truth, and nothing but the truth." By selectively leaving out studies that are crucial to some particular question, the psychologists may be failing to perform according to the oath. The "whole truth" is not being told. For this reason, some social scientists have suggested that the expert may have an obligation to bring up research evidence that runs counter to the thrust of his or her testimony. . . .

POSSIBLE GUIDES TO ETHICAL DECISIONS

Laws of Evidence

The law itself does not require "full disclosure." More specifically, the Federal Rules of Evidence (1975) do not require an expert to disclose facts or data that underlie the opinion or inference being offered. Rule 705 says:

> The expert may testify in terms of opinions or inference and give his reasons

From *Law and Human Behavior, 10*, 63–78. Copyright 1986 by Plenum Publishing. Adapted with permission of the author and publisher.

therefore without prior disclosure of underlying facts or data, unless the court requires otherwise. The expert may in any event be required to disclose the underlying facts or data on cross-examination. (p. 84)

In other words, counsel can disclose the underlying facts (including supportive and contradictory facts) when presenting its case, but is not necessarily obligated to do so. The revealing of underlying facts could, however, be forced on cross-examination. Some have argued that it is unfair to require the cross-examiner to bring out the weaknesses in the expert testimony, but the legal commentary on Rule 705 disagrees. Those who cross-examine are assumed to have advance knowledge, typically through traditional procedures of discovery, necessary for effective challenging of expert testimony. This safeguard is reinforced by the discretionary power of the judge to require preliminary disclosure of the identity of the experts and their findings. Even if this information is not discovered in advance of trial, the opposing attorney is always free to ask the right questions, such as "Do you know of any studies that show the opposite result?"

How should a psychologist decide what role to play? . . .

Ethics of Psychological Practice

It is natural to ask what role the legal principles (that do not require full disclosure) should play in a psychologist's decision. If the legal principles permit less than full disclosure, is this sufficient justification for the expert to adopt the advocate's role; or must ethical principles independent of the legal criteria be taken into account?

A reasonable position is that the ethics of one's own field should govern the choice. In considering the ethics of psychology as a means of resolution, we must turn to the set of ethical standards for the profession of psychology. . . . (Ethical Principles of Psychologists, 1981). . . . As Fersch (1980) has noted, these standards do not go far toward resolv-

ing the troubling ethical issues that psychologists might face when they find themselves in court. And it is easy to see why. Foremost among the difficulties is the question of who the client is. If psychologists are to protect "fundamental human rights," whose rights are we to protect—the rights of the defendant in a criminal case to present the strongest case possible, or the rights of citizens to see the guilty convicted of crimes they have committed? If we are committed to the "promotion of human welfare," whose welfare? If psychologists must "make every effort to protect the welfare of those who seek their services," does this imply a duty to the defendant who has hired the psychologist to help in the advocacy role? Fersch (1980) has stated rather explicitly that when a defendant has hired a psychologist to point out the unreliability of eyewitness identification (or to help pick a jury or offer some other service), the psychologist "has but one client—the defendant—and owes responsibility solely to him or her" (1980, p. 54). But, taking into account the ethical principles, how far should the psychologist go in satisfying this responsibility? Adding fuel to these troubled waters is another one of the ethical principles, which states:

> Psychologists present the science of psychology and offer their services, products, and publications fairly and accurately, avoiding misrepresentation through sensationalism, exaggeration, or superficiality. Psychologists are guided by the primary obligation to aid the public in developing informed judgments, opinions, and choices (p. 635).[1]

What does the psychologist do, then, if the needs of the client (such as the defendant) run somewhat counter to the needs of the public? In short, the Ethical Principles, while usually useful concerning the matter of responsibility to clients seen in a clinical setting, provide little help to the expert in court.

If the Ethical Principles do not provide the necessary guidance, we must tackle the problem in an-

---

[1] *Ed. note:* See Standards 1.06, 3.03, and 7.04 of the APA's current (1992) Ethical Principles.

other way. Does the expert have an obligation to present both sides of the case? As a start, it seems fruitful to ask this question: Does the case have two "reasonable" sides? If there is contrary evidence to the major thrust of the expert's testimony, it can be of two sorts:

1. Contradictory evidence that calls into question the general rule being proffered, and
2. An exception that still maintains the general rule.

The second case is the easier one, for the expert could decide that a minor exception need not be discussed since it will only confuse the jury and prolong the testimony needlessly. The first case, by contrast, is the more difficult one for it presumes that the case has two reasonable sides. The psychologist could still choose the advocacy or the education path. Whatever the choice, trouble may lurk ahead. In any given case, or when it comes to any given issue within a case, neither the advocacy nor the education path is likely to be straight and easy.

Problems With the Advocacy Option

Suppose the psychologist decides that it is ethically responsible to be an advocate. Several problems will still arise. Say, for example, the expert is testifying that cross-racial identifications are more difficult for witnesses, and suppose that 99% of all investigations support this conclusion. Here, the expert may have little problem. He or she could easily decide that any discussion of the other 1% of the studies would simply confuse the jury and prolong the testimony unduly. On the other hand, suppose that 51% of the investigations support the expert's conclusions. Or even a mere 25%. The expert must decide whether selective presentation of this research would seriously distort and misrepresent the available psychological research. In good conscience, the expert could decide that the supportive studies are solid and reliable while the unsupportive ones are shoddily conducted and must be discarded from consideration. But when this happens, it is conceivable that the expert will become immersed in a battle involving opposing experts that could be rather unpleasant.

Indeed, the advocacy position may have one discomforting side effect. It could lead to a battle of

the experts similar to that which exists in the psychiatric area. . . . Several experimental psychologists have already suggested that such a battle in the area of eyewitness reliability is practically a foregone conclusion (Egeth & McCloskey, 1984).

Problems With the Education Option

Suppose the psychologist decides that it is ethically responsible to be an impartial educator. Several problems will arise in this case too. After all, the psychologist is working within an adversary system, the essence of which is that one side of the case is presented, and subsequently challenged by the other. As Schofield (1956) noted almost 30 years ago, there is something in the very nature of this system, and in a court trial in particular, that "arouses the adrenals" (p. 2). During cross-examination, attorneys will try to portray witnesses as "ignorant, irresponsible, or biased" (Brodsky, 1977). Based upon his own participation and observations of trials, Schofield came to believe that only a superhuman person could avoid becoming identified with one of the sides, and avoid the sense of wanting his or her side to win. Thus motivated, the person may become guilty of distorting testimony and potentially frustrate the process of justice.

Whether knowingly or not, psychologists may find that "the whole truth" is not revealed, or worse, a distorted truth is given, because of the procedures required by law. For example, when testifying on the reliability of eyewitness accounts, an expert cannot necessarily control the specific questions posed to elicit information and opinions. If questions that might reveal weaknesses in the testimony are never asked, the information may never reach the jury. Thus, even when a psychologist wants to present more information, or a less distorted picture of the psychological research, it may in practice, be impossible to do so.

Even more likely is the probability that the "impartial educator" will never get the chance to participate in the case. One distinguished trial lawyer who spoke to a conference for lawyers on the subject of "relations with the expert witness" warned his colleagues about the so-called impartial educator:

Many people are convinced that the expert who really persuades a jury is the independent, objective, nonarticulate type. . . . I disagree. I would go into a lawsuit with an objective, uncommitted, independent expert about as willingly as I would occupy a foxhole with a couple of non-combatant soldiers. (Meier, 1982)

. . .

References

Brodsky, S. L. (1977). The mental health professional on the witness stand: A survival guide. In B. D. Sales (Ed.), *Psychology in the legal process*. New York: Spectrum.

Egeth, H., & McCloskey, M. (1984). Expert testimony about eyewitness behavior: Is it safe and effective? In G. Wells and E. Loftus (Eds.), *Eyewitness testimony: Psychological perspectives*. London: Cambridge University Press.

Ethical Principles of Psychologists. (1981). *American Psychologist, 36*, 633–638.

Federal Rules of Evidence for United States Courts and Magistrates. (1975). St. Paul, Minnesota: West.

Fersch, E. A., Jr. (1980). Ethical issues for psychologists in court settings. In J. Monahan (Ed.), *Who is the client? The ethics of psychological intervention in the criminal justice system*. Washington, DC: American Psychological Association.

Meier, P. (1982). *Damned liars and expert witnesses*. Presidential Address. American Statistical Association, Annual Meeting.

Rivlin, A. (1973). Forensic social science. *Harvard Educational Review, 43*, 61–75.

Schofield, W. (1956). Psychology, law and the expert witness. *American Psychologist, 11*, 1–7.

◆ ◆ ◆

Commentary: *Elliott criticized Loftus's position. Specifically, he remarked that the notion that*

> *as between the expert as educator–scientist and the expert as advocate we can settle claims to merit by waiting to see which survives seems to me to be both misplaced Darwinism and bad advice. Lawyers and other policy actors will almost always choose advocates over impartial scientists, which only means that the adversary system is not a fit environment for science. Why let the world of policy be the touchstone of the value of science? (pp. 433–434)*

See Elliott, R. (1993). Expert testimony about eyewitness identification. Law and Human Behavior, 17, 423–448.

Psychologists and the Judicial System: Broader Perspectives

Donald N. Bersoff

. . .

. . . In June 1980, Judge John Grady of the federal district court in northern Illinois, issued his opinion in *PASE v. Hannon* (1980). The plaintiffs had challenged the use of individual intelligence scales to place black children in classes for the educably mentally retarded. A disproportionate number of black children had been misclassified as retarded, they claimed, because the tests upon which the determinations were based were racially and culturally biased. During the three-week trial on this controversial issue, Judge Grady heard the testimony of several prominent psychologists, including a past president of the American Psychological Association, a former member of its Board of Directors, and other acknowledged experts who would comprise a veritable Who's Who of American Measurement, if such a compendium existed. Some of the experts agreed with the plaintiffs that, indeed, there were data to support the assertion that the tests unduly favored those from the white middle-class culture; others concurred with the defendant school system that there was no evidence that the tests disfavored blacks because of inherent bias in their construction.

Actually, the gathering of the experts in *PASE* was something of a reunion. Many of these same witnesses had appeared earlier in San Francisco in a much more heralded case, *Larry P. v. Riles* (1972; 1979). There Judge Robert Peckham found in favor of the minority plaintiffs on both statutory and constitutional grounds. He concluded the tests were culturally biased and permanently enjoined the defendant state of California "from utilizing, permitting the use of, or approving the use of any standardized tests . . . for the identification of black EMR children or their placement into EMR classes, without first securing prior approval by this court" (p. 989).

The plaintiffs in *PASE* apparently expected a replay of the trial in *Larry P.* However, rather than ruling that the tests in question were culturally biased, Judge Grady held that individual intelligence tests "do not discriminate against black children in the Chicago public schools" (p. 883). Judge Grady's reference to *Larry P.* occupied a bit less than one page of his 52-page opinion and he virtually rejected its tenability out of hand. "The witnesses and the arguments," Judge Grady said, "which persuaded Judge Peckham have not persuaded me" (p. 882).

One of the most intriguing aspects of Judge Grady's decision was his almost utter rejection of the testimony of expert psychologists who testified on behalf of both parties. The reason for this rejection is, at the same time, illuminating, instructive, and very troublesome:

> None of the witnesses in this case has so impressed me with his or her credibility or expertise that I would feel secure in basing a decision on his or her opinion. In some instances, I am satisfied that the opinions expressed are more the result of doctrinaire commitment to a preconceived idea than they are the result of scientific inquiry. I need something more than the conclusions of the witnesses in order to arrive at my own conclusions. (p. 836)

From *Law and Human Behavior, 10,* 151–165. Copyright 1986 by Plenum Publishing. Adapted with permission of the author and publisher.

This perception of the behavior of the expert witnesses who testified before Judge Grady raises some formidable and disturbing, if not painful, ethical issues. If he is correct in that perception, each of the psychologists who offered opinions out of a "doctrinaire commitment to a preconceived idea" rather than as a "result of scientific inquiry" may be guilty of violating several important provisions of the Ethical Principles of Psychologists. . . .

These are genuinely serious concerns. If the ethical integrity and scientific objectivity of experimental psychologists begin to be questioned, the significant and potentially useful information they produce may be permanently neglected by the judicial system. This will be detrimental not only to the just resolution of legal disputes between parties that involve empirical issues, but to the advancement of social policy in general. It is imperative, therefore, that social scientists remain true to the primary role they serve in society. . . .

[W]hile unbridled advocacy may be a moral imperative for attorneys, it may be directly antagonistic to the ethical principles that control the behavior of psychologists. Social scientists must continually be conscious of the fact that their data, interpretations, and opinions will be tested in the crucible of courtroom cross-examination whose very purpose it is to destroy credibility and evoke evidence of bias. Although the distillation of that process may yield testimony of great consequence and weight to the court, it can be highly anxiety provoking for psychologists who act as injudicious advocates, pleading for a position rather than as cautious scientists presenting data in an evenhanded manner. I am not suggesting that it is inappropriate to testify on behalf of a particular party in a legal dispute, but, in doing so, psychologists should exhibit the prudence of a circumspect, rational, scrupulous scientist.

Through their publications, collaboration with attorneys and judges, participation in the drafting of *amicus* briefs, testimony before legislative committees, and administrative agencies, as well as serving as expert witnesses, there are many ways social scientists can influence public policy effectively. . . . Within the bounds of scientific and professional ethics, these are important, if not crucial roles. But, if experimental psychologists are to be respected by

the courts and treated as more than mere numerologists attempting to convince the judiciary of doctrinaire positions, they must offer more situation-specific, ecologically valid, objective data that serve science, not a particular adversary. In that way, perhaps, courts may finally arrive at, not only judicially sound but, empirically justified decisions that will withstand both appellate and scientific scrutiny.

References

Larry P. v. Riles, 343 F.Supp. 1306 (N.D. Cal. 1972) (order granting preliminary injunction) *aff'd* 502 F.2d 963 (9th Cir. 1974); 495 F.Supp. 926 (N.D. Cal. 1979) *appeal docketed* No. 80–4027 (9th Cir., Jan. 17, 1980).

PASE v. Hannon, 506 F.Supp. 831 (N.D. Ill. 1980).

◆ ◆ ◆

Commentary: Goldman (1986) also asserts that a psychologist can fulfill the function of expert only by testifying in as impartial and objective a manner as possible. See Goldman, A. H. (1986). Cognitive psychologists as expert witnesses: A problem in professional ethics. Law and Human Behavior, 10, 29–45.

Perhaps the most succinct summary of the consensus position comes from Adams, K. M., & Putnam, S. H. (1994). Coping with professional skeptics: Reply to Faust. Psychological Assessment, 6, 5–7:

> Psychologists called to court are best advised to act as psychologists first and best, allowing the legal arena to evolve as it must and will. Psychologists and lawyers are professionals with different goals, cultures, and rules and who operate in epistemologically diverse ways. (p. 6)

As a middle-ground position, consider Hastie's (1986) recommendations:

> I would like to suggest a concrete image in place of Loftus's teacher–advocate dichotomy. I think that the psychologist should assume the role of watchdog. When he or she honestly believes, based on scientific findings, that, for example, eyewitness testimony is unreliable, then he or she should

take the witness stand to testify against the eyewitness. If any other expert improperly applies scientific findings to impugn eyewitness testimony, then the psychologist should testify against the expert. My watchdog image is meant to exclude two other roles. The psychologist should not be a timid lapdog who never believes there is sufficient reason to leave the comfort of the laboratory to challenge an unreliable eyewitness or misleading expert in the courtroom. Nor should the psychologist be a rabid attack dog who assaults every eyewitness who appears in the courtroom. (p. 80)

Hastie, R. (1986). *Notes on the psychologist expert witness.* Law and Human Behavior, 10, 79–82.

In any event, despite attempts to seek help from the then-current version of the APA code of ethics to resolve the advocacy–educator issue, by the 1980s there began to be a call for specific guidance to be provided for psychologists who enter the legal arena:

As a profession psychology must decide for itself the standards and level of quality that should apply to its forensic assessments. The most important reason for doing this is consumer and public welfare.

Moreover, every industry knows that a high level of internally imposed standards and quality control is important to ensure a high-quality product and to avoid personal and corporate liability.

Both APA's Division 41 and the ABFP can play a role in the development of such standards. The standards should reflect the values not only of psychological practitioners, but also of researchers in psychology and law and scientific psychology in general. The standards should reflect these values because psychologists who perform forensic assessments represent psychology—not merely forensic clinical psychology—when they enter the courtroom. Furthermore, as noted earlier, experimental psychologists themselves are entering the courtroom in increasing numbers. They are facing the same questions regarding the limits of their testimony. (p. 837)

See Grisso, T. (1987). *The economic and scientific future of forensic psychological assessment.* American Psychologist, 42, 831–839.

Four years later, the call was answered.

Specialty Guidelines for Forensic Psychologists

Committee on Ethical Guidelines for Forensic Psychologists

The *Specialty Guidelines for Forensic Psychologists*, while informed by the *Ethical Principles of Psychologists* (APA, 1990) and meant to be consistent with them, are designed to provide more specific guidance to forensic psychologists in monitoring their professional conduct when acting in assistance to courts, parties to legal proceedings, correctional and forensic mental health facilities, and legislative agencies. The primary goal of the *Guidelines* is to improve the quality of forensic psychological services offered to individual clients and the legal system and thereby to enhance forensic psychology as a discipline and profession. The *Specialty Guidelines for Forensic Psychologists* represent a joint statement of the American Psychology–Law Society and Division 41 of the American Psychological Association and are endorsed by the American Academy of Forensic Psychology. The *Guidelines* do not represent an official statement of the American Psychological Association.

The *Guidelines* provide an aspirational model of desirable professional practice by psychologists, within any subdiscipline of psychology (e.g., clinical, developmental, social, experimental), when they are engaged regularly as experts and represent themselves as such, in an activity primarily intended to provide professional psychological expertise to the judicial system. This would include, for example, clinical forensic examiners; psychologists employed by correctional or forensic mental health systems; researchers who offer direct testimony about the relevance of scientific data to a psycholegal issue; trial behavior consultants; psychologists engaged in preparation of *amicus* briefs; or psychologists, appearing as forensic experts, who consult with, or testify before, judicial, legislative, or administrative agencies acting in an adjudicative capacity. Individuals who provide only occasional service to the legal system and who do so without representing themselves as *forensic experts* may find these *Guidelines* helpful, particularly in conjunction with consultation with colleagues who are forensic experts.

While the *Guidelines* are concerned with a model of desirable professional practice, to the extent that they may be construed as being applicable to the advertisement of services or the solicitation of clients, they are intended to prevent false or deceptive advertisement or solicitation and should be construed in a manner consistent with that intent.

I. PURPOSE AND SCOPE

A. Purpose

1. While the professional standards for the ethical practice of psychology, as a general discipline, are addressed in the American Psychological Association's *Ethical Principles of Psychologists*, these ethical principles do not relate, in sufficient detail, to current aspirations of desirable professional conduct for forensic psychologists. By design, none of the *Guidelines* contradicts any of the *Ethical Principles of Psychologists*; rather, they amplify those *Principles* in the con-

From *Law and Human Behavior,* 15, 655–665. Copyright 1991 by Plenum Publishing. Adapted with permission of the author and publisher. Footnotes 1 and 2 have been omitted.

The *Specialty Guidelines for Forensic Psychologists* were adopted by majority vote of the members of Division 41 [American Psychological Association] and the American Psychology–Law Society. They have also been endorsed by majority vote by the American Academy of Forensic Psychology. The Executive Committee of Division 41 and the American Psychology–Law Society formally approved these *Guidelines* on March 9, 1991.

text of the practice of forensic psychology, as herein defined.

2. The *Guidelines* have been designed to be national in scope and are intended to conform with state and Federal law. In situations where the forensic psychologist believes that the requirements of law are in conflict with the *Guidelines*, attempts to resolve the conflict should be made in accordance with the procedures set forth in these *Guidelines* [IV(G)] and in the *Ethical Principles of Psychologists*.

B. Scope

1. The *Guidelines* specify the nature of desirable professional practice by forensic psychologists, within any subdiscipline of psychology (e.g., clinical, developmental, social, experimental), when engaged regularly as forensic psychologists.

   a. "Psychologist" means any individual whose professional activities are defined by the American Psychological Association or by regulation of title by state registration or licensure, as the practice of psychology.

   b. "Forensic psychology" means all forms of professional psychological conduct when acting, with definable foreknowledge, as a psychological expert on explicitly psycholegal issues, in direct assistance to courts, parties to legal proceedings, correctional and forensic mental health facilities, and administrative, judicial, and legislative agencies acting in an adjudicative capacity.

   c. "Forensic psychologist" means psychologists who regularly engage in the practice of forensic psychology as defined in I(B)(1)(b).

2. The *Guidelines* do not apply to a psychologist who is asked to provide professional psychological services when

the psychologist was not informed at the time of delivery of the services that they were to be used as forensic psychological services as defined above. The *Guidelines* may be helpful, however, in preparing the psychologist for the experience of communicating psychological data in a forensic context.

3. Psychologists who are not forensic psychologists as defined in I(B)(1)(c), but occasionally provide limited forensic psychological services, may find the *Guidelines* useful in the preparation and presentation of their professional services.

C. Related Standards

1. Forensic psychologists also conduct their professional activities in accord with the *Ethical Principles of Psychologists* and the various other statements of the American Psychological Association that may apply to particular subdisciplines or areas of practice that are relevant to their professional activities.

2. The standards of practice and ethical guidelines of other relevant "expert professional organizations" contain useful guidance and should be consulted even though the present *Guidelines* take precedence for forensic psychologists.

II. RESPONSIBILITY

A. Forensic psychologists have an obligation to provide services in a manner consistent with the highest standards of their profession. They are responsible for their own conduct and the conduct of those individuals under their direct supervision.

B. Forensic psychologists make a reasonable effort to ensure that their services and the products of their services are used in a forthright and responsible manner.

III. COMPETENCE

A. Forensic psychologists provide services only in areas of psychology in which they have specialized knowledge, skill, experience, and education.

B. Forensic psychologists have an obligation to present to the court, regarding the specific matters to which they will testify, the boundaries of their competence, the factual bases (knowledge, skill, experience, training, and education) for their qualifications as an expert, and the relevance of those factual bases to their qualification as an expert on the specific matters at issue.

C. Forensic psychologists are responsible for a fundamental and reasonable level of knowledge and understanding of the legal and professional standards that govern their participation as experts in legal proceedings.

D. Forensic psychologists have an obligation to understand the civil rights of parties in legal proceedings in which they participate, and manage their professional conduct in a manner that does not diminish or threaten those rights.

E. Forensic psychologists recognize that their own personal values, moral beliefs, or personal and professional relationships with parties to a legal proceeding may interfere with their ability to practice competently. Under such circumstances, forensic psychologists are obligated to decline participation or to limit their assistance in a manner consistent with professional obligations.

IV. RELATIONSHIPS

A. During initial consultation with the legal representative of the party seeking services, forensic psychologists have an obligation to inform the party of factors that might reasonably affect the decision to contract with the forensic psychologist. These factors include, but are not limited to

  1. the fee structure for anticipated professional services;

  2. prior and current personal or professional activities, obligations, and relationships that might produce a conflict of interests;

  3. their areas of competence and the limits of their competence; and

  4. the known scientific bases and limitations of the methods and procedures that they employ and their qualifications to employ such methods and procedures.

B. Forensic psychologists do not provide professional services to parties to a legal proceeding on the basis of "contingent fees," when those services involve the offering of expert testimony to a court or administrative body, or when they call upon the psychologist to make affirmations or representations intended to be relied upon by third parties.

C. Forensic psychologists who derive a substantial portion of their income from fee-for-service arrangements should offer some portion of their professional services on a *pro bono* or reduced fee basis where the public interest or the welfare of clients may be inhibited by insufficient financial resources.

D. Forensic psychologists recognize potential conflicts of interest in dual relationships with parties to a legal proceeding, and they seek to minimize their effects.

  1. Forensic psychologists avoid providing professional services to parties in a legal proceeding with whom they have personal or professional relationships that are inconsistent with the anticipated relationship.

  2. When it is necessary to provide both evaluation and treatment services to a party in a legal proceeding (as may be the case in small forensic hospital settings or small communities), the forensic psychologist takes reasonable steps to minimize the potential negative effects of these circumstances on the rights of the party, confidentiality, and the process of treatment and evaluation.

E. Forensic psychologists have an obligation to ensure that prospective clients are informed of their legal rights with respect to the anticipated forensic service, of the purpose of any evaluation, of the nature of procedures to be employed, of the intended uses of any product of their services, and of the party who has employed the forensic psychologist.

1. Unless court ordered, forensic psychologists obtain the informed consent of the client or party, or their legal representative, before proceeding with such evaluations and procedures. If the client appears unwilling to proceed after receiving a thorough notification of the purposes, methods, and intended uses of the forensic evaluation, the evaluation should be postponed and the psychologist should take steps to place the client in contact with his/her attorney for the purpose of legal advice on the issue of participation.

2. In situations where the client or party may not have the capacity to provide informed consent to services or the evaluation is pursuant to court order, the forensic psychologist provides reasonable notice to the client's legal representative of the nature of the anticipated forensic service before proceeding. If the client's legal representative objects to the evaluation, the forensic psychologist notifies the court issuing the order and responds as directed.

3. After a psychologist has advised the subject of a clinical forensic evaluation of the intended uses of the evaluation and its work product, the psychologist may not use the evaluation work product for other purposes without explicit waiver to do so by the client or the client's legal representative.

F. When forensic psychologists engage in research or scholarly activities that are compensated financially by a client or party to a legal proceeding, or when the psychologist provides those services on a *pro bono*

basis, the psychologist clarifies any anticipated further use of such research or scholarly product, discloses the psychologist's role in the resulting research or scholarly products, and obtains whatever consent or agreement is required by law or professional standards.

G. When conflicts arise between the forensic psychologist's professional standards and the requirements of legal standards, a particular court, or a directive by an officer of the court or legal authorities, the forensic psychologist has an obligation to make those legal authorities aware of the source of the conflict and to take reasonable steps to resolve it. Such steps may include, but are not limited to, obtaining the consultation of fellow forensic professionals, obtaining the advice of independent counsel, and conferring directly with the legal representatives involved.

V. CONFIDENTIALITY AND PRIVILEGE

A. Forensic psychologists have an obligation to be aware of the legal standards that may affect or limit the confidentiality or privilege that may attach to their services or their products, and they conduct their professional activities in a manner that respects those known rights and privileges.

1. Forensic psychologists establish and maintain a system of record keeping and professional communication that safeguards a client's privilege.

2. Forensic psychologists maintain active control over records and information. They only release information pursuant to statutory requirements, court order, or the consent of the client.

B. Forensic psychologists inform their clients of the limitations to the confidentiality of their services and their products (see also Guideline IV E) by providing them with an understandable statement of their rights, privileges, and the limitations of confidentiality.

C. In situations where the right of the client or party to confidentiality is limited, the forensic psychologist makes every effort to maintain confidentiality with regard to any information that does not bear directly upon the legal purpose of the evaluation.

D. Forensic psychologists provide clients or their authorized legal representatives with access to the information in their records and a meaningful explanation of that information, consistent with existing Federal and state statues, the *Ethical Principles of Psychologists, the Standards for Educational and Psychological Testing*, and institutional rules and regulations.

VI. METHODS AND PROCEDURES

A. Because of their special status as persons qualified as experts to the court, forensic psychologists have an obligation to maintain current knowledge of scientific, professional, and legal developments within their area of claimed competence. They are obligated also to use that knowledge, consistent with accepted clinical and scientific standards, in selecting data collection methods and procedures for an evaluation, treatment, consultation, or scholarly/empirical investigation.

B. Forensic psychologists have an obligation to document and be prepared to make available, subject to court order or the rules of evidence, all data that form the basis for their evidence or services. The standard to be applied to such documentation or recording *anticipates* that the detail and quality of such documentation will be subject to reasonable judicial scrutiny; this standard is higher than the normative standard for general clinical practice. When forensic psychologists conduct an examination or engage in the treatment of a party to a legal proceeding, with foreknowledge that their professional services will be used in an adjudicative forum, they incur a special responsibility to provide the best documentation possible under the circumstances.

1. Documentation of the data upon which one's evidence is based is subject to the normal rules of discovery, disclosure, confidentiality, and privilege that operate in the jurisdiction in which the data were obtained. Forensic psychologists have an obligation to be aware of those rules and to regulate their conduct in accordance with them.

2. The duties and obligations of forensic psychologists with respect to documentation of data that form the basis for their evidence apply from the moment they know or have a reasonable basis for knowing that their data and evidence derived from it are likely to enter into legally relevant decisions.

C. In providing forensic psychological services, forensic psychologists take special care to avoid undue influence upon their methods, procedures, and products, such as might emanate from the party to a legal proceeding by financial compensation or other gains. As an expert conducting an evaluation, treatment, consultation, or scholarly/empirical investigation, the forensic psychologist maintains professional integrity by examining the issue at hand from all reasonable perspectives, actively seeking information that will differentially test plausible rival hypotheses.

D. Forensic psychologists do not provide professional forensic services to a defendant or to any party in, or in contemplation of, a legal proceeding prior to that individual's representation by counsel, except for persons judicially determined, where appropriate, to be handling their representation *pro se*. When the forensic services are pursuant to court order and the client is not represented by counsel, the forensic psychologist makes reasonable efforts to inform the court prior to providing the services.

1. A forensic psychologist may provide emergency mental health services to a

pretrial defendant prior to court order or the appointment of counsel where there are reasonable grounds to believe that such emergency services are needed for the protection and improvement of the defendant's mental health and where failure to provide such mental health services would constitute a substantial risk of imminent harm to the defendant or to others. In providing such services the forensic psychologist nevertheless seeks to inform the defendant's counsel in a manner consistent with the requirements of the emergency situation.

2. Forensic psychologists who provide such emergency mental health services should attempt to avoid providing further professional forensic services to that defendant unless that relationship is reasonably unavoidable [see IV(D)(2)].

E. When forensic psychologists seek data from third parties, prior records, or other sources, they do so only with the prior approval of the relevant legal party or as a consequence of an order of a court to conduct the forensic evaluation.

F. Forensic psychologists are aware that hearsay exceptions and other rules governing expert testimony place a special ethical burden upon them. When hearsay or otherwise inadmissible evidence forms the basis of their opinion, evidence, or professional product, they seek to minimize sole reliance upon such evidence. Where circumstances reasonably permit, forensic psychologists seek to obtain independent and personal verification of data relied upon as part of their professional services to the court or to a party to a legal proceeding.

1. While many forms of data used by forensic psychologists are hearsay, forensic psychologists attempt to corroborate critical data that form the basis for their professional product. When using hearsay data that have not been corroborated, but are nevertheless utilized, forensic psychologists have an affirmative responsibility to acknowledge the uncorroborated status of those data and the reasons for relying upon such data.

2. With respect to evidence of any type, forensic psychologists avoid offering information from their investigations or evaluations that does not bear directly upon the legal purpose of their professional services and that is not critical as support for their product, evidence, or testimony, except where such disclosure is required by law.

3. When a forensic psychologist relies upon data or information gathered by others, the origins of those data are clarified in any professional product. In addition, the forensic psychologist bears a special responsibility to ensure that such data, if relied upon, were gathered in a manner standard for the profession.

G. Unless otherwise stipulated by the parties, forensic psychologists are aware that no statements made by a defendant, in the course of any (forensic) examination, no testimony by the expert based upon such statements, nor any other fruits of the statements can be admitted into evidence against the defendant in any criminal proceeding, except on an issue respecting mental condition on which the defendant has introduced testimony. Forensic psychologists have an affirmative duty to ensure that their written products and oral testimony conform to this Federal Rule of Procedure (12.2[c]), or its state equivalent.

1. Because forensic psychologists are often not in a position to know what evidence, documentation, or element of a written product may be or may lend to a "fruit of the statement," they exercise extreme caution in preparing reports or offering testimony prior to the defendant's assertion of a mental state claim

or the defendant's introduction of testimony regarding a mental condition. Consistent with the reporting requirements of state or federal law, forensic psychologists avoid including statements from the defendant relating to the time period of the alleged offense.

2. Once a defendant has proceeded to the trial stage, and all pretrial mental health issues such as competency have been resolved, forensic psychologists may include in their reports or testimony any statements made by the defendant that are directly relevant to supporting their expert evidence, providing that the defendant has "introduced" mental state evidence or testimony within the meaning of Federal Rule of Procedure 12.2(c), or its state equivalent.

H. Forensic psychologists avoid giving written or oral evidence about the psychological characteristics of particular individuals when they have not had an opportunity to conduct an examination of the individual adequate to the scope of the statements, opinions, or conclusions to be issued. Forensic psychologists make every reasonable effort to conduct such examinations. When it is not possible or feasible to do so, they make clear the impact of such limitations on the reliability and validity of their professional products, evidence, or testimony.

VII. PUBLIC AND PROFESSIONAL COMMUNICATIONS

A. Forensic psychologists make reasonable efforts to ensure that the products of their services, as well as their own public statements and professional testimony, are communicated in ways that will promote understanding and avoid deception, given the particular characteristics, roles, and abilities of various recipients of the communications.

1. Forensic psychologists take reasonable steps to correct misuse or misrepresentation of their professional products, evidence, and testimony.

2. Forensic psychologists provide information about professional work to clients in a manner consistent with professional and legal standards for the disclosure of test results, interpretations of data, and the factual bases for conclusions. A full explanation of the results of tests and the bases for conclusions should be given in language that the client can understand.

   a. When disclosing information about a client to third parties who are not qualified to interpret test results and data, the forensic psychologist complies with Principle 16 of the *Standards for Educational and Psychological Testing*. When required to disclose results to a nonpsychologist, every attempt is made to ensure that test security is maintained and access to information is restricted to individuals with a legitimate and professional interest in the data. Other qualified mental health professionals who make a request for information pursuant to a lawful order are, by definition, "individuals with a legitimate and professional interest."

   b. In providing records and raw data, the forensic psychologist takes reasonable steps to ensure that the receiving party is informed that raw scores must be interpreted by a qualified professional in order to provide reliable and valid information.

B. Forensic psychologists realize that their public role as "expert to the court" or as "expert representing the profession" confers upon them a special responsibility for fairness and accuracy in their public statements. When evaluating or commenting upon the professional work product or qualifications of another expert or party to a legal proceeding, forensic psychologists represent their professional disagreements with reference to a fair and accurate evaluation of the data, theories, standards, and opinions of the other expert or party.

C. Ordinarily, forensic psychologists avoid making detailed public (out-of-court) statements about particular legal proceedings in which they have been involved. When there is a strong justification to do so, such public statements are designed to assure accurate representation of their role or their evidence, not to advocate the positions of parties in the legal proceeding. Forensic psychologists address particular legal proceedings in publications or communications only to the extent that the information relied upon is part of a public record, or consent for that use has been properly obtained from the party holding any privilege.

D. When testifying, forensic psychologists have an obligation to all parties to a legal proceeding to present their findings, conclusions, evidence, or other professional products in a fair manner. This principle does not preclude forceful representation of the data and reasoning upon which a conclusion or professional product is based. It does, however, preclude an attempt, whether active or passive, to engage in partisan distortion or misrepresentation. Forensic psychologists do not, by either commission or omission, participate in a misrepresentation of their evidence, nor do they participate in partisan attempts to avoid, deny, or subvert the presentation of evidence contrary to their own position.

E. Forensic psychologists, by virtue of their competence and rules of discovery, actively disclose all sources of information obtained in the course of their professional services; they actively disclose which information from which source was used in formulating a particular written product or oral testimony.

F. Forensic psychologists are aware that their essential role as expert to the court is to assist the trier of fact to understand the evidence or to determine a fact in issue. In offering expert evidence, they are aware that their own professional observations, inferences, and conclusions must be distinguished from legal facts, opinions, and conclusions. Forensic psychologists are prepared to explain the relationship between their expert testimony and the legal issues and facts of an instant case.

The Relation Between Ethical Codes and Moral Principles

Donald N. Bersoff and Peter M. Koeppl

[*Ed. note:* This article, from which the following is an excerpt, appeared in a special issue of *Ethics and Behavior* devoted to forensic expert testimony. The article defines the prima facie duties of nonmaleficence, beneficence, fidelity, justice, and autonomy (see chap. 3) and examines how these same duties have been addressed in the 1992 APA Ethical Principles and the Specialty Guidelines for Forensic Psychologists.]

There are two sets of standards that directly address the activities of psychologists who do forensic work and serve as expert witnesses. The first is Part 7 of the APA (1992) code, denominated Forensic Activities. The second is the "Specialty Guidelines for Forensic Psychologists" (CEGFP, 1991) [footnote omitted]. The Forensic Activities section of the code and the specialty guidelines do not embody as explicitly the moral principles we have found in other provisions of the code. But Provision 7.01 reminds forensic psychologists that they "must comply with all other provisions of the Ethics Code" (APA, 1992, p. 1610) and the guidelines' purpose is to "amplify" the provisions of the APA ethics code "in the context of the practice of forensic psychology" (CEGFP, 1991, p. 656). Thus, to the extent that the philosophical duties we described are represented in the other enforceable provisions of the code, they may be said to be incorporated by reference in Part 7 and in the specialty guidelines.

Although less explicit, some allusion to prima facie duties are found in Part 7 of the code (APA, 1992), particularly fidelity, justice, and to some extent autonomy. If one defines *fidelity* not only as faithfulness to one's client but as allegiance to the scientific roots of one's profession (Diener & Crandall, 1978; Kitchener, 1984), then the code's Forensic Activities provisions are particularly salutary. Provision 7.04, for example, requires that "psychologists testify truthfully, honestly, and candidly . . ." (APA, 1992, p. 1610). Similarly, when necessarily compelled to testify with incomplete data, "psychologists clarify the impact of their limited information on the reliability and validity of their reports and testimony, and they appropriately limit the nature and extent of their conclusions or recommendations" (Provision 7.02, p. 1610). This emphasis on acting as a cautious, objective scientists, not as advocates for an empirically unsupported and predetermined position, also, of course, implements the obligation to act justly and equitably.

The requirements in the code (APA, 1992) that "psychologists avoid . . . potentially conflicting roles in forensic matters" (Provision 7.03, p. 1610) and "take into account ways in which . . . prior relationship[s] might affect their professional objectivity" (Provision 7.05, p. 1610) translate the duty of fidelity more traditionally. In addition, these mandates and the corollary responsibilities (i.e., to clarify role expectations and the conflicts that prior relationships with one or more of the parties to a legal proceedings might produce and clarify the limits of confidentiality found in Provisions 7.03 and 7.05) foster the principles of autonomy and justice.

In like manner, the specialty guidelines (CEGFP, 1991) contain translations of the moral obligations found in the prima facie duties. For example, the re-

From *Ethics and Behavior, 3,* 345–357. Copyright 1993 by Erlbaum. Adapted with permission of the author and publisher.

sponsibility to perform forensic tasks in ways that "do . . . not diminish or threaten" the civil rights of the parties (CEGFP, 1991, p. 658) and to decline to participate in activities in which one's competence as a forensic clinician would be impaired as a result of one's "personal values [or] moral beliefs" (p. 658) implement principles of nonmaleficence, justice, and fidelity. Similarly, the duty to refrain from testifying to any incriminating statements made by a criminal defendant during a forensic examination not only comports with constitutional requirements but exemplifies the principle of nonmaleficence as well (see Guideline VI[G], pp. 662–663). The guidelines ubiquitous references to fairness and accuracy in evaluations, testimony, and other public statements and the corollary obligations to avoid bias, partisanship, and misrepresentation are the most salutary translations of the duties of justice and fidelity.

The prima facie duty of autonomy is also well represented in the guidelines (CEGFP, 1991). Forensic psychologists are obligated to "inform the party of factors that might reasonably affect the decision to contract" with them (p. 658). They also have the responsibility to

> ensure that prospective clients are informed of their legal rights with respect to the anticipated forensic service, of the purposes of any evaluation, of the nature of procedures to be employed, of the intended uses of any product of their services, and of the party who has employed [them]. (p. 659)

Similarly, forensic psychologists are to "inform their clients of the limitations to the confidentiality of their services and their products . . . by providing them with an understandable statement of their rights, privileges, and the limitations of confidentiality" (p. 660). On the other hand, the suggested prohibition in the guidelines that potential experts refrain from providing forensic services to parties unrepresented by legal counsel (guideline VI[C], p. 661), although beneficial in its intent, diminishes a party's right to self-determination. A duty to disclose the risks of such undertakings might have satisfied the dual obligations of autonomy and beneficence.

Finally, as a result of their role, expert witnesses will always be confronted with questions of loyalty and concerns about acting as double agents (Monahan, 1980), particularly if they perform court-compelled examinations. Although the code encourages psychologists to "clarify role expectations and the extent of confidentiality in advance to the extent feasible" (APA, 1992, p. 1610) and the specialty guidelines require forensic experts to "recognize potential conflicts of interest in dual relationships" (CEGFP, 1991, p. 659), they will always be faced with moral dilemmas. For instance, to whom do forensic psychologists owe ultimate loyalty, and to what extent do they abide by the duty of nonmaleficence when it is the products of their endeavors that may lead to the conviction and punishment of a defendant? Because many examinees seen by forensic psychologists are referred by a third party such as a court, these referrals raise questions regarding the voluntariness of the client's participation. To which set of moral or professional principles do psychologists hold allegiance in these cases? The moral principle of autonomy assures clients that their choices will be respected. If clients do not agree to undergo a forensic evaluation, do psychologists have the prima facie duty to respect this desire? Or do they owe an overriding duty of fidelity to the referring agency? If the forensic evaluation is mandated by the court, this obligation may not be rescinded, even when the client is opposed to the procedure. As a result, a forensic psychologist may indeed be acting in accordance with the specialty guidelines but yet still be in conflict with the grander moral principles.

References

American Psychological Association. (1992). Ethical principles of psychologists and code of conduct. *American Psychologist, 47,* 1597–1611.

Committee on Ethical Guidelines for Forensic Psychologists. (1991). Specialty guidelines for forensic psychologists. *Law and Human Behavior, 15,* 655–665.

Diener, E., & Crandall, R. (1978). *Ethics in social and behavioral research.* Chicago: University of Chicago.

Kitchener, K. S. (1984). Intuition, critical evaluation and ethical principles: The foundation for ethical decisions in counseling psychology. *The Counseling Psychologist, 12,* 43–55.

Monahan, J. (Ed.). (1980). *Who is the client? The ethics of psychological intervention in the criminal justice system.* Washington, DC: American Psychological Association.

◆ ◆ ◆

Commentary: *Pfeifer and Brigham (1993) surveyed 37 academic forensic psychologists to identify ethical issues that they had encountered while consulting in pretrial phases of litigation or as experts during trials. Every one of the respondents reported that they had never "resolved their current ethical dilemmas by referring either to the APA's ethical principles or the [Committee on Ethical Guidelines for Forensic Psychologists's] specialty guidelines" (pp. 341–342). See Pfeifer, J. E., & Brigham, J. C. (1993). Ethical concerns of nonclinical forensic witnesses and consultants.* Ethics and Behavior, *3, 329–343. Many of the respondents suggested that ethical conflicts should be resolved through personal choice, beliefs, and values. What do these findings say about the utility of these two documents for scientists who serve as experts?*

In 1993, the U.S. Supreme Court issued an opinion that clarified the rules for the admissibility of scientific evidence in federal courts. The decision Daubert v. Merrell Dow Pharmaceutical Co., 509 U.S. 579 *(1993), excerpted in relevant part next, has already had a major impact on the testimony of all psychologists. See Bersoff, D. N., Dodds, L., Glass, D., Eckl, L., & Peters, L. (manuscript in preparation). The admissibility of forensic and social science evidence five years post-Daubert: A quantitative and qualitative analysis.* Psychology, Public Policy, and the Law.

Daubert v. Merrell Dow Pharmaceuticals, Inc.

. . .

[U]nder the [Federal] Rules [of Evidence] the trial judge must ensure that any and all scientific testimony or evidence admitted is not only relevant, but reliable.

The primary locus of this obligation is Rule 702, which clearly contemplates some degree of regulation of the subjects and theories about which an expert may testify: "*If scientific,* technical, or other specialized *knowledge will assist the trier of fact* to understand the evidence or to determine a fact in issue" an expert "may testify *thereto.*" (Emphasis added.) The subject of an expert's testimony must be "scientific . . . knowledge."[8] The adjective "scientific" implies a grounding in the methods and procedures of science. Similarly, the word "knowledge" connotes more than subjective belief or unsupported speculation. The term "applies to any body of known facts or to any body of ideas inferred from such facts or accepted as truths on good grounds." Webster's Third New International Dictionary 1252 (1986). Of course, it would be unreasonable to conclude that the subject of scientific testimony must be "known" to a certainty; arguably, there are no certainties in science. . . . But, in order to qualify as "scientific knowledge," an inference or assertion must be derived by the scientific method. Proposed testimony must be supported by appropriate validation—i.e., "good grounds," based on what is known. In short, the requirement that an expert's testimony pertain to "scientific knowledge" establishes a standard of evidentiary reliability.[9]

Rule 702 further requires that the evidence or testimony "assist the trier of fact to understand the evidence or to determine a fact in issue." This condition goes primarily to relevance. "Expert testimony which does not relate to any issue in the case is not relevant and, ergo, non-helpful." 3 Weinstein & Berger ¶702[02], pp. 702–18. . . . The consideration has been aptly described by Judge Becker as one of "fit." *Ibid.* "Fit" is not always obvious, and scientific validity for one purpose is not necessarily scientific validity for other, unrelated purposes. . . .

Rule 702's "helpfulness" standard requires a valid scientific connection to the pertinent inquiry as a precondition to admissibility.

That these requirements are embodied in Rule 702 is not surprising. Unlike an ordinary witness, see Rule 701, an expert is permitted wide latitude to offer opinions, including those that are not based on firsthand knowledge or observation. See Rules 702 and 703. Presumably, this relaxation of the usual requirement of firsthand knowledge—a rule which represents "a 'most pervasive manifestation' of the common law insistence upon 'the most reliable sources of information,'" Advisory Committee's Notes on Fed. Rule Evid. 602, 28 U.S.C. App., p. 755 (citation omitted)—is premised on an assumption that the expert's opinion will have a reliable basis in the knowledge and experience of his discipline.

Faced with a proffer of expert scientific testimony, then, the trial judge must determine at the

---

From *Daubert v. Merrell Dow Pharmaceuticals, Inc.*, 509 U.S. 579 (1993). Adapted with permission of the author and publisher.

[8] Rule 702 also applies to "technical, or other specialized knowledge." Our discussion is limited to the scientific context because that is the nature of the expertise offered here.

[9] We note that scientists typically distinguish between "validity" (does the principle support what it purports to show?) and "reliability" (does application of the principle produce consistent results?). . . . In a case involving scientific evidence, *evidentiary reliability* will be based upon *scientific validity.*

outset . . . whether the expert is proposing to testify to (1) scientific knowledge that (2) will assist the trier of fact to understand or determine a fact in issue [footnote omitted]. This entails a preliminary assessment of whether the reasoning or methodology underlying the testimony is scientifically valid and of whether that reasoning or methodology properly can be applied to the facts in issue. We are confident that federal judges possess the capacity to undertake this review. Many factors will bear on the inquiry, and we do not presume to set out a definitive checklist or test. But some general observations are appropriate.

Ordinarily, a key question to be answered in determining whether a theory or technique is scientific knowledge that will assist the trier of fact will be whether it can be (and has been) tested. "Scientific methodology today is based on generating hypotheses and testing them to see if they can be falsified; indeed, this methodology is what distinguishes science from other fields of human inquiry." Green 645. See also C. Hempel, Philosophy of Natural Science 49 (1966) ("[T]he statements constituting a scientific explanation must be capable of empirical test"); K. Popper, Conjectures and Refutations: The Growth of Scientific Knowledge 37 (5th ed. 1989) ("[T]he criterion of the scientific status of a theory is its falsifiability, or refutability, or testability") (emphasis deleted).

Another pertinent consideration is whether the theory or technique has been subjected to peer review and publication. Publication (which is but one element of peer review) is not a *sine qua non* of admissibility; it does not necessarily correlate with reliability, . . . in some instances well-grounded but innovative theories will not have been published. . . .

Some propositions, moreover, are too particular, too new, or of too limited interest to be published. But submission to the scrutiny of the scientific community is a component of "good science," in part because it increases the likelihood that substantive flaws in methodology will be detected. . . . The fact of publication (or lack thereof) in a peer reviewed journal thus will be a relevant, though not dispositive, consideration in assessing the scientific validity of a particular technique or methodology on which an opinion is premised.

Additionally, in the case of a particular scientific technique, the court ordinarily should consider the known or potential rate of error . . . and the existence and maintenance of standards controlling the technique's operation. . . .

Finally, "general acceptance" can yet have a bearing on the inquiry. A "reliability assessment does not require, although it does permit, explicit identification of a relevant scientific community and an express determination of a particular degree of acceptance within that community." *United States v. Downing*, 753 F. 2d, at 1238. . . . Widespread acceptance can be an important factor in ruling particular evidence admissible, and "a known technique which has been able to attract only minimal support within the community," *Downing*, 753 F. 2d, at 1238, may properly be viewed with skepticism.

The inquiry envisioned by Rule 702 is, we emphasize, a flexible one. Its overarching subject is the scientific validity—and thus the evidentiary relevance and reliability—of the principles that underlie a proposed submission. The focus, of course, must be solely on principles and methodology, not on the conclusions that they generate.

Institutional Constraints on the Ethics of Expert Testimony

Bruce D. Sales and Leonore Simon

. . .

A dramatic improvement in the quality of expert testimony could occur if experts reflected on their ethical obligations prior to becoming experts witnesses.

For example, Principle A of the *Ethical Principles of Psychologists and Code of Conduct* (APA, 1992) admonishes psychologists to recognize the boundaries of their competencies and the limitations of their expertise. If an expert witness has not kept up with the literature and testifies using out-of-date information, he or she would be violating the responsibility to be competent. And what of clinical psychologists who testify on a topic without training in the area? The issue of competence becomes salient once again.

Principle B of the ethical principles (APA, 1992) suggests that psychologists should promote integrity in psychology. Is the integrity benefitted or harmed by psychologists who assume the hired gun role or advocate their personal values, rather than presenting scientific knowledge? Advocacy that is one sided and intentionally presented to aid the client rather than present accurate scientific information runs afoul of this principle.

Manipulating testimony to achieve a personal goal might also run afoul of Principle F of the ethical principles (APA, 1992). It admonishes psychologists to apply their knowledge to contribute to and improve the society in which they live and work. For example, some testimony on the battered woman syndrome that passes for expertise involves expert witnesses who misuse their profession by failing to raise the existence of professional criticism about the accuracy of the diagnostic classification (e.g., Vidmar & Schuller, 1989). Such expert testimony would thus constitute a violation of the social responsibility ethic.

Similar examples can be found in the ethical standards that set down enforceable rules for conduct. For example, Ethical Standard 1.04 (APA, 1992) mandates that psychologists perform only within their area of competence, whereas Ethical Standard 1.05 requires psychologists to keep abreast of current scientific information to maintain their competence.

Clearly, ethical principles and standards are important to proscribe certain behaviors. But perhaps most important, if studied and applied regularly and consistently in the normal course of activities, ethical principles and standards provide the impetus for potential expert witnesses to evaluate (a) their decision to participate, (b) the way in which they will prepare for participation, and (c) the way in which they will participate. This self-reflection can improve the quality of expert witnessing.

The use of ethical principles and standards is not without its limits, however. By their very nature, ethics documents do not specifically address all issues and conundrums that experts will face in the courtroom. Indeed, ethical principles are typically broadly drawn so that they can be applied to a wide variety of behaviors. For example, Ethical Standard 1.16 (APA, 1992) prohibits psychologists from participating in activities in which their skills or knowledge are misused by others unless corrective mechanisms are available. Does this standard place a duty

From *Ethics and Behavior, 3,* 231–249. Copyright 1993 by Erlbaum. Adapted with permission of the author and publisher.

on psychologists to take reasonable steps to ensure that their testimony is not distorted even by the side that hired them? A potential solution is for the ethical principles to be supplemented by practice standards, such as the "Specialty Guidelines for Forensic Psychologists" (Committee on Ethical Guidelines for Forensic Psychologists, 1991). But whether this document or other practice standards comprehensively address the issues of concern will have to await further analysis. . . . In addition, if not adopted by the entire organization, such standards will have limited applicability. For example, the specialty guidelines was adopted by the American Psychology–Law Society, a Division of the APA. As such, it is applicable to the approximately 1,500 members of this division but not the remaining members of the APA.

There are other limitations as well. Standards of practice, including ethical principles and standards, do not guarantee excellence. They only institutionalize the minimum level of acceptable performance—competence. Competence in some court cases may not be sufficient when people's lives and/or property are at stake, particularly if we take our social responsibility ethic seriously. How then would ethical principles specify the expertise needed for different types of cases? A uniform standard may be too low in some cases and too high in others. The ethical principles should focus on the necessity of having requisite skills and engaging in a process of competent preparation to meet the demands of a task. But future research will need to explore the mechanics of implementing such an approach.

Finally, even if someone's behavior violated the ethical principles and standards, sanctioning the scientist would be a problem. Although the scientific organization that promulgated the ethical principles could enforce them, it could only do so against members. If scientists chose to drop out of the organization, the organization cannot force its rules on them. Even if violators maintained membership, sanctioning the majority of them is unlikely. It takes significant resources to identify and investigate potential violations, hold hearings to give potential violators an opportunity to present their side of the facts, and implement corrective interventions.

Another solution would be to enforce ethical principles and standards through malpractice actions; the principles could be used to designate the acceptable level of practice to which the scientist–consultant would have to adhere. However, expert witness immunity might prevent potential malpractice claims (e.g., *Bruce v. Byrne-Stevens & Associates Engineers, Inc.,* 1989). Even if permissible, the difficulty of this approach is that there would not be a party who would be likely to sue the scientist and have legal standing to do so. The scientist's employer—the lawyer and the client—would not sue if the scientist's testimony included what they hoped to hear; if the scientist was not going to support the lawyer and client's cause, he or she would not have been retained after the initial interview or would not appear in court. The other side would be unlikely to sue because malpractice actions require that the wrong-doer owe the complaining party a duty to adhere to a certain standard. Because the scientist was hired by the opposing side, the duty would be owed to that side. Some creative lawyering might get the courts to make certain that experts understand that they have a duty to both parties to perform competently on the argument that not to do so would hamper the factfinding process in trials or perhaps perpetrate a fraud on the court. We know of no cases that have considered this issue, however, and would not be optimistic that it would be a winning argument.

The truly injured party is an amorphous one—science, most likely as embodied in one of its scientific organizations. Yet, the scientific organization would not have standing to sue. And even if one did, it is unlikely that an organization would use this approach in any but the most flagrant cases because to do so might open up to question and public scrutiny the competence of the professional behaviors of all members. . . .

References

American Psychological Association. (1992). Ethical principles of psychologists and code of conduct. *American Psychologist, 47,* 1597–1611.

Bruce v. Byrne-Stevens & Associates Engineers, Inc., 776 P.2d 666 (Wash. 1989).

Committee on Ethical Guidelines for Forensic Psychologists. (1991). Specialty guidelines for forensic psychologists. *Law and Human Behavior, 15,* 655–665.

Vidmar, N. J., & Schuller, R. A. (1989). Juries and expert evidence: Social framework testimony. *Law and Contemporary Problems, 52,* 133–176.

◆ ◆ ◆

Commentary: *Sales and Simon conjectured that the immunity from lawsuits (but not from perjury) that expert witnesses enjoy regarding their in-court testimony makes it unlikely that incompetent experts will be sanctioned by the legal system. However, a California appeals court upheld the APA's right to censure one of its members for presenting false testimony in a child custody hearing. The court held that, although court-appointed psychologists are protected from liability (such as malpractice) arising from communications made during judicial proceedings or when acting for courts in resolving custody disputes, that did not preclude professional associations from disciplining their members for violating their ethics. See Budwin v. American Psychological Association, 24 Cal. App. 4th 875, 29 Cal. Rptr. 2d 453 (Cal. App. 3d Dist. 1994).*

In an article published contemporaneously with Sales and Simon's, Perrin and Sales (1994) concluded that the 1992 APA Ethical Principles "provides an initial, but modest attempt to address ethical issues related to forensic practice" (p. 380); but they also found many of the forensic provisions to be so vague as to "provide virtually no specific guidance" (p. 379). See Perrin, G. I., &

Sales, B. D. (1994). Forensic standards in the American Psychological Association ethics code. Professional Psychology: Research and Practice, 25, 376–382.

In this same article, Perrin and Sales (1994) stated that

> providers of forensic services must be aware of, and sensitive to, the potential conflicts between the psychological roles of examiner, therapist, and consultant; between the legal roles of expert witness and fact witness; and between the roles of advocate for the client and advocate for the professional opinion.
>
> . . .
>
> The identification of who is the client has important ramifications in the determination of what service is to be provided, who is to have access to the information, what information is to be confidential, what product is to be generated by the psychologist, to whom the psychologist is to report, and who is to pay the fee for the service. (pp. 377–378)

Standard 7.03 (Clarification of Role) provides some guidance on these issues, but they are much more complex than the Standard contemplates. Some of their complexities are addressed in the next set of materials.

Expert Opinion

American Psychology–Law Society

THE QUESTION

You are a psychologist in private practice and have been working in therapy with a client whose complaints include anxiety and depression attributed to a variety of problems, including dissatisfaction at work, problems in her marriage, and unresolved anger toward family members for events that occurred long ago. During the fourth month of therapy you receive a call from an attorney who reports that she is representing the client in a lawsuit against her employer, alleging that the client has been the victim of sexual harassment and a hostile work environment, resulting in emotional disability. The lawyer advises that, as a mental health professional intimately knowledgeable about her client's mental condition, she intends to call you as an expert witness in the upcoming trial in civil court. She inquires about your hourly fee for forensic evaluation and expert testimony, and then asks you to conduct whatever additional evaluations are needed to prepare for court. She also indicates that she will ask you to testify about the client's diagnosis, treatment, and adjustment. The attorney advises that she has already informed your client of this possibility; a faxed release that you receive later in the afternoon confirms that your client is agreeable to this. What should you do?

THE RESPONSE

The response is from Stephen Golding, Ph.D., Professor, Department of Psychology, University of Utah. . . .

First for the easy part. No particular problems with respect to confidentiality exist in that the client has explicitly waived her privilege [EPPCC 5.05, Disclosures]. However, the therapist should discuss this matter with the client and not rely solely upon the client's lawyer to have adequately informed her of what sorts of information would be disclosed at trial. That is, the informed consent obtained at the start of therapy would not ordinarily have included this sort of information, and the therapist should ensure that the client fully understands the nature of the personal disclosures that would be entailed by her testifying [SGFP section IV-E, and V, as well as corresponding sections of EPPCC].

Now for the hard part. In my view, the therapist cannot agree to become an "expert" witness in this case. While she may have detailed professional information about the client's "diagnosis, treatment, and adjustment," this information was obtained in the context of a therapeutic relationship, not in the context of an independent and neutral evaluation of the client's response to the alleged sexual harassment. Thus, according to the EPPCC [7.05], the therapist may testify as a "fact witness," conveying her professional information as to diagnosis, treatment progress, and the like, but she should not agree to offer "expert" testimony on the underlying psycholegal issue, namely, the causative connection between the alleged harassment and any "emotional harm." Clearly, the therapist is in a professional position to offer the former sort of testimony, but should make clear [SGFP III-B, Boundaries of Competence; EPPCC 7.02, Forensic assessments] that she did not undertake, in the course of diagnosing and treating this client, the kind of psycholegal assessment that would be required to address the causation-harm issues. The sort of expert testimony requested would, in my view, require an analysis of the client's level of emotional adjustment prior to the alleged sexual harassment as well as an analysis of her emotional state during and consequent to that harassment. In performing such an analysis competently and independently, a forensic examiner would ordinarily rely upon data from prior records as well as interviews of a number of third parties, and would not base her findings solely upon the self-report of the client. This is a very different data base than that to which the therapist would typically have access. In addition, the therapist's pre-existing relationship with the client would constitute a dual-role which would make it difficult, if not impossible, for her to assume the "neutral" role (and to gather that "additional information") having already formed a therapeutic relationship with the client.

Hence, I see this vignette as primarily involving problems of dual roles, which in turn raise issues about the adequacy of the assessment. In my view, the therapist can testify as a "fact" witness, but not as an "expert." If she has performed an adequate assessment of her client prior to and during their therapeutic relationship, she can greatly assist her client, but she does not have either the objectivity or the data that would be required for her to agree to change from the role of therapist to that of expert.

Commentary: It would be a useful exercise to draft a rebuttal to Golding's analysis. What provisions in the APA Ethical Principles or the forensic guidelines, if any, would support acting in the role of expert in this case? To what extent is a client's request for his or her psychologist to testify as an expert significant? In thinking about this issue, you may want to also consider the following excerpt.

Irreconcilable Conflict Between Therapeutic and Forensic Roles

Stuart A. Greenberg and Daniel W. Shuman

With increasing frequency, psychologists, psychiatrists, and other mental health professionals are participating as forensic experts in litigation on behalf of their patients. . . . [T]his practice constitutes engaging in dual-role relationships and often leads to bad results for patients, courts, and clinicians.

Although there are explicit ethical precepts about psychologists and psychiatrists engaging in these conflicting roles, they have not eliminated this conduct. One important factor contributing to this continued conduct is that psychologists and psychiatrists have not understood why these ethical precepts exist and how they affect the behavior of even the most competent therapists. When the reasons for the ethical precepts are understood, it is clear why no psychologist, psychiatrist, or other mental health professional is immune from the concerns that underlie them.

This article contrasts the role of therapeutic clinician as care provider and the role of forensic evaluator as expert to the court, acknowledges the temptation to engage in these two roles in the same matter, explains the inherent problems and argues strongly against doing so, and discusses the ethical precepts that discourage the undertaking of the dual roles, as well as the legal and professional responses to this dilemma. The specific problem addressed here is that of the psychologist or psychiatrist who provides clinical assessment or therapy to a patient–litigant and who concurrently or subsequently attempts to serve as a forensic expert for that patient in civil litigation.

Expert persons may testify as fact witnesses as well as either of two types of expert witnesses: treating experts and forensic experts. No special expertise beyond the ability to tell the court what is known from first-hand observation is required to be a fact witness. Being an expert person, however, does not preclude one from simply providing to the court first-hand observations in the role of a fact witness. What distinguishes expert witnesses from fact witnesses is that expert witness have relevant specialized knowledge beyond that of the average person that may qualify them to provide opinions, as well as facts, to aid the court in reaching a just conclusion. Psychologists and psychiatrists who provide patient care can usually qualify to testify as treating experts, in that they have the specialized knowledge, not possessed by most individuals, to offer a clinical diagnosis and prognosis. However, a role conflict arises when a treating therapist also attempts to testify as a forensic expert addressing the psycholegal issues in the case (e.g., testamentary capacity, proximate cause of injury, parental capacity). . . .

ROLE CONFLICT

In most jurisdictions, a properly qualified therapist testifies as a fact witness for some purposes, as he or she is expected to testify to information learned first hand in therapy, and as an expert witness for some purposes, as he or she is permitted to testify to opinions about mental disorder that a layperson would not be permitted to offer. Thus, a therapist may, if requested to do so by a patient or ordered to do so by a court, properly testify to facts, observa-

From *Professional Psychology: Research and Practice, 28,* 50–57. Copyright 1997 by the American Psychological Association. Adapted with permission of the author and publisher.

tions, and clinical opinions for which the therapy process provides a trustworthy basis. This testimony may include the history as provided by a patient; the clinical diagnosis; the care provided to a patient; the patient's response to that treatment; the patient's prognosis; the mood, cognitions, or behavior of the patient at particular times; and any other statements that the patient made in treatment. A therapist may properly testify, for example, that Ms. Jones reported the history of a motor vehicle accident (MVA) 2 weeks prior to the start of therapy and that the therapist observed the patient to be bruised, bandaged, tearful, and extremely anxious. The therapist may properly testify that he or she observed, and that Ms. Jones reported, symptoms that led to a diagnosis of posttraumatic stress disorder (PTSD). The therapist may also describe the particular type of treatment used, the patient's response to that treatment, and her prognosis. The therapist may properly testify that the primary focus for the therapy was the MVA, or the PTSD secondary to the MVA. The therapist may even properly testify that, for treatment purposes, the operating assumption was that the MVA rather than her impending divorce or recent job termination or the death of a family member was what caused the patient's distress.

To be admissible, an expert opinion must be reliable and valid to a reasonable degree of scientific certainty (a metric for scrutinizing the certainty of expert testimony as a condition of its admissibility). It is improper for the therapist to offer an expert opinion that the MVA was the proximate cause of her impairments rather than the divorce, job termination, or bereavement. This is true for two reasons. First, the type and amount of data routinely observed in therapy are rarely adequate to form a proper foundation to determine the psycholegal (as opposed to the clinically assumed) cause of the litigant's impairment, nor is therapy usually adequate to rule out other potential causes. Second, such testimony engages the therapist in conflicting roles with the patient. Common examples of this role conflict occur when a patient's therapist testifies to the psycholegal issues that arise in competency, personal injury, worker's compensation, and custody litigation.

These concerns do not apply when the treating expert witness stays within the boundaries of facts and opinions that can be reliably known by the treating professional. Indeed, the treating therapist can be compelled to testify to information perceived during the therapeutic process and to opinions previously formed for the purpose of therapy but cannot be compelled to do a forensic examination or analysis (Shuman, 1983). Clinical, ethical, and legal concerns arise when the treating expert offers psycholegal assessment—an assessment for which the treating expert does not have adequate professional basis, for which there are inherent role conflicts, and for which there will almost certainly be negative implications for continued therapy.

The temptation to use therapists as forensic experts falls on fertile ground because clinical psychology and psychiatry graduate students often do not receive adequate training in forensic ethics. Although graduate training in ethics has vastly improved in general, most graduate ethics courses teach clinicians in training about the dual roles that most often get therapists in difficulties: mainly, sexual and other nonprofessional relationships with patients. The legal arena is sufficiently foreign to most academicians and their students that ethics training primarily focuses on licensing laws and ethical codes for general practice. For example, few psychologists receive training in the Specialty Guidelines for Forensic Psychologists (Committee on Ethical Guidelines for Forensic Psychologists, 1991) because few see themselves as forensic psychologists. When these clinicians eventually testify in court, they see themselves as benignly telling the court about their patients and perhaps even benevolently testifying on behalf of their patients. Therapists are not typically trained to know that the rules of procedure, rules of evidence, and the standard of proof are different for court room testimony than for clinical practice.

The temptation to use therapists as forensic experts on behalf of patient–litigants exists because of erroneous beliefs about efficiency, candor, neutrality, and expertise. Using a therapist to provide forensic assessment appears efficient because the therapist has already spent time with the patient and knows much about him or her that others are yet to learn and not without substantial expenditures of time and money for an additional evaluation. A therapist appears to gain candid information from a patient—

litigant because of the patient's assumed incentive to be candid with the therapist to receive effective treatment. Although litigants may learn much about themselves as a consequence of receiving thorough forensic evaluations (Finn & Tonsager, 1996), the same treatment incentive does not exist in a forensic examination. Thus, the facts forming the basis for a therapist's opinion may initially appear more accurate and complete than the facts that could be gathered in a separate forensic assessment.

In addition, a therapist does not appear to be the attorney's hired gun who came into the case solely to assist in advancing or defeating a legal claim or defense. Thus, a therapist's forensic assessment may appear more neutral and less immediately subject to financial incentives to reach a particular result than does a separate forensic evaluation. And, it is sometimes assumed that if a therapist has the expertise to be trusted to treat the condition for which a patient seeks compensation, surely the therapist has the ex-

pertise to testify about it. Indeed, in many ways it would appear from this analysis that one would have to be foolish not to have therapists also testify as forensic experts. Nevertheless, examining the differences between the therapeutic and forensic relationships, process, and expertise reveals that such foolishness is the mirror image of sensibility.

TEN DIFFERENCES BETWEEN THERAPEUTIC AND FORENSIC RELATIONSHIPS

As can be seen from Table 1, the therapeutic and forensic roles demand different and inconsistent orientations and procedures (adapted from Greenberg & Moreland, 1995). The superficial and perilous appeal of using a therapist as a forensic examiner is debunked by examining the conceptual and practical differences between the therapist–patient relationship and the forensic examiner–litigant relationship.

TABLE 1

Ten Differences Between Therapeutic and Forensic Relationships

		Care provision	Forensic evaluation
1.	Whose client is patient/litigant?	The mental health practitioner	The attorney
2.	The relational privilege that governs disclosure in each relationship	Therapist–patient privilege	Attorney-client and attorney work-product privilege
3.	The cognitive set and evaluative attitude of each expert	Supportive, accepting, empathic	Neutral, objective, detached
4.	The differing areas of competency of each expert	Therapy techniques for treatment of the impairment	Forensic evaluation techniques relevant to the legal claim
5.	The nature of the hypotheses tested by each expert	Diagnostic criteria for the purpose of therapy	Psycholegal criteria for purpose of legal adjudication
6.	The scrutiny applied to the information utilized in the process and the role of historical truth	Mostly based on information from the person being treated with little scrutiny of that information by the therapist	Litigant information supplemented with that of collateral sources and scrutinized by the evaluator and the court
7.	The amount and control of structure in each relationship	Patient structured and relatively less structured than forensic evaluation	Evaluator structured and relatively more structured than therapy
8.	The nature and degree of "adversarialness" in each relationship	A helping relationship; rarely adversarial	An evaluative relationship; frequently adversarial
9.	The goal of the professional in each relationship	Therapist attempts to benefit the patient by working within the therapeutic relationship	Evaluator advocates for the results and implications of the evaluation for the benefit of the court
10.	The impact on each relationship of critical judgment by the expert	The basis of the relationship is the therapeutic alliance and critical judgment is likely to impair that alliance	The basis of the relationship is evaluative and critical judgment is unlikely to cause serious emotional harm

The first and perhaps most crucial difference between the roles is the identification of whose client
the patient–litigant is. As implied by the name, the
patient–litigant has two roles, one as therapy patient
and another as plaintiff in the legal process. The
patient–litigant is the client of the therapist for the
purposes of treatment. The patient–litigant is as well
the client of the attorney for guidance and representation through the legal system.

The nature of each relationship and the person
who chooses to create it differs for therapy and forensic evaluation. The therapist is ultimately answerable to the client, who decides whether to use the
services of a particular therapist; the forensic evaluator is ultimately answerable to the attorney, or the
court in the case of a court-appointed expert, who
decides whether to use the services of a particular
forensic evaluator. The patient retains the therapist
for treatment. The attorney (or the court) retains the
forensic evaluator for litigation. This arrangement allows for the relationship that is most straightforward
and free of conflict of interest. It best protects the
parties' interests as well as the integrity of the therapist and the forensic evaluator.

Second, the legal protection against compelled
disclosure of the contents of a therapist–patient relationship is governed by the therapist–patient privilege and can usually only be waived by the patient
or by court order. Society seeks to further the goal
of treatment through recognition of a privilege for
confidential communications between a therapist
and patient in most jurisdictions under a physician,
psychiatrist–, psychologist–, or psychotherapist–
patient privilege (Shuman & Weiner, 1987).

Legal protection against compelled disclosure of
the contents of the forensic evaluator–litigant relationship is governed by the attorney–client and
attorney–work-product privileges. Because the purpose of a forensic relationship is litigation, not treatment nor even diagnosis for the purpose of planning
treatment, communications between a forensic
examiner and a litigant are not protected under
a physician–, psychiatrist–, psychologist–,
or psychotherapist–patient privilege. The forensic
evaluator, however, having been retained by the attorney, is acting as an agent of the attorney in evaluating the party or parties in the legal matter. This le-

gal agency status puts the forensic evaluator under
the umbrella of the attorney–client privilege and
usually protects privileged information until such
time that the evaluator is declared to be a witness at
trial. Until that time, most states, especially in civil
matters, allow the attorney to prevent access to that
attorney's retained expert by opposing counsel, thus
best protecting the party's interest should the evaluator's independent opinion not favor the party of the
attorney who has retained him or her. Because it
would not be a therapeutic relationship, no such
potential protection is available if the forensic evaluator were to be retained directly by the party,
thereby creating the onus of one's own expert who
was hired to evaluate some potential merit to the
case instead being used to discredit the retaining
side. Because parties, through their attorneys, need
to be able to evaluate the merits of their case candidly without such jeopardy, the attorney–
work-product privilege covers such trial-preparation
use of experts retained by counsel.

The main practice point to be made here is that
the logic, the legal basis, and the rules governing the
privilege that applies to care providers are substantially different from those that apply to forensic evaluators. Given this, the duty to inform forensic examinees of the potential lack of privilege and the
intended use of the examination product is embodied in case law (*Estelle v. Smith*, 1981) and the Specialty Guidelines for Forensic Psychologists (SGFP)
adopted by the American Psychology–Law Society
(APA Division 41) and the American Board of Forensic Psychology in 1991 [see Guideline IV(E)]. . . .

The third difference is evident in the evaluative
attitude of each of the experts. The therapist is a
care provider and usually supportive, accepting, and
emphatic; the forensic evaluator is an assessor and
usually neutral, objective, and detached as to the forensic issues. A forensic evaluator's task is to gain an
emphatic understanding of the person but to remain
dispassionate as to the psycholegal issues being evaluated. For therapists, empathy and sympathy—
generating a desire to help—usually go hand-in-
hand. For forensic evaluators, the task is a dispassionate assessment of the psycholegal issues.

Fourth, to perform his or her task, a therapist
must be competent in the clinical assessment and

treatment of the patient's impairment. In contrast, a forensic evaluator must be competent in forensic evaluation procedures and psycholegal issues relevant to the case. A therapist must be familiar with the literature on diagnoses and treatment interventions, knowing from among which diagnostic categories and treatment interventions the patient's difficulties would be best identified and treated. The forensic evaluator must know the basic law as it relates to the assessment of the particular impairment claimed.

Fifth, a therapist then uses this expertise to test rival diagnostic hypotheses to ascertain which therapeutic intervention is most likely to be effective. For example, a therapeutic diagnostic question might be whether a patient is a better candidate for insight-oriented psychotherapy, systematic desensitization, or psychopharmacologic intervention. A forensic evaluator must know the relevant law and how it relates to a particular psychological assessment. A forensic evaluator then uses this expertise to test a very different set of rival psycholegal hypotheses that are generated by the elements of the law applicable to the legal case being adjudicated. . . .

The sixth difference is the degree of scrutiny to which information from the patient–litigant is subjected. Historical truth plays a different role in each relationship. At least with competent adults, therapy is primarily based on information from the person being treated, information that may be somewhat incomplete, grossly biased, or honestly misperceived. Even when the therapist does seek collateral information from outside of therapy, such as when treating children and incompetent adults, the purpose of the information gathering is to further treatment, not in the pursuit of validating historical truth. In most instances, it is not realistic, nor is it typically the standard of care, to expect a therapist to be an investigator to validate the historical truth of what a patient discusses in therapy. Indeed, trying to do so by contacting family members, friends, or coworkers and by requesting corroborating documentation may frustrate therapy even if the patient has signed a release of information. Further, this corroboration is usually unnecessary. Effective therapy can usually proceed even in the face of substantial historical inaccuracy. For example, a patient's impaired self-esteem, body image, and sexual interest might be effectively treated regardless of the fact that her reported memory of having been sexually abused early in childhood by her maternal uncle was inaccurate and that she was actually abused by her paternal uncle. . . .

The more important question for most psychotherapeutic techniques is how a patient perceives or feels about the world—what is real to that patient—not factual or historical truth (Wesson, 1985). Even for those therapeutic techniques that involve confrontation and challenge of a patient's conceptions of events, therapists rarely conduct factual investigations into circumstances surrounding patient claims in therapy. Thus, the historical truth of matters raised during therapy cannot, simply on that basis alone, be considered valid and reliable for legal purposes. This is not a criticism of therapy. This approach to psychotherapy makes sense given its temporal framework. If a patient report or a diagnostic hypothesis is not borne out, it can be revised in later sessions. This approach to therapy, which is informed and educated but still somewhat trial-and-error, typically does no harm unless the patient is in a high-risk situation, such as being suicidal or in an abusive environment.

In contrast, the role of a forensic examiner is, among other things, to offer opinions regarding historical truth and the validity of the psychological aspects of a litigant's claims. The accuracy of this assessment is almost always more critical in a forensic context than it is in psychotherapy. A competent forensic evaluation almost always includes verification of the litigant's accuracy against other information sources about the events in question. These sources may include collateral interviews with coworkers, neighbors, family members, emergency room personnel, or a child's teacher or pediatrician and a review of documents such as police reports, school records, military records, medical records, personnel files, athletic team attendance, credit card bills, check stubs, changes in one's resume, depositions, witness statements, and any other possible sources of information about the litigant's pre- and postincident thoughts, emotions, and behaviors. However, therapists do face a dilemma regarding the historical accuracy of the information provided by the patient, depending on how they or their patients act on that information. This is illustrated by a case in which a therapist was successfully sued for slander by a father who was identified through memories recovered in therapy as allegedly having abused the therapist's patient as a child every Friday evening. The father offered employment records at the therapist's trial that revealed that he had worked for the railroad and had been working out of town every Friday evening in question (Blow, 1995).

Seventh, the need for historical accuracy in forensic evaluations leads to a need for completeness in the information acquired and for structure in the assessment process to accomplish that goal. Therapeutic evaluation, in comparison, is relatively less complete and less structured than a forensic evaluation. Moreover, a patient provides more structure to a therapeutic evaluation than does a litigant to a forensic evaluation. Ideally, a patient and therapist work collaboratively to define the goals of a therapeutic interaction and a time frame within which to realize them. The time frame and goals of a forensic evaluation are defined by the legal rules that govern the proceeding, and once these are determined, the forensic evaluator and litigant are usually constrained to operate within them. To make maximum use of the time available, forensic evaluators usually conduct highly structured assessments using structured interviews supplemented with a battery of psychological tests and forensically oriented history and impairment questionnaires. Certainly the plaintiff is encouraged to describe the events in question, but it is the forensic evaluator's task to establish a preincident baseline of functioning, a complete description of the incidents alleged in the legal complaint, the subsequent areas of resilience and impairment of the plaintiff's functioning, the proximate cause of any impairment, and the likely future functioning of the plaintiff, if necessary, ameliorated or enhanced by any needed therapy.

Eighth, although some patients will resist discussing emotionally laden information, the psychotherapeutic process is rarely adversarial in the attempt to reveal that information. Forensic evaluation, although not necessarily unfriendly or hostile, is nonetheless adversarial in that the forensic evaluator seeks information that both supports and refutes

the litigant's legal assertions. This struggle for information is also handled quite differently by each expert: The therapist exercises therapeutic judgment about pressing a patient to discuss troubling material, whereas a forensic evaluator will routinely seek information from other sources if the litigant will not provide it or to corroborate it when the litigant does provide information. In the extreme, when presented with excessive underreporting or overreporting of critical information, the forensic evaluator might even decide that the litigant is dissembling.

Ninth, consider the goals of each of these relationships. Therapy is intended to aid the person being treated. A therapist–patient relationship is predicated on principles of beneficence and nonmaleficence—doing good and avoiding harm. A therapist attempts to intervene in a way that will improve or enhance the quality of the person's life. Effective treatment for a patient is the reason and the principal defining force for the therapeutic relationship. . . .

Forensic examiners strive to gather and present objective information that may ultimately aid a trier of fact (i.e., judge or jury) to reach a just solution to a legal conflict. A forensic examiner is obligated to be neutral, independent, and honest, without becoming invested in the legal outcome. A forensic evaluator advocates for the findings of the evaluation, whatever those findings turn out to be. Thus, the results of a forensic examination may well be detrimental to the legal position of an examinee (American Psychiatric Association, 1984) and contrary to basic therapeutic principles.

Tenth, the patient–litigant is likely to feel differently about expert opinions rendered by therapists than those rendered by forensic experts. Consider the role of judgment in therapeutic relationships. There is a robust, positive relationship between the success of the therapist–patient alliance and success in therapy (Horvath & Luborsky, 1993). To develop a positive therapist–patient alliance, a therapist must suspend judgment of the patient so that the therapist can enter and understand the private perceptual world of the patient without doing anything that would substantially threaten that relationship. Indeed, some believe that even a posttherapy disturbance of this therapeutic alliance may cause serious harm to a patient; hence many advocate substantial limitations on personal relationships between former patients and their therapists.

In contrast, the role of a forensic examiner is to assess, to judge, and to report that finding to a third party (attorney, judge, or jury) who will use that information in an adversarial setting. To assess, a forensic examiner must be detached, maybe even skeptical, and must carefully question what the litigant presents. Because a forensic psychologist or psychiatrist has not engaged in a helping relationship with the litigant, it is less likely that his or her judgment-laden testimony would cause serious or lasting emotional harm to the litigant than would that of the psychologist or psychiatrist who has occupied a therapeutic role.

WAIVING THE DUAL-ROLE CONFLICT

These role differences are not merely artificial distinctions but are substantial differences that make inherently good sense. Unless these distinctions are respected, not only are both the therapeutic and forensic endeavors jeopardized for the patient–litigant but as well the rights of all parties who are affected by this erroneous and conflictual choice. Unlike some conflicts of interest, this role conflict is not one that the plaintiff can waive, because it is not the exclusive province of the plaintiff's side of the case. The conflict affects not only the plaintiff but also the defense and the court. This conflict not only poses therapeutic risks to the patient–litigant but also risks of inaccuracy and lack of objectivity to the court's process and to all of the litigants.

[*Ed. note:* The authors now cite principles from various documents that bar dual and conflicting professional roles with patient–litigants, the most relevant of which are already reprinted in this text.] . . .

CONCLUSION

Psychologists, psychiatrists, and other mental health professionals have given and received criticism about the use of expert witnesses whose partisanship appears to overwhelm their professionalism. Engaging in conflicting therapeutic and forensic relationships exacerbates the danger that experts will be more concerned with case outcome than the accuracy of their testimony. Therapists are usually highly invested in the welfare of their patients and rightfully concerned that publicly offering some candid opinions about their patient's deficits could seriously impair their patient's trust in them. They are often unfamiliar with the relevant law and the psycholegal issues it raises. They are often unaware of much of the factual information in the case, and much of what they know comes solely from the patient and is often uncorroborated. What they do know, they know primarily, if not solely, from their patient's point of view. They are usually sympathetic to their patient's plight, and they usually want their patient to prevail.

By failing to recognize the inherent limitations of their work as therapists, as well as the conflicting therapeutic and forensic roles, psychologists, psychiatrists, and other mental health professionals risk harm to their profession, their patients, and the courts. Although therapists frequently enter the forensic arena in their efforts to help, these efforts may not only put therapists in ethical difficulty but may also neutralize the impact both of their testimony and their work as therapists. Therapists need to acknowledge the limits of what they can accurately and reliably say on the basis of therapeutic relationships. Although it is difficult, when asked psycholegal questions, therapists must be willing to testify "I cannot answer that question given my role in this case," "I do not have an adequate professional basis to answer that question," "I did not conduct the kind of evaluation necessary to reliably answer that question," "I can only tell you what I observed," or "I can only tell you what my patient told me." No matter how laudable their motives might be, therapists who venture beyond these limits and into the arena of psycholegal opinion are deceiving themselves and others. Engaging in an irreconcilable role conflict and lacking an adequate professional basis for their testimony, they can be neither neutral, objective, nor impartial.

References

American Psychiatric Association. (1984). *Psychiatry in the sentencing process: A report of the task force on the role of psychiatry in the sentencing process.* Washington, DC: Author.

Blow, S. (1995, January 11). Slander case shakes family. *Dallas Morning News*, p. 25a.

Committee on Ethical Guidelines for Forensic Psychologists. (1991). Specialty guidelines for forensic psychologists. *Law and Human Behavior, 15,* 655–665.

Estelle v. Smith. 451 U.S. 454 (1981).

Finn, S. E., & Tonsager, M. E. (1996). *Therapeutic assessment: Using psychological testing to help clients change.* Manuscript submitted for publication.

Greenberg, S. A., & Moreland, K. (1995). *Forensic evaluations and forensic applications of the MMPI/MMPI-2.* Unpublished manuscript, University of Minnesota, Department of Continuing Education and Conference Services, Minneapolis, and The American Academy of Forensic Psychology.

Horvath, A. O., & Luborsky, L. (1993). The role of the therapeutic alliance in psychotherapy. *Journal of Consulting and Clinical Psychology, 61,* 561–573.

Shuman, D. W. (1983). Testimonial compulsion: The involuntary medical expert witness. *Journal of Legal Medicine, 4,* 419–446.

Shuman, D. W., & Weiner, M. F. (1987). *The psychotherapist–patient privilege: A critical examination.* Springfield, IL: Thomas.

Wesson, M. (1985). Historical truth, narrative truth, and expert testimony. *Wash. L. Rev., 60,* 331–354.

◆　◆　◆

Commentary: *More recently, Shuman, Greenberg, and their colleagues proposed that therapists should be prohibited from testifying about their patients in all legal contexts, arguing that all such dual-relationship testimony harms the judicial system as well as treatment. See Shuman, D. W., Greenberg, S., Heilbrun, K., & Foote, W. E. (1998). An immodest proposal: Should treating mental health professionals be barred from testifying about their patients? Behavioral Sciences and the Law, 16, 509–523. But what if the patient is asserting an insanity defense? Who would know better the mental state of the patient at the time of the crime than the therapist? What about a case in which the patient was injured and this injury made his/her mental status an issue, i.e., he or she suffered psychic trauma as a result of the injury? Perhaps barring the therapist's testimony would prevent the jury from hearing the most professional opinion about the patient's psychological status just prior to the injury and his or her subsequent status. Shuman et al. take on these concerns. See if other counterarguments are persuasive.*

Role Conflicts in Coercive Assessments: Evaluation and Recommendations

Jose M. Arcaya

. . .

BACKGROUND CONSIDERATIONS

Psychologists normally are trained to administer evaluations in situations in which the clients freely present themselves for testing or examination. These settings—for example, mental health clinics, hospitals, and private practice offices—generally operate according to administrative philosophies that are consistent with the psychologist's own ethical standards to respect the client's privacy and confidentiality. . . .

However, when traditionally trained psychologists—who are thus taught to be protective of the client's privacy, freedom, and integrity—are hired by the various agencies of the criminal justice system (e.g., courts, police departments, prisons, community treatment centers) to conduct assessments, they are required to establish a different kind of professional understanding with their client–offenders. These agencies require that psychologists diversify their professional allegiances. They expect the psychologists to be concerned not only about their clients' welfares, but also about the practical exigencies facing these forensic employers (e.g., maintaining institutional order, upholding court-ordered legal standards, fulfilling governmental mandates) and the general safety of the community.

In the criminal justice system, psychologists are necessarily expected to share their assessment results with many more individuals (e.g., lawyers, administrators, probation-parole officers) than in the free-world situation. Because by definition all criminal justice cases are adversarial, the readership of such forensic reports must be inevitably composed of parties opposed to one another, representing the concerns of the client–offender, the criminal justice system, and the community. Therefore, forensic psychologists automatically find themselves in the midst of controversy whenever they submit their results as neutral professionals, having displeased somebody along the way (e.g., displeasing a prosecutor by advocating lenient treatment, the client by recommending the denial of parole).

These two differences—role diversity and role conflict—are the bases for the role confusion of psychologists working in the criminal justice system. As noted by the American Psychological Association's (APA) Task Force Report on the Role of the Psychologist in the Criminal Justice System (American Psychological Association, 1980), "What psychology appears to lack at the present time is an effective way to differentiate obligations owed to organizational as opposed to individual clients" (p. 2). It indicates, for example, that of 203 criminal justice psychologists surveyed by the Task Force, 75% reported that one of the major ethical issues that they faced concerned confidentiality: how much and what kind of information should be revealed to their criminal justice employers. . . .

THE COERCIVE SETTING

The coercive setting differs markedly from the voluntary situation mainly because client–offenders do not hire their psychologists. They are forced to undergo the evaluation under penalty of law or deprivation of certain rights and privileges. These client–offenders, therefore, are in no position to dictate their terms to their examiners. They must submit to their psychologists' tests and inquiries whether they like it or not, knowing that if they refuse, such intransigency might result in possible negative consequences (e.g., denial of parole, more stringent sentencing, loss of institutional perquisites).

Because client–offenders have been pressured to go to their psychologists, they avoid having to take responsibility for this participation and for solving the problems that are the focus of the evaluation. Instead, they tend to approach their psychologists warily and resistively. The psychologists, therefore, have the task of penetrating these facades of self-sufficiency and denial before being able to reliably assess their client–offenders' true strengths and vulnerabilities.

In portraying themselves in as positive a light as possible, client–offenders tend to exclude from view anything that would block them from attaining their goals (e.g., outright freedom, less severe sentencing, day passes from a locked facility to the community). This guardedness arises, of course, because the evaluation results are not confidential but are used to decide important matters about the clients–offenders' lives. Indeed, in many forensic settings the psychologists are required to warn their client–offenders that whatever they divulge may be used against them in court (see Principle 5, *Ethical Standards of Psychologists*; American Psychological Association, 1981).[1]

Because an assessment report is a legal document that is subject to perusal by a variety of individuals in the criminal justice system, the psychologist in the forensic agency has little control over how the findings will be used and understood. Many judges, lawyers, administrators, counselors, and probation officers associated with a particular client–offender's case have the right to read its contents. This fact makes it difficult for psychologists to tailor their comments to particular individuals or suit the needs of specific referral sources. It also makes it difficult to establish rapport with their client–offenders. However, because forensic psychologists are paid to conduct their evaluations by their agency employers, there exists less incentive to build a working alliance with the typical criminal justice client than with the voluntary subject. Such forensic evaluations are conducted primarily for the benefit of various criminal justice personnel, insofar as they, not the examinees, are the main critics of the psychologists' work.

Despite this reality, forensic psychologists are typically still concerned about their client–offenders' plights. However, they worry about the social institutions with which client–offenders might eventually become involved (such as employers in the case of employment screening), the safety of the community (in the case of probation or parole evaluations), and the well-being of other involved third parties (such as the offspring of mothers charged with child neglect). Thus divided in their concern—to their client–offenders (e.g., "How will my decision affect the long-term interest of this person?"), the community (e.g., "Will this individual pose a threat to other people?"), and the criminal agency for which they are employed (e.g., "Is this agency properly equipped to handle this kind of individual?")—thoughtful forensic psychologists find themselves forced to consider many more variables in making their determinations than are their free-world counterparts.

Obviously, different kinds of cases tend to demand different kinds of priorities among these competing interests. In some instances, the priority of community safety comes first (e.g., when the client–offender has the potential for violence); in others, needs of client–offenders become more central (e.g., when they seem to be good prospects for education or rehabilitation and are not dangerous to others); and in still others, the requirements concerning the institution or agency entrusted to care for client–offenders assumes maximum importance (e.g., avoiding recommending a facility that is overcrowded and understaffed). However, sometimes forensic psychologists can adopt one way of approach-

---

[1] *Ed. note: See* Standard 1.07 of the APA's current (1992) Ethical Principles.

ing all criminal justice clients. When such a way is predictable and habitual, it can stem from unconscious motives and is analogous to the kinds of countertransference encountered in psychotherapy. . . .

THE HELPER BIAS

. . . This stance leads the psychologist to side with the client–offender in practically every instance. According to this person-centered, humanitarian perspective, the needs of the client–offender are more important than the agency's needs or the concerns of the community. The helper bias is based on a kind of antibureaucratic and antiorganizational philosophy, and its followers tend to be oblivious to dimensions of the evaluation other than the offenders' viewpoints. . . .

THE PROSECUTORIAL BIAS

The prosecutorial bias is relatively rare in comparison with the helper bias; the psychologist adopting the prosecutorial bias considers client–offenders with suspicion and tends to make negative value judgments about their conduct. This position is identified closely with the feelings of the community, and the client–offender is considered more from a moral than from a humanitarian perspective. This bias is prosecutorial because the psychologist is assumed to be an extension of the judicial system. The psychologist is more likely to consider the offender's behavior in a condemning rather than a clinical fashion. Reflecting a "law and order" attitude, psychologists operating from this bias are minimally empathetic with their client–offenders' plights.

Because the prosecutorial evaluators tend to adopt a negative view about the future of the client–offender, their recommendations are likely to be conservative and guarded. These evaluators predictably tend to favor the interests of the community over the welfare of their client–offenders. . . .

THE UNCOMMITTED BIAS

This bias reflects the classic bureaucratic mentality. It is more responsive to the implicit demands of the

institution for which the evaluator works than to the needs of the client–offender or of the community. These psychologists avoid taking risks because they dislike conflict and controversy. Psychologists personifying this attitude tend to write their evaluations in terms of the preferences of the agency administrators reading their reports, rather than in terms of their true convictions. . . .

ADVERSARIAL MODEL

The adversarial model is proposed to help avoid the biases inherent in the previous stances. . . .

Following the same rationale as the legal system itself, the adversarial evaluator assumes that final judgments and recommendations about forensic clients are best decided after all opposing viewpoints have been considered. In effect, the adversarial model extends this rationale into the assessment process itself; the report is to be organized and communicated as though it were a courtroom debate between hypothetical psychologists representing opposed vested interests (i.e., the defendant, the prosecutor). Only after these viewpoints are fully discussed could psychologists present their final recommendations.

This model requires psychologists to act as "devil's advocates" who, instead of trying to fit disparate findings about their client–offenders into a consistent narrative (possibly because they want to convey a sense of scientific certainty to the reader), disclose these contradictions honestly. Because evaluators are charged with multiple role responsibilities anyway (to the client–offender, the institution, and the community), there is no reason why all of their judgments, findings, and opinions should be in total agreement. Indeed, as a result of exposure to diverse and opposed information, the readers of reports written from this perspective would be in a better position to evaluate the merits of the evaluator's final recommendations.

Rather straightforward in its format, this model requires forensic psychologists to subdivide their reports into as many sections as there are legal perspectives on their client–offenders. They would then consider their clients from each one of these viewpoints. Most often the typical client–offender would be evaluated from only two perspectives: one favoring the client–offender's interests (the defendant's viewpoint) and one opposing them (the prosecutor's viewpoint). However, in more complex cases, involving other parties with different claims (such as the children in child custody or neglect evaluations), the psychologist would add other viewpoints as well (e.g., how the children might be affected were they to be separated from client–offender) to the report. Each division would contain any information believed to be pertinent to the particular perspective under consideration. After presenting all of the relevant information appropriate to these subsections, psychologists would then make their final recommendations and conclusions.

The standard forensic assessment format, on the other hand, makes it easy for psychologists to present their data impersonally, thereby obscuring their biases. It helps them to avoid dealing with the legal context in which the assessment takes place, in which there is no single truth . . . and in which radically different views of reality are in contention. Modeled to fit a setting in which role conflict or professional ambiguity is absent, the standard forensic assessment format does not dignify the multiperspectival nature of legal proceedings. The adversarial model, in contrast, forces psychologists to be more reflective and to think through their rationales before reaching their conclusions. . . .

References

American Psychological Association (1980). *Who is the client? The psychological intervention in the criminal justice system.* Washington, DC: Author.

American Psychological Association (1981). Ethical principles of psychologists. *American Psychologist, 36,* 633–638.

Role Conflict in Forensic Clinical Psychology: Reply to Arcaya

Dewey G. Cornell

. . .

The various roles of clinical psychologists in the criminal justice system cannot be characterized in the same way. Psychologists who conduct pretrial evaluations of criminal defendants typically deal with very different legal and clinical issues than do psychologists employed in prison settings. Psychologists who are regular employees of a court- or state-administered clinic experience a different relationship with defendants than do psychologists in independent practice who may be hired by the defendant. Also, psychologists whose contact with a defendant is limited to a forensic evaluation have different goals, ethical obligations, and clinical responsibilities than do psychologists involved in a treatment relationship. Arcaya's concerns about the psychologist–client relationship need more careful explication for each different role. The issue of role conflict at a minimum must be examined separately with regard to defendant versus convict status, the interaction of employer and client, and whether the professional relationship is for assessment or treatment purposes.

For purposes of this discussion, attention will be focused on psychologists who conduct pretrial evaluations of criminal defendants. Typically, these evaluations concern one or both of two legal issues: competency to stand trial or criminal responsibility (legal insanity). An evaluation of competency to stand trial concerns the defendant's present mental state: whether the defendant suffers from a mental condition that impairs his or her ability to defend himself or herself at the trial. Criminal responsibility concerns the defendant's mental state at the time of the alleged offense: whether the defendant suffered from a mental condition that would exculpate him or her from criminal charges. Specific legal criteria and guidelines for these evaluations vary from state to state.

However, the psychologist–defendant/client relationship differs in important ways for these two legal issues. For example, in Michigan . . . a defendant has no choice about submitting to an evaluation of competency to stand trial. Although the evaluation is usually conducted on an outpatient basis, the defendant could be committed for inpatient evaluation. If adjudicated incompetent to stand trial, the defendant could be committed involuntarily for a period as long as 15 months.

The circumstances are quite different for evaluations of criminal responsibility. Here the defendant is the one initiating the claim of insanity, and the defendant retains complete authority to refuse or cancel an evaluation. Contrary to Arcaya's global characterization of forensic evaluations, there are important differences according to the legal issue involved, and the defendant does retain voluntary status in some circumstances. Last, the defendant who disagrees with a psychologist's clinical opinion in a pretrial evaluation retains the right to request an independent evaluation by another professional.

As this example indicates, it is misleading for Arcaya to contrast evaluations conducted for the criminal justice system with all other evaluations by describing the former as "coercive" and the latter as "free-world" evaluations. Moreover, many evaluations

From *Professional Psychology: Research and Practice, 18,* 429–432. Copyright 1987 by the American Psychological Association. Adapted with permission of the author and publisher.

outside the criminal justice system are far from fully voluntary. Probably the most "coercive" evaluation in mental health today occurs when an individual is evaluated for involuntary commitment, a civil court matter. A close second would be evaluations of adolescent minors whose parents are seeking to have them admitted for inpatient treatment. Psychologists also face less-than-willing subjects when they conduct child custody evaluations or when they are hired by the defense to examine the complainant in personal injury cases. These examples are not to minimize the difficulties of conducting evaluations with criminal defendants; however, many of the ethical problems, role conflicts, and potential biases that Arcaya described are not specific to criminal forensic work. Perhaps a broader recognition of these problems would facilitate identifying possible solutions.

. . .

PROPOSALS FOR CHANGE

Arcaya's (partial) solution to the problem of psychologist bias was to modify the format for psychological reports. He proposed that psychologists write their reports in a manner more consistent with the legal system's adversarial model. Evidence supporting each side of the case would be presented and weighed before the psychologist expressed a final opinion.

There are several problems with this approach. First, if Arcaya was correct in stating that psychologists are biased because of unconscious personality conflicts and countertransference reactions to the defendant, it is highly unlikely that any change in report format would be effective. . . .

If bias is primarily a result of institutional pressures and professional role conflict, again it seems that merely changing report format would be too weak an intervention. The legal system, rather than the individual, would be the appropriate target for intervention. . . .

Last, many of Arcaya's concerns about bias and role conflict can be addressed from the standpoint of the Ethical Principles of the American Psychological Association (APA, 1981; see also Keith-Spiegel & Koocher, 1985). Psychologists are *already* obligated

to assume an objective and evenhanded approach in their report of psychological findings. . . .

ALTERNATIVES

Psychologists should not attempt to cope with the adversarial pressures of the legal system by mimicking an adversarial approach in their report writing. Instead, psychologists need to resist being co-opted by the system and to reassert their professional identity as scientist-practitioners. Forensic psychologists need to make clear, as often as is necessary, that their role is objective and neutral, and that although they may reach clinical opinions favorable to either defense or prosecution, they are never advocates of one side or the other in legal proceedings. . . .

References

American Psychological Association (1981). Ethical principles of psychologists (revised). *American Psychologist, 36,* 633–638.

Keith-Spiegel, P., & Koocher, G. (1985). *Ethics in psychology: Professional standards and cases.* Hillsdale, NJ: Erlbaum.

◆ ◆ ◆

Commentary: Despite their differences, Arcaya and Cornell did agree that forensic clinicians experience significant role conflicts, particularly when they conduct court-compelled evaluations in criminal prosecutions. These role conflicts not only create the potential for ethical violations but may impair the defendant's rights under the U.S. Constitution as well. The Fifth Amendment states in relevant part: "no person shall be compelled in any criminal case to be a witness against himself." Also the Sixth Amendment provides that "in all criminal prosecutions, the accused shall enjoy the right . . . to have the assistance of counsel for his defense." Consider how these constitutional protections might be endangered under the following scenario:

> *When Smith was indicted for murder, the state announced that it would seek the death penalty. The trial judge ordered Dr. Grigson, a psychiatrist, to evaluate whether Smith was competent to stand*

trial. After a 90-minute interview, Dr. Grigson determined that Smith was competent. Smith was then tried and convicted of murder. Subsequently, a separate sentencing proceeding was held before a jury to decide whether Smith should be executed. One of the issues the jury had to determine in the positive, if it were to give Smith a death sentence, was the probability that Smith would commit violent criminal acts again. At the sentencing hearing,

Dr. Grigson was called by the state to testify about Smith's proclivity toward future violence. Basing his testimony on the pretrial competency evaluation, Dr. Grigson stated that Smith would be a danger to society. The jury then sentenced Smith to death. Smith charged this procedure violated his rights under the Fifth and Sixth Amendments. The Supreme Court agreed to review his claims, with the following result.

Estelle v. Smith

. . .

. . . [W]e turn first to whether the admission of Dr. Grigson's testimony at the penalty phase violated respondent's Fifth Amendment privilege against compelled self-incrimination because respondent was not advised before the pretrial psychiatric examination that he had a right to remain silent and that any statement he made could be used against him at a sentencing proceeding. . . .

The fact that respondent's statements were uttered in the context of a psychiatric examination does not automatically remove them from the reach of the Fifth Amendment. . . . The state trial judge, *sua sponte*, ordered a psychiatric evaluation of respondent for the limited, neutral purpose of determining his competency to stand trial, but the results of that inquiry were used by the State for a much broader objective that was plainly adverse to respondent. Consequently, the interview with Dr. Grigson cannot be characterized as a routine competency examination restricted to ensuring that respondent understood the charges against him and was capable of assisting in his defense. Indeed, if the application of Dr. Grigson's findings had been confined to serving that function, no Fifth Amendment issue would have arisen.

Nor was the interview analogous to a sanity examination occasioned by a defendant's plea of not guilty by reason of insanity at the time of his offense. When a defendant asserts the insanity defense and introduces supporting psychiatric testimony, his silence may deprive the State of the only effective means it has of controverting his proof on an issue that he interjected into the case. Accordingly, several Courts of Appeals have held that, under such circumstances, a defendant can be required to submit to a sanity examination conducted by the prosecution's psychiatrist. . . .

Respondent, however, introduced no psychiatric evidence, nor had he indicated that he might do so. Instead, the State offered information obtained from the court-ordered competency examination as affirmative evidence to persuade the jury to return a sentence of death. Respondent's future dangerousness was a critical issue at the sentencing hearing, and one on which the State had the burden of proof beyond a reasonable doubt. . . . To meet its burden, the State used respondent's own statements, unwittingly made without an awareness that he was assisting the State's efforts to obtain the death penalty. In these distinct circumstances, the Fifth Amendment privilege was implicated.

. . . *Miranda v. Arizona* . . . held that "the prosecution may not use statements, whether exculpatory or inculpatory, stemming from custodial interrogation of the defendant unless it demonstrates the use of procedural safeguards effective to secure the privilege against self-incrimination." . . . Thus, absent other fully effective procedures, a person in custody must receive certain warnings before any official interrogation, including that he has a "right to remain silent" and that "anything said can and will be used against the individual in court." . . .

The considerations calling for the accused to be warned prior to custodial interrogation apply with no less force to be the pretrial psychiatric examination at issue here. Respondent was in custody at the Dallas County Jail when the examination was ordered and when it was conducted. That respondent was questioned by a psychiatrist designated by the trial court to conduct a neutral competency examination, rather than by a police officer, government informant, or prosecuting attorney, is immaterial. When Dr. Grigson went beyond simply reporting to the court on the issue of competence and testified

From *Estelle v. Smith*, 451 U.S. 459 (1981). Adapted with permission of the author and publisher.

for the prosecution at the penalty phase on the crucial issue of respondent's future dangerousness, his role changed and became essentially like that of an agent of the State recounting unwarned statements made in a postarrest custodial setting. During the psychiatric evaluation, respondent assuredly was "faced with a phase of the adversary system" and was "not in the presence of [a] perso[n] acting solely in his interest." . . . Yet he was given no indication that the compulsory examination would be used to gather evidence necessary to decide whether, if convicted, he should be sentenced to death. He was not informed that, accordingly, he had a constitutional right not to answer the questions put to him. . . .

A criminal defendant, who neither initiates a psychiatric evaluation nor attempts to introduce any psychiatric evidence, may not be compelled to respond to a psychiatrist if his statements can be used against him at a capital sentencing proceeding. Because respondent did not voluntarily consent to the pretrial psychiatric examination after being informed of his right to remain silent and the possible use of his statements, the State could not rely on what he said to Dr. Grigson to establish his future dangerousness. If, upon being adequately warned, respondent had indicated that he would not answer Dr. Grigson's questions, the validly ordered competency examination nevertheless could have proceeded upon the condition that the results would be applied solely for that purpose. In such circumstances, the proper conduct and use of competency and sanity examinations are not frustrated, but the State must make its case on future dangerousness in some other way.

"Volunteered statements . . . are not barred by the Fifth Amendment," but under *Miranda v. Arizona* we must conclude that, when faced while in custody with a court-ordered psychiatric inquiry, respondent's statements to Dr. Grigson were not "given freely and voluntarily without any compelling influences" and, as such, could be used as the State did at the penalty phase only if respondent had been apprised of his rights and had knowingly decided to waive them. . . . These safeguards of the Fifth Amendment privilege were not afforded respondent and, thus, his death sentence cannot stand [footnote omitted].

When respondent was examined by Dr. Grigson, he already had been indicted and an attorney had been appointed to represent him. The Court of Appeals concluded that he had a Sixth Amendment right to the assistance of counsel before submitting to the pretrial psychiatric interview. . . . We agree. . . .

Here, respondent's Sixth Amendment right to counsel clearly had attached when Dr. Grigson examined him at the Dallas County Jail [footnote omitted], and their interview proved to be a "critical stage" of the aggregate proceedings against respondent. . . . Defense counsel, however, were not notified in advance that the psychiatric examination would encompass the issue of their client's future dangerousness [footnote omitted], and respondent was denied the assistance of his attorneys in making the significant decision of whether to submit to the examination and to what end the psychiatrist's findings could be employed. . . .

Therefore, in addition to Fifth Amendment considerations, the death penalty was improperly imposed on respondent because the psychiatric examination on which Dr. Grigson testified at the penalty phase proceeded in violation of respondent's Sixth Amendment right to the assistance of counsel [footnote omitted]. . . .

◆ ◆ ◆

Commentary: *Shuman & Greenberg (1998) quoted a 1995 news release from the American Psychiatric Association (No. 95–25, July 20, 1995) that stated that the Association voted to expel Dr. Grigson from membership "for arriving at a psychiatric diagnosis without first having examined the individual in question, and for indicating, while testifying in court as an expert witness, that he could predict with 100 [per cent] certainty that the individual would engage in future violent acts" (p. 6) in connection with his testimony in Barefoot v. Estelle, 463 U.S. 880 (1983), among other cases. See Shuman, D. W., & Greenberg, S. A. (1998, Winter). The role of ethical norms in the admissibility of expert testimony. The Judges' Journal, 37, 4–9; 42–43.*

Apparently, the American Medical Association (AMA) is going even further. According to the online site of the journal, Lawyer's Weekly, *the AMA has ruled* that physicians are practicing medicine when they testify as experts and that they are subject to reprimand or revocation of their AMA membership if their testimony is judged to fall outside accepted scientific standards. Subsequent to a judgment that the testimony is unsound, the AMA will register violations in a national databank that is discoverable by attorneys and hospitals where physicians apply for privileges.

If a psychologist were to act as Grigson did, what provisions of the APA's 1992 Ethical Principles would the clinician violate? What sections of the Specialty Guidelines would be implicated?

Is it not the psychologist's duty to disclose at the initiation of therapy such important information as limits to confidentiality (i.e., in a manner equivalent to the police officer's Miranda warnings)? As chapter 4 illustrated, the legal system compels psychologists at times to act as agents of the state, such as when they are required to report child abuse or to protect a private third party from a patient's violent threats. In instances like these, should not psychologists, regardless of the setting in which they work, inform their clients of those situations in which they feel obligated to serve society and in which, like Grigson, they determine that the duty of fidelity has shifted from their clients to the state?

Role conflicts are an inevitable fact of life for academicians and practitioners, but they occur more often—as *Estelle v. Smith* proves—when the client is an involuntary participant in assessment or treatment. In many such cases, the forensic clinician is asked to predict whether the involuntary client might engage in an act of violence. Such predictions are not restricted to death penalty cases but are also requested in more commonplace instances, with regard to civil commitment, bail and parole hearings, detention of juveniles, and child abuse.

Is It Unethical to Offer Predictions of Future Violence?

Thomas Grisso and Paul S. Appelbaum

For many years, scholars have been warning mental health professionals that the results of our research on predictors of future violence set serious limits for experts who testify about future dangerous behavior (e.g., Cocozza & Steadman, 1976; Ennis & Litwack, 1974; Monahan, 1981). Megargee's (1981) conclusion is representative: "The identification of the potentially violent individual with sufficient accuracy to warrant preventative detention . . . is an impossible quest" (p. 181).

Recognition of these predictive limits often has given rise to recommendations that clinicians should not render opinions about "dangerousness" or future violence in legal forums. For example, the American Psychiatric Association (1974) long ago suggested that "clinicians should avoid 'conclusory' judgments" (p. 33) about such matters in expert testimony. This recommendation seems to have been reached most often with regard to testimony in criminal cases (Brody, 1990), although Stone's (1975) review of the empirical evidence led him to recommend that violence prediction should be placed outside the clinician's role in civil commitment as well.

More recently, some analysts of the state of the art in violence prediction have stated outright that which earlier writers may only have implied: It is unethical to do what our research says we cannot do reliably. Melton, Petrila, Poythress, and Slobogin (1987), after concluding that "there is no specialized clinical knowledge that permits categorical, or even relative, conclusions about dangerousness" (p. 204), observed that "in view of this research, clinicians may decide that they cannot ethically offer predic-

tion testimony" (p. 205). Ethicist Philippa Foot (1990) stated the point more forcefully in the context of capital sentencing, admonishing clinicians to refuse to offer predictive testimony that they know is unreliable: "Such a refusal," she observed, "seems right in the center of the area of professional ethics" (p. 213).

Ewing's (1983, . . . , 1991) statements of this position have been the most sweeping: "[There] is good reason to conclude that psychologists and psychiatrists act unethically when they render predictions of dangerousness that provide a legal basis for restricting another person's interest in life and liberty" (Ewing, 1991, p. 162). The foundation for this assertion is that "such predictions cannot be said to be founded on a scientific basis. . . . The psychiatrist or psychologist who makes a prediction of dangerousness violates his or her ethical obligation to register judgments that rest on a scientific basis" (Ewing, 1983, pp. 417–418).

Ewing's conclusions were reached after his review of research on clinical judgment, expert testimony, and legal considerations in delinquency and criminal cases involving questions of detention and sentencing. But the broad reference to violence predictions affecting restrictions of liberty suggests, as have others (e.g., Stone, 1975), that predictions in matters concerning juvenile and adult offenders are not the only ones that are being condemned. Emergency and involuntary admissions to mental hospitals, as well as decisions about discharge, also involve violence predictions and potential restrictions of liberty. So do the decisions of psychotherapists who fulfill

From *Law and Human Behavior, 16*, 621–633. Copyright 1992 by Plenum Publishing. Adapted with permission of the author and publisher.

legal obligations to protect children or other persons when they become aware of potential violence by their clients. Therefore, it would appear that a broad-based conclusion that predictions of future violence are unethical indicts most mental health professionals in general clinical or forensic work of unethical behavior at least some time in their careers, and a substantial proportion of them on a daily basis.

We believe that a more differentiated analysis of predictive testimony about future violence . . . does not support an assertion that experts' judgments about violent behavior are necessarily or always unethical, even in legal cases involving potential loss of liberty [footnote omitted]. We submit that there may be several ethically significant dimensions along which predictions of future violence can be differentiated, which are not taken into account by a blanket condemnation of predictive testimony. . . .

THE NATURE OF THE PREDICTIVE TESTIMONY

Let us presume that when critics have spoken against "predictions of dangerousness," they have been referring to "predictions of future violent behavior." Expert testimony about future violence can take several forms, all of which might be considered predictions as the term is used broadly in the behavioral and social sciences. We can cite no authority for the forms of testimony that such predictions take, but the following are examples from our experience:

a. *Dichotomous:* Statement that a particular behavior (or type of behavior) will or will not occur in the future. ("In my opinion, he will engage in serious violent behavior in the future.")

b. *Dichotomous With Qualified Confidence:* Dichotomous statement, with additional testimony concerning expert's confidence in his or her opinion. ("In my opinion, he will engage in a serious violent behavior in the future, and I believe that it is more likely than not [or 'reasonably certain' or 'very certain'] that my judgment would prove accurate.")

c. *Risk, Individual-Based:* Statement of the degree of likelihood that this individual will engage in a particular behavior (or type of behavior) in the future.

("In my opinion, there is a 40% probability that he will engage in serious violent behavior in the future.")

d. *Risk, Class-Based:* Statement of likelihood or probability, but offered in reference to a class of persons of which the individual is alleged to be a member. ("In my opinion, about 25% of people with this individual's characteristics engage in violent behavior after release from a mental hospital.") May be combined with individual-based. (". . . but I believe that he presents somewhat greater/less risk than that group" [e.g., based on future environmental circumstances].)

All of these forms of testimony may be construed as predictions [footnote omitted]. They attempt to inform the listener about the clinician's professional opinion concerning behaviors that may occur in the future. Statements of risk are no less predictions than statements in dichotomous form; they simply provide additional information concerning the likelihood that others will be right or wrong in drawing their own dichotomous conclusion.

Broad arguments for a ban on predictions of violent behavior appear not to have been limited to dichotomous statements of prediction, but would prohibit all types of predictive testimony involving questions of future violence and restriction of liberty. The scope of the applicable definition of *prediction* may be significant in evaluating arguments such as Ewing's (1991). If one intends to condemn all forms of predictive testimony as unethical, and if the basis for this conclusion is inadequate scientific support for predictions, then the conclusion is wrong if there is reasonable scientific support for any of the above forms of predictive testimony. It would seem that there is.

Let us consider first the evidence as it relates to dichotomous predictive testimony, our types *a* and *b*. Research demonstrating the lack of scientific support for the validity of predictions of future violence is derived primarily from publications in the 1970s, which have been reviewed extensively (e.g., Monahan, 1981; Webster & Menzies, 1987). Collectively, those studies demonstrated that even for groups with characteristics that often are associated with violent behavior, no more than 20%–40% of individuals, at best, were identified later (e.g., on parole) as engaging in violent acts resulting in recidivism. Reviews of the literature concluded that clinicians have no ability, or no special ability, to predict whether or not a person will engage in a violent act in the future and that they would be right in at best about one in three cases in which they made such predictions (e.g., Cocozza & Steadman, 1976, 1978; . . . Ennis & Litwack, 1974) [footnote omitted].

In a thoughtful, critical review of this literature, Litwack and Schlesinger (1987) have argued that "none of these statements has been established by the relevant research findings and, in all probability, they are simply wrong" (p. 206). Their primary argument was that the design of the studies simply did not allow such sweeping conclusions. Given that some studies demonstrated a high number of false-positive predictions in certain circumstances with certain populations, it still did not follow that there were no circumstances in which clinicians might make more accurate predictions or might have something more to offer than lay persons. . . .

In one sense, Litwack and Schlesinger's observations appear to challenge the conclusion that all dichotomous predictions are unethical. Research on the invalidity of such predictions has focused only on certain populations and circumstances; one might argue, therefore, that the impropriety of dichotomous predictions in those types of cases need not extend to other types of cases for which validity has not yet been challenged. This reasoning is less persuasive, however, if it is also unethical (as some critics have claimed: Dix, 1980) to make dichotomous predictions when we *do not know* their validity for the type of case at hand because of the *absence* of relevant research. Dichotomous predictions of future violence, therefore, remain vulnerable to arguments that they violate ethical propriety.

Turning now to predictive testimony of types *c* and *d*, some of the same studies of the 1970s that challenged the validity of dichotomous predictions provided the earliest scientific support for offering predictive testimony in the form of probabilistic or comparative risk statements. For example, the State of Michigan's (1978) Parole Risk Study identified a small class of parolees with a 40% rate of violent recidivism. Accurate classification of a parole candidate in that group, therefore, would allow scientifically supported predictive testimony that the risk of violent recidivism was much greater for this person than for most parolees (for whom the baserate was shown to be about 10%).

Much more sophisticated research during the 1980s significantly augmented the scientific support for identification of groups with relatively high baserates of future violence (e.g., Binder & McNiel, 1988; Klassen & O'Connor, 1988, 1990; Link, Cullen, & Andrews, 1990; Swanson, Holzer, Ganju, & Jono, 1990). For example, studies identified hospitalized groups, based on a combination of background and demographic characteristics, for which the risk of subsequent violent behavior in the community was over 50% (Klassen & O'Connor, 1988), as well as groups identified merely by a reliable diagnosis (alcohol or drug abuse/dependence) for which prior-year baserates of violence in the community were 25%–35%, or 12–17 times greater than for persons with no DMS-III diagnosis (Swanson et al., 1990).

These newer studies, of course, do not provide scientific evidence with which to claim validity for predictive testimony in dichotomous form (predictive testimony of types *a* and *b* in our characterization above). They merely provide research support, in some cases, for predictive testimony that offers courts a sense of the relative risk of violence associated with individuals in question (predictive testimony of types *c* and *d*). Yet this is enough to contradict the generalized assertion that *all* predictive testimony regarding future violence is unethical for lack of a scientific basis. . . .

THE FOUNDATION OF THE PREDICTIVE TESTIMONY

[T]he scientific basis for predictions of future violence is derived from studies identifying particular characteristics of research subjects who subsequently engaged in violent behavior. This suggests three important limitations on the appropriateness even of predictive risk statements, consistent with a general standard of competence in clinicians' performance of evaluations (Section I: American Psychiatric Association, 1989; Principle 1: American Psychological Association, 1981).

First, the person about whom the estimate of risk is being made must be similar to the research subjects in the studies from which the predictive model is derived. Second, the estimate of risk must be based on types of data comparable to those available in the studies that are being relied upon. Third, the expert's evaluation process and methods by which data are gathered must be sufficiently reliable to assure accurate identification of the relevant characteristics of the individual in question.

Many of the arguments against the use of predictions by mental health professionals have focused on a single type of situation in which none of these limiting conditions has been respected: the prediction of a defendant's future violent behavior at the sentencing phase of a capital trial (Ewing, 1983). In that situation, mental health professionals have testified routinely about the likelihood of future violence when there were no data about comparable groups of subjects (Dix, 1980), or when such data began to be available (Marquart, Ekland-Olsen, & Sorenson, 1989; Marquart & Sorenson, 1989), often in disregard of them. Moreover, such testimony often has been based on evaluation procedures or methods that manifest little regard for a reliable description of the defendant's characteristics. Such is the case when predictions are offered on the basis of information provided in a hypothetical question posed by the prosecutor, typically without the expert having had an opportunity to examine the defendant or to become acquainted with documentary evidence relevant to the defendant's history (Appelbaum, 1984).

The ethics of predictions of future violence in such a context indeed are questionable. But it is not clear that one can generalize from these troublesome practices to all other predictive testimony. For example, predictive testimony may be ethically appropriate when a mental health professional who has examined a potential patient offers testimony at a commitment hearing about an increased risk of future violence, based on (a) data suggesting that certain diagnostic groups, or persons manifesting certain symptoms, are at increased risk for violent behavior, and (b) data indicating that the prospective patient reliably can be associated with those groups. The closer the match between the characteristics of the subject of the prediction and the data

available about those characteristics in the studies on which the predictive statement is based, the less problematic such testimony will be. . . .

THE LEGAL CONSEQUENCES OF THE PREDICTION

. . .

We sometimes have the necessary research support and assessment data to state a probability of violence in a given case. That probability usually will be less than 0.5. [T]his probability may be sufficient to lead the fact-finder to conclude that the identified level of risk satisfies a sociolegal definition of dangerousness for purposes of restricting liberties. When decision makers are satisfied that a level of risk below 0.5 warrants the restriction of liberty, however, across cases the majority of persons about whom the decision is being made will be the "victims" of a high false-positive rate.

Society may believe that it is justified in "mistakenly" restricting the liberties of a majority in order to achieve the proper objectives in relation to the minority who are "correctly" restricted. Yet that which society can justify for itself may not always satisfy the ethical obligations of clinicians, as interpreted individually or by their professional organizations. . . . Therefore independent of that which is accepted by society or the law, professionals have an obligation to consider the potential effects of their testimony about risk statements with high false-positive rates and to question whether the law's use of their testimony violates their professional ethical standards.

When we participate in legal proceedings in which our predictive testimony results in decisions with high false-positive rates and their consequences, do we practice unethically? There are at least three ways that one might address the question.

First, one can argue that *any* restriction of liberty based on predictive testimony about risk involving large false-positive rates constitutes a misuse of psychological or psychiatric information by the legal system. This position would be based on either of two views: (1) that it is wrong for society to restrict liberties on the basis of less than 0.5 probability of future violence, and that to do so demeans the rights of the individual, is "unjustifiable," and does not "promote human welfare" (e.g., American Psychological Association, 1981: Preamble, and Principle 3(b)); or (2) that even with an expert's attempts to inform the court about the limits of testimony based on probabilities with high false-positive rates, there is an unacceptable potential for misunderstanding or misuse of the information in the legal forum. Experts who testify about risk probabilities with high false-positive rates, therefore, would be perceived as participating unethically in the process.

A second approach would leave questions of justification to the courts and society to determine, not the mental health professional. Statutes and procedures of law define the conditions under which society "justly" restricts the liberties of its citizens. The expert who provides reliable risk probability information (and clearly explains its limitations) to courts within that legal framework engages in ethical practice, according to this view, even if the legal outcome deprives the individual of liberty "mistakenly." The duties of the forensic expert are different in this regard from those of the clinician in a doctor–patient relationship, wherein the obligation to maximize the welfare of the patient is paramount. Therefore, the consequences of a court's restrictions of liberty present no ethical burden for the expert beyond that of presenting reliable testimony and clearly explaining its limitations.

A third position is intermediate in relation to the other two. It would not leave questions of justification only to the courts. On the other hand, it would observe that not all types of liberty restrictions are of equal consequence, especially given variability across circumstances (e.g., civil commitment vs. capital sentencing) in potential, counterbalancing benefits to the person whose liberty is restricted. This position might also recognize variability in the qual-

ity of legal justice across jurisdictions (e.g., known patterns of racial bias in sentencing in certain jurisdictions). This perspective would see predictive testimony about risk probabilities with high false-positive rates as neither ethical nor unethical per se. Instead, it would encourage professional debate regarding the circumstances (e.g., degree and type of liberty restrictions associated with the legal questions, types of benefits that may accrue) in which the various magnitudes of false-positive error resulting from risk probability testimony would be ethically acceptable or unacceptable in relation to the balance of consequences for the individual and society.

Our purpose here is not to evaluate, endorse, or refine any of these approaches. We merely observe that they reach different answers to the questions of ethical propriety in predictive testimony about risk probabilities. The second approach would not consider such predictive testimony unethical, and the third might consider it unethical for certain types of legal proceedings, but not for all.

The first approach would, indeed, see all such testimony as unethical. If it is to be used as a basis for arguing that risk-related predictive testimony should be banned because it contributes to unjust legal decisions, then its proponents should make explicit the assumptions and unanswered questions underlying the position so that it can be debated on its merits. For example, on what basis are our professional associations to determine that society's justifications for restrictions of liberty (based partly on our testimony) are wrong? What is the foundation for the argument that our testimony, if carefully presented, will be misunderstood or misused by legal fact-finders? Do the gains in "human welfare" associated with a prohibition on risk-related testimony outweigh the potential negative effects on "human welfare?"[1] . . .

---

[1] Two examples of potential negative consequences of the first position may be offered. *First*, a blanket prohibition of risk probability testimony involving high false-positive rates would disallow not only predictions of violence, but also predictions of nonviolence. According to past research, our predictions that individuals will *not* engage in future violence are quite likely to be accurate (low false-negatives). Therefore, testimony about nonviolence is immune to consequentialist arguments that focus on unjust restrictions of liberty as a result of the effects of testimony on legal dispositions. Prohibiting risk-related predictive testimony could deprive individuals of testimony that might reduce the likelihood of liberty restrictions due to alleged violence potential. *Second*, additional questions are raised by the apparent limitation of the argument (that testimony on future violence is unethical) to situations in which "liberty" is at stake (e.g., Ewing, 1991). If cases involving restrictions on liberty are construed narrowly as only referring to decisions about detention or release, we arrive at the paradoxical argument

References

American Psychiatric Association. (1974). *Clinical aspects of the violent individual.* Washington, DC: Author.

American Psychiatric Association. (1989). *Principles of medical ethics with annotations especially applicable to psychiatry.* Washington, DC: Author.

American Psychological Association. (1981). *Ethical principles of psychologists.* Washington, DC: Author.

Appelbaum, P. (1984). Hypotheticals, psychiatric testimony, and the death sentence. *Bulletin of the American Academy of Psychiatry and the Law, 12,* 169–177.

Binder, R., & McNiel, D. (1988). Effects of diagnosis and context on dangerousness. *American Journal of Psychiatry, 145,* 728–732.

Brody, B. (1990). Prediction of dangerousness in different contexts. In R. Rosner & R. Weinstock (Eds.), *Ethical practice in psychiatry and the law* (pp. 185–196). New York: Plenum.

Cocozza, J., & Steadman, H. (1976). The failure of psychiatric predictions of dangerousness: Clear and convincing evidence. *Rutgers Law Review, 29,* 1084–1101.

Cocozza, J., & Steadman, H. (1978). Prediction in psychiatry: An example of misplaced confidence in experts. *Social Problems, 25,* 265–276.

Dix, G. (1980). Clinical evaluation of the "dangerousness" of "normal" criminal defendants. *Virginia Law Review, 66,* 523–581.

Ennis, B., & Litwack, T. (1974). Psychiatry and the presumption of expertise: Flipping coins in the courtroom. *California Law Review, 62,* 693–752.

Ewing, C. (1983). "Dr. Death" and the case for an ethical ban on psychiatric and psychological predictions of dangerousness in capital sentencing proceedings. *American Journal of Law and Medicine, 8,* 407–428.

Ewing, C. (1991). Preventive detention and execution: The constitutionality of punishing future crimes. *Law and Human Behavior, 15,* 139–163.

Foot, P. (1990). Ethics and the death penalty: Participation of forensic psychiatrists in capital trials. In R. Rosner and R. Weinstock (Eds.), *Ethical practice in psychiatry and the law* (pp. 207–217). New York: Plenum.

Klassen, D., & O'Connor, W. (1988). A prospective study of predictors of violence in adult male mental health admissions. *Law and Human Behavior, 12,* 143–158.

Klassen, D., & O'Connor, W. (1990). Assessing the risk of violence in released mental patients: A cross-validational study. *Psychological Assessment, 1,* 75–81.

Link, B., Cullen, F., & Andrews, H. (1990, August). *Violent and illegal behavior of current and former mental patients compared to community controls.* Paper presented at the meeting of the Society for the Study of Social Problems.

Litwack, T., & Schlesinger, L. (1987). Assessing and predicting violence: Research, law, and application. In I. Weiner & A. Hess (Eds.), *Handbook of forensic psychology* (pp. 205–257). New York: Wiley.

Marquart, J., Ekland-Olsen, S., & Sorenson, J. (1989). Gazing into the crystal ball: Can jurors accurately predict dangerousness in capital cases? *Law and Society Review, 23,* 449–468.

Marquart, J., & Sorensen, J. (1989). A national study of the *Furman*-committed inmates: Assessing the threat to society from capital offenders. *Loyola of Los Angeles Law Review, 23,* 5–28.

Megargee, E. (1981). Methodological problems in the prediction of violence. In J. Hays, T. Roberts, & K. Solway (Eds.), *Violence and the violent individual* (pp. 179–191). New York: Spectrum.

Melton, G., Petrila, J., Poythress, N., & Slobogin, C. (1987). *Psychological evaluations for the courts.* New York: Guilford.

Monahan, J. (1981). *The clinical prediction of violent behavior.* Rockville, MD: National Institute of Mental Health.

State of Michigan, Department of Corrections (June 29, 1978). *The parole risk study.* Unpublished manuscript.

Stone, A. (1975). *Mental health and law: A system in transition.* Rockville, MD: National Institute of Mental Health.

Swanson, J., Holzer, C., Ganju, V., & Jono, R. (1990). Violence and psychiatric disorder in the community: Evidence from the Epidemiologic Catchment Area Surveys. *Hospital and Community Psychiatry, 41,* 761–770.

Webster, C., & Menzies, R. (1987). The clinical prediction of dangerousness. In D. Weisstub (Ed.), *Law and mental health: International perspectives,* Vol. 3 (pp. 158–208). New York: Pergamon.

that the same testimony about a child abuser's future violence that could not be offered at a parole hearing could be tendered at a custody proceeding. On the other hand, if liberty is construed broadly, such that, for example, denial of access to one's child consequent to a custody determination infringes liberty, then testimony on future violence would never be permissible. We question whether proponents of the view that predictions of future violence are unethical truly desire to exclude testimony from child custody hearings (presuming the testimony meets scientific standards that a parent has a 40% likelihood of harming his or her child).

On the Ethics of Dangerousness Assessments

Thomas R. Litwack

. . . I am writing to point out . . . that (1) Grisso and Appelbaum's article did not come to grips with the *key* issue regarding the ethics of dangerousness assessments—whether such assessments are ethical when they are *not* based on actuarial data, and (2) although they disclaim any such intent, Grisso and Appelbaum's article may be too readily *taken* to support the position that assessments of dangerous without what they define as "scientific" support are *not* ethical.

. . .

The problems with Grisso and Appelbaum's formulations are, I believe, as follows: (1) Many—if not most—of the most important *and most necessary* assessments of dangerousness by mental health professionals are not, *and cannot be*, based on meaningful actuarial data. (2) To regard such assessments as "lacking a scientific foundation" requires a very limited view of the word *scientific*. (3) If such assessments are not scientific, the authors do not explain how it can possibly be ethical for mental health professionals to offer such assessments as "expert" testimony.

. . .

[I]s the clinical discernment of the facts relevant to a risk assessment and the logical weighing of those facts not a "scientific" enterprise? Are attempts to classify mental disorders into diagnostic categories based on *observable, reportable, checkable* (and therefore refutable and/or reclassifiable) data—however imperfect those attempts—not "scientific" enterprises? Is psychoanalysis—as a means for investigating human functioning—not a "scientific" enterprise? Obviously, it depends on how one defines *science* and *scientific*.

Regardless of how one defines the terms *science* and *scientific*, however, what *ethical* principle is violated if, in making a risk assessment, a mental health professional makes a conscientious effort to obtain and analyze all relevant data (both clinical and actuarial, when the latter is available), is forthright in describing and explaining the facts and logical inferences upon which her or his risk assessment is based, and is careful not to knowingly exaggerate (or minimize) the degree of risk the person being assessed appears to pose? And is a risk assessment not an "expert" assessment—even if nevertheless a fallible assessment—if it is based on interviewing techniques, other assessment methods, and/or a general body of knowledge not within the ken of the general population?

From *Law and Human Behavior, 17,* 479–482. Copyright 1993 by the American Psychological Association. Adapted with permission of the author and publisher.

Structuring the Debate About Ethical Predictions of Future Violence

Thomas Grisso and Paul S. Appelbaum

Professor Litwack correctly asserts that our article (Grisso & Appelbaum, 1992) did not "come to grips" with the question of the ethical propriety of risk assessments that have no actuarial base. Our purpose was narrower. We wished simply to find the strongest argument to refute the proposition that *all* testimony based on assessments of future violence is unethical. That argument required only that we successfully defend one type of testimony. Therefore, we focused only on that type that was most easily defended: testimony based on actuarial indicators offering probability estimates of future violence for persons manifesting various measurable characteristics.

If one accepts that at least this type of testimony is ethically proper, Litwack's question is the next one with which the field should struggle. Testimony that relies on actuarial base rates is an ideal that we can achieve only sometimes. How far short of that ideal can we fall while remaining within ethical boundaries?

We completely agree with Litwack that our professions' ethical guidelines may accept other types of testimony. Whatever our text might have "implied" or been "too readily taken to support," nowhere in our article did we close the door on other types of testimony. . . . [W]e even suggested that in the absence of any actuarial data, testifying about future violence even to a high degree of certainty might not be unethical in some circumstances.

In other instances, we referred to testimony without a "scientific basis" as ethically "problematic," "questionable," or "troublesome." We chose these words carefully. Testimony that raises a problem or is ethically questionable is not necessarily unethical; it is simply a subject for inquiry and debate concerning its ethical propriety. We welcome that debate, and we expect that our professions will find room for some types of non-actuarially-based testimony in our ethical standards.

In that debate, it will be important to distinguish what is meant by terms like "actuarial" and "scientific." "Actuarial" sometimes is used narrowly to refer to a probability estimate based on a formulaic combination of the statistical relations of several variables to a criterion. Several examples used in our article presumed this type of actuarial foundation. The term "actuarial" is sometimes used more broadly, however, to refer to the statistical relations between single variables and a criterion. This potentially offers a different type of "scientific" base for testimony about risk of future violence.

. . .

[W]e can offer evidence from empirical research (presumably meeting scientific standards) indicating that the variables we are using in forming our clinical judgment about degree of risk do bear some relationship to future violent behavior. Therefore, we would not be without an "actuarial" (empirically derived correlational) base for our risk assessment and our testimony in this case.

We believe that risk estimates and testimony of this type can be within ethical bounds, especially if we do not lead legal decision makers to believe that our estimates should be given more weight than they warrant. . . . We would also caution that testimony of this type in some cases could be considered *unethical*, depending on how one chooses to weigh the issues that we raise in the final section of our three-part analysis ("The Legal Consequences of the Prediction").

. . .

[P]ending further debate, we are reluctant to accept the notion that reliable data collection and logical thinking are enough to satisfy ethical standards for assessments and testimony regarding risk estimates.

◆ ◆ ◆

Commentary: There is a growing literature on the assessment of the risk of violence, what Grisso & Tomkins (1996), call "a required professional ability for every clinical psychologist" (p. 928). See Grisso, T., & Tomkins, A. J. (1996). Communicating violence risk assessments. American Psychologist, 51, 928–930. Much of this literature has been supported and promulgated by the Research Network on Mental Health and the Law of the John D. and Catherine T. MacArthur Foundation. For recent reviews (containing valuable references) see

Borum, R. (1996). Improving the clinical practice of violence risk assessment: Technology, guidelines, and training. American Psychologist, 51, 945–956.

Heilbrun, K. (1997). Prediction versus management models relevant to risk assessment: The importance of legal decision-making context. Law and Human Behavior, 21, 347–360.

Litwack, T. R. (1994). Assessments of dangerousness: Legal, research, and clinical developments. Administration and Policy in Mental Health, 21, 361–378.

Monahan, J., & Steadman, H. J. (Eds.). (1994). Violence and mental disorder: Developments in risk assessment. Chicago: University of Chicago Press.

Monahan, J., & Steadman, H. J. (1996). Violent storms and violent people: How meteorology can inform risk communication in mental health law. American Psychologist, 51, 931–938.

Schopp, R. F. (1996). Communicating risk assessments: Advocacy, efficacy, and responsibility. American Psychologist, 51, 939–944.

In discussing the scientific bases for risk assessment and whether predictions of violence are ethical, are scholars neglecting fundamental moral issues? Contrast

the preceding series of articles with the following, from Goldman (1986):

> *The psychologist ought to weigh directly the probable moral consequences of his testimony and use his full powers of moral reasoning in deciding whether and how to testify as an expert. It is not sufficient from a moral point of view that he tell the truth and do what the court asks of him. He must also desist from contributing directly to outcomes to which he is morally opposed on good grounds.*
>
> *There are many areas in which psychologists might be called as experts. A preliminary example that can be cited here relates to the predictability of violent behavior. Suppose that methods for prediction improve until a high degree of reliability is achieved and that courts increasingly use such predictions as bases for imposing the death penalty (the example is from Loftus & Monahan, 1980). In my view a psychologist who is morally opposed to capital punishment cannot rightly agree to provide testimony that will lead to its imposition on grounds that he is only telling the truth and providing "ethically neutral" scientific knowledge that the judge has the authority to seek and use. Rather than usurping the role of the judge, the psychologist who refuses to testify in such a case is taking a stand as an individual against what he perceives to be unjustifiable homicide. Since individual psychologists cannot themselves determine the law on the matter, such input into the system does not represent the usurpation of lawmaking authority. Just as citizens in general need not support on moral grounds or contribute to the enforcement of laws they consider seriously unjust, so here the psychologist need not aid the imposition of a morally abominable sentence. (p. 37)*

Goldman, A. H. (1986). Cognitive psychologists as expert witnesses: A problem in professional ethics. Law and Human Behavior, 10, 29–45.

Goldman raised the final question to be considered in this chapter: Are there some functions that an ethical psychologist should refuse to perform? This question has been broached most poignantly in the debate over implementation of the death penalty. Specifically, in Ford v. Wainwright (477 U.S. 399, 1986), the U.S. Supreme Court held that the execution of a psychotic and incompetent death row inmate would violate the Eighth Amendment ban on cruel and unusual punishment. Do mental health professionals act unethically if they participate in treating seriously mentally ill criminals so that they may become competent enough to be executed? The American Medical Association has advised physicians that they should not take part in legally authorized executions. And, the Louisiana Supreme Court has held that it is unconstitutional for the state to forcibly medicate condemned inmates with antipsychotic drugs so that they can become competent enough to be executed.

With the exception of a few clinicians in the military and in Guam, psychologists are not yet entitled to prescribe psychotropic medication, but they are qualified to either assess whether a death row inmate is competent to be executed or design and implement psychotherapeutic and behavioral interventions to achieve competency. Should psychologists participate in such endeavors? Read-

ers whose immediate reaction is no should consider this: What about prisoners who choose to be executed rather than live in a psychotic state during a lifetime in prison? For a variety of perspectives on these issues, see

Bonnie, R. (1990). Dilemmas in administering the death penalty: Conscientious abstention, professional ethics, and the needs of the legal system. Law and Human Behavior, 14, 67–90.

Brodsky, S. L. (1990). Professional ethics and professional morality in the assessment of competence for execution: A response to Bonnie. Law and Human Behavior, 14, 91–97.

Heilbrun, K., Radelet, M. L., & Dvoskin, J. (1992). The debate on treating individuals incompetent for execution. American Journal of Psychiatry, 149, 596–605.

Salguero, R. G. (1986). Medical ethics and competency to be executed. Yale Law Journal, 96, 167–186.

White, W. S. (1987). Defendants who elect execution. University of Pittsburgh Law Review, 48, 853–877.

What guidance, if any, do the APA Ethical Principles and the Specialty Guidelines give the forensic practitioner about these issues? What are the relevant provisions in these documents? What moral principles, described in chapter 3 (e.g., justice and nonmaleficence), should prevail? Is there any place for virtue ethics here?

On Being Ethical in Legal Places

Patricia Anderten, Valerie Staulcup, and Thomas Grisso

. . .

SAFEGUARDING ETHICAL STANDARDS

Given that the courtroom presents ethical difficulties and professional conflicts for psychologists, one need not conclude that psychologists should avoid either the courtroom or consultation to attorneys and their clients. A weighing of the potential benefits and liabilities of placing psychological information at the disposal of courts would probably find the potential benefits weighing heavier in the balance. The focus, then, should be on how we can offer our services within the legal system in the most effective and professional manner. An examination of the dynamics of the situations we have discussed suggests several general recommendations for psychologists who would wish to reduce the chances of ethical malfeasance in their participation in legal cases.

First, knowledge of the legal process and of the problems inherent in psychological testimony is essential to maintaining competent and ethical practice as an expert witness. Acquiring this knowledge is presently a matter of individual initiative. Few graduate courses on professional and ethical issues deal more than cursorily with the complexities of psychologist–attorney relationships or the expert witness role. However, workshops in these areas are increasing in number. . . .

Second, especially if one is inclined to actively seek involvement in legal cases, it is important to examine seriously one's needs and motives in relation to this intent. . . . [E]xcessive influence by altruistic motives and self-serving motives alike can easily cloud one's judgment. Clinical psychologists will recall similar admonitions by their supervisors in the early stages of psychotherapy training. For most psychologists, the role of expert witness is as foreign and complex as was the psychotherapist's role in their earlier training and, therefore, requires no less by way of awareness of personal motivations if competent and ethical practice is to prevail.

Third, psychologists who have passed beyond that period of professional development in which they obtained case consultation from another psychologist may wish to reinstate that practice. Peer review of assessment data can provide a hedge against bias during one's initial explorations into legal casework when the threat to autonomous objectivity may be greatest because of one's initial insecurity in a new professional situation.

Finally, we urge psychologists to be assertive concerning the establishment of a truly collaborative relationship with the attorney and the client (be this an individual or a court). . . . Careful joint preparation will reduce the number of "surprises" encountered by psychologists in the courtroom and allow the psychologists to avoid various ethical pitfalls. It is also through active involvement with the attorney that the psychologist can best educate the attorney regarding ethical problems as they arise and can attend closely to events that may unduly jeopardize the psychological well-being of the client.

As more psychologists take the witness stand, the courtroom may become a major source of information with which the public forms its impressions of psychology as a science and a profession. There is a commensurate responsibility for psychologists to ad-

From *Professional Psychology, 11,* 764–773. Copyright 1980 by the American Psychological Association. Adapted with permission of the author and publisher.

equately prepare themselves to meet the special ethical demands of the expert witness role, not only because they represent the profession in the public's eye but also for the welfare of the clients who are served.

◆ ◆ ◆

Commentary: As the final substantive words in this chapter, I can find no more eloquent or elegant summary than this, by Butcher and Pope (1993):

> *The psychologist who conducts forensic assessments holds a sometimes overwhelming power over the lives of others. The results of a forensic assessment may influence— perhaps even determine—whether a person receives custody of his or her child, is forced to pay damages to another litigant, returns home from the courtroom, or spends years in prison. In some cases, the assessment results may literally determine whether a person accused of a capital crime lives or dies. Whatever other implications this power has, it mandates that we never take it for granted or treat it carelessly. The explicit ethical and professional standards reviewed . . . are the profession's attempt to ensure that this power is used competently, carefully, appropriately, and responsibly. Our responsibility as forensic practitioners includes not only upholding these standards in our own work of conducting assessments but also constantly rethinking the nature of these standards, their presence in our education and training, the degree to which the profession ensures accountability or, alternatively, passively tolerates and tacitly accepts or encourages violations, and the care with which we spell out responsibilities that fit the current and constantly evolving demands of forensic assessment. (p. 285)*

See *Butcher, J. N., & Pope, K. S. (1993). Seven issues in conducting forensic assessments: Ethical responsibilities in light of new standards and new tests.* Ethics and Behavior, 3, 267–288.

The literature in forensic psychology is burgeoning. Although this chapter was devoted to examining ethical issues, other recent material is available for readers interested in more intensive knowledge about forensic mental health testimony, including the sharp controversies in the field:

Ackerman, M. J. (1995). Clinician's guide to child custody evaluations. *New York: Wiley.*

Ackerman, M. J., & Kane, E. (1998). Psychological experts in divorce, personal injury, and other civil actions *(2nd ed., Vols. 1–2). New York: Aspen Law & Business.*

Brodsky, S. L. (1991). Testifying in court: Guidelines and maxims for the expert witness. *Washington, DC: American Psychological Association.*

Brodzinsky, D. M. (1993). On the use and misuse of psychological testing in child custody evaluations. Professional Psychology: Research and Practice, 24, 213–219.

Dawes, R., Faust, D., & Meehl, P. (1989). Clinical versus actuarial judgment. Science, 243, 1668–1674.

Glassman, J. B. (1998). Preventing and managing board complaints: The downside risk of custody evaluation. Professional Psychology: Research and Practice, 29, 121–124.

Hagen, M. A. (1997). Whores of the court: The fraud of psychiatric testimony and the rape of American justice. *New York: Harper Collins.*

Heilbrun, K. (1992). The role of psychological testing in forensic assessment. Law and Human Behavior, 16, 257–272.

Lykken, D. T. (1993). Predicting violence in the violent society. Applied and Preventive Psychology, 2, 13–20.

Ogloff, J. R. P., Roberts, C. F., & Roesch, R. (1993). The insanity defense: Legal standards and clinical assessment. Applied and Preventive Psychology, 2, 163–178.

Roesch, R., Ogloff, J. R. P., & Golding, S. L. (1993). Competency to stand trial: Legal and clinical issues. Applied and Preventive Psychology, 2, 43–51.

Sales, B. D., & VandenBos, G. R. (Eds.). (1994). Psychology in litigation and legislation. *Washington, DC: American Psychological Association.*

Shapiro, D. L. (1991). Forensic psychological assessment. *Boston: Allyn & Bacon.*

Skinner, L. J., & Berry, K. K. (1993). Anatomically detailed dolls and the evaluation of child sexual abuse allegations. Law and Human Behavior, 17, 399–421.

Wolfner, G., Faust, D., & Dawes, R. M. (1993). The use of anatomically detailed dolls in sexual abuse evaluations: The state of the science. Applied and Preventive Psychology, 2, 1–11.

Ziskin, J. (1998). Coping with psychiatric and psychological testimony *(5th ed., Vols. 1–3). Beverly Hills, CA: Law and Psychology Press.*

CHAPTER 10

THE BUSINESS OF PSYCHOLOGY

During the time that I first wrote this chapter, there was a joke being bandied about by disgruntled mental health professionals. Relating it to the reader in an attempt at humor may be a dubious reward for wending one's way through the world of ethics reflected in this book, but it will also serve a useful purpose in making the point of this chapter.

Three physicians happened to die on the same day and arrived at the proverbial Pearly Gates, waiting to be interviewed by St. Peter to determine whether they would be allowed to enter the Kingdom of Heaven.

"And who are you? asked St. Peter of the first candidate.

"I'm Jonas Salk," he replied meekly.

"Oh, the discoverer of the vaccine that saved so many children from the perils of polio. Come right in."

Turning to the second healer, St. Peter asked the same question. "I'm Benjamin Spock. I wrote a book on children's health and development," the second physician responded authoritatively.

"Ah, yes, and a wise counselor to millions of otherwise anxious and worried parents. We welcome you to Heaven for the remainder of eternity." He then turned to the third supplicant, saying "And who might you be?"

"Well, I'm Gordon Smiley."

"Don't think I recognize the name. What have you done?"

"I," Smiley said proudly, "invented the concept of managed health care."[1]

"Really?" St. Peter said, "Okay. You're approved for 3 days."

The logistics of doing professional psychology no longer simply involves renting an office; buying an oriental rug, an aquarium, and comfortable couches and chairs; and exercising independent professional discretion. Psychology is becoming, and will very likely be for the foreseeable future, a business. Psychologists are no longer therapists or doctors; they are health service providers (or, worse yet, vendors). Those who receive treatment are no longer patients or clients; they are consumers of psychological services. Patients no longer remit

---

[1]For those still innocent, managed health care involves, among other things, attempts by health care systems and third-party payors (like insurance companies) to control costs. They do this in a variety of ways, including requiring permission before certain procedures, such as surgery or psychotherapy, are undertaken and determining length of treatment, such as limiting a hospital stay to 1 day or therapy to 8–10 sessions.

fees; bills are submitted for reimbursement to third-party payors. For good or ill, and regardless of this kind of "new speak," these are the realities that psychologists face.

The changing world of professional psychology confronts the concerned clinician with an array of ethical issues. The modern psychologist must traverse the metaphorical minefield in which are hidden such explosive and competing values as controlling the quickly rising costs of health care, exercising proper professional autonomy, and serving what are perceived to be the needs and best interests of the patient. Even more generally, the health care revolution raises the question of what effects the commercialization of psychology will have on such fundamental moral principles as beneficence, autonomy, fidelity, and justice.

Another part of the new environment for psychologists is the specter of malpractice. Although psychologists rarely are successfully sued for professional negligence, the threat still looms. Performing incompetent child custody evaluations, invading the boundaries of professional relationships through sexual relationships with clients, damaging patients by improperly administering psychotropic medication (increasingly possible as prescription privileges for psychologists become more likely), and committing other vagaries of practice all may lead to malpractice claims. In an attempt to prevent such claims from succeeding and to alert readers to the concurrent ethical problems that may arise from malpractice suits, this chapter presents material on such important issues as proper record keeping and keeping one's finanical "house" in order.

Finally, because the federal government views the provision of psychological services as a commercial, competitive enterprise, it has sought to regulate both the profession and its professionals. In particular, the Federal Trade Commission (FTC) has scrutinized ethical principles of such associations as APA to see if they restrict competition inappropriately. As a result, there are now fewer controls on setting fees, advertising, and soliciting clients. These changes may increase competition within and between professions (e.g., psychology and psychiatry), but they may also lead to dubiously ethical conduct. I hope that the material in this chapter helps readers to discern the differences among sleazy behavior, bad form, illegal actions, and unethical conduct.

The Commerce of Professional Psychology and the New Ethics Code

Gerald P. Koocher

No one will dispute the notion that the practice of professional psychology demands both clinical competence and up-to-date scientific knowledge. Increasingly, however, successful practice demands a sophisticated understanding of commercial issues not routinely addressed in graduate training. The increasing prevalence of managed mental health care, the range of payment mechanisms, and economic hard times contribute to compounding the complexity of the business aspects of running a mental health practice, whether it is done on a solo basis or as part of a large agency. This article focuses on the impact of the new American Psychological Association (APA) ethics code (APA, 1992) with respect to the commercial aspects of the professional practice of psychology . . . .

RECORDS

New specifics on record maintenance (Standard 5.04), preservation (Standard 5.09), ownership (Standard 5.10), and withholding records for nonpayment (Standard 5.11) are provided in the new code. It is now clear, for example, that protection of the confidentiality of records demands consideration of all media (e.g., magnetic, electronic, and optical computer storage, as well as paper and ink records). The new code reiterates the obligation of clinicians to plan in advance for the protection of confidential records in the event of their death or incapacity. Similarly, psychologists must ensure the continuing availability of records and data that may be needed to serve the best interests of their clients (Standard 5.10). The new code also clearly addresses the issue of withholding records solely because of nonpayment (Standard 5.11). Although the code provides a loophole (i.e., "except as otherwise provided by law"; APA, 1992, p. 1607), it is clear that records that are needed to serve the client's imminent welfare cannot be held hostage to unpaid bills. At the same time, however, there is no clear requirement that the psychologist prepare reports or summaries that require additional professional work to produce when a bill for prior services remains unpaid. The new code addresses only preexisting records under this provision. . . .

New *Record Keeping Guidelines* (APA, 1993), adopted at the APA Council meeting immediately following the one at which the new code was approved, are not technically a part of the new code. They do, however, provide an important set of instructions regarding the minimum acceptable standards for psychologists' records. It will always be necessary to monitor special statutes or regulations governing medical and psychological records in one's own legal jurisdiction, as state and local laws may exceed the APA (1993) specifications or have special features demanding particular care. . . .

Although not specifically cited in the new code, the so-called electronic superhighway of communications calls for special cautions. The dissemination of records (discussed in Standard 1.24) by electronic mail and facsimile requires special caution. For example, confidential records should not be transmitted to E-mail accounts or fax destinations that are not secure or appropriately monitored. Similarly, it is important to recognize that conversations on cellular or cordless telephones are not quite as private as those on standard wired phones. . . .

Some psychotherapists have occasionally asserted with misguided pride that they keep no records other than those needed to issue bills (e.g., dates of appointments, charges, and payments). One such psychologist attempted to argue to a state licensing board investigating concerns about her record keeping practices that case records would be of little use to anyone else because, in her opinion, the only truly important aspect of the treatment was the transference, and that could not be picked up using written notes. The standards explicit in both the new code and the *Record Keeping Guidelines* ensure that her practice of not keeping more detailed notes would be deemed negligent (Standards 1.23 and 1.24). . . .

FEES AND FINANCIAL ARRANGEMENTS

[T]he key point in the ethics of financial arrangements, aside from basic honesty and fairness as discussed in Standard 1.25(b), is disclosure. As stated in Standard 1.25(a), the client should know from the initiation of the professional relationship what to expect in terms of fees and payments. In addition, the psychologists are warned in Standard 1.25(c) that they must be mindful that their practices (even solo practices) are businesses and, as a result, are regulated by many state and local laws. For example, a psychologist might think it is a good idea to charge interest or late payment penalties on client bills; however, such practices may well run afoul of state debtor and creditor laws without special legally approved credit agreements. . . .

Discussing fees up front and taking into account the client's ability to pay, restrictions imposed by third-party payers, and similar issues are very important matters. The psychologist's goal should be to thoughtfully avoid the risk of abandoning the client for financial reasons, to obey applicable laws on financial matters, to be nonexploitative, to make no misrepresentation, to anticipate limitations, to discuss collection practices, and to make accurate reports to payers (Standard 1.26). Although not mentioned in the code, it would be wise for

psychologists' special fee requirements (e.g., billing for missed appointments or appointments that were cancelled late) to secure clients' agreement on this point at the start of the relationship. . . .

Providing bribes or kickbacks in exchange for referrals has never been acceptable. However, from the FTC's perspective, some ethics panels or licensing boards interpreted such prohibitions as forbidding participation in health maintenance organizations, preferred provider organizations, or certain referral services. The FTC regards referral services as pro-competitive, and barring them per se was regarded as a significant problem. Unfortunately, what constitutes a bribe, as opposed to a legitimate fee reduction or membership payment, is open to a wide range of opinion. The key to discriminating between an appropriate and an inappropriate payment will depend on the rationale and justification for the charges or fee reductions and the openness of information on these arrangements to the consumers of the services.

In the new code it is clear that payments for referrals and dividing of fees must be based on services rather than the referral per se (Standard 1.27). It is also very important that any referral be justified principally on the basis of the client's best interests, rather than on some financial arrangement between the referral source and the service provider (Standard 1.20). Both their payers and recipients of referral fees should be prepared to document the actual costs of services provided (e.g., office space rental, secretarial costs, or utilities) and the qualifications of the recipient of the referral to meet the particular needs of the client. . . .

Fraud or lying about services actually provided is illegal under most circumstances and has always been unethical. In Standard 1.26, the new code, however, specifically addresses the issue of accuracy in reporting to payers and funding sources. This would include giving accurate accounts of fees charged and copayments made. Similarly, it is clearly unethical to misrepresent the identity of the actual service provider (e.g., failing to disclose that a service was provided by an assistant) or the actual diagnosis (e.g., exaggerating symptoms to ensure insurance coverage). . . .

The most common business issue that leads to

ethical disputes between colleagues involves departures from a practice. This may mean leaving an institution for private practice, leaving a partnership or group practice to strike out on one's own, or simply moving on. Often such career transitions are either not entirely voluntary or not uniformly welcomed by those departing and those staying behind. At such times clients can too often be lost in the shuffle or used as pawns with each side claiming to righteously respect the needs of the client with its own proposed solution.

The new code addresses this issue in Standard 4.08 by focusing appropriately on the client's needs with respect to interrupted services. Psychologists are cautioned to carefully consider how they will resolve their clinical responsibilities on departure at the time they propose to enter an employment or contractual relationship. In this way, the client's best interests can be focused on hypothetically (i.e., before they are actually the new hire's clients), and the sensitive issue of parting can be addressed during a period of maximal goodwill between employer and employee.

The paramount issue to be considered is client welfare. The client's needs must never be held hostage to a practitioner's business or personal interests. A reasonable plan should be in place to define procedures for notifying clients, providing freedom of choice, and ensuring their best interests whenever a disruption in services or continuity of care occurs. . . .

References

American Psychological Association. (1992). Ethical principles of psychologists and code of conduct. *American Psychologist, 47,* 1597–1611.

American Psychological Association. (1993). *Record keeping guidelines.* Washington, DC: Author.

◆　◆　◆

Commentary: In their survey, Fulero and Wilbert (1988) found wide variability in psychologists' record-keeping policies and practices. They strongly recommended the promulgation of "a specific set of guidelines propounded under the auspices of the APA" that, they speculated, "could help to reduce the variability in record-keeping practices found in [their] study" (p. 660). Fulero, S. M., & Wilbert, J. R. (1988). Record-keeping practices of clinical and counseling psychologists: A survey of practitioners. Professional Psychology: Research and Practice, 19, 658–660. In 1993, the APA responded to this and similar suggestions with its Record-Keeping Guidelines (1993; see the next article). Review these guidelines, and consider to what extent they provide concrete guidance to practitioners.

Record Keeping Guidelines

Committee on Professional Practice and Standards, Board of Professional Affairs

INTRODUCTION[1]

The guidelines that follow are based on the General Guidelines, adopted by the American Psychological Association (APA) in July 1987 (APA, 1987). The guidelines receive their inspirational guidance from specific APA *Ethical Principles of Psychologists and Code of Conduct* (APA, 1992).

These guidelines are aspirational and professional judgment must be used in specific applications. They are intended for use by providers of health care services.[2,3] The language of these guidelines must be interpreted in light of their aspirational intent, advancements in psychology and the technology of record keeping, and the professional judgment of the individual psychologist. It is important to highlight that professional judgment is not preempted by these guidelines; rather, the intent is to enhance it.

UNDERLYING PRINCIPLES AND PURPOSE

Psychologists maintain records for a variety of reasons, the most important of which is the benefit of the client. Records allow a psychologist to document and review the delivery of psychological services. The nature and extent of the record will vary depending upon the type and purpose of psychological services. Records can provide a history and current status in the event that a user seeks psychological services from another psychologist or mental health professional.

Conscientious record keeping may also benefit psychologists themselves, by guiding them to plan and implement an appropriate course of psychological services, to review work as a whole, and to self-monitor more precisely.

Maintenance of appropriate records may also be relevant for a variety of other institutional, financial,

---

From *American Psychologist*, 48, 984–986. Copyright 1993 by the American Psychological Association. Adapted with permission of the author and publisher.

[1] In 1988 the Board of Professional Affairs (BPA) directed the Committee on Professional Practice and Standards (COPPS) to determine whether record keeping guidelines would be appropriate. COPPS was informed that these guidelines would supplement the provisions contained in the *General Guidelines for Providers of Psychological Services*, which had been amended two years earlier. The Council of Representatives approved the General Guidelines records provisions after extended debate on the minimum recordation concerning the nature and contents of psychological services. The General Guidelines reflect a compromise position that psychologists hold widely varying views on the wisdom of recording the content of the psychotherapeutic relationship. In light of the Council debate on the content of psychological records and the absence of an integrated document, BPA instructed COPPS to assess the need for such guidelines, and, if necessary, the likely content.

COPPS undertook a series of interviews with psychologists experienced in this area. The consensus of the respondents indicated that practicing psychologists could benefit from guidance in this area. In addition, an APA legal intern undertook a 50-state review of laws governing psychologists with respect to record keeping provisions. The survey demonstrated that while some states have relatively clear provisions governing certain types of records, many questions are often left unclear. In addition, there is a great deal of variability among the states, so that consistent treatment of records as people move from state to state, or as records are sought from other states, may not be easy to achieve.

Based on COPPS' survey and legal research, BPA in 1989 directed COPPS to prepare an initial set of record keeping guidelines. This document resulted. [These guidelines were adopted as APA policy by the Council of Representatives in February 1993.]

[2] These guidelines apply to Industrial/Organizational psychologists providing health care services but generally not to those providing non-health care I/O services. For instance, in I/O psychology, written records may constitute the primary work product, such as a test instrument or a job analysis, while psychologists providing health care services may principally use records to document non-written services and to maintain continuity.

[3] Rather than keeping their own record system, psychologists practicing in institutional settings comply with the institution's policies on record keeping, so long as they are consistent with legal and ethical standards.

and legal purposes. State and federal laws in many cases require maintenance of appropriate records of certain kinds of psychological services. Adequate records may be a requirement for receipt of third party payment for psychological services.

In addition, well documented records may help protect psychologists from professional liability, if they become the subject of legal or ethical proceedings. In these circumstances, the principal issue will be the professional action of the psychologist, as reflected in part by the records.

At times, there may be conflicts between the federal, state, or local laws governing record keeping, the requirements of institutional rules, and these guidelines. In these circumstances, psychologists bear in mind their obligations to conform to applicable law. When laws or institutional rules appear to conflict with the principles of these guidelines, psychologists use their education, skills, and training to identify the relevant issues, and to attempt to resolve it in a way that, to the maximum extent feasible, conforms both to law and to professional practice, as required by ethical principles.

Psychologists are justifiably concerned that, at times, record keeping information will be required to be disclosed against the wishes of the psychologist or client, and may be released to persons unqualified to interpret such records. These guidelines assume that no record is free from disclosure all of the time, regardless of the wishes of the client or the psychologist.

1. Content of Records

a. Records include any information (including information stored in a computer) that may be used to document the nature, delivery, progress, or results of psychological services. Records can be reviewed and duplicated.

b. Records of psychological services minimally include (a) identifying data, (b) dates of services, (c) types of services, (d) fees, (e) any assessment, plan for intervention, consultation, summary reports, and/or testing reports and supporting data as may be appropriate, and (f) any release of information obtained.

c. As may be required by their jurisdiction and circumstances, psychologists maintain to a reasona-

ble degree accurate, current, and pertinent records of psychological services. The detail is sufficient to permit planning for continuity in the event that another psychologist takes over delivery of services, including, in the event of death, disability, and retirement. In addition, psychologists maintain records in sufficient detail for regulatory and administrative review of psychological service delivery.

d. Records kept beyond the minimum requirements are a matter of professional judgment for the psychologist. The psychologist takes into account the nature of the psychological services, the source of the information recorded, the intended use of the records, and his or her professional obligation.

e. Psychologists make reasonable efforts to protest against the misuse of records. They take into account the anticipated use by the intended or anticipated recipients when preparing records. Psychologists adequately identify impressions and tentative conclusions as such.

2. Construction and Control of Records

a. Psychologists maintain a system that protects the confidentiality of records. They must take reasonable steps to establish and maintain the confidentiality of information arising from their own delivery of psychological services, or the services provided by others working under their supervision.

b. Psychologists have ultimate responsibility for the content of their records and the records of those under their supervision. Where appropriate, this requires that the psychologist oversee the design and implementation of record keeping procedures, and monitor their observance.

c. Psychologists maintain control over their clients' records, taking into account the policies of the institutions in which they practice. In situations where psychologists have control over their clients' records and where circumstances change such that it is no longer feasible to maintain control over such records, psychologists seek to make appropriate arrangements for transfer.

d. Records are organized in a manner that facilitates their use by the psychologist and other authorized persons. Psychologists strive to assure that record entries are legible. Records are to be completed in a timely manner.

e. Records may be maintained in a variety of media, so long as their utility, confidentiality, and durability are assured.

3. Retention of Records

a. The psychologist is aware of relevant federal, state, and local laws and regulations governing record retention. Such laws and regulations supersede the requirements of these guidelines. In the absence of such laws and regulations, complete records are maintained for a minimum of 3 years after the last contact with the client. Records, or a summary, are then maintained for an additional 12 years before disposal.[4] If the client is a minor, the record period is extended until 3 years after the age of majority.

b. All records, active and inactive, are maintained safely, with properly limited access, and from which timely retrieval is possible.

4. Outdated Records

a. Psychologists are attentive to situations in which record information has become outdated, and may therefore be invalid, particularly in circumstances where disclosure might cause adverse effects. Psychologists ensure that when disclosing such information that its outdated nature and limited utility are noted using professional judgment and complying with applicable law.

b. When records are to be disposed of, this is done in an appropriate manner that ensures non-disclosure (or preserves confidentiality) (see Section 3a).

5. Disclosure of Record Keeping Procedures

a. When appropriate, psychologists may inform their clients of the nature and extent of their record keeping procedures. This information includes a statement on the limitations of the confidentiality of the records.

b. Psychologists may charge a reasonable fee for review and reproduction of records. Psychologists do not withhold records that are needed for valid health care purposes solely because the client has not paid for prior services.

References

American Psychological Association. (1987). General guidelines for providers of psychological services. *American Psychologist, 42,* 712–723.

American Psychological Association. (1992). Ethical principles of psychologists and code of conduct. *American Psychologist, 47,* 1597–1611.

---

[4]These time limits follow the APA's specialty guidelines. If the specialty guidelines should be revised, a simple 7 year requirement for the retention of the complete record is preferred, which would be a more stringent requirement than any existing state statute.

Thorough Record Keeping: A Good Defense in a Litigious Era

Ellen L. Soisson, Leon VandeCreek, and Samuel Knapp

. . .

DOCUMENTATION OF SIGNIFICANT DECISIONS AND EVENTS

The record should provide an explanation of significant treatments as well as patient–therapist decisions. Klein, Macbeth, and Onek (1984) recommended that for each significant decision, the record should include (a) what the choice is expected to accomplish, (b) why the clinician believes it will be effective, (c) any risks that might be involved and why they are justified, (d) what alternative treatments were considered, (e) why they were rejected, and (f) what steps were taken to improve the effectiveness of the chosen treatments.

Forensically significant events such as involuntary commitments and possible malpractice suits should be anticipated, and the record should be written from the perspective of future readers (Gutheil & Appelbaum, 1982). For example, in the case of a suicidal client, psychotherapists should document an assessment of the risk, the options considered for the prevention of suicide, and possible treatments of the client (including advantages and disadvantages).

Psychotherapists should record the details of emergencies with special care because they result in a disproportionate number of malpractice suits (Gutheil & Appelbaum, 1982). Consultation and its documentation in such cases can be invaluable. In emergencies and in standard practice, it may also help to document the cooperation or resistance of significant others to an individual's treatment so that the responsibility can be placed where it ought to be if malpractice is claimed (Cohen, 1979). In addition, when a clinician is about to take a calculated risk or make a nonroutine intervention, it is appropriate to "think out loud for the record." According to Gutheil (1980), thinking for the record "stacks the deck heavily in favor of a finding of error in judgment rather than negligence" (p. 482).

DECIDING WHAT NOT TO DOCUMENT

Some members of the medical profession have argued that "no amount of documentation is too much and no detail is too small" ("Physician team," 1985, p. 2). However, the principle of extreme inclusiveness does not necessarily hold true for psychological records. The developing right of clients to gain access to their records and the widespread release of records to third-party payers and others emphasize that records should focus on facts and not hunches or value judgments (Cohen, 1979). As a result, records should exclude emotional statements and other personal opinions. Information about illegal behavior, sexual practices, or other sensitive information that may embarrass or harm the client or others is rarely appropriate for the record.

CLIENT ACCESS TO RECORDS

Psychiatric and psychological records are considered to be the property of the health care provider. The consumer controls its dissemination, although the right of patients to have direct access to their records varies from state to state (Hirsh, 1978). The

From *Professional Psychology: Research and Practice, 18,* 498–502. Copyright 1987 by the American Psychological Association. Adapted with permission of the author and publisher.

trend, however, is toward increasing patient access to records. Patients may request that information be altered or corrected, and agency policies frequently afford a process for appeal if the correction request is denied. The right of client access to the records further increases the professional's accountability, heightening the pressure to write records as clearly and accurately as possible. Access may be denied in cases in which disclosure could be harmful to the patient, but psychologists generally should assume that one's clients will eventually review their records.

Despite the fears of professionals, researchers examining the impact of allowing patients access to their records have found favorable patient responses. Research with psychiatric inpatients (Roth, Wolford, & Meisel, 1980; Stein, Furedy, Simonton, & Neuffer, 1979) who were granted access to their records indicated that many records contained errors. Nonetheless, both patients and staff believed that client access improved treatment.

In states without access statutes, patients may often obtain access to their records by authorizing their release to another professional or to an attorney by initiating a lawsuit against the psychologist (*Palmer v. Durso*, 1977).

That records pose a threat to clients was dramatically reaffirmed by the court in *Wolfe v. Beal* (1978), in which an ex-client successfully brought suit to expunge and destroy the records of her hospitalization on the grounds that the record resulted from an illegal commitment. The court agreed that the continued existence of the record, even though held in confidence by the facility, posed a continual threat to her reputation.

DUAL RECORDS

Some psychologists keep a separate record of material of a sensitive or speculative nature that does not become a part of the client's formal record but remains in the clinician's possession (Brown, 1982). State law is not always clear in regard to the status of such records. In Illinois, however, the term *personal notes* is a part of the Mental Health and Developmental Disabilities Confidentiality Act of 1979. Such notes are not considered to be part of the patient's record, and they are immune from subpoena

[Mental and Developmental Disabilities Confidentiality Act, 1979, ¶802, §2(4)].

The concept of maintaining dual records is controversial. Pollack (1977) warned that a double set of records could lead to an embarrassing legal confrontation if they came to light. However, an ethics code for health professionals proposed by the American Orthopsychiatric Association (Schuchman, Nye, Rafferty, & Freedman, 1982) suggested that a dual record system is appropriate. In general, the distinction between the patient's record and personal notes is considered defensible and potentially analogous to the work product privilege that protects lawyers' records (Klein et al., 1984). The Illinois statute has been upheld twice in court tests (Shutz, 1982).

We are aware of no court tests of dual records in states without explicit protection. However, in a related matter, a court (*White v. United States*, 1986) recently found that a "therapist–administrator split" for treatment and record keeping of a hospital patient was an acceptable practice. This arrangement entailed keeping individual psychotherapy independent of other forms of hospital treatment in order to ensure a trusting relationship. The best solution would be for states to clarify in the statutes the status of personal notes and dual records.

RECORD RETENTION

. . .

In the event of the death or incapacitation of the psychotherapist in independent practice, special provisions must be made for the retention or transferral of the records and for continuity of services. Ideally, the psychotherapist should have a written set of instructions incorporated into a will or into the records of the practice that specify the disposition of the records. The Specialty Guidelines (American Psychological Association, 1980) suggest that if no provisions have been made for records, it is appropriate for another psychologist, acting under the auspices of a local professional standards review committee, to review the records with patients and to recommend a course of action. To facilitate such a process psychotherapists should keep their records current and in good order. It would not be wise for the records to contain inflammatory material that might lead a reviewing patient to initiate a lawsuit against the deceased psychotherapist's estate. . . .

References

American Psychological Association. (1980). Specialty guidelines for delivery of services by clinical psychologists. *American Psychologist, 36,* 652–663.

Brown, S. (1982). Record content. In H. Schuchman, L. Foster, S. Nye, E. Brown, J. Gutman, R. Lanman, & S. Pettee (Eds.), *Confidentiality of health records* (pp. 45–64). New York: Gardner.

Cohen, R. J. (1979). *Malpractice: A guide for mental health professionals.* New York: The Free Press.

Gutheil, T. G. (1980). Paranoia and progress notes: A guide to forensically informed psychiatric record keeping. *Hospital and Community Psychiatry, 13,* 479–482.

Gutheil, T. G., & Appelbaum, P. S. (1982). *The clinical handbook of psychiatry and the law.* New York: McGraw-Hill.

Hirsh, H. L. (1978). Will your medical records get you into trouble? *Legal Aspects of Medical Practice, 6,* 46–51.

Klein, J. L., Macbeth, J. E., & Onek, J. N. (1984). *Legal issues in the private practice of psychiatry.* Washington, DC: American Psychiatric Press.

Mental Health and Developmental Disabilities Confidentiality Act, (1979, January). *Ill. Stat. Ann.,* CA 91 ½, ¶801 et. seq.

Palmer v. Durso, 90 Misc. 2d 110, 393 N.Y.S. 2d 898 (1977).

Physician team studies OB claims. (1985, June). *Malpractice Digest, 12,* 2.

Pollack, S. (1977). Psychiatric–legal problems of office practice. *Current Psychiatric Therapies, 1977,* 31–46.

Roth, L. H., Wolford, J., & Meisel, A. (1980). Patient access to records: Tonic or toxin. *American Journal of Psychiatry, 137,* 592–596.

Schuchman, H., Nye, S., Rafferty, F. T., & Freedman, L. (1982). Appendix II: Ethics codes for health professionals. In H. Schuchman, L. Foster, S. Nye, E. Brown, J. Gutman, R. Lanman, & S. Pettee (Eds.), *Confidentiality of health records* (pp. 199–224). New York: Gardner.

Shutz, B. M. (1982). *Legal liability in psychotherapy.* San Francisco: Jossey-Bass.

Stein, E. J., Furedy, R. L., Simonton, M. J., & Neuffer, C. H. (1979). Patient access to medical records on a psychiatric inpatient unit. *American Journal of Psychiatry, 136,* 327–329.

White v. United States, 780 F.2d 97 (D.C. Cir. 1986).

Wolfe v. Beal, 384 A.2d 1187 (Pa. 1978).

◆ ◆ ◆

Commentary: In recent years, the FTC has scrutinized the business practices of health care entities. It has charged that these entities have placed restrictions on professionals that both reduce competition among practitioners and reduce the free flow of truthful information to consumers. Among the entities scrutinized are state boards that license health care professionals and professional associations that regulate the ethical conduct of their members. As the APA ethics committee noted in the following excerpt from its annual report, the APA has not been immune to FTC scrutiny:

> In July 1986, the Federal Trade Commission (FTC) began an investigation charging that APA's Ethical Principles of Psychologists *were in violation of the federal antitrust laws. In particular, the Federal Trade Commission expressed concern about Principles 4.b.iii, 4.b.v, 4.b.vi, 4.b.vii, 4.b.viii, and portions of Principles 6.d and 7.b. The APA voluntarily placed a moratorium on the adjudication of complaints of unethical conduct under the challenged principles and informed the APA membership of this action. Thereafter, a long series of letter exchanges took place between APA and the FTC, and in June 1989, the APA Board of Directors, on advise[sic] of legal counsel, declared an emergency and voted to rescind the challenged ethical principles. In October 1989, on the advise[sic] of legal counsel, the Board of Directors authorized APA to sign the renegotiated complaint, consent agreement, and order.*
>
> In the opinion of expert legal counsel, the portions of APA's Ethical Principles of Psychologists *in question were clearly in violation of the antitrust laws. Similar principles to those rescinded by the APA Board of Directors contained in the American Medical Association's ethical code were declared in violation of the antitrust laws*

by the federal district and appellate courts. (p. 874)

See APA Ethics Committee. (1990). *Report of Ethics Committee, 1988*. American Psychologist, 45, 874. For a more complete history, see also Koocher, G. P. (1994). *APA and the FTC: New adventures in consumer protection*. American Psychologist, 49, 322–328 (some of which is reprinted on the following pages).

As a result of negotiations with the FTC, the following sections from the 1981 ethics code were deleted in 1989:

> 4(b)(iii) [*Public statements by psychologists do not contain*] *a testimonial from a patient regarding the quality of a psychologists' services or products . . .; (v) a statement implying unusual, unique, or one-of-a-kind abilities; (vi) a statement intended or likely to appeal to a client's*

fears, anxieties or emotions concerning the possible results of failure to obtain the offered services; (vii) a statement concerning the comparative desirability of offered services; (viii) a statement of direct solicitation of individual clients.

> 6(d) [*Psychologists*] *neither give nor receive any remuneration for referring clients for professional services.*

> 7(b) *If a person is receiving similar services from another professional, psychologists do not offer their own services directly to such a person.*

In what ways could these deleted standards be said to restrict competition and the free flow of information to the clients of psychologists? In what ways do the deletion of these standards disserve client welfare and interfere with the goals of effective assessment, therapy, and research?

APA and the FTC: New Adventures in Consumer Protection

Gerald P. Koocher[1]

. . .

THE NATURE OF RESTRICTIONS ON ADVERTISEMENTS

If the general goals of the FTC were to make useful information available to the general public, it is understandable that clinging to vestiges of sameness in public statements for the sake of a sense of professionalism would not survive. However, some limits on advertising may well serve legitimate public interests. This is especially true in professions such as psychology, in which the consumers are often particularly vulnerable to undue influence because of their intellectual or emotional status. . . .

Is Commercial Speech Free Speech Too?

Do restraints imposed by professional association restrictions on advertising violate commercial free speech? Although it is not the same as political free speech, in the constitutional sense, the concept is still highly relevant and has often been an issue in efforts to limit advertising by lawyers. Commercial speech is protected under the First and Fourteenth Amendments, just as political speech is protected (*Virginia State Board of Pharmacy*, 1975); however, the courts have ruled that it is still reasonable to demand substantiation in the face of alleged false or deceptive advertising. The FTC's thrust has been to expand access to truthful information in the marketplace, although there are some exceptions that are discussed later as "in-your face" solicitations. A good example of the commercial free speech argument involved an enterprising Kentucky lawyer named Shapero.

In *Shapero v. Kentucky Bar Association* (1988), the Supreme Court dealt with the case of a young lawyer who wanted to solicit business by sending truthful, nondeceptive letters to potential clients known to be confronting certain legal problems. The letter in question was to go to "potential clients who have had a foreclosure suit filed against them" and advised "you may be about to lose your home" and that "federal law may allow you to . . . ORDER your creditor to STOP." Potential clients were invited to "call my office for FREE information . . . it may surprise you what I may be able to do for you" (p. 1919).

Mr. Shapero had the foresight to ask the Kentucky state bar whether his proposed letter to people facing foreclosure was acceptable. Although the state bar commissioners ruled that the letter was not misleading, they said no to Shapero, citing a then-existing Kentucky Supreme Court rule prohibiting the direct solicitation of individuals (i.e., as opposed to members of the general public) as a directed result of some specific event. Shapero appealed to the U.S. Supreme Court and won. The key point in the decision was that the content of his notice was not false or deceptive and held genuine potential interest for the intended recipients—which they could then choose to act on or ignore.

[1] For the author's latest discussion of this topic see Koocher, G. P., & Keith-Spiegel, P. (1998). *Ethics in psychology: Professional standards and cases* (2nd ed., pp. 259–283). New York: Oxford University Press.

"In-Your-Face" Solicitation

What if the nature of the commercial exercise of free speech involves a more intense approach than Attorney Shapero's letter or takes advantage of a client in a vulnerable position? The bottom line seems to be that so-called in-your-face solicitation of clients, especially vulnerable ones, will not be tolerated.

Consider the case of an enterprising attorney named Ohralik from Montville, Ohio (*Ohralik v. Ohio State Bar Association*, 1978). . . .

. . .

[*Ed. note*: Ohralik visited two young women who had been injured in an auto accident. One was still in the hospital; the other had just been released. He was sanctioned by the state bar and appealed to the state's highest court, which agreed that direct solicitation was inconsistent with the ideals of the legal profession. He then appealed to the U.S. Supreme Court.]

[T]he U.S. Supreme Court (*Ohralik v. Ohio State Bar Association*, 1978) ruled that Ohralik's conduct posed "dangers that the state has a right to prevent" (p. 449), noting that the "appellant not only foisted himself upon these clients; he acted in gross disregard for their privacy" (p. 469).

Testimonials

The use of testimonials by "satisifed users" has a kind of inherent face validity that appeals to the FTC. Unfortunately, like many forms of face validity, the true predictive potential of a testimonial endorsement is far more complex so far as psychological services are concerned. If psychotherapy research has taught us anything, it is that any given psychotherapist is not equally efficacious with all potential clients.

One ironic inconsistency in the latest version of the *EP* [Ethical Principles] is obvious when one contrasts the two-year interval during which sexual intimacies with former psychotherapy clients are absolutely proscribed (Section 4.07) with the instant availability of the client as a testimonial provider upon the moment of terminating therapy. Psychotherapists know very well that their influence in the life of their clients does not end at the close of the last treatment session. The FTC did allow APA to bar the use of testimonials from "current psychotherapy patients" or from "persons who because of their particular circumstances are vulnerable to undue influence." Apparently, the FTC does not regard the lingering influence of the transference relationship and its potential consequences as an automatic barrier to testimonial advertising (e.g., potentially unfair and deceptive endorsements provided in the glow of a positive transference).

Although most private practitioners know that satisfied clients and the people who referred those clients are their best sources of future referrals, there are few data to suggest that the public will rely on commercially advertised testimonials in selecting medical care providers. The one exception may be plastic and cosmetic surgery, in which the concept of "face" validity takes on a unique meaning to the viewer.

Appeals to Fear

Many psychologists wondered why the FTC would object to APA's ban of advertising that appealed to potential clients' fears. After all, some of our clients are emotionally insecure and may be even more vulnerable to inappropriate duress than [the young women in *Ohralik*]. From the FTC's perspective, global bans on advertising that "appeals to fear if services are not obtained" were simply unacceptable in general. Lots of effective advertising appeals to emotions and fears at some level (e.g., fear of tooth decay if you don't brush, fear of accidental injury or death if you ride in a car without benefit of seat belts and air bags, or fear of AIDS as a result of not practicing "safe sex"). In fact, social psychology has taught us that an "appeal to fear" coupled with a designated course of action is highly effective in evoking attitude change.

How might an ethics committee have become involved in such complaints? In one instance, actual complaints were filed when consumers objected to advertising by psychologists running programs to help people quit smoking. The advertisements powerfully cited potential death from lung cancer and other pulmonary diseases. A more troubling example is the coupling of an appeal to fear with so-called in-your-face solicitation. . . . Imagine the situation in which a psychologist arrives unsolicited at the home of a child who witnessed a playground shooting and urges the parents to subscribe to a course of therapy to prevent inevitable posttraumatic stress syndrome in their as-yet asmptomatic child.

It is interesting that FTC Commissioner Azcuenaga disagreed with her colleagues on this point. She supported APA's wish to continue a ban on scare advertising, noting that the justification for banning such advertising by psychologists was plausible and that the FTC ought not to substitute its judgment on the matter without having a sound basis for doing so. She cited the FTC's lack of expertise concerning psychotherapy and noted that "nothing, even hypothetically, suggests that the [APA's] justification is either implausible or invalid" (Azcuenaga, 1990, p. 2). She was outvoted.

Fee Splitting

Providing bribes or kickbacks in exchange for referrals was never an acceptable practice, but from the FTC's perspective some ethics panels or licensing boards were interpreting prohibitions on this point as forbidding psychologists' participation in health maintenance organizations, preferred provider organizations, or referral services during the 1980s. The FTC regards referral services as procompetitive, and barring them per se was regarded as a significant problem. Unfortunately, what constitutes a bribe, as opposed to a legitimate fee reduction or membership payment, is open to a wide range of opinion. The FTC consent order does permit APA to issue "reasonable" principles requiring disclosures to consumers regarding fees paid to referral services or similar entities. The key to discriminating between reasonable and inappropriate payment will have to depend on the rationale for the charges or fee reductions and the openness of information on these arrangements to the consumers of the services.

1992 APA ETHICS CODE

. . .

For the reader interested in reviewing the relevant sections of the current version of the *EP* (APA, 1992) most directly covered by the FTC order are the following:

Standard 1.27 Referrals and Fees, which

prohibits improper payments between professionals based on referrals;

Standard 3.01, which defines what is considered a "Public Statement";

Standard 3.02, which requires reasonable efforts to correct misstatements made about or on behalf of the psychologist by others and prohibits compensation of media personnel to get publicity;

Standard 3.03, which deals with avoiding "False or Deceptive Statements" regarding psychologists' credentials and the scientific bases for claims of efficacy;

Standard 3.05, which bars psychologists from soliciting testimonials from current therapy clients or other persons who are vulnerable to "undue influence" by virtue of their particular circumstances;

Standard 3.06, which bars the uninvited, in-person solicitation for psychotherapy of persons vulnerable to undue influence (except for collateral contact with significant others of existing patients); and

Standard 4.04, which adds back specific requirements to be followed when considering whether to offer services to a client already receiving them elsewhere.

Indirectly, *Standard 1.20*, Sections a and c, which deal with consultation and referral practices (focus on clients' best interests and obeying the law); *Standard 1.25*, Sections a, b, c, and d, which deal with specifying financial, billing, compensation, and fee arrangements, and nonexploitation in that regard, are also relevant. Also Section 4.01, which addresses structuring the therapeutic relationship, so far as fee information is concerned, applies.

Did the FTC–APA interaction lead to an improved ethics code? I believe that some improvements resulted by directing the APA and other professional associations concerned with advertising to focus on substance, rather than on style. On the other hand, I also believe that the FTC failed to fully accept the principle that the relationships between mental health professionals and their clients are qualitatively different from those that exist in many other professions. The result will be a greater reluctance on the part of ethics enforcement groups in psychology to tackle complaints in this arena. What does all of this mean for the psychologist who wants to consider advertising in light of the current code? How about the state licensing board that wants to impose restrictions greater or more specific than those adopted by APA?

The following guidelines summarize the key factors to focus on.

1. Advertising by psychologists is clearly acceptable and cannot be banned, although the content of advertisements should ideally focus on facts of meaningful interest to the potential consumer.

2. One must take great care when listing affiliations, degrees, and other data so as to assure that the public is not misled, confused, or otherwise deceived. Both intentional deception and inadvertent errors that are not corrected can be prosecuted.

3. Once completely prohibited, soliciting testimonials or quotes from "satisfied users" is now permissible, so long as they are not solicited from current psychotherapy clients or others subject to "undue influence." The effectiveness of such advertising for psychologists is unknown.

4. The uninvited, direct, in-your-face solicitation of individuals as clients is also prohibited to the extent that it subjects the potential client to "undue influence," as opposed to mass solicitation through media advertising. However, this does not include barriers to inviting the significant others of current clients for collateral treatment.

5. Psychologists who serve organizational or industrial clients are entitled to broader latitude than those who serve individuals (e.g., current organizational clients could be solicited for endorsements), lay groups, and families; however, they too must observe factual validity-based criteria and avoid deception in their advertising claims.

6. Fees may be mentioned in advertisements but must also be reasonably honored for the reasonable life of the announcement.

7. Referral services may ethically charge a fee to clients, therapists, or both, although this should not be secret from the client, and the fee should not be the primary basis for making the specific referral. When portions of fees are paid to others parties, such fees should be in payment for services actually rendered (e.g., referral service, consultation, supervision, office space rental).

8. Although there is no longer any prohibition to offering treatment to a client who is receiving services from another professional, specific discussion with the client of the potential risks and conflicts is now required. It would also be wise to seek authorization from the client to contact the other professional and to consult with that person.

9. Psychologists must consider their style of presentation-of-self and public statements carefully in any public context, whether or not advertising per se is involved.

10. States may impose more stringent restrictions on professional advertising than do professional associations, so long as a legitimate state's interest is documented and so long as that state's interest does not violate a customer's access to useful information.

References

American Psychological Association. (1992). Ethical principles of psychologists and code of conduct. *American Psychologist, 47,* 1597–1611.

Azcuenaga, M. L. (1990). *Separate statement of Commissioner Mary L. Azcuenaga concurring in part and dissenting in part in American Psychological Association File 861–0082.* Washington, DC: Federal Trade Commission.

Ohralik v. Ohio State Bar Association, 436 U.S. 447 (1978).

Shapero v. Kentucky Bar Association, 486 U.S. 466 (1988).

Virginia State Board of Pharmacy et al. v. Virginia Citizens Consumer Council, Inc., et al., 425 U.S. 747 (1975).

◆ ◆ ◆

Commentary: Koocher correctly stated that the 1992 Ethical Principles bar uninvited in-person solicitation of actual or potential psychotherapy clients who are vulnerable to undue influence (see Standard 3.06). The FTC approved Standard 3.06 on the basis of the Supreme Court's decision in Ohralik v. State Bar Association, 436 U.S. 447 (1978), concerning in-person solicitation by lawyers of clients suffering personal injuries (such as in auto accidents, like the case summarized by Koocher in the preceding excerpt). However, in 1993, the Supreme Court struck down a Florida rule precluding certified public accountants from engaging in direct in-person solicitation. The Court noted that it had not banned all such attempts to garner business and that distinctions among professions were significant in assessing whether such bans were reasonable and constitutional. In Edenfield v. Fane, 507 U.S. 761 (1993), the Court ruled that solicitation by certified public accountants was different than solicitation by lawyers because lawyers are trained in the art of persuasion whereas accountants' training emphasizes independence and objectivity, not advocacy. Who are psychologists more like— lawyers or accountants? Should not the proper analysis involve examining the nature of the client, not the nature of the profession? From that perspective, is the APA's Standard 3.06 appropriate?

Consider the following advertisement:

> Premature ejaculation, impotence and vaginismus, cured by World's Who's Who psychotherapist. Ninety-five percent success, revolutionary short term program, compassionate, scientific, sincere. All anxieties treated between 11:00 a.m. and 1 p.m. Area code . . . .

This ad, quoted by Frisch and Rebert (1991, p. 176), in their article, appeared in the Village Voice in 1989. The authors argued that such self-advertising is not in the best interest of psychology. Instead, they advocated "that psychology should, in fact, expand its efforts to advertise the profession as a whole, bringing the public information about the use of psychological services and where to find those services" (p. 179). Such collective public education programs, they believed, offer a more positive image of the profession. See Frisch, G. R., & Rebert, D. (1991). Effects of advertising on psychology. Canadian Psychology, 32, 176–180. In any event, is the ad that they quoted in violation of the APA Ethical Principles?

With regard to another controversial matter, Koocher correctly stated that Standard 1.27 of the 1992 Ethical Principles does not bar referral fees as long as the fees are based on services provided and are not simply "kick-

backs" for the referral itself. But the line between a kickback and a proper referral fee may be difficult to draw. Furthermore, under the statutes regulating Medicare (nationwide health insurance for the elderly) and Medicaid (state medical assistance programs for the poor), "whoever knowingly and willfully solicits or receives any remuneration" or "whoever knowingly and willfully offers to pay any remuneration (including any kickback, bribe, or rebate) directly or indirectly, overtly or convertly, in cash or in kind in return for referring an individual to a person for the furnishing of [Medicare or Medicaid] service" is guilty of a felony, punishable by a fine of up to $25,000 and imprisonment of up to 5 years. See Social Security Spending Reduction Act of 1984, 42 U.S.C. § 1320a–7b(b). Thus, although some referral-fee practices may be ethical, they may be illegal within federal health systems. Furthermore, some state ethics codes, incorporated into their licensure laws, may be more restrictive than the APA code of ethics. The APA Ethics Committee has issued a statement intended to clarify Standard 1.27. It says that the Standard

> does not prohibit an independent contractor from paying a percentage of a fee to a colleague as long as the payment is within a reasonable range of the fair market value of the services provided. Services are broadly defined and include, for example, mentoring and promotional activities. (p. 713)

See APA Ethics Committee. (1995). Report of the Ethics Committee, 1994. American Psychologist, 50, 706–713. Although this clarification is helpful, the prudent practitioner will obtain sound legal advice before offering or receiving referral fees. For an informative and cautionary article concerning fraud in federal programs generally, see Geis, G., Pontell, H. N., Keenan, C., Rosoff, S. M., O'Brien, M. J., & Jesilow, P. D. (1985). Peculating psychologists: Fraud and abuse against Medicaid. Professional Psychology: Research and Practice, 16, 823–832.

Finally, in reviewing the 1981 APA code of ethics, Faustman (1982) raised another difficult money-related concern:

> The ethical standards seem somewhat

vague on the act of referring [delinquent accounts] to an external collection service. Under the intent of the standards, the use of a collection agency may be ethical if the therapist, prior to the initiation of therapy, obtains the expressed consent (e.g., written and/or verbal consent) of the client to release information should the client not pay the fee. (p. 209)

See Faustman, W. O. (1982). Legal and ethical issues in debt collection strategies of professional psychologists. Professional Psychology, 13, 208–214.

Standard 1.25f of the 1992 Ethical Principles is much clearer on this issue. Psychologists planning to use collection agencies may do so, provided that they "first [inform] the person that such measures will be taken and [provide] that person an opportunity to make prompt payment." However, a collection agency's "aggressive attempts to obtain payment . . . may result in the client's bringing suit against the therapist" (Faustman, 1982, p. 210). For a helpful guide to all these knotty matters, see Yenney, S. L., & American Psychological Association Practice Directorate. (1994). Business strategies for a caring profession. Washington, DC: American Psychological Association.

When the first edition of this book was published, President Clinton's attempt to revolutionize health care delivery and achieve health insurance coverage for all Americans had just failed. As this is being written in late 1998, Clinton's goals remain unrealized.

The complexities of health care reform are far beyond the scope and intent of this text. For two good background pieces, however, the reader may profit from reviewing:

Higuchi, S. A., & Newman, R. (1994). Legal issues for psychotherapy in a managed care environment. Psychoanalysis and Psychotherapy, 11, 138–153.

Petrila, J. (1996). Ethics, money, and the problem of coercion in managed behavioral health care. Saint Louis University Law Journal, 40, 359–405.

The relevant question for practitioners is whether the provision of mental health services under the rubric of managed care will create a significant number of ethical conflicts for psychologists and other mental health professionals. Many practitioners appear to think so. In a 1997 survey sponsored by Division 42 of APA (Independent Practice), 57.8% of 442 respondents (of 1,000 surveyed) reported experiencing ethical dilemmas in managed care organizations not addressed in the 1992 ethics code, and 60.6% stated that the code inadequately helped psychologists solve ethical issues encountered in managed care organizations. See Murphy, M. J., DeBernardo, C. R., & Shoemaker, W. E. (1998). Impact of managed care on independent practice and professional ethics: A survey of independent practitioners. Professional Psychology: Research and Practice, 29, 43–51. See also Field, R. I. (1998). New ethical relationships under health care's new structure: The need for a new paradigm. Villanova Law Review, 43, 467–498.

Whatever the eventual course of health care legislation and whatever attempts are made to reform managed care, it is clear, as Kiesler & Morton (1988) presciently observed, that "health policy is in a state of upheaval in the United States. . . . The rapid evolution of health policy has potentially dramatic implications for psychologists, as scientists, professionals, and advocates" (p. 993). Kiesler, C. A., & Morton, T. L. (1988). Psychology and public policy in the "health care revolution." American Psychologist, 43, 993–1003. What was true a decade ago is decidedly more true today.

The following set of materials provides some education concerning the emotional nature of the debate concerning managed mental health care structures. It also provides some guidance for resolving ethical conflicts to those who provide mental health services in these uncertain and changing times. It may be helpful while reading these materials to consider the obligations of psychologists in temporal terms. That is, what should be the responsibilities of therapists prior to becoming involved with managed care companies, to the patient before therapy begins, and to the patient during the course of therapy?

Legal Liability and Managed Care

Paul S. Appelbaum

...

OVERVIEW OF MANAGED CARE

Managed care as a generic term subsumes a wide variety of practices designed to regulate the utilization of health care (Dorwart, 1990; Tischler, 1990; Zimet, 1989). The key element shared by all managed care approaches, however, is the prospective or concurrent review of care provided to individual patients, with the power to deny payment for care thought to be unnecessary or not cost-effective. Although managed care programs often maintain that their efforts will lead to an improvement in the quality of care—for example, through the elimination of unnecessary procedures or treatments—it is clear that the goal of reducing health care costs lies at the heart of managed care systems (Institute of Medicine, 1989).

Management of care now takes place as part of every type of payment system for health care. In traditional indemnity programs, under which patients select their own providers who are reimbursed on a fee-for-service basis, preadmission or pretreatment authorization with continuing periodic review is often required. Preferred provider organizations (PPOs), in which patients are limited to predetermined panels of providers (or at least have economic incentives to select a provider from the panels), may also require prospective or concurrent review, and in addition may recruit practitioners on the basis of their predisposition to use lower-cost treatments (e.g., short-term psychotherapies) and their willingness to cooperate with cost-control measures (Dorwart, 1990; Tischler, 1990).

In health maintenance organizations (HMOs), in which care is delivered by a preset group of providers for a fixed annual fee, designated gatekeepers (e.g., primary care physicians) may serve the prescreening role, and selection of treatment modalities may be governed by uniform protocols that restrict provider discretion. Providers' compensation may be affected by their abilities to control costs, either directly, through bonuses or penalties, or indirectly, through payments linked to the overall profit of the organization (Bennett, 1988). New organizational forms for financing and delivering health care are evolving rapidly, often combining elements of two or more of the indemnity, HMO, or PPO models. Almost all, however, have some managed care component (Task Force on Managed Health Care, 1991). Even public health insurance programs, such as Medicare and Medicaid, are rapidly embracing managed care models (Hadley & Langwell, 1991).

Oversight of clinical care in managed systems may be performed by health insurers themselves, using in-house reviewers. In the past decade, however, there has been explosive growth of independent companies providing managed care services to insurers (Goleman, 1991; Tischler, 1990). Whether these companies, which usually have financial incentives to hold down utilization, inappropriately deny coverage to the detriment of patients is the subject of fierce controversy (Borenstein, 1990; Gabbard, Takahashi, Davidson, Bauman-Bork, & Ensroth, 1991; Moran, 1991)....

LIABILITY IMPLICATIONS FOR CLINICIANS

Managed Care: The Clinician's Dilemma

Since the growth of employer-provided health insurance after World War II, health professionals gener-

From *American Psychologist, 48,* 251–257. Copyright 1993 by the American Psychological Association. Adapted with permission of the author and publisher.

ally have been free to order for their patients any accepted diagnostic procedure or treatment, knowing that third-party payers would cover the costs. Thus, clinicians had both the obligation to determine what care their patients reasonably required and the power to provide or otherwise obtain that care (Morreim, 1991).

Although this situation obtained for health care generally, it was not always strictly true for mental health treatment, because many policies limited the amount of coverage by dollars, hospital days, or outpatient visits, or imposed copayment requirements. Nonetheless, benefits were adequate for many patients, and when they were not, there was often the possibility of shifting more severely ill patients into public-sector mental health systems, in which insurance coverage was typically not an issue. At a minimum, treatment was always available up to the limits imposed by the insurance policy.

In a managed care system, however, clinicians are not always able to provide or obtain care that they believe is necessary for patients, even when that care would appear to be covered by patients' insurance. If a reviewer for the entity managing the insurer's mental health benefits concludes that the recommended care is not "medically necessary" (the standard ordinarily applied), coverage may be denied, despite the patient's not having exhausted available benefits (Hall & Anderson, 1992). Although mental health professionals have always had to deal with the problem of limited benefits, denial of coverage is now a potential problem for every insured patient, and may occur early in the course of treatment.

To demonstrate the issues that can arise for clinicians in such circumstances, consider the following hypothetical (but, as will be seen, not unimaginable) case. A depressed, suicidal patient is hospitalized, then followed in psychotherapy for two months by an outpatient clinician. The clinician believes long-term treatment is indicated to help the patient remain stable, even though the acute symptoms of depression have resolved. Adequate coverage remains under the patient's insurance plan, but the patient has no personal resources to pay for further care. An employee of the managed care entity overseeing the treatment, on the basis of a record review and a tel-

ephone discussion with the clinician, determines that further treatment is not medically necessary. Because of recent cutbacks in state funding, no public sector resources are available for patients of this sort.

What should a clinician do in a case like this? Should one continue treatment of the patient without compensation? If one is expected to extend free care to this patient, how much of one's caseload must be nonpaying before it is permissible to decline to offer such services? Or should one simply terminate the patient's care, despite one's belief that further treatment is needed to prevent relapse? If so, who will bear responsibility if the patient again becomes suicidal and injures himself or herself severely?

Such questions are usually answered by reference to the *standards of care* of the mental health professions, which evolve from the collective experience of clinicians, shaped by the recommendations of educators and experts in the field. Failure to conform to a recognized standard of care can be the basis for a finding of malpractice. Thus, clinicians concerned about reducing risks of liability naturally will want to know what their colleagues and the courts have accepted as reasonable standards of practice in situations like these.

The task of identifying appropriate standards in this case, however, is complicated by the limited opportunities clinicians and the courts have had to deal with these questions. Standards addressing previously unprecedented situations often crystallize at an agonizingly slow pace, with both the professional literature and appellate court decisions taking a decade or more to catch up to changes in practice. Moreover, standards of care are not static, but are modified continuously as new treatment techniques are developed and innovations are introduced in the delivery of care. Early data suggest that the introduction of managed care itself has led to modifications in professional standards, included marked shifts from inpatient to outpatient treatment (Thompson, Burns, Goldman, & Smith, 1992) and reductions in the number of outpatient sessions per episode of treatment (Norquist & Wells, 1991). As the approaches to mental health treatment reflected in these data become widely practiced, it is likely that the professions and the courts will recognize them as constituting legitimate alternative standards of care (Hall, 1989; Hirshfeld, 1990a).

. . .

Duty to Appeal Adverse Decisions

At a minimum, a clinician whose patient has been denied payment for care that he or she believes is indicated may have an obligation to contest, on the patient's behalf, the decision of the managed care entity. All such systems have some appellate procedures, and the new generation of state statutes regulating managed care practices often sets certain parameters for their availability and speed of response (American Medical Association, 1990) . . . .

Even if one accepts a general obligation to advocate for patients' needs, however, several questions remain. How far must appeals be pursued? Managed care companies and insurers usually have several levels of review. Must every case be taken through the entire process? Because managed care entities are often accused of creating time-consuming procedural obstacles to discourage appeals, does the extent of a caregiver's obligation to spend uncompensated time on this process depend on the amount of time required?

Must appeals be taken in every case? Is this obligation limited to urgent or emergent situations, or does it include cases in which treatment merely would be beneficial to the patient? Perhaps most important, does the likelihood of success affect the duty? If previous appeals have always, or almost always, been rejected . . . , is a clinician obligated to try again every time? In Virginia, for example, Blue Cross/Blue Shield has a 4.6% rate of approving appeals (Task Force on Managed Health Care, 1991). Is that sufficiently high to justify a requirement that appeals always be pursued?

The answers to these questions are unclear, but there does seem to be an evolving belief that clinicians are obligated to undertake at least some efforts to obtain approval for needed treatment. Moreover, lawyers advising managed care entities on how to avoid liability for their actions (discussed more fully below) recommend that they never discontinue coverage when caregivers feel adamantly that further care is needed. Instead, they suggest the reviewers

authorize care for an interim period while additional review (perhaps by a neutral third party) takes place (Hinden & Elden, 1990). If this advice is followed, appeals are likely to have greater potency, at least over the short term, making imposition of a duty to appeal more meaningful.

What constitutes a reasonable approach from a clinician's point of view? At least an initial appeal of adverse decisions should be undertaken when a clinician believes that the treatment in question is necessary for a patient's well-being. Further levels of appeal probably should be pursued only after consultation with the patient, taking into consideration the likelihood of success, whether the patient still desires to proceed with treatment, and the availability of alternative means of paying for care. Clinicians, to this point, generally have assumed the burden of these procedures without directly seeking compensation for their time, although that may change in the future, particularly with patients who can afford to defray the cost of exceptional periods of time spent contesting adverse decisions. Many mental health professionals, in response to the greater bureaucratic demands of working with managed care systems, including appellate procedures, have shortened the standard length of treatment sessions (e.g., treatment "hours" have dropped from 50 to 45 minutes in many places) while maintaining fees at a constant level.

Duty to Disclose

Morreim (1991) has suggested that the entry of managed care into the clinical setting creates an additional obligation on caregivers to discuss with patients the economic implications of their treatment. This duty could be based on clinicians' fiduciary duties, contractual obligations, or the underlying duty to disclose information relevant to obtaining patients' informed consent.

What might such a duty include? At the initiation of therapy, clinicians might want to discuss with patients the potential effects of managed care on the course of treatment, including the possibility that payment for therapy might be terminated before either the patient or the clinician believes that the goals of treatment have been achieved. Patients who are about to embark on therapy involving painful self-disclosure and the activation of disturbing affects might well find such information important to their decision to proceed. Disclosure of the nature and extent of information that may have to be released to managed care reviewers may also be useful to patients.

When further coverage is denied, clinicians will probably need to enter into a full discussion of patients' options. Denial of coverage does not in itself mean that treatment must end. Patients may elect to pay for care out of pocket, or to proceed with therapy during the appeals process, risking in the interim being held responsible for charges accrued. Referral to alternative sources of care that are free or less expensive may also be an option.

The duty to disclose this information to patients seems neither onerous nor unreasonable. Nonetheless, it is not a duty that the courts have yet had an opportunity to rule on, and thus its legal status remains unclear.

Duty to Continue Treatment

When coverage for further treatment has been denied by a managed care entity, a clinician always retains the option of continuing to care for a patient without payment or at a reduced rate. This is obviously not an attractive option from the clinician's perspective, but there may be circumstances in which it is required, and others in which its status is unclear.

Most authorities would probably agree that when clinicians believe an emergency exists—such as in the case example above, if the patient had been acutely suicidal—there is an obligation to continue with treatment until the emergent state resolves or until an alternative provider of care can be found (Appelbaum & Gutheil, 1991). The same is true when insurance coverage is exhausted completely ("Court Finds," 1992). In principle, these situations should arise infrequently, because coverage should not be refused in such cases.

The nature of clinicians' obligations in nonemergent siutations, such as in the case example, is less evident. Some court cases dating from before the managed care era indicate that, once accepting a patient for treatment, clinicians and hospitals must provide all necessary care (Marsh, 1985). Such lan-

guage can be found in more recent cases as well. One opinion, rejecting the attempt of a group of psychiatrists to abrogate a managed care agreement because of alleged negative effects on patient care, noted, "Whether or not the proposed treatment is approved, the physician retains the right and indeed the ethical and legal obligation to provide appropriate treatment to the patient" (*Varol v. Blue Cross and Blue Shield of Michigan*, 1989, p. 833).

As a matter of public policy, however, this approach makes no sense, and it is clearly not sustainable over the long run. Clinicians and hospitals cannot simply be required to provide unlimited amounts of uncompensated care. What then of the duty not to abandon patients whose care one has undertaken? It should be evident that this duty is not absolute, particularly in nonemergent situations. As has always been the case when insurance benefits expired and patients could not or would not assume responsibility for the costs of care, clinicians' obligations are limited to referral (if free or low-cost care is available) or appropriate termination. Depending on the length of time that therapy has gone on, termination may require from one to several sessions to wrap up and consolidate the gains of treatment. Inpatients, of course, will need enough time to make discharge plans. No more can be reasonably required, although it is noteworthy that this is another issue that the courts have yet to address.

The new economic realities embodied in managed care in all likelihood have created a new set of obligations for clinicians, including advocacy of their patients' interests and disclosure of the economic consequences of their treatment decisions. Unlimited responsibilities for the provision of uncompensated care, however, are not likely to be part of clinicians' duties. . . .

References

American Medical Association. (1990). Utilization review. *State Health Legislation Report, 18*(2), 30–35.

Appelbaum, P. S., & Gutheil, T. G. (1991). *Clinical Handbook of Psychiatry and the Law* (2nd ed.) Baltimore: Williams & Wilkins.

Bennett, M. J. (1988). The greening of the HMO: Implications for prepaid psychiatry. *American Journal of Psychiatry, 145,* 1544–1549.

Borenstein, D. B. (1990). Managed care: A means of rationing psychiatric treatment. *Hospital and Community Psychiatry, 41,* 1095–1098.

Court finds Charter negligent in discharge of suicidal teen: Hospital will appeal. (1992, March 20). *Psychiatric News,* p. 1.

Dorwart, R. A. (1990). Managed mental health care: Myths and realities in the 1990s. *Hospital and Community Psychiatry, 41,* 1087–1091.

Gabbard, G. O., Takahashi, T., Davidson, J., Bauman-Bork, M., & Ensroth, E. (1991). A psychodynamic perspective on the clinical impact of insurance review. *American Journal of Psychiatry, 148,* 318–323.

Goleman, D. (1991, October 24). Battle of insurers vs. therapists: Cost control pitted against proper care. *New York Times,* pp. D1, D9.

Hadley, J. P., & Langwell, K. (1991). Managed care in the United States: Promises, evidence to date and future directions. *Health Policy, 19,* 91–118.

Hall, M. A. (1989). The malpractice standard under health care cost containment. *Law, Medicine, and Health Care, 17,* 347–355.

Hall, M. A., & Anderson, G. F. (1992). Health insurers' assessment of medical necessity. *University of Pennsylvania Law Review, 140,* 1637–1712.

Hinden, R. A., & Elden, D. L. (1990). Liability issues for managed care entities. *Seton Hall Legislative Journal, 14,* 1–63.

Hirshfeld, E. B. (1990a). Economic considerations in treatment decisions and the standard of care in medical malpractice litigation. *JAMA: The Journal of the American Medical Association, 264,* 2004–2012.

Institute of Medicine. (1989). *Controlling costs and changing patient care? The role of utilization management.* Washington, DC: National Academy Press.

Marsh, F. H. (1985). Health care cost containment and the duty to treat. *Journal of Legal Medicine, 6,* 157–190.

Moran, M. (1991, May 17). Report criticizes managed care firm. *Psychiatric News,* pp. 1, 20.

Morreim, E. H. (1991). Economic disclosure and economic advocacy: New duties in the medical standard of care. *Journal of Legal Medicine, 12,* 275–329.

Norquist, G. S., & Wells, K. B. (1991). How do HMOs reduce outpatient mental health care costs? *American Journal of Psychiatry, 148,* 96–101.

Task Force on Managed Health Care, Board of Health Professions. (1991). *Report to the Commission on Health Care for all Virginians.* Richmond: Virginia Department of Health Professions.

Thompson, J. W., Burns, B. J., Goldman, H. H., & Smith, J. (1992). Initial level of care and clinical status in a managed mental health program. *Hospital and Community Psychiatry, 43,* 599–603.

Tischler, G. L. (1990). Utilization management of mental health services by private third parties. *American Journal of Psychiatry, 147,* 967–973.

Varol v. Blue Cross and Blue Shield of Michigan, 708 F. Supp. 826 (E.D. Mich. 1989).

Zimet, C. N. (1989). The mental health care revolution: Will psychology survive? *American Psychologist, 44,* 703–708.

Managed Outpatient Mental Health Plans: Clinical, Ethical, and Practical Guidelines for Participation

Leonard J. Haas and Nicholas A. Cummings

THE RISE OF MANAGED OR LIMITED MENTAL HEALTH BENEFITS

The continued emphasis on cost containment in health care, and in mental health care in particular, has stirred strong feelings (both pro and con) among psychologists in recent years. With regard to outpatient psychological treatment, it is increasingly the case that "psychotherapy" is coming to be synonymous with brief or time-limited psychotherapy. For individual providers who examine "managed" mental health outpatient care options carefully, three questions arise forcefully: (a) Does managed mental health care present some unique set of problems for providers or patients?; (b) How can psychologists make sensible decisions about participation in the "new" mental health care plans?; and (c) For psychologists who are providers in managed care environments, are there ethical or clinical considerations in deciding who should or should not be provided treatment? . . .

. . .

THE RESPONSE OF PSYCHOLOGIST PROVIDERS

Strong emotions are generated on both sides of the issue when psychologists consider the rise in managed mental health care plans. Interestingly, the focus is almost entirely on the issue of limitations to outpatient treatment, or the institution of some sort of benefit cap that might tend to shorten the length of psychotherapy. Thus, the debate seems primarily to center on time-limited [footnote omitted] or brief psychotherapy versus long-term treatment. Reaction in the professional literature ranges from suggestions that psychologists have made a mistake in opting to be considered health care providers, to suggestions that those who fail to embrace the new systems are "dinosaurs." Even the old "symptom substitution" argument, not much in evidence since the heyday of the psychodynamic–behavioral wars, is periodically heard (e.g., time-limited treatment cannot really treat the underlying problem, but will inevitably lead to a recurrence of symptoms).

THE CHANGING FACE OF PSYCHOTHERAPY ECONOMICS

. . . Psychologists are primarily in the business of offering outpatient mental health services, and almost all consumers of such services except for the very poor and the very wealthy depend in part on some third party to help them to afford such services. Increasingly, those third parties are imposing limits on outpatient psychotherapy to attempt to contain costs. Initially, these efforts took the form of "benefit design," or alterations in the amount of money patients must pay as they receive longer treatment (e.g., first 5 visits at no copayment, next 10 visits at 20% copayment, and the next 20 visits at 50% copayment). More recently, these efforts have taken the form of "management" of treatment, which inserts the third-party payor into a more active role in the treatment planning or monitoring. And, among some plans (notably, but not exclusively, certain health maintenance organizations [HMOs]), there is

From *Professional Psychology: Research and Practice, 22,* 45–51. Copyright 1991 by the American Psychological Association. Adapted with permission of the author and publisher.

the feature of treatment limitation, which caps the number of sessions, not simply the number of dollars, that will be reimbursed. Although we will argue against the notion of treatment limitation by third parties, we are enthusiastic about the practitioner's use of brief methods. The ideal environment in which to contain costs would be one in which providers well trained in the rapid treatment of disorder were free to use their professional discretion in the service of their patients' welfare.

MANAGED MENTAL HEALTH CARE: UNIQUE THREAT?

. . .

There are various means to limit the access of prospective insurance policyholders or patients to a plan or to a service. These means may be examined from clinical, fiscal, and ethical perspectives, because these are the usual types of concerns expressed about such policy decisions. That is, the clinician is most concerned about the clinical aspects of delivering quality care. The plan administrator has the clearest concern for the financial realities, because they directly affect whether the plan may survive. And both "stakeholders" (Haas & Malouf, 1989) should be concerned about the ethical dimension of their policy, in part to make it consistent with psychologists' ethical principles and in part to make it morally sound on more general grounds. A description of the options and relevant ethical concerns follows:

1. A plan may simply impose limitations on treatment. These limitations are for the present purposes being called *time limits,* although they are most clearly so primarily in HMOs. In other plans, time limits are translated into dollar limits. Thus, a plan could offer (as many do) a $2,000 yearly maximum for outpatient mental health coverage, occurring in a maximum of 50 sessions. In many HMOs, the limit is 20 sessions annually, with annual and lifetime cost caps. From a clinical perspective, this policy may be risky: Patients may be denied needed care that extends beyond their benefits. From a fiscal perspective, this policy is sensible. There is a known cap on the amount of financial risk the program takes (although there is the fiscal risk that pa-

tients may, justly or unjustly, accuse the program of depriving them of needed care). From an ethical perspective, the policy is problematic: It shifts the risk to the therapist, because therapists are ethically bound to care for their patients and not abandon them. Thus, to provide care to patients whose benefits have been exceeded puts the therapist in the position of needing to make a referral of the patient if continued treatment is appropriate. Alternatively, therapists could provide *pro bono* service, although doing this frequently might eventually lower the therapist's income to an unacceptable level.

2. A plan may institute no time limits but may carefully select its policyholders so that they are unlikely to exceed some (actuarially derived) time limits or expenditure limits. This is called *skimming* (McGuire, 1989), or selecting to insure those individuals who are least likely to make a claim. Although no managed-care program would admit to selecting patients in this manner, careful marketing (Nelson, Clark, Goldman, & Schore, 1989) may accomplish the same end. For example, plans may only be open to retired persons, teachers, or military dependents. However, despite the fears of critics (e.g., Nelson et al., 1989) in practice it is almost impossible to select low-utilization policyholders. One strategy that may work involves adverse selection: Lowering premiums and benefits carefully will attract those who perceive themselves to have low need for the service and to have low risk for the noncovered condition and thus expect not to need the benefits and wish to save the money. However, even if the plan administrator is judicious, this may be a relatively risky strategy in terms of financial exposure. Clinically, if it can actually be implemented, this is a relatively low-risk strategy, because it tends to amount to offering treatment to those who do not need it. Ethically, the primary problem involves informed consent; as long as the program gives policyholders clear information on the limits of coverage and they are free to choose other plans, there is no coercion into inappropriate service. However, there is the more abstract ethical concern that by selecting only low-utilization patients, the plan unfairly burdens other health insurers with higher utilization patients.

3. A plan may opt for the policy of limiting ac-

cess to treatment, and limiting access to the policy itself through selection criteria or marketing strategies. There is little data on this option; however, it is likely to be fiscally the safest; a clearly known financial risk is involved. It is, on the other hand, clinically risky: Unless very clear diagnostic criteria are specified, the situation is similar to Paragraph 2, just discussed; it poses the danger that a patient who needs treatment will be denied it. Such a plan is potentially ethically problematic in the same way as other treatment limits are, because it changes the therapist's role to one of resource rationer and restricts his or her ability to act in the best interests of the patient.

4. A program may impose no limitations on outpatient treatment and may offer reimbursement (minus the copayment) to any policyholder. Although this is not a widespread policy (Cummings, 1988), it has proven viable when carefully implemented. Presumably, most plans avoid this arrangement out of fear that it expands their risks uncontrollably. This policy option is clinically safe (patients who need more extensive treatment will get it); it is economically risky (the plan has no way of limiting the amount of expenses it is exposed to); and it is ethically sound (the competent and ethical provider decides in conjunction with the patient what treatment is indicated).

. . .

CONSIDERATIONS BEFORE JOINING A MANAGED-CARE SYSTEM

First and foremost, the prospective provider in a managed-care plan must know exactly what the plan involves and what constraints it will impose. Beyond this, several features of mental health care plans should raise questions.

1. *Who takes the risks?* In the usual arrangement, the insurer takes the risks: The plan and its benefits assume a probability of particular treatment needs, and if the patient should need more treatment, the plan reimburses for it. In managed-care plans, some of this risk is shifted to the patient: If costs go above a certain level, the patient pays. In other plans, notably HMOs, some of the risk is shifted onto providers: If costs go above the limits, or if re-

ferrals to specialists become necessary, the provider's reimbursement drops. One side effect of the shifting of risk to providers is that this tempts them to hoard resources (Morreim, 1988), in the sense that they may be reluctant to refer or extend treatment if it costs them too much.

2. *How much does the plan intrude into the patient–provider relationship?* The professional who agrees to participate in a mental health care plan incurs obligations both to the plan provider and to the patient. In the traditional doctor–patient relationship, there is substantial contractual freedom. The prototypical consumer experiences a need for a service, chooses a provider from among some alternatives, and has some degree of participation in the treatment planning process (e.g., selection of procedures if alternatives are available, agreement to follow the doctor's orders if called on to do so, and informing provider if treatment appears to be working). For the prototypical provider, the relationship involves loyalty to the patient; that is, the provider has the freedom to accept or decline to treat the patient, to select appropriate treatment or treatments from among those in which he or she is competent, and then to honor his or her duty to treat the patient until the presenting problem is resolved, a referral is made, or the patient discontinues treatment. In theoretical terms, the principles of beneficence, autonomy, and justice are relevant (Beauchamp & Childress, 1988). In more conventional language, the relationship is marked by freedom and responsibility; freedom to treat as the provider sees fit, and responsibility, primarily to the patient, to resolve the presenting problem. Although some commentators have argued that this arrangement provides incentives to offer more care than necessary, others (e.g., Nelson et al., 1989) argue that it also highlights the primary loyalty of provider to consumer. The risk to the clinician participating in managed-care arrangements becomes that of balancing loyalty to the patient with responsibilities as an agent of the mental health program. If the program takes on undue risks from a particular case (e.g., the patient's care becomes too costly), the program may suffer damage, as may the therapist and other potential patients of the program.

3. *What provisions exist for exceptions to the rules?*

A provider who is willing to incur the financial risk (or who works in a noncapitated arrangement) may want to continue providing treatment to a particular patient who has exceeded benefits. The provider may be tempted to change the diagnosis or the description of treatment so that the patient can be reimbursed. These maneuvers are possible in any third-party paid arrangement, of course. However, they illustrate that tightening limits on benefits may simply challenge the creativity of clinicians loyal to their patients and that the risks of altering that loyalty extend beyond simply the escalation of costs.

4. *Are there referral resources if patient needs should exceed plan benefits?* Psychologists, like other mental health professionals, have a duty to treat the patient until the presenting problem is resolved, a referral is made, or the patient discontinues treatment. To do otherwise is to abandon the patient, and this is unethical (American Psychological Association, 1990). Thus, a key question before joining a plan that limits benefits may well become, How do practitioners avoid abandoning their patients without going bankrupt?

5. *Does the plan provide assistance or training in helping the provider to achieve treatment goals?* An alternative to the dilemma just mentioned involves the clinician in becoming more knowledgeable about short-term treatment options.... If prospective providers have not been trained in these approaches, plans should either not select them or should make provisions to train them appropriately.

6. *Does the plan minimize economic incentives to hospitalize patients?* The "perverse incentives" noted above operate in many plans. Providers should carefully investigate their existence and perhaps lobby for alternative incentive systems.

7. *Are there ways in which the plan is open to provider input?* Given the proliferation of benefit options and plan arrangements, it is essential that some feedback mechanisms be built into these plans. Otherwise, the provider becomes simply an employee rather than a professional treating patients.

8. *Do plans clearly inform their policyholders of the limits of benefits?* Just as providers have loyalties to both other parties in the system, they should avoid being trapped in the middle, having to explain benefit limits to naive patients after the benefit limits have been reached.

Of course, the ideal policy for a managed mental health care program is one that does not create dual loyalties among therapists and that provides benefits both to specific patients in need of services and to potential patients who may require program resources in the future. This is a difficult policy option to implement because pressing immediate needs are those most likely to claim our loyalties even though alleviating present needs may increase the suffering of patients who will have needs in the future....

ADDITIONAL ETHICAL ISSUES

Consideration of additional ethical issues in managed mental health care plans brings several to the forefront. First ... the issue of competence is crucial. Consistent with the ethical obligation to offer services within the domain of their competence, psychologists must be capable of delivering service in a time-limited context if they are to be involved in managed-care plans.

Second is the issue of informed consent. The prospective patient must be given clear information about the benefits to which he or she is entitled and clear information about the limits of treatment as the clinician envisions them.

A third issue of ethical importance concerns divided loyalties. Third-party payment arrangements always elicit such issues, but never so clearly as in managed mental health care plans. The principal of fidelity (Beauchamp & Childress, 1988) demands that the provider or professional be loyal to those with whom he or she has a contractual relationship. Thus, if a therapist agrees to work in a managed health care program, he or she should believe in the service philosophy it endorses. If the therapist agrees to work with a particular patient, he or she should be loyal to that patient's interests (this is part of what is meant by a fiduciary relationship). The Ethical Principles of Psychologists (APA, 1990) focuses on fidelity in Principle 6, in terms of the psychologist's obligation to obtain informed consent from consumers, and on avoiding relationships in which there is a conflict of interest that may impair his or her objectivity. On this last point, the Ethical Principles of Psychologists (APA, 1990) is also clear. When demands of an organization conflict with the ethics code, psychologists attempt to bring the conflict to the attention of relevant parties and resolve it. In this case, the conflict would likely be between the demands of the plan that reimbursement for treatment cease or change versus the needs of the patient and the psychologist's ethical responsibility to act for the benefit of the client ("welfare of the consumer"). Psychologists may have a corollary obligation to ensure that plans with which they are associated have mechanisms to receive their input and recommendations for change. . . .

References

American Psychological Association. (1990). Ethical principles of psychologists (amended June 2, 1989). *American Psychologist, 45,* 390–395.

Beauchamp, T., & Childress, W. (1988). *Principles of biomedical ethics* (3rd ed.). Baltimore, MD: Johns Hopkins University Press.

Cummings, N. A. (1988). Emergence of the mental health complex: Adaptive and maladaptive responses. *Professional Psychology: Research and Practice, 19,* 308–315.

Haas, L. J., & Malouf, J. L. (1989). *Keeping up the good work: A practitioner's guide to mental health ethics.* Sarasota, FL: Professional Resource Exchange.

McGuire, T. G. (1989). Outpatient benefits for mental health services in medicare: Alignment with the private sector? *American Psychologist, 44,* 818–824.

Morreim, E. H. (1988). Cost containment: Challenging fidelity and justice. *Hastings Center Report, 18,* 20–25.

Nelson, L. J., Clark, H. W., Goldman, R. L., & Schore, J. E. (1989). Taking the train to a world of strangers: Health care marketing and ethics. *Hastings Center Report, 19,* 36–43.

Ethical and Liability Issues Concerning Invisible Rationing

Ivan J. Miller

Managed care companies reduce the cost of mental health services by substituting brief therapy for longer term treatment. When the shorter treatment is as beneficial as the longer treatment, the substitution is advantageous to consumers and the company. If, however, the briefer treatment is only partially effective, substituting brief therapy to save money becomes a form of rationing treatment services.

Unfortunately, the arguments offered by brief therapy proponents and the policies of managed care combine to obscure that brief therapy is often a tool for rationing mental health services. The result is *invisible rationing*, a treatment allocation process that reduces mental health services without informing the client of the reduction (Miller, 1994). However, consumers have a right to know when their health care services are being rationed, and invisible rationing raises serious ethical and liability problems. . . .

ETHICAL ISSUES

Psychologists' Ethics Require Disclosure of Rationing

Multiple aspects of the American Psychological Association (1992) Ethical Principles of Psychologists and Code of Conduct indicate that psychologists should inform their clients of the rationing of psychotherapy services:

Principle B: Integrity

The principle of integrity instructs psychologists to attempt to clarify for relevant parties the roles they are performing. Because the roles of rationing treatment and providing therapy are both relevant to the psychotherapy client, the psychologist should clarify all relevant information about each role.

1.21 Third-Party Requests for Services

Section 1.21 states that "when a psychologist agrees to provide services . . . at the request of a third party, the psychologist clarifies to the extent feasible, at the outset of the service, the nature of the relationship with each party." Whereas rationed treatment is conducted through a contractual request from a third party, the psychologist has an obligation to inform the client of the contract. Because the details of the contract impinge on the treatment and constitute the nature of the relationship with the third party, all contract details and associated policies, including actual and potential rationing, should be available to clients on request.

3.03 Avoidance of False or Deceptive Statements

Section 3.03 prohibits psychologists from making "public statements that are false, deceptive, misleading, or fraudulent, either because of what they state, convey, or suggest or because of what they omit, concerning their research, practice, or other work activities or those persons or organizations with which they are affiliated." Whereas the psychotherapy relationship implies that there are only two parties, the client and the therapist, and does not imply that the therapist is responsible for rationing resources, the omission of a description of the thera-

From *Professional Psychology: Research and Practice, 27,* 583–587. Copyright 1996 by the American Psychological Association. Adapted with permission of the author and publisher.

pist's role in rationing would be misleading and deceptive.

4.02 Informed Consent to Therapy

Section 4.02 explains that part of obtaining informed consent to treatment requires providing clients with "significant information concerning" treatment. The fact that treatment has been rationed is significant information that should be disclosed as part of informed consent.

In general, informed consent is presumed to include information about treatment alternatives as well as the recommended treatment....

The principle underlying this disclosure is the right of self-determination. A self-determining client may choose to self-pay for whatever treatment is unavailable as a consequence of rationing. To exercise this choice, the client must be informed about the alternative treatments that have been eliminated by rationing. Furthermore, the obligation to inform clients of alternative treatments is greater when the therapist is involved in the dual and conflicting roles of both providing psychotherapy and implementing treatment rationing policies.

4.09 Terminating the Professional Relationship

Section 4.09(c) requires that prior to termination, psychologists suggest alternative service providers as appropriate. Whereas substantial research has shown that brief therapy often is not as effective as longer term therapy, the brief therapist has an obligation to refer all clients who have not achieved the desired results at the time of termination.

. . .

LIABILITY ISSUES

The use of brief therapy raises two potential liability issues.

Consequences of Undertreatment and Abandonment

The psychotherapist who uses brief therapy that provides only partial treatment and does not refer the client for further treatment may be liable for consequences of undertreatment. Such a combination of actions could be construed to be abandoning the client according to Section 4.09 of the Ethical Principles of Psychologists and Code of Conduct (American Psychological Association, 1992).

Consequences of Not Informing Clients About Rationing

If brief therapy is presented as the most effective treatment, and the impact of rationing is not explained, the client can be misled to believe that all possible effective treatment has been exhausted at the end of the brief therapy episode. The consequence is that the client's right to self-determination is abridged because of the lack of information about alternative treatment through self-payment.

References

American Psychological Association. (1992). Ethical principles of psychologists and code of conduct. *American Psychologist, 47,* 1597–1611.

Miller, I. J. (1994). *What managed care is doing to outpatient mental health: A look behind the veil of secrecy.* Boulder, CO: Boulder Psychotherapists' Press.

Commentary: For a critical rejoinder that pays particular attention to the issue of disclosure and consent, see the provocative article, Cummings, N. A., Budman, S. H., & Thomas, J. L. (1998). Efficient psychotherapy as a viable response to scarce resources and rationing of treatment. Professional Psychology: Research and Practice, 29, 460–469.

Implications of the 1992 Ethics Code for the Practice of Individual Psychotherapy

Melba J. T. Vasquez

Standard 4.09, Terminating the Professional Relationship, expands the previous code's Principle 6e, which presented the importance of terminating a relationship when the consumer was not benefitting from it and of offering to help locate alternative sources of assistance. The new standard explicitly states, "psychologists do not abandon patients or clients" (APA, 1992, p. 1606). Standard 1.25(e), under Fees and Financial Arrangements, is cross-referenced here as well. Standard 1.25(e) addresses the importance of discussing limitations of services, which might be anticipated because of limitations in financing, as early as is feasible. However, these two standards are potentially in conflict. The proscription to not abandon clients or patients could conflict with Standard 1.25(e), which could be construed by some as permission to terminate on the basis of having previously discussed limitations of services because of finances, regardless of potential abandonment. Simply addressing the limits of services in managed care, for example, does not preclude one from the proscription to not abandon patients or clients. Although abandonment is not defined, we can imagine various dilemmas that arise.

> Case example: A client contacts a psychologist who is a provider for her managed care insurance. She is allowed only eight sessions. When the psychologist requests extension of services, the administrators of the managed care insurance agree to do so only in the case of a major mental disorder or if the patient is a danger to self or others. The client's diagnosis, dysthymia, does not qualify. The client's financial status is restricted, so the psychologist agrees to provide services on an as-needed basis for the client on a sliding scale fee. A month later, the psychologist is dropped as a provider by the managed care company, presumably because the managed care company is changing to a format in which only a few specific providers see their insured employees. Two months later, the client contacts the psychologist through the emergency answering service and indicates that she has overdosed. The psychologist quickly takes action and calls Emergency Medical Services, who gets the client to an emergency room. After the client is physically stabilized, the psychologist makes arrangements for the client to be moved to a psychiatric hospital.

The psychologist is no longer a provider for the client's managed care company. What are this psychologist's continued responsibilities? According to Standard 4.09(a), psychologists are required to not abandon patients or clients. At a minimum, the psychologist should continue to provide therapeutic services until the client is stabilized and less suicidal. At that point, the client and the psychologist would likely negotiate either referral to a new provider through the client's managed care program, continu-

From *Professional Psychology: Research and Practice, 25,* 321–328. Copyright 1994 by the American Psychological Association. Adapted with permission of the author and publisher.

ation of the therapeutic relationship on a sliding scale basis, or renegotiation with the managed care company to allow the psychologist to continue as a provider possibly on the basis of legal liability responsibilities. Under no circumstances would it be acceptable for the psychologist to assume lack of responsibility just because the client's insurance company discontinued granting the psychologist provider status. Situations such as this are unfortunately likely to occur more frequently, and revisions of the current code might include guidelines that would support psychologists' advocacy efforts on behalf of clients.

References

American Psychological Association. (1992). Ethical principles of psychologists and code of conduct. *American Psychologist, 47,* 1597–1611.

The Value and Utility of the 1992 Ethics Code

Celia B. Fisher and Jeffrey N. Younggren

. . .

Managed care. The 1992 APA ethics code requires that psychologists discuss with prospective clients the "nature" (i.e., the general goals and strategies) of the therapeutic techniques that will be used, the "anticipated course" of psychotherapy (e.g., how long treatment is anticipated to last), fees, and confidentiality (Standard 4.01: Structuring the Relationship; [APA, 1992], p. 1605). Some have raised legitimate concerns about the ability of these standards (or any ethics code) to address the difficult informed consent issues raised by managed care (Haas & Cummings, 1991; Newman & Bricklin, 1991; Vasquez, 1994). We concur with this concern and also believe that Standard 4.01 is a helpful guide in this controversial area.

Within the context of managed care, Standard 4.01 can be interpreted as requiring the psychotherapist to discuss the type of treatment he or she can provide within the parameters set by (a) the type of diagnoses and number of sessions that the client's insurer may be expected to reimburse and (b) the ability of the client to engage in psychotherapy without insurance coverage or to continue treatment once the insurance coverage has been exhausted. Under this standard, psychotherapy providers also are required to discuss at the outset of treatment the limits of client–therapist confidentiality that can be expected from working within the specific managed care company's rules and regulations (see also Standard 1.25: Fees and Financial Arrangements; Standard 5.01: Discussing the Limits of Confidentiality). The next revision of the code may provide more adequate guidance in this area. At present, psychologists need to be alert to the complex ethical problems inherent within managed care and inform clients of the clear limitations this system creates.

. . .

References

American Psychological Association. (1992). Ethical principles of psychologists and code of conduct. *American Psychologist, 47,* 1597–1611.

Haas, L. J., & Cummings, N. A. (1991). Managed outpatient mental health plans: Clinical, ethical, and practical guidelines for participation. *Professional Psychology: Research and Practice, 22,* 45–51.

Newman, R., & Bricklin, P. M. (1991). Parameters of managed mental health care: Legal, ethical, and professional guidelines. *Professional Psychology: Research and Practice, 22,* 26–35.

Vasquez, M. J. T. (1994). Implications of the 1992 ethics code for the practice of individual psychotherapy. *Professional Psychology: Research and Practice, 25,* 321–328.

The Rape of Psychotherapy

Ronald E. Fox

... We are witness to a corporatization of health care on a scale that many of us would have thought inconceivable only a decade ago. Corporate take-overs, mergers, and buyouts are so common that most of us have difficulty remembering "who's on first." Big fish are eaten by larger fish who, in turn, are eaten by still larger fish until in many markets all that are left are a few hungry sharks warily circling each other. . . . It is the corporate executive, not the provider, who is dominant in today's health care market, and the change is unsettling to say the least. Surely we are in the hands of the money lenders and the Philistines. I do not like what they are doing to our profession and to our patients.

. . .

[L]et me turn to changes that are implemented in the name of cost efficiency that, in my opinion, pose real threats to our practices and to the proper conduct of psychotherapeutic treatment. Of the many issues that could be discussed, I will focus on five that pose particularly ominous implications for psychotherapy, for the profession of psychology, or for both.

First, there is the problem of confidentiality. There is little need to remind the readers ... about the importance of confidentiality to psychotherapeutic treatment. This is a concept, however, that is proving very difficult to maintain in today's environment. Practitioners are being forced by some firms to choose between signing a provider panel contract that takes unnecessary liberties with the confidentiality of patient records and being excluded from a needed source of patient referrals. The dilemmas are not minor. Recently I talked with an experienced practitioner who had built a successful practice in a midwestern city. He initially refused to sign on to panels of managed care firms that moved into his area because of differences over confidentiality (as well as a number of other issues). Recently, he discovered that two managed care companies now have contracts covering 70% of his patients. He has less than 1 year to terminate or transfer his patients to providers on the panels, and the panels are closed; he could not be a panel provider member even if he chose to go along with their requirements!

How are we to protect ourselves and our patients from such eventualities? The only effective solutions of which I am aware involve the passage of laws defining the proper limits of intrusiveness into a patient's confidentiality. Such regulations are being heavily resisted by the managed care industry. They have a lot of money to spend on lobbying efforts, which means that we have our work cut out for us. The issues here are incredibly important, and events are unfolding in ways that are astonishing to even the most jaded observer.

. . .

A second issue is the built-in bias that exists in most markets against long-term, intensive psychotherapy. Maintenance treatment of the seriously mentally ill, or supportive treatment to prevent hospitalization or the use of more expensive care, and relatively infrequent ongoing treatment for certain conditions such as borderline personality disorders are sometimes available; but treatment of character disorders, or the correction of personality flaws, or treatment of the long-term and devastating effects of traumas, are simply not available in any but indemnity type policies that make up a steadily shrinking share of the market. Here we are faced with a problem that is partly of our own making. I was trained in psychoanalysis, and I happen to believe that it is a powerful technique that is the preferred treatment in certain situations. The data on treatment outcomes and my own experience, however, do not support the widespread use of psychoanalytic treatment as the intervention of choice for the broad array of problems that come to our offices. It is a treatment that has been overprescribed, and we are the ones who did it. It is clear from patterns of practice in various regions of the country that intensive psychotherapy is widely used in urban areas, particularly those in which there are a number of psychoanalytic training institutes. Practice patterns in most regions of the country are quite different, with much less frequent use of intensive psychotherapeutic interventions. Clearly, we are dealing with treatment preferences on the part of providers rather than with patient needs. Obviously, we have much work to do as a profession if we intend to preserve intensive psychotherapy as a viable treatment option. We must clearly differentiate or identify the indicators for such treatment and then work to see that they are used in practice. It is in our best interests as professionals to see that long-term, intensive care does not disappear from the treatment landscape. Our success in doing so is likely to hinge on the recognition that we ourselves have been a part of the problem.

In addition to the bias against intensive, depth-oriented psychotherapy as a simple cost-cutting measure and the problem of the overuse of that treatment by some providers, there is another matter that must be addressed: Where do we stand with respect to legislation that proposes less coverage for the many versus that which proposes more extensive coverage for the few? These are the kinds of practical trade-offs that we confront in the legislative arena. Here we have what is in effect a conflict of values. None of us want to deny treatment to patients in need of intensive care, but neither do we want to deprive others of the kind of preventive, supportive, crisis, and brief treatment that is needed by the vast majority of those who suffer from mental illnesses. Obviously, we need both, but in the practical world of politics, we cannot always have all that we want. What must our stance be? Which value do we choose?

A third issue that constitutes a threat to our profession is the strong bias against psychological assessment that exists in virtually all managed care firms. Managed care officials maintain that we have not made the case that psychological assessments contribute anything toward improving or shortening psychotherapy. Some evidence is starting to come in, but the fact of the matter is that the case has yet to be made, and we must make it effectively if we are to preserve a truly unique psychological service.

. . .

A fourth threat we face in the market today is the bias that exists against specialists. The pressure and financial incentives strongly encourage the use of less well-qualified providers in the belief that the services delivered are comparable. I do not dispute the fact that various providers without a doctoral degree can and do provide some services that are equal to those provided by well-trained doctoral providers in many instances. However, that is different from saying that psychologists are simply higher-priced versions of social workers or counselors of various types. The approach to understanding the total patient in context, the breadth of the providers' knowledge base, and the range of available skills are very different for the doctoral provider—and the differences are ones that matter.

. . .

A fifth feature of the managed care-dominated market that poses a threat to providers is their attempts to avoid responsibility for the adverse effects of their decisions on patients. Not only do they refuse to accept such responsibility (except where laws have dictated otherwise), but they also shift the entire burden of risk to the clinician and his or her malpractice insurance. As though this were not enough, clinicians who attempt to lower their own risk by advocating for patients who are not receiving proper care face the real prospect of being dropped from the provider panel at the next renewal period. Truly this is the business mentality gone seriously awry. Where are the moral values in such decisions? What is the proper accountability for such actions?

Is it really acceptable for firms holding the health of others in their hands to turn a deaf ear to legitimate needs for care in the name of extra profits?

. . .

The possible courses of action available to us (other than doing nothing) that come to mind are not original, but they are important:

1. Psychology should vigorously support "any willing provider" legislation. Opening provider panels to all qualified practitioners who wish to be included and who agree to the operative conditions would go a long way toward addressing the power differential that now exists between providers and managed care firms. Legislation to create a more level playing field should be a top priority at both the federal and state levels.

2. We must exert unrelenting pressure in support of improved confidentiality statutes and rules.

3. We must support current and future health care reform initiatives that allow psychologists to be truly integrated into the system and to be able to function to the full extent of their qualifications.

4. We must support initiatives to fix responsibility for clinical decisions on all of those who are in the decision loop rather than on some. Providers make decisions for which they should be held accountable, but some decisions are now made for them. Mechanisms must be developed to spread responsibility to all of those who are involved.

5. We must address the master's issue in a realistic and straightforward manner. It is unlikely that we will be successful, ultimately, in denying them access to practice (just as we have not been able to stop other master's-level providers). However, we may be able to develop and promulgate (for use in the legislative arena) psychological practice definitions that are tied to the doctoral level and that restrict the title of psychologist to such practitioners.

6. We must develop practice guidelines that explicate when, how, and under what conditions various types of services, such as long-term psychotherapy and psychological assessment, are appropriate.

Parameters of Managed Mental Health Care: Legal, Ethical, and Professional Guidelines

Russ Newman and Patricia M. Bricklin

. . .

APA POLICY ON MANAGED CARE

Although some legislative, ethical, professional, and common law parameters for providing treatment within managed care settings do exist, they are considered by many in organized psychology to be either slow in developing or insufficient to deal with the unique characteristics of the newly emerging health care system. As a result, the American Psychological Association's Council of Representatives promulgated a policy statement in 1988 designed to articulate organized psychology's concerns about the potential effects of managed care on psychological services. Furthermore, the policy was intended to offer some recommendations to providers and consumers, in an attempt to minimize the potential for managed care's adverse effects on services (APA, Council of Representatives, 1989). Since that time, APA boards and committees have taken various steps to implement the spirit of the council policy statement, which remains as APA policy to the present.

Background and Policy Development

In the early 1980s, as a result of activities at the federal level and the emergence of new alternative health care delivery models, many psychologists in practice approached the APA through individual letters expressing interest and concern about these new service delivery systems. In response APA, through its Board of Professional Affairs (BPA), began to ex-

plore managed care in the context of future markets for psychological practice. At that time, there was both a growing excitement about the possibility of managed care as a creative solution to service delivery problems and a concern about the possible legal and ethical issues presented by such an alternative model.

Between 1982 and 1984, BPA sponsored a major APA convention program to review the issues, and as a result established a Subcommittee on Future Markets. . . . Additionally, other APA governance groups associated with public interest expressed particular concern over access-to-care and quality-of-care needs of special populations within these systems.

In response, the BPA approved the development of a manual to educate the APA membership about the opportunities and challenges facing psychologists interested in joining HMOs and PPOs. The manual, *Marketing Psychological Services: A Practitioner's Guide* (APA, 1986) was completed in late 1985 and published in 1986.

During the same time period, the APA Committee on Women, the Committee on Gay and Lesbian Concerns, and the Board of Social and Ethical Responsibility reviewed managed care issues with respect to care and quality-of-care needs of special populations within managed care systems. . . . The particular concern for public interest groups, especially those that work with minority populations, is that the majority of managed care systems designate care providers. In a managed care model the patient generally has the choice only of providers who are

From *Professional Psychology: Research and Practice, 22,* 26–35. Copyright 1991 by the American Psychological Association. Adapted with permission of the author and publisher.

part of the system. These providers may or may not be sensitive to minority issues. In a really free enterprise system, the client is free to choose a provider who is sensitive to his or her specific minority concerns. It is critically important that clients who enter into managed care systems be aware that they may be limited in the choice of service provider. This is a real truth in packaging issue.

The issues of psychologists' participation in alternative managed health care delivery systems continued to be of concern to various APA groups, including public interest and practice oriented constituencies. With the creation of the Office of Professional Practice within APA, its Interim Advisory Committee became a coordinating mechanism for consideration of managed care.

The Interim Advisory Committee (later Committee for the Advancement of Professional Practice) expressed concern over additional issues in managed care in 1988 (APA, Interim Advisory Committee, 1988). The concern that cost containment would be the major driving force in treatment decisions at the expense of the consumer was a major issue. It affirmed that it is especially important that decisions regarding quantity and quality of care be based on consumers' needs as well as on the economic interest of the health care delivery system. A proposed policy statement developed by the Interim Advisory Committee was circulated to all interested APA governance groups, including the BPA, and appropriate public interest groups. . . . This culminated in a document unanimously agreed upon by all of the participating groups, which was presented to the Council of Representatives in August 1988 and became APA policy at that time.

Policy Statement by the Council of Representatives

WHEREAS, many mental health problems are reflective of profound problems of living, substantial intrapsychic disorganization or severe physical and psychological disruption; and

WHEREAS, some psychological services are specifically focused on the alleviation of the personal distress attendant thereto; and

WHEREAS, managed care or other health care delivery systems should not unduly discriminate against those consumers who need intensive care, against those who need specialty care, and should not systematically endorse short-term or biomedical intervention as the treatment of choice for all patients at the expense of individual needs; and

WHEREAS, managed care delivery programs, by their very nature, frequently impose artificial and/or economic barriers to consumer access to health care services and, as such, are as subject to mismanagement as are traditional funding and delivery systems; and

WHEREAS, many managed health care programs may unfairly exclude those with the greatest need from adequate care and/or otherwise put both consumer and participating professional at substantial economic/psychological risk; and

WHEREAS, it is important that mental health care delivery programs provide appropriate and equally high quality services to all persons in diverse client and undeserved populations; and

WHEREAS, providers and patients should be informed of the limitations and restrictions to types and access of psychological services prior to subscribing to a plan (i.e., truth in advertising or explicit statements regarding any financial disincentives to treat and refer patients in need of psychological services),

THEREFORE, BE IT RESOLVED that the American Psychological Association urges consumers, subscribers and psychologists to review carefully the mechanisms, procedures, practices and policies of managed care programs before deciding to participate. Although such programs may offer the potential to expand access to appropriate mental health care, they may also restrict the availability of necessary psychological services.

It is further recommended that providers may wish to require as a condition of their participation that such managed health care delivery systems adequately and concretely demonstrate provisions to serve the consumer's interest with sufficient quantity and highest quality of health care based on the available scientific evidence of efficacy.

It is further recommended that consumers, subscribers and psychologists, as a condition of their participation, require that these programs practice truth in advertising regarding the range and duration of psychological services available through the plan and that these programs provide patients access to diversity of psychological health care competencies based on the available scientific evidence of efficacy.

It is also recommended that providers require that such systems operate in accordance with prevailing standards of care and prevailing scientific knowledge, applicable ethical principles, and that the systems have sufficient economic resources to cover the delivery system's liability.

Finally, individual members, state psychological association and divisions are strongly urged to monitor and inform themselves of the legal and regulatory requirements imposed on managed health care systems and to advocate that such requirements meet the principles enumerated herein. (APA, Council of Representatives, 1989 p. 1024)

This alternative health care delivery policy continues to be APA policy into the 1990s. . . .

References

American Psychological Association. (1986). *Marketing psychological services: A practitioners guide*. Washington, DC: Author.

American Psychological Association, Council of Representatives. (1989). Proceedings of the American Psychological Association, Incorporated, for the year 1988. *American Psychologist, 44,* 996–1028.

American Psychological Association, Interim Advisory Committee. (1988, January 8–10). *Managed care systems*. Washington, DC: American Psychological Association, Practice Directorate.

◆ ◆ ◆

Commentary: *In an effort to provide a unified response to managed care, under the leadership of then APA President Dorothy Cantor, nine major organizations representing mental health practitioners made the following set of principles into policy in 1996.*

Mental Health Bill of Rights Project

A Joint Initiative of Mental Health Professional Organizations

PRINCIPLES FOR THE PROVISION OF MENTAL HEALTH AND SUBSTANCE ABUSE TREATMENT SERVICES

A Bill of Rights

Our commitment is to provide quality mental health and substance abuse services to all individuals without regard to race, color, religion, national origin, gender, age, sexual orientation, or disabilities.

Right to Know

Benefits. Individuals have the right to be provided information from the purchasing entity (such as employer or union or public purchaser) and the insurance/third party payer describing the nature and extent of their mental health and substance abuse treatment benefits. This information should include details on procedures to obtain access to services, on utilization management procedures, and on appeal rights. The information should be presented clearly in writing with language that the individual can understand.

Professional Expertise. Individuals have the right to receive full information from the potential treating professional about that professional's knowledge, skills, preparation, experience, and credentials. Individuals have the right to be informed about the options available for treatment interventions and the effectiveness of the recommended treatment.

Contractual Limitations. Individuals have the right to be informed by the treating professional of any arrangements, restrictions, and/or covenants established between third party payer and the treating professional that could interfere with or influence treatment recommendations. Individuals have the right to be informed of the nature of information that may be disclosed for the purposes of paying benefits.

Appeals and Grievances. Individuals have the right to receive information about the methods they can use to submit complaints or grievances regarding provision of care by the treating professional to that profession's regulatory board and to the professional association.

Individuals have the right to be provided information about the procedures they can use to appeal benefit utilization decisions to the third party payer systems, to the employer or purchasing entity, and to external regulatory entities.

Confidentiality

Individuals have the right to be guaranteed the protection of the confidentiality of their relationship with their mental health and substance abuse professional, except when laws or ethics dictate otherwise. Any disclosure to another party will be time limited and made with the full written, informed consent of the individuals.

Individuals shall not be required to disclose confidential, privileged or other information other than: diagnosis, prognosis, type of treatment, time and length of treatment, and cost.

Entities receiving information for the purposes of benefits determination, public agencies receiving information for health care planning, or any other organization with legitimate right to information will maintain clinical information in confidence with the same rigor and be subject to the same penalties for violation as is the direct provider of care.

Information technology will be used for transmission, storage, or data management *only* with methodologies that remove individual identifying information and assure the protection of the individual's privacy. Information should not be transferred, sold or otherwise utilized.

Choice

Individuals have the right to choose any duly licensed/certified professional for mental health and substance abuse services. Individuals have the right to receive full information regarding the education and training of professionals, treatment options (including risks and benefits), and cost implications to make an informed choice regarding the selection of care deemed appropriate by individual and professional.

Determination of Treatment

Recommendations regarding mental health and substance abuse treatment shall be made only by a duly licensed/certified professional in conjunction with the individual and his or her family as appropriate. Treatment decisions should not be made by third party payers. The individual has the right to make final decisions regarding treatment.

Parity

Individuals have the right to receive benefits for mental health and substance abuse treatment on the same basis as they do for any other illnesses, with the same provisions, co-payments, lifetime benefits, and catastrophic coverage in both insurance and self-funded/self-insured health plans.

Discrimination

Individuals who use mental health and substance abuse benefits shall not be penalized when seeking other health insurance or disability, life or any other insurance benefit.

Benefit Usage

The individual is entitled to the entire scope of the benefits within the benefit plan that will address his or her clinical needs.

Benefit Design

Whenever both federal and state law and/or regulations are applicable, the professional and all payers shall use whichever affords the individual the greatest level of protection and access.

Treatment Review

To assure that treatment review processes are fair and valid, individuals have the right to be guaranteed that any review of their mental health and substance abuse treatment shall involve a professional having the training, credentials and licensure required to provide the treatment in the jurisdiction in which it will be provided. The reviewer should have no financial interest in the decision and is subject to the section on confidentiality.

Accountability

Treating professionals may be held accountable and liable to individuals for any injury caused by gross incompetence or negligence on the part of the professional. The treating professional has the obligation to advocate for and document necessity of care and to advise the individual of options if payment authorization is denied.

Payers and other third parties may be held accountable and liable to individuals for any injury caused by gross incompetence or negligence or by their clinically unjustified decisions.

Participating Groups:
American Association for Marriage and Family Therapy (membership: 25,000)
American Counseling Association (membership: 56,000)
American Family Therapy Academy (membership: 1,000)
American Nurses Association (membership: 180,000)
American Psychological Association (membership: 142,000)
American Psychiatric Association (membership: 42,000)
American Psychiatric Nurses Association (membership: 3,000)
National Association of Social Workers (membership: 155,000)
National Federation of Societies for Clinical Social Work (membership: 11,000)

Supporting Groups:
  National Mental Health Association
  National Depressive and Manic Depressive Association

American Group Psychotherapy Association
American Psychoanalytic Association
National Association of Alcoholism and Drug Abuse Counselors

Index